IBM Smalltalk:
The Language

The Benjamin/Cummings Series
in Object-Oriented Software Engineering

Grady Booch, Series Editor

Booch, *Object-Oriented Analysis and Design with Applications, Second Edition* (1994)
Booch, *Object Solutions: A Sourcebook for Developers* (1995)
Booch/Bryan, *Software Engineering with Ada, Third Edition* (1994)
Collins, *Designing Object-Oriented User Interfaces* (1995)
LaLonde, *Discovering Smalltalk* (1994)
Pohl, *Object-Oriented Programming Using C++* (1993)
Smith, *IBM Smalltalk: The Language* (1995)
Tkach/Puttick, *Object Technology in Application Development* (1994)
White, *Using the Booch Method* (1994)
White, *Rational Rose Essentials: Using the Booch Method* (1994)

Other Titles of Interest

Fischer/LeBlanc, *Crafting a Compiler in C* (1991)
Kelley/Pohl, *A Book on C, Third Edition* (1995)
Kelley/Pohl, *C by Dissection: The Essentials of C Programming, Second Edition* (1992)
Pohl, *C++ for C Programmers* (1994)
Pohl, *Object-Oriented Programming Using C++* (1993)
Sebesta, *Concepts of Programming Languages, Second Edition* (1993)
Sobell, *A Practical Guide to the UNIX System, Third Edition* (1994)
Weiss, *Data Structures and Algorithm Analysis in C++* (1992)

IBM Smalltalk: The Language

David N. Smith
IBM T. J. Watson Research Center
Hawthorne, NY

The Benjamin/Cummings Publishing Company, Inc.
Redwood City, California • Menlo Park, California
Reading, Massachusetts • New York • Don Mills, Ontario
Wokingham, U.K. • Amsterdam • Bonn • Sydney
Singapore • Tokyo • Madrid • San Juan

Acquisitions Editor: *J. Carter Shanklin*
Executive Editor: *Dan Joraanstad*
Editorial Assistant: *Melissa Standen*
Text Design Consultant: *London Road Design*
Book Design: *BusiSoft Services*

Production Editor: *Ray Kanarr*
Copy Editor: *MaryBeth Lorence*
Proofreader: *Chris Grisonich*
Cover Design: *Yvo Riezebos Design*
Photo Credit: *Courtesy of International Business Machines*

IBM, VisualAge, OS/2, Presentation Manager, and IBM Smalltalk are a trademarks of the International Business Machines Corporation. X Window System and X-WINDOWS are trademarks of the Massachusetts Institute of Technology. UNIX is a trademark of AT&T Bell Laboratories. Other trademarks are the properties of their respective owners.

Many of the designations used by manufacturers and sellers to distinguish their products are claimed as trademarks. Where those designations appear in this book, and Benjamin/Cummings was aware of a trademark claim, the designations have been marked with ® or ™ after the trademark.

Disclaimer of Warranty for Merchantability
The following paragraph does not apply to the United Kingdom or any country where such provisions are inconsistent with the local law:

INTERNATIONAL BUSINESS MACHINES CORPORATION PROVIDES THE PUBLICATION "AS IS" WITHOUT IMPLIED WARRANTY OF ANY KIND, EITHER EXPRESS OR IMPLIED, INCLUDING BUT NOT LIMITED TO, THE IMPLIED WARRANTIES OF MERCHANTABILITY OR FITNESS FOR A PARTICULAR PURPOSE. Some states do not allow disclaimers of express or implied warranties in certain transactions, therefore, this statement may not apply to you.

IBM assumes no responsibility for any infringement of third-party rights that may result from use of this publication or from the manufacture, use, lease, or sale of the programs created using this publication.

Instructional Material Disclaimer
The examples presented in this book have been included for their instructional value. They have been tested with care but are not guaranteed for any particular purpose. The publisher does not offer any warranties or representations, nor does it accept any liabilities with respect to the programs or examples.

The material in this book is for instructional purposes. The author does not offer any warranties or representations, nor does he accept any liabilities with respect to the programs, examples, or other material in this book.

Library of Congress Cataloging-in-Publication Data
Smith, David N.
     IBM Smalltalk: The Language / David N. Smith.
        p.   cm. — (The Benjamin/Cummings series in object-oriented software engineering)
     Includes index.
     ISBN 0-8053-0908-X
     1. Smalltalk (Computer language program) 2. Object-oriented programming
     I. Title. II. Series
QA76.73.S59S65   1994
005.13'3--dc20
                                                94-24584
                                              CIP

ISBN 0-8053-0908-X
1 2 3 4 5 6 7 8 9 10 - DOC - 98 97 96 95 94

The Benjamin/Cummings Publishing Company, Inc.
390 Bridge Parkway
Redwood City, CA, 94065

For Carol, Charles, Katrina, and Noel

Table of Contents

Short

Table of Contents

Expanded

Building Blocks

Examples

Preface

The IBM Smalltalk system is an industrial-strength Smalltalk for the rapid development of business and scientific applications for both in-house use and for software product delivery.

The IBM Smalltalk language is delivered in several products, as *VisualAge* which emphasizes visual construction of interfaces and applications, and as *IBM Smalltalk* which emphasizes a more traditional textual programming approach. Each comes with two levels of development support: team and individual. Each of these runs on a number of platforms, including IBM OS/2, Microsoft Windows, and AIX.

This is a language book. It describes the IBM Smalltalk language and class libraries. Like most books for other languages, this book does not describe the development environment, the compiler, editors, or debuggers, to any great degree. The environment in which Smalltalk programs are written looks, feels, and acts in different ways in VisualAge than in IBM Smalltalk, is different in the team and individual versions, and is different in look and feel across the various implementation platforms. This book concentrates on the language and core libraries, because they are common to and uniform across all products and platforms. This book thus applies to all of the IBM Smalltalk and VisualAge products.

Information specific to a platform is omitted since the book (and IBM Smalltalk) is platform independent. There are no live screen shots, no platform-specific operating system or graphics calls, and no information on installing or starting Smalltalk. Detailed information on the development environment is likewise omitted, since the subject is large, details vary by platform, and the topic deserves a book of its own. Graphics and windowing are introduced in this book, but will be described in detail in a companion volume.

It is assumed that readers know how to program in some language, know the concepts of variable, procedure, parameter, loop, array, number, and so on, and have some experience writing programs for others to use.

If you are already a Smalltalk programmer, you will know most of the material in the early chapters. However, there are some extensions and changes, and it will be worthwhile skimming these chapters.

Goals

The author set out to write a book that was to be specifically for the IBM Smalltalk language. Five goals were set:

- To be a *programmer's* Smalltalk book, practical and for everyday use, and not a theoretical description, or an overview;
- To *support all IBM Smalltalk and VisualAge platforms* by including only portable interfaces, by defining and describing where portability problems are, and by not describing platform-dependent details;
- To be a *reference*, by being complete and useful enough to be keep at hand while programming;
- To emphasize *examples,* from short expressions to code fragments through full programs; and
- To make it easy to *find things* by indexing and cross-referencing extensively.

Parts

The book is divided into four parts: an introduction to concepts and features, more advanced topics, sample programs, and the encyclopedia of classes.

Chapters in Part I introduce the concepts of object-oriented programming, the beginnings of interaction with the Smalltalk system, language elements, blocks and methods, basic classes, collections, and how to write classes.

Part II describes more advanced topics, including graphics, windowing, files and streams, details on variables and scoping, memory management, exception handling, and processes.

Part III contains sample Smalltalk programs.

Part IV is an encyclopedia of Smalltalk classes. It contains more detailed information about the classes and a full description of the public interface to the classes.

Typographic Conventions

Fonts

Text in this book is set in the typeface you are reading right now.

Programs are set in this typeface and are indented.

Words in the program (or code) typeface that appear in body text refer to actual items in a program or in Smalltalk itself. For example:

A SortedCollection keeps it elements in some sorted order.

Numbers

Floating-point numbers in examples are not necessarily shown to the precision readers will see when evaluating the example, since such precision depends on that of the native floating-point hardware and the number formatting code in various releases.

Special Paragraphs

••• Paragraphs marked with three bullets indicate a topic more advanced than the surrounding material; it can be safely skipped on first reading.

Names

All class names start with a capital letter:

SortedCollection
Orbit
Integer
PayrollLedger

Instances of classes are often referred to with class names, but with a leading lower-case letter, with compound names split at word boundaries, and prefaced with *a* or *an*:

- a sorted collection *or* aSortedCollection
- an integer *or* anInteger
- a payroll ledger *or* aPayrollLedger.

Parameters to methods and blocks usually name the expected class of data.

anInteger	An instance of Integer
aString	An instance of String
aPayrollLedger	An instance of PayrollLedger

Sometimes, the instance can be one of any subclass of an abstract class, such as a subclass of Number.

aNumber	An instance of some kind of number

Sometimes, the parameter can be one of several kinds of objects. When possible, the classes are named, as in:

anIntegerOrString	Can be an instance of Integer or of String
aFloatOrFraction	Can be an instance of Float or of Fraction

In other cases, the parameter is simply named for its usage and a note in the text will describe what kind of things it can be.

Acknowledgments

The author would like to thank all those without whom this book would not be possible:

- First and always, the readers of various drafts: Larry Smith and Tony Cianchetta of the IBM Cary Lab; John Prager of IBM T. J. Watson Research Center; Dave Collins formerly of the Watson Center, and now an OOP consultant; and the readers selected by the publisher: David Chapman; Jim Fulton; Herky Gottfried; Mamdouh Ibrahim, EDS/Object-Oriented and AI Services; Mark Kunichika, SABRE Decision Technologies; Junsheng Long, University of North Carolina; Lloyd Martinson, Synergistic Soultions Inc.; Jeff McKenna; and Alok Sharma.

- The IBM Smalltalk and VisualAge teams in Cary, NC, and Dave Thomas and his team in Ottawa, who worked very long weeks for years to make it all possible.

- Skip McGaughey and Chris Weatherly, also of the IBM Cary Lab; Skip suggested this book, and moved unmoveable objects to make it happen; and Chris provided invaluable support.

- My manager, John Richards, whose support and encouragement over the years has been invaluable.

- My editor, Carter Shanklin, who stuck it out even when the mountain looked unmoveable; Jan, of London Road Design, who got a size 18 book into a size 12 cover and made it look better in the process; and Ray Kanarr, my production editor, who saved me from self-inflicted bodily harm during the final weeks before delivery.

And, of course, I can't forget Archie, our Labrador Retriever, who curled up under my feet and slept while I wrote.

Any bugs, glitches, or misunderstandings that might remain are, of course, the sole responsibility of the author.

The author would very much like feedback from readers about any bugs that crept in, about places that were hard to understand, and comments about the book in general. Address them to the author care of the publisher, to the Internet address dnsmith@watson.ibm.com, or to 70167,2274 on CompuServe.

David N. Smith

IBM Smalltalk:
The Language

Part I

Foundations

Part I introduces the concepts of object-oriented programming, the Smalltalk language, control flow, interaction, basic kinds of data, and classes.

Chapter 1: The Landscape
Smalltalk; images; source programs; class libraries; platforms.

Chapter 2: Introduction to Concepts
What objects are; how objects are defined; how objects are used; polymorphism; data hiding; hierarchy; typing data; messages; abstraction; classes.

Chapter 3: Introduction to the Environment
Workspaces; text; selecting text; evaluating text; inspecting objects; simple expressions and interaction; sample code; the transcript.

Chapter 4: Language Elements
The character set; constants; tokens; messages; variables; expressions; statements; conditionals; looping; return; cascaded messages; methods, method formats; blocks; block format; scope of names.

Chapter 5: Basic Classes
Numbers; integers; floating-point; fractions; characters; true and false; dates; times; points; rectangles.

Chapter 6: Collections and Iteration
Creating collections; iteration; fixed-size collections; arrays; strings; ordered collections; sorted collections; bags; dictionaries; sets.

Chapter 7: Creating Classes
Defining classes; access methods; new instances; inheritance; abstraction; self; super; external class format; class Object.

The Landscape

The IBM Smalltalk system is large and rich with function. The language and the base class library, the subject of this book, is but a part of an integrated development system. This chapter surveys the parts of Smalltalk, the platforms on which it runs, and the Smalltalk image, where all development is performed.

The Parts

IBM Smalltalk is broken up into the logical parts in the list below. This book concentrates on those shown in bold.

1) The ***Smalltalk Language*** constants, variables, expressions, conditionals, loops, methods (subroutines), classes (programs), etc.

2) The *Class Libraries*, which come in six parts.

    a) ***Common Language Data Types*** (CLDT): Defines numbers, characters, collections (arrays, strings, and more), common core functions, etc. CLDT is based on the "Blue Book"† and the "Red Book"‡.

    b) ***Common File System*** (CFS): Defines file access. CFS is based on POSIX.1§ and the Blue Book.

---

† A. Goldberg and D. Robson, *Smalltalk-80: The Language and its Implementation*, Addison-Wesley, Reading, MA, 1983.

‡ IBM, *Smalltalk Portability: A Common Base*, IBM International Technical Support Center, Boca Raton, FL, September 1992, order number GC24-3903-00.

§ F. Zlotnick, *The POSIX.1 Standard, A Programmers Guide*, Benjamin/Cummings, Redwood City, CA, 1991.

c) ***Common Process Model*** (CPM): Defines processes and their control. CPM is based on the Blue Book.

d) *Common Language Implementation* (CLI): The compiler, classes, methods, and 'magic' that lets classes be instances of classes. CLI is based on the Blue Book and the Red Book.

e) *Common Graphics* (CG): Drawing on the screen, text, fonts, color, etc. CG is based on X-Windows.††

f) *Common Widgets* (CW): Windows, sub-windows, dialog boxes, controls, buttons, etc. CW is based on OSF/Motif.‡‡

3) The *Development Environment* or the *Multiuser Development Environment* and *Application Delivery Tools*.

4) *Low-Level Interfaces*: user primitives, calling C code, platform dependencies.

5) In *VisualAge*, the visual development environment.

This volume covers the Smalltalk Language, Common Language Data Types, Common File System, and the Common Process Model (1, 2a, 2b, 2c), introduces Common Graphics and Common Widgets (2e, 2f), and very small portions of the development environment (3).

A companion volume, tentatively titled *IBM Smalltalk: Applications and Interfaces*, will cover Common Graphics and Common Widgets (2e and 2f) and other topics. It is planned for 1995 from Benjamin/Cummings.

Details of implementation, the development environment and tools, low-level interfaces, and application delivery tools are covered in product documentation and may be platform specific.

The Platforms

IBM Smalltalk and IBM VisualAge run on a number of platforms, such as IBM OS/2, Microsoft Windows, and IBM's AIX. These platforms differ a lot in both their internals and their visual presentation. A Smalltalk program written on one platform will run on all others, provided that platform dependencies are avoided. Such avoidance is easy, since such portability is intended and system documentation covers the platform-independent interfaces only.

IBM Smalltalk uses the look and feel of the host platform. Windows, buttons, scroll bars, menus, and cursors all have the host system's look and feel.

Code written to the documented interfaces will mainly be portable; now and then some detail will hinder portability and this book points many of these out. These can be differences in function in the operating systems of different platforms, like ways that files are locked for sharing, or the precision of floating-point numbers, which need careful handling if your application depends on them.

---

†† Scheifler and Gettys, *X Window System*, Third Edition, Digital Press, 1992; and A. Nye, ed., *Xlib Programming Manual*, Volumes One and Two, O'Reilly & Associates, Sebastopol, CA, 1988.

‡‡ A. Nye and T. O'Reilly, *X Toolkit Intrinsics Reference Manual*, Volumes Four and Five, O'Reilly & Associates, Sebastopol, CA, 1990-91.

The Image

All Smalltalk programming and execution takes place in an *image.* An image is analogous to a workspace in some languages. The image allows complete integration of programs, tools, the compiler, debuggers, editors, and the process of writing and debugging. Everything is an object in the image, including compiled programs, the debugger itself, and data. The normal process of writing and debugging is completely changed because of the image: running programs are often stopped, traced, data is modified or examined, code is modified, and then execution is resumed. In fact, modifying a running program is the normal way that Smalltalk programs are written, extended, and debugged.

Applications are images from which all development tools and other unneeded things have been removed.

Developing Programs

Smalltalk programs typically live in the image or in an image-owned file, encoded in a special way. Programs can be exported to a regular text file using a *fileout* operation, and imported into the image using a *filein* operation. Exported files have a special format that is human-readable but is not intended to be created by humans.

There is no syntax for certain things for which conventional languages have syntax. The largest entity with its own syntax is a subroutine (Smalltalk calls them *methods*). There is no syntax for a class, or a Smalltalk program, which are defined using interactive tools and are remembered in the image.

The Smalltalk compiler is one of the tools that lives in the image. It is invoked to compile a method when the code is saved, after it is created or modified. Such units of code are typically small in Smalltalk, usually not more than 8-12 lines; the pause for compilation is usually so short that it is not noticed.

The debugger shows the source program and traces execution by highlighting the portion of the source currently active. Variables are shown by name, and they can be examined using an inspector tool; virtually the whole system can be examined while debugging, since it's mainly written in Smalltalk.

The Class Library

The Smalltalk language is really quite small, consisting of very few statements and features. Most of the language is actually written in Smalltalk as class libraries which are collections of objects and procedures that work together.

Objects in Smalltalk include things as simple as numbers and characters, accumulations of objects called collections, more specialized objects such as points, rectangles, dates or times, and many others, including programs and windows.

These are all implemented as classes and, together, form the basic class library that comes with Smalltalk. This library is very rich; most of this book is spent describing this library.

Additional class libraries can be developed, or purchased, and added to the image.

Class libraries tend to be rich in function, usually providing not just the basic functions needed to do something, but a large number of convenience functions that make it easy to do things. As a result, the study of Smalltalk is mainly the study of class libraries.

Further Reading

The Blue Book, the 'Purple Book', and the Red Book:

- A. Goldberg and D. Robson, *Smalltalk-80 The Language and its Implementation*, Addison-Wesley, Reading, MA, 1983.

  This is the original Smalltalk book, often called the Blue Book, since its cover is blue, and it's worth having a copy if you're interested in a high-level description of the implementation of a Smalltalk system. The book may, however, be out of print.

- A. Goldberg and D. Robson, *Smalltalk-80 The Language*, Addison-Wesley, Reading, MA, 1989.

  This is the Blue Book, less the part on implementation. It's cover is purple and it is sometimes called the Purple Book.

- *Smalltalk Portability: A Common Base*, IBM International Technical Support Center, Boca Raton, FL, September 1992, order number GC24-3903-00.

  This IBM publication is a proposal for the core of a standard Smalltalk. It is often called the Red Book.

2

Introduction to Concepts

Object-oriented programming (OOP) is a programming technology. It is not a user interface technology, program design technique, data base technology, or user interaction technique. Each of these other technologies uses the term *object-oriented* in different ways.

OOP, the programming technology, differs from 'traditional' programming technologies in four ways:

Data hiding	Data hiding, sometimes called *encapsulation*, hides data except from a set of routines that belong to the data.
Hierarchy	A hierarchy is a set of hierarchical definitions in which encapsulated data and code inherit code and data from more general sets of encapsulated data and code. Lower-level sets of data and code are said to inherit from higher levels.
Polymorphism	Polymorphism means multiple names; in a program, it simply means that multiple subprograms can have the same name.
Typing of data	Typing data, rather than variables, means that the data itself has a type. Variables can be considered to have no type or can be considered to have but a single type, an object.

This chapter will discuss these four principles, and will introduce simple object-oriented programming using a pseudo-language. When first reading this chapter, it is more important to learn the terms and obtain some idea of the concepts than to study it in detail. The concepts will be addressed again, using Smalltalk syntax, in Chapter 7, 'Creating Classes', on page 85.

Pseudo-code

Throughout this chapter, code will be written in a made-up language that has the concepts of Smalltalk in a syntax similar to C or Pascal.

- Procedures, called *methods*, are invoked by naming them. There is no call keyword nor are parentheses required (as in C when there are no parameters). Methods are called using a *dot* notation: the method crash in an object named car would be invoked by car.crash.

- Variable declarations in the body of a method use the var keyword. A parameter list is a list of argument names.

```
aMethod( arg1, arg2 );
    var a, b, pi;
    var x, y;
```

- Assignment uses colon-equal (:=) and comparison uses equal (=).

```
a := 2 + 3;
if ( a = 5 ) then a := 0;
```

- The fatalError keyword issues a message and terminates the program.
- There is no end statement; if a procedure is written with another following it, then the second ends the first.

Example:

```
computePay( gross );
    var deductions;
    deductions := self.deductions(gross);
    return gross - deductions;
```

object . method

Objects

Objects are simply some grouping of related data with the code that operates on that data. The data can be accessed only from the associated code.

Figure 1 illustrates an object that represents a simple time value of money calculation and its data.

The variables are shown on the left; they are not accessible to code outside of the object. On the right are the methods that *can* access the data. All calculations involving access to the data must occur in these methods. Code can be written, as in setPeriod(), to allow an outsider to provide a value for the variable.

In this particular case, all of the variables can be set from the outside, since methods that set the three variables are provided. No methods are provided for reading the values that are set. Thus, these variables are write-only to outside users.

The future value is calculated and returned by the getFutureValue method; there is no associated variable (but the caller does not know that). The remaining method, calculate, is private. Private methods are for the use of other methods in the object, but are not for outsiders.

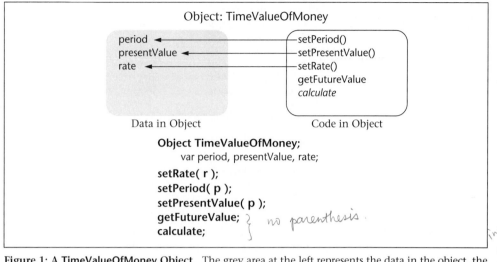

Object: TimeValueOfMoney

period	setPeriod()
presentValue	setPresentValue()
rate	setRate()
	getFutureValue
	calculate

Data in Object   Code in Object

Object TimeValueOfMoney;
    var period, presentValue, rate;

setRate(r);
setPeriod(p);
setPresentValue(p);
getFutureValue; } *no parenthesis.*
calculate;

Figure 1: A TimeValueOfMoney Object. The grey area at the left represents the data in the object, the three variables period, presentValue, and rate. The outlined area at the right represents the methods of the object. Arrows show which methods set which variables. At the bottom is the pseudo-code definition for the object, excluding the body of the methods.

inside of objects there could be several variables.

The methods that allow a variable to be set or read from the outside are called *access methods*; they can perform whatever checks they need on the data before setting it.

    setRate(r);
        if(r <= 0) fatalError('Invalid interest rate');
        rate := r / 100.0;

The method setRate has a parameter r which is checked for validity; if valid, the object's rate value is set.

The method getFutureValue calls calculate and returns the future value.

    getFutureValue;
        if(rate = 0 or period = 0 or presentValue = 0)
            then fatalError('Not all values have been set.');
        return self.calculate; *the current object*

First, if all variables have not been set, a fatal error is raised. Otherwise, the private method calculate is called to perform the calculations.

Invoking a method is called *sending a message;* self.calculate means to send the calculate *message to self.* This invokes a method with the same name as the message, calculate. The name self refers to the current object, the one that owns the code currently being run. (That is, *my* calculate method.) Other objects might also have calculate methods; self indicates which one to call.

The whole TimeValueOfMoney object looks like this:

    Object TimeValueOfMoney;
        var period, presentValue, rate;

    setRate(r);
        if(r <= 0) fatalError('Invalid interest rate.');
        rate := r / 100.0;
    setPeriod(p);
        if(p <= 0) fatalError('Invalid period.');

```
        period := p;
setPresentValue( p );
        if( p <= 0 ) fatalError( 'Invalid present value.' );
        presentValue := p;
getFutureValue;
        if( rate = 0 or period = 0 or presentValue = 0 )
            then fatalError( 'Not all values have been set.' );
        return self.calculate;
calculate;
        return presentValue * exp(period * rate);
```

The object might be used this way by some code outside of the object:

```
...
TimeValueOfMoney.setPeriod( 360 );
TimeValueOfMoney.setPresentValue( 10000.00 );
TimeValueOfMoney.setRate( 5.0 );
value := TimeValueOfMoney.getFutureValue;
```

The TimeValueOfMoney object is asked to setPeriod, setPresentValue, and setRate to the given values. Then it is asked for the future value.

Protocol

The list of methods that is implemented by an object is called the *protocol* of the object. One speaks of the protocol of an object when referring to the whole list of methods. When speaking of some logical subset of the methods, one speaks of, say, the access protocol or the initialization protocol. In any event, 'protocol' is a fancy way to refer to a coherent list of methods.

Classes and Instances

The TimeValueOfMoney example has one set of code and one set of data, but typically applications need one set of code and many sets of data; each identical object should not need to have its own copy of the code.

The obvious solution is to separate the data from the code, so that each set of data refers to the associated code in some way. This lets many instances of the data share one set of code. Smalltalk, and the pseudo-language used here, both make this split, and name the parts *class* and *instance*.

A *class* is the code and the *definition* of the data.

An *instance* is the actual *allocation* of the data. When the term *object* is used, it refers to an instance.

A class is defined very much as was done with the TimeValueOfMoney example. An instance of the class can then be allocated to hold the data; this instance then refers to the class and its procedures. Instances are obtained from the system using a new operator, such as TimeValueOfMoney.new. Obtaining a new instance is sometimes called *instantiation*.

The code for a TimeValueOfMoney class that allows instances is identical to the prior version. The keyword Object is replaced by Class to emphasize the difference.

```
Class  TimeValueOfMoney;
    var period, presentValue, rate;
```

The rest of the definition is the same. Variables defined with the class, period, presentValue, and rate are called *instance variables*. They are unique to each instance of the class.

Instances make TimeValueOfMoney more useful. In the example below, two instances are obtained and used to calculate two different answers. The new keyword gets a new instance each time it is used. Messages are then sent to these instances, rather than to TimeValueOfMoney. Figure 2 illustrates the class and its two instances.

```
1)   var value1, value2, difference, tvm1, tvm2;

2)   tvm1 := TimeValueOfMoney.new;
3)   tvm1.setPeriod( 360 );
4)   tvm1.setPresentValue( 10000.00 );
5)   tvm1.setRate( 5.0 );
6)   value1 := tvm1.getFutureValue;

7)   tvm2 := new( TimeValueOfMoney );
8)   tvm2.setPeriod( 360 );
9)   tvm2.setPresentValue( 10000.00 );
10)  tvm2.setRate( 7.0 );
11)  value2 := tvm2.getFutureValue;

12)  difference := value2 - value1;
```

Line 1 declares variables. Line 2 obtains a new instance of TimeValueOfMoney. In line 3, the setPeriod method is invoked, passing a value of 360. This invocation sends the setPeriod message to the instance held in tvm1.

Line 4 sends the setPresentValue message to the instance in tvm1, passing 10000.00.

Line 6 sends the getFutureValue message to tvm1; the value is returned and saved in value1.

In lines 7-11, the identical process is followed for a new instance which is held in tvm2. Finally, in line 12, a difference is calculated.

Abstraction and Refinement

Classes model something: a concept like time value of money, real objects like stocks or bonds, cars, windows on a display screen, aircraft engines, or optical fiber interconnections in a network.

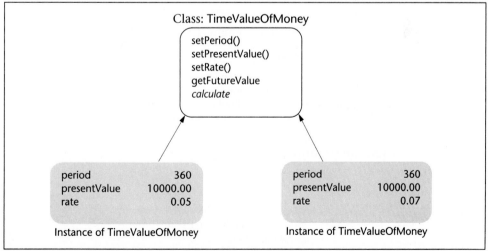

Figure 2: Instances and Their Class. The class, TimeValueOfMoney, is shown at the top. Two instances, the grey shapes at the bottom, hold two sets of data; each instance refers to the class. When a messages are sent to an instance, the system thus knows which code is associated with the instance.

Frequently, the things modeled are very similar, such as various financial instruments that pay interest, various kinds of vehicles for transportation, or interconnections between many kinds of things.

Classes can be defined in terms of other, more general classes. Such definitions form a *hierarchy,* which is sometimes called a *class tree.* Hierarchies are outlines, like an author might make for an article she is about to write. The top is the most general concept; lower levels in the outline add more detail to the level immediately above.

Hierarchies are used in object-oriented programming to define a general concept, and then to refine it to a level of detail which matches the problem at hand.

Stocks and bonds might be parts of the general concept of a financial instrument.

```
FinancialInstrument
    Stock
    Bond
    Mortgage
    TreasuryBill
```

Stocks and bonds come in many types, each with somewhat different characteristics. A hierarchy should reflect such distinctions when they are important.

```
Financial Instrument
    Stocks
        Common
        Preferred
    Bonds
        TaxFree
        Taxable
    Mortgage
    TreasuryBill
```

Engines might be defined in a hierarchy that classifies many kinds of engines. Turbines and reciprocating engines are two very different types of mechanism.

```
Engine
    Turbine
    ReciprocatingEngine
```

Turbines and reciprocating engines come in different types.

```
Engine
    Turbine
        SteamTurbine
        GasTurbine
    ReciprocatingEngine
        ExternalCombustionEngine
        InternalCombustionEngine
```

These can be further classified.

```
Engine
    Turbine
        SteamTurbine
            FixedSpeedSteamTurbine
            VariableSpeedSteamTurbine
        GasTurbine
            AircraftEngine
            MarineTurbine
    ReciprocatingEngine
        ExternalCombustionEngine
```

```
                        SteamEngine
                 InternalCombustionEngine
                     DieselCycleEngine
                     OttoCycleEngine
                     TwoCycleEngine
```

The structure, detail, and depth of the hierarchy depends upon the needs of the application designer. This Engine hierarchy would be inappropriate for a jet engine manufacturer, providing detail where it is not needed and leaving out structure that is important. It might be quite useful to a student learning about engines.

Layers of abstractions provide the structure on which classes are based. Each level in a hierarchy defines a new class. In this example, there would be an Engine class, a Turbine class, a GasTurbine class and an AircraftEngine class. Each class will define data and methods that are applicable to its level of detail. The class FinancialInstrument will define data and methods that are common to all kinds of financial instruments, while Stock defines additional data and/or methods that refine FinancialInstrument into a model of a stock.

A Turbine is very different from a ReciprocatingEngine, and the data and methods each defines reflects those differences. A SteamTurbine and a GasTurbine are more similar, but still differ in detail. AircraftEngine and MarineTurbine are even more similar, but differ in lesser details.

At each level of a class hierarchy, the concepts are a *refinement* of the concepts of the next higher level. A SteamTurbine is a refinement of the concept of Turbine. A SteamTurbine differs from its sibling GasTurbine in how the concept of Turbine is refined. A steam turbine runs by expanding hot, pressurized steam. A gas turbine expands a hot, pressurized (and possibly still burning) mixture of air, fuel, and combustion products. These differences cause many details to vary: the pressures are different, the blade angles are different, the materials are different, and as a result some of the code must be different.

The parent, Turbine, encapsulates those concepts and calculations of a turbine that are common to all turbines. The children refine the concepts and calculations for a particular kind of turbine.

But, if all we want is an aircraft engine or a common stock, why do all this work? There are several reasons:

- It helps us understand the problem.

- It is rare that a given organization, or large computer program for that matter, has just single, unrelated concepts to work with. A financial institution works with many kinds of financial instruments, many of which are very complex and differ from others only in certain details. Payroll systems have many kinds of employees, deductions and financial institutions to work with.

- Writing code in a hierarchy lets it be reused in a natural way. Adding a new kind of bond or a new kind of engine takes much less work, because the code in higher-level classes can be immediately reused.

- Observation of well-designed hierarchies shows that it is quite common for there to be a significant amount of code at surprisingly high levels of the hierarchy, and often relatively little at lower levels. Design and coding in a hierarchy produces more abstract designs and thus more general code.

An Example

Employees of a corporation come in different types: hourly, salaried, part time, executive, temporary, retired, etc. This example will abstract the concept of employee to just hourly and salaried employees.

It is often the case that classes higher in the hierarchy are not intended to have instances. They are called *abstract classes*. Classes lower in the hierarchy, which are intended to have instances, are called *concrete classes*. Class Employee will be an abstract class, while classes Hourly and Salaried will be concrete classes. Abstract classes are often shown in italics.

> *Employee*
> Hourly
> Salaried

Each class in the hierarchy will have some data associated with it. Class Employee defines five variables. Class Hourly defines two new variables, and class Salaried defines one new variable.

each variable represents a feature of the class.

Class	Variables
Employee	name address id crUnionDeduct taxRate
Hourly	hourlyRate hours
Salaried	annualSalary

Class Hourly and class Salaried inherit the five variables of Employee. This means, each instance of Hourly actually has seven variables: name, address, id, crUnionDeduct, taxRate, hourlyRate, and hours.

Each employee has deductions for the credit union and for taxes, and these calculations can be based on data held just in Employee, so a deductions method would go in the class Employee. The techniques for calculating pay depend on the type of employee, and use data specific to Hourly and Salaried, so these methods go with these *subclasses*.

Class	Methods
Employee	deductions
Hourly	computePay
Salaried	computePay

The code for deductions in Employee looks like this:

```
deductions( gross );                    /* Class Employee */
     return gross * taxRate + crUnionDeduct;
```

This deductions method takes one parameter, the gross pay, and computes the amount of deductions. It refers to two instance variables, taxRate and crUnionDeduct, which are part of the class definition. Both Salaried and Hourly are said to *inherit* this method; it will act just as if it were written explicitly for, and in, these classes.

The method for computePay in Salaried is:

```
computePay;                             /* Class Salaried */
     var gross;
     gross := annualSalary / 52;
     return gross - self.deductions(gross);
```

The method for computePay in Hourly is:

```
computePay;                              /* Class Hourly */
    var gross;
    gross := hourlyRate * hours;
    return gross - self.deductions(gross);
```

The method in Hourly starts by calculating gross from hourlyRate and hours, which are instance variables. It then sends the deductions message to self. While deductions was written higher in the hierarchy, it acts as if it were a part of Hourly, and it is invoked just as if it were.

The definition of all three classes is shown below, with subclasses indented to show the hierarchy. (Methods to access instance variables are not shown to keep down the amount of code in the example.) The Class statement is extended to show the *parent* class. Figure 3 shows the relationship of the three classes and of two possible instances.

```
Class Employee;
    var name, address, id, crUnionDeduct, taxRate;
    deductions( gross );
        return gross * taxRate + crUnionDeduct;

    Class Salaried of Employee;
        var annualSalary;
    computePay;
        var gross;
        gross := annualSalary / 52;
        return gross - self.deductions(gross);

    Class Hourly of Employee;
        var hourlyRate, hours;
    computePay;
```

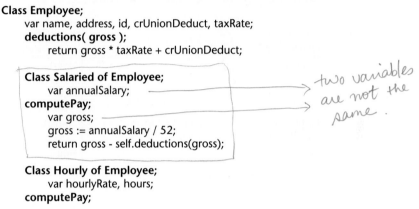

two variables are not the same.

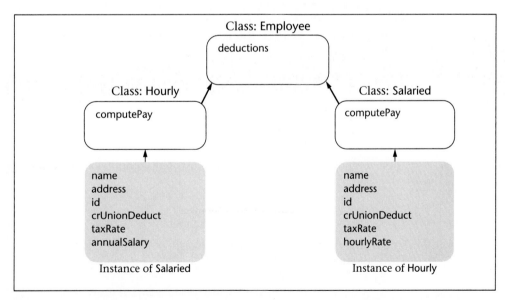

Instance of Salaried   Instance of Hourly

Figure 3: Class Employee and its Subclasses. The two subclasses of class Employee, Hourly and Salaried, each have an instance (in grey). The darker arrows are pointers from a subclass to its parent. The lighter arrows are pointers from an instance to its class.

```
var gross;
gross := hourlyRate * hours;
return gross - self.deductions(gross);
```

Some other method in another object, partly shown below, will send the computePay message to an instance of Hourly or Salaried held in the variable anEmployee. This variable is filled in (by code not shown) with the appropriate instance for the next employee to be processed.

The sending code will not know whether it is sending the computePay message to an instance of Hourly or to an instance of Salaried.

```
pay := anEmployee.computePay.
...
```

Figure 4 shows the execution of the computePay message for both salaried and hourly employees.

Employee is Salaried		Employee is Hourly	
Class: Method	Code	Class: Method	Code
Salaried: computePay	gross := annualSalary / 52;	Hourly: computePay	gross := hourlyRate * hours;
Salaried: computePay	self.deductions(gross)	Hourly: computePay	self.deductions(gross);
Employee: deductions	return gross*taxRate + crUnionDeduct	Employee: deductions	return gross*taxRate + crUnionDeduct
Salaried: computePay	return gross - *returnedValue*	Hourly: computePay	return gross - *returnedValue*

Figure 4: Execution of Message computePay.

Generalizing

The two computePay methods differ only in the one line where the calculation of the gross pay is made. If gross pay were calculated in a separate method, computeGross, then computePay could be the same for both classes. Figure 5 illustrates the result.

The method for computeGross in Salaried is:

```
computeGross;
    return annualSalary / 52;
```

The method for computeGross in Hourly is:

```
computeGross;
    return hourlyRate * hours;
```

Then computePay can call computeGross. The computePay method now looks like this:

```
computePay;
    var gross;
    gross := self.computeGross;
    return gross - self.deductions(gross);
```

Since computePay is now the same for both subclasses, it can be moved up to Employee. The class now looks like this:

```
Class Employee;
    var name, address, id, crUnionDeduct, taxRate;
    deductions( gross );
        return gross * taxRate + crUnionDeduct;
    computePay;
        var gross;
```

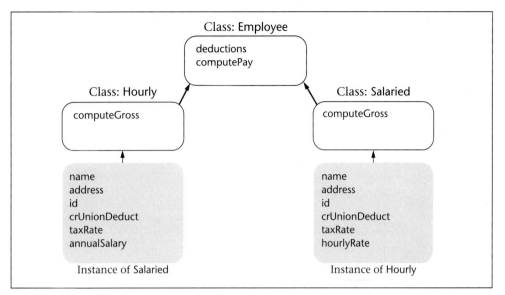

Figure 5: Updated Employee and its Subclasses. The two subclasses of class Employee, Hourly and Salaried, updated to share the computePay method. The darker arrows are pointers from a subclass to its parent. The lighter arrows are pointers from an instance to its class.

```
        gross := self.computeGross;
        return gross - self.deductions(gross);

    Class Salaried of Employee;
        var annualSalary;
    computeGross;
        return annualSalary / 52;

    Class Hourly of Employee;
        var hourlyRate, hours;
    computeGross;
        return hourlyRate * hours;
```

could be the same name since in different class.

Now, when the computePay message is sent to, say, an instance of Hourly, there isn't a computePay method in Hourly, but the new method in Employee is inherited and it is invoked. It immediately sends the computeGross message to self. But what is self? Is it Employee?

The name self always refers to the current instance, and that is an instance of Hourly, so the computeGross message belonging to Hourly is invoked.

Figure 6 shows the execution of a computePay message for Hourly and Salaried.

While all of the code being executed is done on behalf of a particular instance of Salaried or Hourly, almost all of the code is general to both. Only short calculations in computeGross make the two classes different.

Adding a Subclass

Executives get paid too; an Executive class will have an additional deduction for a stock plan. Since executives are also salaried employees, the concept of executive is a refinement of salaried employee, so a class that represents executives is best placed under **Salaried**.

Employee is Salaried		Employee is Hourly	
Class: Method	*Code*	**Class: Method**	*Code*
Employee: computePay	gross := self.computeGross;	**Employee:** computePay	gross := self.computeGross;
Salaried: computeGross	return annualSalary / 52;	**Hourly:** computeGross	return hourlyRate * hours;
Employee: computePay	self.deductions(gross)	**Employee:** computePay	self.deductions(gross);
Employee: deductions	return gross*taxRate + crUnionDeduct	**Employee:** deductions	return gross*taxRate + crUnionDeduct
Employee: computePay	return gross - *returnedValue*	**Employee:** computePay	return gross - *returnedValue*

Figure 6: Execution of Message computePay.

Class	*Variables*
Employee	name address id crUnionDeduct taxRate
Hourly	hourlyRate hours
Salaried	annualSalary
Executive	**stockDeduct**

Executive will need a new deductions method.

Class	*Methods*
Employee	deductions computePay
Hourly	computeGross
Salaried	computeGross
Executive	**deductions**

The computeGross method of Salaried works fine for executives since executives are salaried employees. The new deductions method for Executive could look like this:

```
deductions( gross );
    return pay * taxRate + crUnionDeduct + stockDeduct
```

It is just a copy of the deductions method from Employee with one change (shown in bold). It does, however, copy code; it is better if details, such as how the tax deduction is computed, are done in one place. What we want is to call the method in Employee that knows how to calculate deductions, and then modify the resulting value. A better deductions method for Executive is then:

```
deductions( gross );
    return super.deductions( gross ) + stockDeduct
```

The name super refers to the same object as self, but causes a message-send to look upwards in the class hierarchy for the deductions method. If self were used here, the same deductions method would be invoked over and over. Figure 7 shows how super is executed.

loop forever

In this case, the deductions method in Employee is invoked and computes the deductions. When it returns, the additions for Executive are made.

The class now looks like this:

```
Class Employee;
    var name, address, id, crUnionDeduct, taxRate;
deductions( gross );
```

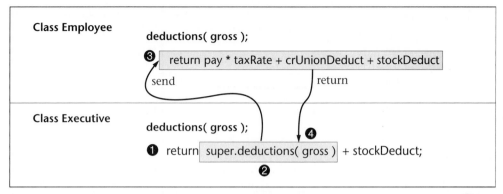

Figure 7: Using super in an Expression. The execution of deductions in Executive (bottom) ❶, encounters a message send to super ❷. The message name is deductions, the name of the current method; instead of reinvoking the current method, super looks in the parent, and in the parent's parent, and so on, until another deductions method is found (in Employee). ❸. That one is invoked; when it returns, its return value is used ❹.

```
            return gross * taxRate + crUnionDeduct;
computePay;
    var gross;
    gross := self.computeGross;
    return gross - self.deductions(gross);

    Class Salaried of Employee;
        var annualSalary;
    computeGross;
        return annualSalary / 52;

        Class Executive of Salaried;
            var stockDeduct;
        deductions( gross );
            return super.deductions( gross ) + stockDeduct;

    Class Hourly of Employee;
        var hourlyRate, hours;
    computeGross;
        return hourlyRate * hours;
```

Figure 8 compares the invocation of computePay for a salaried employee and an executive, assuming that the code is invoked with aSalaried computePay and anExecutive computePay.

Four Principles

The four principles of object-oriented languages have been illustrated by the hierarchies and code developed in this chapter.

Employee is instance of *Salaried*		Employee is instance of *Executive*	
Class: Method	*Code*	*Class: Method*	*Code*
Employee: computePay	gross := self.computeGross;	**Employee:** computePay	gross := self.computeGross;
Salaried: computeGross	return annualSalary / 52;	**Salaried:** computeGross	return annualSalary / 52;
Employee: computePay	self.deductions(gross)	**Employee:** computePay	self.deductions(gross);
Employee: deductions	return gross*taxRate + crUnionDeduct	**Executive:** deductions	... super.deductions(gross) ...
		Employee: deductions	return gross*taxRate + crUnionDeduct
		Executive: deductions	return returnedvalue + stockDeduct
Employee: computePay	return gross - *returnedvalue*	**Employee:** computePay	return gross - *returnedvalue*

Figure 8: Execution of Message **computePay**.

Encapsulation (Data Hiding)

Data hiding is an old concept, and has been implemented in several more conventional languages, most famously the Modula languages and their follow-on, Oberon, in Ada and even in Fortran-90. Data hiding is often called *encapsulation*.

Encapsulation means that access to data is controlled by the 'owner' of the data and that access only occurs by using a method belonging to the owner to perform that access. Users of class TimeValueOfMoney can access all of the data, but only to set it. Users of class Employee and its subclasses cannot access any data in the classes since there are no access methods. (Access methods should have been provided for all data but were omitted to keep the example smaller.)

Encapsulation has both advantages and disadvantages.

The important disadvantage is:

• It is harder for non-owners to change data. One cannot simply fetch a value from a global data structure, or modify it. One has to ask: 'Hey! Ms. Data Owner, please give me that value.'

The advantages are:

• It is harder for non-owners to change data. One cannot simply fetch a value from a global data structure, or modify it. One has to ask: 'Hey! Ms. Data Owner, please give me that value.'

   All access to data from outside the object is controlled; there are no hidden accesses that someone put in one day, in a routine far away, when in a hurry to fix a bug. Access to data can be monitored (does anyone use this data anymore?). Access to data that doesn't need exposure can be prevented.

• The data structures can be changed at any time in the future, without major impact on other classes, since no one but the owners see the data structure anyway.

Polymorphism

(1). lower level share the intance variables with higher level
(2)   4 ↝ inherit methods in upper level.
(3) The use of "self" to "super".

Conventional languages allow just one subroutine with a given name. Smalltalk, and other OOP languages, allow multiple methods with the same name. This is possible because different objects (each with its own set of methods) define different contexts, and each context can have methods with the same name.

Polymorphism is useful because it allows refinement: a deductions method in a parent can be refined in a child. Both will have the same name. Both do what the name suggests, but in different contexts the specific actions differ.

Polymorphism also prevents name clashes between two methods in completely unrelated classes.

Hierarchy, Inheritance, and Refinement

Hierarchies are outlines (or trees) of definitions. Inheritance is a property of a hierarchy in which definitions higher in the hierarchy become properties of lower definitions. Classes lower in the hierarchy are said to *inherit* data and methods from their *superclasses*.

The FinancialInstrument, Engine, and Employee hierarchies illustrate refinement in action.

Inheritance provides several benefits:

- More general code: code written for higher and often quite abstract levels does not know about refinements at lower levels, and cannot inadvertently use them.
- While it is not always true, it is typical that lower levels often have very little code; much of the code ends up being written higher up in the hierarchy.
- It is usually easy to reuse the code higher in the hierarchy simply by adding a new lower level with additional characteristics.

There is one small caveat: learning to program well in a hierarchy is non-trivial. It requires a lot of forgetting of old techniques, and learning of new ones, but it is worth the effort.

Single Variable Type

Smalltalk variables have no type. While variable names must be declared, the declaration is simply a list of names. In Smalltalk, data is typed instead. One object might be an integer, and another a RetiredEmployee. Or, the same variable might 'hold' an integer for a while, and then a RetiredEmployee, or a floating-point number.†

The following code illustrates this (again in pseudo-code):

```
x = 2;
x = sqrt(x);
```

The first value in x is an integer, 2. The second value is a floating-point number with a value of 1.4142... .

Other authors call this fourth property by other names, such as 'typed data', or 'everything is an object'.

---

† Strictly speaking, variables usually don't hold the instance; they hold pointers to it.

Summary

In Smalltalk, everything is an object; all code is associated with data and all data has its associated code. No method can exist except in conjunction with its data; there is no concept of a stand-alone function that calculates, say, the square root of a number or a check-digit for an ISBN.

Methods are invoked by sending a message to an object. The name of the message is the name of the method that is to be invoked.

Abstraction and refinement are the process of developing a hierarchy of classes, and filling it in with methods and data.

The four concepts defined herein (encapsulation, polymorphism, hierarchy and inheritance, and a single variable type) work together:

- Encapsulation provides a clean concept of data and code.

  The other three build on encapsulation and interact with each other.

- Inheritance encourages abstractions, the definition of a general idea and then, in subclasses, more refined or specific abstractions, until finally a concrete representation is realized.

  Class Employee is such a general idea; its subclasses refine and make concrete its concepts.

- Polymorphism makes hierarchical definitions more useful; it allows various lower-level definitions, which inherit a characteristic, to refine or replace the definition of that characteristic; otherwise each enhancement would require a different name and code would be much less general.

  Both the computeGross and deduction methods in class Employee and its subclasses illustrate polymorphism.

- A variable that holds anything is required for polymorphism to work, since otherwise the variable would have to be typed with the kind of object, and that would directly specify the name to use.

Further Reading

If you would prefer a more gentle introduction to Smalltalk and OOP, this book of the author's may be for you:

- Smith, David N. *Concepts of Object Oriented Programming*, McGraw-Hill, 1991.

  This book introduces object oriented programming slowly, showing why it is useful, and introducing each concept slowly and carefully using Smalltalk. It is small, just 160 small-format pages of text, heavily illustrated, and provides numerous examples.

A less detailed and broader-scoped introduction to OOP is:

- Taylor, David A., *Object-Oriented Technology: A Manager's Guide*, Addison-Wesley, 1991.

  A guide for managers that explains object-oriented technology in simple, direct terms, and shows the business benefits.

3

Introduction to the Environment

Small examples proliferate throughout this book. They are intended to be evaluated and explored as you read the book. This chapter introduces interaction with the Smalltalk development environment, showing how to evaluate small bits of code, look inside objects, find and view the files that contain the examples and sample programs from the book, and how to write to the system transcript.

These examples are gathered together into files so that they can be evaluated directly. This file of machine-readable materials is available across Internet and other networks and services, and by mail. See access and ordering information at the very back of the book.

Because IBM Smalltalk and IBM VisualAge are available for a number of platforms, it is not possible to show a screen image that will look familiar to all users. Screen illustrations herein are generic, and are simplified by removing unneeded detail.

Chapter 10, 'Programming Interaction', on page 119 contains some additional information on the development environment. Since details vary, depending on which product is being used, the best source of information on the development environment is the documentation that comes with a particular IBM VisualAge or IBM Smalltalk product.

Workspaces

A workspace is a special window that contains text. Workspaces can be opened on any text file and can contain any text whatsoever. Empty workspaces can also be opened and any desired text entered.

Text is selected with the mouse in the usual way; see platform documentation for information. Once text is selected, it can be cut, pasted, etc. It can be operated on as

Smalltalk code; there are three slightly different commands that are selected from menus or the keyboard.

Display	Evaluate the selection as a Smalltalk expression, and display the result immediately after the selection in the workspace.
Evaluate	Evaluate the selection as a Smalltalk expression, but do not show the result.
Inspect	Evaluate the selection as a Smalltalk expression, and open an Inspect window on the result.

Paragraphs of code will be flagged to indicate which way to evaluate an expression. The machine-readable materials contain each of the expressions below, and both the example number and the corresponding page number where they are found.

" **Evaluate the expression;** *display* **the object that results.**"
2 + 3

Example 1, Display

" **Evaluate the expression; do not display or inspect** "
2 + 3

Example 2, Execute

" **Evaluate the expression;** *inspect* **the object that results** "
2 + 3

Example 3, Inspect

Sample Code Files

The numbered examples in this book are held in files in the machine-readable materials. Those for Part I are in a file named IBMSTEX1.ST. A workspace can be opened on this file by using the File menu of any window, and then selecting open. (See Figure 9).

The items in the file are listed by the page number where they are defined and by example number. Once you find the example in the file, select the example, including its comments if you wish, and display, inspect, or execute it.

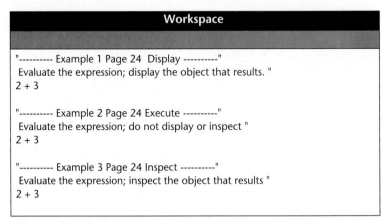

Figure 9: Workspace Showing Examples. This workspace is open on the file that holds the machine-readable materials for Part I of this book.

Simple Evaluations

Open a workspace and type in:

> 2 + 3

Select the expression. The workspace should look something like this.

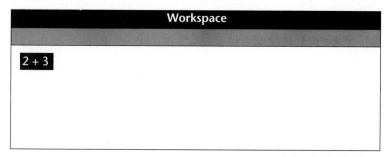

Choose Display. After evaluation, the expression is deselected, and the result is displayed and automatically selected. The workspace should now look like this:

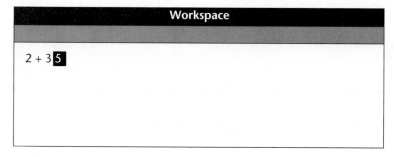

On most platforms it is easy to delete the result by doing a cut or by pressing the delete key.

Evaluate the expression in Example 4. (Double quotes delimit comments.)

> " **Evaluate 10 factorial** "
> 10 factorial
> " Answer: 3628800 "

Example 4, Display

Factorial is the name of a method, used here like a function name; such names come behind the expression they apply to.

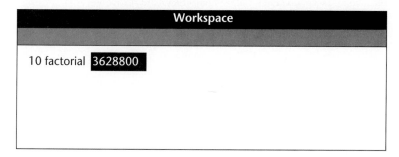

Try this:

> " **Square root of the sum of the squares** "
> (3 squared + 4 squared) sqrt
> " Answer: 5.0 "

Example 5, Display

Now try:

> " **Concatenate two strings** "
> 'This is a ', 'string'
> " Answer: 'This is a string' "

Example 6, Display

The comma between the two strings is the concatenation operator.

Errors and Debugging

If a runtime error occurs while an expression is being evaluated, a debugger window will appear. It looks like Figure 10. The error message will be displayed in the top left corner (where 'ERROR MESSAGE' appears in the figure). It may be necessary to scroll right to see it all.

Smalltalk Debugger	
'ERROR MESSAGE' in UIProcess:5398{suspended,3}	no variables selected

```
[ ] in ExceptionEvent class>> #initializeSystemExecption
ExceptionEvent>>#applyDefaultHandler:
... more lines ...
UndefinedObject>>#Doit
... more lines ...
... more lines ...
... more lines ...
```

Into	Over	Return	Resume

```
UIProcess
    Name: 5398
    Process State: suspended
    Priority: 3
    Executing in: ExceptionalEvent class>>#initializeSystemExceptions

    Error string: halt encountered
```

Figure 10: The Debugger Window.

The window just below contains a traceback of execution, including calls to get from the expression that caused the error into the debugger. Somewhere in this list is a line that looks like:

> UndefinedObject>>#Doit

It may be necessary to scroll down to see it. Select this line to display the expression that caused the error. The last expression executed will be highlighted. See the section on 'Debugging' on page 130 for additional information on the debugger.

Inspecting Objects

Inspecting is very similar to displaying, except that after evaluation a window appears. In simple cases it may just show the same information that would have been displayed in the workspace, but when the object is more complex, the variables in the object can be seen, and inspected themselves.

Points are objects that hold *x* and *y* values representing a coordinate on an *x-y* plane. They are created by writing the *x* value, an at-sign (@), and the *y* value: 4@7 is a point with an *x* value of 4 and a *y* value of 7.

    " **Make a point; inspect it** "
    4.225 @ 7.185

Example 7, Inspect

Select the expression and inspect it. A window will pop up:

Inspect Point	
self	4.225@7.185
x	
y	

The list at the left shows the internal variables of the object, just self, x, and y in this case. The name self is highlighted and its value, the value of the object, is displayed in the text area at the right. Selecting the next variable, typically by clicking on it or by pressing the down arrow key, displays its value in the text area.

Inspect Point	
self	4.225
x	
y	

Now try inspecting this array constant:

    " **Inspect an array constant** "
    #(3.1415927 1776 1970 2001)

Example 8, Inspect

The list area now holds numbers that are the indexes into the array, and the text area holds values. The first element is selected and displayed below.

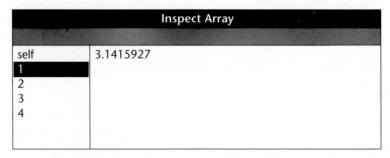

Example 9 produces a rectangle from two points.

" **Create a rectangle and inspect it**"
(2 @ 3) corner: (4 @ 5)   *Example 9, Inspect*

The inspector will show self, origin, and corner. The variables origin and corner are points.

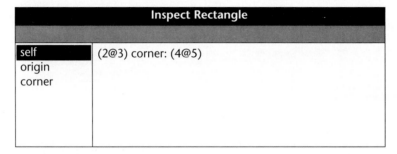

Double-click on origin (or select it, then choose Inspect from a menu) to open another inspect window. It shows the origin point 2@3.

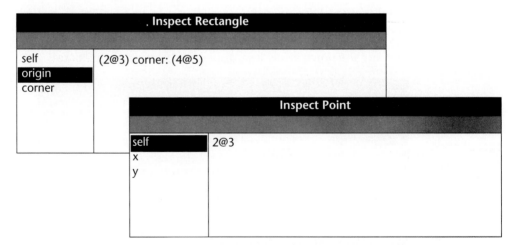

Transcript

The Transcript is a special kind of workspace that is always open in the development environment; closing it exits the Smalltalk system. The transcript initially holds copyright information. It is used to log activities and some kinds of errors. Programs can write to it, and it is a simple and useful place to display 'printed' output from sample programs.

```
" Hello, World! in Smalltalk "
Transcript show: 'Hello, World!'
```
Example 10, Execute

This text looks like this in the Transcript.

Transcript
This Product Release 9.7.1g (C) Copyright whenever by...
Hello, World!

The Transcript is an object, and show: is a message to it. Another message, cr, starts a new line.

```
" Continuing Hello World "
Transcript cr.                          " Move down to next line "
Transcript show: 'How y''all doin''?'
```
Example 11, Execute

Transcript
This Product Release 9.7.1g (C) Copyright whenever by...
Hello, World! How y'all doin'?

Summary

The basics of interaction with a Smalltalk system includes using workspaces to evaluate small bits of code or as viewers or editors of files on a disk. Objects answered by the evaluation of expressions can be viewed using inspectors.

Simple terminal-like output can be directed to the Transcript window from within running programs.

points:
1) minus sign
2) 3 ways of sending message
3) no operator precedence. all from left to right.
4) first unary, then binary, then keyword

4

Language Elements

This chapter describes the syntax of basic elements of the IBM Smalltalk language, including the character set, comments, names, constants, messages, variables, expressions, statements, conditional execution, looping, methods, and blocks.

Basic Elements

The Character Set

Smalltalk uses the following characters:

abcdefghijklmnopqrstuvwxyz	Lower-case letters
ABCDEFGHIJKLMNOPQRSTUVWXYZ	Upper-case letters
1234567890	Numbers
, + / \ * ~ < > = @ % | & ?	Special characters
[ ] { } ( ) ^ ; $ _ : !	Special characters
blank, tab, return, form feed, line feed	White space
"	Comment beginning and end

Other characters that may be available on a given platform can be used in strings.

Comments

Smalltalk comments are enclosed in double quotes; comments may not be nested and may not contain double quotes. Comments may be placed wherever white space is allowed.

```
" HI! I am a Smalltalk comment! "
volume := height * width * depth.  " Calculate volume of box "
```

Names

Names are composed of upper- and lower-case letters, numbers, and underscores, with a leading letter or underscore. It is common to use imbedded upper-case letters to enhance readability. There is no practical limit on the length of names.

```
a
_2
rate
CheckBook
amortizedAnnualMortgageRate
listOfRiversAndStreamsAndFloodsOnThemInThisCentury
list_of_rivers_and_streams_and_floods_on_them_in_this_century
```

Constants

Smalltalk has number, string, character, and boolean constants, plus constants for a special kind of string, called a symbol, and for constant arrays. Constants are objects and are instances of some class.

Some constants are collections of other constants: string literals are collections of characters, and array constants are collections of any constant. Constant collections are forced to be read-only, and any attempt to change them results in a runtime error.

Numeric Constants

Smalltalk has constants for integer numbers, floating-point numbers, and fractions. Fractions have two integer values, a numerator and a denominator. This section describes these constants. A detailed summary of numeric constants is in the section on 'Numeric Constants Summary' on page 457.

Integer Constants

Integer numbers have no practical limit on the size of the numbers. While most languages limit integers to 16 or 32 bits (2 or 4 bytes), Smalltalk allows integers to grow to a very large size. On some platforms, the maximum size can be tens of thousands of *bytes* or more. This means that the largest number that can be represented could be 2^{100000} or larger. While the maximum size is platform dependent, it is guaranteed to be huge.

```
1
-176
234
265252859812191058636308480000000   "30 factorial"
```

Scientific notation can be used for integers:

```
2e1              "Has the value 20"
10e8             "Has the value 100000000"
```

Integer constants cannot have a plus sign; while -8 is allowed, +8 is not.

Integers of other bases are written using the format:

> base **r** *digits*

(but without blanks), where *base* is a decimal integer number, 'r' is the lowercase letter 'r', and *digits* are one or more digits from the string below, with 10 being A, 11 being B, etc. Only upper-case letters may be used.

'0123456789ABCDEFGHIJKLMNOPQRSTUVWXYZ'.

```
" Integer constants with radix; evaluate each line separately  † "
16rFF                    "Has the value 255"
16r10                    "Has the value 16"
16r-10                   "Has the value -16"
36rZ                     "Has the value 35"
10r129                   "Has the value 129"
8r1                      "Has the value 1"
8r-10                    "Has the value  -8"
3r1210                   "Has the value 48"
2r1000                   "Has the value 8"
36rSMALLTALK             "Has the value 80738163270632"        Example 12, Display
```

Floating-Point Constants

Floating-point numbers have the same basic formats as integer numbers, but also have a decimal point. The decimal point cannot be the last character in the constant, since a trailing period means the end of a Smalltalk statement.

```
        -1.0
        234.321
```

Floating-point constants may also have exponents; the exponent is indicated by a lower-case 'e' and a following positive or negative integer.

```
" Floating-point numbers with exponents; evaluate each line separately "
2.0e1                    "Has the value 20.0"
10.0e8                   "Has the value 1.0e9"
-10.0e-8                 "Has the value -0.0000001"            Example 13, Display
```

In addition, floating-point constants may be written in other radixes by prefacing the constant with a radix indicator.

```
" Floating-point numbers with a radix; evaluate each line separately "
16rF.0                   "Has the value 15.0"
16rF.0e1                 "Has the value 240.0"
16r2E1                   "Has the value 737 (The 'E1' is not an exponent!)"
16r2e1                   "Has the value 32 (The 'e1' is an exponent)"
16r2E1e1                 "Has the value 11792 (The 'e1' is an exponent)"
2r10.0                   "Has the value 2.0"
2r1.0e1                  "Has the value 2.0"
36rZ.0                   "Has the value 35.0"
36rSMALL.TALK            "Has the value 48069417.81373362"     Example 14, Display
```

Fraction Constants

Fraction objects are a ratio of two integers: 2/3 is an expression that produces a fraction. The fraction has a numerator of 2 and a denominator of 3.

The only fraction constants are integers with negative exponents.

```
" Fraction constants; evaluate each line separately "
2e-1                     "The value 2/10, which is simplified to 1/5"
12e-3                    "The value 12/1000, which is simplified to 3/250"   Example 15, Display
```

---

† "Evaluate each line separately" makes most sense when you read it in the machine-readable file of examples; it's shown here so that the book and the files are identical. Throughout the book there will be occasional notes intended mainly for users of the machine-readable materials.

String Constants

String constants consist of zero or more characters enclosed within single quote marks. String constants may include any character representable on the host system, including all of the characters that make up the tokens of the Smalltalk language. Single-quote characters in a string are represented by two successive single-quote characters. There is no practical limit on the length of string constants. String constants are read-only; attempts to change them result in a runtime error.

```
'a'
'abcdefghijklmnopqrstuvwxyz'
'0123456789'
'it isn''t'
```

Character Constants

Character constants consist of a dollar sign followed by one other character. The character may be any character representable on the host system, including all of the characters that make up the tokens of the Smalltalk language. A blank character is thus a dollar sign followed by a blank, and a dollar sign character is represented by a dollar sign followed by a dollar sign.

```
$a $b $c $d $x $y $z
$A $B $C $D $X $Y $Z
$1 $@ $* $& $-
$$
```

Boolean Constants

Smalltalk has special reserved names for boolean values: true and false. Arithmetic expressions and numeric constants do not evaluate to booleans.

```
true
false
```

Symbol Constants

Symbol constants are special strings starting with a number sign (#). They have two formats:

1) The body of the symbol is any valid variable name or message name.

```
#size
#<=
#at:put:
```

2) The body of the symbol is a string containing any characters.

```
#'size'
#'<='
#'at:put:'
#'123'
```

Symbols, while similar to strings, are used only under special circumstances defined later. Symbol constants are read-only; attempts to change them result in a runtime error.

Array Constants

Array constants are a list of elements surrounded with parentheses and prefixed with a number sign (#). Array constants are read-only; an attempt to change them results in a runtime error.

```
" Array constants; evaluate each line separately  "
#( 1 2 3 4 5 6 7 8 9 10 )           "A 1 at position 1, a 2 at 2, ..."
#( $a $b $c $d $e )                 "An array of characters"
#( 'abe' 'def' 'xyz' )              "An array of strings"
#( 1 'abc' $a #( 2 'xyz' $z) )      "An array holding a mixture of elements"
#(abc def)                          "An array of symbols"
#( #abc #'abc' abc )                "Array with three identical symbols "
```

Example 16, Inspect

Elements in array constants can be any other constant. Names in the list become symbols. See Figure 79, 'Elements Allowed in Array Constants', on page 337, for full details on elements in array constants.

Byte Array Constants

Byte arrays are arrays of integers with positive values in the range 0 to 255. Byte array constants are one or more such integers surrounded by square brackets and starting with a number sign. Byte array constants are read-only.

```
" ByteArray constant "
#[ 1 2 3 4 5 6 7 8 9 10 ]           "A 1 at position 1, a 2 at 2, ..."
```
Example 17, Inspect

```
"Constant array of byte array constants"
#( #[1 2] #[ 3 4] )
```
Example 18, Inspect

Periods

Periods are used in floating-point constants and to separate statements. A period is a statement separator only when it is not part of a constant. A floating-point constant cannot start or end with a period: 0.3 is valid, while .3 is not, and 2.0 is valid, while 2. is not. Periods that occur in strings, and in the character constant $., do not act as statement separators.

Minus Signs

Minus signs are used in constants and as a binary operator. A minus sign that is part of a constant must immediately precede it; that is, there is no white space between it and the constant. All other uses indicate a binary operator. Thus: 3-4 and 3 -4 are not valid expressions, since the minus sign is interpreted as part of the constant, but 3- 4 and 3 - 4 are valid expressions involving two positive integers.

White Space

At any boundary between tokens, any combination of the white space characters, blank, tab, return, line feed, or form feed, and/or comments is allowed.

The following are equivalent:

```
2+3.
2 + 3.
2
    +   3 .
```

The following are equivalent:

```
2- 3.
2 - 3.
2-"minus"3.
```

Messages

Procedures or subroutines are called *methods*, and calling them is referred to as *sending a message*. This terminology emphasizes important differences from traditional languages.

However, there is a strong parallel with traditional languages too. Consider a procedure named next and a method named next; they are invoked like this:

Steps to Invoke	Traditional Language	Smalltalk
Find procedure	linker does it	done at run time
Set up parameters	yes	yes
Branch to procedure	yes	yes

The only difference is in the first step, finding the method. In traditional languages this is done by the linker, and requires no work at execution time. In Smalltalk, the method is found at run time.

This is one of the critical differences between OOP languages and all other languages; it provides Smalltalk with significant power.

Sending Messages

There are three ways to request that a message be sent to an object; they are named *unary*, *binary*, and *keyword*. These are syntactic differences only; the concept is the same for all.

In each case, the name of the message to be sent is the same as that of the method that will be run. That is, sending the computePay message always invokes a method named computePay.

Returning Values

All methods return values and thus all message-sends result in some value. By default, a method that does not explicitly return a value, returns self (the object to which the message was sent).

Unary Messages

Unary messages, Smalltalk's equivalent of a single-parameter function call, consist of a message name and an operand. The object appears first, before the message name.

Smalltalk Unary Message	Traditional Language
x sin	sin(x)
7 factorial	factorial(7)
'abcde' size	size('abcde')

Binary Messages

Binary messages are like binary operators in traditional languages. They consist of one or two special characters, which are written between two operands.

The expression 2+4 has three pieces: a number object (2), a binary message name (+), and a number object (4). When it is executed, the plus (+) message is sent to the 2 object, passing the 4 object as a parameter. The 2 object adds the 4 to itself and returns a 6 object as the answer.

Smalltalk Binary Message	Traditional Language
2 + 4	2 + 4
2 * x + 6	2 * x + 6
'abc', 'def'	concatenate('abc', 'def')
4 @ 3	newPoint(4, 3)

••• Smalltalk allows the creation of methods that respond to binary messages. The message names can be formed from any one or two of the set of special characters below.

, + / \ * ~ - < > = @ % | & ?

Keyword Messages

Keyword messages are equivalent to procedure calls with two or more parameters; however, the syntax is completely different.

Smalltalk Keyword Message	Traditional Procedure Call
box1 overlaps: box2	overlaps(box1, box2)
dict includesKey: key	includesKey(dict, key)

The object to which the message is sent is written first, then the name of the message (the method name), and then a parameter to be passed to the method.

Target object	Message name	Parameter
box1	overlaps:	box2
dict	includes:	key

The colon is a part of the name of the message and of the method.

When there is more than one parameter, the message name has more than one part and there is one parameter for each part.

The message breaks down this way:

Target	name part 1	parameter 1	name part 2	parameter 2
a	between:	2	and:	8

First comes the target object, a, the one to which the message will be sent. Then comes between:, the first part of the message name, and its associated parameter, 2. Then comes and:, the second part of the message name, and its associated parameter, 8.

Saying it another way, this expression sends the message between:and: to the object referred to by a and passes 2 and 8 as parameters.

Keyword messages are order-dependent. The name between:and: is not equivalent to and:between:.

Example keyword messages:

setOfThings add: aNewThing

gadget displayAt: middlePoint

creditCardStatement addCharge: description forAmount: value
    "The message name is addCharge:for:'

Variables

Variables are not typed in Smalltalk. Variables in most traditional languages are typed with the kind of data that the memory location is to hold. Variables in Smalltalk are simply names of memory locations.

Smalltalk variable names are often long; imbedded capital letters are used to enhance readability.

```
bondYield
statesAverageIncomePerCapita
gasTurbineExhaustFlowRate
```

Leading letters can be lower-case or upper-case, depending on the usage. By convention, only global variables and class names start with upper-case letters, and they must do so. Other variables, including instance variables, parameters, and local variables, as well as method names, can start with an upper-case letter, but typically they are not so written.

Unary message names must be valid variable names. Keyword message names must be valid names with a colon appended to each part.

For detailed information on variables and the scope of variable names, see Chapter 8, 'Variables', on page 101.

Special Variables

There are six special variables in Smalltalk: nil, true, false, super, self, and Smalltalk.

nil

The value of the variable nil represents nothing. Most allocated memory in Smalltalk objects is initialized to nil.

true and false

The variables true and false hold special values. These same values are returned by relational operators.

self and super

The variables self and super refer to the object on behalf of which a method is running. The variable super is a variant of self and will be described later.

Smalltalk

The dictionary Smalltalk holds global variables.

Expressions

Smalltalk expressions are made up of one or more message sends. Unary, binary, and keyword messages can be combined into longer expressions.

Expressions can be enclosed in parentheses to force a particular order of evaluation.

Unary Expressions

One effect of writing unary message names after the object is to allow several unary messages be written back-to-back. The second message is sent to the value returned from the first message send, the third to the result of the second, and so on.

Smalltalk Unary Message	Traditional Function Call
x parent name	name(parent(x))
payCheck employee name	name(employee(payCheck))
widget boundsRect height	height(boundsRect(widgit))

In general, as many unary messages may be sent in a row as makes sense. They are always evaluated left to right, with the next message sent to the result of the previous message.

Binary Expressions

Binary messages are also be written left to right, with as many messages sent as make sense. The expression is evaluated left to right, regardless of which binary message is sent. There is no operator precedence for binary operators.

Smalltalk Binary Message	Equivalent to
2 + 3	2 + 3
2 * 3 + 4	(2 * 3) + 4
2 + 3 * 4	(2 + 3) * 4
2 + (3 * 4)	2 + (3 * 4)
7+6+5+4+3*2	(((((7+6)+5)+4)+3)*2

Mixed Unary and Binary Expressions

Unary messages are evaluated before binary messages.

Smalltalk Mixed Messages	Equivalent to
a size + b size	(a size) + (b size)
2 * x sin	2 * (x sin)
(2 * x) sin	(2 * x) sin
employee name size + 1	((employee name) size) + 1
1 + employee name size	1 + ((employee name) size)

Keyword Expressions

Keyword messages are evaluated last. Parameters to keyword messages can be any mixture of unary, binary, or parenthesized keyword messages.

Smalltalk Mixed Messages	Equivalent to
bob age: bob age + 1	bob age: ((bob age) + 1)

car weight:
  body weight +
  engine weight
	car weight:
	  ((body weight) +
	  (engine weight))

Multiple keyword message expressions cannot be written back to back, since they would look like one longer keyword message. This:

employee raise: amount effective: date

is the raise:effective: message sent to employee, but what was intended was:

(employee raise: amount) effective: date

which is the raise: message sent to employee and then the effective: message sent to the result of the first message. The effects of parentheses are further illustrated in the following table.

Expression	First message	Second message
a rotateby: b offsetby: c	rotateby:offsetby:	
(a rotateby: b) offsetby: c	rotateby:	offsetby:
a rotateby: (b offsetby: c)	offsetby:	rotateby:

Cascaded Messages

Sometimes it is useful to send multiple messages to the same object in one expression. This is called cascading, and is indicated by a semicolon. The general format is:

anObject messageAndArguments; messageAndArguments; …

The first message is sent to anObject (passing any arguments, of course); then the next message is sent to anObject, and so on. For example, this code:

```
Transcript cr.
Transcript show: 'Value: '.
Transcript show: '7'
```
Example 19, Display

looks like this when cascading is used:

```
Transcript cr;
    show: 'Value: ';
    show: '7'
```
Example 20, Display

The cr message is sent to Transcript. Each semicolon indicates that the following message will also be sent to Transcript; thus, the show: messages will be sent to Transcript also, one after the other.

The object that receives the cascaded messages is the object to which the *previous* message was sent. That message is the one in the expression just before the first semicolon. Cascaded messages are not necessarily sent to the first object in the expression. For example:

```
aircraft engine ⊖ ⟶   no semicolon here.
    temperature: temp;
    oilPressure: pres.
```

The object to which temperature: is sent is the object returned by the engine message to aircraft; that is the same object that the oilPressure: message is sent to. It is equivalent to:

```
eng := aircraft engine.
eng temperature: temp.
eng oilPressure: pres.
```

Cascading should only be used where it makes the resulting code clearer.

Assignments

Assignments have this format:

variablename := expression

Examples:

```
a := 7.
a4 := a * 4.

daysOld := Date today subtractDate: employee birthDate.
ageInYears := daysOld / 365.
```

Assignments are special operations that assign and then return the value assigned. Thus it is valid to write:

```
" Assignment within an expression "
| a b |
a := 2.0 + (b := 0.5 sin) + 7.
^ b + a
    " Answers: 9.95885108
```

Example 21, Display

or:

```
" Multiple assignment "
| a b c |
a := b := c := 0
```

Example 22, Display

Assignments must either be first in a statement, as in the last example above, or must be enclosed in parentheses, as shown in Example 21, to delimit the scope of the assignment.

Statements

Smalltalk has statements for evaluating expressions, conditionals, looping, and returning from methods.

Format and Separation

Smalltalk expressions and statements can be written without regard to line boundaries. Line breaks can occur wherever white space can occur, and a statement can cover many lines. Many statements can also be placed on a single line.

Statements are separated by a period. There does not need to be a period following the last statement in a method, but there can be. Two periods in a row are an error.

Expressions

Any expression can be written as a statement, simply by separating it from surrounding statements by periods.

```
bond clipCoupon.
auditor notify.
2 + 3.
```

Values returned by such expressions are ignored; thus the last statement is relatively useless.

Blocks

Blocks are square brackets containing zero or more expressions or statements that enclose code for looping, iterating, or conditional expressions.

```
[ a + 3 ]
[    x := a sin * a sin.
     y := x + 1.0 ]
```

Blocks can have parameters; parameters are named first in the block, each prefaced with a colon, and the list of variables ends with a vertical bar. The variable a, below, is a parameter.

> [:a | a + 3]

Blocks can be evaluated with the value or value: messages; value evaluates a parameterless block, value: evaluates a block with one parameter; related messages can evaluate blocks with any number of parameters.

> [2 + 3] value   "Send value to the block; answer a 5"
> [:a | a + 3] value: 2   "Send value: to the block passing 2; answer a 5"

Blocks are covered in more detail later in this chapter.

Return

The return statement in Smalltalk is a caret followed by an expression; the value of the expression is returned as the result of the method.

> ^ massOfCar * velocityOfCar

Returns are covered in more detail later in this chapter.

Control Flow

The flow of control in a method is linear from top to bottom, interrupted only by the transfer of control to other methods, by the selective or repetitive invocation of blocks by conditional and looping statements, and by returning.

Conditionals can be used either as statements, when actions are themselves statements, or as parts of an expression when the actions are, or end with, an expression. Conditionals are messages to boolean values.

ifTrue:

Format:

> booleanExpression **ifTrue:** aBlock

If booleanExpression returns true, evaluate aBlock and answer its value; if it returns false, do not evaluate ablock but answer nil instead.

Example:

> n < 0 ifTrue: [n := 0]

Example:

> n := n < 0 ifTrue: [0]   " If n>=0, n := nil "

Example:

> distance > minOperatingDistance
>   ifTrue:
>   [airplane advanceOnePosition]

ifFalse:

Format:

> booleanExpression **ifFalse:** aBlock

If booleanExpression returns false, evaluate aBlock and answer its result; if it returns true, do not evaluate ablock but answer nil.

Example:

> n >= 0 ifFalse: [n := 0]   "If true, answer nil"

Example:

> distance <= minOperatingDistance
> > ifFalse:
> > > [airplane advanceToStartPosition]

ifTrue:ifFalse:

Format:

> booleanExpression **ifTrue:** trueBlock **ifFalse:** falseBlock

If booleanExpression returns true, evaluate block trueBlock; if it returns false, evaluate block falseBlock. Answer the result of the block evaluated.

Example:

> n < 0 ifTrue: [n := 0] ifFalse: [n := n + 1]

or:

> n := n < 0 ifTrue: [0] ifFalse: [n + 1]

if n<0
then n:=0
else n:=n+1 .

Example:

> distance >= minOperatingDistance
> > ifTrue:
> > > [airplane advanceOnePosition]
> > ifFalse:
> > > [airplane advanceToStartPosition]

ifFalse:ifTrue:

Format:

> booleanExpression **ifFalse:** falseBlock **ifTrue:** trueBlock

If booleanExpression returns false, evaluate block falseBlock; if it returns true, evaluate block trueBlock. Answer the result of whichever block is evaluated.

Example:

> n < 0 ifFalse: [n := n + 1] ifTrue: [n := 0]

or:

> n := n < 0 ifFalse: [n + 1] ifTrue: [0]

Example:

> distance >= minOperatingDistance
> > ifFalse:
> > > [airplane advanceToStartPosition]
> > ifTrue:
> > > [airplane advanceOnePosition]

Looping and Iterating

Messages to blocks and integers are used for looping and iterating.

whileTrue:

Format:

aBlock **whileTrue:** trueBlock

Evaluate aBlock; if it evaluates to true, then evaluate trueBlock. Repeat for as long as aBlock evaluates to true.

Example:

[a < 0] whileTrue: [a := a + 1]

Example:

[airplane isFlying]
    whileTrue: [
        airplane flySimulationStep]

whileFalse:

Format:

aBlock **whileFalse:** falseBlock

Evaluate aBlock; if it evaluates to false, then evaluate falseBlock. Repeat for as long as aBlock evaluates to false.

Example:

[a >= 0] whileFalse: [a := a + 1]

Example:

[airplane notFlying]
    whileFalse: [
        airplane flySimulationStep]

timesRepeat:

Format:

anInteger **timesRepeat:** aBlock

Evaluate aBlock repeatedly for anInteger times; anInteger must be a positive integer.

Example:

a := 0.
5 timesRepeat: [a := a + 1].
"a is now 5"

to:do:

Format:

start to: end do: aOneParameterBlock

Evaluate aOneParameterBlock once for each value in a series of numbers, passing the value to the block at each evaluation. The series starts with start. Each successive value is obtained by adding one to the previous value. The series ends with the highest value that does not exceed end. At each step, the current value is passed to the block as a loop index.

The table below shows the individual steps for various values of start and end.

Expression	Steps
1 to: 10 do: [ ]	1 2 3 4 5 6 7 8 9 10
1/2 to: 2 do: [ ]	1/2 3/2
-2 to: -10 do: [ ]	(none)
-2 to: 2 do: [ ]	-2 -1 0 1 2
1 to: 3.0 do: [ ]	1 2 3
1.1 to: 3.4 do: [ ]	1.1 2.1 3.1

Example:

```
" A series from 5 to 10 "
Transcript cr.
5 to: 10
    do: [ :k |
        Transcript show: k printString; cr ]
```

parameter in the block which is more like in C:
for (k := 5; k ≤ 10; k++)

Example 23, Display

Example:

```
1 to: array size
    do: [ :n |
        array at: n put: 0 ]  "Set each element to zero"
```

Example:

```
1 to: invoice numberOfItems
    do: [ :n | invoice shipProduct: n ]
```

to:by:do:

Format:

start **to:** end **by:** step **do:** aOneParameterBlock

Evaluate aOneParameterBlock once for each value in a series of numbers, passing the value to the block at each evaluation. The series starts with start. Each successive value is obtained by adding step to the previous value. The series ends with the highest value that does not exceed end. At each step, the current value is passed to the block as a loop index.

The table below shows the individual steps for various values of start, end, and step.

Expression	Steps
1 to: 10 by: 1 do: [ ]	1 2 3 4 5 6 7 8 9 10
1 to: 10 by: 2 do: [ ]	1 3 5 7 9
1.0 to: 3.0 by: 0.6 do: [ ]	1.0 1.6 2.2 2.8
1/2 to: 2 by: 1/2 do: [ ]	1/2 1 3/2 2
-2 to: -10 by: -1 do: [ ]	-2 -3 -4 -5 -6 -7 -8 -9 -10
1 to: 3.0 by: 1/2 do: [ ]	1 3/2 2 5/2 3
1.0 to: 3.0 by: 1/2 do: [ ]	1.0 1.5 2.0 2.5 3.0

Example:

```
1 to: array size by: 2
    do: [ :n | array at: n put: 0 ]
```

Example:

```
1.2 to: 7.6 by: 0.1
        do: [ :x | airplane engineThrustTest: x ]
```

Example:

```
" Series of fractions "
Transcript cr.
1/2 to: 5/2 by: 1/4
      do: [ :index |
            Transcript
                  show: index printString, ' ' ]
"The Transcript shows:
(1/2) (3/4) 1 (5/4) (3/2) (7/4) 2 (9/4) (5/2) "
```

Example 24, Execute

Methods

Methods in Smalltalk are roughly equivalent to value-returning procedures, or functions, in traditional languages. There is no equivalent in Smalltalk to a procedure that does not return a value; methods always return values, but such values can be ignored when not wanted. There is also no equivalent of a stand-alone function; all methods belong to some object.

The steps involved in invoking a method are:

1) Find the method;

2) Associate each parameter value in the invoking message with an argument name in the method header. This association depends on the kind of message.

   a) Keyword messages associate values to arguments in left-to-right order.

   b) Binary messages associate the right-hand value with a single argument.

   c) Unary messages have no parameters.

3) The built-in variables self and super are associated with the object to which the message is being sent; self and super can be thought of as hidden parameters.

4) The execution of the method starts.

Methods are fully recursive; recursion is commonly used in Smalltalk programs.

Method Format

A method has the following parts:

1) A *method header*, sometimes called the *message pattern*, which defines the name and arguments of the method. The method header is required.

2) A comment describing the purpose of the method. The comment is optional.

3) A list of local variables that will exist for the duration of one execution of the method. Local variables must be listed before they can be used.

4) One or more statements, separated by periods. Statements are optional.

5) An optional return statement.

These parts have this format:

1) messageHeader
2) "Method comment"
3) | local variables |
4) statements. ...
5) ^ expression

While it is typical to have the message header on one or more lines by itself, the local variable list on one or more lines by itself, and statements each on a separate line, there is no requirement that this must be done.

Method Headers

The format of message headers depends on the type of the message.

Unary Message Headers

Unary message headers consist of just the name of the method. A method to implement the amount method would have this header:

amount

Binary Message Headers

Binary message headers have two parts, the binary message selector made up of one or two of these special characters:

, + / \ * ~ - < > = @ % | & ?

and the name of the argument.

A message header for a method named >>, and with an argument name dependent, looks like this:

>> dependent

This might be invoked by the expression:

employee >> spouse

The value in spouse would be associated with dependent; the value in employee would be associated with self (and super).

Keyword Message Headers

Keyword message headers have one or more pairs of keyword and argument pairs. The names of the keywords must match in order and capitalization between the sending message and the method header.

A message header for a method named addDependent:, and with an argument dependent, looks like this:

addDependent: dependent

This might be invoked by the expression:

employee addDependent: spouse

The value in spouse would be associated with dependent; the value in employee would be associated with self (and super).

The message send:

employee raiseSalaryTo: 95000 starting: date

might invoke a method with the following header:

raiseSalaryTo: sizeOfRaise starting: startDate

The value 95000 would be associated with sizeOfRaise, the value in date would be associated with startDate, and the value in employee would be associated with self.

Local Variables

Local variables are listed after the method header. They are enclosed between vertical bars. There may be as few as zero variables and there is no practical limit on the number of local variables. If there are no local variables, the vertical bars can be omitted.

```
| age zilch bandito |
```

Statements

Statements follow next; they are separated by periods.

Method Examples

Unary Methods

A unary method with all parts present:

```
piSquared
    "Return the value PI squared"
    | pi  sq |
    pi := 3.1415927.
    sq := pi * pi.
    ^ sq
```

However, there is no need in this case to assign to local variables, so here is an equivalent unary method with no local variables:

```
piSquared
    ^ 3.1415927 * 3.1415927
```

Binary Methods

A binary method -> might specify how two objects are connected.

```
-> nextObject
    " Connect this object to nextObject "
    connector := nextObject
```

It might be invoked like this:

```
throttleLinkage -> fuelInjectorController
```

The value in fuelInjectorController will be associated with nextObject, and throttleLinkage with self and super.

Keyword Methods

A keyword method:

```
raise: amount
    "implement a raise for an employee; return true if successful"
    amount <= 0
        ifTrue: [ ^ false ].
    self performSalaryAdjustment: amount.
    ^ true
```

Public and Private

Methods can be declared to be public or private using the development environment tools. Public methods are intended for users of the class; they are documented, and appear in code in other classes.

Private methods are intended only for use within the class that defines them, and with subclasses of that class.

Evaluating Code

When a text selection is evaluated, it is made into a method named Doit and temporarily inserted into a system class. Doit differs from other methods only in that the last expression is returned as the value of the method by default, rather than self.

Blocks

Blocks are objects that are also fragments of Smalltalk code. They can be executed, assigned to variables, put into another object's private storage, or passed as parameters. Blocks answer values; the last expressions value is the block value. Blocks are fully recursive.

Block Format

Blocks consist of an optional list of arguments, an optional set of local variables, and an expression, statement, or set of statements. Figure 11 shows the format of a block.

Arguments are names prefaced with a colon in the argument list, but not in the body of the block.

```
[ :index | index + 1 ]
```

The following code illustrates a two-argument block with two local variables. The last line is the expression whose value becomes the block value.

```
[ :x :y |
    "Find the hypotenuse of a right triangle with sides x and y"
    | xx yy |
    xx := x * x.
    yy := y * y.
    (xx + yy) sqrt ]
```

statements are seperated by period.

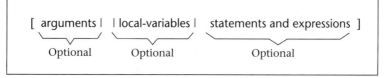

Figure 11: Format of a Block. Each of the three parts is optional: arguments and its ending vertical bar are omitted if there are no arguments; local-variables and the two vertical bars are omitted if there are no local variables, and the statements and expressions portion is also optional. The simplest block is thus a pair of square brackets.

Block Execution

A block is executed by sending a message to it. If a block has no arguments, then the message to send is value. If a block has one argument, then the message to send is value:, if two, the message is value:value:, if three, the message is value:value:value:. The valueWithArguments: message allows any number of parameters.

When a block terminates, the last value computed or assigned is returned as the value of the block.

```
" Simple block "
^ [ 2 + 3 ] value
" Result: 5 "
```
Example 25, Display

```
" Block with parameter "
^ [ :a | 2 + a ] value: 3
" Result: 5 "
```
Example 26, Display

```
" Block with two parameters "
^ [ :a :b | a + b ] value: 2 value: 3
" Result: 5 "
```
Example 27, Display

```
" Longer block with two parameters "
| value |
value := [ :a :b |
      | r |
      r := a + b.
      r * 2 ]  value: 2 value: 3.
^ value
" Result: 10 "
```
local variable
Example 28, Display

Since the value of a block is the value of the last expression evaluated within the block, this result can be assigned or used for calculations.

```
" Expression of blocks "
^ [ 2 ] value + ( [ :a | 2 + a ] value: 3)
"Result: 7 "
```
Example 29, Display

Block Assignment and Block Parameters

Blocks are objects and can be assigned to variables. In Example 30, a one-parameter block is assigned to the variable aBlock; then the block is evaluated and the result is returned.

```
" Block assignment and parameters "
| aBlock |
aBlock := [ :p | p * p * 3 ].
^ aBlock value: 2
    " Answer: 12 "
```
Example 30, Display

Blocks may be passed to methods as parameters.

> aircraft nextPositionWith: [:pos :delta | pos + delta]

A two-parameter block is passed to a method; presumably the method will evaluate the block at some point.

For detailed information on blocks, see Chapter 25, 'Blocks', on page 297.

^ (Return)

A return in a block terminates both the block and the method; if blocks are nested, all nested blocks in the method are terminated and the method is exited.

Format:

```
^ expression
```

Example:

```
^ 4
```

Example:

```
^ todaysBondPrice * factor
```

If execution of a method ends before encountering a return, that is, if execution runs off the end of the method, the method is considered to have this statement invisibly appended to its end:

```
^ self
```

Scope of Names

Parameter and local variables defined in methods are local to that invocation of the method. They are accessible in blocks defined within the method.

Parameters and local variables of a block are local to one invocation of that block and cannot be referenced outside the block. They are, however, accessible to another block nested within the block.

For detailed information about the scope of names, see Chapter 8, 'Variables', on page 101.

Summary

While the syntax of Smalltalk is surely different, Smalltalk statements and constructs directly parallel statements in traditional languages.

Smalltalk has constants for various kinds of numbers, for strings, characters, and arrays. It has looping and conditional statements, variables, expressions, assignments, and returns. It can invoke 'subprograms'.

The syntax is not different just to be different; it comes from the basic object oriented nature of Smalltalk. Smalltalk is all about messages to objects. Even its syntax for looping and conditional statements is based on message sends to blocks, booleans, or numbers (or to collections, as will be seen in a later chapter).

Methods are just procedures that belong to their owner objects: they take parameters, have local variables, perform calculations, invoke blocks and other methods, and return values.

Blocks are similar to functions or procedures: they take parameters, have local variables, perform calculations, invoke other methods and blocks, and answer values. In addition, they are full-fledged objects and can be assigned to variables, stored in arrays, and passed as parameters.

5

Basic Classes

The basic classes of data described in this chapter include magnitudes, booleans, and geometric quantities. Magnitudes are values that can be compared with less-than or greater-than, and include all kinds of numbers, characters, dates, and times. Booleans are the values true and false. Geometric quantities are points and rectangles.

Each of these basic classes has, of course, a set of messages that operate on it. This section surveys many of these messages. Part IV, 'Encyclopedia of Classes', describes these messages, and many more, in detail.

Classes in Smalltalk are defined in a hierarchy. The top of the hierarchy is an abstract class named Object. All other classes inherit from it. Object provides protocol related to being an object. The class hierarchy for the objects described in this chapter is shown below. Classes in italics are abstract; their instances are not useful.

Class	Page
Object	54
Boolean	61
False	61
True	61
Magnitude	54
Association	58
Character	58
Date	58
Number	55
Float	57
Fraction	57
Integer	57
Time	60
Point	61
Rectangle	62
UndefinedObject	54

Object

Class Object defines methods related to just being an object; all other classes are subclasses of Object. These subclasses refine the idea of object to be various more useful things.

Object implements a number of methods. These compare two objects for equal values or equality of object.

Message	Description	Example	Result
=	Do two objects have equal values?	2 = 3	false
==	Are two objects the same object?	2 == 2	true
~=	Do two objects have unequal values?	2 ~= 3	true
~~	Are two objects not the same object?	2 ~~ 2	false

These messages test the class of an object.

Message	Description	Example	Result
isCharacter	Is the object a character?	$a isCharacter	true
isFloat	Is the object a floating point number?	2 isFloat	false
isInteger	Is the object an integer number?	2 isInteger	true
isNil	Is the object nil? Answer false.	nil isNil	true
isString	Is the object a string?	'abc' isString	true
isSymbol	Is the object a symbol?	#abc isSymbol	true
notNil	Is the object anything but nil? Answer true.	2 notNil	true

The following messages obtain the class of an object, copy an object, raise errors, halt and enter the debugger, inspect, convert to a string, and answer the size of objects.

Message	Description	Example	Result
class	The class of an object	$A class	Character
copy	Copy an object	#(1 2 3) copy	1 2 3
error: string	Raise an error	self error: 'bad'	
halt	Enter the debugger	self halt	
halt: string	Enter the debugger	self halt: 'Uh Oh!'	
inspect	Inspect the object	$A inspect	
printString	Answer a string representing the object	2.3 printString	'2.3'
size	The size of the object	#(1 2 3) size	3

For detailed information on class Object see Chapter 24, 'Class Object', on page 281.

Undefined Object

The class UndefinedObject has just one instance. It is globally available as the special variable nil.

Message	Description	Example
isNil	Is the object nil? Answer true	nextClient isNil
notNil	Is the object anything but nil? Answer false.	nextClient notNil

Magnitudes

Magnitudes are values that can be compared with relations. Each must respond to these messages, plus those inherited from Object, including =, ==, ~=, and ~~.

Message	Description	Example	Result
<	Less than	2 < 3	true
<=	Less than or equal	2 <= 3	true
>	Greater than	3 > 2	true
>=	Greater than or equal	3 >= 2	true
between:and:	Between two values	3 between: 1 and: 7	true
min:	Lowest of two values	2 min: 3	2
max:	Highest of two values	2 max: 3	3

For detailed information on magnitudes see Chapter 32, 'Magnitudes', on page 425.

Numbers

There are three kinds of numbers: integers, floats, and fractions. All numbers respond to a large set of messages which are summarized in this section.

Binary messages to numbers may involve mixed kinds of numbers; integers may be added to floating-point numbers which can be multiplied by fractions, etc. Values returned may be of different kinds than the operands. For example, the division of two integers will result in a fraction if the result is not integral, and trigonometric functions of integers return floating-point numbers.

Common messages are described briefly in the following tables.

Message	Description	Example	Result
+	Addition	2 + 3	5
-	Subtraction	5 - 2.0	3.0
*	Multiplication	2 * 3	6
/	Division	7 / 2	7/2
//	Division with integer result	7 // 2	3
\\	Remainder after // division	7 \\ 2	1

The arithmetic unary messages are equivalent to common one-argument functions in other languages.

Message	Description	Example	Result
abs	Absolute value	-5 abs	5
ceiling	Next highest integer	2.3 ceiling	3
floor	Next lowest integer	-2.3 floor	-3
negated	Flip sign	7 negated	-7
reciprocal	One divided by value	2 reciprocal	1/2
rounded	Nearest integer	2.47 rounded	2
sign	1 if pos, -1 if neg, 0 if zero	-4 sign	-1
truncated	Next integer nearer 0	-3.9 truncated	-3

Conversions between various kinds of numbers are supported by explicit conversion messages.

Message	Description	Example	Result
asFloat	Floating-point number	2 asFloat	2.0
asFraction	Fraction	0.3 asFraction	3/10
asInteger	Integer, rounded	6.6 asInteger	7

Trigonometric messages can be sent to any kind of number, but always return floating-point numbers. Angle values are in radians; two messages allow conversion between radians and degrees.

Message	Description	Example
arcCos	Arccosine	a arcCos
arcSin	Arcsin	a arcSin
arcTan	Arctangent	a arcTan
cos	Cosine	x cos
sin	Sine	x sin
tan	Tangent	a tan
radiansToDegrees	Convert radians to degrees	a radiansToDegrees
degreesToRadians	Convert degrees to radians	a degreesToRadians

Power and logarithmic messages can be sent to any kind of number, but usually return a floating point number.

Message	Description	Example	Result
exp	Raise e to a power	4 exp	54.59815003
ln	Logarithm to base e	5 ln	1.60943791
raisedTo	Raise to power	2.0 raisedTo: 2.0	4.0
raisedToInteger:	Raise to integer power	2 raisedToInteger: 2	4
sqrt	Square root	4 sqrt	2.0

Comparisons can be made on mixed kinds of numbers, say a float and a fraction.

Message	Description	Example	Result
<	Less than	2 < 4	true
<=	Less then or equal	2 <= 4.0	true
>	Greater than	2 > 4	false
>=	Greater than or equal	2 >= 4	false
=	Equal	2 = 2.0	true
~=	Not equal	2 ~= 2	false
==	Are both objects the same object?	2 == 2.0	false
~~	Are both objects different objects?	2 ~~ 2	false

Maximum and minimum messages return one of two values. The values can be any kind of number.

Message	Description	Example	Result
max:	Pick highest operand	2 max: 7/3	7/3
min:	Pick smallest operand	2 min: 7.0	2

For detailed information on numbers see Chapter 33, 'Numbers', on page 449. The forms of constants and their size ranges are described in the section on 'Numeric Constants Summary' on page 457.

Integers

Integer numbers have messages that are unique to integers. Messages supported by integer numbers exclusively include even and odd, which return true or false.

Message	Description	Example	Result
even	Test integer for evenness	3 even	false
odd	Test integer for oddness	3 odd	true

Integers support a number of bit-oriented operations such as masking, *and*ing, *or*ing, and shifting. Bits are numbered from the right (low-order bit) starting with one. The bit operations on integers include the following messages:

Message	Description	Example	Result
<<	Shift left	2r10 << 2	2r1000
>>	Shift right	2r1000 >> 1	2r100
&	Logical *and*	2r 1101 & 2r0111	2r0101
|	Logical *or*	2r1101 | 2r0111	2r1111
bitInvert	Invert bits	2r1010 bitInvert	2r-1011
bitXor:	Exclusive *or*	2r1010 bitXor: 2r0111	2r1101
clearBit:	Clear one bit at an index	2r1111 clearBit: 2	2r1101
highBit	Bit index of highest bit	2r001000 highBit	4
isBitSet:	Test one bit at an index	2r0101 isBitSet: 3	true
setBit:	Set one bit at an index	2r0101 setBit: 2	2r0111

For detailed information on integers, and for the full set of bit operations, see class Integer on page 474, and the section on 'Inside Integers and Floats' on page 454.

Floating-Point Numbers

Floating-point numbers in Smalltalk are typically long or double-precision. Exact results depend on the hardware implementation of floating-point numbers.

Floating-point numbers respond to fractionPart and integerPart, which return the respective parts of the number.

For detailed information on floating-point numbers, see Chapter 33, 'Numbers', on page 449.

Fractions

Fractions are the ratio of two integers; both integers are part of the value of the fraction. The messages numerator and denominator extract these values.

Fractions are created automatically when two integers are divided and the result is non-integral: the expression 7/4 produces a fraction. Fractions are also created when some arithmetic operation is done with an integer and a fraction. Fractions are always reduced to their simplest terms.

Fractions do not lose precision, because they are always stored as the ratio of two integers, and integers have an effectively unlimited length. If a result of an integer division with a non-integral result is converted to a floating-point value or truncated to an integer, then precision could be lost.

```
" Example of fraction arithmetic "
| q r |
q := 16 / 6.                    " q is the fraction (8/3) "
r := q * (3 / 2).               " r := (8/3) * (3/2) = (8/2) =  4 "
^ r        " Answers: 4 "
```

Example 31, Display

For detailed information on fractions, see Chapter 33, 'Numbers', on page 449.

Characters

Characters are the individual parts of strings. Characters with an internal value from 0 to 127 are encoded in the ASCII character set; characters with internal values greater than 127 are platform dependent. Characters can be compared, converted, and tested.

Characters may be compared only with other characters. Character comparisons, except equal and not-equal, ignore case.

```
" Character comparisons (Evaluate one line at a time) "
$a < $b                                    " true "
$a >= $b                                   " false "
$a > $4                                    " true "
$a > $A                                    " false "
$A > $a                                    " false "              Example 32, Display
```

Characters may be converted to other characters with the messages asLowercase and asUppercase, and to an integer that represents the ASCII encoding, with value.

```
" Character conversions (Evaluate one line at a time) "
$A asLowercase                             " $a "
$a value                                   " 97 "                Example 33, Display
```

Characters answer to a number of other messages including the following.

Message	Description	Example	Result
isDigit	Is the character a numeric digit?	$4 isDIgit	true
isLetter	Is the character a letter?	$R isLetter	true
isVowel	Is the character a vowel?	$A isVowel	true
isLowercase	Is the character a lowercase letter?	$a isLowercase	true
isUppercase	Is the character an uppercase letter?	$Z isUppercase	true
isAlphaNumeric	Is the character a digit or letter?	$6 isAlphaNumeric	true
between:and:	Is the character between two others?	$c between: $a and: $f	true

For detailed information on characters, see class Character on page 434.

Associations

Associations are magnitudes that hold pairs of values; one is called the key and the other the value. Associations are used in dictionaries (see the next chapter) to hold the index, the key, and the value. Associations are sometimes used in other contexts.

An association is created by the key:value: message to Association.

```
" Create an Association "
Association key: 'Duke' value: 'Edward Kennedy Ellington'
```

The key and value can be accessed with key, key:, value, and value:.

For detailed information, see class Association on page 431.

Dates

Dates represent the day, month, and year of a calendar date. Dates are created by sending messages to class Date. Messages to class Date include the following:

Examples:

```
" Fetch today's date "
Date today                                                      Example 34, Display
```

Message	Description	Example	Result
dateAndTimeNow	Array with new data and time	Date dateAndTimeNow	An array
daysInMonth:forYear:	Number of days in a month	Date daysInMonth: #March forYear: 1995	31
daysInYear:	The number days in a year	Date daysInYear: 1995	365
newDay:month:year:	Create a new date	Date newDay: 22 month: #Feb year: 1995	A date: 02-22-95
newDay:year:	Create a new date	Date newDay: 143 year: 1995	A date: 05-23-95
today	Today's date	Date today	A date

Figure 12: Examples of Messages to Class Date.

```
" Build a date for a given month, day, and year "
Date newDay:  6
     month: #February
     year: 1995
" Answer the date: 02-06-95 "
```
Example 35, Display

```
" Build a date for a given day number and year "
Date newDay: 37
     year: 1995
" Answer the date: 02-06-95 "
```
Example 36, Display

The instance protocol of dates includes the messages shown in Figure 13.

Message	Description	Example
addDays: n	A new date n days from now	aDate addDays: 12
asSeconds	As seconds from 00:00 on 1Jan1901	aDate asSeconds
dayName	Name of the day	aDate dayName
dayOfMonth	Number of the day in the month	aDate dayOfMonth
dayOfYear	Number of the day in the year	aDate dayOfYear
daysInMonth	Number of days in this month	aDate DaysInMonth
daysInYear	Number of days in this year	aDate daysInYear
daysLeftInMonth	Number of days after today in this month	aDate daysLeftInMonth
daysLeftInYear	Number of days after today in this year	aDate daysLeftInYear
firstDayOfMonth	A new date for the first day in this month	aDate firstDayOfMonth
monthIndex	Number of this month	aDate monthIndex
monthName	Name of this month	aDate monthName
subtractDate: aDate	Number of days between this date and aDate	aDate subtractDate: d
subtractDays: anInteger	A new date n days ago	aDate subtractDays: n
year	The year number	aDate year

Figure 13: Examples of Messages to a Date.

Try this:

```
" Various messages to dates "
| d |
d := Date newDay: 29 month: #April year: 1995.
Transcript show: 'Date: ', d printString; cr.
Transcript show: 'As seconds: ', d asSeconds printString; cr.
Transcript show: 'Day name: ', d dayName; cr.
Transcript show: 'Month name: ', d monthName; cr.
Transcript show: 'Days left in year: ', d daysLeftInYear printString; cr.
Transcript show: 'First day of month: ', d firstDayOfMonth printString; cr.
```

```
Transcript show: 'Ten days from now: ', (d addDays: 10) printString; cr.

"The Transcript will show (details will vary by locale):
Date: 04-29-95
As seconds: 2976566400
Day name: Saturday
Month name: April
Days left in year: 246
First day of month: 04-01-95
Ten days from now: 05-09-95   "
```

Example 37, Execute

For detailed information, see class Date on page 439.

Time

Times represent the time of day to an accuracy of one second. Times are created by messages to class Time.

```
" Fetch the time right now "
Time now
```
Example 38, Display
```
" Get a time that is 45 seconds after midnight "
Time fromSeconds: 45
```
Example 39, Display

Time instances respond to the messages in Figure 14, among others.

Message	Description	Examples
addTime: aTime	Add a time and a time offset	aTime addTime: t
asSeconds	The number of seconds since midnight	aTime asSeconds
hours	The hours since midnight	aTime hours
hours:minutes:seconds:	Set hour, minute, and second	aTime hours: h minutes: m seconds: s
minutes	The minutes in this hour	aTime minutes
seconds	The seconds in this minute	aTime seconds
setFromSeconds:	Set the time from seconds since midnight	aTime setFromSeconds: 421
subtractTime: aTime	Subtract another time to get a time offset	aTime subtractTime: t

Figure 14: Messages to Instances of Time.

Time offsets are also instances of Time, but the values of hour, minute, and second are the differences between two times.

Try these examples:

```
" Time offsets "
| t1 t2 offset |
t1 := Time new hours: 4 minutes: 2 seconds: 22.
t2 := Time new hours: 5 minutes: 4 seconds: 14.
^ t2 subtractTime: t1
" Answers a time for: 01:01:52 AM "
```
Example 40, Display
```
" Several messages to times "
| d |
d := Time fromSeconds: 14*3600 + (35*60) + 42.   "02:35:42 PM"
Transcript show: 'As seconds: ', d asSeconds printString; cr.
Transcript show: 'Hours: ', d hours printString; cr.

" The Transcript will show:
As seconds: 52542
Hours: 14   "
```
Example 41, Display

Millisecond Clock

Higher accuracy can be obtained from the millisecond clock, which answers values based on system or image startup time.

Time also returns integers that represent the number of milliseconds in a day, and the number of milliseconds to run a block.

" **Answer how many milliseconds per day; a constant (86400000)** "
Time millisecondsPerDay   *Example 42, Display*

" **Answer the millisecond clock value** "
Time millisecondClockValue   *Example 43, Display*

" **Answer the number of milliseconds it takes to run a block** "
Time millisecondsToRun: [1000 factorial]
" Answer on authors platform: 2410 "   *Example 44, Display*

For detailed information, see class Time on page 445.

Booleans

The special variables, true and false, and the results returned by relational operators, which are the values held in true and false, have a set of messages for comparing and for logical boolean operations. These include logical and (&), logical or (|), exclusive or (xor:), negation (not), and comparison (=).

" **Examples of boolean expressions (evaluate each line separately)** "
true & true   " true "
true & false   " false "
true | true   " true "
true | false   " true "
true xor: false   " true "
true not   " false "   *Example 45, Display*

Points

Points are objects that hold two numbers representing a position on an *x-y* plane.

Points are created with one of the following messages:

" **A point with an x of 4 and a y of 5** "
4 @ 5   *Example 46, Display*

" **A point with an x of 4 and a y of 5** "
Point x: 4 y: 5   *Example 47, Display*

Points can be compared with the usual cast of relational messages. The protocol of instances of Point includes the messages in Figure 15.

Try these:

" **Add a constant 2 to each element of a point** "
(2 @ 3) + 2
" Answers: 4 @ 5 "   *Example 48, Display*

Message	Description	Example	Result
*	Multiply a point by a number	(2@3) * 2	(4@6)
+	Add a number or point to a point	(2@3) + 1	(3@4)
-	Subtract a number or point from a point	(2@3) - 1	(1@2)
/	Divide a point by a number	(4@6) / 2	(2@3)
dist:	Distance between two points	(0@0) dist: (3@4)	5.0
transpose	Swap *x* and *y* values	(6@3) transpose	(3@6)

Figure 15: Examples of Messages to Points.

```
" Add a point to a point "
(2 @ 3) + ( 1 @ 1)
" Answers: 3 @ 4
```
Example 49, Display

```
" Multiply a point by a constant "
(2 @ 3 ) * 2
" Answers: 4 @ 6 "
```
Example 50, Display

For detailed information on points, see Chapter 34, 'Points', on page 485

Rectangles

Rectangles are pairs of points that define an axis-aligned rectangle on an *x-y* plane. Rectangles are created with the origin:corner: or origin:extent: messages to Rectangle.

```
" Create a new rectangle with origin:corner: "
Rectangle origin: 2@3 corner: 5@6
" Answer: 2@3 corner: 5@6 "
```
Example 51, Display

```
" Create a new rectangle with origin:extent: "
Rectangle origin: 2@3 extent: 3@3.
" Answer: 2@3 corner: 5@6 "
```
Example 52, Display

Rectangles can also be created using messages to points.

```
" Create a rectangle from two points with corner: "
2@3 corner: 5@6
" Answer: 2@3 corner: 5@6 "
```
Example 53, Display

```
" Create a rectangle from two points with extent: "
2@3 extent: 3@3
" Answer: 2@3 corner: 5@6 "
```
Example 54, Display

Rectangle instances have a large set of messages, much of which involves accessing and modifying its values. Other messages scale, move, offset, translate, merge, intersect, and inset rectangles. Selected messages are shown in the following tables.

For detailed information on rectangles see Chapter 36, 'Rectangles', on page 509.

Access operations on corners are shown in Figure 16.

Message	Description	Example
bottomLeft	Answer the point at the bottom left corner	aRect bottomLeft
bottomLeft:	Set the point at the bottom left corner	aRect bottomLeft: (3@7)
bottomRight	Answer the point at the bottom right corner	aRect bottomRight
bottomRight:	Set the point at the bottom right corner	aRect bottomRight: (3@7)

Figure 16: Corner Access Messages of Rectangles. Part 1 of 2

Message	Description	Example
corner	Answer the point at bottom right corner	aRect corner
corner:	Set the point at bottom right corner	aRect corner: (3@7)
origin	Answer the origin (the top left corner)	aRect origin
origin:	Set the origin (the top left corner)	aRect origin: (3@7)
topLeft	Answer the point at the top left corner	aRect topLeft
topLeft:	Set the point at the top left corner	aRect topLeft: (3@7)
topRight	Answer the point at the top right corner	aRect topRight
topRight:	Set the point at the top right corner	aRect topRight: (3@7)

Figure 16: Corner Access Messages of Rectangles. Part 2 of 2

Testing operations are shown in Figure 17.

Message	Description	Example
contains:	True if one rectangle contains another	aRect contains: r
containsPoint:	True if a rectangle contains a point	aRect containsPoint: 2@5
intersects:	True if one rectangle intersects another	aRect intersects: r

Figure 17: Testing Methods of Rectangles.

Scaling and translation operations are shown in Figure 18.

Message	Description	Example
expandBy:	New rectangle expanded from another	aRect expandBy: 2@4
insetBy:	New rectangle inset from another	aRect insetBy: 2@4
intersect:	New rectangle that's an intersection of both	aRect intersect: r
merge:	New rectangle just big enough to hold both	aRect merge: r
moveBy:	Move rectangle by a delta	aRect moveBy: 2@4
moveTo:	Move rectangle to a new origin	aRect moveTo: 2@4
scaleBy:	New rectangle scaled in x and y	aRect scaleBy: 2@4
translateBy:	New rectangle translated by x and y	aRect translateBy: 2@4

Figure 18: Scaling and Translation Methods of Rectangles.

Access operations on edges, extents, and center points are shown in Figure 19.

Message	Description	Example
bottom	Answer y-coordinate of the bottom edge	aRect bottom
bottom:	Set the y-coordinate of the bottom edge	aRect bottom: 2@4
center	Answer a point at the center	aRect center
extent	A point holding the height and width	aRect extent
extent:	Set the height and width relative to the origin	aRect extent: 2@4
height	Answer the height	aRect height
height:	Set the height relative to the origin	aRect height: 2@4
left	Answer the x-coordinate of the left edge	aRect left
left:	Set the x-coordinate of the left edge	aRect left: 2@4
right	Answer the x-coordinate of the right edge	aRect right
right:	Set the x-coordinate of the right edge	aRect right: 2@4
top	Answer the x-coordinate of the top edge	aRect top

Figure 19: Edge Access Methods of Rectangles. Part 1 of 2

Message	Description	Example
top:	Set the *x*-coordinate of the top edge	aRect top: 2@4
width	Answer the width	aRect width
width:	Set the width relative to the origin	aRect width: 2@4

Figure 19: Edge Access Methods of Rectangles. Part 2 of 2

Summary

The most fundamental basic class, Object, is the parent of all other Smalltalk classes. It implements protocol related to the object nature of objects. Subclasses, such as Magnitude, refine the concept of object. Magnitudes add the concept of ordering of values, and its subclasses add concepts such as number and time.

Magnitudes illustrate the refinement process. (Collections, in the next chapter, provide another interesting illustration).

Class	What it defines
Object	Defines the idea of object, including testing for equality or identity, printing a string representation, and finding the size.
Magnitude	Defines the idea of objects with a magnitude, or values that can be compared with relationals.
Number	Defines the abstract idea of number, an object that supports counting, addition, subtraction, etc. Number is still abstract though, since no internal computer representation is specified.
Float	Defines a concrete representation of a number using the platform's floating-point hardware.
Integer	Defines a concrete representation of a number using the platform's integer hardware.
Fraction	Defines a concrete representation of a number using a pair of integers.

6

Collections and Iteration

Collections are objects whose purpose is to hold other objects. In traditional languages, arrays are typically the only collections. Smalltalk has a number of different kinds of collections including arrays, sets, bags of unordered items, strings, dictionaries, sorted collections, and symbols.

As is true with virtually all objects in Smalltalk, a collection is dynamically allocated when a new one is requested, and space occupied by it is automatically reclaimed for reallocation when its use ends.

Collections check all indexed accesses to assure that the bounds are not exceeded.

For detailed information, see Chapter 27, 'Collections', on page 309, and Chapter 28, 'Collections: Sequenceable', on page 331.

Kinds of Collections

Collections are categorized by these characteristics:

Fixed	The size of the collection is fixed when it is allocated. It cannot be extended. *just like in C*
Variable	New elements can be added to the collection; it will grow as needed. The initial allocation can be specified or will default to something appropriate.
Ordered	The collection has some ordering to the elements; this can be a simple index, as in an array, or a key in a dictionary, or enforced by some internal ordering such as sorting.

Unordered	The collection has no ordering; the elements cannot be indexed.
Indexed	The collection can be indexed by an integer; indexed collections are always ordered.
Values	Some collections can hold any object including collections. Some collections hold only special objects; strings hold just characters, for example.

The classes described in this chapter, along with their abstract parents, are:

```
Object
    Collection
        Bag                                          79
        Dictionary                                   82
        SequenceableCollection
            AdditiveSequenceableCollection
                OrderedCollection                    76
                SortedCollection                     78
            ArrayedCollection
                Array                                71
                ByteArray                            73
                String                               73
                    Symbol                           74
                Interval                             79
        Set                                          80
```

Figure 20 summarizes the concrete classes in this chapter and their characteristics.

Indexed by	Class	Ordering	Size	Holds
Integer	Array	Index	Fixed	Any object
	ByteArray	Index	Fixed	Integers: 0-255
	Interval	Internal	Fixed	Computed sequence
	OrderedCollection	Index	Variable	Any object
	SortedCollection	Internal	Variable	Any object
	String	Index	Fixed	Characters
	Symbol	Index	Fixed	Characters
Key	Dictionary	Key, =	Variable	Key + any object
	IdentityDictionary	Key, ==	Variable	Key + any object
None	Bag	None	Variable	Any object but nil
	Set	None	Variable	Any object but nil

Figure 20: Comparison of Concrete Collection Subclasses.

Arrays have a fixed number of elements and are indexed by an integer. The elements can be any object.

Byte arrays are very similar to arrays but hold integers in the range 0 to 255.

Bags are unordered collections that act like containers into which things can be placed and withdrawn; bags grow as needed. There is no ordering of items in the bag. Multiple items with the same value can be placed in the bag. Bags can hold any object except nil.

Dictionaries hold key-value pairs which are instances of Association, and will grow as needed to hold new key-value pairs. Only one value with a given key can be in the dictionary. Values can be any object.

Identity dictionaries are identical to dictionaries except that the == message is used (instead of =) when comparing keys.

Intervals are collections that have computed values in some range of numbers such as 3 to 32, or 1.0 to 10.0 in steps of 0.2.

Ordered collections are similar to arrays; they are indexed by integers and can hold any object. However, the size of an ordered collection is not fixed, and can change as elements are added or removed. They also can be used as stacks or queues.

Sets are very similar to bags, except that they only hold one of any given object. Sets are unordered collections and are not indexable; they grow to hold additional elements. Sets can hold any object except nil.

Sorted collections can hold any object, and can grow as elements are added. The elements are maintained in a sorted order which can be defined by the user.

Strings are like arrays, fixed in size and indexed by integers, but hold just characters.

Symbols are a refinement of strings. It is guaranteed that any two symbols with the same value are also the same object.

Creating Collections

Collections are created by asking a collection class for a new instance. The new: message asks for a new instance with a given number of elements; the new message asks for a new instance with a default number of elements.

> " **Allocate a new array** "
> Array new: 27   *Example 55, Inspect*

> " **Allocate a new ordered collection** "
> OrderedCollection new   *Example 56, Inspect*

The new method allocates a new instance of a collection having a default size of some small integer. For variable-size collections, the size method answers the number of elements actually added to the collection, not the available space. Thus Bag new size is always zero.

The new: method allocates a new instance with a specified size. It should always be used for fixed-size collections, and for variable-size collections when a size is known. The size message of fixed-size collections always returns the allocated size for fixed-size collections. Thus (Array new: 10) size answers 10; for variable-size collections, size answers the number of elements, initially zero.

Another way to create collections is by converting one kind of collection to another. A common way is to write a constant array and convert it:

> " **Convert an array to a set** "
> #(1 2 3 4 5) asSet   *Example 57, Inspect*

Iterating Through Collections

In most conventional languages, it is necessary to write a loop of some kind to iterate through arrays. There is always the possibility of the loop being off by one and accessing the wrong values (and possibly exceeding the array size). In Smalltalk, it is not possible to run off the end; collection boundaries are checked and an error is raised if an index is outside the bounds. Further, collections will iterate over themselves, eliminating the need to use indexes at all in many cases.

All collections provide a number of messages that perform the iteration across the collection. The simplest is do:.

do:

The do: message simply passes each element of a collection to a one-parameter block, the loop 'body'.

aCollection do: [:element | do-something]

Example:

```
" Max element of an array "
| a coll |
a := 0.
coll := #( 7 9 5 3 1 ).
coll do: [ :elem | a := a max: elem ].
^ a
    " Answer: 9"
```
Example 58, Display

collect:

The collect: message produces a new collection with one element for each element in the original collection.

Each element is passed to a block. The value of the block is returned and becomes the value added to the new collection.

In Example 59, an array in someIntegers holds integers. A new collection is formed and contains someInteger size elements. Each element value is one larger than the original element.

```
" Collect incremented elements "
| someIntegers |
someIntegers := #(0 1 2 3 4 5 ).
^ someIntegers collect: [ :e | e + 1 ]
    "Result: 1 2 3 4 5 6"
```
Example 59, Display

conform:

The conform: message returns true if each element passes some test.

The array in someIntegers is tested for non-negative elements:

```
" See if all array elements are non-negative "
| someIntegers |
someIntegers := #(0 1 2 3 4 5 ).
^ someIntegers conform: [ :e | e >= 0 ]
    " Result: true "
```
Example 60, Display

detect:

The detect: message returns the first element that meets some criteria.

```
" Detect element greater-than zero "
| someIntegers |
someIntegers := #( -6 2 0 9 ).
^ someIntegers detect: [ :e | e > 0 ]   "Result: 2"
```

The array in someIntegers is searched for the first element greater than zero; the expression returns a 2.

detect:ifNone:

The detect:ifNone: message returns the value of the second block if no match is found.

```
" Detect element less-than zero; answer block value if none "
| someIntegers |
someIntegers := #( 1 2 3 4 5 ).
^ someIntegers detect: [ :e | e < 0 ] ifNone: [ 0 ]   "Result: 0"
```
Example 62, Display

inject:into:

The inject:into: message iterates across a collection, carrying some result forward to the next iteration.

Format:

aCollection **inject:** initialValue **into:** [:injectedValue :element | ...]

The first execution of the block passes initialValue as the value of injectedValue and the first element of aCollection as element. The result of the block is then passed to the block as the new injectedValue, along with the second element, and so on.

In Example 63, an array of numbers is iterated across. The initial value is 0. In the first execution of the block, the 0 is added to the first element, producing a 1. In the second iteration, the 1 is passed as inj and is added to the second element, a 2. This process continues until the collection is exhausted. The final answer is 15, the sum of the values in the collection.

```
" Simple inject:into: to sum elements in an array "
| sum |
sum := #( 1 2 3 4 5 )
        inject: 0
        into: [ :inj :ele | inj + ele ]
        " Answers: 15 "
```
Example 63, Display

In Example 64, an array contains strings; the loop concatenates the strings, with a blank between each.

```
" Concatenating strings with inject:into: "
| string strs |
strs := #( 'When' 'in' 'the' 'course' ' of' 'human' 'events' ).
strs inject: ''
        into: [ :inj :ele | inj, ele, ' ' ]
        " Answers: 'When in the course of human events ' "
```
Example 64, Display

Finally, Example 65 calculates a factorial using inject:into:.

```
" Factorial with inject:into: "
| n nfact |
n := 12.
nfact := (2 to: n)
    inject: 1
    into: [ :inj :ele | inj * ele ].
^ nfact
    " Answers: 479001600 "
```
Example 65, Display

reject:

The reject: message produces a new collection, with one element for each element in the collection that fails a given test.

```
" Collect elements rejected by even test "
| someIntegers |
someIntegers := #(0 1 2 3 4 5 ).
^ someIntegers reject: [ :e | e even ]
    " Answers: 1 3 5"
```
Example 66, Display

A new collection is returned that holds just the odd integers in someIntegers.

select:

The select: message produces a new collection, with one element for each element in the collection that passes a given test.

In Example 67, a new collection is returned, holding just the odd integers in someIntegers.

```
" Collect elements selected by even test "
| someIntegers |
someIntegers := #(0 1 2 3 4 5 ).
^ someIntegers select: [ :e | e even ]
    " Answers: 0 2 4 "
```
Example 67, Display

In Example 68, a new collection is returned, holding just the non-blank characters in a string.

```
" Select blanks out of a string "
'I am not a crook!' select: [ :ch | ch ~= $  ]
    " Answers: 'Iamnotacrook!' "
```
Example 68, Display

Testing

A collection can be tested for emptiness (isEmpty, or the converse, notEmpty), number of occurrences of some element (occurrencesOf:), for the existence of an element (includes:), and for its number of elements (size).

```
" Count 3s in collection "
^ #(1 2 3 4 5) occurrencesOf: 3        "Result: 1"
```
Example 69, Display

```
" How many 6s in collection "
^ #(1 2 3 4 5) occurrencesOf: 6        "Result: 0"
```
Example 70, Display

```
" Get collection size "
^ #(1 2 3 4 5) size                    "Result: 5"
```
Example 71, Display

```
" See if collection is empty "
^ #(1 2 3 4 5) isEmpty                    "Result: false"                    Example 72, Display
```

Conversions

Collections can be converted to other kinds of collections with the messages:

asArray	To an array
asBag	To a bag
asByteArray	To a byte array
asOrderedCollection	To an ordered collection
asSet	To a set
asSortedCollection	To a sorted collection
asSortedCollection:	To a sorted collection giving a sort block

---

Fixed-Size Collections

Fixed-size collections, also called *arrayed collections*, are collections such as arrays and strings. They have a fixed number of elements that are indexed by integers. The index of the first element of the collection is always one. The size is specified when the collection is created, and cannot be changed thereafter. It is an error if the index is not within the bounds of the collection. Fixed-size collections do not support adding or deleting elements.

Arrays

Arrays are fixed-size collections that can hold any kind of object.

```
Array new: 100     "Create a new array with 100 elements"
```

New arrays are initialized with the value nil.

Arrays can be created with specified elements using the with: family of messages. From one to four with:'s can be used. In the following a new array with four elements is created.

```
fourItems := Array with: 2 with: 3 with: 4 with: 5
```

Accessing Elements

Elements of arrays are retrieved with the at: message; the parameter is an index into the array. Thus the expression fourItems at: 1 would return the first element of fourItems, a 2.

```
fourItems at: 1                       "Returns the first element, a 2"
```

Unlike traditional languages, in which an element of a collection is set with an assignment statement, Smalltalk uses a message to set elements of a collection. Elements are set using the at:put: message.

```
fourItems at: 1 put: 6                "Set element 1 to 6. Contents: 6 3 4 5"

fourItems at: 2                       "Put 4th item into 2nd place"
    put: (fouritems at: 4)            "Contents: 6 5 4 5"
```

All elements in an array can be set at one time with atAllPut:, and selected elements can be set to a single value with atAll:put:.

```
" Zero new array; set some elements to 1 "
| a |
a := Array new: 10.                    "All elements are initialized to nil"
a atAllPut: 0.                         "Initialize all to zero"
a atAll: #(2 5 9 1) put: 7.            "set elements 2, 5, 9, and 1 to 1"
^ a
    " Answers: 7 7 0 0 7 0 0 0 7 0 "
```

Example 73, Display

Additional messages allow searching for a given element, creating new arrays by copying parts or all of an array in a variety of ways, and replacing portions of the elements in an array.

Arrays of Collections

Array elements can be other collections. Arrays of arrays are the way that Smalltalk implements multidimensional arrays. The following example creates an array with four elements, each of which is itself an array with five elements.

```
" Initialize 2-D array "
| a2d |
a2d := Array new: 4.
a2d at: 1 put: (Array new: 5).
a2d at: 2 put: (Array new: 5).
a2d at: 3 put: (Array new: 5).
a2d at: 4 put: (Array new: 5).
^ a2d
```

Example 74, Inspect

This can obviously be generalized by looping.

```
" Initialize 2-D array by looping "
| a2d m n |
m := 4.
n := 5.
a2d := Array new: m.
1 to: a2d size
    do: [ :i |
        a2d at: i put: (Array new: n) ].
^ a2d
```

Example 75, Inspect

This example creates a four-element array (Array new: m) and then loops across the new collection, adding a new five-element (Array new: n) array at each position.

The indexing of arrays in arrays requires multiple at: messages.

```
        (a2d at: 3) at: 2
```

The first at: message returns the array in the third element of a2d. The second is sent to the extracted five-element array, and returns the second element of it. (Remember that, without the parentheses, this would attempt to send the at:at: message to a2d.)

The array in a2d is a four-by-five array. However, there is nothing that requires that arrays of arrays be rectangular. It is quite possible to have arrays with triangular or other shapes.

```
" Initialize triangular array "
| tri |
tri := Array new: 4.
tri at: 1 put: (Array new: 1).
tri at: 2 put: (Array new: 2).
tri at: 3 put: (Array new: 3).
tri at: 4 put: (Array new: 4).
^ tri
```

Example 76, Inspect

or:

```
" Initialize triangular array by looping "
| tri |
tri := Array new: 4.
1 to: (tri size)
        do: [ :n |
                tri at: n put: ((Array new: n) atAllput: 0) ].
^ tri
```

Example 77, Inspect

The resulting array has this shape:

```
tri at: 1   is   0
tri at: 2   is   0  0
tri at: 3   is   0  0  0
tri at: 4   is   0  0  0  0
```

Arrays can also hold other collections such as strings, bags, sets or ordered collections (and these other collections can hold arrays or bags or whatever.)

For detailed information, see class Array on page 360.

Byte Arrays

The elements in byte arrays must be integers in the range 0 to 255. Byte arrays are otherwise identical to arrays.

For detailed information, see class ByteArray on page 361.

Strings

Strings are fixed-size collections of characters. The size is specified when the string is created, and cannot be changed thereafter.

```
String new: 100     "Create a new string with 100 characters"
```

New strings are initialized to character values of zero; that is, each character is:

```
0 asCharacter
```

Strings can be created with specified elements with the with: messages. From one to four with: messages can be used. In the following, a new string with three characters is created.

```
" Create 'the' string with with: "
^ String with: $t with: $h with: $e
    " Answers: 'the' "
```

Example 78, Display

Typically, however, strings are either literals, are returned from some conversion or input operation, or are formed from several strings with the concatenation operator comma (,).

```
" Create a string by concatenation of other strings "
| the sent |
the := 'the'.
sent := the, ' cat ate ', the, ' food.'.
^ sent
    "Answers: 'the cat ate the food.' "
```

Example 79, Display

String Comparisons

Strings can be compared with the relational operators <, <=, =, >, >=, ~~, and ~=. While = and ~= perform exact comparisons, including case, the other relationals ignore case. Thus both 'the'<'The' and 'the'>'The' are false.

Accessing Elements and Substrings

Elements of strings are retrieved with the at: message; the parameter is an index into the string. The expression (the at: 1) will return the first element of the, a $t.

          'the' at: 1   " returns the 1st element, a $t"

Elements are set using the at:put: message. (It is necessary to copy the literal string before making a change to it, since literals are read-only.)

          'the' copy at: 1 put: $T   "change 'the' to 'The' "

Substrings are extracted with copyFrom:to: (and a number of related messages). An index can be found using indexOf: which returns the first occurrence of a character in the string.

```
" Extract substrings "
| a cat1 cat2 |
a := 'The cat ate the food.'.
cat1 := a copyFrom: 5 to: 7.              "cat1 holds the string 'cat'"
cat2 := a copyFrom: (a indexOf: $c)
           to: (a indexOf: $t)."cat2 holds the string 'cat'"
^ cat1, ' ', cat2
     " Answer: 'cat cat' "
```
                                                                    Example 80, Display

Additional messages allow searching for a given element, creating new arrays by copying parts or all of an array in a variety of ways, and replacing portions of the elements in an array.

For detailed information, see class String on page 362.

Symbols

Symbols are strings with one additional property; two symbols that have the same value when compared with = will always compare true with ==.

          ('abc', 'def') asSymbol == #abcdef   " Answers true"   *Example 81, Display*

Symbols are used for special purposes, such as holding method names, and should not be used as a general replacement for strings. Symbols cannot be changed, such as by at:put:.

For detailed information, see class Symbol on page 370.

Intervals

Intervals are computed collection-like objects in which the elements are numbers that are calculated when referenced. Intervals are created with the to: and to:by: messages. Intervals act like collections and respond to the same messages, except that elements cannot be changed.

Format:

          start **to:** end

The collection starts with start. Each successive value is obtained by adding one to the previous value. The series ends with the highest value that does not exceed end. The table below shows the individual steps for various values of start and end.

Expression	Calculated elements
1 to: 10	1 2 3 4 5 6 7 8 9 10
1/2 to: 2	1/2 3/2
-2 to: -10	(empty)
0 to: 3.0	0 1 2 3
1.0 to: 3.0	1.0 2.0 3.0

Example:

```
" An Interval from 5 to 10 "
Transcript cr.
Transcript show: (5 to: 10) printString
```
Example 82, Display

Format:

start **to:** end **by:** step

The collection starts with start. Each successive value is obtained by adding step to the previous value. The series ends with the highest value that does not exceed end. The table below shows the individual steps for various values of start, end, and step.

Expression	Steps
1 to: 10 by: 1	1 2 3 4 5 6 7 8 9 10
1 to: 10 by: 2	1 3 5 7 9
1.0 to: 3.0 by: 0.6	1.0 1.6 2.2 2.8
1/2 to: 2 by: 1/2	1/2 1 3/2 2
-2 to: -10 by: -1	-2 -3 -4 -5 -6 -7 -8 -9 -10
1 to: 3.0 by: 1/2	1 3/2 2 5/2 3
1.0 to: 3.0 by: 1/2	1.0 1.5 2.0 2.5 3.0

Example:

```
" An Interval With Fractions "
Transcript cr.
Transcript show: (1/2 to: 5/2 by: 1/4) printString
    "The Transcript shows:
        (1/2) (3/4) 1 (5/4) (3/2) (7/4) 2 (9/4) (5/2) "
```
Example 83, Execute

Intervals can be used to initialize other collections with numeric values, as in:

(1 to: 100) asArray

Or, as an alternative to Example 63 on page 69:

```
" Simple inject:into: to sum elements in an interval "
| sum |
sum := (1 to: 5)
    inject: 0
    into: [ :inj :ele | inj + ele ]
    " Answers: 15 "
```
Example 84, Display

Creation messages for intervals look similar to, but are distinct from, the to:do: and to:by:do: messages used for looping.

Variable-Size Collections

Variable-size collections grow as needed to hold whatever is placed in them. The initial extent can be specified when the collection is created, or it can default to a system provided value.

In either case, the extent and the size of variable-size collections are different. The size, as retrieved by the size message, is the count of the number of elements placed in the collection. It is, of course, never bigger than the extent, but can be as small as zero.

Ordered Collections

Ordered collections are variable-size collections that can hold any kind of object. The initial extent can be specified when the collection is created, but will increase if more elements are added.

"**Collection with room for 20 elements**"
OrderedCollection new: 20   *Example 85, Inspect*

Since ordered collections grow, they can be created with new.

"**Collection with room for a default number of elements**"
OrderedCollection new   *Example 86, Inspect*

New ordered collections have no contents; the size is zero.

Adding Elements

Elements are added to ordered collections with one of several add messages. The basic add: message adds one element at an unspecified position. The messages addFirst: and addLast: specify to add a new element at the front or back of the collection. The messages add:before: and add:after: add elements before or after specified elements in the collection.

```
" Create a collection using add:, addFirst:, and addLast: "
| oc |
oc := OrderedCollection new: 20.
oc add: 7.                          "Holds: 7"
oc addLast: 9.                      "Holds: 7 9"
oc addFirst: 3.                     "Holds: 3 7 9"
oc addLast: 'The End'.              "Holds: 3 7 9 'The End' "
oc add: 22 before: 'The End'.       "Holds: 3 7 9 22 'The End' "
^ oc
```
Example 87, Inspect

The addAll: message adds the contents of some collection to an ordered collection.

```
" Create a collection using addAll: "
| oc |
oc := OrderedCollection new: 20.
oc addAll: #( 3 7 9 22 'The End').
^ oc
    " Answers: 3 7 9 22 'The End' "
```
Example 88, Display

Removing Elements

The following examples each assume that oc holds: 3 7 9 22 'The End'.

Elements can be removed from ordered collections in a variety of ways. The simplest way removes the first element with a given value.

oc remove: 9   "Holds: 3 7 22 'The End' "

A group of elements can be removed too.

oc removeAll: #(7 22)   "Holds: 3 9 'The End' "

The messages removeFirst, removeLast, and removeAtIndex: remove specific elements.

If an element is not present, the remove: message generates an error. The remove:ifAbsent: message lets some corrective action be taken by invoking a block passed as a parameter instead of raising an error.

oc remove: 3 ifAbsent: [ ]   "If 3 is missing, do nothing"

Accessing Elements

The following examples each assume that oc holds: 3 7 9 22 'The End'.

Elements of ordered collections can be retrieved with the at: message; the parameter is an index into the active elements of the collection.

oc at: 3   "returns the 3rd element, a 9"

If the second element is removed, the expression above will still return the third element of the collection, now a 22.

oc remove: 7.   "removes the element '7' "
oc at: 3   "answers the 3rd element, a 22"

Elements can be set with the at:put: message.

oc at: 1 put: 6   "change element 1 from 3 to 6"
oc at: 2 put: (oc at: 4)   "put 4th item into 2nd place"

All elements in an ordered collection can be set at one time with atAllPut:, and selected elements can be set to a single value with atAll:put:.

Additional messages allow searching for a given element, creating new ordered collections by copying parts or all of an ordered collection in a variety of ways, and replacing portions of the elements in an ordered collection.

Using Ordered Collections

As Arrays

Since ordered collections can be indexed, and since they can grow and shrink, they are often used in programs instead of arrays.

As Queues

Ordered collections can act like queues. Queues are data structures in which new elements are added sequentially and removed in the same order in which they were added.

Use the addFirst: message to add elements and the removeLast message to remove them, or addLast: and removeFirst. The size message gives the size of the queue.

As Stacks

Ordered collections can act like stacks. Stacks are data structures in which new elements are added, and then removed in the inverse order in which they were added.

Use the addLast: message to add elements and the removeLast message to remove them. The size message gives the size of the stack.

For detailed information, see class OrderedCollection on page 351.

Sorted Collections

Sorted collections are variable-size collections of objects that are kept in some sort order. The initial extent is specified when the collection is created; it specifies the number of elements that can be added before the extent has to be increased.

```
"Create a new collection with room for 20 elements"
SortedCollection new: 20
```

New sorted collections contain no elements; the size is zero. The default sort order is ascending, but can be changed as needed.

Sorted collections are frequently created by the asSortedCollection message sent to some other kind of collection.

```
s := someCollection asSortedCollection
```

Adding Elements

Elements are added to sorted collections with one of several add messages. The basic add: message adds one element at its appropriate sorted position, and addAll: adds a collection of elements in sorted order.

```
" Add elements to a sorted collection "
| sc |
sc := #(50 10 40 20 30)
        asSortedCollection.          "Holds: 10 20 30 40 50 "
sc add: 25.                          "Holds: 10 20 25 30 40 50 "
sc addAll: #( 55 5 35 ).             "Holds: 5 10 20 25 30 35 40 50 55"
^ sc                                          Example 89, Inspect
```

Removing Elements

The following examples each assume that sc holds: (5 10 20 25 30 35 40 50 55).

Elements can be removed from sorted collections with remove: and removeAll:.

```
sc remove: 25              "Holds: 5 10 20 30 35 40 50 55"
```

Group of elements can also be removed.

```
sc removeAll: #(35 55 5)        "Holds: 10 20 25 30 40 50"
```

If an element is not present, the remove message generates an error. The remove:ifAbsent: message lets some corrective action be taken, by invoking a block passed as a parameter, instead of raising an error

```
sc remove: 3 ifAbsent: [ ]        "If 3 is missing, do nothing"

sortie remove: aircraftJustTargeted
    ifAbsent: [ self error: 'Targeted something else!' ].
```

Accessing Elements

The following examples all assume that sc holds: (10 20 30 40 50).

Elements of sorted collections can be retrieved with the at: message; the parameter is an index into the active elements of the collection.

```
sc at: 3                        "returns the 3rd element, 30"
```

If the second element is then removed, the expression above will still return the third element of the collection, now a 40.

```
sc remove: 20.
sc at: 3                        "returns the 3rd element, 40"
```

If an element is not present, the remove: message generates an error. The remove:ifAbsent: message gives control over missing elements.

> sc at: 3 ifAbsent: [nil]　　　　　　　　"If 3 is missing, return nil"

Note: It is an error to attempt to set elements with the at:put: message.

Additional messages allow searching for a given element, and replacing portions of the elements in an array.

Sort Blocks

By default, sorted collections are sorted in ascending order and elements must respond to less-than (<) by answering a boolean. The sort order can be overridden by specifying a sort block. Sort blocks take two parameters and return true if the first parameter should come before the second parameter in the sorted collection.

Sort blocks can be specified when the sorted collection is created. In the following, a new collection is created with a sort block which specifies ascending order, the default.

> sc := SortedCollection sortBlock: [:a :b | a < b]

In the following, the sort order is descending.

> sc := SortedCollection sortBlock: [:a :b | a > b]

Both of these assume that the object can be compared using relationals. If the objects do not respond to less-than (<), then the sort block must be changed to compare something in or about the object.

In the following, some employee objects respond to the message name by returning a string. These strings are then compared.

> sc := SortedCollection
> 　　sortBlock: [:emp1 :emp2 |
> 　　　　emp1 name < emp2 name]

Sort blocks can be changed as needed to resort a collection.

> sc sortBlock: [emp1: emp2: |
> 　　　　emp1 name > emp2 name]

For detailed information, see class SortedCollection on page 356.

Bags

Bags are variable-size collections of objects that are not kept in any kind of order. The values in bags can be any kind of object. The number of elements that can be added before the collection is expanded is specified when the bag is created, but the number can increase if more elements are added. Bags cannot hold the value nil.

> b := Bag new: 20　　　　　　　　"Create a new Bag with 20 elements"

Since bags grow, they can be created with new.

> oc := OrderedCollection new

New bags contain no elements; the size is zero.

Bags store just one copy of a given object. If more then one identical object is added, just the count of the number of such objects is remembered. Thus adding 250 instances of a single object takes up no more space than a single occurrence.

Adding Elements

Elements are added to bags with one of several add messages. The basic add: message adds one element and addAll: adds a collection of elements. In this book, the notation 2:5 means that the bag holds 2 elements with the value 5; bold type shows changes.

```
| bag |
bag := #( 1 1 1 3 5 5 8 ) asBag.      " Holds: 3:1 1:3 2:5 1:8 "
bag add: 7.                           " Holds: 3:1 1:3 2:5 1:7 1:8 "
bag addAll: #( 1 7 $a $a ).           " Holds: 4:1 1:3 2:5 2:7 1:8 2:$a"
^ bag
    " Answer: Bag( 1 1 1 1 $a $a 3 5 5 7 7 8 )"                    Example 90, Inspect
```

Removing Elements

The following examples each assume that bag holds: (4:1 1:3 2:5 2:7 1:8 2:$a).

Elements can be removed from bags with remove: and removeAll:.

```
        bag remove: 8                  " Holds: 4:1 1:3 2:5 2:7 2:$a"
```

Groups of elements can be removed in the same way.

```
        bag removeAll: #(1 1 $a)       " Holds: 2:1 1:3 2:5 2:7 1:8 1:$a"
```

If an element is not present, the remove message above generates an error. The remove:ifAbsent: message gives control over missing elements.

```
        bag remove: 3 ifAbsent: [ ]     " If 3 is missing, do nothing"
```

Accessing Elements

Elements in bags cannot be accessed directly: the at: and at:put: messages are not supported. The existence of an element can be tested with includes:.

```
    " Test a bag for the existence of a specific element "
    | bag |
    bag := #( 1 1 1 3 5 5 8 ) asBag." Holds: 1 1 1 3 5 5 8 "
    ^ bag includes: 5
        " Answers: true"                                          Example 91, Display
```

Bags can, of course, be iterated through with the various iteration messages.

Using Bags

Bags are useful for tallying things, since the bag maintains a count of how many identical objects are added.

For detailed information, see class Bag on page 320.

Sets

Sets are variable-size collections of objects that are not kept in any kind of order. The values in sets can be any kind of object except nil. A new set is created by the new message.

```
        s := Set new.
```

The initial extent can be specified when the set is created; the extent will increase if more elements are added.

```
        s := Set new: 100               " Create a Set with room for 100 elements"
```

New sets contain no elements; the size is zero.

Sets hold just one copy of a given object. Attempts to add more than one element with the same value are ignored.

Adding Elements

Elements are added to sets with one of several add messages. The basic add: message adds one element, and addAll: adds a collection of elements.

```
" Add elements to a set "
| set |
set := #( 1 1 1 3 5 5 8 ) asSet.          " Holds: 1 3 5 8 "
set add: 7.                               " Holds: 1 3 5 8 7 "
set addAll: #( 1 7 $a $a ).               " Holds: 1 3 5 8 7 $a"
^ set
```
Example 92, Display

Removing Elements

In each of the examples below, set is assumed to contain: (1 3 5 7 8 $a.)

Elements can be removed from sets with remove: and removeAll:.

```
set remove: 8                             " Holds: 1 3 5 7 $a"
```

A collection of elements can be removed.

```
set removeAll: #(1 $a)                     " Holds: 3 5 8 7"
```

If an element is missing, the remove: and removeAll: messages raise errors. To prevent this, the message remove:ifAbsent: is passed a block which is invoked if the element is absent. It can either take some special action or do nothing.

```
set remove: 22 ifAbsent: [ self error: 'The absence is unsettling!' ]
```

Accessing Elements

Elements cannot be accessed directly with at: or at:put: but the existence of an element can be tested with includes:.

```
" Test a set for the existence of a specific element "
| set |
set := #( 1 1 1 3 5 5 8 ) asSet.          " Holds: 1 3 5 8 "
^ set includes: 5                          " Returns true"
```
Example 93, Display

Sets can, of course, be iterated through with the various iteration messages.

Using Sets

Sets are useful for finding out how many unique elements some other collection holds, or for keeping track of which of a set of unique objects have been seen.

If collection zips holds one ZipCode† for each customer, then converting it to a set produces a collection with just one of each ZipCode.

```
ncust := zips size.         "ncust holds the number of customers"
nzips := zips asSet size.   "nzips holds the number of different zip codes"
```

A tally of how many customers are in each zip code area can be determined by converting zips into a bag, which will provide the count of occurrences of each element, and then by iterating on zips as converted to a set, which assures that the loop will execute only once for each unique element.

---

† ZipCode is the U.S. Postal Service trademark for a postal code.

```
" Tally ZipCodes "
| zips tally count |
zips := #( 10598 99987 10598 63476 10019 10598 99987 ).
tally := zips asBag.
zips asSet do: [ :azip |
    count := tally occurrencesOf: azip.
    Transcript
        show: azip printString;
        show: ' ';
        show: count printString;
        cr ]
" The result in the transcript is:
99987 2
63476 1
10019 1
10598 3  "
```

Example 94, Execute

If a sorted collection holds duplicate elements, they can be removed by converting to a set and back, like this:

```
coll := coll asSet asSortedCollection: coll sortBlock
```

For detailed information, see class Set on page 329.

Dictionaries

Dictionaries are variable-size collections of objects that are accessed by a specified key. The keys and values in dictionaries can be any kind of object, but the keys are often some kind of magnitude, such as a string or symbol. The initial extent can be specified when the collection is created, but the extent can increase if more elements are added.

Dictionaries are used wherever a value is associated with a key. Uses include symbol tables with string keys or sparse arrays with integer keys and array values, or many other things.

```
" Create a new dictionary with space for a default number of elements "
Dictionary new
```
Example 95, Inspect

```
" Create a new dictionary with space for 20 elements "
Dictionary new: 20
```
Example 96, Inspect

New dictionaries contain no elements but have room for some number of elements that can be added before the dictionary has to be expanded. The initial size is zero.

The key/value pairs are instances of class Association. When a value is changed the change is made to the value part of the association.

Adding Elements

Elements are added to dictionaries with the at:put: message, that puts a value at a position named by the first parameter, the key. If the key already exists in the dictionary then the value is changed.

82 Collections and Iteration

```
" Create dictionary; add new elements "
| ages |
ages := Dictionary new: 30.
ages at: 'Dave' put: 42;
    at: 'Carol' put: 35;
    at: 'Archie' put: 4.
^ ages
```

Example 97, Inspect

Removing Elements

Key/value pairs can be removed from dictionaries with removeKey: and removeAllKeys:.

```
ages removeKey: 'Archie'
```

A collection of elements can be removed in the same way.

```
ages removeAllKeys: #( 'Archie' 'Carol' )
```

If an element is missing, removeKey: raises an error condition; removeKey:ifAbsent: is passed a block which is invoked if the element is absent. It can either take some special action or do nothing.

```
ages removeKey: 'Fido' ifAbsent: [ ]
```

Accessing Elements

The following examples each assume that ages holds the values:

```
'Dave':42
'Carol':35
'Archie':4
```

(This notation is used in this book to describe an Association. The part before the colon is the key and the part after the colon is the value.)

Elements can be accessed directly using the key.

```
d := ages at: 'Dave'              "d holds 42"
```

Elements can be updated with at:put:. In the following, the age of 'Dave' is increased by one.

```
ages at: 'Dave' put: (ages at: 'Dave') + 1
```

If an element is missing, at: raises an error condition. To prevent this, the message at:ifAbsent: can be used. It is passed a block which is invoked if the element is absent. The value it returns becomes the result of the expression. In the following, a zero is returned if the key is missing.

```
fido := ages at: 'Fido' ifAbsent: [ 0 ]
```

In the following, if 'Fido' is present, its value is answered; if absent, it is added and a zero is returned.

```
dog := ages at: 'Fido'               "Index ages at key 'fido'"
       ifAbsent: [                    "If the key is missing"
           ages at: 'Fido' put: 0 ]   "Add key and some value"
```

In addition, dictionaries can be searched for a key corresponding to some element, collections with just the keys or values extracted, the existence of a given key queried, and other functions can be performed.

Example:

```
" Build dictionary of names and ages; extract ages and calculate sum "
| ages |
ages := Dictionary new.
ages at: 'Archie' put: 4.
ages at: 'Carol' put: 44.
ages at: 'Dave' put: 39.
ages at: 'Total' put: (
        (ages at: 'Archie') + (ages at: 'Carol') + (ages at: 'Dave')  ).
^ ages at: 'Total'
"Answers: 87"
```
                                                                          Example 98, Display

For detailed information on dictionaries, see class Dictionary on page 321 and class IdentityDictionary on page 328.

Global Variables

The reserved name, Smalltalk, is an instance of a special subclass of Dictionary. It holds keys that must be variable names starting with an upper-case letter. Whenever such a name occurs in Smalltalk code, the value from the Smalltalk dictionary is used. Class names are the most common thing in the Smalltalk dictionary.

Pool dictionaries, which are instances of Dictionary, hold variable names and associated values too, and are also accessed by writing the variable names in code. Pool dictionaries are specified as a part of a class definition and apply to that class and all of its subclasses.

For detailed information on dictionaries see Chapter 8, 'Variables', on page 101.

Summary

Collections come in many colors and flavors, not just an array as in most traditional languages. A variety of fixed-size and variable-size collections provide quite different ways to hold objects.

The fixed-size collection, Array, is a general-purpose workhorse. Instances of String, Symbol, and ByteArray take specialized objects, characters, and integers from 0 to 255. Instances of Interval don't store values at all, but generate numbers in a sequence upon demand.

Intervals are fixed-size collections where the collection is not stored, but the elements are calculated as they are referenced.

The variable-size, indexed collection OrderedCollection is, in essence, an array that can grow and which can be added to at the front, back, or between elements. They can act like arrays, queues, and stacks.

SortedCollection instances, too, are variable-size collections, but can only be indexed by integers when reading values.

Set and Bag are unordered, variable-size collections that are identical except that sets keep just one of each element with a given value and bags keep a count of elements with the same value.

Instances of Dictionary are unordered, variable sized collections that can be indexed by keys. Pool dictionaries are dictionaries used to hold constants for methods in selected classes.

7

Creating Classes

This chapter will describe how to create new classes, how messages work in a hierarchy, how to use self and super, and will show several examples of new classes. It revisits material that was first presented in Chapter 2, 'Introduction to Concepts', on page 7.

An Employee Class

A general-purpose employee class should hold just that information that is common to all kinds of employees, and no more. Not all employees have salaries (hourly workers or contract employees, for example), not all have a position (retirees, for example).

Class Employee will have four instance variables, empID, name, address, and startDate.

> Class:
> > Employee
>
> Variables:
> > empID
> > name
> > address
> > startDate

Class Employee might have the following subclasses:

> *Employee*
> > SalariedEmployee
> > HourlyEmployee
> > RetiredEmployee
> > Contractor
> > Executive

Each of these subclasses will have data associated with it; potential instance variables are shown in Figure 21.

Class Name	Instance Variables
Employee	empID, name, address, startDate
SalariedEmployee	salary, position
Executive	salary, position, bonus
HourlyEmployee	payRate, position
Contractor	payRate, contractNum
RetiredEmployee	pension, dateRetired

Figure 21: Definition of **Employee.**

This outline means, for example, that a SalariedEmployee is a logical extension, or a subclass, of Employee, and it has all of the instance variables shown for Employee and those shown for SalariedEmployee:.

Note that both SalariedEmployee and Executive have two common data items, salary and position. HourlyEmployee and Contractor also have common items, payRate and position. It is best to have just one instance variable for a given purpose, since that means just one set of access methods, and one place to find to make changes.

The solution for Executive is easy; since executives are also salaried employees, class Executive is a refinement of SalariedEmployee, shown in Figure 22.

Class Name	Instance Variables
Employee	empID, name, address, startDate
SalariedEmployee	salary, position
Executive	bonus
HourlyEmployee	payRate, position
Contractor	payRate, contractNum
RetiredEmployee	pension, dateRetired

Figure 22: Definition of **SalariedEmployee** with Executive subclass.

The solution for Contractor is logically harder, since a contractor is definitely *not* a refinement of the concept of HourlyEmployee; it also means that, if it were a subclass of HourlyEmployee, Contractor would have a variable, position, that it wouldn't use. However, the data fields almost match, and it *might* be decided to share these data fields, as in Figure 23.

Class Name	Instance Variables
Employee	empID, name, address, startDate
SalariedEmployee	salary, position
Executive	bonus
HourlyEmployee	payRate, position
Contractor	contractNum
RetiredEmployee	pension, dateRetired

Figure 23: Definition of **HourlyEmployee** with Contractor subclass.

A better solution, which maintains the logic of the hierarchy, adds a new abstract class, Hourly, and makes both HourlyEmployee and Contractor subclasses of it; it is shown in Figure 24.

Class Name	Instance Variables
Employee	empID, name, address, startDate
SalariedEmployee	salary, position
Executive	bonus
Hourly	payRate
HourlyEmployee	position
Contractor	contractNum
RetiredEmployee	pension, dateRetired

Figure 24: **Employee with Instance Variables.**

This refinement is based mainly on instance variable usage; there are other factors, such as the logic of the hierarchy (which guided the addition of class Hourly). The design of classes and hierarchies is a subject that has been much studied and debated. See the references for further reading at the end of the chapter.

Methods

Methods to access the variables are shown in Figure 25.

Class Name	Instance Variables	Methods
Employee	empID	empID, empID:
	name	name, name:
	address	address, address:
	startDate	startDate, startDate:
SalariedEmployee	salary	salary, salary:
	position	position, position:
Executive	bonus	bonus, bonus:
Hourly	payRate	payRate, payRate:
HourlyEmployee	position	position, position:
Contractor	contractNum	contractNum, contractNum:
RetiredEmployee	pension	pension, pension:
	dateRetired	dateRetired, dateRetired:

Figure 25: **Employee with Subclasses and Method Names.**

Class Employee

The code for class Employee, including access methods, would look like this:

```
Class:
      Employee
Subclass of:
      Object
Variables:
      empID name startDate
Class Methods:
  new
        ^ super new initialize
Instance Methods:
  empID: n
        empID := n
  empID
```

```
                        ^ empID
            name
                        ^ name
            name: aString
                name := aString
            address
                        ^ address
            address: anAddress
                address := anAddress
            startDate: aDate
                aDate > Date today
                    ifTrue: [ self error: 'Invalid start date ', aDate printString ].
                startDate := aDate
            startDate
                        ^ startDate
```

Obtaining a New Instance

A new Employee object is created by writing Employee new. A new method is often used to initialize instance variables, and most often looks just like the following.

```
        Private Class Methods:
        new
            ^ super new initialize
```

A new instance of the class is obtained (from super); then the initialize message is sent to that new instance.

```
        Private Instance Methods:
        initialize
            address := Address new.
            empID := EmployeeIDAllocator newID.
            startDate := Date today
```

Three variables of Employee are initialized: address is set to an instance of class **Address**; empID is set to the next available employee ID by some employee identification manager; and the startDate is set to today.

Private Methods

The initialize and new methods are examples of what are called private methods. Private methods are not documented for users, and are only seen in the development environment if asked for explicitly. By convention, it is agreed that no code outside the class and its subclasses will call a private method.

SalariedEmployee Subclass

The methods of the subclass SalariedEmployee are:

```
        Class:
            SalariedEmployee
        Variables:
            position salary
        Subclass of:
            Employee
```

Instance Methods:
position: aString
    position := aString
position
    ^ position
salary: n
    salary := n
salary
    ^ salary

Messages in a Hierarchy

A new salaried employee object is defined like this:

    newHire := SalariedEmployee new.

Then messages like these are sent to this new instance.

    newHire salary: 58234.
    newHire position: 'Programmer'.

Messages defined in Employee can also be sent to instances of SalariedEmployee.

    newHire startDate: aDate

How does this work? When a message is sent to an object, the object is first examined for a method that implements the message. If found, as in position:, it is invoked. However, if one is not found, the parent class is examined. If found there, as in startDate:, it is invoked. If one is not found, its parent is examined, and so on until there are no more parents; then an error is raised.† See Figure 26.

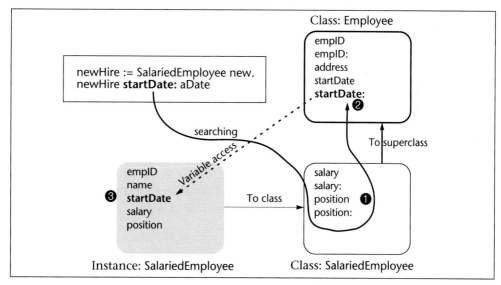

Figure 26: Searching for Inherited Methods. In the second line of the code in the box the empID: message is sent to a new instance of SalariedEmployee. The search for empID: begins at ❶ but there is no empID:. The search then goes to the parent, Employee at ❷. There is an empID: method there so it is invoked; the method sets the variable startDate in the instance of SalariedEmployee, at ❸.

---

† In practice, methods are not found by searching, except possibly the first time, but by va[...] that give direct access to the method.

Creating Classes

Classes are created in the development environment using one of the class or application browsers. The steps are:

1) Select the class that is to be the parent of the new class.

2) Ask that a subclass be added.

3) When prompted for the name, enter one; don't forget that the first character must be upper-case.

4) When prompted for the type of subclass, select subclass. (See the section on 'Indexed Memory' on page 117 for information on the other kinds of classes).

When finished, the browser window will hold an expression in the text area. This expression was just used to create the class; it can be modified to change and extend the class. The expression for a new class, TrainSet, would look like the following.

```
Object subclass: #TrainSet
    instanceVariableNames: ' '
    classVariableNames: ' '
    poolDictionaries: ' '
```

Instance variables are added by adding names to the quoted string following instanceVariableNames:.

```
Object subclass: #TrainSet
    instanceVariableNames: 'engine cars caboose track crossings '
    classVariableNames: ' '
    poolDictionaries: ' '
```

If TrainSet has a pool dictionary or a class variable, they are added in a similar way.

```
Object subclass: #TrainSet
    instanceVariableNames: 'engine cars caboose track crossings '
    classVariableNames: 'TrackLayout '
    poolDictionaries: 'Trains'
```

This expression is also present in the external format of a class.

External Class Format

Class definitions in IBM Smalltalk are created with interactive tools. While methods have a text format, classes do not. However, it is possible to save a class definition to a text file. The text file contains messages and text that will recreate the class in another ᵗalk image.

nainder of this book will show class definitions in this external format. The pre-
ᵉfinition of SalariedEmployee looks like the following, except for emphasis, in
ʳnal format.

```
"A subclass of Employee that adds protocol
needed for employees with salaries."

Employee subclass: #SalariedEmployee
    instanceVariableNames: 'position salary'
    classVariableNames: ''
    poolDictionaries: '' !

ariedEmployee publicMethods !
```

```
    position: aString
        position := aString !
    position
        ^ position !
    salary: n
        salary := n !
    salary
        ^ salary !  !
```

The expression starting with Employee subclass: defines the class Employee. This is the same expression found in class or application browsers in the development environment.

The first two lines define a new class, SalariedEmployee, as a subclass of Employee, and define two instance variables. The next two lines define any class variables or pool dictionaries; these are described in Chapter 8, 'Variables', on page 101. The exclamation point, often called a *bang*, ends the definition.

The next line starts and ends with a bang; it specifies the class and the type (public or private) of methods that follow.

Then come the methods, each ending with a bang. After the last method, another bang indicates the end.

No one ever has to write code in this format; it is the export/import format used by IBM Smalltalk.‡ It is used in this book since it is the only reasonably standard textual form of a class, and thus is preferable to something created just for this book.

Examples

Two small but complete examples will be developed. The first is a very simple investment object; the second models a number of related writing instruments.

Single Deposit

This section will develop a simple investment object. The object has a concept of value invested, an evaluation of that value across time, and some kind of interest calculation.

    Class:
        SingleDeposit
    Variables:
        value, interestRate
    Class Method:
        deposit: startAmount atRate: percent
    Instance Methods:
        value
        interestRate
        valueAfter: years

---

‡ This export format differs slightly from that of other vendors in that it identifies public and private methods. IBM Smalltalk can read the other format and, with an option properly set, can also export it.

Private Instance Methods:
initialize: startAmount atRate: percent

SingleDeposit is a simple object, assuming a single deposit and a fixed interest rate. As a result of the single deposit and fixed interest rate, it is not desirable to have a way to set the value or rate for an existing object, but that the value and rate only be set when the object is created.

One way to do this is to have a class method that allocates and initializes new objects instead of using new or new:. It can be named in a descriptive manner, say deposit:atRate:. The deposit:atRate: method needs to be the only way to set the value of the deposit or rate. The values can be queried with value and interestRate methods.

> **deposit: amount atRate: percent**
> ^ super new initialize: amount atRate: percent

Initialization takes place in the instance method initialize:atRate:.

> **initialize: amount atRate: percent**
> value isNil
>   ifTrue: [
>   value := amount.
>   interestRate := percent / 100.0]
>   ifFalse: [
>   self error: 'Cannot reinitialize a SingleDeposit instance']

All instance variables are automatically initialized to the value nil (which is, in effect, a value that indicates that no value is present). This is tested for; if it is nil, the initialization has not yet taken place.

If it is not nil, initialization has taken place; an error message is issued by sending an error: message to self.

The interest rate is seen by the user as a percentage; it is stored as a decimal number. This choice is simply a user interface issue. Rates are thought of by humans as percentages. The interest calculation needs a decimal number. It is simpler to make the conversion as it is set.

The values of the deposit and the interest rate can be requested.

> **value**
> ^ value
> **interestRate**
> ^ interestRate * 100.0

Finally comes the calculation of interest and the value of the deposit after some number of years.

> **valueAfter: years**
> ^ value * (1.0 + interestRate) raisedToInteger: years

Putting the class all together, it looks like this.

> " **SingleDeposit** "
> " A class representing a financial instrument with
> one initial deposit and a fixed interest rate across its life."
>
> **Object** subclass: **#SingleDeposit**
>   instanceVariableNames: '**value interestRate**'
>   classVariableNames: ''
>   poolDictionaries: '' !

```
! SingleDeposit class publicMethods !
deposit: amount atRate: percent
        ^ super new initialize: amount atRate: percent ! !


! SingleDeposit publicMethods !
value
        ^ value !
interestRate
        ^ interestRate * 100.0 !
valueAfter: years
        ^ (value * (1.0 + interestRate raisedToInteger: years) ) rounded ! !


! SingleDeposit privateMethods !
initialize: amount atRate: percent
        value isNil
            ifTrue: [
                value := amount.
                interestRate := percent / 100.0 ]
            ifFalse: [
                self error: 'Cannot reinitialize a SingleDeposit instance' ] ! !
```

Example 99, FileIn

Now, deposit 10,000 at 5 percent and determine the value after 10 years.

```
" SingleDeposit Example "
| investment |
investment := SingleDeposit deposit: 10000 atRate: 5.25.
^ investment valueAfter: 10
        "Answer: 16681"
```

Example 100, Display

Writing Instruments

Imagine a simple model of a fountain pen. It holds ink, uses so much ink per character written, and has a maximum capacity. Operations upon a pen would include asking is it empty, is it full, what quantity of ink remains, and to fill the pen.

Many of these characteristics hold for other kinds of writing instruments. A mechanical pencil is quite similar. It uses a stick of graphite instead of ink, but the other characteristics are the same. A felt tip or ball point pen is also quite similar, except that the capacity is higher and they cannot be refilled.

When defining new objects in Smalltalk, it is always wise to consider the general case, and to define a general concept first; then to use refinement to make the object that is needed. Similar objects are quite likely to be needed in the future and the structure will be present for them. The process of refinement also helps think through the problem.

A Design

A class tree showing five concrete writing instruments and their abstract parents along with a single instance variable, is shown below. Issues such as paper absorption or surface roughness are ignored, and capacities are thought of in terms of the number of characters that can be written. Thus a pen refill might be 1/3 fluid ounce or 10 cubic centimeters, but the capacity is thought of as, say, 5,000 written characters, thus simplifying the problem.§

Class	Instance Variables
WritingInstrument	quantity
RefillableWritingInstrument	
FountainPen	
MechanicalPencil	
DisposableWritingInstrument	
DisposablePen	
BallPointPen	
FeltTipPen	
WoodPencil	

Potential methods to access data and perform operations are:

Class	Instance Methods
WritingInstrument	howFull isEmpty isFull quantity write:
RefillableWritingInstrument	fill
FountainPen	
MechanicalPencil	
DisposableWritingInstrument	
DisposablePen	
BallPointPen	
FeltTipPen	
WoodPencil	

All but one method can be defined in the top level of the hierarchy. Since all these writing instruments have some quantity of ink or graphite, methods that operate on the remaining quantity are placed there. The howFull message requires knowledge of the maximum capacity; since it is fixed per type of writing instrument, it was decided to make a class method that returned this constant.

Class	Class Methods
WritingInstrument	capacity
RefillableWritingInstrument	refillable
FountainPen	capacity
MechanicalPencil	capacity
DisposableWritingInstrument	refillable
DisposablePen	
BallPointPen	capacity
FeltTipPen	capacity
WoodPencil	capacity

§ There are other ways to design a hierarchy of writing instruments. One might think the writing medium more important, and base a hierarchy on it. Other approaches might consider how the instrument works: mechanical, gravity feed, pressure feed, consumable instrument, etc. The approach used in the text seems useful when the writing instrument is going to be used to write characters.

The definition of the class method capacity in WritingInstrument specifies that all subclasses either must inherit or override the methods. Since capacity returns a class-specific constant, each concrete class must override it and specify an appropriate value.

With this constant available, methods such as howFull or write: can operate quite independently of the specific class they are inherited by; each will evaluate the expression self class capacity to obtain the capacity.

> **howFull**
> "Answer a value from 0 to 1 indicating quantity remaining"
> ^ quantity / self class capacity!

The refillable class method is used in the same way; it is defined in WritingInstrument to specify that all subclasses must implement or inherit it. It is redefined in RefillableWritingInstrument to answer true and in DisposableWritingInstrument to answer false. It is accessed with the expression self class refillable.

An Implementation

It is not necessary to implement the whole design, especially since it was only a fountain pen that was needed to begin with. The following hierarchies shows only FountainPen and its two abstract parents. First, the instance methods:

Class	Instance Methods
WritingInstrument	quantity howFull isEmpty IsFull write:
RefillableWritingInstrument	fill
FountainPen	

and then the class methods:

Class	Class Methods
WritingInstrument	capacity refillable
RefillableWritingInstrument	refillable
FountainPen	capacity

Class WritingInstrument

Some methods of WritingInstrument can be implemented in full; two cannot. Implementation of these is deferred by coding a method that sends the subclassResponsibility message to self. This message raises an error if it is sent. It forces subclasses to reimplement the message with a concrete implementation.

> **capacity**
> self subclassResponsibility!

Several methods, such as howFull, are generally applicable to all subclasses because they refer to information of the subclass indirectly. The howFull method uses the expression self class capacity to obtain the capacity of the specific subclass on behalf of which it is running. The alternative is to have a howFull method for each concrete class tha references the class name directly. For fountain pen this would be:

> **howFull**   " Less General Implementation "
> ^ quantity / FountainPen capacity!

The write: method is completely general and refers only to the current quantity remaining in the instrument.

```
" Writing Instrument   "
Object subclass: #WritingInstrument
    instanceVariableNames: 'quantity '
    classVariableNames: ''
    poolDictionaries: ''
!
!WritingInstrument class publicMethods !
capacity
        self subclassResponsibility!
new
        "Answer a new and full instrument"
        ^ super new initialize!
refillable
        self subclassResponsibility! !


!WritingInstrument publicMethods !
howFull
        "Answer a fraction from 0 to 1 indicating quantity remaining"
        ^ quantity / self class capacity!
isEmpty
        "Answer true if instrument is empty"
        ^ quantity = 0!
isFull
        "Answer true if the instrument is full"
        ^ quantity = self class capacity!
write: nchars
        "Answer the number of characters left to write after writing nchars
          characters. If zero, all characters were written; if greater, the quantity
          is zero"
        | need |
        need := nchars.
        quantity >= need
            ifTrue: [
                quantity := quantity - need.
                need := 0 ]
            ifFalse: [
                need := need - quantity.
                quantity := 0  ].
        ^ need
        " Answer number of characters yet to write (or 0)." ! !


!WritingInstrument privateMethods !
initialize
        "Set the quantity in a new instrument"
        quantity := self class capacity! !
```

Example 101, FileIn

Class RefillableWritingInstrument

Class RefillableWritingInstrument is trivial to write since it only needs one class method
which specifies that its subclasses are refillable, and one instance method to refill the
writing instrument.

```
" Refillable Writing Instrument   "
WritingInstrument subclass: #RefillableWritingInstrument
    instanceVariableNames: ' '
    classVariableNames: ''
    poolDictionaries: ''
!
!RefillableWritingInstrument class publicMethods !
```

refillable
        ^ true ! !

```
!RefillableWritingInstrument publicMethods !
fill
        quantity := self class capacity ! !                              Example 102, FileIn
```

Class FountainPen

Class FountainPen is trivial also; it only needs one class method which defines the capacity of the pen to hold ink; the units of capacity are the number of characters that can be written.

```
" Fountain Pen   "
RefillableWritingInstrument subclass: #FountainPen
    instanceVariableNames: ' '
    classVariableNames: ''
    poolDictionaries: ''
!
!FountainPen class publicMethods !
capacity
        ^ 500! !                                                         Example 103, FileIn
```

Example 104 obtains a new pen, writes some characters, and returns the percentage full.

```
" FountainPen example: simple writing "
| f s |
s := 'Fountain pens are wet inside.'.
f := FountainPen new.
f write: s size.
^ f howFull        " Result is: 471/500 "                                Example 104, Display
```

If the string is long and the pen runs out of ink, then the example above will not write the remaining characters. Example 105 loops, filling the pen as needed, until the whole string is written.

```
" FountainPen example: writing and refilling "
| f s n |
s := 'Fountain pens are wet inside.'.
f := FountainPen new.
n := s size.
[ (n := f write: n) > 0
            and: [self class refillable] ]       "Loop while not finished writing"
                whileTrue: [ f fill ].            "Fill pen when it gets empty"
^ f howFull
    " Answers: 471/500"                                                  Example 105, Display
```

Note how all of the writing is done in the first block of whileTrue:. Only if the pen runs dry is the second block ever executed.

Summary

Three examples of new classes are developed, illustrating both refinement of concepts in a hierarchy and information hiding and access control.

The employee hierarchy refines the concept of employee into three subclasses for salaried, hourly, and retired employees. Employees are further refined into executives, and hourly workers are refined into hourly employees and contractors.

The external, and only, textual format of classes is described.

A simple, non-hierarchical example implementing a basic long-term deposit with interest illustrates how to limit access to variables and private and public methods.

Finally, a longer example develops a hierarchy for writing instruments and implements a portion of the hierarchy for fountain pens. Abstractions are important in this example and illustrate the common tendency to have most of the code end up at the higher levels of the hierarchy, and very little at lower levels.

Further Reading

The design of larger object-oriented programs is well beyond the scope of this book. All of these references are highly recommended by Smalltalk design specialists and are suitable places to start learning about OOP design.

Grady Booch has published several books on object-oriented design and analysis; he is widely known from his lectures on the subject. His early books used Ada, but the first one below use C++ for examples.

- G. Booch, *Object-Oriented Analysis and Design with Applications*, Second Edition, Benjamin/Cummings, 1994.

  Covers the concepts (object model, classes, and objects), the Booch method (notation and process), and five examples.

- I. White, *Using the Booch Method: A Rational Approach*, Benjamin/Cummings, 1994.

  A short how-to book on using the Booch methodology. Does not use any particular object-oriented language.

Other design books include the following.

- R. Wirfs-Brock, B. Wilkerson, and L. Wiener, *Designing Object-Oriented Software*, Prentice-Hall, 1990.

  Emphasizes the design of classes, their subclasses, and groups of classes that work together. Describes how to 'find classes', assign responsibilities to classes, identify abstract classes, design collaborations between classes, build good hierarchies, and specify protocols.

- I. Jacobson, *Object-Oriented Software Engineering*, Addison-Wesley/ACM Press, Revised fourth printing, 1993.

  While covering lower-level issues, as Wirfs-Brock does, this book stresses larger system issues including the system life cycle, general architecture, real-time issues, database issues, testing, management of development, and real industrial applications.

The development process is the subject of this next book.

- M. Lorenz, *Object-Oriented Software Development: A Practical Guide*, Prentice-Hall, 1993.

  Describes the development of object-oriented software in a real-life context. Covers iterative development, presents a simple design methodology, describes the software development phases, and covers testing and integration.

Part II

Building Blocks

Part II covers additional language topics, including files and file streams, graphics and widgets, memory management, pool dictionaries, exception handling, and processes.

Chapter 8: Variables
> Names, kinds, lifetime, scope; variables in class definitions; variables in methods and blocks; side effects.

Chapter 9: Memory, Pointers, and Copying
> Identity and immutable objects; memory management; pointers; copying; memory objects.

Chapter 10: Programming Interaction
> Prompters; workspaces; transcript.

Chapter 11: Introduction to Debugging
> System code; tracing execution.

Chapter 12: Streams and File Streams
> Read and write streams; file streams; random number streams.

Chapter 13: Files
> Files; directories; disks; paths; locking; sharing.

Chapter 14: Handling Exceptions
> Exceptions; signals; exception handlers; kinds of exceptions.

Chapter 15: Processes and Synchronization
> Starting; stopping; priorities; control; semaphores.

Chapter 16: Building User Interfaces
> Widgets and graphics; windows and window layout, drawing, text, cursor tracking.

8

Variables

This chapter discusses variable naming, kinds of variables, special variables, side effects involving variables, and the scope of variables. It also describes how to create pool dictionaries.

Kinds of Variables

There are ten kinds of variables in Smalltalk.

Smalltalk Global variables	Global to all classes; all are entries in Smalltalk
Class variables	Global to a class
Pool variables	Global to classes that use the pool dictionary
Special variables	nil, true, false, self, super, and Smalltalk

The instance and method variables are:

Instance variables	Specific to each instance
Class instance variables	Specific to class methods and subclasses
Method parameters	Local to the method
Method local variables	Local to the method
Block parameters	Local to the block
Block local variables	Local to the block

In a given method, instance variable names, method parameters and locals, and block parameters and locals must be unique, and none must duplicate a special variable. Separate blocks in a method may have the same variable names as other blocks do in the same method.

Global variable, class variable, and pool variable names are resolved in the following order:

1) Class variables,
2) Pool dictionaries in the order listed in the class description, and
3) The system dictionary, Smalltalk.

Remember that this search occurs at compile time, and that any changes should always be followed by recompilation.

Variables In Class Definitions

There are four kinds of variables that are defined along with the class.

Instance Variables

Instance variables are names of data items within instances of a class. Each instance allocates its own memory for instance variables. Thus, while the variable names are common to all instance methods of a class, and are accessible by subclasses, the values are not shared between instances of the class.

Class Variables

Class variables are special global variables that can be used by all methods in a class, and in all subclasses, both instance and class methods. They belong to the class, and will hold their values even if there are no instances. Class variable names must start with a capital letter.

Class Instance Variables

Class instance variables are like instance variables but belong to classes. Class instance variables are accessible only to class methods, and to class methods of subclasses, and hold their values as long as the class remains defined.

Pool Variables

Pools are special dictionaries that typically contain named constants. Entries in pool dictionaries become global variables to all classes that declare them, and are called pool variables. Pool variable names must start with a capital letter. Pool dictionaries are inherited by all subclasses. Any user-created dictionary with appropriate keys can be used as a pool dictionary. See the section on 'Pool Dictionaries' on page 107 for more information.

Variables In Methods and Blocks

Methods have parameters and local variables; their scope is the defining method and all nested blocks. Blocks also have parameters and local variables; their scope is the defining block and all nested blocks. Figure 27 illustrates the scope of all class, method, and block variables.

Blocks can live longer than the block in which they are created if the are returned to the caller, or are placed in a collection. Such blocks continue to reference local variables and parameters of the method, thus extending their lifetime. Figure 29 on page 105 summarizes variable lifetimes.

Method Parameters

Parameters to methods are declared in method headers. Such names may be used in the method, and in blocks defined in the method. They may not be assigned to. The variables are local to one method and hold values only for the duration of execution of the method, or the lifetime of blocks defined in the method, whichever is longer.

Block Parameters

Parameters to blocks are declared in block headers. Such names may be used in the block only, and may not be assigned to. The variables are local to one block and hold values only for the duration of execution of the block. Textually nested blocks can use block parameter names from outer blocks.

See the section on 'Blocks and Returns' on page 298 for further information.

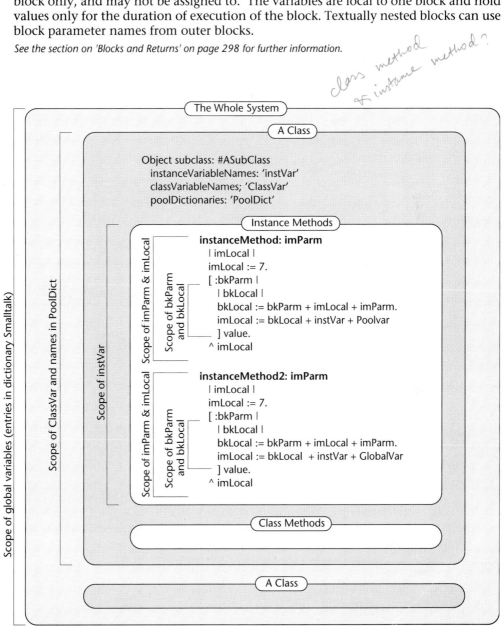

Figure 27: Scope of Names. The scope of all variable types is shown. The sample methods have one of each kind of variable. The names start with an abbreviation that identifies their origin: im for instance method, *bk* for blocks, Global for items in dictionary Smalltalk, Pool for items in pool dictionaries, etc.

Local Variables in Methods

Local variables are declared in method headers. Names defined in method headers may be used anywhere in the method, including blocks. The variables are local to one method and hold values only for the duration of execution of the method, or the lifetime of blocks defined in the method, whichever is longer.

Local Variables in Blocks

Local block variables are declared in block headers. The variables are local to one block and hold values only for the duration of execution of the current invocation of the block. Textually nested blocks can use block local and parameter names from outer blocks.

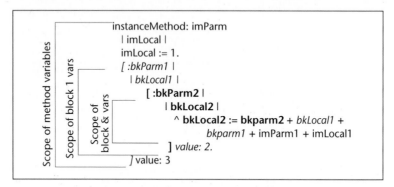

Figure 28: Scope of Local Variables in Nested Blocks. Scope of variables in a method and nested blocks are shown. Variables defined in the inner block are local to that block. Variables in the outer block are visible to the inner block. Variables in the method are visible in both blocks.

There is a significant difference between local variables in a block, and local variables defined just for use within blocks. In Example 106, the scope of the variable apple is the whole method since it is defined in the method.

```
" Illustrating scope of local variable 'apple' "
| apple |
[ :x |
    apple := 4. apple * x ] value: 2.
[ :y |
    apple := 2. apple * y ] value: 3.
^ apple
    "Answers: 2 "                                         Example 106, Display
```

In Example 107, the scope of the variable apple in the first block is just the inside of the first block. The scope of the variable a in the second block is just the inside of the second block. The reference to apple in the last line is invalid, since there is no variable apple for the method.

```
" Invalid reference to variable 'a' in last line "
[ :x |
    | apple |
    apple := 4. apple * x ] value: 2.
[ :y |
    | apple |
    apple := 2. apple * y ] value: 3.
^ apple              "Undefined reference "              Example 107, Display
```

Scope and Lifetime

Figure 29 summarizes the scope and lifetime of variables. Each type of variable is shown on the left, some listed twice with the conditions in which they might be used. The remaining columns specify the scope of the variable, whether or not it can be assigned to, how long the value persists, the scope of the value, and whether or not the leading character must be an upper-case letter.

Variable type	Scope	Lifetime of a value	One value for	Assign to?	Leading upper-case
Global Variable	Whole system	Can be forever	Whole system	Yes	Required
Class Variable	All class and instance methods in one class and its subclasses	Life of class	A class and its subclasses	Yes	Required
Pool Variable	Classes where declared	Life of dictionary	Dictionary	Yes	Required
Instance Variable	All instance methods in one class and its subclasses	Life of instance	Each instance	Yes	Optional
Class Instance Variable	All *class* methods in one class and its subclasses	Life of class	A class and its subclasses	Yes	Optional
Method Parameter (*no* block lives after return)	One method	One invocation of block	Each invocation	No	Optional
Method Local Variable (*no* block lives after return)				Yes	Optional
Method Parameter (*some* block references parameter and lives after return)		Until returned block(s) become garbage		No	Optional
Method Local Variable (*some* block references variable and lives after return)				Yes	Optional
Block Parameter (*no* block lives after return)	Block	One invocation of block	Each invocation	No	Optional
Block Local Variable (*no* block lives after return)				Yes	Optional
Block Parameter (*the* block lives after return)		Until returned block becomes garbage		No	Optional
Block Local Variable (*the* block lives after return)				Yes	Optional

Figure 29: Scope and Lifetime of Variables.

Names in Blocks

Names in blocks that belong to the method or instance, continue to refer to the same variable when passed to another method, even though a variable with the same name might be in the second method.

In the following, a block in meth1 (line 4) contains a reference to variable x. The block is passed to meth2 which also has a variable x (line 6). The block is evaluated (line 8). The x referred to in the block is the x defined on line 2, and the value returned is a 1.

```
1)   meth1
2)      | x |
3)      x := 1.
4)      ^ self meth2: [ x ]
```

```
5)    meth2: aBlock
6)        | x |
7)        x := 2.
8)        ^ aBlock value
```

In Example 108, the value of r1 might be expected to be 4 and r2 to be 8, but both are 12.

```
" External variable references within blocks "
| a b1 b2 r1 r2 |
a := 2.  b1 := [ :x | a * x ].
a := 4.  b2 := [ :y | a * y ].
a := 6.
r1 := b1 value: 2.
r2 := b2 value: 2.
^ Array with: r1 with: r2
    " Answers: (12 12 )
```
Example 108, Inspect

The value of a that is used in the evaluation of the blocks is the last one set, not the one in effect when the block is assigned. The first two assignments to a are irrelevant.

Global Variables

Global variables are known to all methods in the system. They are defined as names in the special dictionary named Smalltalk. Global variable names start with an upper-case letter. The dictionary Smalltalk is like a pool dictionary that is automatically declared for all classes. While global variables are sometimes useful, their use in applications is strongly discouraged. Instead, use class variables, class instance variables, or pool dictionaries for data that needs a lifetime longer than one instance.

The system uses Smalltalk to hold classes. The expression (Smalltalk at: #Bag) answers the class Bag, as does simply writing Bag in an expression. Whenever the name of a class is given in a method, it is found by the compiler in Smalltalk.

Special Variables

There are six special variables in Smalltalk: nil, true, false, super, self, and Smalltalk. They may not be the targets of assignment.

nil
The variable nil represents "nothing". All newly allocated variables in Smalltalk objects are initialized to nil, as are elements of all new collections that can hold any object.

true and false
The variables true and false are the only two instances of classes True and False. These same values are produced by the relational operators.

self and super
The variables self and super refer to the object on behalf of which a method is running.

Smalltalk
The dictionary Smalltalk holds global variables. Its name is reserved. Smalltalk is essentially a pool dictionary, except that it does not have to be explicitly named. It normally contains classes, pool dictionaries, and global variables; when programs name classes, the compiler will find them in Smalltalk.

Side Effects

Consider the following:

```
" No side effects "
| x |
x := 1.
x := (x:=2) + 2.
     " Always answers: 4  (it's OK) "
```
Example 109, Display

The assignment in the parentheses will be executed and answer a 2. However, consider this:

```
" Bad side effects "
| x |
x := 1.
x := (x:=2) + x.
     " Sometimes answers: 4 (it's NOT OK) "
```
Example 110, Display

The difference is that the value of x is referenced in the expression, but it is not guaranteed which value the last (bold) x refers to. It could be 1 or 2.

A similar problem can occur with instance variables; consider this, where iv is an instance variable:

```
aMethod
     iv := 1.
     iv := iv + (self iv: 2).
iv: value
     iv := value.
     ^ iv
```

There is no guarantee which value of iv is referenced in line 3 (bold); it could be a 1 from line 2, or a 2 from the execution of the iv: method. On the author's machine the result of running aMethod is 3.

Pool Dictionaries

Pool dictionaries are ordinary dictionaries that have special keys and are used to hold constant values; these values can be referenced directly in methods by using the key as a variable name. This section describes the pool dictionaries that come with IBM Smalltalk, and shows how to build new pool dictionaries.

Pool dictionaries are declared for a class in the class definition. A given pool dictionary can be declared in one or many classes as needed. (See the section on 'External Class Format' on page 90 for information on how to declare pool dictionaries for a class.)

Values in pool dictionaries can be changed as needed; they can be used as global variables between all those classes that declare them, but such usage is discouraged. Typically, values are set once. They are used to hold constants in one place for use in multiple separate compilations, as included header files are in many traditional languages.

Keys in pool dictionaries must be valid variable names. They must start with an uppercase character. They are created by sending the asPoolKey message to a string or symbol.

...l not be deleted from pool dictionaries (or the Smalltalk dictionary) so long as ...fers to that entry. While values in associations in a dictionary can be changed ...ing an association may cause unpredictable results, even if another with the ...immediately added.†

...es are not accessible in methods unless the method is compiled after the ...e is in the pool dictionary. The following will get a compile error complain-...Key is not defined.

```
MyPoolDict at: 'NewKey' asPoolKey put: 7.
NewKey := NewKey + 1.
```

...vay is to first add an entry in a pool dictionary, possibly using an initial-ization method in a class or using evaluated code in a workspace. Then write and compile the code that references it.

Evaluate:

```
MyPoolDict at: 'NewKey' asPoolKey put: 7
```

Then compile code with references:

```
NewKey := NewKey + 1.
```

Pool dictionary entries in a class definition are inherited by subclasses.

Provided Pool Dictionaries

Smalltalk comes with several pool dictionaries of constants that are used in classes of various types. These are:

CfsConstants	Constants used by file system calls
CgConstants	Constants used by graphics calls
CldtConstants	Characters often used in printable strings
CwConstants	Constants used by widgets calls
SystemExceptions	Values used in exception handling

CfsConstants

CfsConstants are used in message-sends to common file system objects. See Chapter 29, 'Common File System', on page 373 or Chapter 31, 'File Streams', on page 407. To examine the names and their values, do this:

```
" See inside pool dictionary CfsConstants "
CfsConstants
```
Example 111, Inspect

Names in CfsConstants include the following:

ORDONLY	Open the file for reading only
OWRONLY	Open the file for writing only
ORDWR	Open the file for both reading and writing
FREG	Match regular files
FDIR	Match directories

CgConstants

The CgConstants dictionary contains values that are used in message sends to common graphics objects. See Chapter 16, 'Building User Interfaces', on page 179.

---

† Compiled code contains a pointer to the association in the dictionary, rather than a reference to the value. Even when the association is removed from the dictionary, the compiled code still points to it, and its last value will continue to be used.

CldtConstants

CldtConstants contains characters that represent the unprintable characters of the ASCII character set, including Cr, Tab, and Lf, and strings that represent platform-dependent combinations of these characters including PMLineDelimiter, UNIXLineDelimiter, WINLineDelimiter, and the value for the current platform, LineDelimiter. Figure 30 shows the contents of CldtConstants on the author's platform.

Key	Value	Key	Value	Key	value
Ack	16r1	Eot	16r4	Si	16rF
Bell	16r9	Esc	16r1B	So	16rE
Bs	16r8	Etb	16r17	Soh	16r1
Can	16r18	Etx	16r3	Space	16r20
Cr	16rD	Ff	16rC	Stx	16r2
Dc1	16r11	Fs	16r1C	Sub	16r1A
Dc2	16r12	Gs	16r1D	Syn	16r16
Dc3	16r13	Lf	16rA	Tab	16r9
Dc4	16r14	LineDelimiter	*Cr Lf*	UNIXLineDelimiter	*Lf*
Del	16r7F	Nak	16r15	Us	16r1F
Dle	16r10	Nul	16r0	Vt	16rB
Em	16r19	PMLineDelimiter	*Cr Lf*	WINLineDelimiter	*Cr Lf*
Enq	16r5	Rs	16r1E		

Figure 30: Sample Contents of CldtConstants. The key column shows the name of the constant in the dictionary, while the value column shows either the integer value of the character, or the characters in the string.

CwConstants

CwConstants are used in message-sends to common widgets objects. See Chapter 16, 'Building User Interfaces', on page 179.

SystemExceptions

SystemExceptions are used in the exception-handling feature. See Chapter 14, 'Handling Exceptions', on page 157.

System exception names are:

ExAll	The most general exception
ExError	The exception signalled by error:
ExHalt	The exception signalled by halt:
ExUserBreak	The exception signalled by a user break

Building Pool Dictionaries

Pool dictionary creation involves four steps:

1) Create a dictionary;

2) Insert values with appropriate keys, which must be variable names with a leading upper-case letter; keys are converted from strings or symbols to the appropriate platform-specific class with the asPoolKey message;

3) Add the new dictionary to the Smalltalk dictionary, thus making it accessible through a global variable; its name must be a valid variable name and start with an upper-case letter; and

4) Add the new pool dictionary name to the pool dictionary list of one or more class-

es.

**" Create a new pool dictionary for mathematical constants
and add it to Smalltalk "**
| pool |
pool := Dictionary new.   " Allocate a new dictionary "
" Add values and keys; make the precision higher than what a float will hold "
pool at: 'Pi' asPoolKey   put: 3.1415926535897932384626434.
pool at: 'Sqrt2' asPoolKey   put: 1.4142135623730950488016887.
pool at: 'PiInverse' asPoolKey   put: 0.3183098861837906715377675.
pool at: 'E' asPoolKey   put: 2.7182818284590452353602874.
pool at: 'PiSquared' asPoolKey   put: 9.8696044010893586188344909.
" Add the pool dictionary as a global variable "
Smalltalk at: 'FloatConstants' asGlobalKey put: pool.   *Example 112, Execute*

The contents of the dictionary can be seen by inspection.

" Inspect contents of FloatConstants "
FloatConstants   *Example 113, Inspect*

Now that the dictionary is created, it can be added to the pool dictionary list in one or more class definitions as shown in the section on 'External Class Format' on page 90.

The variables in the dictionary can be referenced in methods, provided the class or a parent references the pool dictionary.

areaOutsideCircle: radius
    " Area outside circle but inside enclosing square (uses FloatConstants) "
    | circleArea squareArea |
    circleArea := **Pi** * radius squared.
    squareArea := (2*radius) squared.
    ^ squareArea - circleArea

Summary

Smalltalk has ten kinds of variables: global, class, pool, special, instance, class instance, method parameter, block parameter, method local, and block local.

Global, class, and pool variables are global to one or more classes. The special variables nil, true, false, and Smalltalk are also global, but self and super have different values in different contexts. All other variables are local to a class, method or block.

9

Memory, Pointers, and Copying

Smalltalk memory management is quite different than that in traditional languages. The biggest difference is that there is little for programmers to do, since memory allocation happens when a new object is requested, and memory deallocation is automatic.

A Smalltalk variable holds a pointer to an object, not the actual object itself.† Usually this distinction is invisible, but in a few cases it is not.

This chapter will cover memory management, garbage collection, pointers, immutable objects, the copying of objects, and objects with indexed memory.

Identity and Immutable Objects

Identity objects always compare true with == when they compare true with =. Since = answers true when the values are the same, and == answers true when the two objects are the same, operations on identity objects must always produce the same object no matter how derived or calculated. Small integer numbers have this property. Adding 2 and 2 always produces the object 4 and thus (2+2)==4 is always true.

Identity objects include small integers, characters, symbols, and true and false.

Always true	*Always true*
2 = 2	2 == 2
(1+2) = 3	(1+2) == 3
$a = $A asLowercase	$a == $A asLowercase
true = true	true == true
#ab = 'ab' asSymbol	#ab == 'ab' asSymbol

---

† There are several exceptions for performance reasons, such as small integers and characters.

But:

<table>
<tr><td>*Always true*</td><td>*Always false*</td></tr>
<tr><td>(1.5 + 1.5) = 3.0</td><td>(1.5 + 1.5) == 3.0</td></tr>
<tr><td>'ab', 'cd' = 'abcd'</td><td>'ab', 'cd' == 'abcd'</td></tr>
<tr><td>(1@1) + 1 = (2@2)</td><td>(1@1) + 1 == (2@2)</td></tr>
</table>

Immutable objects cannot be modified internally. All operations on immutable objects that answer a different value also answer a different instance. Most objects are not immutable. Immutable objects include numbers, characters, and symbols. Identity objects are always immutable, but the converse is not true.

Copies of identity objects and of other immutable objects always return the same object.

<table>
<tr><td>*Always true*</td><td>*Always true*</td></tr>
<tr><td>2 copy = 2</td><td>2 copy == 2</td></tr>
<tr><td>$a copy = $a</td><td>$a copy == $a</td></tr>
<tr><td>true copy = true</td><td>true copy == true</td></tr>
</table>

But:

<table>
<tr><td>*Always true*</td><td>*Always false*</td></tr>
<tr><td>(2@3) copy = (2@3)</td><td>(2@3) copy == (2@3)</td></tr>
<tr><td>'abc' copy = 'abc'</td><td>'abc' copy == 'abc'</td></tr>
</table>

Memory Management

Objects are allocated with the new, new:, basicNew, and basicNew: messages. These messages perform calculations to determine how much memory is needed, then allocate it, and return a pointer to the object just allocated. (The basicNew: and basicNew messages are identical to new: and new except that it is agreed that they will never be overridden by subclasses.).

In Example 114, two new objects are allocated, and pointers to them are assigned, the first to a variable and the second to an array element.

```
" Allocate two objects; at end they become garbage "
| array |
array := Array new: 10.
array at: 1 put: (2@3 corner: 6@5)                    Example 114, Execute
```

So long as these pointers are in some variable or collection element, the objects remain allocated and accessible. When the code ends, the objects are no longer pointed to by anything, and they become *garbage*. Garbage objects take up memory, but are not accessible.

Garbage collection is an automatic process that reclaims the garbage, and makes the memory available for reuse. Garbage collection is incremental, it happens a bit at a time as other code executes, and has very low overhead.

Garbage collection is invisible and fast. It allows a style of programming impossible in conventional languages, and it makes virtually all coding much simpler.

```
" How many digits in some integer, expressed in decimal radix? "
| anInt |
anInt := Time millisecondClockValue.   "Some arbitrary integer"
^ anInt printString trimBlanks size                    Example 115, Display
```

In Example 115 an integer is obtained from the millisecond clock (a place to get an arbitrary integer). Then:

1) The message printString is sent to anInt and answers a string;‡

2) This string is sent the message trimBlanks and answers a different string; the first string is now garbage; and

3) The second string is sent the size message which answers an integer; the second string becomes garbage. See Figure 31.

Expression	Answer	Becomes garbage	Result name
anInt printString	a String	anInt	result1
result1 trimBlanks	a String	result1 (String)	result2
result2 size	an Integer	result2 (String)	

Figure 31: Garbage Generated by Example 115.

The garbage generated is just a by-product of the execution of the expression, and very normal and usual in Smalltalk. There was no worry about how much room to allocate for the two strings, nor about how big the integer result from the clock was.

Optimizations

Once a program is written and running, a source code profiler can identify 'hot spots' in the code, places where a little optimization can make a big difference.

One of these optimizations is to eliminate unneeded allocations by reusing an allocated object rather than obtaining a new one. Allocations take more cycles than not allocating at all. Individual blocks of code can be timed with the bench: message which times the block and prints a message along with the time onto the Transcript.

```
" Reusing a Point "
| p x y |
x := 6.
y := 8.
p := Point new.
[ 100000 timesRepeat: [ p x: x; y: y ] ]     bench: 'Reusing a point: '.
[ 100000 timesRepeat: [ x @ y] ]             bench: 'Allocating a new point: '.
[ 100000 timesRepeat: [ ] ]                  bench: 'Empty loop: '

" On the authors platform, the results in the Transcript are:
  Reusing a point: 1220
  Allocating a new point: 2590
  Empty loop: 94  "
```
Example 116, Execute

This difference represents a factor of about two, and can be critical in an inner loop.

Pointers

All variables, and elements in general-purpose collections (arrays, bags, sets, etc.), hold pointers to the objects they represent. Under some circumstances, this is semantically

---

‡ The integer becomes garbage, but since integers are implemented in a special way there is no need to reclaim the memory. More precisely, this is true for small integers only; see the section on 'Kinds of Numbers' on page 449.

equivalent to having the variable hold the object itself, and programmers don't see or have to be aware of the distinction.

The exception comes when more than one variable or element 'holds' the same object. The presence of pointers is then visible (it's obvious that things wouldn't work otherwise), but typically no problems arise by ignoring the issue.

There are, however, situations in which an awareness of pointers is mandatory, typically appearing as a bug that a new programmer finds inexplicable.

Everyone's First Pointer Bug

Everyone who programs Smalltalk is apt to run into this bug either of their own creation or from a friend. There are many variations, but most boil down to a loop that initializes a collection.

```
" Everyone's First Pointer Bug "
| array point |
point := Point new.
array := Array new: 10.
1 to: array size do: [ :n |
    array at: n put: (point x: n; y: n) ].
^ array at: 1
" Expected answer:  1@1
  Actual Answer:  10@10"
```
                                                                              Example 117, Display

Example 117 takes advantage of the trick learned earlier in this chapter, it tries to optimize the running time of the loop by reusing a point and just assigning new values to its components.

But therein lies the problem: each element of the array points to the same point. When the internal values of the point are changed, the previous values are simply overwritten. At the end of the loop, all elements point to the same point which then holds 10 and 10 for the x and y values.

But consider this one:

```
" ... but this one works ... "
| array |
array := Array new: 10.
1 to: array size do: [ :n |
    array at: n put: n  ].
^ array at: 1
" Expected answer:  1
  Actual Answer:  1"
```
                                                                              Example 118, Display

Why did this work? In this case the value was an integer, which is an identity object, and thus is a different object for each loop. The correction for the bug is to make the value that is put in the array be different each time. When the object is not an identity object, this means the a new instance must be obtained for each array element.

```
" Everyone's First Pointer Bug FIXED "
| array |
array := Array new: 10.
1 to: array size do: [ :n |
    array at: n put: n@n  ].          " Each array element gets a new instance "
^ array at: 1
" Expected answer:  1@1
  Actual Answer:  1@1"
```
                                                                              Example 119, Display

Copying Objects

Since variables hold pointers, and objects can point to objects that point to objects, (sometimes, endlessly since a can point to b, which can point to a), how can objects be meaningfully copied? How may levels of pointers is it necessary to copy?

Object defines three methods for copying: copy, shallowCopy, and deepCopy. The copy method simply calls shallowCopy, which makes a copy of an object but not of objects to which it refers. The deepCopy method makes a copy of the object and a shallow copy of its contents.

Shallow Copying

Shallow copying makes a copy of the object, but not of its contents.

In Example 120, an array is constructed, copied, and the first element of the original is changed. (The string literals must be copied to make them ordinary strings since the second version of this example will modify one of them; literals are read-only and cannot be modified.) The first element of the copy is then returned. It holds the value that was in the original, showing that it is indeed a copy. Figure 32 shows both the state just after the copy and the final state.

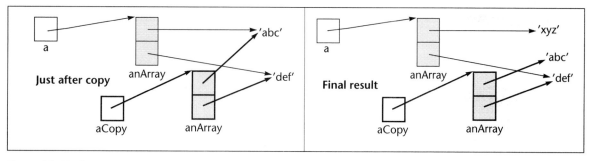

Figure 32: Shallow Copy of an Array, #1. Just after the copy, variables a and aCopy each point to different arrays, but the arrays point to common elements. At the end, the first element of a has been changed to point to a new string. The copy is not affected.

```
" Shallow copying an array, #1 "
| a aCopy |
a := Array with: 'abc' copy with: 'def' copy.   "Make a new array with 2 elements"
aCopy := a copy.                    "Copy it"
a at: 1 put: 'xyz'.                 "Replace the first element of the original"
^ aCopy at: 1                       "Return first element of copy"
   " Answer: 'abc' "
```
Example 120, Display

But consider this:

```
" Shallow copying an array, #2 "
| a aCopy |
a := Array with: 'abc' copy with: 'def' copy.   " Make a new array with 2 elements "
aCopy := a copy.                    " Copy it "
(a at: 1) at: 1 put: $Z.            " Replace the first char of the first element "
^ aCopy at: 1                       " Return first element of copy "
   " Answer: 'Zbc' "
```
Example 121, Display

The line in bold type modifies the string held in the first position. While the arrays are copies, they hold pointers to identical elements, and a change to an element is visible in both arrays. Figure 33 shows the objects at the end of execution.

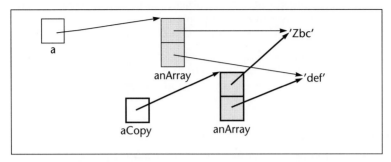

Figure 33: Shallow Copy of an Array, #2. Variables a and aCopy each point to different arrays, but the arrays point to common elements.

Deep Copying

Deep copying makes a copy of the object and of its contents.

In Example 122, which is identical to Example 120 except for deepCopy, an array is copied and the first element of the original is changed. The first element of the copy is then returned. It holds the value that was in the original, showing that it is indeed a copy.

```
" Deep copying an array, #1 "
| a aCopy |
a := Array with: 'abc' copy
          with:  'def' copy.          "Make a new array with 2 elements"
aCopy := a deepCopy.                   "Copy it"
a at: 1 put: 'xyz'.                    "Replace the first element of the original"
^ aCopy at: 1                          "Return first element of copy"
     " Answer: 'abc' "
```
Example 122, Display

But consider Example 123 (which is identical to Example 121 except for **deepCopy**). While the line in bold type modifies the string held in the first position, the returned value is unmodified. The arrays are copies, but now they hold pointers to copies of the elements, as would be expected from the definition of a deep copy. Figure 34 shows the result of the deep copy operation.

```
" Deep copying an array, #2 "
| a aCopy |
a := Array with: 'abc' copy
          with:  'def' copy.          "Make a new array with 2 elements"
aCopy := a deepCopy.
(a at: 1) at: 1 put: $Z.
^ aCopy at: 1
     " Answer: 'abc' "
```
Example 123, Display

Making Copies

While IBM Smalltalk does implement deepCopy, both shallowCopy and deepCopy are private methods in Object; only copy is public. This is intended to discourage use of deepCopy, while having an implementation of a traditional Smalltalk function.

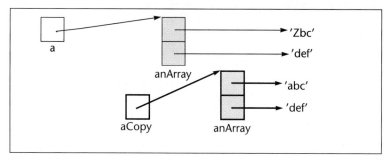

Figure 34: Deep Copy of an Array. Variables a and aCopy each point to different arrays, but the arrays point to common elements.

The use of deepCopy is discouraged because it rarely does just the right thing, and it can introduce subtle bugs. The best way to make copies, if copy is not sufficient, is to override copy and make a proper copy of your objects yourself. Often, this may involve copying some parts of the objects deeper than others.

Consider some object that has a dictionary, itemDictionary, that is shared between all instances, and a collection, layout, of collections of numbers that are private to each instance. It might have a copy method like the following.

```
copy
    | newMe coll |
    newMe := self class new.
    newMe itemDictionary: itemDictionary.
    coll := layout class new: layout size.
    coll size timesRepeat: [ :n |
        coll at: n put: (layout at: n) copy].
    ^ newMe
```

A new instance of the object is obtained. The itemDictionary is set to be the same object as in the original. Then a new array is obtained and filled in with copies of the numbers, for which copy is sufficient.

Indexed Memory

Not all memory is in instance variables. Arrays, for instance, do not hold their values in instance variables, but in indexed memory that belongs to an instance and that has no name. This memory is accessible by use of at: and at:put:. Objects comes in five shapes and sizes. These are:

subclass	A standard subclass, as used in most examples in this book. Its only data is in instance variables.
variableSubclass	A subclass that has some number of indexed instance variables; these variables can hold pointers to any other object. It may also have named instance variables. Arrays, sets, and other collections that hold any other object are variable subclass objects (or have an instance variable that points to a variable subclass object).

variableByteSubclass	A subclass that has some number of indexed bytes (8-bit values) that can hold arbitrary bit values. It may also have named instance variables. Strings, byte strings, floats, and symbols are variable byte subclasses.
variableWordSubclass	A subclass that has some number of indexed words (16-bit values) that can hold arbitrary bit values. It may also have named instance variables.
variableLongSubclass	A subclass that has some number of indexed long words (32-bit values) that can hold arbitrary bit values. It may also have named instance variables.

The memory characteristics of a class are specified when the class is created. Virtually all user-created classes are simple subclasses with no indexed memory. Objects with indexed memory are created with the new: message giving the number of indexed elements in the indexed memory. The memory is accessed with at: and at:put:.

Several system collections use indexed memory:

Array	A variableSubclass
String	A variableByteSubclass
LargeInteger	A variableLongSubclass. Large integers are made up of a collection of 32-bit values.

Summary

Smalltalk is really a pointer language, not unlike C, but with a great difference: the pointers are hidden, cannot be arbitrarily dereferenced, and pose no threat to system integrity. Only rarely do programmers even need to be aware of Smalltalk's pointers. However, pointers are the basis for memory management; whenever an object is no longer pointed to by anything, its memory can be reclaimed.

Pointers show up vividly when initializing collections or variables where copies, or new allocations, are needed.

Finally, objects with indexed memory are alternative ways to keep certain kinds of data and are used by collections classes.

Further Reading

While garbage collection is an esoteric subject, and understanding how it works is not necessary for an understanding of Smalltalk, the following book, an ACM Distinguished Dissertation, contains an excellent description of the generation scavenging algorithm, the technique that is the basis for most modern garbage collection systems.

- D. Ungar, *The Design and Evaluation of a High Performance Smalltalk System*, MIT Press, 1987.

useful chapter

Programming Interaction

This chapter describes how to program simple interaction using prompters, how to issue error and informative messages, and how to program interfaces to workspaces and the Transcript.

More advanced interface programming is covered in Chapter 16, 'Building User Interfaces', on page 179.

Simple Interaction

Prompters can ask permission for a pending action or accept some value from the user. There are three kinds:

1) a *message prompter,* which returns true or false (or sometimes nil);

2) a *text prompter,* which displays a string and asks for another string to be entered; and

3) a *file selection prompter,* which displays a 'file open' dialog and waits for a file to be selected.

In addition, there are quick ways to invoke common versions of the prompters.

Quick Interaction

Messages can be sent to an object named System to perform simple interaction with a minimum of coding. These include:

confirm:	Ask question; wait for Yes or No
confirmYesNoCancel:	Ask question; wait for Yes, No, or Cancel
errorMessage:	Beep, then display a message; wait for OK

message:	Display a message; wait for OK
prompt:	Ask for text; wait for OK
prompt:answer:	Ask for text; provide default; wait for OK

In each case, pressing the Enter key will select the default button.

Confirmations

The message confirm: is sent to System with a string. A dialog is displayed that displays the string. Two buttons, Yes and No, are shown; pressing Yes terminates the dialog and answers true; pressing No answers false.

System confirm: 'Update the master list?'   *Example 124, Execute*

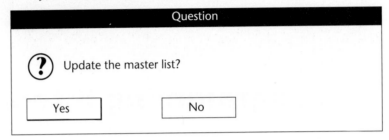

The message confirmYesNoCancel: adds another button, Cancel, which when pressed causes nil to be answered.

System confirmYesNoCancel: 'Replace existing file?'   *Example 125, Execute*

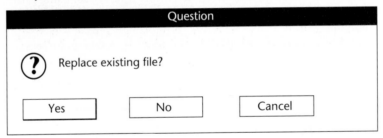

Messages

The message message: is sent to System with a string. A dialog is displayed which displays the string. One button, OK, is shown; pressing it terminates the dialog and answers nil to the program.

System message: 'Update was successful.'   *Example 126, Execute*

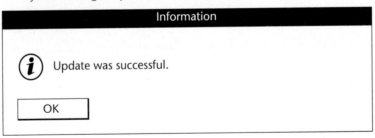

Error Messages

The message errorMessage: is sent to System with a string. A beep is sounded and a dialog is displayed which displays the string. One button, OK, is shown; pressing it terminates the dialog and answers nil to the program.

System errorMessage: 'File open error'

Example 127, Execute

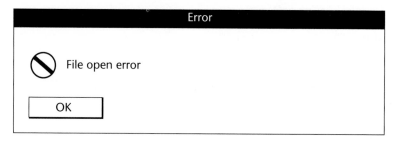

Prompts

The message prompt: is sent to System with a message string. A dialog is displayed which displays the string and asks for a line of input; two buttons, OK and Cancel, are also displayed. Pressing OK terminates the dialog and answers whatever is typed by the user, or an empty string if nothing was typed. Pressing Cancel terminates the dialog and answers nil.

System prompt: 'Enter your mother''s birth name spelled backwards.'

Example 128, Display

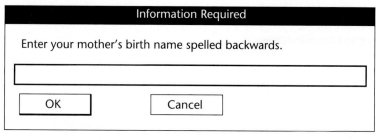

The message prompt:answer: is similar, but adds a default answer; the user can simply press OK for the default, or replace the text and then press OK.

(System
   prompt: 'Enter your mother''s birth name spelled backwards.'
   answer: 'klatllamS') reverse

Example 129, Display

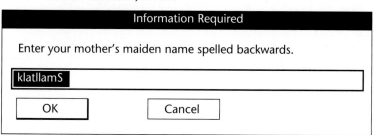

Message Prompter

Message prompters are used to build prompters like the message and confirm prompters above. The simplest form of the message prompter is created with the title: and messageString: messages.

```
( CwMessagePrompter new
    title: 'Confirm or Deny';
    messageString: 'Begin Phase II?'
    ) prompt
```
Example 130, Display

Example 130 will popup a dialog similar to this:

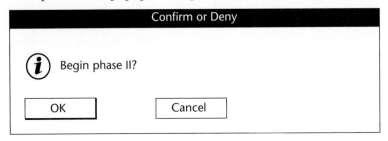

If the OK button is pressed, a value of true is returned, but if the Cancel button is pressed, a value of nil is returned.

Two messages, buttonType:, and iconType:, set the styles of button and icon. (Values passed as parameters are described after Example 132.) Changes from Example 130 are shown in bold type in Example 131.

```
( CwMessagePrompter new
    title: 'Confirm or Deny';
    messageString: 'Begin Phase II?';
    buttonType: XmYESNOCANCEL;
    iconType: XmICONQUESTION
    ) prompt
```
Example 131, Display

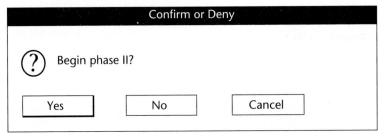

If the Yes button is pressed, a value of true is returned; if the No button is pressed, a value of false is returned; and if the Cancel button is pressed, a value of nil is returned.

In Example 132, a prompter is created and stored in the variable prompter. It is then activated with the prompt message.

```
| prompter |
prompter := ( CwMessagePrompter new
    title: 'Prompter';
    buttonType: XmYESNOCANCEL;
    defaultButtonType: XmDEFAULTBUTTON3;
    iconType: XmICONQUESTION;
```

messageString: 'Please press a button.').
^ prompter prompt

Example 132, Display

Button and Icon Types

The arguments to buttonType: can be:

XmOK	OK button only
XmOKCANCEL	OK and CANCEL buttons (default setting)
XmRETRYCANCEL	RETRY and CANCEL buttons
XmABORTRETRYIGNORE	ABORT, RETRY, and IGNORE buttons
XmYESNO	YES and NO buttons
XmYESNOCANCEL	YES, NO, and CANCEL buttons

The arguments to the defaultButtonType: message are:

XmDEFAULTBUTTON1	The first button is the default (default setting)
XmDEFAULTBUTTON2	The second button is the default
XmDEFAULTBUTTON3	The third button is the default

The icon can be changed with the iconType: message:

XmNOICON	No icon
XmICONINFO	Info icon (default setting)
XmICONWARNING	Warning icon
XmICONERROR	Error icon
XmICONQUESTION	Question icon

The prompt message returns one of the following values, depending on which button was pressed:

true	The OK, YES, or RETRY button was pressed
false	The NO or ABORT button was pressed
nil	The CANCEL or IGNORE button was pressed

Text Prompter

A text prompter displays a message, usually a question, and waits for the user to type a string in reply. The reply area can be initialized with either a standard reply or instruction, or it can be blank. It answers nil if Cancel is pressed, it answers the default string if the user made no changes, otherwise it answers the string entered by the user.

```
( CwTextPrompter new
        title: 'Query';
        messageString: 'Enter color palette name.';
        answerString: 'RichEarthTones'
        ) prompt
```
Example 133, Display

Example 133 will pop-up a dialog similar to this:

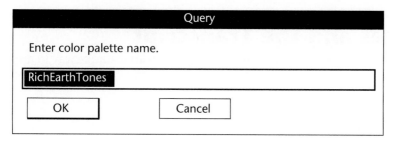

The suggested reply is highlighted; it can be deleted and another string entered.

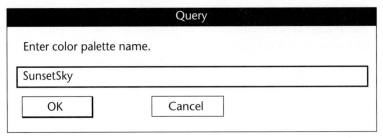

File Selection Prompters

File prompters display a file selection dialog from which a user can select a file in some directory in the system. The simplest file selection prompter is:

" **Simple file selection prompter** "
^ CwFileSelectionPrompter new prompt   *Example 134, Display*

Options can specify the title of the window, the initial search path, a search mask, and a default file name.

title:	The window title
searchPath:	The path to view first.
searchMask:	A string that describes which files to see

Example 135 prompts for all files ending with '.ST' in the path 'E:\'.

```
" Open a file selection prompter "
| prompter |
prompter := CwFileSelectionPrompter new
    title: 'Select file to open';
    searchPath: 'E:\';
    searchMask: '*.ST'.
^ prompter prompt.
```
Example 135, Display

Prompters in Code

Each of the prompters can be used in code evaluated in a workspace. When used in a class, the pool dictionary CwConstants must be specified in the class definition.

Pool dictionaries are described in the section on 'Pool Dictionaries' on page 107.

Workspaces and the Transcript

Workspaces can be created by programs. They are a simple way to display textual data. The Transcript is a special kind of workspace and responds to the same messages as a workspace, once the workspace is open.

Workspaces

Workspaces are simple to open from within programs; they are instances of class Et-Workspace; simply get a new instance, send it the open message to create it, and the show: message to put text into it.

```
" Pop up a workspace on a string "
EtWorkspace new open;
    show: 'I want to be in a workspace, please!'
```
Example 136, Display

Messages to workspaces include:

confirmClose: false	Say it's OK to close without confirming
cr	Move down to the next line
label: aString	Set the window label (before using open)
open	Open a workspace on the screen
show: aString	Display aString at the end
tab	Output a tab
tab: anInteger	Output anInteger tabs

```
                    My Own Workspace


Line 1 of some text.
   Line 2 of some text.
      Line 3 of some text.
         Line 4 of some text.
            Line 5 of some text.
```

Try this:

```
" Open a workspace on some text "
| workspace |
workspace := EtWorkspace new
    label: 'My Own Workspace';
    open.
1 to: 5 do: [ :n |
    workspace
        show: 'Line ', n printString, ' of some text.';
        cr;
        tab: n ].
workspace confirmClose: false
```
Example 137, Execute

Also see Chapter 17, 'Example: Stereograms', on page 205, for an example of building a workspace.

Log Files

A log file, that can be used in a manner similar to the Transcript, can be created with a workspace. This log file can be used instead of the Transcript as a place to write messages; it can also be saved to disk as a text file.

This example will put the log into a global variable, Log.

```
" Initialize the global variable Log to a workspace "
Smalltalk at: 'Log' asGlobalKey
    put: (EtWorkspace new label: 'Application Log'; open)
```
Example 138, Execute

The following code will put text into the log:

```
" Use Log created in Example 138 "
Log cr;
    show: 'Hello, world!!'
```
Example 139, Execute

It is not necessary to make the log be global if you only need to access it within one class.

The Transcript

The Transcript global variable holds an instance of a subclass of EtWorkspace. Only one can be open at a time, and the system opens it at startup. The following messages to Transcript are often useful.

cr	Move down to next line
show: aString	Display aString next
tab	Output a tab
tab: anInteger	Output anInteger tabs

Summary

IBM Smalltalk provides a number of easy-to-use facilities for interacting with the user.

Message prompters are used to confirm actions, inform of errors, or simply display information and wait for a response.

Text prompters ask the user for a string of text; a default can be provided.

File selection prompters ask the user to select a file for processing; the prompter lets the user browse the file system hierarchy to find the file, or to type in a name.

Finally, workspaces can be created from within methods, and can be written to. Both workspaces and the Transcript respond to a common set of messages.

11

Introduction to Debugging

This chapter shows how to view source code, how to trace execution with the debugger, and presents additional details on the evaluation of text in workspaces and other places.

Viewing System Code

Each Smalltalk system comes with much of the Smalltalk code that is used to implement the system. You can open a *browser* and look at how arrays work, or see the code for numbers, or examine how workspaces operate.

Typically, the Transcript window will have a menu which has an item 'Browse Classes'. Select that menu item; a multipaned window will open that resembles Figure 35.

The top left subwindow (or pane) displays the class hierarchy in its entirety. The list will contain a number of classes not documented in this book; many of these are classes that implement the various system tools (such as this browser), interface with the platform, or implement graphics and widgets.

Note: When writing Smalltalk applications, the application management tools† should be used, rather than the general-purpose class browser, since the tools provide many useful aids. The class browser shows all of the code; it the tool to use to look inside to see how it all works. It will show how collections and magnitudes work, look at the mechanisms that make classes be classes, or even see how processes work inside.‡

---

† See the documentation that came with the product you are using.

‡ Some parts of the implementation are not present in source code form for proprietary or other reasons; in particular, the compiler and some low-level graphics code may be missing. These omissions may vary by platform.

Classes Browser			
Object ApplicationSwapper... Behavior... Block... Boolean... CfsDirectoryDescriptor CfsError			
	Default: (some application)	instance	public

NameOfSuperclass subclass: #NameOfClass
  instanceVariableNames: 'instVarName1 instVarName2'
  classVariableNames: 'ClassVariableName1 ClassVarName2'
  poolDictionaries: ' PoolDictName1 PoolDictName2 '			

Figure 35: Class Browser.

The center pane displays the applications or subsystems that are involved in implementing a given class. Text appears here when a class is selected. (Some platforms and versions may have two center panes; see your system documentation.)

The right pane displays method names. There are four lists possible; the default is instance/public. By pressing the buttons just below this pane, the list of methods can show instance/private, class/public, and class/private.

The bottom pane can show an expression that creates or modifies a class, or it can show the text of a method. The method can be changed, and then saved to make the change to the class. Class definitions can also be changed.

Exploring Magnitude

Scroll the class pane down to 'Magnitude...'. The three dots indicate that there are hidden subclasses. Make the subclasses visible (usually just by double-clicking the class name). The browser will look similar to Figure 36.

The name of the class, Magnitude, is highlighted as is CLDT, which stands for Common Language Data Types and is the 'application' in which the common data types are implemented. Sometimes this pane holds more than one such name and only the first one is selected by default; if there are more than one, you should select them all. (If there are two center panes on your system, select everything in both; the second holds categories of messages.)

The bottom pane shows the expression that was used to define Magnitude; there are no instance or class variables and no pool dictionaries are used.

The top right pane shows method names depending on the buttons selected.

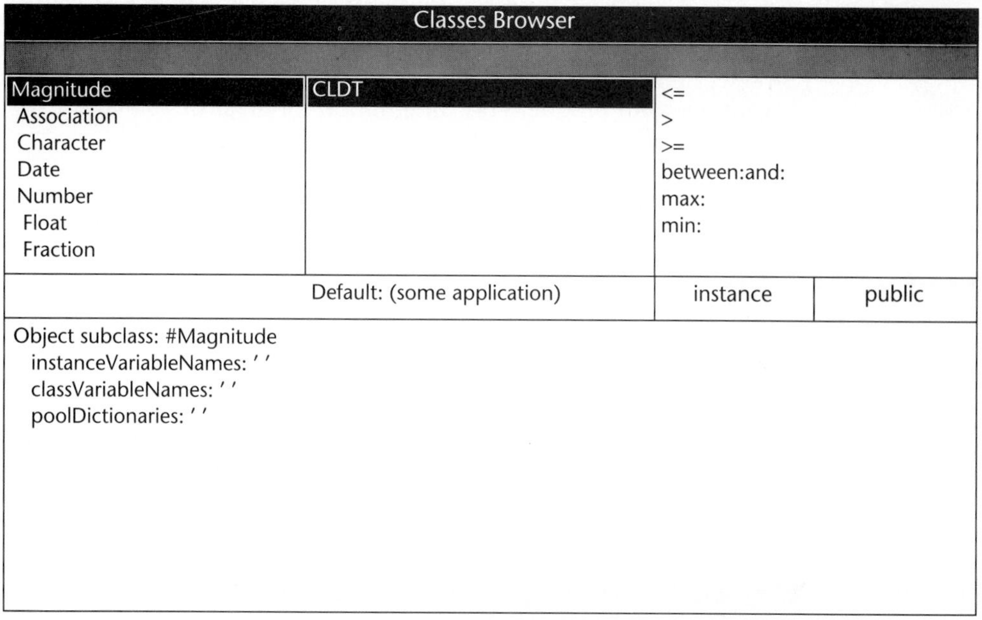

Figure 36: Class Browser on Magnitude.

Select between:and: as in Figure 37. The source code for the method is now displayed in the bottom pane.

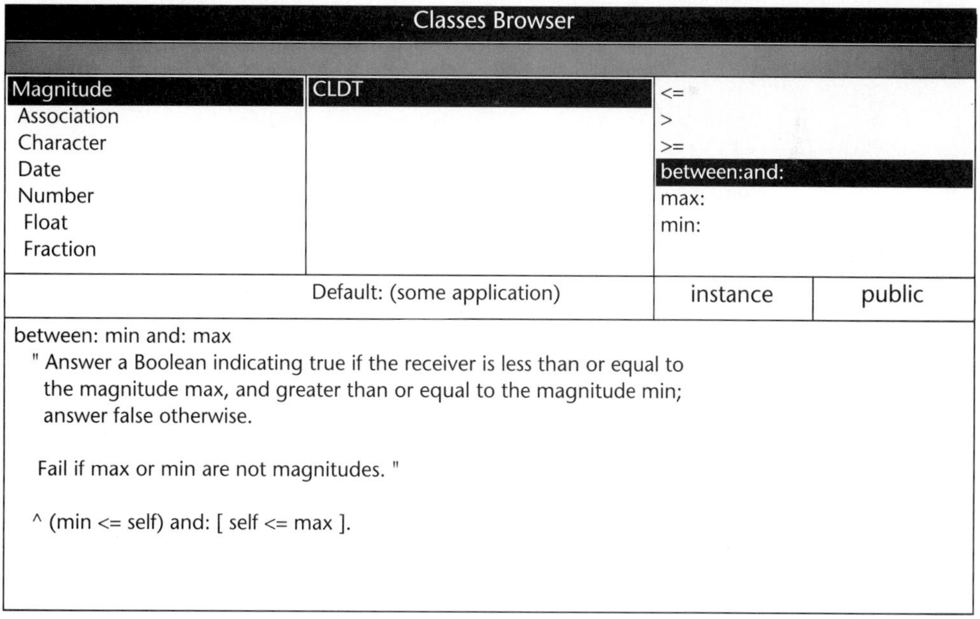

Figure 37: Class Browser on between:and: in Magnitude.

It is possible to interactively cross-reference the code in a number of ways. You can ask for all implementations of a given method, or all its senders, or all of the messages sent by a given method, among others. After you learn the various options in the class browser menus, it is easy to take a look at an appropriate 'cross-section' of the code. (Again, see your product's documentation for details.)

Debugging

The Smalltalk debugger can be used to watch expressions execute. Try this:

" **Invoke debugger then run factorial method** "
self halt. 10 factorial

Example 140, Display

Smalltalk Debugger				no variables selected
'halt encountered' in UIProcess:5398{suspended,3}				
[ ] in ExceptionEvent class>> #initializeSystemExecption				
ExceptionEvent>>#applyDefaultHandler:				
... more lines ...				
UndefinedObject>>#Doit				
... more lines ...				
... more lines ...				
... more lines ...				
Into	Over	Return	Resume	

UIProcess
   Name: 5398
   Process State: suspended
   Priority: 3
   Executing in: ExceptionalEvent class>>#initializeSystemExceptions

   Error string: halt encountered

Figure 38: Debugger: First Encounter.

The halt message to self starts up the debugger. A window similar to Figure 38 will appear. It will show you more than you ever wanted to know about what is going on. If you look down the pane of gobbledegook§ (the *traceback* pane) near the top left corner, you will find a line that looks like this:

UndefinedObject>>#Doit

---

§ Named after Hendrick Wilhelm van Gobble de Gook, an early resident of Dutch New York (ca. 1602), and possibly the first programmer in the new world. He was known for his ebullience, being a man of many words, but he tended to lecture and ramble. On social occasions he was a near disaster, not being at all good at small talk. (Dietrich Knickerbocker, *History of New-York*, New York, 1808.)

Select this line. The window should change and be similar to Figure 39.

Smalltalk Debugger			

'halt encountered' in UIProcess:5398{suspended,3}	self	nil

|] in ExceptionEvent class>> #initializeSystemExecption
ExceptionEvent>>#applyDefaultHandler:
... more lines ...
UndefinedObject>>#Doit
... more lines ...
... more lines ...
... more lines ... | | |

Into	Over	Return	Resume

Doit self halt. 10 factorial

Figure 39: Debugger: Doit is Selected.

The source code for the expression in the workspace is visible in the debugger; it is prefaced with the word 'Doit', its temporary method name. Smalltalk compiles workspace code and installs it as a temporary method for long enough to run it.

There are four buttons below the traceback pane: Into, Over, Return, and Resume.

Into	Trace execution one message send at a time, *always* tracing into message sends.
Over	Trace execution one message send at a time, *never* tracing into message sends.
Return	Skip to the next return statement, or the end of the method.
Resume	End tracing and resume normal execution.

Press the Into button. The window will change to look like Figure 37. The traceback pane shows a highlighted line, which names the class and method displayed in the bottom pane. In the bottom pane an expression is selected; this is the current point of execution, and self > 1 is about to be executed.

From this point, simply press Into to watch the execution step by step, or press Over to skip a message send. Press Resume when you are tired of watching factorial execute.

The top right corner is a mini-inspector with a list of variables and a value pane. Local variables show up in this list. Instance variables can be seen by inspecting self.

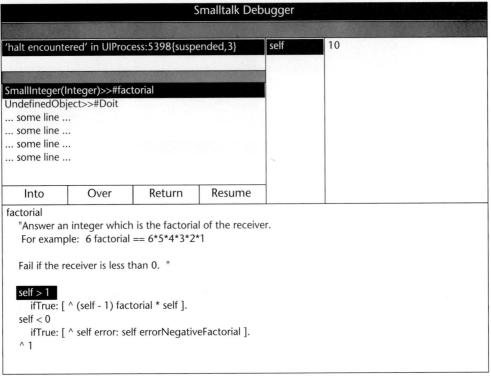

Smalltalk Debugger			

'halt encountered' in UIProcess:5398{suspended,3} | self | 10

SmallInteger(Integer)>>#factorial
UndefinedObject>>#Doit
... some line ...
... some line ...
... some line ...
... some line ...

Into	Over	Return	Resume

```
factorial
    "Answer an integer which is the factorial of the receiver.
     For example:  6 factorial == 6*5*4*3*2*1

     Fail if the receiver is less than 0.  "

    self > 1
        ifTrue: [ ^ (self - 1) factorial * self ].
    self < 0
        ifTrue: [ ^ self error: self errorNegativeFactorial ].
    ^ 1
```

Figure 40: Debugger: After Pressing Into.

Try tracing the following:

```
" Trace example "
self halt. Bag new add: #( 1 1 3 5 3 )
```
Example 141, Display

```
" Trace example "
self halt. Date today
```
Example 142, Display

```
" Trace example "
self halt. 2 / 3
```
Example 143, Display

Text Evaluation

Text can be evaluated in places other than workspaces, such as in the midst of code for a method, in an inspector, or anywhere else that a general text pane is used.

The selected text is turned into a method named Doit which is then compiled, installed, executed, and deleted. When evaluated in a workspace, the method is installed in UndefinedObject, the class of which nil is the only instance. However, when text is evaluated in an inspector or the debugger, it is run as part of the class of the instance being inspected or viewed. It can reference instance variables of the instance and send messages to the instance.

If the class definition contains pool dictionaries, they can be used in the selected text. The standard pool dictionaries, CldtConstants, CfsConstants, CwConstants, and CgConstants are defined in UndefinedObject and can be used in expressions evaluated in workspaces.

The Doit method differs slightly from other methods in the way that it returns values. Normally a method with no return statement answers self; but, Doit answers the last value evaluated, like blocks do. Most examples of evaluated text in this book use a return statement, but it is often not required.

Debugger and Errors

Using the debugger for errors is much like using it for tracing, except that the debugger is opened automatically when an error occurs. Not all errors can be resumed, but many can be.

It is, in fact, not only possible to correct a problem and restart the method that contained the problem, but is a common way of working. Smalltalk applications are typically debugged by starting them, interacting with them, detecting a bug (either with the debugger or by observing some incorrect action), correcting the problem, and resuming execution.

Summary

Browsers are used to view system code and applications. Depending on the IBM Smalltalk product, the browser might be the class browser described in this chapter, or another browser.

Classes can be debugged with the system debugger simply by executing self halt as a part of starting up the code. The debugger can step one expression at a time through the methods as they execute.

Text in any text window or pane can be evaluated, and, depending on where the pane is, instance method and variables can be referenced.

12

Streams and File Streams

Streams are objects that return successive items from some source of sequential data. Streams can be open on sequenceable collections of any kind of object, on a source of random numbers, or on files.

There are two separate sets of stream classes, one for streams on files, and one for streams on collections.

Streams on collections are instances of ReadStream, WriteStream, or ReadWriteStream, which are subclasses of PositionableStream, which is a subclass of Stream. The other sub-class of Stream is EsRandom.

Streams on files are instances of CfsReadFileStream, CfsWriteFileStream, or CfsReadWrite-FileStream, which are subclasses of CfsFileStream.

The two stream hierarchies are not physically related, as is shown in the class hierarchy below, but they work on the same principles and respond to almost the same set of messages, differing only in the kinds of objects that can be used, and differences due to the objects, files, or collections, over which the stream operate.

Streams

All streams respond to three messages.

atEnd	Has the final item been consumed?
do:	Iterate through a stream
next	Answer the next item n the stream

These are the only messages that random number streams answer to.

For detailed information on stream classes, see Chapter 37, 'Streams', on page 527.

Streams on Collections

Streams are devices that provide sequential access to collections. While they are usually used on strings, they work regardless of the kind of objects that the collection contains. They are particularly useful when multiple items (*elements*) need to be fetched or added to a collection.

Positionable Streams

Streams on collections are all subclasses of the abstract class PositionableStream which provides a common protocol.

close	Close the stream
contents	Answer the whole contents of the stream
isEmpty	Is the stream empty?
position	Get the current position of the stream
position: n	Set the current position of the stream
reset	Set the position to the front of the collection
setToEnd	Set the position to the end of the collection
upToEnd	Answer all items up to the stream's end

Read Streams

Read streams are instances of class ReadStream. They are created by sending the on: message to the class with some sequenceable collection.

ReadStream on: 'Mary had a little laptop, its screen was white as snow'

(Subclasses of SequenceableCollection include String, Array, OrderedCollection, SortedCollection, and ByteArray).

Items are taken from the stream with these messages:

next	Answer the next element
next: n	Answer the next n elements as a collection
nextLine	Answer up to the next line delimiter
nextMatchFor: anObject	Answer all elements up to anObject
skip: n	Skip n items
skipTo: item	Skip items to the next occurrence of item
skipToAll: aCollection	Skip items to aCollection
upTo: item	Return items up to next occurrence of item
upToAll: aCollection	Skip items up to aCollection

The next message is used when the stream needs to be processed one item at a time.

```
" Next character from a read stream "
| rs |
rs := ReadStream on: 'Mary had a little laptop, its screen was white as snow'.
^ rs next
    "Answers: $M "
```
Example 144, Display

Larger amounts of data are often useful though.

```
" Next word from a read stream "
| rs |
rs := ReadStream on: 'Mary had a little laptop, its screen was white as snow'.
^ rs upTo: $         " Get up to the next blank "
    "Answers: 'Mary' "
```
Example 145, Display

```
" Next line from a read stream "
| rs |
rs := ReadStream on: 'Mary had a little laptop,', LineDelimiter, 'its screen was white as snow'.
^ rs nextLine
"Answers:  'Mary had a little laptop,' "
```
Example 146, Display

Write Streams

Write streams are instances of class WriteStream. They are created by sending the on: message to the class, passing a fixed-size sequenceable collection such as a String, Array, or ByteArray.

```
        WriteStream on: String new
```

or:

```
        WriteStream on: Array new
```

The output collection will be automatically extended when it gets full.

Items are written to the stream with messages such as:

nextPut: item	Put a single item
nextPutAll: collection	Put a collection
next: n put: item	Put n copies of item
cr	Put a line delimiter
space	Put a space
tab	Put a tab

Example 147 writes two lines to a stream, and then uses the contents message to retrieve a copy of the elements written to the stream.

```
" Simple Write Stream "
| ws |
ws := WriteStream on: String new.
ws nextPutAll: 'Mary had a little laptop,'; cr.
ws nextPutAll: 'it''s screen was white as snow;'; cr.
ws nextPutAll: 'and everywhere that Mary went;'; cr.
ws nextPutAll: 'her laptop was sure to go.'; cr.
^ ws contents
    " Answers:
'Mary had a little laptop,
it's screen was white as snow;
and everywhere that Mary went,
her laptop was sure to go.' "
```
Example 147, Display

Read and Write Streams

A ReadWriteStream combines the above protocols and adds messages for setting the position in the stream. Thus, random access is allowed.

ReadWriteStream answers to the same messages as ReadStream and WriteStream.

Line Delimiters

Line delimiters are platform-dependent sequences of one or more characters which are output by the cr message and used when reading to delimit input lines. The line delimiter defaults to the one that is used by the native operating system of the platform. Line delimiters are used in both streams and file streams.

The line delimiter can be changed in various ways to match other supported platforms (by name) or to other sequences. The line delimiters are in the pool dictionary CldtConstants (see the section on 'CldtConstants' on page 109). The default is named LineDelimiter.

The two examples below are the same, provided that the default line delimiter has not been changed.

```
aStream cr.                         " Output a line delimiter "
aStream nextPutAll: LineDelimiter   " Output a line delimiter "
```

Line delimiters are defined for platforms on which IBM Smalltalk operates (and possibly other platforms to allow data interchange). These include WinLineDelimiter, PMLineDelimiter, and UNIXLineDelimiter. Line delimiters are set with the lineDelimiter: message to a stream.

File Streams

File streams are very similar to streams over collections, but operate upon files in the platform file system. File streams read and write characters or bytes only. The naming of files and directories is constrained by the platform operating system; the details are given in the section on 'Paths' on page 144.

For detailed information on stream classes, see Chapter 29, 'Common File System', on page 373.

There are three kinds of file streams:

CfsReadFileStream	Reads files only
CfsWriteFileStream	Writes files only
CfsReadWriteFileStream	Reads and writes files

Errors

Errors are reported by answering a special object, an instance of CfsError, instead of the normal returned value†. In some cases, the returned value is always an instance of CfsError or an instance of CfsErrorProxy, a special object that indicates that no error occurred.

All objects in Smalltalk respond to the isCfsError message; all objects except instances of CfsError answer false. When isCfsError answers true, either some corrective action should be taken, or an error message issued. Instances of CfsError contain an error message that describes what happened, and this text can be used in a message.

```
" Perform some file operation; detect an error and issue an error message "
| result |
(result := some file operation) isCfsError
    ifTrue: [ ^ self error: result message ].
```

Opening

File streams are opened with the open: or openEmpty: messages, and are closed with the close message.

Example 148 illustrates how to open an existing file for reading and properly check for open errors.

```
" Open existing file for reading; check for open errors "
| file |
(file := CfsReadFileStream open: 'existing.txt') isCfsError
    ifTrue: [ ^ self error: file message ].
file close
```
Example 148, Execute

Example 149 illustrates how to open an existing file for reading and writing and properly check for open errors.

```
" Open existing file for reading and writing; check for open errors "
| file |
(file := CfsReadWriteFileStream open: 'existing.txt') isCfsError
    ifTrue: [ ^ self error: file message ].
file close
```
Example 149, Execute

Example 150 illustrates how to open an existing file for writing only, using the openEmpty: message, and properly check for open errors.

```
" Open file for writing (empty it if it exists); check for open errors "
| file |
(file := CfsWriteFileStream openEmpty: 'new.txt') isCfsError
    ifTrue: [ ^ self error: file message ].
file close
```
Example 150, Execute

Once a file stream is open, it is operated upon with the same set of messages used for streams, including, for reading:

next	Answer the next element
next: n	Answer the next n elements as a collection
nextLine	Answer up to the next line delimiter
nextMatchFor: anObject	Answer all elements up to anObject
skip: n	Skip n items

---

† Some CFS messages have no normal returned value; they return instances of a class named CfsErrorProxy when there is no error. These instances only respond to isCfsError and always answer false, and are never directly visible except in the debugger or inspector.

skipTo: item	Skip items to the next occurrence of item
skipToAll: aCollection	Skip items to aCollection
upTo: item	Return items up to next occurrence of item
upToAll: aCollection	Skip items up to aCollection

and for writing:

nextPut: item	Put a single item
nextPutAll: collection	Put a collection
next: n put: item	Put n copies of item
cr	Put a line delimiter
space	Put a space
tab	Put a tab

Reading and Writing

Example 151 is Example 147 modified to write to a file stream.

```
" Simple Write File Stream "
| ws text |
(ws := CfsReadWriteFileStream openEmpty: 'maryslap.txt') isCfsError
    ifTrue: [ ^ self error: ws message ].
ws nextPutAll: 'Mary had a little lamp,'; cr.
ws nextPutAll: 'it''s light was white as snow;'; cr.
ws nextPutAll: 'and everywhere that Mary went;'; cr.
ws nextPutAll: 'that lamp was sure to glow.'; cr.
text := ws contents.
ws close.
^ text


" Answers:
'Mary had a little lamp,
it's light was white as snow;
and everywhere that Mary went,
that lamp was sure to glow.' "
```
Example 151, Display

Example 152 shows how to open an existing file for reading, another for writing, and then write the input file's entire contents to the output file. After two opens, the expression old contents reads the whole contents of the open file old into memory; then nextPutAll: outputs it all to new.

```
" Copy a file all at once; prompt for file names "
| old new |
(old := CfsReadFileStream
    open: (CwFileSelectionPrompter new prompt) ) isCfsError
        ifTrue: [ ^ self error: old message ].
(new := CfsWriteFileStream
    openEmpty: (System prompt: 'Output file name') ) isCfsError
        ifTrue: [ ^ self error: new message ].
new nextPutAll: old contents.
old close.
new close
```
Example 152, Execute

Examples

Changing Line Delimiters

Files with one kind of line delimiter are often moved to platforms where the line delimiter is different. This example shows a simple utility which will convert a DOS, Windows or OS/2 file to a UNIX file.

The actual copy is done line by line in a simple loop. The message nextLine, used to read a line, removes line delimiters; the line delimiters for UNIX are added by the cr message.

```
" Convert DOS file to UNIX file "
| input output str |
str :=  CwFileSelectionPrompter new
        title: 'Enter name of DOS format input file'; prompt.
(input := CfsReadFileStream open: str) isCfsError
        ifTrue: [ ^ self error: input message ].
input lineDelimiter: PMLineDelimiter.

str := System prompt: 'Enter name of UNIX format output file'.
(output := CfsWriteFileStream open: str) isCfsError
        ifTrue: [ ^ self error: output message ].
output lineDelimiter: UNIXLineDelimiter.

[ input atEnd ]
        whileFalse: [ output nextPutAll: (input nextLine); cr ].
input close.
output close
```
Example 153, Execute

Adding Uppercase Letters

This example reads a text file and changes the first lower case character which follows a period, possibly with separating white space, into an upper case character. It will take text such as:

> the dog ran up the tree. the cat barked. the boy laughed.

and convert it to:

> The dog ran up the tree. The cat barked. The boy laughed.

```
" Capitalize first letter past a period in a file "
| input output str period |
period := true.

str := CwFileSelectionPrompter new title: 'Select input file'; prompt.
(input := CfsReadFileStream open: str) isCfsError
    ifTrue: [ ^ self error: input message ].

str := System prompt: 'Enter name of output file'.
(output := CfsWriteFileStream open: str) isCfsError
        ifTrue: [ ^ self error: output message ].

[ input atEnd ]
    whileFalse: [  |char|
            char := input next.
            period & char isLowercase
                ifTrue: [ output nextPut: char asUppercase ]
```

```
                    ifFalse: [ output nextPut: char ].
            char isSeparator
                    ifFalse: [ period := char == $. ] ].
    input close.
    output close
```
Example 154, Display

Random Streams

Instances of EsRandom answer an endless stream of floating-point numbers in the range 0.0 through, but not including, 1.0. Random streams answer to these messages:

atEnd	Always answers false
do:	Iterate through a stream; never terminates
next	Answer the next random number

Random streams are automatically seeded and the seed cannot be changed. Each instance of EsRandom is seeded differently, and thus answer a different sequence of random numbers.

Random Stream Example

Shuffle a 'deck' of 'cards' using random numbers. The cards are represented by integers from 1 to 52 in an ordered collection; removal is random. Removed cards are placed into a second array.

```
" Shuffle a deck of cards "
| deck rand shuf n |
rand := EsRandom new.                    "Get new generator"
deck := (1 to: 52) asOrderedCollection.  "Init deck to integers 1 to 52"
shuf := OrderedCollection new: deck size. "Put shuffled cards here"
deck size timesRepeat: [                 "Loop on initial deck size"
    n := (deck size * rand next)
            floor asInteger + 1."Rand range 1 to cur deck size"
        shuf addLast: (deck removeAtIndex: n) ]. "Move card to shuffled deck"
shuf size = 52 ifFalse:
    [ self error: 'This better not ever happen!' ].
^ shuf
```
Example 155, Display

Summary

Streams provide an alternative way to read and write files and collections, and are especially useful when the reading or writing involves multiple items at one time or when reading involves scanning the input for a particular element of sequence of elements.

Streams on collections and on files are very similar; each allows reading, writing, or both, and each responds to essentially the same messages.

Random streams are a convenient source for random numbers.

13

Files

This chapter describes lower-level file access, including opening and closing file descriptors, reading and writing data, random access, errors, locking and sharing, testing and querying file and directory information, and platform file and directory issues.

File streams, described in Chapter 12, 'Streams and File Streams', on page 135, are the preferred way to read and write files. It is possible to use low-level access for finding and opening a file, then use a file stream for reading or writing.

Two pool dictionaries are needed for file access.

CldtConstants	Holds names and values for various unprintable ASCII characters, and for line delimiters.
CfsConstants	Holds flags and error codes used with both low-level access and file streams.

Class descriptions for lower level file access are in Chapter 29, 'Common File System', on page 373.

File Names

The names of files are held in strings, usually along with a valid path to a directory. File names can include any character that the platform supports, but, for portability, names should be limited to an eight-byte name, and an optional period followed by an optional three byte name. Characters should be limited to upper-case and lower-case letters, numbers, and the hyphen. For portability, do not assume that filenames are either case sensitive or case insensitive. A safe technique is to force all filenames to lowercase.

Some valid portable filenames are:

        readme.txt   May be the same file as README.TXT
        readme
        payroll.log

File System Roots

Some platforms have a single file system that spans all drives, and others have a separate file system for each drive; information on the name or names of root directories is available. UNIX systems have just one string, '/'; OS/2 and Windows systems have several strings which are qualified drive and path names, such as:

        'A:\' 'B:\' 'C:\' 'D:\' 'E:\'

The expression in Example 156 answers an array that holds one string for each root directory.

" **Ask for the platform's root directory(s)** "
CfsDirectoryDescriptor rootDirectories
" Answer on the author's platform:
    ('A:\' 'B:\' 'C:\' 'D:\' 'E:\' 'F:\' 'G:\') "

Example 156, Display

Paths

Path names are held in strings, and usually contain platform-specific delimiters. Path names are absolute (fully qualified) or relative.

Absolute path names uniquely identify a directory or file within the system or complex of systems and networks that make up a user's environment. Such paths will contain drive specifications on systems that have individually identifiable drives.

Absolute OS/2 directory:	'C:\smalltlk\examples\'
Absolute OS/2 file:	'C:\smalltlk\examples\tictac.st'
Absolute UNIX directory:	'/usr/dave/smalltlk/examples/'
Absolute UNIX file:	'/usr/dave/smalltlk/examples/tictac.st'

Relative path names uniquely describe a directory or file based on some separately specified current working directory. Relative path names can start with a dot-dot ('..') to base the relative path on the parent of the current working directory, a dot ('.') to base the relative path on the current working directory, or can simply be the name of a directory or file in the current working directory.

Relative OS/2 directory:	'..\examples\'
Relative OS/2 file:	'..\examples\tictac.st'
Relative OS/2 file:	'tictac.st'
Relative UNIX directory:	'../examples/'
Relative UNIX file:	'../examples/tictac.st'
Relative UNIX file:	'tictac.st'

Fully qualified directory paths start with a root, and have zero or more directory names, each followed by a path separator character. Fully qualified file names are a fully qualified directory path name followed by the name of a file from a directory.

For portability, the directory names should either be determined by interaction with the user, or the platform, or should not exceed eight bytes in length. Characters should be limited to upper- and lower-case letters and numbers. For portability, do not assume that directory names are either case sensitive or case insensitive.

A path separator character is a platform-specific character used to separate directory names in a path. This character is a backslash on OS/2 and Windows, and a slash on UNIX. The pathSeparator and pathSeparatorString messages to CfsDirectoryDescriptor answer the current platform's separator as a character or as a one character string.

```
" See if a path ends with a path separator character "
| path |
path := 'C:\sources\c\includes\'.
^ path last = CfsDirectoryDescriptor pathSeparator
    " Answers true on the authors platform "
```
Example 157, Display

```
" Build a path name "
| parts root sep path |
root := CfsDirectoryDescriptor rootDirectories at: 1.
parts := #( 'sources' 'c' 'includes' ).
sep := CfsDirectoryDescriptor pathSeparatorString.
path := root.
1 to: parts size do: [ :n |
    path := path, (parts at: n), sep ].
^ path
    "Answer on OS/2: 'A:\sources\c\includes\' "
```
Example 158, Display

Current Directory

The current working directory can be obtained with the expression in Example 159.

```
" Get the current working directory "
CfsDirectoryDescriptor getcwd
" Possible answer: 'C:\IBMST\PMIMAGE' "
```
Example 159, Display

The expression returns a string containing the fully qualified path name to the directory, such as:

```
'C:\IBMST\PMIMAGE'
```

The current working directory can be changed with the chdir: message.

```
" Change the working directory to the C: drive (OS/2 or Windows) "
CfsDirectoryDescriptor chdir: 'C:\'.
```
Example 160, Execute

```
" Change the working directory to the last (or only) root "
CfsDirectoryDescriptor chdir:
    CfsDirectoryDescriptor rootDirectories last
```
Example 161, Execute

Creating and Removing Directories

Directories are created by sending the mkdir: message. Directories can be removed by sending the rmdir: message.

```
" Create a new directory "
CfsDirectoryDescriptor mkdir: 'Examp162'
```
Example 162, Execute

```
" Remove a directory "
CfsDirectoryDescriptor rmdir: 'Examp162'
```
Example 163, Execute

Deleting the current working directory (CWD) can cause platform-specific errors, possibly unrecoverable ones. Platforms with drives maintain separate working directories for each drive; simply changing the working directory to another drive will not necessarily solve the problem. Instead, change the working directory to the root of the current drive.

```
" Removing a directory the wrong way; cwd is 'C:\pascal' "
CfsDirectoryDescriptor chdir: 'D:\smalltlk'.
CfsDirectoryDescriptor rmdir: 'C:\pascal'   "might still be CWD on C:"
```

```
" Removing a directory the right way; cwd is 'C:\pascal' "
CfsDirectoryDescriptor chdir: 'C:\'.
CfsDirectoryDescriptor rmdir: 'C:\pascal'.   "Cannot be CWD on C:"
CfsDirectoryDescriptor chdir: 'D:\smalltlk'
```

Deleting and Renaming Files

Files are deleted with the remove: message, and renamed with the rename: message.

```
CfsFileDescriptor remove: '1981rate.dat'
```

```
CfsFileDescriptor remove: '../rates/1981rate.dat'
```

```
CfsFileDescriptor rename: 'oldname.fil' new: 'newname.fil'
```

Some platforms support renaming directories.

```
CfsFileDescriptor rename: '../rates' new: '../values'
```

The rename: method performs a move operation if the target path is different from the source path.

```
CfsFileDescriptor
    rename: '..\mom\oldname.fil'
    new: '..\dad\newname.fil'
```

Properties

Instances of three common file system classes return information about directories and files.

CfsStat	CfsStat instances answer information about a file from its directory entry, including its size, date of last change, and its type.
CfsDirectoryDescriptor	CfsDirectoryDescriptor instances can read entries in a directory, selecting just those that match some pattern, and answer instances of CfsDirectoryEntry.

CfsDirectoryEntry   CfsDirectoryEntry instances describe one directory en-
                                     try; the instance responds to the same messages as do
                                     instances of CfsStat.

The stat: message to class CfsStat answers an instance from which file properties can
be obtained.

" **Obtain an instance of CfsStat for a file** "
| aStat |
aStat := CfsStat stat: 'IBMSTEX2.TXT'   *Example 164, Inspect*

If a file or directory does not exist, the stat: message returns an instance of CfsError.

" **See if a file exists** "
^ (CfsStat stat: 'IBMSTEX1.TXT') isCfsError not   *Example 165, Display*

Caution: Do not fail to check for errors when opening files; while a file might exist
when tested as above, it might be deleted by another process between this test and the
time the file is opened.

The instance of CfsStat can be sent a number of messages, including:

isDir	Is this a directory?
isReg	Is this a regular file?
stFtime	The date and time created (or nil)
stMtime	The date and time last modified (never nil)
stSize	File size as in directory entry

Some messages, such as stFtime, are platform dependent; they answer nil if the current
platform does not support them.

" **Determine characteristics of a file** "
| aStat |
aStat := CfsStat stat: (CwFileSelectionPrompter new title: 'Obtain info on file'; prompt).
aStat isCfsError ifTrue: [self error: aStat message].
Transcript cr; show: 'Directory: ', aStat isDir printString.
Transcript cr; show: 'Created: ', aStat stFtime printString.
Transcript cr; show: 'Last modified: ', aStat stMtime printString.
Transcript cr; show: 'Size: ', aStat stSize printString.

" The Transcript will show something like:
Directory: false
Created: nil
Last modified: (07-05-95 12:48:42 PM)
Size: 20318 "   *Example 166, Execute*

Check For Directory

The isDir message is used to determine if a path names a file, or names a directory.

" **See if a path names a directory** "
| stat |
stat := CfsStat stat: (CfsDirectoryDescriptor rootDirectories at: 1).
stat isCfsError
        ifTrue: [^ false]
        ifFalse: [^ stat isDir]
            "Answer: true "   *Example 167, Display*

Searching Directories

The class CfsDirectoryDescriptor has methods that read the contents of directories. The contents can be filtered by a pattern that each name must match.

Patterns

Patterns are strings made up of three kinds of characters:

*	Matches zero or more arbitrary characters.
?	Matches one and only one arbitrary character.
All others	Other characters match themselves.

A nil pattern matches all files.

Patterns can be simple or complex:

*	Matches all names.
*.TXT	Matches all names that end with '.TXT'.
V2*.ST	Matches all names that start with 'V2' and that end with '.ST'.
V?*.ST	Matches all names that start with 'V', that have a required second character, possibly more characters, and that end with '.ST'.
*.???	Matches all names that have three characters behind the period.
???.*	Matches all names that have three characters, and a period with zero or more characters behind it.
A*B.TXT	Matches all names that start with 'A' followed by zero or more characters and then a 'B.TXT'.

Caution: Not all patterns will necessarily handled by all platforms; for example, the last pattern above ('A*B.TXT') has an imbedded asterisk, and some platforms do not handle them. For portability, use asterisks by themselves, as the name or extension in an 8+3 name, or as a trailing character in either the 8 or 3 part of the name.

Reading Entries

A directory is opened for searching with the opendir:pattern:mode: message sent to CfsDirectoryDescriptor. It answers an instance of itself to which messages are sent to step through the entries; this instance is called a directory stream, but has a different protocol than other streams.

The opendir:pattern:mode: message takes three arguments; the first is a string holding the path to the directory, the second is a string holding the pattern, and the third is one of three search mode flags, or two or more inclusive ored together, as shown below.

Flag	Description
FREG	Match regular files.
FDIR	Match directories.
FSPECIAL	Match files that are neither regular files nor directories.

Figure 41: Directory Search Flags.

There are three methods that read directory information from an instance of CfsDirectoryDescriptor:

readdir

Answers a new instance of CfsDirectoryEntry that represents the next directory entry that matches the pattern and mode; these instances understand the same querying messages as do instances of CfsStat.

readdir: aCfsDirEnt

Takes an old instance of CfsDirectoryEntry and fills it in with information from the next directory entry that matches the pattern and mode.

readdirName

Answers a string with the name of the next directory entry that matches the pattern and mode.

In each case, the operation moves the directory stream forward one entry. After the last entry is read, the operations answer nil. The rewinddir message resets the stream back to the beginning, and has the same effect as closing the stream with closedir and then reopening the stream.

Note: For best performance with readdirName, ask for all modes by *or*ing FREG, FDIR, and FSPECIAL together.

Caution: Do not use readdirName to get a file name and then use the CfsStat message stat: to get file information; it is never faster, and on some platforms it causes the directory to be searched twice.

Example 168 and Example 169 show how to use directory streams.

```
" Open a directory stream on all files in the current directory "
| stream |
stream := CfsDirectoryDescriptor
     opendir: '.'      " Open current directory "
     pattern: '*'
     mode: FREG | FDIR | FSPECIAL.
stream isCfsError ifTrue: [ ^ self error: stream message ].
stream closedir
```
Example 168, Execute

```
" Open directory stream on all .BAT files in the parent directory "
| stream |
stream := CfsDirectoryDescriptor
     opendir: '.'
     pattern: '*.BAT'
     mode: FREG | FDIR | FSPECIAL.
stream isCfsError  ifTrue: [ ^ self error: stream message ].
stream closedir
```
Example 169, Execute

Example 170 shows how to read directory entries.

```
" Make collection of directory entries in a root directory "
| roots root stream entry collection |
collection := OrderedCollection new.
roots := CfsDirectoryDescriptor rootDirectories.
roots size > 1
     ifTrue: [ root := roots at: 3 ]          " roots at: 3  gets the C:\ drive root "
     ifFalse: [ root := roots at: 1 ].
stream := CfsDirectoryDescriptor
     opendir: root
     pattern: '*'
     mode: FDIR.
```

```
        stream isCfsError  ifTrue: [ ^ self error: stream message ].
        [ (entry := stream readdir) notNil ]
            whileTrue:
                [ collection add: entry ].
        stream closedir.
        ^ collection
```
Example 170, Inspect

Example 171 shows how to use readdirName.

```
    " Display on the Transcript  the names of all files  and directories in the CWD"
    | stream name |
    stream := CfsDirectoryDescriptor
        opendir: '.'
        pattern: '*'
        mode: FREG | FDIR | FSPECIAL.
    stream isCfsError ifTrue: [ ^ self error: stream message ].
    [ (name := stream readdirName) isNil ]
        whileFalse:
            [ Transcript cr; show: name ].
    stream closedir
```
Example 171, Execute

Opening Files

Files are opened by sending the open:oflag: message to CfsFileDescriptor, which answers a new CFS file descriptor, through which file operations are performed. The two parameters are the path to the file and open flags, which specify how to open a file; they are described in Figure 42. Only one of the first three flags can be given, but any of the last four can be *inclusive or*ed to it.

Flag	*Description*	*Usage*
ORDONLY	Open the file for reading only.	Choose just one of these flags.
OWRONLY	Open the file for writing only.	
ORDWR	Open the file for both reading and writing.	
OAPPEND	Set the file offset to the end of the file before *each* write.	*Inclusive or* zero or more of these flags to the one chosen above.
OCREAT	If the file does not exist, create a new one; if the file exists, just open it (unless OEXCL is also given; see below).	
OEXCL	Cause the open to fail if the file exists and OCREAT and OEXCL are both specified.	
OTRUNC	Truncate the file to a length of zero if it is successfully opened ORDWR or OWRONLY.	

Figure 42: File Open Flags.

Some examples:

```
    " Open an existing file for reading; fail if it does not exist "
    | file |
    file := CfsFileDescriptor
        open: 'examp172.txt'
        oflag: ORDONLY.
    file isCfsError ifTrue: [ ^ self error: file message ].
    file close
```
Example 172, Execute

CfsFileDescriptor answers an instance of CfsError when something goes wrong; this can be checked with the isCfsError message and some action taken. Error handling will be covered in more detail later in this chapter.

```
" Open a new file for writing; fail if it exists
  (which it will the 2nd time this is run, since 1st time creates it) "
| file |
file := CfsFileDescriptor
      open: 'examp173.txt'
      oflag: OWRONLY | OCREAT | OEXCL.
file isCfsError ifTrue: [ ^ self error: file message ].
file close
```

Example 173, Execute

```
" Open a file for reading and writing; create it if it doesn't exist "
| file |
file := CfsFileDescriptor
      open: 'examp174.txt'
      oflag: ORDWR | OCREAT.
file isCfsError ifTrue: [ ^ self error: file message ].
file close
```

Example 174, Execute

```
" Open empty file; if it exists, truncate its contents "
| file |
file := CfsFileDescriptor
      open: 'examp175.txt'
      oflag: ORDWR | OCREAT | OTRUNC.
file isCfsError ifTrue: [ ^ self error: file message ].
file close
```

Example 175, Execute

Files must be closed when all file activity has ended. If not closed, operating system resources may remain allocated, and may eventually prevent further file access.

Reading and Writing Files

Data is transferred between a file and a buffer with the read:startingAt:nbyte: and write:startingAt:nbyte: messages to a file descriptor on an open file. The first argument, a string or byte array, is the buffer. The second specifies the position in the *buffer* from or to which data is to be transferred. The last argument specifies the number of bytes to transfer. The message answers the number of bytes that were actually transferred, or answers an instance of CfsError.

Example 176 copies a file using buffers.

```
" Copying a file using buffers "
| rbytes wbytes from to buf toName |
buf := ByteArray new: 32768.

from := CfsFileDescriptor
      open: (CwFileSelectionPrompter new title: 'Input file'; prompt)
      oflag: ORDONLY.
from isCfsError ifTrue: [ ^ self error: from message ].

toName := CwFileSelectionPrompter new title: 'Output file'; prompt.
to := CfsFileDescriptor
      open: toName
      oflag: OWRONLY | OCREAT | OTRUNC.
```

```
to isCfsError ifTrue: [ ^ self error: to message ].

[ rbytes := from read: buf startingAt: 1 nbyte: buf size.
  rbytes > 0 ]
    whileTrue: [
        wbytes := to write: buf startingAt: 1 nbyte: rbytes.
        rbytes > wbytes
            ifTrue: [  "Less written than read; disk full?"
                from close.
                to close.
                CfsFileDescriptor remove: toName.
                ^ self error:  'Unable to copy; file system may be full.' ] ].
from close.
to close
```
Example 176, Execute

Random Access

The lseek:whence: message to a CFS file descriptor that is opened on a file will set and query the file position. The first parameter is an integer byte offset into the file, and the second argument is one of the constants Figure 43. It always answers the new file position.

Flag	Description
SEEKSET	Set the position relative to the start of the file.
SEEKCUR	Set the position relative to the current position.
SEEKEND	Set the position relative to the end of the file.

Figure 43: File Positioning Constants.

Example 177 illustrates how to use lseek:whence:.

```
" Using lseek:whence: to set and query file positions "
| file pos |
"Open an existing file"
file := CfsFileDescriptor
        open: (CwFileSelectionPrompter new title: 'File to read'; prompt)
        oflag: ORDONLY.
file isCfsError ifTrue: [ ^ self error: file message ].

"Get current file position"
pos := file lseek: 0 whence: SEEKCUR.
Transcript cr; show: 'Starting file position: ', pos printString.

"Position near the end"
pos := file lseek: -20 whence: SEEKEND.
Transcript cr; show: 'Position 20 ahead of end: ', pos printString.

"Position near the front"
pos := file lseek: 50 whence: SEEKSET.
Transcript cr; show: 'Position 50 from front: ', pos printString.

"Position back 30 bytes"
pos := file lseek: -30 whence: SEEKCUR.
Transcript cr; show: 'Position -30 from prior position: ', pos printString.

file close.
```
Example 177, Execute

Other File Operations

Other messages to a CFS file descriptor are rewind, which sets the position back to the front of the file; size, which answers the current size of the file in bytes; and flush, which forces all changes made to the file to be written to disk.

These messages are described in Chapter 29, 'Common File System', on page 373.

Error Handling

If an error occurs in any low level file operation, a file stream class method, or a CfsStat operation, an instance of CfsError is answered instead of the usual answer; it contains information about the error. To determine if an error has occurred, send the isCfsError message to the returned value. All objects except instances of CfsError answer false; those answer true.

The errors that can be returned are summarized in Figure 84 in the section on 'File Error Constants' on page 376.

An instance of CfsError responds to three messages:

errno	The platform dependent error number
identifier	The symbolic name of the error
message	A short text description of the error

Identifiers are the names in the CfsConstants pool dictionary; the associated values are platform dependent error numbers. The error number should be used only for comparison with values defined in CfsConstants, and should never be hard coded.

```
" How to use error numbers from CfsError "
| fd |
fd := CfsFileDescriptor
        open: 'existing.fil'
        oflag: ORDWR | OCREAT | OEXCL.
fd isCfsError
    ifTrue: [
            fd errno = EEXIST  ifTrue: [ ... ... ... ].
            fd errno = EROFS  ifTrue: [ ... ... ... ].
            fd errno = ENOSPC ifTrue: [ ... ... ... ].
            ^ self error: fd message.  "Else use the default message" ].
    fd close
```

File Sharing and Locking

The Common File System provides uniform file sharing and locking mechanisms across the various platforms.

Locking

There are two approaches to locking:

Advisory locking	Has no effect on clients that do not explicitly check for locks.
Mandatory locking	All clients must check for locking.

Mandatory locking presents a performance or reliability risk, since essential resources can be locked and such locks can disrupt operations. However, it also provides better locking control and data security, since it can be assured that no other users can interfere. A platform usually supports just one of these approaches.

Locking constants are defined in the pool dictionary CfsConstants and are described in Figure 44.

Flag	*Description*
FRDLOCK	Specifies a shared (read) *advisory* lock, which prevents any other client from setting an exclusive advisory lock on any portion of the protected area. Noncooperating clients can read or write in protected areas.
FWRLOCK	Specifies an exclusive (write) *advisory* lock. An exclusive advisory lock prevents any other client from setting a shared *or* exclusive advisory lock on any portion of the protected area. Noncooperating clients can read or write in protected areas.
FMDLOCK	Specifies an exclusive *mandatory* lock, which prevents any other client from reading, writing, or locking any portion of the protected area.

Figure 44: File Locking Constants.

The supportsLockType: message can be sent to CfsFileDescriptor passing one of the lock constants to determine if that lock type is supported on the current platform.

```
" Answer the best exclusive lock type available "
(CfsFileDescriptor supportsLockType: FMDLOCK)   "Ask for mandatory"
    ifTrue: [ ^ FMDLOCK ].
(CfsFileDescriptor supportsLockType: FWRLOCK)   "Ask for exclusive advisory"
    ifTrue: [ ^ FWRLOCK ].
^ self error: 'No exclusive locks available on this platform.'           Example 178, Display
```

Caution: On some platforms, locking may have no effect unless the file is being accessed from different processes, and on some networks locking can be effective only if the file is accessed from different machines. These are limitations present in the operating system or the network code on specific platforms.

Regions

The lock:start:len: message to an instance of CfsFileDescriptor sets a segment lock on the file. The first argument is one of the file locking constants, the second is an integer with the region's offset from the front of the file, and the third is the length of the region. If the file cannot be locked because the lock type is not supported, an instance of CfsError is answered. Unlocking is done with unlock:start:len:, which takes the same arguments.

```
" Perform various lock operations "
| file lockType len |

"Determine best exclusive lock type"
(CfsFileDescriptor supportsLockType: FMDLOCK)   "Ask for mandatory"
    ifTrue: [ lockType := FMDLOCK ].
(CfsFileDescriptor supportsLockType: FWRLOCK)   "Ask for exclusive advisory"
    ifTrue: [ lockType :=  FWRLOCK ].
```

```
lockType isNil
     ifTrue: [ ^ self error: 'No exclusive locks available on this platform.' ].

"Open a file"
file := CfsFileDescriptor
     open: 'examp179.fil'
     oflag: ORDWR | OCREAT | OTRUNC.
file isCfsError ifTrue: [ self error: file message ].

"Put some data into the file"
file write: (1 to: 100) asByteArray startingAt: 1 nbyte: 100.

"Lock 10-14"
file lock: lockType start: 10 len: 5.

"Release the lock"
file unlock: lockType start: 10 len: 5.

"Lock the current extent of the whole file"
file lock: lockType start: 0 len: (len := file size).

"Write more to file"
file write: (101 to: 120) asByteArray startingAt: 101 nbyte: 20.

"Unlock it"
file unlock: lockType start: 0 len: len.

"Close the file"
file close
```

Example 179, Execute

Note that the unlock, just above, cannot be:

```
"Unlock it"
file unlock: lockType start: 0 len: **file size**.
```

which asks the file for its current size, because the size has changed. The unlock would attempt to unlock more than it locked, and unpredictable behavior could result.

In general, locked regions should not overlap, and regions that have not been locked should not be unlocked. All locks should be explicitly released before closing the file.

Sharing Files

Sharing is similar to locking, but applies to the whole file at once. Sharing mode constants are defined in the pool dictionary CfsConstants, and are described in Figure 45.

Flag	Description
ODENYNONE	Other processes can open the file for any type of access: read-only, write-only, or read-write.
ODENYRD	Other processes can open the file only for write access.
ODENYWR	Other processes can open the file only for read access.
ODENYRDWR	Other processes cannot open the file for any kind of access; it is unspecified whether the current process can open it a second time.

Figure 45: File Sharing Constants.

As with file locking, platforms do not support sharing uniformly; some will combine open modes and share modes. If a file is opened ORDONLY, it might have the effect of applying the ODENYWR share mode, and OWRONLY might imply ODENYRDWR.

Some platforms do not support share modes at all; when this is the case, sharing requests are ignored.

The supportsShareMode: message can be sent to CfsFileDescriptor to determine if a particular mode is supported.

```
" Determine if this platform supports ODENYWR "
^ CfsFileDescriptor supportsShareMode: ODENYWR
```
Example 180, Display

Shared files are opened with the open:oflag:share: message to CfsFileDescriptor. The first two arguments are the same as for open:oflag:. The share argument is one of the file-sharing constants.

```
" Open a file with exclusive read and write access "
| file |
file := CfsFileDescriptor
     open: CwFileSelectionPrompter new prompt
     oflag: ORDWR | OCREAT
     share: ODENYRDWR.
file isCfsError
          ifTrue: [ ^ self error: file printString ].
file close
```
Example 181, Execute

```
" Open a file with read access; deny write access "
| file |
file := CfsFileDescriptor
     open: CwFileSelectionPrompter new prompt
     oflag: ORDONLY
     share: ODENYWR.
file isCfsError
     ifTrue: [ ^ self error file printString ].
file close
```
Example 182, Execute

Summary

File support in Smalltalk provides access to files, directories, locking, and sharing facilities of the underlying platform.

File and directory names, directory roots, and path separators can be manipulated in a platform-independent manner. Directories and files can be found by searching; they can be created, deleted, and renamed. Files can be read or written. Properties of files and directories can be examined.

Files can be shared with users on other machines, and portions of files can be locked so that updates can be performed.

14

Handling Exceptions

Exception handling provides control over error conditions; it allows recovery from system errors and conditions, as well as user-defined exceptions.

Survey of Classes and Concepts

Exceptions are raised by errors that occur while running code, such as divide-by-zero or exceeding an array bound, or by explicitly signalling an exception. Exceptions are caught by running a block of code in a special way that specifies which exceptions to watch for.

Exception handling involves four classes: ExceptionalEvent, Signal, Block, and ExceptionalEventCollection.

Instances of ExceptionalEvent describe a particular kind of error and provide default code to handle the error. Smalltalk provides four exceptional events, ExAll, ExError, ExHalt, and ExUserBreak; new exceptional events are created as children of one of these.

Instances of Signal describe a particular error. Instances of ExceptionalEventCollection hold more than one instance of ExceptionalEvent.

For detailed information about exception handling classes, see Chapter 30, 'Exception Handling', on page 395.

Exceptional Events

IBM Smalltalk comes with several defined instances of ExceptionalEvent. They include:

ExAll   The most general exception; catches all exceptions.
ExError   The exception signalled by error:.

| ExHalt | The exception signalled by halt: or halt. |
| ExUserBreak | The exception signalled when the user presses the break key (or its equivalent). |

These exceptions are all instances of class ExceptionalEvent, and are held in the pool dictionary SystemExceptions.

Exceptional events are defined in a *containment hierarchy*, a hierarchy built from instances that point to other instances. The system provided exceptional events are arranged in the hierarchy shown below. User-created exceptional events are always children of one of the provided exceptional events.

```
ExAll
    ExError
    ExHalt
    ExUserBreak
```

All new exceptions must be children of one of these, typically ExAll. Additional instances of ExceptionalEvent are created by asking an existing instance to create a child of itself. This child handles some new exception; if it cannot handle it, the exception is passed on to the parent. Hierarchies of exceptions can be built.

The following example shows the context in which exceptions are used. A new exception, named exTankEmpty, is created (lines 2-4). A block of code (lines 5-7) is run by the when:do: message (lines 8-9). The block signals the exception (line 6) which causes the block after the do: (line 9) to run; it refills the tank and exits so that execution continues after the signal (line 7). The remainder of this chapter will fill in details of how this works.

```
1)    | exTankEmpty |
2)    exTankEmpty := ExAll newChild
3)        description: 'Feed tank is empty.';
4)        resumable: true.
5)    [ ... do something with tanks ...
6)        exTankEmpty signal: tankTwo.
7)        ... do more with tanks ... ]
8)        when: exTankEmpty
9)        do: [ ... refill the tank ... ]
```

Signals

There are two uses of the term 'signal'. One is a message sent to an exceptional event which causes the event to be raised. The second refers to instances of class Signal, which are passed to exception handling blocks, and which describe the particular exception that was raised.

Instances of Signal have messages that provide various information about the exception that was signalled, including parameters passed at the time of the signal.

argument	The first argument passed by a signal message
arguments	All arguments passed by a signal message
description	The text description of the exception
exitWith:	Return a value as the result of when:do:
resumeWith:with:	Resume execution
retry	Re-execute the receiver of when:do:

Other messages to signals are described later in the chapter.

Blocks

Blocks take special messages, the when:do: messages, that cause them to process exceptions. Exceptions are handled by handlers, blocks which are passed a description of a particular exception as a parameter.

Format:

```
[ block of code that might signal an exception ]
    when: anException
    do: [ :aSignal |
        contents of exception handler block ]
```

Messages to blocks for exception handling are:

atEndOrWhenExceptionDo:	Capture control at the end of the execution of a block or when an exception occurs (but before it is handled).
when:do:	Run a block and handle one exception.
when:do:when:do:	Run a block and handle two exceptions.
when:do:when:do:when:do:	Run a block and handle three exceptions.
when:do:when:do:when:do:when:do:	Run a block and handle four exceptions.
when:do:when:do:when:do:when:do:when:do:	Run a block and handle five exceptions.
whenExceptionDo:	Capture control when an exception occurs (but before it is handled).

Exceptional Event Collections

Instances of ExceptionalEventCollection group multiple instances of ExceptionalEvent. To combine ExHalt and ExError so that both can be handled by one when:do:, create an exceptional event collection like this:

```
ExHalt | ExError
```

The collection is used like this:

```
[ … do some work … ]
    when: ExHalt | ExError
    do: [ process exception … ]
```

Handling Exceptions

A simpler exception handler looks like this:

```
" A simple exception handler for ExError "
[ #(1) at: 2 ]                        " Cause an error "
    when: ExError                     " Specify to catch errors "
    do: [ :signal |                   " When the error occurs, signal holds info on it "
        System message:               " Issue error message "
            signal argument.          " Message text is held in signal "
        signal exitWith: nil ]        " Terminate the when:do: "
```

Example 183, Execute

The code to be executed is in the first block; here it is an obvious bounds error. The when:do: message is sent to the block, passing an exception, ExAll, and a block to handle any exceptions that might occur. The first block is evaluated by when:do:.

When the exception occurs, the second block (the handler), is evaluated, passing a new instance of Signal. It holds several values, including the description of the error (which is usually very general), and the arguments passed as a part of signalling the event. The first argument for errors is a detailed message, which is displayed using System Message:. The last expression in the block ends the handler.

The ExAll exceptional event could have been used as well, since it captures everything that its children capture.

Exceptional Events

Exceptions are instances of class ExceptionalEvent, and are created by sending the new-Child message to an existing instance. Commonly, ExAll is the parent of new children, since ExAll is the most general exception.

Exceptional events have four important variables: a description, the parent, a default handler, and a flag indicating whether or not execution can be resumed. These are accessed by the following messages:

description	Answer the exception's description
description:	Set the description
defaultHandler	Answer the default handler
defaultHandler:	Set the default handler
parent	Get the parent, or nil
resumable	Answer true or false
resumable:	Set resumable to true or false

New children are created by the newChild message.

newChild	Answer a new instance of ExceptionalEvent

For example:

```
" Define a resumable communications line exception "
| commLineError |
commLineError := ExAll newChild
    description: 'Error on communications line';
    resumable: true.
```

or:

```
" Define an 'aircraft out of range' exception "
| aircraftOutOfRange |
aircraftOutOfRange := ExAll newChild
    description: 'Aircraft out of range';
    resumable: false.
```

Signalling Events

Signals are messages sent to exceptions and are said to *raise* the exception. One of four signal messages can be used.

signal	Raise an exception
signalWith:	Raise an exception; pass one value
signalWith:with:	Raise an exception; pass two values
signalWithArguments:	Raise an exception; pass zero or more values

A simple signal looks like this:

ExError signalWith: 'Two paychecks for: ', name.

Signals are handled by a block known as an exception *handler*. Handlers are created with the when:do: message to a block. The handler is passed an instance of Signal; a signal responds to the following messages:

argument	The first argument passed by a signal message
arguments	All arguments passed by a signal message
description	The text description of the exception
exitWith:	Return a value as the result of when:do:
handlesByDefault	Exits when:do: handler; uses default handler
resumeWith:with:	Resume execution with values
retry	Re-execute the receiver of when:do:
signal	Terminate this handler; search for another
signalWith:	Same, with one argument
signalWith:with	Same, with two arguments
signalWithArguments:	Same, with arguments

A simple situation is shown in the example below: an error message is displayed, then when:do: terminates with a value; execution continues after the when:do:. (The variable violation is an instance variable.)

endOfWeekProcessing
        violation := ExAll newChild description: 'Two checks to one person'.
        [self computePayroll]
            when: violation
            do: [:aSignal |
                System errorMessage: aSignal argument.
                aSignal exitWith: 'Where is **my** extra check?']

computePayroll
        ...
        violation signalWith: someData.
        ...

Figure 46 illustrates the handling of an exception by a when:do:.

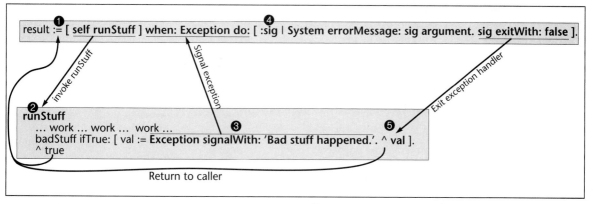

Figure 46: Execution of Exception Handling. The line at top ❶ invokes when:to: to execute method runStuff ❷, and to watch for the exception named Exception. After doing some work, runStuff finds that some bad stuff happened and signals Exception ❸. The signalWith: message searches through prior message sends until if finds one for when:do: that specifies Exception. The associated handler block ❹ is evaluated. It displays a message and then exits, with the value false, back to runStuff ❺. Now, runStuff returns the returned value. If no badStuff happens, runStuff returns true. In either case, this value is assigned to result ❶.

Building Exceptions

There are many ways to build exceptions. They can contain a default handler or not; the default can do all expected processing or not; the exception can be resumable, continuing where the exception was signalled, or not; the exception can be retried, re-executing the block that failed; or the handler can abort processing. It's even possible to signal some exceptions without having an active when:do: construct.

Example 184 defines a simple exception and then signals it. The handler pops up an error message dialog containing the description string, and then exits the when:do: with the value 'done'.

```
" Simple exception; no default handler; no resume or retry "
| zing |
(zing := ExAll newChild)                    "Define exception"
     description: 'zing signalled'.
[ zing signal ]                              "Signal Exception"
     when: zing
     do:[ :aSignal |
          System errorMessage: aSignal description.
          aSignal exitWith: 'done' ]
```
Example 184, Execute

Example 185 is similar; it defines an exception and then signals it. The exception has a default handler that does just what the handler in Example 184 did. The when:do: handler specifies that the default handler is to be run. The result is the same. Bold type shows new code

```
" Exception has a default handler; no resume or retry "
| zing |
(zing := ExAll newChild)
     description: 'zing signalled';
     defaultHandler: [ :sig |
          System errorMessage: sig description.
          sig exitWith: 'done' ].
[ zing signal ]
     when: zing
     do:[ :sig | sig handlesByDefault ]
```
Example 185, Execute

Since the when:do: really adds nothing, and since the default handler does all the work, why not eliminate it? Example 186 attempts to remove that seemingly redundant when:do: and simply signal the exception directly. It doesn't work because exitWith: requires a when:do: to exit from.

```
" This doesn't work since when:do: is not used "
| zing |
(zing := ExAll newChild)
     description: 'zing signalled';
     defaultHandler: [ :sig |
          System errorMessage: sig description.
          sig exitWith: 'done' ].
zing signal
```
Example 186, Execute

There is one circumstance in which when:do: can be omitted; that is when the exception is resumable and is always resumed.

Example 187 is similar to Example 186, but the exception is now marked as resumable and execution is resumed. The arguments to resumeWith:with: are arbitrary; any values can be used. An association holding the two values, the first as the key, and the second as the value, becomes the result of the signal: message.

```
" Don't need when:do: if block resumable and resumeWith: is used "
| zing |
(zing := ExAll newChild)
    description: 'zing signalled';
    resumable: true;
    defaultHandler: [ :sig |
        System errorMessage: sig description.
        sig resumeWith: #zing with: sig argument ].
zing signal
```
Example 187, Execute

Example 188 is similar to Example 187, but a when:do: is used to invoke the default handler with the handlesByDefault: message. The when:do: handler could take other actions.

```
"  Resumes after when:do:   "
| zing |
(zing := ExAll newChild)
    description: 'zing signalled';
    resumable: true;
    defaultHandler: [ :sig |
        System errorMessage: sig description.
        sig resumeWith: #zing with: sig description ].
^ [ zing signal ]
    when: zing
    do: [ :sig | sig handlesByDefault ]
" Answers an association:   #zing -> 'zing signalled'  "
```
Example 188, Display

Default handlers can be ignored. Example 189 bypasses the default handler and immediately exits when:do:.

```
" Exits handler but default is not run "
| zing |
(zing := ExAll newChild)
    description: 'zing signalled';
    resumable: true;
    defaultHandler: [ :sig |
        System errorMessage: sig description.
        sig resumeWith: #zing with: sig description ].
[ zing signal ]
    when: zing
    do: [ :sig | sig exitWith: 'done' ]
" Answers:  'done'  "
```
Example 189, Display

Capturing User Breaks

The exception ExUserBreak will capture system interrupt key presses. (System interrupt keys vary by platform; sometimes it is the Break key, sometimes Alt-SysRq is held down until a beep is heard, and sometimes other keys.)

The following example runs String new: 100000 repeatedly 10,000 times; on the author's platform this runs about 30 seconds, more than long enough to reach for the system interrupt key.

```
" Trapping User Breaks "
System message: 'After exiting this dialog, press user break key'.
[ 10000 timesRepeat: [ String new: 100000 ] ]
    when: ExUserBreak
    do: [ :aSignal |
        System message: aSignal description, ' at ', Time now printString.
        aSignal exitWith: 'Broken!' ]
```
Example 190, Display

Capturing Halts

Messages to halt and halt: can be captured with the ExHalt exception. Halts are inherently resumable.

Example 191 captures a halt and shows a message.

```
" Captures a halt and shows a message "
[ self halt. System message: 'resumed' ]
    when: ExHalt
    do: [ :signal |
        System message: signal description ]
```
Example 191, Execute

Example 192 also captures a halt and shows a message; if the user presses Yes, then the block that caused the exception is retried, causing another exception. When the user presses No, the code terminates.

```
" Captures a halt; retries block when user responds Yes "
[ self halt. System message: 'resumed' ]
    when: ExHalt
    do: [ :signal |
        (System confirm: signal description)
            ifTrue: [ signal retry ] ]
```
Example 192, Execute

Capturing Errors

Messages to error:, whether sent by the system or by Smalltalk code, can be trapped with the ExError exception. Example 193 captures a bounds error on an array and provides a default result.

```
" Provide a default value if index out of range "
| a |
a := [ #(1) at: 2 ]
    when: ExError
    do: [ :signal |
        signal exitWith: 0 ].
^ a
" Answers: 0 "
```
Example 193, Display

Example 194 captures a divide by zero and provides a default result.

```
" Capture error: message "
| a |
a := [ 3 / 0 ]
    when: ExError
    do: [ :signal |
        System message: signal argument.
        signal exitWith: 1.0e100 ].
^ a
```
Example 194, Display

Example 195 captures a 'does not understand' error.

```
" Capture 'does not understand' error "
[ 2 ++ 3 ]
    when: ExError
    do: [ :signal |
        System message: signal argument.
        signal exitWith: nil ]
```
Example 195, Execute

Example 196 captures a user-issued error: message. The argument message to signal returns the text from the error: message.

```
" Capture user-issued error: message "
[ self error: 'Too many notches in frammus' ]
    when: ExError
    do: [ :signal |
        System message: signal argument.
        signal exitWith: nil ]
```
Example 196, Execute

Block Termination Cleanup

Two messages to blocks allow for block termination cleanup. The first, whenExceptionDo: invokes a termination block only if some exception occurred in the block. The second, atEndOrWhenExceptionDo: is always invoked. These messages do not handle exceptions, but sneak in ahead and allow a bit of cleanup before the exception is raised.

In Example 197, the stream is closed even if an exception occurred.

```
"Make sure stream is closed if error occurs"
| name stream s |
s := ''.
name := CwFileSelectionPrompter new title: 'File to open'; prompt.
stream := CfsReadFileStream open: name.
stream isCfsError
    ifTrue: [ self error: stream message ].
[   [ stream atEnd ] whileFalse: [ s := s, stream next asString ].
    stream close ]
        whenExceptionDo: [ stream close ].
^ s
```
Example 197, Display

In Example 198 the stream is closed by the termination block whether or not an exception occurred. This is equivalent to Example 197 but is shorter and simpler.

```
"Make sure stream is closed no matter what"
| name stream s |
s := ''.
name := CwFileSelectionPrompter new title: 'File to open'; prompt.
stream := CfsReadFileStream open: name.
stream isCfsError
    ifTrue: [ self error: stream message ].
[   [ stream atEnd ] whileFalse: [ s := s, stream next asString ] ]
        atEndOrWhenExceptionDo: [ stream close ].
^ s
```
Example 198, Display

Example

Example 199 defines two exceptions, doorBell and burp, both things that might interrupt a mother feeding her baby. The first block of when:do: randomly signals the events, which display a message and resume execution. Both exceptions are specified after when: by the expression:

        doorBell | burp

which builds an ExceptionalEventCollection. Either of the exceptions can be signalled and the one when:do: handler will be run.

```
" Baby Burps & Doorbells "
| burp doorBell randy |

" Get a new random number generator "
randy := EsRandom new.

" Define a 'doorBell' exception "
doorBell := ExAll newChild
    resumable: true;
    description: 'The doorbell rang.';
    defaultHandler: [ :sig | System message: 'Ding, dong.' ].

" Define a burp exception "
burp := ExAll newChild
    resumable: true;
    description: 'Baby had to burp.';
    defaultHandler: [ :sig | System message: 'Belch, burble...  gurgle' ].

" Repeatedly and randomly signal an exception "
[ 6 timesRepeat:
    [ randy next < 0.5
        ifTrue: [burp signal]
        ifFalse: [doorBell signal] ] ]
    when: burp | doorBell
    do: [ :signal | signal handlesByDefault ]
```
Example 199, Display

Summary

Exception handling allows the capture of errors, user interrupts, halts, and signalled events. The events can be processed in various ways, including terminating the method(s) that caused the exception or correcting something and restarting the method(s).

User-defined exceptions can be defined many ways, both to allow exception handling of application errors and to integrate exception handling into the basic logic of the application.

15

Processes and Synchronization

Smalltalk processes allow execution of multiple blocks of code at the same time. The apparent simultaneous execution is simulated by moving from one process to another at small increments of time

Four classes are described in this chapter. Instances of class Delay are used to pause for a period of time. Instances of class Semaphore are used to synchronize separate processes. Instances of class Process run blocks of code in parallel, and a single instance of class ProcessorScheduler, named Processor, decides which process is to be run at any given time.

Many algorithms have been developed that use semaphores to coordinate multiple processes. This chapter will discuss some simpler cases of coordination. See the section on 'Further Reading' on page 178, for references that contain information and algorithms for more complex cases.

For detailed information on process classes, see Chapter 35, 'Processes', on page 497.

Delaying

Instances of class Delay are used to delay execution for a period of time. An instance is obtained with the forSeconds: message to Delay, but no delay occurs until this instance is sent the wait message.

    " **Delay for 5 seconds** "
    (Delay forSeconds: 5) wait   *Example 200, Execute*

The delay can also be specified in milliseconds.

    " **Delay for 5000 milliseconds** "
    (Delay forMilliseconds: 5000) wait   *Example 201, Execute*

Creating Processes

Processes are created by sending messages to blocks. In Example 202 a process is created to execute the block and is made active. It delays for five seconds and then pops up a message prompter. When the block ends, the process ends.

```
" Start a process and run it "
[ (Delay forSeconds: 5) wait.
        System message: 'Hello!' ] fork
```
Example 202, Execute

Process related messages to blocks include:

fork	Start a new process to run the block; answer the process. The process has a default priority.
forkAt: priority	Start a new process to run the block; answer the process. The process has a specified priority.
newProcess	Answer a new, suspended process which is ready to run the code in the block.
newProcessWith: anArray	Answer a new, suspended process which is ready to run the block with the values in the array anArray as the block parameters.

Processes respond to the following messages:

priority	Get the priority of a process.
priority:	Set the priority of a process.
resume	Resume execution of a suspended process.
suspend	Halt execution of a process; it can be resumed.
terminate	Terminate a process; it cannot be resumed.

Processes can thus be created without running them immediately; they are placed in a suspended state. The resume message ends the suspended state and executes the process.

```
" Create a suspended process and resume it "
| p |
p := [ :n | (Delay forSeconds: n) wait.
        System message: 'Hello!'
            ] newProcessWith: #( 5 ).
p resume.
```
Example 203, Execute

Priorities

Priorities are integer numbers that indicate the order in which processes will be executed. Higher priorities run before lower priorities. Each process has a priority with one of seven possible values, as shown in Figure 47.

Priority 3, the user scheduling priority, is the default priority for new processes. Users can set process priorities to 4, for higher priority user processes, or to 2 for background user processes. Users should only set processes to one of the three priorities shown in bold.

Priority	Priority Name	Description
1	systemBackgroundPriority	System background processes
2	**userBackgroundPriority**	**User background processes**
3	**userSchedulingPriority**	**User scheduling priority**
4	**userInterruptPriority**	**User interrupt priority**
5	lowIOPriority	Low priority IO processes
6	highIOPriority	High priority IO processes
7	timingPriority	Timing processes

Figure 47: Process Priorities.

The priority names in the table are actually message names of an object named Processor. The expression, Processor userSchedulingPriority, is the preferred way to refer to priority 3.

Blocks can be forked with a different priority.

```
" Start a process and run it at a given priority"
[ (Delay forSeconds: 5) wait.
     System message: 'Hello!'
          ] forkAt: Processor userBackgroundPriority
```
Example 204, Execute

Process priorities can be queried with the priority message or set with the priority: message.

```
" Create a suspended process and run it at a given priority"
| p b |
b := [ :delay :msg |
     ( Delay forSeconds: delay ) wait.
     System message: msg ].
p := b newProcessWith: #( 5 'Hello!' ).
p priority: Processor userBackgroundPriority.
p resume
```
Example 205, Execute

Process Scheduler

Class ProcessScheduler has one instance that is in a global variable named Processor. It manages all of the processes in the system, deciding which gets run next and which have to wait.

Processor answers to several messages including:

activeProcess	Answer the current process, the one that is sending this message.
activePriority	Answer the current processes' priority, the priority of the process that sends this message. This is equivalent to Processor activeProcess priority.
signal: sem at: time	Signal semaphore sem at time time, where time is a future value of the millisecond clock. The clock starts at an arbitrary point (often system startup) and ticks every millisecond.

See the method 'millisecondClockValue' on page 446, and the section on 'Millisecond Clock' on page 61 for more information on the millisecond clock.

Semaphores

Processes can be coordinated by the use of semaphores, which are instances of class Semaphore. Sending wait to a semaphore causes the process sending the wait to be suspended until the semaphore is signalled. Sending signal to a semaphore indicates to resume execution of a process that is waiting on that semaphore. If the signal gets to the semaphore before the wait, the semaphore remembers the signal and doesn't make the process wait for another one.

A semaphore is conceptually both a counter and a queue. It counts the number of times it has been signalled, and it queues processes that need a signal to continue execution.

The counter is simply an integer, and it can be negative, zero, or positive. It is negative when there are processes waiting to run, positive when processes attempting to wait can run immediately, and zero otherwise. A semaphore can be created with either a count of zero or a count of one.

A semaphore responds to two basic messages, signal and wait. The signal message increments the counter by one. If it was negative, which means that some process was waiting, then the highest priority process (or one of them if more than one has the same priority) is removed from the wait queue and made ready to run. Whether or not it runs immediately depends on other factors, such as the priority of other running processes.

The wait message decrements the counter by one. If it was positive, nothing more happens and the process that sent the wait message continues to execute. If the semaphore's counter was zero or negative, the process sending the wait is placed into the semaphore's queue and stops executing. It will not execute again until a signal message releases it from the queue.

Figure 48 shows the life of a semaphore (from the semaphore's viewpoint), which is variously waited upon and signalled by processes.

Time	Before		Message to Semaphore	After		Notes
	Sema-phore	Processes Queued		Sema-phore	Processes Queued	
1	0	0	wait	-1	1	Process waiting
2	-1	1	wait	-2	2	Second process waiting
3	-2	2	signal	-1	1	A process released
4	-1	1	signal	0	0	Other process released
5	0	0	signal	+1	0	Count goes positive
6	+1	0	wait	0	0	Process does not wait

Figure 48: Life of a Semaphore.

Figure 49 shows the effects of signal and wait at various priorities.

Process Coordination

While it is sometimes useful to have processes that just run along by themselves, most uses for processes require coordination between processes in order to share a single re-

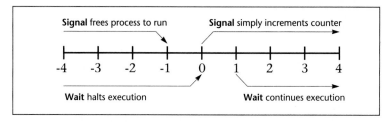

Figure 49: Wait and Signal at Various Priorities. The arrows show the ranges of priority numbers for which wait and signal differ in their actions.

source, such as a source of data, or to coordinate activities. This section describes the process coordination features in IBM Smalltalk and introduces some basic process programming concepts.

Mutual Exclusion

Semaphores are used to coordinate the use of resources, such as shared data, or input from an external source.

Multiple processes should not update the same data without coordination. The portion of the code that does the update is called the *critical section*; a semaphore is used to prevent concurrent execution of critical sections in multiple processes.

```
... ... ...
semaphore wait.
... update data ...        " Critical Section "
semaphore signal.
... ... ...
```

The first operation is a wait. If the semaphore count is a zero, then the process will wait. If all processes wait first then none will ever get to run the critical section. However, if the semaphore was initialized with a value of one, then the first process to encounter the critical section will send a wait which sets the semaphore value to zero, but doesn't stop the process; a second process sending a wait would be stopped and queued. The first process can then update the data and signal the semaphore, which restores the semaphore's value to one. The second process is then able to run the critical section.

A semaphore initialized to a value of one can be obtained with the forMutualExclusion message.

```
mutex := Semaphore forMutualExclusion.
```

An semaphore initialized to a value of zero can be obtained with the new message.

```
semi := Semaphore new.
```

Semaphores initialized to a value of one can be used with a special message, critical:, to synchronize access to one resource.

Example 206 illustrates how critical: is used. A new semaphore initialized with a count of one is obtained. Then five processes are started, each of which waits some seconds and then tries to enter a critical region, in this case a block that updates some information.

```
" Mutual exclusion: Update of shared data "
I sema k I
k := 0.
sema := Semaphore forMutualExclusion.
5 to: 1 by: -1 do: [ :n |
    [ sema critical: [ k := k + 100 factorial ] ] fork ]
```
Example 206, Execute

The expression k := k + 100 factorial is not an *atomic* operation. That is, it does not necessarily complete before another process is run. Even the expression k := k + 1 is not
atomic.† While a program might run for long periods and seem to work, it is necessary
to coordinate all updates of shared data so that the processes always work. Thus, in example Example 206, the update of k is placed in a critical region.

It is usually desired to minimize the amount of time in a critical region. The factorial
calculation is lengthy and it can be split out of the critical region, as in Example 207.

```
" Mutual exclusion: minimizing time in critical region "
I sema k I
k := 0.
sema := Semaphore forMutualExclusion.
5 to: 1 by: -1 do: [ :n |
    | fact |
    fact := 100 factorial.
    [ sema critical: [ k := k + fact ] ] fork ]
```
Example 207, Execute

Critical regions do not solve all synchronization problems, but when they do solve a
problem they are exceptionally easy to use and do not involve any direct waiting or
signalling of semaphores.

Each critical bit of data should have its own semaphore, since the amount of processing done within a critical section should be kept to a minimum. This often means that
several semaphores are necessary to finish a long transaction.

Coordination

Semaphores can be used for other kinds of process coordination in which no data is
necessarily shared, but in which the timing of events is controlled.

Example 208 illustrates how one semaphore might be used to coordinate two processes. The first process waits on the semaphore; when the semaphore is signalled it will
say *Hello!* and again wait on the same semaphore; when it wakes up the second time it
says *Again!* and terminates.

The second process delays for five seconds and signals the semaphore, causing the first
process to wake up and speak. The second process waits for five more seconds, again
signals the semaphore, and then terminates.

```
" Coordinate two processes with a semaphore "
I sema I
sema := Semaphore new.
" Create and run first process "
[    sema wait.                              " Process One"
     System message: 'Hello!'.
     sema wait.
     System message: 'Again!' ] fork.
```

---

† Typically, it is at least three operations: get k, increment k, and store k. A switch to another process can occur
between any of the operations.

```
              " Create and run second process "
        [      (Delay forSeconds: 5) wait.              " Process Two "
               sema signal.
               (Delay forSeconds: 5) wait.
               sema signal ] fork.
```
Example 208, Execute

Depending on the whims of the process scheduler, the whims of the operating system, and various other unpredictable events, the first process may or may not start running immediately; it may or may not even run before the second process runs.

This makes it somewhere between hard and impossible to predict what will happen, but semaphores make it all work regardless of the order in which the processes really run.

Two cases, one in which process one runs first, and one in which process two runs first, will be examined.

Case One

Process one starts and immediately waits on the semaphore (Figure 50, time 1). Then process two starts and delays for five seconds (2).

Process two wakes up after five seconds (7), and signals the semaphore. This signal wakes up process one, which speaks (8); meanwhile process two has started waiting for five more seconds. Process one waits on the semaphore again (9).

At time (13), the delay has ended and process two signals the semaphore. Then it terminates, while process one again speaks (14). Process one then terminates.

Time	Process One	Process Two	Semaphore	Notes
1	Waiting	Not started	-1	One blocked, waiting on a semaphore
2	Waiting	Delay 5	-1	
7	Waiting	Signal	0	
8	Running	Delay 5	0	*Hello!*
9	Waiting	Delaying	-1	
13	Waiting	Signal	0	
14	Running	Terminates	0	*Again!*
15	Terminates	Terminated	0	

Figure 50: Example 208, Case 1.

Case Two

Case two is similar but the events happen in a different order. Process two starts (Figure 51, time 1) and signals the semaphore, leaving it with a count of 1 (2), and then starts delaying for five seconds (3).

Process one then starts up (4) and sends a wait to the semaphore (5); since the semaphore has a positive count, process one can immediately continue. It then speaks (6), and again sends a wait to the semaphore (7). This time, the semaphore is zero so process one has to wait.

Process two wakes up (8), signals the semaphore, and terminates (9). Process one wakes up (9), speaks, and terminates (10).

Time	Process One	Process Two	Semaphore	Notes
1	Not started	Starting	0	
2	Not started	Signal	1	
3	Not started	Delay 5	1	
4	Starting	Delaying	1	
5	Sends wait	Delaying	0	No wait necessary
6	Running	Delaying	0	*Hello!*
7	Waiting	Delaying	-1	
8	Waiting	Signal	0	
9	Running	Terminates	0	*Again!*
10	Terminates	Terminated	-1	

Figure 51: Example 208, Case 2.

Producers and Consumers

A common problem involves one or more producers of data, and one or more consumers of data. The producers can produce more data only if the place into which the data is placed contains room for it. The consumers can consume data only so long as there is data to consume. Both producers and consumers must coordinate access to the data.

In the examples below, an OrderedCollection will be used as a queue; new data will be placed at the end and data will be removed from the front. Input events will be simulated randomly.

One Producer and One Consumer

Example 209 starts three processes, a producer of data, a consumer of data, and a terminator, which is used to end the example.‡ It attempts to solve the problem with one semaphore.

The producer waits for some random number of seconds (in the range 0 to 10) and then adds a random number to the end of the ordered collection oc. The ordered collection is protected here by a critical region. The consumer delays for four seconds and then removes the first element in the queue (if any).

The terminator waits for 60 seconds and then terminates the producer and the consumer.

```
" One producer, one consumer; poor solution "
| producer consumer terminator randy queue critex size |
size := 10.
queue := OrderedCollection new: size.
randy := EsRandom new.
critex := Semaphore forMutualExclusion.

producer := [
    10 timesRepeat: [
        (Delay forSeconds: (randy next *10) asInteger) wait.
        critex critical: [ queue addLast: randy next ] ].
    ] fork.
```

---

‡ Terminators are not a part of the solution to the problem but an artifice used in these examples to stop execution after a short time. Terminators do have the advantage of keeping the producers and consumers code simpler and easier to read, since they do not needed to contain termination code. Note that the terminator runs at a higher priority than the processes it will terminate.

```
consumer := [ | n |
    10 timesRepeat: [
        critex critical: [
            queue size > 0
                ifTrue: [ n := queue removeFirst ]
                ifFalse: [ n := -1] ].
        (Delay forSeconds: 4) wait.
        n ~= -1
            ifTrue: [ Transcript cr; show: 'Consumed: ', n printString ] ]
    ] fork.

terminator := [
    (Delay forSeconds: 60) wait.
    producer terminate.
    consumer terminate.
    Transcript cr; show: 'Terminated!'.
    ] forkAt: Processor userInterruptPriority

" The Transcript shows:
Consumed: 0.83805749
Consumed: 0.89503169
Consumed: 0.43712475
Consumed: 0.77217044
Terminated!
"
```

Example 209, Execute

This example has some real problems.

- To make it run, delays were adjusted so that the average time it takes the consumer to consume data is less than the average time that it takes to produce it.

- The consumer wakes up and consumes nothing if there is no data in the queue. The consumer should wake up only when the queue has data.

- There is no guarantee that the queue will not grow endlessly; typically, it is desired that the queue be no bigger than is needed to keep the consumer from having to wait.

This is not a real-world solution, and none is possible with one semaphore.

With Two Semaphores

Example 210 solves these problems by using two semaphores, items and spaces, and by limiting the amount of data that can be queued. Differences are shown in bold. (There is still a bug in this solution; it really takes three semaphores for a correct solution.)

The items semaphore is initialized to the number of items that are in the queue, initially a zero. The spaces semaphore is initialized to the number of empty slots or spaces that are in the queue; this initialization is done by signalling the semaphore as many times are there are spaces. The critex semaphore is dropped.

```
" One producer and one consumer; two semaphores; one bug "
| producer consumer terminator randy queue items spaces size |
size := 10.
queue := OrderedCollection new: size.
randy := EsRandom new.
items := Semaphore new.
spaces := Semaphore new.
size timesRepeat: [ spaces signal ].

producer := [
    100 timesRepeat: [
```

```
            (Delay forSeconds: (randy next *2) asInteger) wait.
            spaces wait.
            queue addLast: randy next.
            items signal ]
        ] fork.

    consumer := [
        | n |
        100 timesRepeat: [
            items wait.
            n := queue removeFirst.
            spaces signal.
            (Delay forSeconds: 4) wait.
            Transcript cr;
                show: 'Consumed: ', n printString;
                show: '; Queue size: ', queue size printString ]
        ] fork.

    terminator := [
        (Delay forSeconds: 60) wait.
        producer terminate.
        consumer terminate.
        Transcript cr; show: 'Terminated!'.
        ] forkAt: Processor userInterruptPriority

    " The Transcript shows:
    Consumed: 0.01082735; Queue size: 7
    Consumed: 0.45639298; Queue size: 10
    Consumed: 0.79664858; Queue size: 10
    Consumed: 0.13829488; Queue size: 10
    Consumed: 0.7808214; Queue size: 10
    Consumed: 0.87194006; Queue size: 10
    Consumed: 0.48129267; Queue size: 10
    Consumed: 0.43329155; Queue size: 10
    Consumed: 0.16598859; Queue size: 10
    Consumed: 0.7925899; Queue size: 10
    Consumed: 0.723287; Queue size: 10
    Consumed: 0.75988516; Queue size: 10
    Consumed: 0.05960155; Queue size: 10
    Terminated!  "
```

Example 210, Execute

The producer waits on the spaces semaphore and when the count is positive, which it will be initially, it adds data to the data queue, oc. It can run endlessly without waiting if the consumer is fast enough at removing data. When a new item has been added, the producer signals the items semaphore, indicating that the consumer has data to operate upon.

The consumer waits on the items semaphore. When the producer signals the items semaphore, it releases the consumer to consume the data. When the data is removed, the consumer signals the spaces semaphore, indicating that there is another free space. Further processing of the data is assumed to take four seconds.

With Three Semaphores
The two-semaphore solution assures that the producer runs only when there is space in which to put new data, and that the consumer runs only when there is data to consume; it assumes that operations on the data queue are atomic. But this is not true at all; sooner or later one of these processes will be part way through adding or removing

data from the queue and the other process will be started, and it will operate on the queue also. The results are unpredictable, and *very* hard to debug.

The solution is to add a critical region in each process when it touches the queue.

```
" One producer and one consumers; three semaphores"
| producer consumer terminator randy queue items spaces size guard |
size := 10.
queue := OrderedCollection new: size.
randy := EsRandom new.
items := Semaphore new.
spaces := Semaphore new.
guard := Semaphore forMutualExclusion.
size timesRepeat: [ spaces signal ].

producer := [
    100 timesRepeat: [
        (Delay forSeconds: (randy next *2) asInteger) wait.
        spaces wait.
        guard critical: [ queue addLast: randy next ].
        items signal ]
    ] fork.

consumer := [ | n |
    100 timesRepeat: [
        items wait.
        guard critical: [ n := queue removeFirst ].
        spaces signal.
        (Delay forSeconds: 4) wait.
        Transcript cr;
            show: 'Consumed: ', n printString;
            show: '; Queue size: ', queue size printString ]
    ] fork.

terminator := [
    (Delay forSeconds: 60) wait.
    producer terminate.
    consumer terminate.                 " Omit to let consumer clean up all transactions "
    Transcript cr; show: 'Terminated!'.
    ] forkAt: Processor userInterruptPriority

" The Transcript shows:
Consumed: 0.51383915; Queue size: 4
Consumed: 0.17248556; Queue size: 7
Consumed: 0.59491614; Queue size: 9
Consumed: 0.30676517; Queue size: 10
Consumed: 0.89878786; Queue size: 10
Consumed: 0.93144918; Queue size: 10
Consumed: 0.0169994; Queue size: 10
Consumed: 0.37284549; Queue size: 10
Consumed: 0.25208081; Queue size: 10
Consumed: 0.99050874; Queue size: 10
Consumed: 0.82604111; Queue size: 10
Consumed: 0.68851651; Queue size: 10
Consumed: 0.12972095; Queue size: 10
Terminated!
```

Example 211, Display

Finally, this is a correct solution!

The time delays, used to simulate processing time, can be varied to see quite different results; these examples all show producers running faster than consumers, and they always operate with a full queue, once steady-state conditions are reached.

Summary

Processes allow the apparent simultaneous execution of blocks of code. The priorities of the processes can be changed to favor certain processes over others.

Semaphores provide a mechanism for coordination between processes and for the control of access to shared resources.

Further Reading

The first book is dedicated to the subject of concurrency of all types. Process coordination is covered in depth.

- J. Bacon, *Concurrent Systems*, Addison-Wesley, 1993.

  Covers concurrency of all types; lengthy discussion of semaphores and monitors.

These next two books are about operating systems. Since processes and concurrency are a major part of an operating system, they are covered in depth.

- A. Silberschatz and P. Galvin, *Operating System Concepts*, Addison-Wesley, 1994.
- A. Tannenbaum, *Modern Operating Systems*, Prentice-Hall, 1992.

16

Building User Interfaces

Widgets are parts that are combined in various ways to create user interfaces. Widgets are sometimes called controls; they are user interface components such as top-level windows (shells), buttons, or lists. A user interface is built by combining these widgets into a tree, or containment hierarchy, of widgets.

The graphics and widgets interfaces are large and rich. The first part of this chapter describes a subset of the facilities for building widgets and windows. This subset can be used for a large variety of interactive applications. The second part of the chapter describes graphics methods for drawing within a window.

There are no Encyclopedia chapters for widgets or graphics. Full coverage of widgets plus the encyclopedia chapters can be found in the companion volume (see page 4). This chapter is a cookbook for building interfaces: start with some fresh window widgets, stir in some button widgets, spread out evenly on a form, draw the decorations, and bake until open.

Many graphics and widget methods are passed values that are contained in the pool dictionaries CwConstants and CgConstants. These pool dictionaries must be specified for all classes that use graphics or widgets.

For information on these pool dictionaries, see the section on 'Pool Dictionaries' on page 107.

Widget Types

This section describes a number of widget classes. Programmers rarely send messages directly to these classes, instead sending messages to existing widget instances to return new instances or other kinds of widgets.

The shell widget works with the window manager to determine the screen area, title bar, border, close box, and other window decorations.

All widgets are subclasses of CwPrimitive, CwComposite, or CwShell.

Object
   CwWidget
      CwBasicWidget
         CwPrimitive
         CwComposite
         CwShell

Primitive Widgets

Primitive widgets are the simplest building blocks; they are always child widgets. Primitive widgets include:

Class	Displays
CwArrowButton	Arrow button
CwComboBox	Choice of items and last selected item
CwLabel	Static label, either icon or string
CwCascadeButton	Button from which menu appears
CwDrawnButton	Button custom drawn by the application
CwPushButton	Push button
CwToggleButton	Radio or checkmark button
CwList	List of strings from which selection is made
CwScrollBar	Vertical or horizontal scroll bar
CwSeparator	Single or double line in menus
CwText	Text; allows editing of the text

Composite Widgets

Composites can have zero or more children, and the children can be either primitive or composite widgets. Composite widget classes include:

Class	Provides
CwBulletinBoard	Application-defined child widget positioning
CwForm	Constraint-based mechanism for layout
CwDrawingArea	Drawing area for graphics operations
CwFrame	Frame around its child widget
CwRowColumn	Layout widgets in rows or columns
CwScrolledWindow	Scrollbars to scroll child widget
CwMainWindow	Layout for menu bar and optional scrolling

Shell Widgets

Shells provide the interface between the application and the window manager. The shell widgets, all subclasses of CwShell, include:

Class	Responsibility
CwTopLevelShell	A normal window with standard appearance
CwTransientShell	A pop up shell
CwDialogShell	Dialog boxes

Widget Concepts

To build an interactive interface, applications must build a *containment hierarchy,* or tree, of various kinds of widgets. All windows start with a CwTopLevelShell, which contains the window frame, the title bar, and a contents area. The contents area holds an instance of CwMainWindow. A CwForm is placed into the main window and it is the place where all other widgets are placed.

When the widgets are displayed, child widgets are displayed on top of parent widgets, and are prevented from drawing outside the bounds of the parent.

Figure 52 shows such a structure with a CwDrawingArea in the form into which drawing can be done, and a CwList from which selections can be made.

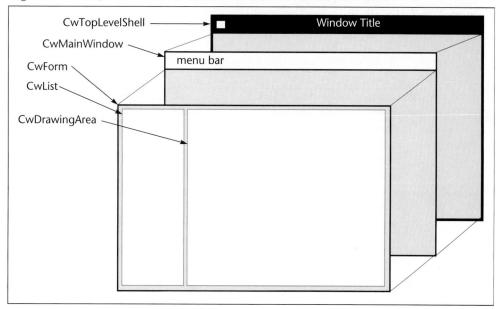

Figure 52: Drawing Area and Parent Widgets.

A widget hierarchy is a containment hierarchy; that is, it consists of one object that contains another, which might contain another, etc. Each contained object has a parent. Since no object can be a parent of itself, the result is a tree structure; this can be represented as a hierarchy similar to, but not related to, the class hierarchy. The containment hierarchy for Figure 52 is:

```
aCwTopLevelShell
    aCwMainWindow
        aCwForm
            aCwList
            aCwDrawingArea
```

Creating Widgets

A widget hierarchy is created from the top down. First, a top level shell is created. Then additional widgets are created and placed within it.

Create

Widgets can be most easily created by *convenience methods,* messages sent to the widget which will become the parent. Convenience methods do most of the work of creation, which would otherwise require several other calls, and provide the commonly needed defaults.

Figure 53 lists common convenience methods. The first parameter is always a string naming the widget; the second is always nil or an *argument block,* such as:

```
[ :widget |
    widget
        height: 100;
        width: 200 ].
```

The block sets resources of the widget.

Convenience Method	Notes
createApplicationShell:argBlock:	Create the top level shell
createDrawingArea:argBlock:	A place in which to draw
createForm:argBlock:	The form in the main window
createMainWindow:argBlock:	The main window
createScrolledText:argBlock:	Editable, scrolled text
createSimpleMenuBar:argBlock:	A menu bar
createSimplePulldownMenu:argBlock:	A pull down menu
createList:argBlock:	A list of selectable items
createRowColumn:argBlock:	A container for other widgets
createSimplePopupMenu:argBlock:	A popup menu

Figure 53: Selected Convenience Methods.

Once created, widgets must be managed, mapped, and realized.

Manage

A widget is managed by sending it the message manageChild. This method asks the parent to manage a new child (rather than asking the new child to manage its children). The position and size of widgets are managed by the parent widget. Any changes in position or size of the parent will be recursively propagated to child widgets, and changes to child widgets are propagated to the parents. Typically, a widget is managed as soon as it is created, and never unmanaged.

Map

Mapping a widget specifies that it should be displayed once it has been realized. The default is to map a widget when it is realized, so mapping is typically invisible. It is possible to unmap a widget to quickly make it invisible.

Realize

Sending the realizeWidget message to the top widget in the widget tree causes the whole widget tree to be managed, mapped, and made visible on the screen.

Destroying Widgets

Widgets can be destroyed explicitly, but are typically destroyed by closing the window.

Resources

Widget resources are values that specify things about a widget. They are *hot*, that is, when changed the effect is immediate. All widgets have width and height resources, and each has resources specific to its function. Default values are provided for all resources.

Resources can be set or retrieved at different times as indicated by one of the letters C, S, or G; these letters are used in descriptions in the pages to come.

C   The resource can be set at creation only, using the argument block. The argument block is invoked before the widget is fully created.

S   The resource can be set at any time including in the argument block.

G   The resource can be retrieved after the widget is created.

Resource methods are flagged with these letters to indicate when they can be used. If no designation is given, then the method is a *function* and can only be used after the widget is created. Functions are simply methods that perform some action.

After a widget is created, the setValuesBlock: message can be sent to the widget to set multiple resources at one time. The block has the same structure as an argument block.

When possible, set multiple resources in the arguments block. Otherwise, set them all at once in one *set values block*, rather than one for each resource, since changing one resource can cause unexpected changes to others, thus causing unpleasant surprises. When all are set at the same time, all get set as specified.

Common Resources of Common Widgets

Resources of all widgets include:

backgroundColor:	The background color. (CSG)
borderWidth:	The width of the border that surrounds the widget's windows on all four sides. (CSG)
foregroundColor:	The foreground color. (CSG)
height:	The height of the widget's window in pixels, not including the border. (CSG)
width:	The width of the widget's window in pixels, not including the border. (CSG)
x:	The x-coordinate of the widget's upper-left corner, excluding the border, in relation to its parent widget. (CSG)
y:	The y-coordinate of the widget's upper-left corner, excluding the border, in relation to its parent widget. (CSG)

Resources of text widgets include:

editable:	When true, the user can edit the text. (CSG)
scrollHorizontal:	When true, a scroll bar allows horizontal scrolling. (CG)
scrollVertical:	When true, a scroll bar allows vertical scrolling. (CG)

getString	Get the contents of the text widget.
setString:	Set the contents of the text widget.
setHighlight:mode:	Highlight or unhighlight the text between two character positions passed as a point in the first parameter. The second parameter is one of: † XmHIGHLIGHTNORMAL, XmHIGHLIGHTSELECTED, or XmHIGHLIGHTSECONDARYSELECTED.

The example below highlights the text from the character at index 2 through the character at index 7.

    wig setHighlight: 2@7 mode: XmHIGHLIGHTSELECTED

Resources of row-column widgets include:

orientation:	The orientation of the widget: XmVERTICAL (the default) or XmHORIZONTAL. (CSG)

Resources of list widgets include:

items:	An array of strings that are to be displayed as list items. (CSG)
selectionPolicy:	Various values; for single selection specify XmSINGLESELECT; other policies are not described in this book. (CSG)

Resources of simple pull-down menu widgets include:

buttons:	An array of strings that are the labels on the menu items. A dummy entry, and empty string, must be present for each separator as well. (C)
buttonType:	An array holding constants defining the menu item type; values may be XmPUSHBUTTON or XmSEPARATOR. (C)
buttonMnemonics:	An array of characters, one for each menu item or separator, to be used for keyboard shortcuts. For menu items the character must be present in the menu item name; it will be underscored. If a menu item is, say, 'Close' then a mnemonic of $C would produce a menu item of <u>C</u>lose and if the mnemonic is $e then the menu item is Clos<u>e</u>. (C)
postFromButton:	The number of the pull-down menu in the menu bar; the first is numbered 0, the second is 1, etc. (C)

A Very Simple Application

This 'application' simply displays a window and draws a rectangle in it.

1)   Create a top-level shell to interact with the window manager.

```
| shell main form drawArea gc drawable color |
shell := CwTopLevelShell
        createApplicationShell: 'Drawing Area Example'
        argBlock: nil.
```

---

† Constant names in this chapter are held in the pool dictionaries CwConstants or CwConstants.

The shell is named 'Drawing Area Example'.

2) Create a main window as the single child of the shell.

```
main := shell
    createMainWindow: 'main'
    argBlock: nil.
main manageChild.
```

A main window named 'main' is created and is sent the **manageChild** message. Nothing has happened on the screen yet.

3) Create a form as the only child of the main window.

```
form := main
    createForm: 'form'
    argBlock: nil.
form manageChild.
```

as soon as create a widget. send "manageChild" msg

4) Create a drawing area as the only child of the form.

```
drawArea := form
    createDrawingArea: 'drawing'
    argBlock: [ :w |
        w width: 300; height: 300; borderWidth: 1 ].
drawArea manageChild.
```

The dimensions of the drawing area are specified along with its border width. The parameter w is the widget being created (the drawing area); the argument block is not invoked until later in the creation process.

5) Finally, *realize* the shell and its children. Realization causes the display of the whole widget tree.

```
shell realizeWidget.
```

A window is now visible on the screen, but it has no contents.

The shell and window sizes are calculated from the drawing area size; in general, sizing of widgets starts with the bottom of the widget tree and works upwards, with the parents sizing themselves to hold the children.

Example 212 contains the code above.

```
" Create and display simple window "
| shell main form drawArea gc drawable color |
shell := CwTopLevelShell
    createApplicationShell: 'Drawing Area Example'
    argBlock: nil.
main := shell
    createMainWindow: 'main'
    argBlock: nil.
main manageChild.
form := main
    createForm: 'form'
    argBlock: nil.
form manageChild.
drawArea := form
    createDrawingArea: 'drawing'
    argBlock: [ :w |
        w width: 300; height: 300; borderWidth: 1 ].
    drawArea manageChild.
shell realizeWidget.
```

Example 212, Execute

Drawing

It is easy to extend the example to draw into its drawing area. (Several methods below invoke graphics methods that are described in more detail later in the chapter.)

6) Ask the drawArea for its window.

```
drawable := drawArea window.
```

7) Obtain a graphics context. Graphic contexts are a place where characteristics of drawing areas can be stored; things like color, line width, scaling, etc. can be placed in a graphics context. (Graphics contexts are described in detail later in the chapter.)

```
gc := drawable createGC: None values: nil.
gc setForeground: drawArea screen blackPixel.
```

8) Now, finally, the drawArea is ready for drawing. Draw a rectangle in it:

```
drawable fillRectangle: gc
    x: 100 y: 100 width: 50 height: 50.
```

9) Finally, free the graphics context:

```
gc freeGC.
```

Example 213 contains the code from steps 6 to 9 appended to Example 212.

```
" Create and display simple window "
| shell main form drawArea gc drawable color |
shell := CwTopLevelShell
    createApplicationShell: 'Drawing Area Example'
    argBlock: nil.
main := shell
    createMainWindow: 'main'
    argBlock: nil.
main manageChild.
form := main
    createForm: 'form'
    argBlock: nil.
form manageChild.
drawArea := form
    createDrawingArea: 'drawing'
    argBlock: [ :w |
        w width: 300; height: 300; borderWidth: 1 ].
    drawArea manageChild.
shell realizeWidget.

" Window is on screen; now do things to it.  "
drawable := drawArea window.
gc := drawable createGC: None values: nil.
gc setForeground: 0.  "Black"
drawable fillRectangle: gc
    x: 100 y: 100 width: 50 height: 50.
gc freeGC.
```

Example 213, Execute

Colors

A rich set of colors and many methods that provide a great degree of control over colors are supported. Colors can be specified with values from 0 to 65535 for each of the red, green, and blue components. Palettes of colors can be constructed and used for full-color, photograph-quality images.

There is, however, a simple default palette which provides 16 basic colors. This default will be used in examples in this book. Figure 54 shows the colors and associated pixel values. These values are used in resource calls.

Pixel Value	Color		Pixel Value	Color
0	Black		8	Gray
1	Dark Red		9	Red
2	Dark Green		10	Green
3	Dark Yellow		11	Yellow
4	Dark Blue		12	Blue
5	Dark Cyan		13	Cyan
6	Dark Magenta		14	Magenta
7	Light Gray		15	White

Figure 54: Colors in the Default Palette.

There are no constants in the pool dictionaries CgConstants or CwConstants for these colors; however, there are entries with names that match these colors that are for use in a different context. The following pool dictionary definition provides names for these basic colors.

```
" Create a pool dictionary for basic color names "
| pool |
pool := Dictionary new.                    " Allocate a new dictionary "

" Add values and keys "
pool at: 'BasicBlack' asPoolKey put: 0.
pool at: 'BasicDarkRed' asPoolKey put: 1.
pool at: 'BasicDarkGreen' asPoolKey put: 2.
pool at: 'BasicDarkYellow' asPoolKey put: 3.
pool at: 'BasicDarkBlue' asPoolKey put: 4.
pool at: 'BasicDarkCyan' asPoolKey put: 5.
pool at: 'BasicDarkMagenta' asPoolKey put: 6.
pool at: 'BasicLightGray' asPoolKey put: 7.
pool at: 'BasicGray' asPoolKey put: 8.
pool at: 'BasicRed' asPoolKey put: 9.
pool at: 'BasicGreen' asPoolKey put: 10.
pool at: 'BasicYellow' asPoolKey put: 11.
pool at: 'BasicBlue' asPoolKey put: 12.
pool at: 'BasicCyan' asPoolKey put: 13.
pool at: 'BasicMagenta' asPoolKey put: 14.
pool at: 'BasicWhite' asPoolKey put: 15.

" Add the pool dictionary as a global variable "
Smalltalk at: 'BasicColors' asGlobalKey put: pool.
```

Example 214, Execute

The contents of the dictionary can be seen by inspection.

```
" Inspect contents of BasicColors "
BasicColors
```

Example 215, Inspect

Chapter 21, 'Example: Chalkboard', on page 247, will use this pool dictionary.

Callbacks

A *callback* tells an application when some action is performed on a window, such as a button press, menu selection, or close. Figure 55 lists some common widget types and the callbacks they support.

Callback Description	Callback Constants	Widget Type						
		drawing areas	*forms*	*lists*	*main window*	*menus*	*row column*	*text*
Destroy	XmNdestroyCallback	X	X	X	X	X	X	X
Expose	XmNexposeCallback	X						
Resize	XmNresizeCallback	X	X	X	X		X	X
Simple	XmNsimpleCallback					X	X	
Single Selection	XmNsingleSelectionCallback				X			
Value Changed	XmNvalueChangedCallback							X

Figure 55: Selected Widget Callbacks. The callback constants are used to specify which callback is requested. X's indicate supported callbacks.

A callback invokes a user defined method, that is 'called-back' by Smalltalk to perform some action at a specified place.

A callback might look like this:

```
drawing addCallback: XmNdestroyCallback
    receiver: self
    selector: #destroy:clientData:callData:
    clientData: nil.
```

The application is to be called-back when the drawing area, drawing, is being destroyed. The receiver of the callback is typically self, the object that sets up the callback, but can be any object. The user written method to invoke is destroy:clientDate:callData:. Data can be passed to the callback, but is nil here.

Events

An *event* tells an application that a mouse or keyboard event has happened. Events include mouse down, up, and move, and keyboard presses and releases. An event handler method that will be called when the event occurs, is specified when a widget is created. The event method is passed a mask which indicates which event or events happened. Figure 56 shows these masks.

Caution: Some platforms can generate a button release event without a corresponding button press event. Portable code should match button up events with a previous button down event, and ignore other button up events.

Note: On platforms with two-button mice, button one is typically the left button, and button three is typically the right button.

In the following method fragment, a drawing area, drawing, is asked to notify self when either button 1 or button 3 is held and the pointer is moved.

Event mask name	Description
KeyPressMask	Keyboard key went down
KeyReleaseMask	Keyboard key went up
ButtonPressMask	Mouse button went down
ButtonReleaseMask	Mouse button went up
PointerMotionMask	All pointer motion events
Button1MotionMask	Pointer moved with button 1 down
Button2MotionMask	Pointer moved with button 2 down
Button3MotionMask	Pointer moved with button 3 down
ButtonMotionMask	Pointer moved with any button down
ButtonMenuMask	Button menu requests

Figure 56: Event Masks.

```
drawing
    addEventHandler: Button1MotionMask | Button3MotionMask
    receiver: self
    selector: #movement:clientData:event:
    clientData: nil
```

The object notified of the event can be any object, but it is typically self. The client data can be any data that the event handler would find useful.

When the event handler method is executed, it is passed three arguments:

- The widget to which the handler was attached;
- the client data, if any; and
- an event object describing the event.

The event handler for the example above might be:

```
movement: widget clientData: clientData event: event
    event button = 1 ifTrue: [ ^ self drawTo: event point ].
    event button = 3 ifTrue: [ ^ self dragTo: event point ].
```

Client data is data passed when the callback is created; it is passed to the callback method when it is invoked. Chapter 19, 'Example: The DoIt Browser', on page 223, uses client data.

Event handlers are typically used for drawing in a drawing area, dragging objects, or for handling popup menus.

Event Object

Event objects respond to various messages, including the following.

For all events:

type   Answers the type of event that occurred; values can be: ButtonPress, ButtonRelease, Expose, KeyPress, KeyRelease, or MotionNotify.

window   The instance of CgWindow associated with the event.

For expose events:

count	The number of additional expose events which remain for the window. A simple application might want to ignore all expose events with a non-zero count and just redraw the window when the count is zero (or just draw it for each expose event).
rectangle	A rectangle describing the part of the area that needs to be redrawn in the coordinates of the window, in pixels.
x, y	The origin of rectangle.
height, width	The extent of rectangle.

For input events (buttons, keys, and motion):

state	A mask giving the state of modifier keys and pointer buttons just prior to the event. Values can include ControlMask, ShiftMask, LockMask, Button1Mask, Button2Mask, Button3Mask, or the *inclusive-or* of these.
x, y	The position of the pointer.
point	The position of the pointer.
xRoot, yRoot	The position of the pointer relative to the screen.
pointRoot	The position of the pointer relative to the screen.
time	The time, in milliseconds from the millisecond clock, at which the event occurred.

For mouse button events:

button	The number of the button that was pressed or released (1, 2, or 3).

For key events:

keysym	A constant describing the keyboard key that was pressed or released. These constants are found in the CwConstants pool dictionary prefixed with XK.
character	The character describing the keyboard key that was pressed or released, or nil if it does not represent a valid character.

Geometry

Widget layout, or geometry, specifies the sizes, positions, and connections of widgets in a window using special layout resources. These resources allow connecting widgets to each other, to the background, or to the forms edges.

Layout can be specified in the argument block but is best specified separately in a set values block; it is also best to do all of the geometry specification in one place, or in separate methods called from one place. Ordering is important in specifying connections. It is an error for attachments to be circularly defined. If widget A is attached to widget B, then widget B cannot be attached to widget A.

Geometry resources include the following. (Indentation is used for visual grouping and is not otherwise significant.)

leftAttachment:	What the edge attaches to; see values below.
leftOffset:	An optional number of pixels to offset the edge.
leftPosition:	An integer from 0 through 100 that specifies the position of the edge relative to the parent; use only when XmATTACHPOSITION is specified.
leftWidget:	The widget this edge attaches to; use only when XmATTACHWIDGET is specified.
rightAttachment:	What the right edge attaches to; see values below.
rightOffset:	An optional number of pixels to offset the edge.
rightPosition:	An integer from 0 through 100 that specifies the position of the edge relative to the parent; use only when XmATTACHPOSITION is specified.
rightWidget:	The widget this edge attaches to; use only when XmATTACHWIDGET is specified.
topAttachment:	What the top edge attaches to; see values below.
topOffset:	An optional number of pixels to offset the edge.
topPosition:	An integer from 0 through 100 that specifies the position of the edge relative to the parent; use only when XmATTACHPOSITION is specified.
topWidget:	The widget this edge attaches to; use only when XmATTACHWIDGET is specified.
bottomAttachment:	What the bottom edge attaches to; see values below.
bottomOffset:	An optional number of pixels to offset the edge.
bottomPosition:	An integer from 0 through 100 that specifies the position of the edge relative to the parent; use only when XmATTACHPOSITION is specified.
bottomWidget:	The widget this edge attaches to; use only when XmATTACHWIDGET is specified.

Attachment constants include:

XmATTACHWIDGET	Attach this side of the widget to another widget.
XmATTACHFORM	Attach this side of the widget to the form.
XmATTACHNONE	Do not attach this side of the widget.
XmATTACHPOSITION	Attach this side of the widget to a relative position in the form. The values, specified by the leftPosition: or rightPosition: resource, range from 0 to 100, with 0 being the left edge and 100 the right. A value of 50 means the attachment is in the middle. It works the same for topPosition: and bottomPosition: except that the values apply vertically.
XmATTACHSELF	Attach this side of the widget to its initial position in the form.

One Widget Example

Attachments are specified with sets of resources, typically one for each edge. This example simply attaches a widget to the edges of the form. The width and height are the initial size.

```
widget setValuesBlock: [ :w | w
    width: 400; height: 200;
    leftAttachment: XmATTACHFORM;
    rightAttachment: XmATTACHFORM;
    topAttachment: XmATTACHFORM;
    bottomAttachment: XmATTACHFORM ]
```

Two Widgets Example

Two widgets are attached left and right of each other in this example. The first specifies no attachment for its right side; the second, w2, specifies a left attachment of w1. Figure 58 shows the attachments.

Form

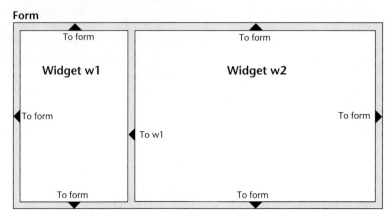

Figure 57: Attachments of Widgets w1 and w2 in Two Widgets Example.

The height is specified only for w1; w2 is forced to be the same height since both are attached to the form at top and bottom.

In general, the geometry manager examines widgets from the bottom of the containment hierarchy and then works upwards. Containing widgets, such as forms and windows, are sized to fit their contents.

```
w1 setValuesBlock: [ :w | w
    width: 200; height: 200;
    leftAttachment: XmATTACHFORM;
    topAttachment: XmATTACHFORM;
    bottomAttachment: XmATTACHFORM ]
w2 setValuesBlock: [ :w | w
    width: 100;
    leftAttachment: XmATTACHWIDGET;
    leftWidget: w1;
    rightAttachment: XmATTACHFORM;
    topAttachment: XmATTACHFORM;
    bottomAttachment: XmATTACHFORM ]
```

The example does not specify where to place the boundary between the two widgets when the window is resized. The results are platform and release dependant.

Relative Positions Example

The example with two widgets can be modified so that resizing does something predictable. One possibility is to make w1 take up some percent of the space available. Since the left edge of w2 is already specified to attach to w1, the relative position of the right edge of w1 is set to 33. The width for w2 no longer has to be set. Figure 58 shows these attachments. When the window is resized, the proportions are used to determine the new sizes.

The width of w2 is forced to be about 400 since w1 is 33/100 of the width and w1 is 200 wide.

```
w1 setValuesBlock: [ :w | w
        width: 200; height: 200;
        leftAttachment: XmATTACHFORM;
        rightAttachment: XmATTACHPOSITION;
        rightPosition: 33;
        topAttachment: XmATTACHFORM;
        bottomAttachment: XmATTACHFORM ]
w2 setValuesBlock: [ :w | w
        leftAttachment: XmATTACHWIDGET;
        leftWidget: w1;
        rightAttachment: XmATTACHFORM;
        topAttachment: XmATTACHFORM;
        bottomAttachment: XmATTACHFORM ]
```

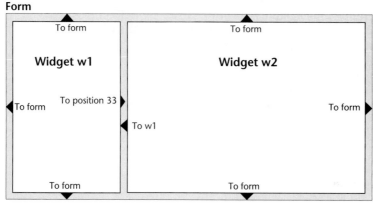

Figure 58: Attachments of Widgets in Relative Positions Example.

Graphics

Graphics operations include the display of text, drawing of lines (including dashed and wide lines), control of line endings and joins, filling shapes and fill patterns, clipping, and the drawing or arcs, circles, pie shapes, and rectangles and general polygons.

The Drawing Process

Graphics operations draw into a *drawable*, an object that represents a window (or a *pixel map*). Conceptually, drawables are contained in a *graphics server*, which might be another workstation, a graphics engine in the same workstation, or code directly in the workstation itself.

All graphics operations require a *graphics context*, or GC, which is an object that contains attributes such as foreground and background colors, line widths, line styles, and fill styles. Various graphics contexts can be used with one drawable and one graphics context can be used with multiple drawables.

Basic Steps

Most drawing operations follow the steps below.

- Before drawing:
  - Create one or more graphics contexts.
  - *Create any required pixelmaps.*
- During drawing:
  - Set the graphics context attributes, as needed.
  - Issue the drawing requests.
- After drawing:
  - Free graphics contexts.

This final step releases any operating system resources that may have been allocated.

An Example

The following example is a copy of Example 212 on page 185. The lines in bold draw a rectangle. In the following pages, replacements will be given for these bold lines that illustrate the use of other drawing methods.

```
" Create and display simple window "
| shell main form drawArea gc drawable color |
shell := CwTopLevelShell
      createApplicationShell: 'Drawing Area Example'
      argBlock: nil.
main := shell
      createMainWindow: 'main'
      argBlock: nil.
main manageChild.
form := main
      createForm: 'form'
      argBlock: nil.
form manageChild.
drawArea := form
      createDrawingArea: 'drawing'
      argBlock: [ :w |
            w width: 300; height: 300; borderWidth: 1 ].
      drawArea manageChild.
shell realizeWidget.

drawable := drawArea window.
gc := drawable createGC: None values: nil.
gc setForeground: 0. "Black"

drawable
      fillRectangle: gc
      x: 100
      y: 100
      width: 50
      height: 50.

gc freeGC.
```

Example 216, Execute

Graphics Contexts

A basic graphics context is created with the createGC message to a drawable.

```
| gc |
gc := drawable createGC: None values: nil.
```

The parameter None indicates to set all values to their defaults.

Values can be set when creating a GC by specifying an instance of CgGCValues. Such an instance holds the same values as does a graphics context; portions of the values are copied to a GC by specifying the flags, GCForeground, and GCLinewidth, which indicate which portions to copy.

```
| gc values drawable |
...
drawable := ...
values := CgGCValues new
        foreground: 0; "Black"
        lineWidth: 2.
gc := drawable
        createGC: GCForeground | GCLineWidth
        values: gcValues.
...
```

or simply:

```
| gc drawable |
...
drawable := ...
gc := drawable
        createGC: GCForeground | GCLineWidth
        values:
            ( CgGCValues new
                foreground: 0; "Black"
                lineWidth: 2 ).
...
```

Values can be changed in a similar manner:

```
| gc drawable lw |
...
gc   changeGC: GCForeground | GCLineWidth
        values:
            ( CgGCValues new
                foreground: 0; "Black"
                lineWidth: 2 ).
...
```

Continuing the above example, values can be retrieved from a GC:

```
...
gc getGCValues: GCLineWidth
        valuesReturn: values.
lw := values lineWidth.
...
```

Figure 59 shows selected value masks, associated messages to an instance of CgGCValues instance to set or retrieve the value, valid values, and defaults.

Value Mask	Messages to CgGCValues	Values and Notes		Default
GCForeground *The foreground color*	foreground foreground:	anInteger	- Index into color map	0
GCBackground *The background color*	background background:	anInteger	- Index into color map	1
GCLineWidth *Thickness of the line*	lineWidth lineWidth:	anInteger	- Line width in pixels	1
GCLineStyle *Dashed lines*	lineStyle lineStyle:	LineSolid LineOnOffDash LineDoubleDash	- Uses foreground color - Uses foreground color - Uses foreground and background colors	LineSolid
GCCapStyle *How to end lines*	capStyle capStyle:	CapNotLast CapButt CapRound CapProjecting	- No cap on end - Blunt, straight ends - Rounded ends - Blunt, projecting past end	CapButt
GCJoinStyle *How lines are joined*	joinStyle joinStyle:	JoinMiter JoinRound JoinBevel	- Square join - Rounded join - Bevel join	JoinMiter
GCFillStyle *How to fill shapes*	fillStyle fillStyle:	FillSolid	(Other values are not described in this book)	FillSolid
GCFillRule *How to fill polygons*	fillRule fillRule:	EvenOddRule WindingRule	- Hollow intersection - Solid intersection	EvenOddRule
GCArcMode *How to draw an arc*	arcMode arcMode:	ArcChord ArcPieSlice	- Connect start-end points - Draw pie shape	ArcChord
GCFunction *Draw inverted or not*	function function:	GXcopy GXhighlight	- Draw exactly as described - Fore/back colors swapped	GXcopy

Figure 59: Selected Graphics Context Attributes.

Convenience methods allow directly setting certain values into a GC. These include:

setArcMode: flag	Set arc drawing mode. Flag values are: ArcPieSlice ArcChord
setBackground: n	Set background color.
setDashes: dashOffset dashList: anArray	Set both an offset (initial gap) and an array of dash/gap pairs.
setForeground: n	Set foreground color.
setLineAttributes: lineWidth lineStyle: lineStyle capStyle: capStyle joinStyle: joinStyle	Set many line attributes at once.

Graphics contexts must be explicitly freed since they represent system resources possibly distributed across several machines.

gc freeGC

Caution: Do *not* write gc free. On some platforms there is a private free message to graphics contexts, which means something else.

Using Graphics Contexts

A graphics context can be used on any drawable that is on the same screen and that has the same *depth* as the drawable for which the GC was created. This means, for example, that a GC created for a window on a 256-color screen (a depth of 8) can be used for another window (on the same screen) which also has 256 colors, but it cannot be used for drawing on a pixmap of depth 1 (black and white).

Note that the screen depth is independent of the number of colors in the current palette, which can be smaller or larger than 256. This book assumes use of the default palette, which has sixteen colors.

Drawing

Various messages draw points, lines, segments, rectangles, filled rectangles, arcs, filled arcs, and polygons. All drawing messages are sent to drawables. Figure 60 summarizes the drawing methods.

Message to a Drawable	Parameters	Description
drawPoint: gc x: anInt y: anInt	- A graphics context - X and Y coordinates	Draw one point at x@y.
drawPoints: gc points: anArray mode: CoordModeOrigin	- A graphics context - An array of points - Relative to what?	Draw each of the points in anArray. CoordModeOrigin draws relative to the origin; CoordModePrevious draws remaining points relative to the first point in the array.
drawLine: gc x1: x1 y1: y1 x2: x2 y2: y2	- A graphics context - Starting X & Y-coord - Ending X & Y-coord	Draw a single line from x1@y1 to x2@y2.
drawLines: gc points: anArray mode: CoordModeOrigin	- A graphics context - An array of points - Relative to what?	Draw lines connecting the first through the last points in anArray. CoordModeOrigin draws relative to the origin; CoordModePrevious draws remaining points relative to the first point in the array.
drawRectangle: gc x: x y: y width: widthInteger height: heightInteger	- A graphics context - X and Y coordinates - Width - Height	Draw an unfilled rectangle.
fillRectangle: gc x: x y: y width: widthInteger height: heightInteger	- A graphics context - X and Y coordinates - Width - Height	Draw a filled rectangle.
fillPolygon: gc points: anArray shape: Complex mode: CoordModeOrigin	- A graphics context - An array of points - Shape complexity - Relative to what?	Draw a closed polygon in order through the points in anArray. Use Complex unless the shape is known to be Convex or Nonconvex. CoordModeOrigin draws relative to the origin; CoordModePrevious draws remaining points relative to the first point in the array.
drawArc: gc x: x y: y width: widthInteger height: heightInteger angle1: angle1 angle2: angle2	- A graphics context - X and Y coordinates - Width - Height - Starting angle - Ending angle	Draw an unfilled arc in the rectangle x@y extent: widthInteger@heightInteger starting at angle1 and sweeping through angle2; angle1 is measured CCW from 3 o'clock. Angles are 1/64th of a degree.
fillArc: gc x: x y: y width: widthInteger height: heightInteger angle1: angle1 angle2: angle2	- A graphics context - X and Y coordinates - Width - Height - Starting angle - Ending angle	Draw a filled arc in the rectangle x@y extent: widthInteger@heightInteger starting at angle1 and sweeping through angle2; angle1 is measured CCW from 3 o'clock. Angles are 1/64th of a degree. Connect end points according to GcArcMode settings.
drawString: gc x: anInt y: anInt string: aString	- A graphics context - X and Y coordinates - A string	Draw a string. The bottom left corner of the first character is at x@y. Use the default system font from the graphics context.

Figure 60: Drawing Methods.

The following examples logically replace the bold code in Example 212 on page 185, which draws a rectangle. If you are using the machine readable materials, copy Example 212 into a workspace and then replace the rectangle code with one of the examples.

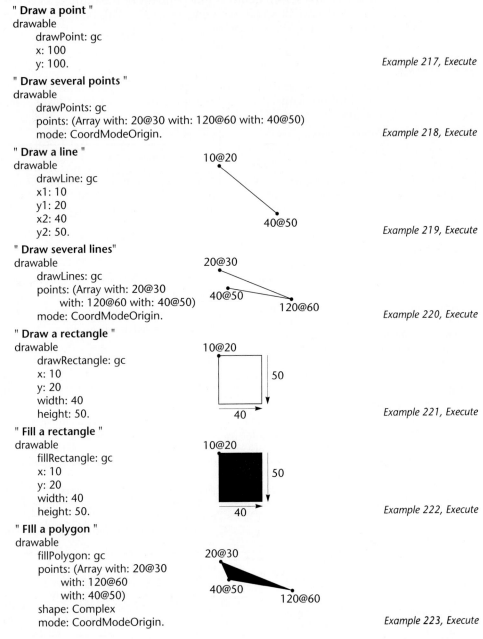

" **Draw a point** "
drawable
    drawPoint: gc
    x: 100
    y: 100.

Example 217, Execute

" **Draw several points** "
drawable
    drawPoints: gc
    points: (Array with: 20@30 with: 120@60 with: 40@50)
    mode: CoordModeOrigin.

Example 218, Execute

" **Draw a line** "
drawable
    drawLine: gc
    x1: 10
    y1: 20
    x2: 40
    y2: 50.

Example 219, Execute

" **Draw several lines**"
drawable
    drawLines: gc
    points: (Array with: 20@30
        with: 120@60 with: 40@50)
    mode: CoordModeOrigin.

Example 220, Execute

" **Draw a rectangle** "
drawable
    drawRectangle: gc
    x: 10
    y: 20
    width: 40
    height: 50.

Example 221, Execute

" **Fill a rectangle** "
drawable
    fillRectangle: gc
    x: 10
    y: 20
    width: 40
    height: 50.

Example 222, Execute

" **FIll a polygon** "
drawable
    fillPolygon: gc
    points: (Array with: 20@30
        with: 120@60
        with: 40@50)
    shape: Complex
    mode: CoordModeOrigin.

Example 223, Execute

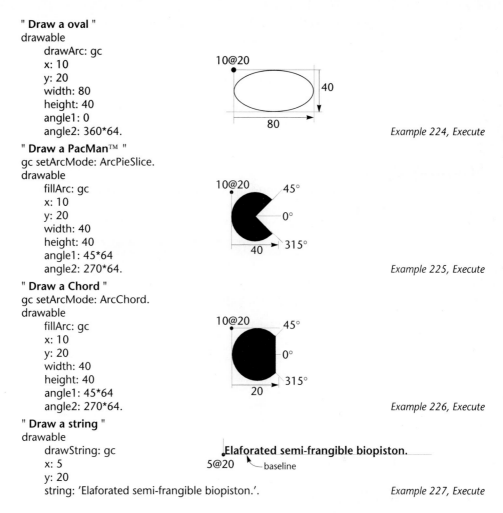

```
" Draw a oval "
drawable
    drawArc: gc
    x: 10
    y: 20
    width: 80
    height: 40
    angle1: 0
    angle2: 360*64.
```
Example 224, Execute

```
" Draw a PacMan™ "
gc setArcMode: ArcPieSlice.
drawable
    fillArc: gc
    x: 10
    y: 20
    width: 40
    height: 40
    angle1: 45*64
    angle2: 270*64.
```
Example 225, Execute

```
" Draw a Chord "
gc setArcMode: ArcChord.
drawable
    fillArc: gc
    x: 10
    y: 20
    width: 40
    height: 40
    angle1: 45*64
    angle2: 270*64.
```
Example 226, Execute

```
" Draw a string "
drawable
    drawString: gc
    x: 5
    y: 20
    string: 'Elaforated semi-frangible biopiston.'.
```
Example 227, Execute

Fonts

Smalltalk supports a number of fonts; fonts can be queried to see which are available, and then some can be loaded and used. The system has a default (current) font which will be used in this book.

The current font can be queried for its characteristics by asking a graphics context for its font, asking the resulting font for its fontStruct, and then asking the fontStruct for various bits of information. Figure 61 lists common messages to a font structure.

CgFontStruct Access Methods	Answers
font	An instance of CgFont
name	The font name
ascent	The integer height above the baseline
descent	The integer distance below the baseline
height	Ascent + descent, the font height
numChars	The number of the characters in the font
textWidth: aString	An integer holding the drawing width of aString in pixels

Figure 61: Messages to Instances of CgFontStruct.

Code to access the default font and to query it is:

```
| gc values font fontStruct fontName |
…
gc getGCValues: GCFont
    valuesReturn: (values := CgGCValues new).
font := values font.
fontStruct := font queryFont.
fontName := fontStruct name.
…
```

Shaping Up

This example draws four different colored shapes in a window and draws text in each naming the color. The non-bold code is from Example 212 on page 185, and the bold code is new to this example. Figure 62 shows a representation of the final result.

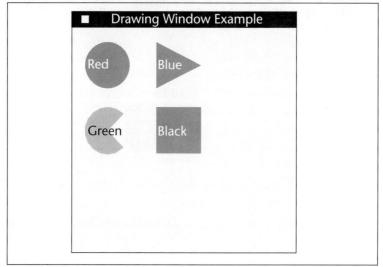

Figure 62: Result of Example 228.

```
" Create and display simple window with named, colored shapes "
| shell main form drawArea gc drawable color |
shell := CwTopLevelShell
    createApplicationShell: 'Drawing Area Example'
    argBlock: nil.
main := shell
    createMainWindow: 'main'
    argBlock: nil.
main manageChild.
form := main
    createForm: 'form'
    argBlock: nil.
form manageChild.
drawArea := form
    createDrawingArea: 'drawing'
    argBlock: [ :w |
        w width: 300; height: 300; borderWidth: 1 ].
    drawArea manageChild.
shell realizeWidget.
```

```
drawable := drawArea window.
gc := drawable createGC: None values: nil.
gc setForeground: 0. "Black"

gc setForeground: 0 "black".
drawable fillRectangle: gc
        x: 100 y: 100 width: 60 height: 60.

gc setForeground: 9 "red".
drawable fillArc: gc
        x: 20 y: 20 width: 60 height: 60
        angle1: 0 angle2: 360*64.

gc setForeground: 12 "blue".
drawable fillPolygon: gc
        points: (Array with: 100@20 with: 100@80 with: 160@50)
        shape: Convex mode: CoordModeOrigin.

gc setForeground: 10 "green".
gc setArcMode: ArcPieSlice.
drawable fillArc: gc
        x: 20 y: 100 width: 60 height: 60
        angle1: 45*64 angle2: 270*64.

gc setForeground: 15 "white".
drawable drawString: gc x: 105 y: 135 string: 'Black'.
drawable drawString: gc x: 25 y: 55 string: 'Red'.
drawable drawString: gc x: 105 y: 55 string: 'Blue'.
gc setForeground: 0  "Black".
drawable drawString: gc x: 25 y: 135 string: 'Green'.

gc freeGC.
```

Example 228, Execute

Using Graphics and Widgets

There are two examples of widgets, one of which uses graphics, in Part III:

- Chapter 19, 'Example: The DoIt Browser', on page 223, creates a window with two text areas and a set of buttons. Text entered into the top text area can be evaluated; the result is shown in the lower text area. It illustrates the use of text areas, buttons, menu bars, and pop-up menus.

- Chapter 21, 'Example: Chalkboard', on page 247, creates three drawing programs that illustrate how to use drawing areas, lists for selection, geometry for positioning, and redrawing when the window is resized and uncovered.

Summary

Widgets are windows, scroll bars, buttons, menus, and related objects, including compositions of other widgets. Top level windows are container widgets that hold a main window, which holds a form, which holds widgets like buttons, lists, drawing areas, etc.

Widgets are usually created with convenience methods. Widgets are managed, mapped, and realized to get them properly displayed. Widget have resources that include colors, border widths, position, and (for specific types) such things as orientation, button type, or highlight. Drawing is done in a widget with functions such as draw a line, a filled rectangle, an oval, or a pie shape.

Callbacks give control to an application when the user does certain things, such as close the window, expose a window by moving or closing one on top, resize a window, or select from a list.

Events are similar, but work at a lower level; they include keyboard key down and up, and mouse button press, release, and movement.

Geometry management allows the specification of connections between various widgets, or how widgets are attached to the background or containing form. Sizes of widgets can also be specified. When a window is opened or resized the geometry manager resolves geometry specification.

Further Reading

The following works describe X-Windows and graphics and widgets programming in C.

- Scheifler and Gettys, *X Window System*, Third Edition, Digital Press, 1992.
- Nye, ed., *Xlib Programming Manual*, Volumes One and Two, O'Reilly & Associates, Sebastopol, CA, 1988.
- Nye and O'Reilly, *X Toolkit Intrinsics Reference Manual*, Volumes Four and Five, O'Reilly & Associates, Sebastopol, CA, 1990-91.

The design of object-oriented user interfaces using object-oriented languages is the subject of this last book.

- D. Collins, *Designing Object-Oriented User Interfaces*, Benjamin/Cummings, Redwood City, CA, 1995.

Part III

Examples

Part III contains several longer examples of Smalltalk code. These examples use the full range of capabilities of Smalltalk; some may use messages not yet documented. Refer to the class descriptions in Part IV in these cases.

Chapter 17: Example: Stereograms
Stereograms are flat pictures that are transformed into 3-D images by the human visual system. A simple random character stereogram class is developed.

Chapter 18: Example: Block Streams
Block Streams are a kind of stream in which numbers are generated from a block and a starting value. A BlockStream class is developed. Block streams illustrate the power of blocks, and show one way that new iterative constructs can be created.

Chapter 19: Example: The DoIt Browser
The DoIt Browser is an interactive application that evaluates an expression entered in one pane of a window and displays the result in another. It illustrates the use of text areas, buttons, menu bars, and pop-up menus.

Chapter 20: Example: Stream Filters
Stream filters are streams that operate on other streams and act in an analogous manner to Unix pipes. A hierarchy for building filters that examine or modify read and write streams is developed, and several examples of the use of stream filters are given.

Chapter 21: Example: Chalkboard
Three versions of a drawing program illustrate how to use drawing areas, lists for selection, geometry for positioning, and redrawing when the window is resized and uncovered.

Chapter 22: Long Numbers
Two aspects of long precision numbers are covered: first, conversion from and to string representations illustrates string handling and provides useful code; second, calculations of roots and of π to one-hundred and more digits.

17

Example: Stereograms

Stereograms are two-dimensional flat pictures which can appear in full 3-D. Several top-selling books† have popularized stereograms. This chapter surveys stereograms briefly and shows how to implement simple stereograms in Smalltalk.

The stereograms example is a fairly simple Smalltalk class with no inheritance and only ten methods, making it a good first example. If you can see the 3-D effect, and some people cannot, they are also fun to play with.

Stereograms

Stereograms coerce the human visual system into 'seeing' a full fledged three-dimensional image in a flat 2-D image. They come in many forms.

Stereopairs. A very popular item in the late 1800s and early 1900s; stereopairs are a postcard-sized card containing two photographs taken from slightly different positions. The card is viewed in a special viewer. A more modern version is the ViewMaster™.

Stereograms. A single drawing or image with information for both eyes combined into one illustration.

Text Stereogram. A text stereogram consisting of rows of text. Some rows or parts of rows seem to stand out when viewed just right. Figure 63 shows a text stereogram that consists of readable text aligned such that a real 3-D effect can be seen. Once you see

---

† See Further Reading at the end of the chapter.

```
                    •             •
    Pascal       Pascal       Pascal       Pascal       Pascal
  Smalltalk Smalltalk Smalltalk Smalltalk Smalltalk
    C++          C++          C++          C++          C++
  IBM ST    IBM ST    IBM ST    IBM ST    IBM ST    IBM ST
    Ada          Ada          Ada          Ada          Ada
  Smalltalk Smalltalk Smalltalk Smalltalk Smalltalk
    C++          C++          C++          C++          C++
  IBM ST    IBM ST    IBM ST    IBM ST    IBM ST    IBM ST
    Ada          Ada          Ada          Ada          Ada
  Smalltalk Smalltalk Smalltalk Smalltalk Smalltalk
    C++          C++          C++          C++
  IBM ST    IBM ST    IBM ST    IBM ST    IBM ST    IBM ST
    Ada          Ada          Ada          Ada          Ada
  Smalltalk Smalltalk Smalltalk Smalltalk Smalltalk
   Fortran       Fortran       Fortran       Fortran
```

Figure 63: Character Stereogram. Defocus your eyes (or move the page slowly away from your face) until the dots at the top become three dots. You should see a background layer of alternate lines, Pascal, C++, Ada, etc. Standing out from this is the Smalltalk level and above that is the IBM ST level.

the effect, note how words on lines on different levels have different interword spacing. This spacing causes the 3-D effect.

Random Stereograms. A stereogram in which the flat picture is not related to the stereo picture but is made up of random elements of characters, dots, or distorted images.

Random Character Stereogram. A random stereogram composed of random characters. It too has character offsets, but they are hidden in a field of randomness. It is conceptually similar to a random dot stereogram, but is simpler to make. Figure 64 is a random character stereogram generated with the code in this chapter. Look carefully, and a rectangle will float above the page.

The Implementation

A complete implementation of random character stereograms is presented. It takes 64-column images and produces 80-column stereograms in a workspace. Each character in the image is either a dash or not; dashes mean background and anything else means foreground. Foreground characters will float above the background.

Note: The font of any workspace in which stereograms are displayed must be monospace. A workspace menu item lets the font be selected; Courier is a good choice.

```
                    *                    *
MTNLSEFLAAJATCMKMTNLSEFLAAJATCMKMTNLSEFLAAJATCMKMTNLSEFLAAJATCMKMTNLSEFLAAJATCMK
YOSDYNEFDBLXGNJNYOSDYNEFDBLXGNJNYOSDYNEFDBLXGNJNYOSDYNEFDBLXGNJNYOSDYNEFDBLXGNJN
TAFMBXUEWCCETXCNTAFMBXUEWCCETXCNTAFMBXUEWCCETXCNTAFMBXUEWCCETXCNTAFMBXUEWCCETXCN
GGWBYAOPPOAJOVQYGGWBYAOPPOAJOVQYGWBYAOPPOAJOVQYGWBYAOPPOAJOVQYGWNBYAOPPOAJOVQYGW
ORZOQELQVRMNPAETORZOQELQVRMNPAETRZOQELQVRMNPAETRZOQELQVRMNPAETRZYOQELQVRMNPAETRZ
DMOGGDRIAYSHYVTHDMOGGDRIAYSHYVTHMOGGDRIAYSHYVTHMOGGDRIAYSHYVTHMOBGGDRIAYSHYVTHMO
WPLZAHWQMNATBKQKWPLZAHWQMNATBKQKPLZAHWQMNATBKQKPLZAHWQMNATBKQKPLKZAHWQMNATBKQKPL
JUOCYLUZSHZZVCQAJUOCYLUZSHZZVCQAUOCYLUZSHZZVCQAUOCYLUZSHZZVCQAUORCYLUZSHZZVCQAUO
FJTBPTTTBBUTOMUCFJTBPTTTBBUTOMUCJTBPTTTBBUTOMUCJTBPTTTBBUTOMUCJTYBPTTTBBUTOMUCJT
WWFTBFIUYJYMGNFOWWFTBFIUYJYMGNFOWFTBFIUYJYMGNFOWFTBFIUYJYMGNFOWFGTBFIUYJYMGNFOWF
YRUNTSVSVRWZOLNLYRUNTSVSVRWZOLNLRUNTSVSVRWZOLNLRUNTSVSVRWZOLNLRUINTSVSVRWZOLNLRU
XOBMDXKIJQIZRKJUXOBMDXKIJQIZRKJUOBMDXKIJQIZRKJUOBMDXKIJQIZRKJUOBLMDXKIJQIZRKJUOB
JUENOHMHKWYQNUVAJUENOHMHKWYQNUVAUENOHMHKWYQNUVAUENOHMHKWYQNUVAUEJNOHMHKWYQNUVAUE
ZFAHOZHLTEVVESAGZFAHOZHLTEVVESAGFAHOZHLTEVVESAGFAHOZHLTEVVESAGFAUHOZHLTEVVESAGFA
DCMFIZRMLQHDGEASDCMFIZRMLQHDGEASCMFIZRMLQHDGEASCMFIZRMLQHDGEASCMTFIZRMLQHDGEASCM
KVHSHLOJPPDMJVJWKVHSHLOJPPDMJVJWVHSHLOJPPDMJVJWVHSHLOJPPDMJVJWVHKSHLOJPPDMJVJWVH
PLKFTWHADBEQAXJSPLKFTWHADBEQAXJSLKFTWHADBEQAXJSLKFTWHADBEQAXJSLKLFTWHADBEQAXJSLK
NTQYCYXKWRWNQAMONTQYCYXKWRWNQAMOTQYCYXKWRWNQAMOTQYCYXKWRWNQAMOTQWYCYXKWRWNQAMOTQ
BBIIAEFEFABESMUUBBIIAEFEFABESMUUBIIAEFEFABESMUUBIIAEFEFABESMUUBINIAEFEFABESMUUBI
SOXDNDHFQODWABQRSOXDNDHFQODWABQROXDNDHFQODWABQROXDNDHFQODWABQROXNDNDHFQODWABQROX
CCYCCYZIXVFMKRRBCCYCCYZIXVFMKRRBCYCCYZIXVFMKRRBCYCCYZIXVFMKRRBCYRCCYZIXVFMKRRBCY
DRQFQAKJFINRUCVNDRQFQAKJFINRUCVNDRQFQAKJFINRUCVNDRQFQAKJFINRUCVNDRQFQAKJFINRUCVN
DXSCICTXWMSZGXVEDXSCICTXWMSZGXVEDXSCICTXWMSZGXVEDXSCICTXWMSZGXVEDXSCICTXWMSZGXVE
MMKMVUILQEJABJHAMMKMVUILQEJABJHAMMKMVUILQEJABJHAMMKMVUILQEJABJHAMMKMVUILQEJABJHA
WWMNHORANXMDWQRWWWMNHORANXMDWQRWWWMNHORANXMDWQRWWWMNHORANXMDWQRWWWMNHORANXMDWQRW
```

Figure 64: Random Character Stereogram of a Rectangle. Defocus your eyes (or move the page slowly away) until the two dots appear as three dots and the rectangle appears floating out from the page. The rectangle is similar to the one in the small picture at right.

Core Algorithm

Class Definition

The StereoView class has one variable, randy, a random number generator.

Object subclass: **#StereoView**
    instanceVariableNames: '**randy** '
    classVariableNames: ' '
    poolDictionaries: '**CldtConstants** '

Instance: Main †

The main instance method, stereoViewOf:, accepts the image array, **arrayOfStrings**, as a parameter. First, a new workspace is defined and opened. Then the *alignment line* is displayed; this is the pair of dots at the top. Then buildOneFrom: is invoked to convert

---

† Paragraph titles describe what the following method(s) are for. These titles are similar to categories used in some development environment browsers. The first word is always Instance or Class, and the names describes the methods that follow.

each line of the image, and the result is displayed in the workspace. Finally, the workspace is set so that it won't grumble when it is closed.

```
stereoViewOf: arrayOfStrings
    " Build a random character stereogram and show it in a new workspace.
      Usage:  StereoView of: anArrayOf64LongStrings "
        | workspace |
        workspace := EtWorkspace new
            label: 'Stereo Viewer';
            open.
        workspace show: StereoView alignmentLine; cr.
        1 to: arrayOfStrings size do: [ :n |
            workspace show:
                (self buildOneFrom:
                    (arrayOfStrings at: n)); cr ].
        workspace confirmClose: false
```

Instance: Core Algorithm

The key method, buildOneFrom:, initializes the result string with 80 characters of blanks, and replaces the first 16 characters with random characters. These 16 characters will be copied over and over to fill out 80 positions.

Then it scans the input line from the image, with the initial state of the algorithm set to background. The index, k, starts 17 characters into the result string.

- If the next character in the input (k-16) is a foreground character, the character at k-15 is moved to the result string and the flag is set to foreground.

- Otherwise, the new character is a background character. If the state is foreground, a random character is moved to the result string and the state is changed to background. If the state is background, a character is copied from k-16.

Basically, this algorithm copies the random characters from 16 to the left when the image holds a background character, and from 15 to the left when it holds a foreground character. In the transition between foreground and background, a new random character is generated to fill out the full 16 positions. It is this simple offset, 15 versus 16, that makes the image stand out.

```
buildOneFrom: aString
    " Build one line from template string aString (64 long) "
    | flag ans |
    ans := String new: 80.
    1 to: 16 do: [ :n | ans at: n put: self randChar ].
    flag := #back.
    17 to: 80 do: [ :k |
        (aString at: k - 16) ~~ $-
            ifTrue: [
                ans at: k put: (ans at: k - 15).
                flag := #fore ]
            ifFalse: [ flag = #fore
                ifTrue: [
                    ans at: k put: self randChar.
                    flag := #back ]
                ifFalse: [
                    ans at: k put: (ans at: k - 16) ]
            ].
        ].
    ^ ans
```

```
                          *                        *
DIZLHAMFGDEUOMOPDIZLHAMFGDEUOMOPDIZLHAMFGDEUOMOPDIZLHAMFGDEUOMOPDIZLHAMFGDEUOMOP
KFUPHRLNSTVUTGDPKFUPHRLNSTVUTGDPKFUPHRLNSTVUTGDPKFUPHRLNSTVUTGDPKFUPHRLNSTVUTGDP
LHZNWBRLXYALTKGDLHZNWBRLXYALTKGDLHZNWBRLXYALTKGDLHZNWBRLXYALTKGDLHZNWBRLXYALTKGD
CTTGVXJTCISBDBHSCTTGVXJTCISBDBHSCTTGVXJTCISBDBHSCTTGVXJTCISBDBHSCTTGVXJTCISBDBHS
BPSVCJTDVYLSXOQZBPSVCJTDVYLXOQZBPSVCJTDVYLZXOQZBPSVJTDVYLZXOQZBPSVJTDVYWLZXOQZBP
KVEQRSPKONKYCGNBKVEQRSPKONYCGNBKVEQRSPKONYCOGNBKVERSPKONYCOGNBKVERSPKONYTCOGNBKV
HGXBQIZPFXEZPRAIHGXBQIZPFFEZPRAIHGXBQIZPFEZPRYAIHGBQIZPFEZPRYAIHGBQIZPFEZPHRYAIHG
RMPYHXZYJJANDSUMRMPYHXZYJANDGSUMRMPYHXZYJANDGSUMRMPYHXZYJANGSUMRMPYHXZYJANGSUMG
DRHPCGYYKQJFJECMDRHPCGYKQJFZJECMDRHPCGYKQJFJECMDRHPCGYKQJFJECMDRHPCGYKQJFJECMC
ITYCBSTVJXDWUGTSITYCBSTJXDWHUGTSITYCBSTJXDWHUGTSITYCBSTJXDWUGTSZITYCBSTJXDWUGTSZ
CLTGFVCJAVXJAIPDCLTGFVCJVXJAXIPDCLTGFVCJVXJAXIPDLCLTGFVCJVXJXIPDLCLTGFVCJVXJXIPDL
OSFNZCZKMPIZHVLXOSFNZCZKMIZHVLXOSFNZCZKMICZHVLXOSFNZCZKMICZVLXONSFNZCZKMICZVLXON
PBBMWANXZZBFQSOIPBBMWANXZZFQSOIPBBMWANXZZFKQSOIPBBMWANXZZFKSOIPFBBMWANXZZFKSOIPF
NOPCQTVYESGZKNZFNOPCQTVYESGKNZFNOPCQTVYESGKMNZFNOPCQTVYESGKNZFNIOPCQTVYESGKNZFNI
HSWUNFVAINEEAVTDHSWUNFVAINEEAVTDHSWUNFVANEEAEVTDHSWUNFVANEEEVTDFHSWUNFVANEEEVTDF
HXKKSWCWPDPPOEKAHXKKSWCWPDPPOEKAHXKKSWCWPPPOEMKAHXKKSWCWPPPEMKAEHXKKSWCWPPPEMKAE
QOCZDHVKXTBLOARZQOCZDHVKXTBLOARZQOCZDHVKXBLOAURZQOCZDHVKXBLAURZNQOCZDHVKXBLAURZN
RFIDEPSNRZNBNUTFRFIDEPSNRZNBNUTFRFIDEPSNZNBNYUTFRFIDEPSNZNBYUTFPRFIDEPSNZNBYUTFP
BYCIDSOJCNWEJZZPBYCIDSOJNWEJZZPBYCIDSOJNWEJWZZPBYCIDSOJNWEJZZPBMYCIDSOJNWEJZZPBM
TNAGHEAMAIEGFFJUTNAGHEAMAEGFFJUTNAGHEAMAEGKFFJUTNAGHEAMAEGKFJUTYNAGHEAMAEGKFJUTY
SNYISGVDEYQWKCVUSNYISGVDEYWKCVUSNYISGVDEYXWKCVUSNYISGVDEYXWCVUSSNYISGVDEYXWCVUSS
CFVEPDKTCVNAWGDDCFVEPDKTCVNAWGDDCFVEPDKTCVNAWGDDCFVEPDKTCVNAWGDDCFVEPDKTCVNAWGDD
BJEOFTXTDJBUGELHBJEOFTXTDJBUGELHBJEOFTXTDJBUGELHBJEOFTXTDJBUGELHBJEOFTXTDJBUGELH
NDZGXTWZCYCXVPJXNDZGXTWZCYCXVPJXNDZGXTWZCYCXVPJXNDZGXTWZCYCXVPJXNDZGXTWZCYCXVPJX
OWLSVYPHDUBJREZAOWLSVYPHDUBJREZAOWLSVYPHDUBJREZAOWLSVYPHDUBJREZAOWLSVYPHDUBJREZA
```

Figure 65: Stereo 3D Sample Output. Defocus your eyes (or move the page slowly away) until the letters 'ST' appears floating out from the page. The result is similar to the small picture at the right.

Other Methods

Instance: Support

Prepare the pair of dots used for visual alignment. The dots have an offset of 16, which means that the background and the dots are at the same level.

```
alignmentLine
    " Return the top line used for visual alignment "
    | blank |
    blank := $  .   " A blank character "
    ^    ((String new: 31) atAllPut: blank ), '*',
         ((String new: 15) atAllPut: blank ), '*',
         ((String new: 32) atAllPut: blank )
```

Answer a random upper-case ASCII character.

```
randChar
    " Answer a random upper-case character "
    ^ Character value: (randy next * 26) floor + $A value
```

Instance: Access
One method initializes the variable randy.

```
randy: aRandomStream
    randy := aRandomStream
```

Class: Instance Creation
The new and new: methods are overridden so that they do not return uninitialized instances.

```
new
    "Answer a default something"
    self error: 'Use of: to obtain new instances.'

new: arrayOfStrings
    self new
```

The main instance creation method is of:. It performs initialization.

```
of: arrayOfStrings
^ super new
    randy: EsRandom new;
    stereoViewOf: arrayOfStrings;
    yourself !
```

Class: Samples
Two class methods provide sample images. The shapeSquare method produces output as seen in Figure 64 on page 207. The shapeST method, which is shown only in the filein at the end of the chapter, produces the output seen in Figure 65 on page 209.

```
shapeSquare
    | temp |
    temp := Array new: 25.
    temp atAll: (1 to: 3), (temp size - 3 to: temp size)
        put: ( (String new: 64) atAllPut: $-).
    temp atAll: (4 to: temp size - 4)
        put: '---------------================',
             '================----------------'.
    ^ (self  of: temp)
```

Stereogram Filein

```
" Stereo 3-D Pop-ups "
Object subclass: #StereoView
    instanceVariableNames: 'randy '
    classVariableNames: ' '
    poolDictionaries: 'CldtConstants '
!
!StereoView class publicMethods !
new
    "Answer a default something"
    self error: 'Use of: to obtain new instances.'!
new: arrayOfStrings
    self new!
of: arrayOfStrings
 super new
    randy: EsRandom new;
    stereoViewOf: arrayOfStrings !
shapeSquare
    | temp |
```

```
        temp := Array new: 25.
        temp atAll: (1 to: 3), (temp size - 3 to: temp size)
            put: ( (String new: 64) atAllPut: $-).
        temp atAll: (4 to: temp size - 4)
            put: '---------------================',
                '================---------------'.
        ^ (self of: temp)!
shapeST
| t |
t := Array new: 25.
t at:  1 put: '----------------------------------------------------------------'.
t at:  2 put: '----------------------------------------------------------------'.
t at:  3 put: '----------------------------------------------------------------'.
t at:  4 put: '----------------------------------------------------------------'.
t at:  5 put: '-----------zzzzzzzzzzzzzzz--------zzzzzzzzzzzzzzzzzzz---------'.
t at:  6 put: '----------zzzzzzzzzzzzzzzz-------zzzzzzzzzzzzzzzzzzzz--------'.
t at:  7 put: '---------zzzzzzzzzzzzzzzzzz-----zzzzzzzzzzzzzzzzzzzzz-------'.
t at:  8 put: '--------zzzz-------------------------------------zzzz-------'.
t at:  9 put: '-------zzzz--------------------------------------zzzz-------'.
t at: 10 put: '------zzzz----------------------------------------zzzz------'.
t at: 11 put: '-------zzzz---------------------------------------zzzz------'.
t at: 12 put: '--------zzzzzzzzzzzzzzzz--------------------------zzzz------'.
t at: 13 put: '----------zzzzzzzzzzzzzzzz------------------------zzzz------'.
t at: 14 put: '----------zzzzzzzzzzzzzzzz------------------------zzzz------'.
t at: 15 put: '--------------------------zzzz--------------------zzzz------'.
t at: 16 put: '---------------------------zzzz-------------------zzzz------'.
t at: 17 put: '----------------------------zzzz------------------zzzz------'.
t at: 18 put: '---------------------------zzzz-------------------zzzz------'.
t at: 19 put: '--------zzzzzzzzzzzzzzzzzz-------------------------zzzz------'.
t at: 20 put: '---------zzzzzzzzzzzzzzzzz-------------------------zzzz------'.
t at: 21 put: '----------zzzzzzzzzzzzzzzz-------------------------zzzz------'.
t at: 22 put: '----------------------------------------------------------------'.
t at: 23 put: '----------------------------------------------------------------'.
t at: 24 put: '----------------------------------------------------------------'.
t at: 25 put: '----------------------------------------------------------------'.
^ self of: t ! !


!StereoView class privateMethods !
alignmentLine
        " Return the top line used for visual alignment "
        | blank |
        blank := $ .    " A blank character "
        ^    ((String new: 31) atAllPut: blank ), '*',
            ((String new: 15) atAllPut: blank ), '*',
            ((String new: 32) atAllPut: blank )! !


!StereoView publicMethods !
stereoViewOf: arrayOfStrings
        | workspace |
        workspace := EtWorkspace new
            label: 'Stereo Viewer';
            open.
        workspace show: StereoView alignmentLine; cr.
        1 to: arrayOfStrings size do: [ :n |
            workspace show:
                (self buildOneFrom:
                    (arrayOfStrings at: n)); cr ].
            workspace confirmClose: false! !


!StereoView privateMethods !
buildOneFrom: aString
```

```
" Build one line from template string "
| flag ans |
ans := String new: 80.
1 to: 16 do: [ :n |  ans at: n put: self randChar ].
flag := #back.
17 to: 80 do: [ :k |
      (aString at: k - 16) ~~ $-
          ifTrue: [
              ans at: k put: (ans at: k - 15).
              flag := #fore ]
          ifFalse: [ flag = #fore
              ifTrue: [
                  ans at: k put: self randChar.
                  flag := #back ]
              ifFalse: [
                  ans at: k put: (ans at: k - 16) ]
          ].
      ].
^ ans!
randChar
    " Answer a random upper-case character "
    ^ Character value: (randy next * 26) floor + $A value!
randy: aRandomStream
    randy := aRandomStream ! !
```

Example 229, FileIn

Using Stereograms

The two expressions below invoke the two built-in shapes.

" Display a Stereogram of a Square; requires filein of Stereogram "
StereoView shapeSquare

Example 230, Execute

" Display a Stereogram of the letters 'ST' ; requires filein of Stereogram "
StereoView shapeST

Example 231, Execute

Any properly formatted array of strings can be 'stereoized' like this:

StereoView of: anArrayOfStrings

Variations

To explore this example further, try the following variations.

- Design a new shape and add it as a class method. Try both algorithmic shapes, like shapeSquare, and hand-designed shapes, like shapeST.

- Initialization is done in the class method of:. If an initialize instance method had been used for initialization, would it have been necessary to have access methods? Modify the code to initialize instances in a new initialize method rather than in of:.

- Add multiple levels, as in Figure 63 on page 206. Change the text strings to use a '1' for the first floating level and '2' for the second.

- Using graphics, replace random characters with randomly colored rectangles.

Further Reading

Examples of stereograms have appeared in many books, calendars, and posters. The first three references were among the first published in the U.S.A., and provide an good coverage of the field.

- *Magic Eye*, N. E. Thing Enterprises, Andrews and McMeal, Kansas City, 1994. (Also available are *Magic Eye II*, and more.)

  Magic Eye was the first book on random dot stereograms published in the U.S.A. and is probably the best known. *Magic Eye II and III* are continuations. All three contain absolutely gorgeous pictures.

- *3D Wonderland*, Tokuma Shoten Publishing Co., Belleview, WA, 1994

  This book contains both random dot stereograms and various other kinds of flat 3-D pictures.

- *Stereogram*, Cadence Books, San Francisco, CA, 1994.

  In addition to vivid examples of many kinds of 'flat' 3-D pictures, this book includes articles about the history of stereograms, and a long article by the discoverer of the random dot stereogram. At least one sequel is available.

Books with software for making stereograms include this title:

- D. Richardson, *Create Stereograms on Your PC*, Waite Group Press, 1994.

Information and pictures are available across the Internet using anonymous FTP from katz.anu.edu.au in /pub/stereograms. Several interesting files and programs can also be found on CompuServe.†

Advanced information is reported to be available in the following book.

- *Random Dot Stereograms*, Andrew A. Kinsman, Kinsman Physics, P. O. Box 22682, Rochester, NY 14692-2682, US$13.95, 1992.

---

† Try searching the IBM PC files using the 'file finder' menu. Try keywords like 'stereo' and 'stereogram'.

18

Example: Block Streams

Block streams generate a stream of numbers from a user-provided block and an initial value. Block streams are implemented by class BlockStream, which is a subclass of class Stream.

Block streams illustrate one of the ways that blocks can be used, and test how well the reader understands blocks.

Description

BlockStream inherits these messages from Stream:

atEnd	True if at the end of the stream
do:	Iterate through the stream
next	Answer the next value in the stream
size	Answer the size of the stream

Block streams take two initial values, the first value to return, and a block which accepts that value and generates another value. A simple case is a block stream that returns the cardinal numbers.

```
cardinals := BlockStream on: [ :last | last + 1 ] startingAt: 0.
```

The block takes a value, starting with the startingAt: value, and continuing with the last generated value. It performs some action; here it simply adds one. Each successive next value is obtained by sending the next message to the block stream.

```
cardinals next
```

The first next message answers the initial value, as set by startingAt:, but first it generates the value to be returned the next time. It is always one ahead but *only* one ahead. Evaluation is thus 'lazy'; new elements are computed as needed.

The do: message sent to a block stream invokes the do: block once for each remaining element in the stream. If the stream does not terminate, the iteration will never end.

Block streams need not be infinite. Block stream blocks can return nil to indicate the end of the stream. The nil is not returned by next or do: though, but is used internally to indicate that atEnd should answer true.

The next example returns powers of two up to 1024; it then returns a nil to end the stream.

```
powersOf2 := BlockStream
    on: [ :last |
        last <= 1024
            ifTrue: [ last * 2 ]
            ifFalse: [ nil ] ]
    startingAt: [ 2 ].
```

It can answer a collection containing the values, since it is not an infinite stream:

```
powersOf2 contents.
"Answers: 2 4 8 16 32 64 128 256 512 1024 2048 "
```

Short Examples

Positive even numbers:

```
even := BlockStream
    on: [ :last | last + 2 ]
    startingAt: 2.
```

Return one value forever:

```
oneNote := BlockStream
    on: [ :last | last ]
    startingAt: aValue.
```

Class Methods

The class methods of BlockStream are:

on: aBlock startingAt: aNum

> Answer a block stream that returns values that start with aNum, then increments by the value of aBlock. The block takes one parameter, the previous value of the block stream. If aBlock answers nil at any time, the block stream is ended and no more values are calculated.

from: num1 to: num2 by: incNum

> Answer a block stream that returns numbers starting with num1, incrementing each successive number by incNum, and ending with the highest value that is less than or equal to num2. This is a block stream version of an interval.
>
> BlockStream from: 1 to: 10 by: 2
>
> > Answers: 1 3 5 7 9
>
> BlockStream from: 0.1 to: 1.2 by: 0.25
>
> > Answers: 0.1 0.35 0.6 0.85 1.1

from: num1 to: num2 byBlock: aBlock

> Answer a block stream that returns numbers starting with num1, incrementing each successive number by the value of aBlock, and ending with the highest value that is less than or equal to num2. The block must take one parameter, which is the previous value of the block stream.
>
> BlockStream from: 2 to: 20 byBlock: [:p | p]
>> Answers: 2 4 8 16 ...
>
> BlockStream from: 2 to: 10 byBlock: [:p | p - 1]
>> Answers: 2 3 5 9 17 ...

Instance Methods

Block streams answer to these basic messages:

atEnd
> Answer true if there are no more values to return from the stream; answer false otherwise.

contents
> Answer a collection containing the remaining elements from the stream. If the stream is infinite, this method will attempt to loop forever.

do: aBlock
> For each successive remaining item in the stream, invoke aBlock passing the item as the single parameter.

next
> Answer the next item in the stream. It is an error if there are no more elements in the stream.

size
> Answer zero if at the end of the block stream; answer one otherwise. (General-purpose stream code that checks the size of a stream for non-zero before using it will function properly with this definition.)

The Implementation

The core methods of BlockStream are few, small, and quite simple.

The class definitions specifies two variables: block, which holds the generator block, and value, which holds the initial value or the next value.

```
Stream subclass: #BlockStream
    instanceVariableNames: 'block value '
    classVariableNames: ''
    poolDictionaries: ''
```

Core Methods

Paragraph titles, below, describe what the following method(s) are for. These titles are similar to categories used in some development environment browsers. The first word is always Instance or Class, and the names describes the methods that follow.

Class: Creation

Neither new or new: should be used to create new instances, since the instances will not be properly initialized.

new
> ^ self error: 'Use on:startingAt: to create BlockStreams'

new: anObject
> ^ self new

New instances are all created by the on:startingAt: class method. It simply sends the block: and next: messages to a new instance to fill in two instance variables with its parameters.

on: aBlock startingAt: aValue
> ^ super new
> > block: aBlock;
> > next: aValue

Instance, Private: Access

The methods are typical access methods; they set the block and the starting value when an instance is initialized.

block: aBlock
> block := aBlock

next: aValue
> value := aValue

Instance: Access

The key block stream method is next. It performs the steps:

- Fetch and test the initial or saved previous value.
- If the value is nil then raise an error; the user should have called atEnd first.
- Otherwise, invoke the block and pass the previous value; save the new value.
- Answer the previous value.

next
> | prev |
> prev := value.
> prev isNil
> > ifTrue: [self error: 'No more values in block stream.'].
> value := block value: prev.
> ^ prev

Everything else builds on next.

Instance: Testing

Testing for the end of the stream simply involves asking if the saved next value is nil.

atEnd
> ^ next isNil

This is now the complete basic block stream code; all other methods build on this core.

Access and Control

Instance: Iteration

Iteration through the items in a block stream involves these steps:

- If at the end of the stream, stop looping.

- Otherwise, invoke **aBlock**, passing the next value of the stream; and
- Get the next value of the stream with next.

```
do: aBlock
    [ self atEnd ]
        whileFalse: [
            aBlock value: value.
            self next. ]
```

Instance: Accumulation
Building upon do:, the contents of the stream can be accumulated; this will not terminate unless the block returns nil.

```
contents
    | oc |
    oc := OrderedCollection new.
    self do: [ :e | oc add: e ].
    ^ oc
```

Instance: Testing
To allow testing for an empty stream by asking if the size is zero, size answers zero if at the end, and one otherwise.

```
size
    ^ self atEnd ifTrue: [ 0 ] ifFalse: [ 1 ]
```

Additional Creation Methods
These methods build upon on:startingAt: to create useful general-purpose block streams.

Class: Series
Create an instance that answers a series of numbers starting with from, with no value bigger than to, and incremented by inc. This is a stream version of an interval.

```
from: from to: to by: inc
    ^ self
        on: [ :prev |
            | next |
            next := prev + inc.
            next <= to
                ifTrue: [ next ]
                ifFalse: [ nil ] ]
        startingAt: from
```

Class: Series
Create an instance that answers a series of numbers starting with from, with no value bigger than to, and incremented by a value returned from aBlock, which takes one argument, the previous answer.

```
from: from to: to byBlock: aBlock
    ^ self
        on: [ :prev |
            | next |
            next := prev + (aBlock value: prev).
            next <= to
                ifTrue: [ next ]
                ifFalse: [ nil ] ]
        startingAt: from
```

Block Stream Filein

Methods in the filein contain comments that were removed from the versions in the text above.

```
" ========== Block Streams =========="

Stream subclass: #BlockStream
    instanceVariableNames: 'block value '
    classVariableNames: "
    poolDictionaries: "
!
!BlockStream class publicMethods !
from: from to: to by: inc
    " Create an instance that answers a series of numbers starting with
        from, with no value bigger than to, and incremented by inc. This is
        a stream version of an interval. Answers nil when the series is complete."
    ^ self
        on: [ :prev |
            | next |
            next := prev + inc.
            next <= to
                ifTrue: [ next ]
                ifFalse: [ nil ] ]
        startingAt: from!
from: from to: to byBlock: aBlock
    " Create an instance that answers a series of numbers starting with from,
        with no value bigger than to, and incremented by a value returned from
        aBlock, which takes one argument, the previous answer.
        Answers nil when the series is complete."
    ^ self
        on: [ :prev |
            | next |
            next := prev + (aBlock value: prev).
            next <= to
                ifTrue: [ next ]
                ifFalse: [ nil ] ]
        startingAt: from!
on: aBlock startingAt: aValue
    "Create an instance of BlockStream. This is the basic creation method."
    ^ super new
        block: aBlock;
        next: aValue!
new
    ^ self error: 'Use on:startingAt: to create BlockStreams' !
new: anObject
    ^ self new ! !


!BlockStream publicMethods !
atEnd
    " Answer true if the next value to return is nil, which indicates the
        end of the stream; false otherwise."
    ^ value isNil!
contents
    " Return a collection holding all the elements of the block stream.
        WARNING: this will not terminate unless the block returns nil. "
    | oc |
    oc := OrderedCollection new.
    self do: [ :e | oc add: e ].
```

```
        ^ oc!
copy
        self error: 'Block streams cannot be copied' !
do: aBlock
        " Iterate through the block stream using next to get new values;
          stop if the end is ever reached. "
        [ self atEnd ]
              whileFalse: [
                    aBlock value: value.
                    self next. ] !
next
        " This is the method that makes block streams work. Answer the next
          value in the block-stream. If the value to return is nil then raise an error.
          (Use atEnd before sending next to assure there are more values.)"
        | prev |
        prev := value.
        prev isNil
              ifTrue: [ self error: 'No more values in block stream.'].
        value := block value: prev.
        ^ prev!
size
        ^ self atEnd ifTrue: [ 0 ] ifFalse: [ 1 ] ! !

!BlockStream privateMethods !
block: aBlock
        " Set the block stream "
        block := aBlock!
next: aValue
        "Set the next value to return."
        value := aValue! !
```

Example 232, FileIn

Examples

Twiddling the Increment

The from:to:byBlock: method increments by an amount answered by a block. The result is an interesting and unexpected series of numbers in which each successive pair is of the form: n*n, n*(n+1). The first 19 pairs are: 1*1, 1*2, 2*2, 2*3, 3*3, 3*4, ..., 9*9, 9*10, and 10*10, which evaluate to: 1, 2, 4, 6, 9, 12, ..., 81, 90, 100..

```
" BlockStream Example: from:to:byBlock: "
^ (BlockStream
      from: 1 to: 100
      byBlock: [:prev | prev sqrt ceiling ])  contents
"Answer:  OrderedCollection(1 2 4 6 9 12 16 20 25 30 36 42 49 56 64 72 81 90 100 )
```

Example 233, Display

Deferred Mind Bender

For a mind-twisting experience, try to see what the following does:

```
" Mind Twister - Deferred Evaluation "
| b |
b := BlockStream
      on: [ :last |
```

```
        [ last value squared ] ]
    startingAt: [ 2 ].
1 to: 8 do: [ :n |
    Transcript cr; show: n printString, ': ', b next value printString ]

"Transcript shows:
1: 2
2: 4
3: 16
4: 256
5: 65536
6: 4294967296
7: 18446744073709551616
8: 340282366920938463463374607431768211456 "
```
Example 234, Execute

Its effect is to provide the next element in the stream without actually calculating it.

How does it work? Just like Example 235, which is Example 234 without deferred evaluation. The differences are shown in each in boldface. The value in the last line of Example 234 is obvious; that leaves the block:

[last value squared]

which is not evaluated, but is just returned over and over. But, and this is a big but, each time it is returned it is from a slightly different context, one in which the parameter last has a different value, and each time it returns it takes that value with it. When it is evaluated (by that obvious use of value), it is the most recent value of last that is evaluated.

```
" Mind Twister Equivalent without deferred evaluation "
b := BlockStream
    on: [ :last |
        last squared ]
    startingAt: 2.
1 to: 8 do: [ :n |
    Transcript cr; show: n printString, ': ', b next printString ]
```
Example 235, Display

Variations

To explore this example further, try building the following block streams:

- A block stream that answers a stream of random numbers from 1 to 52, representing cards in a deck. When created, the block will return cards until all 52 different cards are gone; the stream then ends. (An earlier example shuffles a deck of cards; see Example 155 on page 142.)

- A block stream that answers the Fibonacci numbers. Each new element in the Fibonacci series is the sum of the previous two elements; the series starts with (1, 1). The next element is obviously a 2, then a 3, then 5, then 8, and so on. The block stream needs to remember two prior values.

    What might be changed in BlockStream to make it easier to handle cases that need to remember more than one prior value?

Example: The DoIt Browser

The DoIt Browser is a simple but functional Smalltalk application. It illustrates how to build an interactive application.

Description

The DoIt Browser has two vertical text widgets and a row of buttons placed between them. Text entered into the top text area can be evaluated, displayed, or inspected. Any result, whether compile error or answer, is placed in the bottom text area. There is a menu bar with two pull-down menus; the top text area also has a pop-up menu. The window looks approximately like Figure 66.

DoitBrowser is a subclass of Object.

```
Object subclass: #DoitBrowser
    instanceVariableNames: 'shell main form rowCol text1 text2
                    menuBar menuEdit menuAction popup '
    classVariableNames: ''
    poolDictionaries: 'CldtConstants CwConstants '
```

The variables are:

shell	The top-level shell
main	The main window
form	The form
rowCol	The widget that holds the row of buttons
text1	The top text area
text2	The bottom text area
menuBar	The menu bar

menuEdit	The edit menu pull-down
menuAction	The action menu pull-down
popup	The pop-up menu

A DoitBrowser is started with the message:

DoitBrowser new open

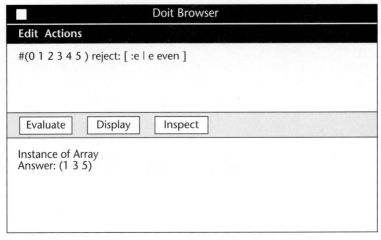

Figure 66: Doit Browser. The top holds an expression for evaluation; the bottom holds the class of the result and whatever printString returns when sent to the result.

The Implementation

Instance: Basic†
The open method sends messages to create the window, buttons, text areas, constraints, and menus, and finally displays the window. It then exits and no application code runs until some interaction with the user occurs.

```
open
    self createWindow: 'Doit Browser'.
    self createButtons.
    self createTopTextArea.
    self createBottomTextArea.
    self text1Constraints.
    self buttonConstraints.
    self text2Constraints.
    self createMenus.
    self displayWindow.   " Window is now on screen "
```

---

† Paragraph titles describe what the following method(s) are for. These titles are similar to categories used in some development environment browsers. The first word is always Instance or Class, and the names describes the methods that follow.

The createWindow: method creates the top-level shell, a main window, and a form. Note that the initial window size is specified here.

createWindow: aStringTitle
    shell := CwTopLevelShell createApplicationShell: aStringTitle argBlock: nil.
    main := shell createMainWindow: 'main' argBlock: nil.
    main manageChild.
    form := main createForm: 'aForm'
        argBlock: [:w | w width: 600; height: 350].
    form manageChild

The displayWindow method simply realizes the shell, which causes the whole widget tree to become visible.

displayWindow
    shell realizeWidget.   " Window is now on screen "

Instance: Buttons

The createButtons method creates three buttons; since they are identical except for their name and the client data, they are created in a loop.

A callback to actions:clientData:callData: is specified; the same callback method will be used for the Actions pull-down menu. The client data is set to 0 for the first button, 1 for the second, and 2 for the third, which matches exactly what the pull-down menu provides for selecting the equivalent functions.

createButtons
    | button labels |
    rowCol := form createRowColumn: 'buttons' argBlock: nil.
    rowCol manageChild.
    names := #('Evaluate' 'Display' 'Inspect').
    1 to: names size do: [:n |
        button := rowCol createPushButton: (names at: n) argBlock: nil.
        button addCallback: XmNactivateCallback
            receiver: self
            selector: #actions:clientData:callData:
            clientData: n - 1.
        button manageChild]

Instance: Menus

The createMenus method sends messages to create the various menus; then the setAreas:horizontalScrollBar:verticalScrollBar:workRegion: message is sent to set up the menus.

createMenus
    self createMenuBar.
    self createEditMenu.
    self createActionMenu.
    self createMenuPopup.
    main
        setAreas: menuBar
        horizontalScrollbar: nil
        verticalScrollbar: nil
        workRegion: form

The simple menu bar has two pull-down menus; each has a mnemonic.

createMenuBar
    menuBar := main createSimpleMenuBar: 'menu bar'
        argBlock: [:w | w

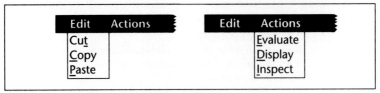

Figure 67: Doit Browser Pull-down Menus.

```
                              buttons: #( 'Edit' 'Actions' );
                              buttonMnemonics: #( $E $A )  ].
            menuBar manageChild
```

The action menu has three items, each of which has a mnemonic; it is menu item number 1. When a menu item is selected, the actions:clientData:callData: method will be called.

```
            createActionMenu
                menuAction := menuBar createSimplePulldownMenu: 'Actions'
                    argBlock: [ :w |
                        w buttons: #( 'Evaluate' 'Display' 'Inspect' );
                            buttonType: ( Array
                                with: XmPUSHBUTTON
                                with: XmPUSHBUTTON
                                with: XmPUSHBUTTON );
                            buttonMnemonics:  #( $E $D $I );
                            postFromButton: 1 ].
                menuAction
                    addCallback: XmNsimpleCallback
                    receiver: self
                    selector: #actions:clientData:callData:
                    clientData: nil.
                menuAction manageChild
```

The edit menu has three items, each of which has a mnemonic; it is menu item zero. When a menu item is selected the editMenu:clientData:callData: method will be called.

```
            createEditMenu
                menuEdit := menuBar createSimplePulldownMenu: 'Edit'
                    argBlock: [ :w | w
                        buttons: #( 'Cut' 'Copy' 'Paste' );
                        buttonType: ( Array
                            with: XmPUSHBUTTON
                            with: XmPUSHBUTTON
                            with: XmPUSHBUTTON );
                        buttonMnemonics:  #( $t $C $P );
                        postFromButton: 0 ].
                menuEdit
                    addCallback: XmNsimpleCallback
                    receiver: self
                    selector: #editMenu:clientData:callData:
                    clientData: nil.
                menuEdit manageChild
```

The pop-up menu performs the same functions as the edit menu. When a menu item is selected, the editMenu:clientData:callData: method will be called just as it was for an edit menu. When the pop-up menu button (mouse button 3) is pressed, the event handler menuButton:clientdata:event: is invoked.

createMenuPopup
```
popup := text1 createSimplePopupMenu: 'popup'
    argBlock: [ :w |
        w buttons: #( 'Cut' 'Copy' 'Paste' ) ].
popup manageChild.
popup
    addCallback: XmNsimpleCallback
    receiver: self
    selector: #editMenu:clientData:callData:
    clientData: nil.
text1
    addEventHandler: ButtonMenuMask
    receiver: self
    selector: #menuButton:clientData:event:
    clientData: nil
```

Instance: Text
The two text creation methods are identical except for the identity of the result.

createTopTextArea
```
text1 := form
    createScrolledText: 'text1'
    argBlock: [ :w | w
        editMode: XmMULTILINEEDIT;
        scrollHorizontal: true;
        wordWrap: false ].
text1 manageChild
```

createBottomTextArea
```
text2 := form
    createScrolledText: 'text2'
    argBlock: [ :w | w
        editMode: XmMULTILINEEDIT;
        scrollHorizontal: true;
        wordWrap: false ].
text2 manageChild
```

Instance: Geometry
The size of the window was specified when the form was created. The geometry methods specify attachments and edge offsets. Figure 68 shows the layout of the widgets.

The top text area, text1, is attached on three sides to the form and the bottom to the rowCol widget that holds the buttons. Messages to set values for text1 (and text2 below) are sent to the parent, an otherwise unseen object that holds the text widget.

text1Constraints
```
text1 parent setValuesBlock: [ :w | w
    leftAttachment: XmATTACHFORM;
    leftOffset: 2;
    bottomAttachment: XmATTACHWIDGET;
    bottomWidget: rowCol;
    bottomOffset: 2;
    rightAttachment: XmATTACHFORM;
    rightOffset: 2;
    topAttachment: XmATTACHFORM;
    topOffset: 2 ]
```

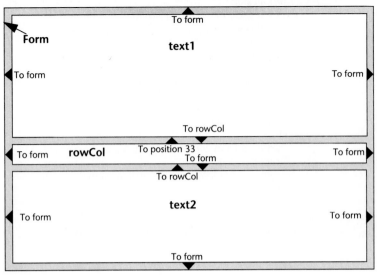

Figure 68: Attachments of Widgets.

The rowCol widget is attached on the left and right to the form, on the top to position 50 (which makes the top text area always be one-half of the size of the form), and the bottom to the text2 widget. The rowCol widget has a fixed height.

buttonConstraints
    rowCol setValuesBlock: [:w | w
        orientation: XmHORIZONTAL;
        bottomAttachment: XmATTACHWIDGET;
        bottomWidget: text2;
        bottomOffset: 2;
        leftAttachment: XmATTACHFORM;
        leftOffset: 2;
        topAttachment: XmATTACHPOSITION;
        topPosition: 50;
        rightAttachment: XmATTACHFORM;
        rightOffset: 2]

The bottom text area, text2, is attached on three sides to the form, and the top is not attached to anything. The top will be attached to the rowCol widget because the rowCol widget specified an attachment to text1.

text2Constraints
    text2 parent setValuesBlock: [:w | w
        rightAttachment: XmATTACHFORM;
        rightOffset: 2;
        leftAttachment: XmATTACHFORM;
        leftOffset: 2;
        bottomAttachment: XmATTACHFORM;
        bottomOffset: 2]

Instance: Interaction, Evaluation

The actions callback fetches the contents of text1. It then asks the compiler to evaluate this string in the context of self.‡ If the compile succeeds, an action is taken depending on the request result.

See the section on 'EsCompiler' on page 551 for information on the evaluate:self:ifFail: message, and the error message object it can provide.

```
actions: widget clientData: clientData callData: callData
    | item str answer |
    str := text1 getString.
    answer := EsCompiler evaluate: str for: self
        ifFail: [ :er | ^ self evaluationError: er ].
    item := clientData + 1.
    item = 1        "Evaluate"
        ifTrue: [ text2 setString: '' ].
    item = 2        "Display"
        ifTrue: [ text2 setString: (self formatAnswer: answer) ].
    item = 3        "Inspect"
        ifTrue: [ answer inspect. text2 setString: '' ]
```

If the compile fails, evaluationError: is invoked to put the error message into text2, and to highlight the first character past where the error occurred in text1. The parameter is a special compiler error message object that responds to three messages: startPosition, endPosition, and message.

```
evaluationError: er
    | start len |
    start := er startPosition - 1.
    text2 setString: er message, LineDelimiter, '(at cursor position)'.
    text1 setHighlight: start@(start+1) mode: XmHIGHLIGHTSELECTED
```

When the result needs to be displayed, formatAnswer: does the work, showing both the class of the answer and the printString of the answer in text2.

```
formatAnswer: answer
    | stream |
    stream := WriteStream on: String new.
    stream
        nextPutAll: 'Instance of ', answer class printString;
        cr;
        nextPutAll: 'Answer: ', answer printString.
    ^ stream contents
```

Instance: Menu and Button Interaction

When an item in one of the edit menus is selected this method performs the appropriate action, a cut, copy, or paste.

```
editMenu: widget clientData: clientData callData: callData
    | item |
    item := clientData + 1.
    item = 1 ifTrue: [ text1 cutSelection ].
    item = 2 ifTrue: [ text1 copySelection ].
    item = 3 ifTrue: [ text1 paste ]
```

When the mouse menu button is pressed, this next method pops up the edit pop-up menu.

```
menuButton: widget clientData: clientData event: event
    event button = 3 ifFalse: [ ^ self ].
    popup
        menuPosition: event;
        manageChild
```

---

‡ This means that variables of the instance of DoitBrowser can be seen and used in expressions. Evaluating self inspect in the top text area will open an inspector on the instance of DoitBrowser.

Doit Browser Filein

```
Object subclass: #DoitBrowser
    instanceVariableNames: 'shell main form title rowCol text1 text2
                    menuBar menuEdit menuAction popup '
    classVariableNames: ''
    poolDictionaries: 'CldtConstants CwConstants '!
!
DoitBrowser publicMethods !
actions: widget clientData: clientData callData: callData
    | item str answer |
    str := text1 getString.
    answer := EsCompiler evaluate: str for: self
        ifFail: [ :er | ^ self evaluationError: er ].
    item := clientData + 1.
    item = 1 ifTrue: [ text2 setString: '' ].          "Evaluate"
    item = 2 ifTrue: [ text2 setString: (self formatAnswer: answer) ]."Display"
    item = 3 ifTrue: [ answer inspect. text2 setString: '' ]  "Inspect"
buttonConstraints
    rowCol setValuesBlock: [ :w | w
        orientation: XmHORIZONTAL;
        bottomAttachment: XmATTACHWIDGET;
        bottomWidget: text2;
        bottomOffset: 2;
        leftAttachment: XmATTACHFORM;
        leftOffset: 2;
        topAttachment: XmATTACHPOSITION;
        topPosition: 50;
        rightAttachment: XmATTACHFORM;
        rightOffset: 2 ]!
createActionMenu
    menuAction := menuBar createSimplePulldownMenu: 'Actions'
        argBlock: [ :w |
            w buttons: #( 'Evaluate' 'Display' 'Inspect' );
                buttonType: ( Array
                    with: XmPUSHBUTTON
                    with: XmPUSHBUTTON
                    with: XmPUSHBUTTON );
                buttonMnemonics:#( $E $D $I );
                postFromButton: 1 ].
    menuAction
        addCallback: XmNsimpleCallback
        receiver: self
        selector: #actions:clientData:callData:
        clientData: nil.
    menuAction manageChild!
createBottomTextArea
    text2 := form
        createScrolledText: 'text2'
        argBlock: [ :w | w
            width: 600; height: 150;
            editMode: XmMULTILINEEDIT;
            scrollHorizontal: true;
            wordWrap: false ].
    text2 manageChild!
createButtons
```

```
    | button labels |
    rowCol := form createRowColumn: 'buttons' argBlock: nil.
    rowCol manageChild.
    names := #( 'Evaluate' 'Display' 'Inspect' ).
    1 to: names size do: [ :n |
        button := rowCol createPushButton: (names at: n) argBlock: nil.
        button addCallback: XmNactivateCallback
            receiver: self
            selector: #actions:clientData:callData:
            clientData: n - 1.
        button manageChild ] !
createEditMenu
    menuEdit := menuBar createSimplePulldownMenu: 'Edit'
        argBlock: [ :w |
            w buttons: #( 'Cut' 'Copy' 'Paste' );
                buttonType: ( Array
                    with: XmPUSHBUTTON
                    with: XmPUSHBUTTON
                    with: XmPUSHBUTTON );
                buttonMnemonics: #( $t $C $P );
                postFromButton: 0 ].
    menuEdit
        addCallback: XmNsimpleCallback
        receiver: self
        selector: #editMenu:clientData:callData:
        clientData: nil.
    menuEdit manageChild!
createMenuBar
    menuBar := main createSimpleMenuBar: 'menu bar'
        argBlock: [ :w |
            w buttons: #( 'Edit' 'Actions' );
                buttonMnemonics: #( $E $A ) ].
    menuBar manageChild!
createMenuPopup
    popup := text1 createSimplePopupMenu: 'popup'
        argBlock: [ :w |
            w buttons: #( 'Cut' 'Copy' 'Paste' ) ].
    popup manageChild.
    popup
        addCallback: XmNsimpleCallback
        receiver: self
        selector: #editMenu:clientData:callData:
        clientData: nil.
    text1
        addEventHandler: ButtonMenuMask
        receiver: self
        selector: #menuButton:clientData:event:
        clientData: nil !
createMenus
    self createMenuBar.
    self createEditMenu.
    self createActionMenu.
    self createMenuPopup.
    main
        setAreas: menuBar
        horizontalScrollbar: nil
        verticalScrollbar: nil
```

```
        workRegion: form!
createTopTextArea
        text1 := form
            createScrolledText: 'text1'
            argBlock: [ :w | w
                editMode: XmMULTILINEEDIT;
                scrollHorizontal: true;
                wordWrap: false ].
        text1 manageChild!
createWindow: aStringTitle
        shell := CwTopLevelShell createApplicationShell: aStringTitle argBlock: nil.
        main := shell createMainWindow: 'main' argBlock: nil.
        main manageChild.
        form := main createForm: 'aForm'
                    argBlock: [ :w | w width: 600; height: 350 ].
        form manageChild !
displayWindow
        shell realizeWidget.   " Window is now on screen "!
editMenu: widget clientData: clientData callData: callData
        | item |
        item := clientData + 1.
        item = 1 ifTrue: [ text1 cutSelection ].
        item = 2 ifTrue: [ text1 copySelection ].
        item = 3 ifTrue: [ text1 paste ].!
evaluationError: er
        | start len |
        start := er startPosition - 1.
        text2 setString: er message, LineDelimiter, '(at cursor position)'.
        text1 setHighlight: start@(start+1) mode: XmHIGHLIGHTSELECTED!
formatAnswer: answer
        | stream |
        stream := WriteStream on: String new.
        stream
            nextPutAll: 'Instance of ', answer class printString;
            cr;
            nextPutAll: 'Answer: ', answer printString.
        ^ stream contents!
initialize
        title := 'Doit Browser'!
menuButton: widget clientData: clientData event: event
        event button = 3 ifFalse: [ ^ self ].
        popup
            menuPosition: event;
            manageChild !
open
        self initialize.
        self createWindow: title.
        self createMenus.
        self displayWindow.   " Window is now on screen "
        self createButtons.
        self createTopTextArea.
        self createBottomTextArea.
        self text1Constraints.
        self buttonConstraints.
        self text2Constraints !
text1Constraints
        text1 parent setValuesBlock: [ :w | w
```

```
                    leftAttachment: XmATTACHFORM;
                    leftOffset: 2;
                    bottomAttachment: XmATTACHWIDGET;
                    bottomWidget: rowCol;
                    bottomOffset: 2;
                    rightAttachment: XmATTACHFORM;
                    rightOffset: 2;
                    topAttachment: XmATTACHFORM;
                    topOffset: 2 ]!
        text2Constraints
            text2 parent setValuesBlock: [ :w | w
                    rightAttachment: XmATTACHFORM;
                    rightOffset: 2;
                    leftAttachment: XmATTACHFORM;
                    leftOffset: 2;
                    bottomAttachment: XmATTACHFORM;
                    bottomOffset: 2 ]! !
```

Example 236, FileIn

Variations

To explore this example further, try the following:

- Save all evaluated expressions and allow browsing through them.
- Add a fourth function, Trace, which inserts the expression self halt into the code, so that the debugger will start immediately.
- Instead of placing both the result and the class of the result into the bottom text area, add a third text widget and put the class into it. Could it go to the right of the buttons?
- Build a new browser that only evaluates collections, then plots the collections in the bottom pane. If the collection holds single numbers, plot them as y values with the index into the collection as the x value. If it holds points, plot the points.

  Do this new browser and the Doit Browser have any code (or concepts) in common? Could there be, or should there have been, an abstract parent class? What might go into it?

Example: Stream Filters

Stream filters are stream-like objects that can be plugged together with a stream to do processing as the stream is read or written. They act a bit like programs piped together in Unix or MS/DOS, and can be used for many of the same kinds of things.

Stream filters illustrate the use of hierarchy and of inheritance.

Stream Filter Classes

The basic hierarchy of stream filters is similar to the hierarchy of streams or file streams:

```
StreamFilter
    StreamDataFilter
        StreamReadFilter
            StreamReadWriteFilter
        StreamWriteFilter
```

One difference is an extra class between StreamFilter and the read/write filter classes; this is StreamDataFilter which is used to separate out operations that are used to filter data.

StreamFilter and its subclasses are all abstract classes. Instances are functional, they do run, but they perform no new actions.

This chapter will implement several concrete subclasses, shown in bold below.

StreamFilter
    StreamDataFilter
        StreamReadFilter
            DropCaseFilter
            FilterExcessBlanks
            WhitespaceCountFilter
        StreamReadWriteFilter
    StreamWriteFilter
        ListingStream
            XrefListingStream

Stream Filter

The core class, StreamFilter, defines a class method to open a stream filter on a stream, or any other stream filter that is open on a stream. It has a dummy initialize method, and two access methods for the instance variable stream.

It also has a doesNotUnderstand: method. The message doesNotUnderstand: is sent from the innards of Smalltalk when a message to some object cannot find a method for that object. It is sent to the object that did not have the method, rather than to the one that sent the message, and an instance of Message is passed as a parameter. Usually, it results in an error: message being sent and the ExError exception being signalled.

If a class implements its own doesNotUnderstand: method, that method will be found before the default implementation in Object.

In StreamFilter, any message sent to a stream filter that is not understood is then passed on to the stream held in the instance variable stream.

The effect is to make StreamFilter and its subclasses respond to all messages of the kind of stream (or stream filter) on which they are opened.

```
Object subclass: #StreamFilter
    instanceVariableNames: 'stream '
    classVariableNames: ''
    poolDictionaries: ''
!
!StreamFilter class publicMethods !
onStream: aStream
    ^ super new initialize
        stream: aStream! !

!StreamFilter publicMethods !
stream
    ^ stream!
stream: aStream
    stream := aStream ! !

!StreamFilter privateMethods !
doesNotUnderstand: aMessage
    ^ stream
        perform: aMessage selector
        withArguments: aMessage arguments!
initialize
    " do nothing " ! !
```

Example 237, FileIn

Stream Data Filter

Class StreamDataFilter refines StreamFilter with methods that will process data from the stream. It does not use these methods, that being left to subclasses. These methods could be placed in StreamFilter and this class eliminated, but that would preclude sub-classing StreamFilter with some class that did not want to filter data the same way.

The methods filterReadCollection: and filterWriteCollection: each take a collection of items from the stream and filter each item by calling the filterReadItem: and filter-WriteItem: methods (which just return their inputs). Many subclasses might find it useful to only override filterReadItem: and filterWriteItem:.

```
StreamFilter subclass: #StreamDataFilter
    instanceVariableNames: ''
    classVariableNames: ''
    poolDictionaries: ''
!
!StreamDataFilter privateMethods !
filterReadCollection: aColl
    ^ aColl collect: [ :e | self filterReadItem: e ] !
filterReadItem: anItem
    ^ anItem!
filterWriteCollection: aColl
    ^ aColl collect: [ :e | self filterWriteItem: e ] !
filterWriteItem: anItem
    ^ anItem! !
```

Example 238, FileIn

Stream Read Filter

Class StreamReadFilter reimplements all of the stream methods that process data. If the data is a single item, then filterReadItem: (and filterWriteItem:) are used; if it is a collection, as in nextLine, then filterReadCollection: (and filterWriteCollection:) are used.

Several methods, including peekFor: and skipTo:, use filterWriteItem: or filterWriteCollection:. It is not obvious why at first, but note that these methods have to look for an item (or collection) in the stream. The item or collection in hand is in terms of the results of the filtering. In these cases, the item or collection has to be 'unfiltered', or converted to the same characters, as are in the stream. The filterReadItem:, filterReadCollection:, filter-WriteItem:, and filterWriteCollection: methods do just this.

```
StreamDataFilter subclass: #StreamReadFilter
    instanceVariableNames: ''
    classVariableNames: ''
    poolDictionaries: ''
!
!StreamReadFilter publicMethods !
copyFrom: start to: end
    ^ self filterReadCollection: (stream copyFrom: start to: end)!
next
    ^ self filterReadItem: stream next!
next: anInteger
    ^ self filterReadCollection: (stream next: anInteger)!
nextLine
    ^ self filterReadCollection: (stream nextLine)!
nextMatchFor: anItem
    ^ stream nextMatchFor: (self filterWriteItem: anItem)!
peek
    ^ self filterReadItem: stream peek!
```

peekFor: anItem
    ^ stream peekFor: (self filterWriteItem: anItem)!
skipTo: anItem
    ^ stream skipTo: (self filterWriteItem: anItem)!
skipToAll: aColl
    ^ stream skipToAll: (self filterWriteCollection: aColl)!
upTo: anItem
    ^ stream upTo: (self filterWriteItem: anItem)!
upToAll: aColl
    ^ stream upToAll: (self filterWriteCollection: aColl)! !   *Example 239, FileIn*

Stream Read/Write Filter

Class StreamReadWriteFilter is a refinement of StreamReadFilter. It adds three new methods.

StreamReadFilter subclass: #**StreamReadWriteFilter**
    instanceVariableNames: ''
    classVariableNames: ''
    poolDictionaries: ''
!
!StreamReadWriteFilter publicMethods !
next: anInteger put: anItem
    ^ stream next: anInteger put: (self filterWriteItem: anItem)!
nextPut: anItem
    ^ stream nextPut: (self filterWriteItem: anItem)!
nextPutAll: aColl
    ^ stream nextPutAll: (self filterWriteCollection: aColl)! !   *Example 240, FileIn*

Stream Write Filter

The class StreamWriteFilter, a subclass of StreamDataFilter, adds just three methods, each of which are identical to those in StreamReadWriteFilter.

StreamDataFilter subclass: #**StreamWriteFilter**
    instanceVariableNames: ''
    classVariableNames: ''
    poolDictionaries: ''
!
!StreamWriteFilter publicMethods !
next: anInteger put: anItem
    ^ stream next: anInteger put: (self filterWriteItem: anItem)!
nextPut: anItem
    ^ stream nextPut: (self filterWriteItem: anItem)!
nextPutAll: aColl
    ^ stream nextPutAll: (self filterWriteCollection: aColl)! !   *Example 241, FileIn*

Applications of Stream Filters

Count White Space

This simple filter counts the number of characters of white space that are read, and provides protocol for accessing the count.

```
StreamReadFilter subclass: #WhitespaceCountFilter
    instanceVariableNames: ' count '
    classVariableNames: ''
    poolDictionaries: ''
!
!WhitespaceCountFilter publicMethods !
count
    ^ count ! !

!WhitespaceCountFilter privateMethods !
initialize
    count := 0 !
filterReadItem: anItem
    anItem isSeparator
        ifTrue: [ count := count + 1 ].
    ^ anItem ! !
```
Example 242, FileIn

In Example 243 a stream on a string is obtained and used as the input to the WhitespaceCountFilter. The stream is read, the data is discarded, and the count extracted and answered.

```
" Count white space "
| str filter count |
str := ' Mary  had  a  little  laptop  '.
filter := WhitespaceCountFilter onStream: (ReadStream on: str).
[ filter atEnd ]
    whileFalse:
        [ filter next ].
count := filter count.
filter close.
^ count
    " Answer: 17 "
```
Example 243, Display

Make All Text Lower-case

This simple filter converts all text in a text stream to lower-case characters. If the input stream contains a mixture of upper-case and lower-case characters, then methods such as peekFor: and skipTo: may fail, since filterWriteItem: forces all text to upper-case.

```
StreamReadFilter subclass: #DropCaseFilter
    instanceVariableNames: ''
    classVariableNames: ''
    poolDictionaries: ''
!
!DropCaseFilter privateMethods !
filterReadItem: anItem
    ^ anItem asLowercase!
filterWriteItem: anItem
    ^ anItem asUppercase! !
```
Example 244, FileIn

In Example 245, a stream on a string is used as the input to the DropCaseFilter.

```
" Filter all upper-case to lower-case; Uses DropCaseFilter "
| str filter count ans |
ans := ''.
str := 'MARY HAD A LITTLE LAPTOP, ITS SCREEN WAS WHITE AS SNOW'.
filter := DropCaseFilter onStream: (ReadStream on: str).
filter skipToAll: 'laptop,'.
[ filter atEnd ]
    whileFalse: [ ans := ans, filter next asString ].
filter close.
^ ans
" Answers: ' its screen was white as snow' "
```

Filter Excess Blanks

The class FilterExcessBlanks removes extra blanks from a text stream. Since blanks are removed, methods that look ahead for more than one blank will fail.

The filterReadCollection: method opens another FilterExcessBlanks instance to process the collection.

```
StreamReadFilter subclass: #FilterExcessBlanks
    instanceVariableNames: ''
    classVariableNames: ''
    poolDictionaries: ''
!
!FilterExcessBlanks privateMethods !
filterReadCollection: aColl
    | st newColl n |
    st := FilterExcessBlanks onStream: (ReadStream on: aColl).
    newColl := aColl class new: aColl size.
    n := 0.
    [ st atEnd ]
        whileFalse: [
            n := n + 1.
            newColl at: n put: st next ].
    ^ newColl copyFrom: 1 to: n!
filterReadItem: anItem
    anItem = $   " a blank "
        ifTrue: [
            [ stream atEnd not and: [stream peek = anItem] ]
                whileTrue:
                    [ stream next ] ].
    ^ anItem! !
```

In Example 247, a stream on a string is obtained and used as the input to FilterExcessBlanks.

```
" Filter Excess Blanks; requires fileins, above "
| str stream filter count ans |
ans := ''.
str := ' Four score and   seven   years ago   '.
stream := ReadStream on: str.
filter := FilterExcessBlanks onStream: stream.
[ filter atEnd ]
    whileFalse: [ ans := ans, filter next asString ].
filter close.
^ ans
" Answers: ' Four score and seven years ago ' "
```

Listing Stream

ListingStream is a write filter that takes lines of text and produces a paginated listing with or without line numbers. All text should be written with nextPutAll:. (Other output methods remain unimplemented, in order to reduce the size of the example.) Figure 69 on page 244 shows, at the left, a line numbered listing.

```
StreamWriteFilter subclass: #ListingStream
    instanceVariableNames: 'heading pageNumber printLine line
                isLineNumbered maxLinesPerPage maxLineLength '
    classVariableNames: ''
    poolDictionaries: 'CldtConstants '
!
!ListingStream class publicMethods !
listFile: filename on: outfilename
    " Example of using ListingStream.
      Takes input and output filenames;

      Opens stream and lists input to output."
    | list in out |
    in := CfsReadFileStream open: filename.
    CfsFileDescriptor remove: outfilename.
    out := CfsWriteFileStream open: outfilename.
    list := ListingStream onStream: out.
    list datedHeading: 'File listing of ', filename, ' '.
    list isLineNumbered: true.
    [ in atEnd not ]
        whileTrue: [
                list nextPutAll: (in nextLine); cr ].
    in close.
    out close! !


!ListingStream publicMethods !
cr
    self countPrintLine.
    stream cr!
datedHeading: aString
    heading := aString, ' ', Date today printString, ' at ', Time now printString!
heading: aString
    heading := aString!
isLineNumbered: bool
    isLineNumbered := bool!
maxLineLength: anInteger
    maxLineLength := anInteger!
maxLinesPerPage: anInteger
    maxLinesPerPage := anInteger!
nextPutAll: aString
    isLineNumbered
        ifTrue: [ self putNumbered: aString ]
        ifFalse: [ self putUnnumbered: aString ]!
startNewPage
    printLine := 0.
    stream nextPut: Ff.
    pageNumber := pageNumber + 1.
    stream nextPutAll: ' Page ', pageNumber printString, '    ', heading.
    stream cr; cr! !

!ListingStream privateMethods !
```

checkPageFull
```
    printLine >= maxLinesPerPage
        ifTrue: [
            self startNewPage ]!
```
countPrintLine
```
    self checkPageFull.
    printLine := printLine + 1!
```
initialize
```
    super initialize.
    heading := 'Listing--- '.
    maxLinesPerPage := 60.
    printLine := 99999.
    maxLineLength := 80.
    line := 0.
    pageNumber := 0.
    isLineNumbered := true!
```
lineNumberString
```
    line := line + 1.
    ^ ' ', (line printStringRadix: 10 padTo: 4), ' | '!
```
printOneLine: str
```
    self checkPageFull.
    stream nextPutAll: str!
```
putNumbered: aString
```
    | str lineNumStr blanks |
    lineNumStr := self lineNumberString.
    str := lineNumStr, aString.
    str size <= maxLineLength
        ifTrue: [
            ^ self printOneLine: str ].
    " Input line is longer than space on one print line "
    blanks := (String new: lineNumStr size) atAllPut: $ .
    [ str size > blanks size ]
        whileTrue: [
            self printOneLine:
                (str copyFrom: 1 to: (str size min: maxLineLength)).
            str := blanks, (str copyFrom: maxLineLength+1 to: str size).
            str size > blanks size ifTrue: [ self cr]
            ]!
```
putUnnumbered: aString
```
    | str |
    str :=aString.
    str size <= maxLineLength ifTrue: [
        ^ self printOneLine: str ].
    " Input line is longer than space on one print line "
    [ str size > maxLineLength ]
        whileTrue: [
            self printOneLine:
                (str copyFrom: 1 to: (str size min: maxLineLength)).
            str := str copyFrom: maxLineLength+1 to: str size.
            str size > 0 ifTrue: [ self cr]
            ]! !
```

Example 248, FileIn

Quick Test

Figure 249 opens a listing stream on a write stream and writes 51 lines to it. The result is displayed in the Transcript.

```
" A dumb but quick test of ListingStream  "
    | st list |
    st := WriteStream on: String new.
    list := (ListingStream onStream: st)
        maxLinesPerPage: 20;
        maxLineLength: 40;
        isLineNumbered: true;
        heading: 'Ugly short test'.
    1 to: 25 do: [ :k |
        list nextPutAll: '======== ', k printString,  '========'; cr ].
    list nextPutAll:  'abcdefghijklmnopqrstuvwxyzabcdefghijklmnopqrstuvwxyz'; cr.
    26 to: 50 do: [ :k |  list nextPutAll: '======== ', k printString, '========'; cr ].
    Transcript show: st contents
Transcript show: st contents


" Transcript shows (some lines omitted):

0001 | ======== 1 ========
0002 | ======== 2 ========
0003 | ======== 3 ========
    ...
0018 | ======== 18 ========
0019 | ======== 19 ========
0020 | ======== 20 ========


Page 2    Ugly short test

0021 | ======== 21 ========
0022 | ======== 22 ========
0023 | ======== 23 ========
0024 | ======== 24 ========
0025 | ======== 25 ========
0026 | abcdefghijklmnopqrstuvwxyzabcdef
     ghijklmnopqrstuvwxyz
0027 | ======== 26 ========
0028 | ======== 27 ========
0029 | ======== 28 ========
    ...
0039 | ======== 38 ========


Page 3    Ugly short test

0040 | ======== 39 ========
0041 | ======== 40 ========
    ...
0050 | ======== 49 ========
0051 | ======== 50 ========  "
```

Example 249, Execute

Cross-Reference Stream

Class XrefListingStream is a subclass of ListingStream. It performs in the same matter as its parent, but builds a table of words and the lines on which they were encountered. After all lines are written, the table is formatted and written to the output stream. Figure 69 shows sample pages from a cross-reference listing of a version of the code from this book.

```
Page 7    Cross-reference listing of file A:\DISKETTE\IBMSTEX1.TXT  10-08-94 at 12:07:27 PM

0358 | "---------- Example 57 Page 69 Inspect ----------"
0359 | " Convert an array to a set "
0360 | #(1 2 3 4 5) asSet
0361 |
0362 | "---------- Example 58 Page 70  Display ----------"
0363 | " Max element of an array "
0364 | | a coll |
0365 | a := 0.
0366 | coll := #( 7 9 5 3 1 ).
0367 | coll do: [ :elem | a := a max: elem ].
0368 | ^ a
0369 | " Answer: 9"
0370 |
0371 | "---------- Example 59 Page 70  Display ----
0372 | " Collect incremented elements "
0373 | | someIntegers |
0374 | someIntegers := #(0 1 2 3 4 5).
0375 | ^ someIntegers collect: [ :e | e + 1 ]
0376 | "Result: 1 2 3 4 5 6"
0377 |
0378 | "---------- Example 60 Page 70  Display ----
0379 | " See if all array elements are non-negative
0380 | | someIntegers |
0381 | someIntegers := #(0 1 2 3 4 5).
0382 | ^ someIntegers conform: [ :e | e >= 0 ]
0383 | " Result: true "
0384 |
0385 | "---------- Example 61 Page 71  Display ----
0386 | " Detect element greater-than zero "
0387 | | someIntegers |
0388 | someIntegers := #( -6 2 0 9 ).
0389 | ^ someIntegers detect: [ :e | e > 0 ]  "Resu
0390 |
0391 | "---------- Example 62 Page 71  Display ----
0392 | " Detect element less-than zero; answer bloc
0393 | | someIntegers |
0394 | someIntegers := #( 1 2 3 4 5 ).
0395 | ^ someIntegers detect: [ :e | e < 0 ] ifNone
0396 |
0397 | "---------- Example 63 Page 71  Display ----
0398 | " Simple inject:into: to sum elements in an
0399 | | sum |
0400 | sum := #( 1 2 3 4 5 )
0401 | inject: 0
0402 | into: [ :inj :ele | inj + ele ]
0403 | " Answers: 15 "
0404 |
0405 | "---------- Example 64 Page 71  Display ----
0406 | " Concatenating strings with inject:into: "
0407 | | string strs |
0408 | strs := #( 'When'  'in'  'the'  'course'
0409 | strs inject: ''
0410 | into: [ :inj :ele | inj, ele, ' ' ]
0411 | " Answers: 'When in the course of human even
0412 |
0413 | "---------- Example 65 Page 72  Display ----
0414 | " Factorial with inject:into: "
0415 | | n nfact |
0416 | n := 12.
0417 | nfact := (2 to: n)
```

```
Page 22     Cross-reference listing of file A:\DISKETTE\IBMSTEX1.TXT   10-08-94 at 12:07:27 PM
run               0291
rZ                0067 0090
s                 0218 0443 0447 0780 0781 0783 0788 0789 0791
Saturday          0249
sc                0582 0583 0585 0586 0587
seconds           0260
seconds:          0239 0248 0266 0267 0275 0279
See               0379 0455
Select            0438
select:           0434 0439
selected          0431
self              0697 0714 0719 0724 0730 0750 0765 0793
sent              0514 0516 0517
separately        0063 0076 0082 0094 0099 0296
Series            0147
series            0140
set               0359 0459 0463 0605 0606 0607 0608 0609 0610 0613 0614
                  0615 0616
Set               0749
Several           0272
show              0246
show:             0052 0057 0118 0119 0124 0125 0144 0152 0238 0239 0240
                  0241 0242 0243 0244 0275 0276 0278 0536 0541 0626 0627
                  0628
shows:            0153 0542
simple            0779
Simple            0157 0398 0546
simplified        0095 0096
sin               0130
SingleDeposit     0669 0673 0678 0682 0690 0697 0700 0702
size              0451 0452 0483 0502 0783 0791
Smalltalk         0051
some              0459
someIntegers      0373 0374 0375 0380 0381 0382 0387 0388 0389 0393 0394
                  0395 0425 0426 0427 0432 0433 0434
sorted            0581
space             0637 0641
specific          0598 0613
sqrt              0030
Square            0029
squared           0030 0030
squares           0029
String            0509
string            0035 0036 0407 0438 0508 0513 0524 0526
strings           0034 0102 0406 0513
strs              0407 0408 0409
subclass:         0673 0707 0754 0769
subclassResponsibil 0714 0719
substrings        0521
subtractTime:     0268
sum               0029 0398 0399 0400 0546 0547 0548 0654
super             0680 0717
symbols           0104 0105
t                 0265 0265 0266 0267 0268 0268 0509 0526
takes             0291
TALK              0091
tally             0620 0622 0624
Tally             0619
Ten               0244 0253
Test              0598 0613
```

Figure 69: Output from Cross-Reference Lister.

```
ListingStream subclass: #XrefListingStream
    instanceVariableNames: 'names offset pad numLen translate '
    classVariableNames: ''
    poolDictionaries: ''
!
!XrefListingStream class publicMethods !
xrefFile: infile on: outfile
    | list input output |
    "Open files and listing stream"
    (input := CfsReadFileStream open: infile) isCfsError
        ifTrue: [ self error: input message ].
    CfsFileDescriptor remove: outfile.
    (output := CfsWriteFileStream open: outfile) isCfsError
        ifTrue: [ self error: output message ].
    list := XrefListingStream onStream: output.
    list datedHeading: 'Cross-reference listing of file ', infile.
    "Read file; list each line"
    [ input atEnd ]
        whileFalse: [
            list nextPutAll: input nextLine; cr].
    list close.
    input close.
    "output close.  (Done by 'list close' above) "! !


!XrefListingStream publicMethods !
close
    self printXref.
    ^ stream close!
nextPutAll: aString
    super nextPutAll: aString.
    ^ self addAllIn: aString !
offset: n
    offset := n! !


!XrefListingStream privateMethods !
addAllIn: str
    (self removeJunk: str) subStrings
        do: [ :word |
            (names at: word ifAbsentPut: [ OrderedCollection new] )
                add: line ]!
initialize
    super initialize.
    names := Dictionary new.
    offset := 20.
    pad := (String new: offset) atAllPut: $ .
    numLen := 4.
    translate := (String new: 256) atAllPut: $ .
    'ABCDEFGHIJKLMNOPQRSTUVWXYZ',
        ':_', 'abcdefghijklmnopqrstuvwxyz'
            do: [ :c | translate at: c value put: c ]!
printLineForKey: key
    | str |
    str := ' ', key asString, pad.
    str := str copyFrom: 1 to: (offset min: str size).
    (names at: key)
        do: [ :elem |
            str size + numLen + 1 >= maxLineLength
```

```
                ifTrue: [
                        super nextPutAll: str; cr.
                        str := pad ].
                str := str, ' ', (elem printStringRadix: 10 padTo: numLen)
                ].
        str size > pad size
                ifTrue: [ super nextPutAll: str; cr ]!
printXref
        self isLineNumbered: false.
        names removeKey: ':' ifAbsent: [ ].
        names keys asSortedCollection do: [ :key |
                self printLineForKey: key ]!
removeJunk: str
        | s |
        s := str copy.
        1 to: s size do: [ :n |
                s at: n
                        put: (translate at: (s at: n) value) ].
        ^ s! !
```

Example 250, FileIn

Evaluate the following to try cross-referencing a file.

```
" Cross-reference a file "
XrefListingStream
        xrefFile: (CwFileSelectionPrompter new title: 'File to XREF'; prompt)
        on: (System prompt: 'Output file name')
```

Example 251, Execute

Variations

To explore this example further, try the following:

- Create a filter that converts all lower-case letters after periods, to upper-case. The period must be followed by at least one white space character.

- Create a filter that breaks a stream of text up into words.

- Create a filter that takes strings, such as words from the stream filter above, and counts the number of words.

  Do another that counts the number of each distinct word. (Hint: consider using a Bag to hold the words.)

- Plugging several filters together requires several lines of code, custom built for the particular filters. Consider building a mechanism that makes it simpler and more like piping programs together in UNIX or DOS. Use any syntax; the following is but a suggestion.

```
| filter aStream |
aStream := ... .
filter := aStream -> DropCaseFilter -> FIlterExcessBlanks.
filter do: [ ... ]
```

21

Example: Chalkboard

The chalkboard is a very simple drawing program. There are three versions, the base class Chalkboard, a subclass named ChalkboardList, that adds a list from which the chalk color can be selected, and its subclass ChalkboardRedraw, which redraws the window when it is resized or uncovered.

The chalkboard classes are:

Class Chalkboard displays one pane in which drawing is done. As the mouse is moved, a small circle is drawn; if movement is slow, the result appears to be a thick line; if faster, the circles space apart and the line becomes individual circles. The class has two problems:

- Resize is inelegant; the drawing area is not attached to the window, and does not resize as the window resizes; and

- There is no redraw; when the window is resized or uncovered, the contents are lost.

Class ChalkboardList fixes the first of these problems, and adds a list of colors for selection.

Class ChalkboardRedraw fixes the second by redrawing the drawing area contents when the window is uncovered or resized.

Figure 70 shows the three classes and all of their methods.

Classes	open	closingDown	createDrawArea:	createWindow:	destroy: clientData:callData:	displayWindow	drawCircle:in:	drawSpot:at:	eventHandler: clientData:event:	initialize	createList	singleSelect: clidntData:callData:	expose:clientData: callData:	redraw
Method Names														
Chalkboard	D	D	D	D	D	D	D	D	D	D				
ChalkboardList				R						R	D	D		
ChalkboardRedraw			R						R	R			D	D

Figure 70: Chalkboard Classes and Methods. Each method is listed across the top and classes down the left side. Where there is a D, a method with the given name is defined; where there is an R, the method is redefined; where there is a blank, the method above is inherited, and where there is grey, the class does not contain the method.

The Simplest Chalkboard

The simplest chalk board uses one callback to capture control as the window is being destroyed, and an event to capture mouse movements. The BasicColors pool dictionary defined in the section on 'Colors' on page 186 is used here; note that it must be the first pool dictionary so that potential name conflicts are resolved with names from it.

```
Object subclass: #Chalkboard
    instanceVariableNames: 'shell main form drawArea
                    gc drawable color title '
    classVariableNames: ''
    poolDictionaries: 'BasicColors CwConstants CgConstants '
```

The chalk board application is started with the expression:

```
Chalkboard new open
```

Instance: Opening†

The open method creates the window and then exits. No application code then runs until some user action triggers an event or callback.

```
open
    self initialize.
    self createWindow: title.
    self displayWindow.   " Window is now on screen "
    drawable := drawArea window.
    gc := drawable createGC: None values: nil
```

Initialization sets the default color and the window title.

---

† Paragraph titles describe what the following method(s) are for. These titles are similar to categories used in some development environment browsers. The first word is always Instance or Class, and the names describes the methods that follow.

```
initialize
    color := BasicRed.
    title := 'Chalk Board'
```

The createWindow: method creates the top-level shell, the main window, and a form within the main window.

```
createWindow: aStringTitle
    shell := CwTopLevelShell
        createApplicationShell: aStringTitle
        argBlock: nil.
    main := shell createMainWindow: 'main' argBlock: nil.
    main manageChild.
    form := main createForm: 'aForm' argBlock: nil.
    form manageChild.
    self createDrawArea: 300@350
```

The drawing area, created by createDrawArea:, is created as a child of the form. The argument block specifies three resources. A destroy callback is specified so that the graphics context can be freed, and an event handler is specified for button 1 motion.

```
createDrawArea: aPoint
    drawArea := form
        createDrawingArea: 'drawing'
        argBlock: [ :w | w
            width: aPoint x;
            height: aPoint y;
            borderWidth: 2 ].
    drawArea addCallback: XmNdestroyCallback
        receiver: self
        selector: #destroy:clientData:callData:
        clientData: nil.
    drawArea addEventHandler: Button1MotionMask
        receiver: self
        selector: #eventHandler:clientData:event:
        clientData: nil.
    drawArea manageChild
```

Finally, the shell is realized, which causes the widgets to be displayed.

```
displayWindow
    shell realizeWidget.
    " Window is now on screen "
```

Instance: Executing

The event handler checks to see if the event was MotionNotify (which it should be, since that's all that was asked for) and, if so, draws a spot on the screen.

```
eventHandler: widget clientData: clientData event: event
    "Handle an input event"
    event type = MotionNotify
        ifTrue: [ self drawSpot: color at: event point ]
```

Spots are circles and drawSpot:at: draws one.

```
drawSpot: spotColor at: aPoint
    " Draw a spot around the point "
    gc setForeground: spotColor.
    self drawCircle: (aPoint - (2@2) extent: 4@4) in: drawable
```

Circles are drawn with the fillArc: method. (Graphics contexts and drawing methods will be described in the next chapter.)

```
drawCircle: aRect in: area
    area fillArc: gc
        x: aRect left
        y: aRect top
        width: aRect extent x
        height: aRect extent y
        angle1: 0
        angle2: 360*64
```

Instance: Closing

Finally, when the user closes the window, the destroy callback is invoked.

```
destroy: widget clientData: clientData callData: callData
    " Shutting Down "
    self closingDown
```

Since things can go wrong when debugging a new window or changing an old one, it is possible a destroy event could occur before a graphics context is defined. It's is wise to check for nil first.

```
closingDown
    gc notNil ifTrue: [ gc freeGC ]
```

Filein

Here is the same code, ready for filein.

```
" Chalkboard Drawing Application
    Evaluate: Chalkboard new open    "
Object subclass: #Chalkboard
    instanceVariableNames: 'shell main form drawArea
                            gc drawable color title '
    classVariableNames: ''
    poolDictionaries: 'CwConstants CgConstants '!

!Chalkboard publicMethods !
open
    self initialize.
    self createWindow: title.
    self displayWindow.   " Window is now on screen "
    drawable := drawArea window.
    gc := drawable createGC: None values: nil ! !

!Chalkboard privateMethods !
closingDown
    gc notNil ifTrue: [ gc freeGC ]!
createDrawArea: aPoint
    drawArea := form
        createDrawingArea: 'drawing'
        argBlock: [ :w |
            w width: aPoint x; height: aPoint y; borderWidth: 2 ].
    drawArea addCallback: XmNdestroyCallback
        receiver: self
        selector: #destroy:clientData:callData:
        clientData: nil.
    drawArea addEventHandler: Button1MotionMask
```

```
              receiver: self
              selector: #eventHandler:clientData:event:
              clientData: nil.
         drawArea manageChild!
    createWindow: aStringTitle
         shell := CwTopLevelShell createApplicationShell: aStringTitle argBlock: nil.
         main := shell createMainWindow: 'main' argBlock: nil.
         main manageChild.
         form := main createForm: 'aForm' argBlock: nil.
         form manageChild.
         self createDrawArea: 300@350!
    destroy: widget clientData: clientData callData: callData
         " Shutting Down "
         self closingDown!
    displayWindow
         shell realizeWidget.    " Window is now on screen "!
    drawCircle: aRect in: area
         area fillArc: gc
              x: aRect left
              y: aRect top
              width: aRect extent x
              height: aRect extent y
              angle1: 0
              angle2: 360*64!
    drawSpot: spotColor at: aPoint
         " Draw a spot around the point "
         gc setForeground: spotColor.
              self drawCircle: (aPoint - (2@2) extent: 4@4)  in: drawable!
    eventHandler: widget clientData: clientData event: event
         "Handle an input event"
         event type = MotionNotify
              ifTrue: [ self drawSpot: color at: event point ]!
    initialize
         color := 9.  "red"
         title := 'Chalk Board' ! !
```

Example 252, FileIn

Evaluate the following expression to run Chalkboard:

```
    " Run Chalkboard "
    Chalkboard new open
```

Example 253, Execute

Chalkboard With a List

The subclass ChalkboardList is identical to its parent Chalkboard except that it adds a second area to the form which holds a list of colors. Selecting one color from the list changes the chalk to that color.

```
              Chalkboard subclass: #ChalkboardList
                   instanceVariableNames: 'list '
                   classVariableNames: ''
                   poolDictionaries: ''
```

Instance: Creation

Creation of the window is mainly handled by the parent, by sending createWindow: to super. When the parent has finished, its work is extended; a list is created. (See the method createList below.)

```
createWindow: aStringTitle
    | items |
    super createWindow: aStringTitle.
    self createList
```

Again, the parent is called to do its initialization, and then the title is changed.

```
initialize
    super initialize.
    title := 'Chalk Board with Function List'
```

Next, a list is created in method createList specifying attachments to the background form; the right attachment is omitted. At the bottom of the method, attachments are given for the drawing area. It too attaches to the background form, except for the left, which is attached to the list. Thus the list is on the left and the drawing area is on the right; when the window is resized, the list will always stay attached to the drawing area.‡

The list is given a width of 150, which will remain fixed as resizing is done; it is also given a height of 350, which will *not* remain fixed as the window is resized. Why? The list is attached to the top and bottom of the form (which itself is attached firmly to the window). As the window changes size the list will thus change height. The 350 is used as the initial height only. On the other hand, the width, 150, stays fixed because, once created, lists maintain a fixed width; while its left edge is attached to the form, its right edge floats free. Since resizing does not affect the width of the list, the drawing area width takes up all of the width changes.

A callback to method singleSelection:clientData:callData: is defined; it will be called whenever a selection is made from the list.

The colors are named in an array in an order such that their position is also their pixel value; that is, Black is 0, Red is 9, and so on. Later on when an item in the list is selected, the list position number is easily changed into a pixel value.

```
createList
    | items |
    items := #(    'Black' 'Dark Red' 'Dark Green' 'Dark Yellow'
                   'Dark Blue' 'Dark Cyan' 'Dark Magenta' 'Light Grey'
                   'Gray' 'Red' 'Green' 'Yellow'
                   'Blue' 'Cyan' 'Magenta' 'White' ).
    list := form createList: 'list'
        argBlock: [:w | w
            selectionPolicy: XmSINGLESELECT;
            items: items;
            width: 150; height: 350;
            bottomAttachment: XmATTACHFORM;
            bottomOffset: 2;
            topAttachment: XmATTACHFORM;
            topOffset: 2;
            leftAttachment: XmATTACHFORM;
```

---

‡ Try resizing a Chalkboard window. While the window does resize, there are two problems. First, and most obviously, any drawing is cleared. Second, the drawing area stays at its 300 by 350 size, even if the window is much larger, since it is not attached to anything.

```
                    leftOffset: 2  ].
            list addCallback: XmNsingleSelectionCallback
                receiver: self
                selector: #singleSelect:clientData:callData:
                clientData: nil.
            list manageChild.

            " Extend drawArea attributes here since they reference 'list' "
            drawArea setValuesBlock: [ :w | w
                leftAttachment: XmATTACHWIDGET;
                leftWidget: list;
                leftOffset: 2;
                bottomAttachment: XmATTACHFORM;
                bottomOffset: 2;
                topAttachment: XmATTACHFORM;
                topOffset: 2;
                rightAttachment: XmATTACHFORM;
                rightOffset: 2 ]
```

The callback simply takes the list's item position, which can range from 1 to 16, subtracts one, and sets that as the color pixel value.

```
            singleSelect: widget clientData: clientData callData: callData
                color := callData itemPosition - 1
```

Filein

The following code is the filein for ChalkboardList.

```
    Chalkboard subclass: #ChalkboardList
        instanceVariableNames: 'list '
        classVariableNames: ''
        poolDictionaries: ''!

    !ChalkboardList privateMethods !
    createList
        | items |
        items := #(    'Black'  'Dark Red'  'Dark Green'  'Dark Yellow'
                       'Dark Blue'  'Dark Cyan'  'Dark Magenta'  'Light Grey'
                       'Gray'  'Red'  'Green'  'Yellow'
                       'Blue'  'Cyan'  'Magenta'  'White' ).
        list := form createList: 'list'
            argBlock: [:w | w
                selectionPolicy: XmSINGLESELECT;
                items: items;
                width: 150; height: 350;
                bottomAttachment: XmATTACHFORM;
                bottomOffset: 2;
                topAttachment: XmATTACHFORM;
                topOffset: 2;
                leftAttachment: XmATTACHFORM;
                leftOffset: 2  ].
        list addCallback: XmNsingleSelectionCallback
            receiver: self
            selector: #singleSelect:clientData:callData:
            clientData: nil.
        list manageChild.

        " Extend drawArea attributes here since they reference 'list' "
```

```
drawArea setValuesBlock: [ :w | w
    leftAttachment: XmATTACHWIDGET;
    leftWidget: list;
    leftOffset: 2;
    bottomAttachment: XmATTACHFORM;
    bottomOffset: 2;
    topAttachment: XmATTACHFORM;
    topOffset: 2;
    rightAttachment: XmATTACHFORM;
    rightOffset: 2 ] !
createWindow: aStringTitle
    | items |
    super createWindow: aStringTitle.
    self createList!
initialize
    super initialize.
    title := 'Chalk Board with Function List'!
singleSelect: widget clientData: clientData callData: callData
    color := callData itemPosition - 1 ! ! !
```
Example 254, FileIn

Evaluate the following expression to run ChalkboardList:

```
" Run Chalkboard List"
ChalkboardList new open
```
Example 255, Execute

Chalkboard With Redraw

The subclass ChalkboardRedraw is identical to its parent ChalkboardList, except that it remembers where spots have been drawn and will redraw them when the window is resized or uncovered.

```
ChalkboardList subclass: #ChalkboardRedraw
    instanceVariableNames: 'spots '
    classVariableNames: ''
    poolDictionaries: ''
```

Instance: Create
An expose callback is added to the drawing area; it is called whenever the drawing area needs to be redrawn.

```
createDrawArea: aPoint
    super createDrawArea: aPoint.
    drawArea addCallback: XmNexposeCallback
        receiver: self
        selector: #expose:clientData:callData:
        clientData: nil.
```

Initialization is extended to create a collection to hold information about each spot that is drawn, and to change the window title.

```
initialize
    super initialize.
    title := 'Chalk Board with Redraw'.
    spots := OrderedCollection new
```

Instance: Execute

The event handler is extended to remember each spot that is drawn; it adds a new element to the spots collection, holding both the color and the point at which the spot is drawn.

```
eventHandler: widget clientData: clientData event: event
    "Handle an input event"
    super eventHandler: widget clientData: clientData event: event.
    event type = MotionNotify
        ifTrue: [
            spots add: (Array with: color with: event point) ]
```

The expose callback first checks to assure that the widget is alive, then calls redraw to do the actual drawing.

```
expose: widget clientData: clientData callData: callData
    "The drawing area has been exposed."
    widget isDestroyed ifTrue: [^self].
    self redraw
```

The redraw method simply calls drawSpot:at: in a loop.

```
redraw
    " Redraw all spots; elements in 'spots' are arrays holding:
            at 1 - the color
            at 2 - the point  "
    spots do: [ :a | self drawSpot: (a at: 1) at: (a at: 2) ]!
```

Filein

The following code is the filein for ChalkboardRedraw.

```
ChalkboardList subclass: #ChalkboardRedraw
    instanceVariableNames: 'spots '
    classVariableNames: ''
    poolDictionaries: ''!


!ChalkboardRedraw privateMethods !
createDrawArea: aPoint
    super createDrawArea: aPoint.
    drawArea addCallback: XmNexposeCallback
        receiver: self
        selector: #expose:clientData:callData:
        clientData: nil.!
eventHandler: widget clientData: clientData event: event
    "Handle an input event"
    super eventHandler: widget clientData: clientData event: event.
    event type = MotionNotify
        ifTrue: [
            spots add: (Array with: color with: event point) ]!
expose: widget clientData: clientData callData: callData
    "The drawing area has been exposed."
    widget isDestroyed ifTrue: [^self].
    self redraw!
initialize
    super initialize.
    title := 'Chalk Board with Redraw'.
    spots := OrderedCollection new!
```

redraw
" Redraw all spots; elements in 'spots' are arrays holding:
    at 1 - the color
    at 2 - the point "
spots do: [:a | self drawSpot: (a at: 1) at: (a at: 2)]! !

Example 256, FileIn

Evaluate the following expression to run ChalkboardRedraw:

" **Run Chalkboard List**"
ChalkboardRedraw new open

Example 257, Execute

Long Numbers

This chapter illustrates how to work with long numbers. It comes in two separate parts: reading and printing numbers, and calculating with long numbers.

The section on reading and printing numbers illustrates string handling and how to extend builtin classes. It shows how to convert to and from string representations of long numbers, and provides useful code for such conversions. The methods handle very long numbers; printing a 100 digit number is quite reasonable.

The section on calculating illustrates some of the power of long integers and fractions, but may not interest all readers. It shows calculations of common constants to very high precision. Before reading this section, it is useful to have read the section on 'Kinds of Numbers' on page 449.

Long Calculations

Smalltalk supports integers of effectively unlimited precision, and fractions which are ratios of such long integers. A fraction can represent the value of any real number. (After all, 3.14159 is simply 314159/100000.)

The calculations in this chapter use fractions instead of floating-point numbers, and will never lose precision due to roundoff or truncation, since all digits are retained.

There is a penalty for very high precision. The run time performance is often (but not always) very slow. This can be bad if such a calculation is in an inner loop of a real-time system, but can be quite acceptable if high precision constants need to be calculated once and used again and again.

With unlimited precision, intermediate results can grow into monsters of thousands of digits and bring calculation to a virtual halt. The author uses a trick to prevent the worst of this problem by simplifying long fractions after each step. This is particularly effective in the calculation of π.

Some releases of IBM Smalltalk do not have methods for printing fractions as long precision decimal numbers. The first two sections of this chapter build tools for printing long precision results and converting numbers from string representations to long precision fractions. In both sections, comments are omitted from the code; comments are present in the versions printed at the end of the chapter.

Strings to Numbers

The method readNumberString converts string representations of numbers to the corresponding numbers. It can be added as a public method of String. The string can have one of the following formats, where D's indicates a string of digits, F's indicates a string of digits in the fraction part, e indicates the character $e, and X's indicates a string of digits in an exponent. The radix cannot be specified and is assumed to be 10.

DDD	-DDD		
DDD.FFF	-DDD.FFF		
DDDeXX	DDDe-XX	-DDDeXX	-DDDe-XX
DDD.FFeXX	DDD.FFe-XX	-DDD.FFeXX	-DDD.FFe-XX

The header and initialization are:

readNumberString
```
| str num sign c n exp wexp esign |
num := n := exp := wexp := esign := 0.
```

The variables are:

str	The input, less blanks, plus a $# character
num	The value being computed
sign	Sign of number as -1 or 1
c	A character
n	Index into str
exp	Number of digits in fraction (negative #)
wexp	Unsigned value of exponent
esign	Sign of exponent as -1 or 1

The string to be converted is stripped of blanks. An invalid character is appended to prevent running off the end; it can be any character not found in a string representation of a number.

Next, the string is checked for a leading sign and the variable sign is set. The string index is also updated.

```
str := self trimBlanks, '#'.
(str at: (n+1)) = $-
    ifTrue: [ n := 1. sign := -1 ]
    ifFalse: [ sign := 1 ].
```

The next character must be a digit or a period; consume leading digits, if any are present, and convert them to binary.

```
[ (c := str at: (n:=n+1)) isDigit ]
    whileTrue: [ num := num*10 + c value - $0 value ].
```

Then scan any period and fractional digits. The number of digits in the fraction is remembered in exp. If there is no period, or no fractional digits, do nothing.

```
c = $. ifTrue: [
    [ (c := str at: (n:=n+1)) isDigit ]
        whileTrue: [
            exp := exp - 1.
            num := num*10 + c digitValue ]  ].
```

If an exponent is present, the next character is 'e'. Scan the exponent, setting esign to -1 if a minus sign is present, or to 1 otherwise. Then convert the exponent to binary.

```
(c = $e)
    ifTrue: [
        (str at: n+1) = $-
            ifTrue: [ n:=n+1. esign := -1 ]
            ifFalse: [ esign := 1 ].
        [ (c := str at: (n:=n+1)) isDigit ]
            whileTrue: [ wexp := wexp * 10 + c digitValue]  ].
```

At this point the index, n, should be at the '#' that was appended, and n should be equal to the size of str. If not true, the input format is incorrect.

```
n ~= str size ifTrue: [ self error: 'Invalid number: ', str ].
```

Finally, the result is built. All numbers so far are integers. The result will be either an integer or a fraction. Thus, the full precision of the input is retained.

```
^ sign * num * (10 raisedToInteger: exp + (esign*wexp))
```

Examples

Figure 71 shows a number of strings and the integers or fractions to which they convert. These fractions would rarely be printed this way, but typically would be printed by one of the number-printing methods described later in this chapter.

Input String	*Resulting Fraction or Integer*
'123'	123
'12.3'	(123/10)
'123e3'	123000
'12.3e3'	12300
'123e-3'	(123/1000)
'-12.3e-3'	(-123/10000)
'123456789012345678901234567 89'	123456789012345678901234567 89
'1234567890.1234567890123456789'	(12345678901234567890123456789/ 10000000000000000000)

Figure 71: Examples of Converted Strings.

Numbers to Strings

Three methods that can be added to class Number to convert numbers of any kind to printable strings are:

printStringDigits:	Convert with a given precision
printStringWidth:	Convert into a given field width
printStringWidth:decimalPlaces:	Convert in a given field width with a specified number of decimal places

Two utility methods (also for Number) that are used in these methods are described first.

Leading Digits

The three conversion methods each will need to know the number of digit positions from the decimal point to the first significant digit. The value can be positive or negative.

The number is first stripped of any sign. If it is less than 1, the number of zeros to the left is counted in a loop that multiplies the number by 10 until it is no longer less than 1.

If it is greater than or equal to 1, a similar loop divides the number by 10 until the number is no longer greater than 1.

In either case, the number of leading digits is produced.

```
! Number privateMethods !
leadingDigits
    | num lead |
    self = 0 ifTrue: [ ^ 1 ].
    lead := 0.
    num := self abs.
    num < 1
        ifTrue: [
            [ num < 1 ]
                whileTrue: [ num := num * 10.  lead := lead - 1 ].
            ^ lead + 1 ].
    [ num >= 1 ]
        whileTrue: [ num := num / 10.  lead := lead + 1].
    ^ lead
```

Extending and Rounding

The conversion methods obtain printable digits by sending printString to an integer that is calculated by roundAndExtendFraction: as follows.

1) Take the absolute value of self, the number. Convert it to a fraction (using asFraction); this conversion is only meaningful if the number is a floating-point number, since fractions don't need converting, and integers are a degenerate form† of a fraction anyway.

2) Multiply that by a power of 10 to make the result, when converted to an integer, contain all significant digits that will be printed.

3) Convert it to an integer using floor; round the integer and return it.

---

† Integers act like fractions that have a denominator of 1:

7 numerator	"Answers 7"
7 denominator	"Answers 1"

```
roundAndExtendFraction: power
    | n nfloor |
    n := self abs asFraction * (10 raisedToInteger: power).
    nfloor := n floor.
    ^ nfloor + ((n - nfloor) * 2) floor
```

Converting Digits

Using a Given Precision

The printStringDigits: method is a new public method of class Number. It converts a number into a string with precision significant digits; the width of the result can be as much as 7 characters longer (even more for huge exponents). When the digits can be displayed without an exponent, the result has the format: 'DDD.FFF'. Otherwise, scientific notation is used: '0.FFFeEE'.

```
printStringDigits: precision
    | s lead sign n nfloor |
```

Invoke leadingDigits, then find the sign of the number.

```
    lead := self leadingDigits.
    sign := (self < 0) ifTrue: [ '-' ] ifFalse: [ '' ].
```

Invoke roundAndExtendFraction: to get an integer that holds the digits to print, and convert it to a string.

```
    n := self roundAndExtendFraction: precision - lead.
    s := n printString.
```

Build the result from these digits, depending upon the number and needed precision. The first form handles cases where an exponent must be used, the second handles the case where the digits are all in the fraction part, and the last is the case where the decimal point is inside the string of digits.

```
    "Form: 0.DDDeXX or Form: 0.DDDe-X"
    (lead > precision) | (lead < 0)
        ifTrue: [ ^ sign, '0.', s, 'e', lead printString ].

    "Form: 0.DDD"
    lead = 0  ifTrue: [ ^ sign, '0.', s ].

    "Form: DDD.FFF"
    ^ sign, (s copyFrom: 1 to: lead), '.', (s copyFrom: lead+1 to: s size)
```

Examples

Figure 72 shows a number of examples of printStringDigits: output. The last example, π to 25 places, is clearly wrong, since π is an irrational constant. What happens is simple however. Floating-point numbers are converted to fractions by taking the full precision of the number as an integer, and dividing by a power of 10 such that the value is unchanged. For π on the author's platform, this is:

```
    314159265358975/100000000000000
```

This is no longer irrational, of course. The author argues that it is better to see a string of zeros than a string of garbage which might be mistaken for reality.

Using a Given Field Width

The printStringWidth: method is a new public method of class Number. It formats numbers into a given field width; the precision depends on the space that is left after

Expression	Resulting String
(13/11) printStringDigits: 40	'1.1818181818181818181818181818181818182'
(13/111) printStringDigits: 40	'0.117117117117117117117117117117171171171'
(13/1111) printStringDigits: 40	'0.1170117011701170117011701170117011701170e-1'
(-13/1111) printStringDigits: 40	'-0.1170117011701170117011701170117011701170e-1'
(111111113/11) printStringDigits: 40	'10101010.27272727272727272727272727272727'
-12345678901234567 printStringDigits: 10	'-0.1234567890e17'
-1.234e2 printStringDigits: 12	'-123.400000000'
Float pi printStringDigits: 25	'3.141592653589750000000000'

Figure 72: Examples of **printStringDigits:**

signs, a decimal point and a possible exponent are formatted. When the digits can be displayed without an exponent, the form DDD.FFF is used. Otherwise, scientific notation is used: **0.FFFeEE**.

printStringWidth: fieldSize
    | s lead sign dig exp n nfloor |

Invoke leadingdigits, then find the sign of the number.

    lead := self leadingDigits.
    sign := (self < 0) ifTrue: ['-'] ifFalse: [''].

Build the result from these digits, depending upon the number and needed precision. The first form handles cases where an exponent must be used, the second handles the case where the digits are all in the fraction part, and the last is the case where the decimal point is inside the string of digits. Note that here the digits from roundAndExtend-Fraction: cannot be obtained until the width of the other parts of the output are determined. If the number that results in the first case exceeds the field width, a string of asterisks is returned.

    "Form: 0.DDDeXX or Form: 0.DDDe-X"
    exp := 'e', lead printString.
    (lead > (fieldSize - sign size - 2)) | (lead < 0)
        ifTrue: [
            dig := fieldSize - exp size - sign size - 2.
            n := self roundAndExtendFraction: dig-lead.
            s := sign, '0.', n printString, exp.
            s size > fieldSize ifFalse: [^ s].
            ^ (String new: fieldSize) atAllPut: $*].

    "Form: 0.FFF"
    lead = 0
        ifTrue: [
            dig := fieldSize - sign size - 2.
            n := self roundAndExtendFraction: dig-lead.
            ^ sign, '0.', n printString].

    "Form: DDD.FFF"
    dig := fieldSize - sign size - 1.
    n := self roundAndExtendFraction: dig-lead.
    s := n printString.
    ^ sign, (s copyFrom: 1 to: lead), '.', (s copyFrom: lead+1 to: s size)!

Examples

Figure 73 contains a number of examples of printStringWidth:.

Expression	Resulting String
(111111113/11) printStringWidth: 9	'0.10101e8'
(111111113/11) printStringWidth: 10	'10101010.3'
(111111113/11) printStringWidth: 11	'10101010.27'
(111111113/11) printStringWidth: 12	'10101010.273'
(13/11) printStringWidth: 12	'1.1818181818'
(13/11) printStringWidth: 13	'1.18181818182'
(13/111) printStringWidth: 12	'0.1171171171'
(13/1111) printStringWidth: 12	'0.1170117e-1'
-12345678901234567 printStringWidth: 10	'-0.1235e17'
-12345678901234567 printStringWidth: 4	'****'
-1.234e2 printStringWidth: 12	'-123.4000000'
Float pi printStringWidth: 20	'3.141592653589750000'

Figure 73: Examples of printStringWidth:

The differences between printStringWidth: and printStringDigits: are illustrated in Figure 74.

Expression	Resulting String
(-13/1111) printStringWidth: 12	'-0.117012e-1'
(-13/1111) printStringDigits: 12	'-0.117011701170e-1'

Figure 74: Differences between printStringWidth: and printStringDigits:

Using a Given Number of Places

The printStringWidth:decimalPlaces: method is a new public method of Number. It converts the receiver to a printable string of width fieldSize with nplaces to the right of the decimal place. The digits are displayed without an exponent: DDD.FFF. If the number of leading digits exceeds the room to hold them, a string of asterisks is answered instead. If the receiver is non-zero, but is so small that it would just print as zeros, the fraction part is replaced with asterisks.

```
printStringWidth: fieldSize decimalPlaces: nplaces
    | s sign lead n nfloor |
    lead := self leadingDigits.
    sign := (self < 0) ifTrue: [ '-' ] ifFalse: [ '' ].

    "Convert n to a string and format output"
    n := self roundAndExtendFraction: nplaces.
    n = 0
        "Either of these formats:  0.0000  or  0.**** "
        ifTrue: [ | c |
            self = 0 ifTrue: [ c := $0 ] ifFalse: [ c := $* ].
            s := sign, '0.', ((String new: nplaces) atAllPut: c) ]

        "This formats all formattable numbers.  Format:  DDD.FFF "
        ifFalse: [ | split whole fraction |
            s := n printString.
            [ lead < 0 ] whileTrue: [ s := '0', s. lead := lead + 1 ].
            split := s size - nplaces.
            whole := s copyFrom: 1 to: split.
            whole size = 0 ifTrue: [ whole := '0' ].
            fraction := s copyFrom: split + 1 to: s size.
            s := sign, whole, '.', fraction ].
```

```
"If string is bigger than field size, return all asterisks: '*******' "
s size > fieldSize
        ifTrue: [ ^ (String new: fieldSize) atAllPut: $* ].

"Pad the result at the left to the field width "
[ s size < fieldSize ] whileTrue: [ s := ' ',s ].
^ s
```

Examples

Figure 75 contains a number of examples of printStringWidth:decimalPlaces:.

Expression	Resulting String
-21212121.345 printStringWidth: 12 decimalPlaces: 3	'************'
-21212121.345 printStringWidth: 12 decimalPlaces: 2	'-21212121.34'
-0.123 printStringWidth: 12 decimalPlaces: 3	' -0.123'
-0.123 printStringWidth: 5 decimalPlaces: 3	'*****'
-0.123 printStringWidth: 6 decimalPlaces: 3	'-0.123'
0.126 printStringWidth: 6 decimalPlaces: 3	' 0.126'
0.0126 printStringWidth: 6 decimalPlaces: 3	' 0.013
0.00126 printStringWidth: 6 decimalPlaces: 3	' 0.001'
0.000126 printStringWidth: 6 decimalPlaces: 3	' 0.***'
0.0 printStringWidth: 6 decimalPlaces: 3	' 0.000'
1234 printStringWidth: 12 decimalPlaces: 3	' 1234.000'
21212121.345 printStringWidth: 12 decimalPlaces: 3	'21212121.345'
21212121.345 printStringWidth: 11 decimalPlaces: 3	'************'

Figure 75: Examples of printStringWidth:decimalPlaces:

The expression:

$$(13/11)\ \text{printStringWidth: 79 decimalPlaces: 77}$$

produces the string:

'1.18181818181818181818181818181818181818181818181818181818181818
1818181818182'

Calculating With Long Numbers

The algorithms in this section are generally basic, and do not necessarily represent optimal solutions to the problems. These implementations are intended to show the feasibility of high-precision calculations in Smalltalk.

Square Root of Two

Compute the square root of two using Newton's Method:

$$r_{n+1} = \frac{(r_n + 2/r_n)}{2}$$

Each new and more accurate value, r_{n+1}, is a simple function of the previous value r_n.

The number of accurate digits more than doubles once the initial guess is approximately correct in its first few digits (i.e., 1.4 or so). Initial guesses can be off a bit, but this example will start with the number 2 itself and work from there. (A better initial guess is calculated in a more general version of this algorithm later in the chapter.)

Three versions will be evaluated. The first uses floating-point arithmetic and is quite fast, but is limited in precision by the floating-point hardware on the platform.

The second version uses fractions, but at the same precision as the first.

The third version is a variation of the second, but with higher precision. It uses the print methods described earlier this chapter.

Floating-Point Version

This is a limited precision calculation, producing just 10 good digits.‡

```
" Calculate the square root of 2 using Float "
| sq2 error |
sq2   := 2.0.                          "guess "
error := 1.0e-10.                      "10 digits of precision"
[ (sq2*sq2 - 2.0) abs > error ]
      whileTrue: [
            sq2 := (sq2 + (2.0/sq2)) / 2.0.
            Transcript show: sq2 printString, ' ';
                  show: sq2 squared printString; cr ].
^ sq2
      " Answer: 1.41421356 "


"The Transcript shows the iteration converging:
1.5                       2.25
1.41666667                2.00694444
1.41421569                2.00000601
1.41421356 "              2.0
```

Example 258, Execute

Fraction Version

This is a limited precision calculation, producing just 10 good digits. Differences from the first version are in bold.

```
"Calculate the square root of 2 using Fraction "
| sq2 error digits |
sq2   := 2.                            " guess "
digits := 10.
error := 1 / (10 raisedToInteger: digits).
[ (sq2*sq2 - 2) abs > error]
      whileTrue: [
            sq2 := (sq2 + (2/sq2)) / 2.
            Transcript cr; show: sq2 printString, ' ';
                  show: sq2 asFloat printString ].
^ sq2
      "Answer: (665857 / 470832) "
```

---

‡ This algorithm should not be used to obtain real floating-point answers; it is for illustration only. Accurate calculations of *floating-point* values to full hardware precision involves steps not shown here.

```
" The Transcript shows the following:
(3/2) 1.5
(17/12) 1.4166667
(577/408) 1.41421569
(665857/470832) 1.41421356  "
```
Example 259, Display

Long-Precision Fraction Version

This revised version of the code shows changes in bold. The needed precision is in the variable digits. The Transcript shows both the improving value and the square of that value; in the latter, it is easier to see how fast the iteration converges. All numbers are printed using printStringDigits: to show their full precision.

```
" Calculate a long-precision square root of 2 using Fraction
 (Requires that printStringDigits: from Example 268 be filed in first) "
| sq2 error digits |
sq2  := 2.                            " guess "
digits := 28.
error := 1 / (10 raisedToInteger: digits).
[ (sq2*sq2 - 2) abs > error]
        whileTrue: [
            sq2 := (sq2 + (2/sq2)) / 2.
            Transcript
                show: (sq2 printStringDigits: digits);
                show: ' ';
                show: (sq2*sq2 printStringDigits: digits); cr].
^ sq2
"Answers:
        (157258404803281863335321717/11119848443498681379381112)


" The Transcript shows the following:
1.5000000000000000000000000000  2.2500000000000000000000000000
1.4166666666666666666666666667  2.0069444444444444444444444444
1.4142156862745098039215686274  2.0000060073048827374086889666
1.4142135623746899106262955579  2.0000000000004510950444942772
1.4142135623730950488016896624  2.0000000000000000000000002544
1.4142135623730950488016887244  2.0000000000000000000000000000
"
```
Example 260, Display

Running with the number of digits set to 200 produces this result:

```
1.4142135623730950488016887242096980785696718753769480731766797379
9073247846210703885038753432764157273501384623091229702492483605585
0737212644121497099935831413222665927505592755799950501152782060557
1470109559971605970274534596862014728517418640889198609552329230484
3087143214508397626036279952514079896872533965463318088296406206152
5835235395054745750287759961729835575220337531857011354374603408498
8471603868999706990048150305440277903164542478230684929369186215805
78463111596668713013015618568987237
```

Square Root of X

Very slight changes in the algorithm will allow calculation of the square root of any integer or fraction. The changes are:

- The method of checking the error is changed to compare the differences between two steps, rather than the difference between the correct answer and the square of the current value.

- The formula is changed to: $r_{n+1} = \dfrac{(r_n + x/r_n)}{2}$.

- The initial guess is improved: $\dfrac{(1 + x)}{2}$.

In addition, the variable sq2 is changed to sq.

The example below calculates the square root of 3. Changes are in bold; output to the Transcript is moved out of the loop.

```
" Calculate the square root of x using Fraction "
| sq psq digits error x |
x := 3.
digits := 40.
error := 1/(10 raisedToInteger: digits).
sq := (1 + x) / 2.
psq := x.
[ (psq - sq) abs > error]
        whileTrue: [
            sq := ((psq:=sq) + (x/sq)) / 2 ].
Transcript
        cr; show: (sq printStringDigits: digits);
        cr; show: (sq*sq printStringDigits: digits).
^ sq
"Answer:
(809573136055783589088877953506025683247929506274957925716465437048789401 7/
467407268030496179016896236014461465044271863627677574165811337072837606 4)

The Transcript shows:
1.7320508075688772935274463415058723 66943
3.0000000000000000000000000000000000000000"
```

Example 261, Display

Sine and Cosine

The power series:

$$\sin x = x - \frac{x^3}{3!} + \frac{x^5}{5!} - \frac{x^7}{7!} + \dots$$

is used to calculate the sine. Rather than recalculate x^n and $n!$ for every loop, two variables, top and nfact, accumulate successive values. The answer is accumulated in sin; the variable sinp holds the previous value of sin; it is initialized to a value that is guaranteed to cause the loop to run the first time.

```
" Calculate sin(x) using Fraction "
| sin sinp digits error n nfact x top |
digits := 40.
error := 1/(10 raisedToInteger: digits).
x := 1.
top := (x*x*x) negated.
sin := x.
sinp := sin - (sin/100).  "Just used in loop test"
n := 3.
nfact := n factorial.
[ (sin-sinp) abs > error ]
    whileTrue: [
        sin := (sinp:=sin) + (top/nfact).
```

```
            nfact := nfact * (n+1) * (n+2).
            n := n + 2.
            top := (top * x * x) negated.
            Transcript
                    show: (sin printStringDigits: digits); cr ].
^ sin

"Answer for x := 1 radian --
(86950441954406624426999828662742289621 49/
10333147966386144929666651337523200000000)

Transcript shows:

0.83333333333333333333333333333333333333333333
  ... 14 lines omitted ...
0.84147098480789650665250232163 02989996227
0.84147098480789650665250232163 02989996226
"
```

Example 262, Display

The power series:

$$\cos x = 1 - \frac{x^2}{2!} + \frac{x^4}{4!} - \frac{x^6}{6!} + \dots$$

can be used to calculate the cosine. The code is not shown, but is very similar. For an *x* of one radian, it produces the answer:

$$0.54030230586813971740093660744297660 37323$$

The results can be tested by taking the answers from the sine and cosine calculations, squaring them, and then adding. The result should always be unity.

```
"Testing:  sin(x)^2 + cos(x)^2 = 1"
(0.84147098480789650665250232163 02989996226 squared
+ 0.54030230586813971740093660744297660 37323 squared)
    printStringDigits: 40
    "Answer: ' 1.0000000000000000000000000000000000000000' "
```
Example 263, Display

Making Pi

The calculation of π is somewhat more difficult, but it is the 'ultimate' test of a long-precision system. If it can't do π to some useless length, well, then it must not be of much use.

The algorithm implemented below uses a series described by Borwein and Borwein§. The following initial values are calculated:

$$X_0 = \sqrt{2}$$
$$\pi_0 = 2 + \sqrt{2}$$
$$Y_0 = \sqrt{\sqrt{2}}$$

Then the successive values are calculated using these equations:

---

§ See *Numerical Recipes in C, Second Edition*, W. H. Press, et al., Cambridge University Press, 1992, pages 915 to 925.

$$x_{i+1} = \frac{1}{2}\left(\sqrt{x_i} + \frac{1}{\sqrt{x_i}}\right)$$

$$\pi_{i+1} = \pi_i\left(\frac{X_{i+1} + 1}{Y_i + 1}\right)$$

$$Y_{i+1} = \frac{Y_i\sqrt{X_{i+1}} + \dfrac{1}{\sqrt{X_{i+1}}}}{Y_i + 1}$$

There are a lot of repeated elements that can be calculated once. But there is also a square root of a fraction, and our only code for high precision square roots (Example 261 on page 267) is not a method. Rather than expand the code inline, it is better to make it into a method.

```
! Number privateMethods !
squareRootTo: digits
    "Fraction square root to 'digits' places"
    | sq psq error x |
    self = 1 ifTrue: [ ^ self ].
    x := self asFraction.
    error := 1/(10 raisedToInteger: digits).
    sq := (1 + x) / 2. "initial guess "
    psq := x.
    [ (psq - sq) abs > error]
        whileTrue: [
            sq := ((psq:=sq) + (x/sq)) / 2.
        sq := sq truncateFractionTo: digits ].
    ^ sq!
```
Example 264, FileIn

This is essentially the same code except for the call to truncateFractionTo: which limits the precision to approximately the given number of digits.

The code for truncateFractionTo: is shown in Example 265; it tests to see if the parts of the fraction are both small integers. This test is not critical, and it is done by comparing against the approximate size of a small integer on most platforms. If either part is long, then the fraction is truncated to the precision (digits) plus a few for padding. No good rationale is given for the length test or the amount of padding (5 digits), except that a great improvement in performance results with no loss of precision.††

```
! Number privateMethods !
truncateFractionTo: digits
    | pow10 |
    (self numerator abs < 1e9) & (self denominator abs < 1e9) ifTrue: [ ^ self ].
    pow10 := 10 raisedToInteger: digits+5.
    ^ (self * pow10) floor / pow10! !
```
Example 265, FileIn

Output from the code for π, below, was run for 100 and 150 digits of precision. The 150-digit case took over 5 minutes on the author's platform. (Most of the time is spent in the gcd: method called by Fraction to reduce each value to its smallest terms.)

---

†† The methods squareRootTo: and truncateFractionTo: should be carefully evaluated before applying them to other problems.

```
" Calculate PI
    Be sure to file in Example 264 and Example 265, above, first "
| pi pip x y xsq digits error |
digits := 100.
error := 1 / (10 raisedToInteger: digits).
x := 2 squareRootTo: digits.
xsq := x squareRootTo: digits.
pi := 2 + x.
pip := 2.
y := xsq.
[ (pi-pip) abs > error ]
    whileTrue: [
        x := (xsq + (1/ xsq))/2 truncateFractionTo: digits.
        xsq := x squareRootTo: digits.
        pip := pi.
        pi := pi * ( (x+1)/(y+1) ) truncateFractionTo: digits.
        Transcript show: (pi printStringDigits: digits); cr.
        y := ( y*xsq + (1/xsq) ) / (y+1) truncateFractionTo: digits ].
^ pi

" Answer for n=100  (Run time 2 minutes, 22 seconds on author's platform):
(49087385212340519350978802863742232565580771865236028452733509254809631 34
82220156035630441459705791 87221/
156250000000000000000000000000000000000000000000000000000000000000000000000
00000000000000000000000000000000)

The Transcript shows a final value for n=100 of:
3.14159265358979323846264338327950288419716939937510582097494459230781 6406
286208998628034825342117068"                                    Example 266, Display
```

The result for 150 digits is shown below with the first 99 digits underlined. The bold digits, above and below, show the rounding.

```
3.1415926535897932384626433832795028841971693993751058209749445923
07816406286208998628034825342117067982148086513282306647093844 6095
5058223172535940813
```

Methods to Filein

Class String

This code includes comments omitted from the version in the text.

```
!String publicMethods !
readNumberString
    " convert string to a fraction; string can have one of the numeric formats:
        DDD  -DDD
        DDD.FFF  -DDD.FFF
        DDDeXX    DDDe-XX   -DDDeXX   -DDDe-XX
        DDD.FFeXX    DDD.FFe-XX    -DDD.FFeXX   -DDD.FFe-XX
    Where 'D' are digits, 'F' are digits in the fractional part,
    and 'X' are digits in the exponent. There is no limit on the
    size of the input number nor on the resulting value "
```

```
| str num sign c n exp wexp esign |
num := n := exp := wexp := esign := 0.

"Append marker so we don't ever run off end "
str := self, '#'.   "Any char not valid in a number will do"

"Check for leading sign"
(str at: (n+1)) = $-
    ifTrue: [ n := 1. sign := -1 ]
    ifFalse: [ sign := 1 ].

"Consume leading digits"
[ (c := str at: (n:=n+1)) isDigit ]
    whileTrue: [ num := num*10 + c value - $0 value ].

"If a period, get fractional digits"
c = $. ifTrue: [
    [ (c := str at: (n:=n+1)) isDigit ]
        whileTrue: [
            exp := exp - 1. num := num*10 + c value - $0 value ]  ].

"Check for exponent; if present, get its value"
(c = $e)
    ifTrue: [
        (str at: n+1) = $-
            ifTrue: [ n:=n+1. esign := -1 ]
            ifFalse: [ esign := 1 ].
        [ (c := str at: (n:=n+1)) isDigit ]
            whileTrue: [ wexp := wexp * 10 + c value - $0 value]  ].

"If n doesn't point to end of string marker, something went wrong "
n ~= str size ifTrue: [ self error: 'Invalid number: ', str ].

"Build resulting number, a fraction"
^ sign * num * (10 raisedToInteger: exp + (esign*wexp))! !
```

Example 267, FileIn

Class Number

This code includes comments omitted from the version in the text.

```
!Number privateMethods !
leadingDigits
    " Answer the number of leading digits needed for printStringDigits:
      and printStringWidth* methods. "
    | num lead |
    self = 0 ifTrue: [ ^ 1 ].
    lead := 0.
    num := self abs.
    num < 1
        ifTrue: [
            [ num < 1 ]
                whileTrue: [ num := num * 10.  lead := lead - 1 ].
            ^ lead + 1 ].
    [ num >= 1 ]
        whileTrue: [ num := num / 10.  lead := lead + 1].
    ^ lead!
roundAndExtendFraction: power
    " Answer the receiver multiplied by 10**power and then
```

rounded to an integer. "
| n nfloor |
" Assure we're a fraction, then do multiply "
n := self abs asFraction * (10 raisedToInteger: power).
" Now, convert to an integer by flooring "
nfloor := n floor.
" Finally, round by taking floor of fractional part times 2 "
^ nfloor + ((n - nfloor) * 2) floor.! !

!Number publicMethods !
printStringDigits: precision
    " Convert the receiver to a printable string with 'precision' digits
      of precision. When the digits can be displayed without an
      exponent, they are: DDD.FFF.
      Otherwise scientific notation is used: 0.FFFeEE "
    | s lead sign n nfloor |

    "Find the number of digits that lead the decimal point"
    lead := self leadingDigits.
    sign := (self < 0) ifTrue: ['-'] ifFalse: [''].

    "Now, multiply the receiver (converted to a fraction and rounded)
      by enough so that the whole of the printed answer is to the left
      of the decimal point. Then make it into a string."
    n := self roundAndExtendFraction: precision-lead.
    s := n printString.

    "Form: 0.DDDeXX or Form: 0.DDDe-X"
    (lead > precision) | (lead < 0)
        ifTrue: [^ sign, '0.', s, 'e', lead printString].

    "Form: 0.FFF"
    lead = 0 ifTrue: [^ sign, '0.', s].

    "Form: DDD.FFF"
    ^ sign, (s copyFrom: 1 to: lead), '.', (s copyFrom: lead+1 to: s size)!

printStringWidth: fieldSize
    " Convert the receiver to a printable string of width 'fieldSize'.
      The number of digits of precision depends on the number format.
      When the digits can be displayed without an exponent,
      they are: DDD.FFF.
      Otherwise scientific notation is used: 0.FFFeEE. "
    | s lead sign dig exp n nfloor |

    "Find the number of digits that lead the decimal point"
    lead := self leadingDigits.
    sign := (self < 0) ifTrue: ['-'] ifFalse: [''].

    "Form: 0.DDDeXX or Form: 0.DDDe-X"
    exp := 'e', lead printString.
    (lead > (fieldSize - sign size - 2)) | (lead < 0)
        ifTrue: [
            dig := fieldSize - exp size - sign size - 2.
            n := self roundAndExtendFraction: dig-lead.
            s := sign, '0.', n printString, exp.
            s size > fieldSize ifFalse: [^ s].

```
            ^ (String new: fieldSize) atAllPut: $* ].

    "Form: 0.FFF"
    lead = 0
        ifTrue: [
            dig := fieldSize - sign size - 2.
            n := self roundAndExtendFraction:  dig-lead.
            ^ sign, '0.', n printString ].

    "Form: DDD.FFF"
    dig := fieldSize - sign size - 1.
    n := self roundAndExtendFraction:  dig-lead.
    s := n printString.
    ^ sign, (s copyFrom: 1 to: lead), '.', (s copyFrom: lead+1 to: s size)!
```

printStringWidth: fieldSize decimalPlaces: nplaces

```
    " Convert the receiver to a printable string of width 'fieldSize' and
    with 'nplaces' to the right of the decimal place.
    The digits are displayed without an exponent: ddd.fffff.
    If the number of leading digits exceeds the room to hold them,
    a string of asterisks is answered instead. If the receiver is so small
    that it would just print as zeros, the fraction part is replaced
    with asterisks.
    "
    | s sign lead n nfloor |
    lead := self leadingDigits.
    sign := (self < 0) ifTrue: [ '-' ] ifFalse: [ '' ].

    "Convert n to a string and format output"
    n := self roundAndExtendFraction:  nplaces.
    n = 0
        "Either of these formats:   0.0000   or   0.****  "
        ifTrue: [  | c |
            self = 0 ifTrue: [ c := $0 ] ifFalse: [ c := $* ].
            s := sign, '0.', ((String new: nplaces) atAllPut: c) ]

        "This formats all formattable numbers.  Format:   DDD.FFF "
        ifFalse: [  | split whole fraction |
            s := n printString.
            [ lead < 0 ] whileTrue: [ s := '0', s. lead := lead + 1 ].
            split := s size - nplaces.
            whole := s copyFrom: 1 to: split.
            whole size = 0 ifTrue: [ whole := '0' ].
            fraction := s copyFrom: split + 1 to: s size.
            s := sign, whole, '.', fraction ].

    "If string is bigger than field size, return all asterisks:  '*******'  "
    s size > fieldSize
        ifTrue: [ ^ (String new: fieldSize) atAllPut: $* ].

    "Pad the result at the left to the field width "
    [ s size < fieldSize ] whileTrue: [ s := ' ',s ].
    ^ s! !
```

Example 268, FileIn

Variations

To explore this example further, try the following:

- Modify printStringWidth: to remove trailing zeros which are exactly zero, but not when the result is rounded.
- Extend the input and output code to handle radix specifications.
- Do the cosine calculation mentioned in the section on 'Sine and Cosine' on page 267.

Further Reading

Two key books covering numerical analysis algorithms are:

- W. H. Press, et al., *Numerical Recipes in C, Second Edition*, Cambridge University Press, 1992.

  This is one of the classic books of numerical analysis algorithms. It is available in editions for various languages including C, Pascal, Fortran, and Basic (but not Smalltalk). Most versions are now available in a much expanded second edition.

- D. Knuth, *The Art of Computer Programming*, in three volumes, Addison-Wesley, Reading, MA.

  If Press is a classic book, then Knuth is the bible. These books should be on the shelf of every serious computer programmer.

There are numerous books on numerical analysis; the first book is oriented towards applications and is recent; the other two are inexpensive. All should be widely available.

- C. F. Gerald, P. O. Wheatly, *Applied Numerical Analysis*, Fifth Edition, Addison-Wesley, Reading, MA, 1994.

  An undergraduate text for engineers and science majors.

- D. Young and R. T. Gregory, *A Survey of Numerical Mathematics*, Volumes I and II, Dover, 1988.

  Originally published by Addison-Wesley in 1972.

- R. W. Hamming, *Numerical Methods for Scientists and Engineers*, Second Edition, Dover, 1986.

  Originally published by McGraw-Hill in 1972; yes, it's *that* Hamming.

Part IV

Encyclopedia of Classes

Part IV describes the Smalltalk class libraries. Each family of classes is described in one or more chapters; the classes, and their messages, are compared and contrasted. Each class is summarized in several ways. Each method is fully described and its use is illustrated with short examples.

23

Using The Encyclopedia

The chapters in Part IV contain detailed information about classes and their methods. Each chapter is defined according to this pattern:

1) A description of a part of the class hierarchy, general information, summary information for each class, and other information about the classes. This includes *protocol tables* which summarize instance and class protocols.

2) A description of each class which contains:
    a) Parents and subclasses;
    b) Class method summary table;
    c) Class method descriptions;
    d) Instance method summary table; and
    e) Instance method descriptions.

At the start of most chapters there is a list of subclasses, a description of the characteristics of each, and how they differ from the parent class and from each other.

Methods are categorized by how they are used, in short summaries showing both the method name and its function.

Protocol Tables

Protocol tables show a portion of the inheritance hierarchy, with several related classes and their instance protocols. The intent is to summarize just what messages can be sent to which classes in one easy-to-read table.

Typically, the highest level in the hierarchy spreads across the page; methods are shown alphabetically in tabbed columns.

Lower levels in the hierarchy are in columns under higher levels.

Methods shown at one level are not repeated at lower levels, even if the lower level overrides the method. If an inherited method is overridden to produce an error (in effect undoing the protocol) it is shown struck through: ~~reMap~~.

Parents of the subject of the chapter are usually incomplete, presenting just that protocol which is useful to the class at hand.

An Example

The table below is a shortened version of the one in Chapter 27, 'Collections', on page 309.

Collection is a subclass of Object; while Object is shown, only that protocol which is of most use to collections is shown.

Object			
= ==	copy	printString	printStream:
Collection			
add: addAll: asArray ...	asSortedCollection asSortedCollection: collect: ...	do: includes: inject:into: ...	remove:ifAbsent: replaceFrom:to:withObject: ...
Bag	**Dictionary**	**SequenceableCollection**	**Set**
add:withOccurrences:	associationAt: associationAt:ifAbsent: ... values	Sequenceable-Collection and its subclasses are described in the next chapter.	No new protocol

A class in the table is a subclass of another when it is below the other. Thus, Set is a subclass of Collection and Object.

In the following, RacingBike is a subclass of Bicycle and Vehicle, and it inherits all of the methods of Bicycle even though it accidentally happens to be below just one.

Vehicle			
wheels	color	weight	maxSpeed
Automobile		**Bicycle**	
fuel	fuel:	hasRinger	height
SportsCar		**RacingBike**	**PopCycle**
hasTrunk			

Method Definition Table

Method definition tables describe the name and parameters of methods, what class it is described in, and where a description of the method can be found. Methods that are new for the class, or ones that have overriding definitions, are shown in bold. Names of methods that are inherited but are not supported are struck through.

The second column shows the classes in which the method is documented. Page numbers in the third column refer to all definitions, and are in the same order as the class names.

Some methods may actually be implemented in platform-specific abstract superclasses that are not shown. Methods may also be implemented in many places in the hierarchy; so long as the function is unchanged, the revised implementation is not shown. (The size method is a prime example; it is reimplemented many places in the hierarchy but always answers the size of the object. It is redocumented only where the details are different.)

In the first line of the table below, extracted from the definition for class Dictionary, the method add: is in bold face, which means that it is either new or redefined, that it is documented in Dictionary and Collection, and the definitions can be found on pages 279 and 323.

The third line in the table below shows that the method detect:, which is not in bold face, is defined in class Collection, and shows the page number where this definition can be found.

Instance Method Summary (*from Dictionary*)

Method	Documented	See page
add: anAssociation	Dictionary Collection	279 323
addAll: aCollection	Dictionary Collection	280 323
size	Collection Object	319 295
values	Dictionary	280

Method Descriptions

Each method description contains a full description of the method header, a textual definition of what the method does, and one or more short examples that show input values, an expression, and a result.

'*See Also*' refers to other related methods including those in other classes. A shorthand notation is used:

| *aMethod* | Refers to *aMethod* in the current class. |
| *aMeth...* | Refers to a set of methods in the current class whose names begin with *aMeth*. |

If the method is not in the same set of methods:

aClass>>aMethod	Refers to *aMethod* in the class *aClass*
class>>aMethod	Refers to the class method aMethod in this class
inst>>aMethod	Refers to the instance method aMethod in this class
super>>aMethod	Refers to aMethod in one or more parent classes.

add: anAssociation
Add anAssociation to the receiver; return anAssociation.

See also: addAll:

Value of a	*Value of b*	*Expression*	*Result in a*	*Answer*
aDictionary: #a:2 #b:3	anAssociation: #c:4	a add: b	aDictionary: #a:2 #b:3 #c:4	anAssociation: #c:4

addAll: aDictionary

Add all of the key/value pairs in aDictionary to the receiver. Answer aDictionary.

Value of a	Value of b	Expression	Result in a	Answer
aDictionary: #x:2 #y:3	aDictionary: #e:6 #f:7	a addAll: b	aDictionary: #x:2 #y:3 #e:6 #f:7	aDictionary: #e:6 #f:7

values

Return a collection holding the values of the key/value pairs in the receiver.

See also: keys.

Value of a	Expression	Result
aDictionary: #a:2 #b:3	a values	aCollection: 2 3

24

Class Object

Class Object is the parent class of all other objects in Smalltalk. It is the last class from which all objects inherit methods.† It provides many basic functions common to all objects.

For an introduction to class Object, *see the section on 'Object' on page 54.*

Categories of Messages

Object implements a number of different kinds of messages: basic messages, error, testing, dependents, symbolic message sends, printing, and processes.

Object-Related

Object-related messages answer values related to the basic nature of objects: the size, the class, inspecting, responding to messages, etc.

basicSize	How big are you? (Never overridden)
class	What is your class?
copy	Copy yourself
inspect	Open a window to view your insides
isKindOf:	Are you an instance of a given class or one of its subclasses?
isMemberOf:	Are you an instance of a given class?
respondsTo:	Do you respond to a given message?
size	How big are you? (Often overridden)
yourself	Answer the receiver

---

† It *is* possible to write classes that do not inherit from Object, but it is rarely needed, and the details are beyond the scope of this book. IBM's *VisualAge* product has classes that are not subclasses of Object.

Dependents

Any object in Smalltalk can have dependents, objects that are notified when the dependee is changed. This first set of messages are used by the 'owner' of the dependents:

addDependent:	Add a new dependent
broadcast:	Send given message to all dependents
broadcast:with:	Send given message with a parameter
changed	Send update: to all dependents
changed:	Send update: to all dependents
dependents	Return a list of the dependents
release	Remove all dependents
removeDependent:	Remove a given dependent

This message is implemented by dependents to receive notice of changes:

update:	In dependent, do something
(specified in broadcast: message)	In dependent, do something

For information on dependents, see the section on 'Dependents' on page 283.

Error Messages

Error messages come in two types, those typically sent by Smalltalk itself when something goes awry (doesNotUnderstand:), and those that are typically sent from Smalltalk code (error:, shouldNotImplement and subclassResponsibility).

doesNotUnderstand:	System sends if a message isn't understood
error:	Basic error message method
shouldNotImplement	Sent when a method is disabled
subclassResponsibility	Sent when a method was not overridden

Printing and Storing

The print messages form a printed representation of the object. The store messages answer a string holding Smalltalk code which, when compiled and executed, will recreate the object.

printOn:	Place printed form of object on a stream
printString	Return printed form of object
storeOn:	Place code form of object on a stream
storeString	Return code form of object

Process Related

Processes in Smalltalk allow apparent simultaneous execution of methods. The two halt messages suspend the currently running process, and enter the debugger.

halt	Halt the current process
halt:	Halt the current process with a message

Symbolic Messages

Given an object, a message name as a symbol, and possibly some parameters, the 'perform' family of messages will send the named message to the object. The name of the method can be determined at execution time.

perform:	Perform with no arguments
perform:with:	Perform with one argument
perform:with:with:	Perform with two arguments
perform:with:with:with:	Perform with three arguments
perform:withArguments:	Perform with some arguments

Testing

Testing consists of basic equality and identity testing, and of convenience methods to ask if any given object is an instance of a frequently used class.

=	Are objects equal?
==	Are objects the same?
~	Are objects not equal?
~~	Are objects not the same?
isCfsError	Are you an instance of CfsError?
isCharacter	Are you an instance of Character?
isClass	Are you a class?
isFloat	Are you an instance of Float?
isInteger	Are you an instance of Integer?
isNil	Are you nil?
isString	Are you an instance of String?
isSymbol	Are you an instance of Symbol?
notNil	Are you not nil?

Dependents

A dependent is an object that needs to be notified when some value changes or some event occurs. Any object can declare that it has dependents.

Dependents are created with the addDependent: message, and are removed with the release or removeDependent: messages.

Dependents are informed of a change with the broadcast:, broadcast:with:, changed, and changed: messages. The broadcast messages send a specified message and the changed messages send the update or update: messages. There is no difference between the broadcast and changed messages except personal preference and the needs of the application.

Each dependent must implement at least one method that can be invoked when a change occurs. If the changed or changed: messages are used to inform dependents, then the dependent should implement update and/or update:.

If broadcast: or broadcast:with: are used to inform dependents, then a method or methods with appropriate names must be implemented in the dependent.

Example

This example of dependents is about the simplest possible. There are two classes, Consumer and Producer. Instances of Consumer gets updated values from instances of Producer at a producer's convenience. When a value is received, it is multiplied by an ID number and displayed on the Transcript. The ID numbers are arbitrarily assigned when a consumer is created.

```
" Class Consumer; companion to Class Provider "
Object subclass: #Consumer
    instanceVariableNames: 'amount id '
    classVariableNames: ''
    poolDictionaries: ''
!
!Consumer class publicMethods !
new: id
        ^ super new id: id! !

!Consumer publicMethods !
id: aNumber
    id := aNumber!
printString
        ^ 'Consumer', id printString, ': ', amount printString!
update: aValue
    amount := aValue * id.
    Transcript cr; show: self printString! !
```
Example 269, FileIn

Providers have 'knobs' that can be twisted by others. When a knob is twisted, a provider prints a message to the Transcript and then informs any dependents of the new value.

```
" Class Provider; companion to Class Consumer "
Object subclass: #Provider
    instanceVariableNames: 'value '
    classVariableNames: ''
    poolDictionaries: ''
!
!Provider publicMethods !
printString
        ^ 'Provider: ', value printString!
reset
    self value: 0!
turnKnob: amount
    self value: amount!
value: v
    value := v.
    Transcript cr; show: self printString.
    self changed: value! !
```
Example 270, FileIn

The code in Example 271 creates three consumers and one provider. It makes the three consumers be dependents of the provider. The knobs are then turned.

```
" Dependents example "
| p c1 c2 c3 |
c1 := Consumer new: 1.
c2 := Consumer new: 2.
c3 := Consumer new: 3.
p := Provider new.
p addDependent: c1.
p addDependent: c2.
p addDependent: c3.
p reset.
p turnKnob: 5.
p turnKnob: 2.
p turnKnob: -3.
p release

" The Transcript shows:
```

```
          Provider: 0
          Consumer1: 0
          Consumer2: 0
          Consumer3: 0
          Provider: 5
          Consumer1: 5
          Consumer2: 10
          Consumer3: 15
          Provider: 2
          Consumer1: 2
          Consumer2: 4
          Consumer3: 6
          Provider: -3
          Consumer1: -3
          Consumer2: -6
          Consumer3: -9  "
```

Example 271, Execute

Protocol Summary

Class Protocol Summary

Object class			
basicNew	canUnderstand:	name	new:
basicNew:	includesSelector:	new	superclass

Instance Protocol Summary

Object			
=	dependents	isKindOf:	printOn:
==	doesNotUnderstand:	isMemberOf:	printString
~=	error:	isNil	release
~~	halt	isString	removeDependent:
addDependent:	halt:	isSymbol	respondsTo:
basicSize	hash	notNil	shouldNotImplement
broadcast:	inspect	perform:	size
broadcast:with:	isCfsError	perform:with:	storeOn:
changed	isCharacter	perform:with:with:	storeString
changed:	isClass	perform:with:with:with:	subclassResponsibility
class	isFloat	perform:withArguments:	update:
copy	isInteger	primitiveFailed	yourself

Class Object

Class Object is an abstract class that defines methods that all other objects inherit.

Class Method Summary‡

Method	Documented	See page
basicNew	Object class	287
basicNew: aNumber	Object class	288
canUnderstand: aSymbol	Object class	288
includesSelector: aSymbol	Object class	288
name	Object class	288
new	Object class	288
new: aNumber	Object class	289
superclass	Object class	289

Instance Method Summary

Method	Documented	See page
= anObject	Object	289
== anObject	Object	289
~= anObject	Object	289
~~ anObject	Object	290
addDependent: dependent	Object	290
basicSize	Object	290
broadcast: aSymbol	Object	290
broadcast: aSymbol with: anObject	Object	290
changed	Object	290
changed: value	Object	290
class	Object	291
copy	Object	291
dependents	Object	291
doesNotUnderstand: message	Object	291
error:	Object	291
halt	Object	291
halt: aString	Object	292
hash	Object	292
inspect	Object	292

Part 1 of 2.

---

‡ These class methods act as if defined in Object, and they are inherited by all subclasses of Object. However, these methods are *not* implemented as Object class methods. The actual implementation techniques used are beyond the scope of this book.

Method	Documented	See page
isCfsError	Object	292
isCharacter	Object	292
isClass	Object	292
isFloat	Object	292
isInteger	Object	292
isKindOf: aClass	Object	293
isMemberOf: aClass	Object	293
isNil	Object	293
isString	Object	293
isSymbol	Object	293
notNil	Object	293
perform: aSymbol	Object	294
perform: aSymbol with: argument	Object	294

perform: aSymbol
    with: argument1
    with: argument2
	Object	294

perform: aSymbol
    with: argument1
    with: argument2
    with: argument3
	Object	294

perform: aSymbol withArguments: aCollection	Object	294
printOn: aWriteStream	Object	294
printString	Object	295
release	Object	295
removeDependent: aDependent	Object	295
respondsTo: aSymbol	Object	295
shouldNotImplement:	Object	295
size	Object	295
storeOn: aStream	Object	295
storeString	Object	296
subclassResponsibility	Object	296
update: anObject	Object	296
yourself	Object	296

Part 2 of 2.

Class Interface

basicNew

Return a new instance of the receiver. Performs exactly the same function as new but, by convention, is never overridden by subclasses.

Expression	Result
Array basicNew	A new instance of Array
Array new	A new instance of Array

Caution: This message should be used only with a thorough understanding of how the particular class works, since using basicNew instead of new can bypass necessary initializations performed by new. The basicNew message can be quite useful when writing versions of new or new: for a new class.

basicNew: aNumber

Return a new instance of the receiver with the specified size. Performs exactly the same function as new: but, by convention, should never be overridden by subclasses.

Expression	Result
Array basicNew: 10	A new instance of Array of size 10
Array new: 10	A new instance of Array of size 10

Caution: This message should be used only with a thorough understanding of how the particular class works, since using basicNew: instead of new: can bypass necessary initializations performed by new. The basicNew: message can be quite useful when writing versions of new or new: for a new class.

canUnderstand: aSymbol

Answer true if instances of the receiver or one of its superclasses understands the message named by aSymbol; answer false otherwise.

See also: inst>>isKindOf:, inst>>isMemberOf:, inst>>respondsTo:

Expression	Result	Note
Bag canUnderstand: #add:	true	Implemented in Bag
Bag canUnderstand: #class	true	Inherited from Class
Bag canUnderstand: #+	false	Does not understand +

includesSelector: aSymbol

Answer true if the receiver itself has a method named by aSymbol; answer false otherwise.

See also: inst>>isKindOf:, inst>>isMemberOf:, inst>>respondsTo:

Expression	Result	Note
Bag includesSelector: #add:	true	Implemented in Bag
Bag includesSelector: #class	false	Inherited from Class
Bag includesSelector: #+	false	Does not understand +

name

Answer a symbol holding the name of the class.

Expression	Result
Array name	A symbol: Array
self class name	The class name of the current object

new

Answer a new instance of the receiver; new is often overridden in subclasses to perform initialization or to change what new means.

Expression	Result
OrderedCollection new	A new instance of OrderedCollection

new: aNumber

Answer a new instance of the receiver with the specified amount of space. It is often overridden in subclasses to perform initialization or to change what new: means.

Expression	Result
Array new: 10	A new instance of Array of size 10
String new: 10	A new instance of String of size 10

superclass

Answer the immediate superclass of the receiver; if there are no superclasses, answer nil.

See also: allSuperclasses

Expression	Result
Number superclass	Magnitude
Number superclass name	A symbol: Magnitude
Object superclass	nil

Instance Interface

= anObject

Compare the receiver with anObject; return true if they have the same value, and false otherwise. In Object, this is implemented as a call to ==; subclasses can override as needed to test for equality of value.

For example, instances of class Point are compared for equality of the values of the x and y coordinates by overriding =. The following code illustrates how this might be implemented.

```
= aPoint
    ^ (x = aPoint x) & (y = aPoint y)
```

Caution: If = is overridden in any subclass, then the hash and ~= methods should also be overridden to reflect the changes made to =. If this is not done, the instances cannot be used as keys in a dictionary, set, bag, or other collection that uses hashing.

The corresponding hash method for the = method above might be:

```
hash
    " Answer the receiver's hash value "
    ^ x hash + y hash
```

== anObject

Compare the receiver with anObject; return true if anObject and the receiver are the same object, and false otherwise.

Expression	Result
objectA == objectA	true
objectA == objectB	true only if objectA and objectB refer to the same object.

~= anObject

Compare the receiver with anObject; return false if equal, and true otherwise. This message is implemented in Object as a call to ~~; subclasses override it as needed to test for equality.

Caution: If ~= is overridden in any subclass, then the hash and = methods should also be overridden to reflect the changes made to ~=. If this is not done, the instances cannot be used as keys in a dictionary, set, bag, or other collection that uses hashing.

~~ anObject
Compare the receiver with anObject; return false if they are the same object, and true otherwise.

Expression	Result
objectA ~~ objectA	false
objectA ~~ objectB	false only if objectA and objectB refer to the same object.

addDependent: dependent
Add dependent to the dependents of the receiver.

Expression
self addDependent: anObject
node addDependent: connection

basicSize
Answer the number of indexed instance variables in the receiver. It is identical to size, except that basicSize should never be overridden in a subclass.

Try 1.2 basic

Expression	Result
#(a b c) basicSize	3

broadcast: aSymbol
Send the unary message aSymbol to each of the receiver's dependents. Both the returned value, and the result (if there are no dependents), are undefined.

Expression	Result
button broadcast: #pressed	Each dependent is sent the pressed message.

broadcast: aSymbol with: anObject
Send the one-parameter message aSymbol to each of the receiver's dependents, passing anObject to each. Both the returned value, and the result (if there are no dependents), are undefined.

Expression	Result
engine broadcast: #throttle: with: 2*x+base	Each dependent is sent throttle: and the value 2*x+base.

changed
Send the message update: to each of the receiver's dependents, passing the receiver as the parameter. It is equivalent to:

anObject changed: anObject

Expression	Result
flowRate changed	Each dependent is sent update:

changed: value
Send the message update: to each of the receiver's dependents, passing value to each.

Expression	Result
pipeline changed: flowRate	Each dependent receives the changed: message and flowRate.

class

Answer the class of the receiver.

Expression	Result
7 class	Integer
'abc' class	String
someObject class new	A new instance of someObject
self class new	A new instance of 'my' class

copy

If the object is an identity or immutable object, answer the object.

Otherwise, answer a new instance of the receiver, initialized to have the same data. Instance variables are shared between the original and the copy; thus, == applied to instance variables in the new and the old will respond true. The old and new objects respond false when compared with ==.

This method can be overridden, and the depth of copies of instance variables can be changed as needed.

See the section on 'Copying Objects' on page 115 for more information.

Expression	Result
a copy	A copy of a

dependents

Answer a collection containing the receiver's dependents.

Expression	Result
self dependents	A collection of dependents

doesNotUnderstand: message

This message is sent by the Smalltalk message lookup mechanism when it cannot find a method which implements a message. The parameter message is an instance of class Message which holds the selector and arguments of the original, failed, message.

The implementation in Object simply raises an error. Subclasses can, in exceptional circumstances, override doesNotUnderstand and take some other action.

See the section on 'Stream Filter' on page 236 for an example of delegation using doesNotUnderstand:.

error: aString

Raise an error and display the message aString. The current process is terminated.

For more information on errors and recovering from them, see Chapter 30, 'Exception Handling', on page 395.

Expression
self error: 'Improper framble became disjuncted'

halt

Suspend the currently executing process, and enter the debugger.

For more information on halts, see Chapter 30, 'Exception Handling', on page 395.

Expression
self halt

halt: aString
Suspend the currently executing process and enter the debugger with aString as the reason.

For more information on halts, see Chapter 30, 'Exception Handling', on page 395.

Expression
self halt: 'I am mad and I am going to hold my breath until I turn red.'

hash
Answer a non-negative integer for the receiver. Objects that are equal (using =) have the same hash value; objects that are not equal (using ~=) may or may not have the same hash value. If the = method is changed, the hash method must also be changed.

inspect
Open an inspector on an object.

See the section on 'Inspecting Objects' on page 27 for an example.

isCfsError
Answer true if the receiver is an instance of CfsError; answer false otherwise.

isCharacter
Answer true if the receiver is a character, false otherwise.

Value of a	Expression	Result
$b	a isCharacter	true
'b'	a isCharacter	false ('b' is a string, not a character)

isClass
Answer true if the receiver is a class, false otherwise.

Value of a	Expression	Result
Number	a isClass	true
4	a isClass	false

isFloat
Answer true if the receiver is a floating-point number, false otherwise.

Value of a	Expression	Result
7.234e3	a isFloat	true
7e3	a isFloat	false (It is an Integer)

isInteger
Answer true if the receiver is an integer; answer false otherwise.

Value of a	Expression	Result
700	a isInteger	true
7.0e3	a isInteger	false
7e3	a isInteger	true

isKindOf: aClass

Answer true if the receiver is an instance of aClass or one of its subclasses; else answer false.

See also: isMemberOf:, respondsTo:, class>>canUnderstand:, class>>includesSelector:

Expression	Result
'abc' isKindOf: Collection	true
4 isKindOf: Number	true

Caution: Significant or frequent use of isKindOf: is probably an indication of a design flaw. Inheritance and polymorphism should be more heavily used.

isMemberOf: aClass

Answer true if the receiver is an instance of aClass; answer false otherwise.

See also: isKindOf:, respondsTo:, class>>canUnderstand:, class>>includesSelector:

Expression	Result	Note
'abc' isMemberOf: Collection	false	It is a String
4 isMemberOf: Number	false	It is an Integer
'abc' isMemberOf: String	true	It is a String

Caution: Significant or frequent use of isMemberOf: is probably an indication of a design flaw. Inheritance and polymorphism should be more heavily used.

isNil

Answer true if the receiver is nil, false otherwise.

Value of a	Expression	Result
nil	a isNil	true
7	a isNil	false

isString

Answer true if the receiver is a string, false otherwise.

Value of a	Expression	Result
'bean'	a isString	true
#rope'	a isString	false

isSymbol

Answer true if the receiver is a symbol, false otherwise.

Value of a	Expression	Result
#Elvis	a isSymbol	true
'John Doe'	a isSymbol	false

notNil

Answer false if the receiver is nil, true otherwise.

Value of a	Expression	Result
nil	a notNil	false
7	a notNil	true

perform: aSymbol

Answer the result of sending the unary message aSymbol to the receiver.

Value of a	Expression	Result
-12	a perform: #abs	12
'asdf'	a perform: #size	4

perform: aSymbol with: argument

Answer the result of sending the one-parameter message aSymbol to the receiver.

Value of a	Expression	Result
12	a perform: #+ with: 2	14
2	a perform: #max with: 3	3

perform: aSymbol with: argument1 with: argument2

Answer the result of sending the two-parameter keyword message aSymbol to the receiver passing argument1 and argument2.

Expression
employee perform: #raiseAmount:when: with: 2000 with: aDate

perform: aSymbol with: argument1 with: argument2 with: argument3

Answer the result of sending the three-parameter keyword message aSymbol to the receiver passing argument1 and argument2 and argument3.

Expression
employee perform: #city:state:zip: with: 'LA' with: 'CA' with: 97120

perform: aSymbol withArguments: aCollection

Answer the result of sending the *n*-parameter keyword message aSymbol to the receiver, passing the *n* elements in aCollection as arguments. If aSymbol represents a binary message, aCollection should be empty.

Expression
employee perform: #city:state:zip: withArguments: #('LA' 'CA' 97120)

printOn: aWriteStream

Write a character string that describes the receiver onto aWriteStream.

Expression	String output to write stream
Object new printOn: aWriteStream	'an Object'

Note: Many subclasses override printOn: and print something more useful than the default. The implementation of printString uses printOn: to format the result; thus just printOn: needs to be provided for new classes.

Expression	Result in aStream
2398 printOn: aStream	'2398'
'2398' printOn: aWriteStream	'''2398'''
(5@8) printOn: aStream	'5@8'
(2/3) printOn: aStream	'(2/3)'

printString

Answer a character string that describes the receiver. The implementation in Object simply returns a or an concatenated with the class name. The answer is identical to the string written with printOn:.

Note: The default implementation of printString uses printOn: to create the answer; overriding printOn: in a new class will thus change the result answered by printString.

Expression	Result
Object new printString	'an Object'

The Display menu item returns the printString of the result of the evaluation.

release

Remove all dependents from the receiver.

Expression	Result
self release	All dependents are removed.

removeDependent: aDependent

Remove one dependent from the receiver.

Expression	Result
self removeDependent: joe	One dependent is removed.

respondsTo: aSymbol

Answer true if the receiver or one of its superclasses implements the message aSymbol; answer false otherwise.

See also: isKindOf:, isMemberOf:, class>>canUnderstand:, class>>includesSelector:

Expression	Result
7 respondsTo: #+	true
anyThing respondsTo: #respondsTo:	true

shouldNotImplement

Display an error message indicating that the receiver does not implement the message. It is used to remove behavior from a class on the rare occasions that a subclass cannot meaningfully override a method of a parent, and the method is not useful in the context of the subclass.

Smalltalk uses shouldNotImplement in several places; one is in Symbol to disable **new** and new: (which are invalid, since new symbols are obtained other ways).

```
new
        self shouldNotImplement
```

See also: subclassResponsibility

Caution: Use of shouldNotImplement should be rare. If a subclass needs to use it many times, it is probable that the subclass is in the wrong place.

size

Return the size of the receiver.

storeOn: aStream

Put a string onto aStream that, when compiled and executed, will recreate the receiver. The result is undefined if the receiver contains references to itself.

See storeString for examples.

storeString

Answer a string that, when compiled and executed, will recreate the receiver. The result is undefined if the receiver contains references to itself.

Expression	Result

#(1 2) storeString	'((Array basicNew: 2)
	    at: 1 put: 1;
	    at:2 put: 2;
	    yourself)'

'isn''t' storeString	'''isn''''t'''
2.3 storeString	'2.3'
Object storeString	'Object'

subclassResponsibility

Raise and error indicating that a method implemented in a superclass should have been reimplemented by the receiver. This message is typically used to define protocol in an abstract class, but to leave the implementation undefined; subclasses are then expected to override with a useful implementation.

See the section on 'Polymorphism in Boolean' on page 308 for an example.

See also: shouldNotImplement

Expression
self subclassResponsibility

update: anObject

The receiver is a dependent of some other object. A change has occurred. Perform the necessary actions as a result of the change. The implementation in Object does nothing. Dependents are expected to override update:.

yourself

Answer the receiver; yourself is used at the end of cascaded messages to cause the value of the entire cascade to be the receiver of the cascade, instead of the result of the otherwise last cascaded message.

Answer the receiver; yourself answers the object to which it is sent. It is often used at the end of a cascaded message to cause the value of the entire cascade to be the receiver of the cascade, instead of the result of the otherwise last cascaded message.

Expression	Result
self yourself	self
(Bag new) add: someStuff	someStuff
(Bag new) add: someStuff; yourself	The bag
2 + 3; yourself	2

25

Blocks

Blocks are objects that are also Smalltalk programs. They are created only by writing block syntax in a program.

Blocks are instances of class Block, or of some subclass of Block. The subclasses are implementation and platform dependent, often representing optimizations performed by the compiler.

For an introduction to blocks, see the section on 'Blocks' on page 49.

The Block classes are:

Class	Page
Object	
Block	300

Categories of Messages

Block methods fall into five categories: evaluation, exceptions, looping, processes, and timing.

Evaluation

Evaluation methods are:

value	Evaluate a zero-parameter block
value:	Evaluate a one-parameter block
value:value:	Evaluate a two-parameter block
value:value:value:	Evaluate a three-parameter block
valueWithArguments:	Evaluate a block

Exceptions

Exception handling methods are:

atEndOrWhenExceptionDo:	Termination cleanup
when:do:	Run block and handle given exception
when:do:when:do:	Run block and handle given exceptions
when:do:when:do:when:do:	Run block and handle given exceptions
when:do:when:do:when:do: when:do:	Run block and handle given exceptions
when:do:when:do:when:do: when:do:when:do:	Run block and handle given exceptions
whenExceptionDo:	Run block and handle all exceptions

These are described further in Chapter 30, 'Exception Handling', on page 395.

Looping

Looping methods are:

whileFalse:	Loop while receiver evaluates false
whileTrue:	Loop while receiver evaluates true

Processes

Process-related methods are:

fork	Create a new process at same priority
forkAt:	Create a new process at a given priority
newProcess	Create a new, suspended process
newProcessWith:	Create a new, suspended process

These are described further in Chapter 35, 'Processes', on page 497.

Timing

The timing method is:

bench:	Print run time on the Transcript

Blocks and Returns

A return statement in a block terminates the method in which the block is written. In the following example, the return statement in the block terminates both the block and the method, and returns zero.

```
aMethod: x
    x ~= 0 ifTrue: [ ^ 0 ].
    ^ x * x
    " Always answers 0 "
```

Blocks with return statements can be passed as parameters, and thus can be invoked in a called method. Any methods called are terminated back to the method in which the block was defined. The return in the passed block immediately terminates the method in which the block is evaluated, any intermediate methods through which the block was passed, and the method in which it was originally defined.

```
Object subclass: #ReturnExample
    instanceVariableNames: ' '
    classVariableNames: ''
    poolDictionaries: ''!

!ReturnExample publicMethods !
meth1
    self meth2: [ ^ 0 ].
    ^ 1!
meth2: aBlock
    self meth3: aBlock.
    ^ 2!
meth3: aBlock
    aBlock value.        "<=== This causes a return from meth1"
    ^ 3! !
```
Example 272, FileIn

A block with a return is passed (by meth1) to two successive methods (meth2 and meth3) and is evaluated in the last (meth3). The block executes a return, which terminates meth3 immediately, and then terminates meth2 immediately, and then returns from meth1 with the value 0.

```
" Send message meth1 to an instance of ReturnExample "
ReturnExample new meth1
    "Answers: 0 "
```
Example 273, FileIn

Saved Blocks

Blocks that are assigned to variables can continue to be referenced after the method in which they are defined has terminated; sort blocks are a prime example of this. Smalltalk saves all information needed to execute the block, including local variables of the method that might be referenced.

However, since blocks can contain return statements, returns performed from within blocks cause a return from the method in which they are defined. But the method may have already been returned from! How can a second return from a now-dead method occur? The honest answer is, it cannot.

Such returns are errors. Smalltalk does catch them and give an appropriate walkback, so finding these bugs isn't that hard.

```
gotcha
    ^ [ ^ 7 ]
```

The method gotcha returns a block that returns a constant 7. The returned block still exists after the method invocation is finished. However, it cannot be validly evaluated, since it will try to return from the terminated method; if it is evaluated, an error message will result. However, the method below is OK.

```
itsOK
    ^ [ 7 ]
```

It returns a block that does not contains a return. The returned block still exists after the method invocation is finished. It *can* be evaluated because there is no return. The result of the evaluation is simply the value 7. The following is thus valid:

```
usingItsOK
    | value |
    value := self itsOK value.
    ...
```

Method Contexts

When a block is returned by a method, the context of the method is saved; it is called a *block context*. The context holds the block, its local variables, and the method's local variables and parameters.

```
Object subclass: #ContextExample
    instanceVariableNames: 'iv '
    classVariableNames: ''
    poolDictionaries: ''!

!ContextExample publicMethods !
returnABlock: mparm
    | mlocal block |
    mlocal := 2.
    block := [ :bparm | mparm + mlocal + bparm ].
    ^ block
runBlock
    | block |
    block := self returnABlock: 1.
    ^ block value: 4 "
```
Example 274, FileIn

The method returnABlock: has a parameter (mparm), a local variable (mlocal), and a block with a parameter (bparm). When the block is returned, the value of mparm and mlocal are remembered in the method context. When the block is evaluated, they are referenced. Such blocks can potentially stay around in an image for a long time after being returned.

```
" Send message runBlock to an instance of ReturnExample "
ContextExample new meth1
    "Answer: 7  (mlocal is 2, mparm is 1, bparm is 4)
```
Example 275, FileIn

Instance Protocol Summary

Object			
==			
Block			
atEndOrWhenExceptionDo:	newProcess	value:value:	when:do:when:do: (etc.)
bench:	newProcessWith:	value:value:value:	whenExceptionDo:
fork	value	valueWithArguments:	whileFalse:
forkAt:	value:	when:do:	whileTrue:

Class Block

Class Block is either a concrete or abstract class, depending upon implementation details. Its instances are created by Smalltalk when code is compiled.

Class	Page
Object	
Block	300

Class Method Summary

There are no new class methods.

Instance Method Summary

Note: The typographic conventions in the following table differ from the standard used elsewhere in this book. While all methods are new to Block, only those documented in this chapter are in boldface. The others are documented in the chapters on processes and exception handling.

Method	*Documented*	*See page*
atEndOrWhenExceptionDo: aBlock	Block	399
bench: aString	Block	301
fork	Block	501
forkAt: anInteger	Block	501
newProcess	Block	501
newProcessWith: aCollection	Block	501
value	Block	302
value: anObject	Block	302
value: obj1 **value: obj2**	Block	302

value: obj1
    value: obj2
    value: obj3
	Block	302

valueWithArguments: aCollection	Block	302
when: exception do: aBlock	Block	399
when: exception1 do: aBlock1 when: exception2 do: aBlock2	Block	400

when: exception1 do: aBlock1
    when: exception2 do: aBlock2
    when: exception3 do: aBlock3
	Block	400

when: exception1 do: aBlock1
    when: exception2 do: aBlock2
    when: exception3 do: aBlock3
    when: exception4 do: aBlock4
	Block	400

when: exception1 do: aBlock1
    when: exception2 do: aBlock2
    when: exception3 do: aBlock3
    when: exception4 do: aBlock4
    when: exception5 do: aBlock5
	Block	401

whenExceptionDo: aBlock	Block	401
whileFalse: aBlock	Block	302
whileTrue: aBlock	Block	302

Instance Interface

bench: aString

Display aString on the Transcript followed by an integer that represents the number of milliseconds that it took to execute the receiver once. This is equivalent to:

```
        Transcript cr;
            show: aString;
            show: (Time millisecondsToRun: receiver) printString
```

Example:

```
" Benchmark 1000 factorial "
[ 1000 factorial ]
        bench: 'Time for 1000 factorial: '
"Transcript shows:
        'Time for 1000 factorial: 2560'  (on the author's machine) "
```

value

Evaluate the receiver, a zero-parameter block. Answer the result of the last statement evaluated. The value of an empty block is nil.

Expression	Result
[2 raisedToInteger: 8] value	256
[la bl a := 7. b := 3. a + b] value	10
[self setUp. 3] value	3
[ ] value	nil

value: anObject

Evaluate the receiver, a one-parameter block, passing anObject as the parameter. Answer the result of the last statement or expression that is evaluated. An error is raised if the block has the wrong number of parameters.

Expression	Result
[:n l 2 raisedToInteger: n] value: 8	256

value: obj1 value: obj2

Evaluate the receiver, a two-parameter block, passing obj1 and obj2 as parameters. Answer the result of the last statement evaluated. An error is raised if the block has the wrong number of parameters.

value: obj1 value: obj2 value: obj3

Evaluate the receiver, a three-parameter block, passing obj1, obj2, and obj3 as parameters. Answer the result of the last statement evaluated. An error is raised if the block has the wrong number of parameters.

valueWithArguments: aCollection

Evaluate the receiver, an *n*-parameter block, passing the *n* objects in aCollection as parameters. Answer the result of the last statement evaluated. If the block takes no parameters, aCollection must be empty. An error is raised if the block has the wrong number of parameters.

whileFalse: aBlock

For each time the receiver answers false when evaluated, evaluate aBlock; repeat until the receiver answers true. Answer nil.

whileTrue: aBlock

For each time the receiver answers true when evaluated, evaluate aBlock; repeat until the receiver answers false. Answer nil.

26

Booleans

Booleans represent true and false values and operations on logic values.

The Boolean classes are:

Categories of Messages

Booleans are created just once by Smalltalk system initialization. One instance of True and one of False are created and remembered; they are retrieved by the variables true and false, and returned by comparison operators such as < or =. No additional instances should be created. These instances are identity objects.

The following are always true:

```
( 1 = 1 ) == true      "Test 1 and 1 for equality; see if the result is true"
( 1 ~= 1 ) == false    "Test 1 and 1 for inequality; see if the result is false"
```

Boolean methods fall into two categories: logic operations and conditionals.

Logic Operations

Logic operations are:

&	The logical-and of two booleans
=	The equality of two booleans
and:	The logical-and of two booleans with deferred evaluation
eqv:	The logical equivalence of two booleans (same as =)
not	Inversion of one boolean
or:	The logical-or of two booleans with deferred evaluation
xor:	The exclusive-or of two booleans with deferred evaluation
|	The logical-or of two booleans

Conditionals

Conditional operations are:

ifFalse:	Evaluate a block if a boolean is false
ifFalse:ifTrue:	Evaluate one of two blocks if a boolean is false or true
ifTrue:	Evaluate a block if a boolean is true
ifTrue:ifFalse:	Evaluate one of two blocks if a boolean is true or false

Boolean Operations

Figure 76 shows all possible boolean input values and results from the eight boolean operations.

Expression	Values of a and b			
	true, true	true, false	false, true	false, false
a & b	true	false	false	false
a | b	true	true	true	false
a = b	true	false	false	true
a == b	true	false	false	true
a and: [b]	true	false	false	false
a eqv: b	true	false	false	true
a or: [b]	true	true	true	false
a xor: b	false	true	true	false

Figure 76: The Whole Truth.

Protocol Summary

Class Protocol Summary

There are no new class methods.

Instance Protocol Summary

<table>
<tr><th colspan="4">Object</th></tr>
<tr><td>=</td><td>==</td><td>~</td><td>~~</td></tr>
<tr><th colspan="4">Boolean</th></tr>
<tr><td>&</td><td>eqv:</td><td>ifTrue:</td><td>or:</td></tr>
<tr><td>|</td><td>ifFalse:</td><td>ifTrue:ifFalse:</td><td>xor:</td></tr>
<tr><td>and:</td><td>ifFalse:ifTrue:</td><td>not</td><td></td></tr>
<tr><th colspan="2">True</th><th colspan="2">False</th></tr>
<tr><td colspan="2">No new protocol</td><td colspan="2">No new protocol</td></tr>
</table>

Class Boolean

Class Boolean describes the protocol of logic values.

Class	*Page*
Object	
Boolean	305
False	307
True	307

Class Method Summary

There are no new class methods.

Instance Method Summary

Method	*Documented*	*See page*
= anObject	Object	289
== anObject	Object	289
~= anObject	Object	289
~~ anObject	Object	290
& aBoolean	Boolean	306
| aBoolean	Boolean	306
and: aBlock	Boolean	306
eqv: aBoolean	Boolean	306
ifFalse: aBlock	Boolean	306
ifFalse: falseBlock ifTrue: trueBlock	Boolean	306
ifTrue: aBlock	Boolean	306
ifTrue: trueBlock ifFalse: falseBlock	Boolean	306
not	Boolean	307
or: aBlock	Boolean	307
xor: aBoolean	Boolean	307

Instance Interface

& aBoolean
Answer the logical-and of the receiver and aBoolean.

| aBoolean
Answer true if the receiver is true, else answer aBoolean.

and: aBlock
Answer false if the receiver is false, else answer the result of evaluating aBlock (which must return a boolean). The block is not evaluated unless the receiver is true; thus the expressions in the block are evaluated only when necessary.

The Boolean & operation can have an evaluation ordering problem:

$$(a \sim= 0) \& (b/a > 2)$$

There is no guarantee that the first comparison will be tested first, nor that if it produces false that the second comparison won't be performed. This problem can be solved by using the and: message:

$$(a \sim= 0) \text{ and: } [b/a > 2]$$

eqv: aBoolean
Answer true if the receiver and aBoolean have the same truth value; answer false otherwise.

ifFalse: aBlock
If the receiver is false, answer the result of evaluating aBlock; else answer nil.

Value of a	Expression	Result
false	a ifFalse: [7]	7
true	a ifFalse: [7]	nil

ifFalse: falseBlock ifTrue: trueBlock
If the receiver is false, answer the result of evaluating falseBlock; else answer the result of evaluating trueBlock.

Value of a	Expression	Result
false	a ifFalse: [1] ifTrue: [2]	1
true	a ifFalse: [1] ifTrue: [2]	2

ifTrue: aBlock
If the receiver is true, answer the result of evaluating aBlock; else answer nil.

Value of a	Value of b	Expression	Result
true	7	a ifTrue: [b]	7
false	9	a ifTrue: [b]	nil

ifTrue: trueBlock ifFalse: falseBlock
If the receiver is true, answer the result of evaluating trueBlock; else answer the result of evaluating falseBlock.

Value of a	Expression	Result
true	a ifTrue: [1] ifFalse: [2]	1
false	a ifTrue: [1] ifFalse: [2]	2

not

Answer true if the receiver is false, and false if the receiver is true.

Value of a	Expression	Result
true	a not	false
false	a not	true

or: aBlock

Answer true if the receiver is true, else answer the result of evaluating aBlock (which must return a boolean). The block is not evaluated unless the receiver is false; thus the expressions in the block are evaluated only when necessary.

xor: aBoolean

Answer true if the receiver and aBoolean have different logical values; answer false otherwise.

Class False

Class	Page
Object	
Boolean	305
False	307
True	307

Class Method Summary

There are no new class methods.

Instance Method Summary

There are no new instance methods.

Class True

Class	Page
Object	
Boolean	305
False	307
True	307

Class Method Summary

There are no new class methods.

Instance Method Summary

There are no new instance methods.

Polymorphism in Boolean

The implementation of methods in True and False illustrates very clearly the power of polymorphism. The following shows how several methods might be implemented; in practice, details vary and optimizations by the compiler might actually put these operations in-line.

& aBoolean

In Boolean
The protocol is defined, but the implementation issues an error message.

> **& aBoolean**
>   self subclassResponsibility

In True
Since the receiver is true, return aBoolean.

> **& aBoolean**
>   ^ aBoolean

In False
Since the receiver is false, return false.

> **& aBoolean**
>   ^ false

ifTrue: trueBlock ifFalse: falseBlock

In Boolean
The protocol is defined, but the implementation issues an error message.

> **ifTrue: trueBlock ifFalse: falseBlock**
>   self subclassResponsibility

In True
Since the receiver is true, it is not necessary to test anything; thus trueBlock is evaluated and the result is returned.

> **ifTrue: trueBlock ifFalse: falseBlock**
>   ^ trueBlock value

In False
Since the receiver is false, it is not necessary to test anything; thus falseBlock is evaluated and the result is returned.

> **ifTrue: trueBlock ifFalse: falseBlock**
>   ^ falseBlock value

27

Collections

Collections are objects that hold other objects. IBM Smalltalk implements arrays, **bags**, byte arrays, dictionaries, intervals, ordered collections (queues and stacks), sets, **sorted** collections, strings, and symbols.

See Chapter 6, 'Collections and Iteration', on page 65 for an introduction to collections.

The collection classes are:

For detailed information on sequenceable collections, see Chapter 28, 'Collections: Sequenceable', on page 331.

The subclasses of Collection differ in how the objects are stored and accessed, and in a few cases differ in what kinds of objects can be held. Various platforms have additional abstract classes, not shown in the hierarchy, that are for internal implementation purposes.

Kinds of Collections

Collections come in two basic types: those that hold any kind of object and those that hold only special kinds of objects. Array and OrderedCollection are examples of collections that can hold any kind of object, including collections. String, Symbol and Byte-

Array hold only special objects; String and Symbol hold characters and ByteArray holds numbers in the range 0 to 255.

All collections support messages to convert to other kinds of collections, to iterate through the elements of the collections one at a time, and to build new collections in a number of different ways from a given collection. Figure 77 summarizes the characteristics of collection classes.

Indexed by	Class	Ordering	Size	Holds	Size answers
Integer	Array	Index	Fixed	Any object	max size
	ByteArray	Index	Fixed	Integers: 0-255	max size
	Interval	Internal	Fixed	Computed sequence	# elements
	OrderedCollection	Index	Variable	Any object	# elements
	SortedCollection	Internal	Variable	Any object	# elements
	String	Index	Fixed	Characters	max size
	Symbol	Index	Fixed	Characters	max size
Key	Dictionary	Key, =	Variable	Key + any object	# elements
	IdentityDictionary	Key, ==	Variable	Key + any object	# elements
None	Bag	None	Variable	Any object but nil	# elements
	Set	None	Variable	Any object but nil	# elements

Figure 77: Comparison of Concrete Collection Subclasses.

Bags

Bags are unordered collections that act like containers into which things can be placed and withdrawn; but like grocery bags, there is no ordering of items in the bag. Multiple items with the same value can be placed in the bag. Bags can hold any object but nil.

Dictionaries

Dictionaries hold key-value pairs that are instances of class Association. Only one value with a given key can be in the dictionary. Items are accessed only by the key value, and equality of keys is determined by using =. Keys can be any object, but are typically strings or symbols. The values can be any object.

Identity Dictionaries

Identity dictionaries are identical to dictionaries, except that the comparison used to determine if keys are the same is ==.

Sets

Sets are very similar to bags, except that they can only hold one of any given object. Sets are unordered collections and are not indexable. Sets can hold any object but nil.

Categories of Messages

The categories below cover class Collection, Bag, Dictionary, and Set. SequenceableCollection and its subclasses are categorized in the next chapter.

Access

Access methods in Collection are concerned with adding and removing objects in ways that do not specify positions or organization of the collection.

add:	Add an object
addAll:	Add objects in a collection
remove:	Remove an object
remove:ifAbsent:	Remove an object; fix up if none
removeAll:	Remove objects in a collection

Bag adds:

add:withOccurrences:	Add multiple copies of one element

Dictionary adds and removes:

associationAt:	Answer association at a key; error if none
associationAt:ifAbsent:	Answer association at a key; fix up if none
at:	Answer value at key
at:ifAbsent:	Answer value at key; fix up if missing
at:put:	Replace value at key; error if missing
at:ifAbsentPut:	Add value at key if key not present
at:ifPresent:	If key present, do a block
keyAtValue:	Answer key for a value; error if none
keyAtValue:ifAbsent:	Answer key for value; fix up if none
~~remove:~~	Cannot remove an object
~~remove:ifAbsent:~~	Cannot remove an object
~~removeAll:~~	Cannot remove collection of objects
removeAllKeys:	Remove some keys; error if any missing
removeAllKeys:ifAbsent:	Remove some keys; fix up if missing
removeKey:	Remove a key; error if missing
removeKey:ifAbsent:	Remove a key; fix up if missing

Conversion

Conversion operations convert collections to other collections.

asArray	Convert to an array
asBag	Convert to a bag
asByteArray	Convert to a byte array
asOrderedCollection	Convert to an ordered collection
asSet	Convert to a set
asSortedCollection	Convert to a sorted collection
asSortedCollection:	Convert, with sort block

Iteration

All iteration methods pass each element of a collection to a block. Some build new collections from the results of the block invocations.

collect:	A new collection, same size, new elements
conform:	Test each element
detect:	Answer first element for which block is true

detect:ifNone:	As in detect: but traps error if none found
do:	Simple iteration across collection
inject:into:	Used for summing, products, etc.
reject:	New collection with elements failing a test
select:	New collection with elements passing a test

Dictionary adds:

| associationsDo: | Pass associations as the element |
| keysDo: | Pass keys as the element |

Testing

Testing methods can detect the presence of an element in a collection, determine how many of a given element are present, test for emptiness, and size.

=	Test contents of two collections for equality
==	Test two collections for identity
detect:	Answer first element for which block is true
detect:ifNone:	As in detect: but traps error if none found
includes:	Is a given element present?
isEmpty	Is the collection empty?
notEmpty	Is the collection not empty?
occurrencesOf:	How many of a given element are present?
size	How many elements in the collection?

Dictionary adds:

| includesKey: | Answer true if a key is present |

Other

From Dictionary:

| keys | Answer a collection holding the keys only |
| values | Answer a collection holding the values only |

Protocol Summary

Class Protocol Summary

Object class			
new	new:		
Collection class			
with:	with:with:	with:with:with:	with:with:with:with:
Bag class	**Dictionary class**	**SequenceableCollection class**	**Set class**
No new protocol	No new protocol	SequenceableCollection class and its subclasses are described in the next chapter.	No new protocol
	IdentityDictionary class		
	No new protocol		

Instance Protocol Summary

Object				
= == -= --	copy	printString	printOn:	size

Collection				
add:	asOrderedCollection	conform:	inject:into:	remove:
addAll:	asSet	detect:	isEmpty	remove:ifAbsent:
asArray	asSortedCollection	detect:ifNone:	notEmpty	removeAll:
asBag	asSortedCollection:	do:	occurrencesOf:	select:
asByteArray	collect:	includes:	reject:	size

Bag	Dictionary			Sequenceable Collection	Set
add:withOccurrences:	associationAt: associationAt:ifAbsent: associationsDo: at: at:ifAbsent: at:ifAbsentPut: at:ifPresent:	at:put: includesKey: keyAtValue: keyAtValue:ifAbsent: keys keysDo: ~~remove:~~	~~remove:ifAbsent:~~ ~~removeAll:~~ removeAllKeys: removeAllKeys:ifAbsent: removeKey: removeKey:ifAbsent: values	Sequenceable Collection and its subclasses are described in the next chapter.	No new protocol
	IdentityDictionary				
	No new protocol				

Class Collection

Class Collection is an abstract class that defines the protocol that all other collections must reimplement or inherit.

Class Method Summary

Method	*Documented*	*See page*
new	Collection class	314
new: count	Collection class	315
with: element1	Collection class	315
with: element1 with: element2	Collection class	315
with: element1 with: element2 with: element3	Collection class	315
with: element1 with: element2 with: element3 with: element4	Collection class	315

Instance Method Summary

Method	Documented	See page
=	Object	289
==	Object	289
add: anObject	Collection	315
addAll: aCollection	Collection	315
asArray	Collection	315
asBag	Collection	316
asByteArray	Collection	316
asOrderedCollection	Collection	316
asSet	Collection	316
asSortedCollection	Collection	316
asSortedCollection: aSortBlock	Collection	316
collect: aBlock	Collection	316
conform: aBlock	Collection	317
copy	Collection Object	317 291
detect: aBlock	Collection	317
detect: aBlock ifNone: errorBlock	Collection	317
do: aBlock	Collection	317
includes: anObject	Collection	317
inject: anObject into: aBlock	Collection	317
isEmpty	Collection	318
notEmpty	Collection	318
occurrencesOf: anObject	Collection	319
printString	Object	295
reject: aBlock	Collection	319
remove: anObject	Collection	319
remove: anObject ifAbsent: aBlock	Collection	319
removeAll:	Collection	319
select: aBlock	Collection	319
size	Collection Object	319 295

Class Interface

new
Answer a new collection with room for a default number of elements.

Expression
OrderedCollection new
Bag new

new: count
Answer a new collection with room for count elements. Depending on the kind of collection, size may or may not return the value count.

Expression
OrderedCollection new: 100
Bag new: (otherBag size * 2)
Array new: 50

with: element1
Answer a new collection with element1 as its only element.

Expression	Result
Array with: 'string'	anArray: 'string'

with: element1 with: element2
Answer a new collection with element1 and element2 as its only elements.

Expression	Result
Array with: 1 with: 2	anArray: 1 2

with: element1 with: element2 with: element3
Answer a new collection with element1, element2, and element3 as its only elements.

Expression	Result
OrderedCollection with: 1 with: 2 with: 3	anOrderedCollection: 1 2 3

with: element1 with: element2 with: element3 with: element4
Answer a new collection with element1, element2, element3, and element4 as its only elements

Expression	Result
Bag with: 1 with: 2 with: 3 with: 2	aBag: 1:1 2:2 1:3

Instance Interface

add: anObject
Add anObject to the receiver; answer anObject.

Value of a	Expression	Result in a	Answer
aSet: 1 2 3 4	a add: 5	aSet: 1 2 3 4 5	5

addAll: aCollection
Add all of the elements in aCollection to the receiver; answer aCollection.

Value of a	Expression	Result in a	Answer
aSet: 1 2 3 4	a addAll: #(4 5 6)	aSet: 1 2 3 4 5 6	#(4 5 6)

asArray
Answer a new array whose elements are the elements of the receiver.

Value of a	Expression	Result
aSortedCollection: 2 5 8 12	a asArray	anArray: 2 5 8 12

asBag

Answer a new bag whose elements are the elements of the receiver.

Value of a	Expression	Result
anArray: 5 1 6 1 1 5	a asBag	aBag: 2:5 3:1 1:6

Caution: Conversion of a collection with some kind of ordering, such as a SortedCollection or Array, to a bag may appear to impose that same ordering on the bag when iterated over. Such ordering is platform and release dependent.

asByteArray

Answer a new byte array whose elements are the elements of the receiver. The receiver's elements must be integers in the range 0 to 255.

Value of a	Expression	Result
anArray: 2 5 8 96 255	a asByteArray	aByteArray: 2 5 8 96 255
aString: 'AB12'	a asByteArray	aByteArray: 65 66 49 50

asOrderedCollection

Answer a new ordered collection whose elements are the elements of the receiver.

Value of a	Expression	Result
anArray: 2 5 8 12	a asOrderedCollection	anOrderedCollection: 2 5 8 12

asSet

Answer a new set whose elements are the elements of the receiver.

Value of a	Expression	Result
anArray: 5 1 6 1 1 5	a asSet	aSet: 5 1 6

Caution: Conversion of a collection with some kind of ordering, such as a SortedCollection or Array, to a set may appear to impose that same ordering on the set when iterated over. Such ordering is platform and release dependant.

asSortedCollection

Answer a new sorted collection whose elements are the elements of the receiver. The collection is sorted by the default sort block:

        [:a :b | a < b]

Value of a	Expression	Result
anArray: 9 2 6 1	a asSortedCollection	aSortedCollection: 1 2 6 9

asSortedCollection: aSortBlock

Answer a new sorted collection whose elements are the elements of the receiver. Use aSortBlock for ordering of elements.

Value of a	Expression	Result
anArray: 9 2 6 1	a asSortedCollection: [:j :k	j > k]	aSortedCollection: 9 6 2 1

collect: aBlock

Answer a new collection of the same size and class as the receiver. The new collection contains one new value for each element in the receiver. The elements are obtained by invoking aBlock, passing each element of the receiver once, in the order of do:, and then inserting the value into the new collection using add:.

Value of a	Expression	Result
anArray: 2 4 6 8 10	a collect: [:e	e + 1]	anArray: 3 5 7 9 11

conform: aBlock

Answer true if aBlock returns true for each element in the receiver; answer false otherwise.

Value of a	Expression	Result
anArray: 2 4 6 9	a conform: [:e	e even]	false
'abcdef'	a conform: [:e	e isLowercase]	true

copy

Answer a new collection of the same size and class as the receiver, and holding the same contents. The new collection is a copy of the collection, but does not hold a copy of each element in the receiver.

For detailed information on copying, see Chapter 9, 'Memory, Pointers, and Copying', on page 111.

detect: aBlock

Answer the first element for which aBlock returns true. Raise an error if no element produces true.

Value of a	Expression	Result
anArray: 2 4 5 6 9	a detect: [:e	e odd]	5
'el Toro'	a detect: [:e	e isUppercase]	$T

detect: aBlock ifNone: errorBlock

Answer the first element for which aBlock returns true. Execute errorBlock if no element produces true.

Value of a	Expression	Result
anArray: 2 4 6 8	a detect: [:e	e odd] ifNone: [1]	1
aString: 'abcdef'	a detect: [:e	e isUppercase] ifNone: [nil]	nil

do: aBlock

Invoke aBlock once for each element in the receiver, passing the element to aBlock.

Value of a	Expression	Value of sum
anArray: 2 4 6 8	sum := 0. a do: [:e	sum := sum + e]	20

includes: anObject

Answer true if the receiver contains anObject; answer false otherwise.

Value of a	Expression	Result
anArray: 2 4 6 8	a includes: 6	true

inject: initialValue into: aBlock

Evaluate aBlock once for each element in the receiver, passing two values to the block. In the first invocation, pass initialValue and the first element of the receiver; in each successive invocation, pass the result of the previous invocation and the next element of the receiver. Answer the result of the last evaluation of aBlock.

Value of a	Expression	Result
anArray: 2 4 6 8	a inject: 0 into: [:v :e	v + e]	20

The example above sums the elements in the array. The steps are shown in the table below.

Iteration	v	e	Returned value (v+e); becomes next v
1	0	2	2
2	2	4	6
3	6	6	12
4	12	8	20 (the final value; becomes block result)

Take the product of a series of numbers using inject:.

```
" Calculate 10 factorial using inject: "
^ (1 to: 10)
    inject: 1
    into: [ :inj :ele | inj * ele ]
" Answer: 3628800 "
```

While inject:into: is often used for summing as shown above, it can be used for other purposes. In Example 278, the injected value is an ordered collection. A new term in the Fibonacci series is formed by taking the previous two terms and adding them; the series is initialized with two 1's.

```
" Fibonacci using inject:into: "
| nterms |
nterms := 10.
^ (3 to: nterms)
    inject: (OrderedCollection with: 1 with: 1)
    into: [ :inj :n |
        inj addLast: ( ( inj at: n - 2) + (inj at: n - 1) ); yourself ].
" Result: 1 1 2 3 5 8 13 21 34 55 "
```
Example 278, Display

Example 279 finds the longest word in a string.

```
" Find the longest word in a string with subStrings and inject:into: "
| str |
str := 'which word is the longest of them all?'.
^ str subStrings              " Break into words at white space "
    inject: 0
    into: [ :count :elem | count max: elem size ]
" Answers: 7 "
```
Example 279, Display

isEmpty
Answer true if the receiving collection is empty; answer false otherwise.

Value of a	Expression	Result
aSet: 2 4 6 8	a isEmpty	false
#()	a isEmpty	true

notEmpty
Answer true if the receiving collection is not empty; answer false otherwise.

Value of a	Expression	Result
aSet: 2 4 6 8	a notEmpty	true
#()	a notEmpty	false

occurrencesOf: anObject
Answer the number of occurrences of anObject in the receiver.

Value of a	Expression	Result
anArray: 2 6 4 9 3 6	a occurrencesOf: 6	2
anArray: 2 6 4 9 3 6	a occurrencesOf: 1	0
aBag: 3 3 3 9 9 9 9 11 11	a occurrencesOf: 9	4

reject: aBlock
Answer a new collection of the same class as the receiver that contains those elements of the receiver that cause aBlock to return false.

See also: select:.

Value of a	Expression	Result
anArray: 1 2 3 4 5	a reject: [:e	e even]	anArray: 1 3 5

remove: anObject
Remove anObject from the receiver, using equal (=) for comparison; answer anObject. If anObject is not found, report an error.

Value of a	Expression	Result in a	Answer
anArray: 1 2 3 4 5	a remove: 3	1 2 4 5	3
anArray: 1 2 3 4 5	a remove: 6	1 2 3 4 5	An error

remove: anObject ifAbsent: aBlock
Remove anObject from the receiver, using equal (=) for comparison; answer anObject. If anObject is not found, return the result of evaluating aBlock.

Value of a	Expression	Result in a	Answer
anArray: 1 2 3 4 5	a remove: 3 ifAbsent: [0]	1 2 4 5	3
anArray: 1 2 3 4 5	a remove: 6 ifAbsent: [self error: 'Whoops!']	1 2 3 4 5	Issues error

removeAll: aCollection
Remove all elements in aCollection from the receiver, using equal (=) for comparison. It is an error if an element in aCollection is not found in the receiver.

Value of a	Expression	Result
anArray: 1 2 3 4 5	a removeAll: #(3 4)	anArray: 1 2 5

select: aBlock
Return a new collection of the same class as the receiver that contains those elements of the receiver that cause aBlock to return true.

Value of a	Expression	Result
anArray: 1 2 3 4 5	a select: [:e	e even]	anArray: 2 4

The following example selects from some collection of an employee object.

    allEmployees select: [:e | e salary < 30000].

See also: reject:

size
Return the number of elements in the receiver.

For collections such as bags and ordered collections, that can have elements added, size returns the number of elements actually present, not the number of potential elements.

For collections such as arrays and strings, that have a fixed size and to which new elements cannot be added, size returns the actual size of the collection (which *is* the number of elements).

Value of a	*Expression*	*Result*
a := OrderedCollection new: 20	a size	0
a := Array new: 20	a size	20

Class Bag

Class Bag is a concrete collection class. Bags are unordered collections of any kind of object; duplicate entries are allowed.

Class	*Page*
Collection	313
Bag	320
Dictionary	321
IdentityDictionary	328
SequenceableCollection	340
...	
Set	329

Class Method Summary

There are no new class methods.

Instance Method Summary

See Collection for a summary of all other methods of Bag.

Method	*Implemented*	*See page*
add: anObject withOccurrences: count	Bag	320

Instance Interface

add: anObject withOccurrences: count
Add anObject to the receiver with count occurrences. Answer anObject.

Value of a	*Expression*	*Result in a*	*Answer*
aBag: 1 1 3 3	a add: 7 withOccurrences: 3	aBag: 1 1 3 3 7 7 7	7

Class Dictionary

Class Dictionary is a concrete collection class whose elements are instances of class Association, which have key/value pairs. Values are accessed only by the key value. Only one key/value pair with the same key (as compared with =) can exist in a dictionary.

Class	Page
Collection	*313*
Bag	320
Dictionary	**321**
IdentityDictionary	
SequenceableCollection	*340*
...	
Set	329

Class Method Summary

Method	Documented	See page
new	Collection class	315
new: count	Collection class	315
with: element1	Collection class	315
with: element1 　with: element2	Collection class	315
with: element1 　with: element2 　with: element3	Collection class	315
with: element1 　with: element2 　with: element3 　with: element4	Collection class	315

Instance Method Summary

Method	Documented	See page
=	Object	289
==	Object	289
add: anAssociation	Dictionary Collection	323 315
addAll: aCollection	Dictionary Collection	323 315
asArray	Dictionary Collection	323 315
asBag	Dictionary Collection	323 316
asByteArray	Dictionary Collection	323 316
asOrderedCollection	Dictionary Collection	323 316
asSet	Dictionary Collection	323 316
associationAt: key	Dictionary	323
associationAt: key 　ifAbsent: aBlock	Dictionary	324
associationsDo: aBlock	Dictionary	324

Part 1 of 2.

Method	Documented	See page
asSortedCollection	Dictionary Collection	324 316
asSortedCollection: aSortBlock	Dictionary Collection	324 316
at: key	Dictionary	324
at: key ifAbsent: aBlock	Dictionary	324
at: key ifAbsentPut: value	Dictionary	325
at: key ifPresent: block	Dictionary	325
at: key put: value	Dictionary	325
collect: aBlock	Dictionary Collection	325 316
conform: aBlock	Dictionary Collection	325 317
detect: aBlock	Dictionary Collection	325 317
detect: aBlock ifNone: errorBlock	Dictionary Collection	325 317
do: aBlock	Dictionary Collection	325 317
includes: anObject	Dictionary Collection	326 317
includesKey: key	Dictionary	326
inject: anObject into: aBlock	Dictionary Collection	326 317
isEmpty	Collection	318
keyAtValue: anObject	Dictionary	326
keyAtValue: anObject ifAbsent: aBlock	Dictionary	326
keys	Dictionary	326
keysDo: aBlock	Dictionary	326
notEmpty	Collection	318
occurrencesOf: anObject	Dictionary Collection	327 319
reject: aBlock	Dictionary Collection	327 319
~~remove: anObject~~	Collection	319
~~removeAll: aCollection~~	Collection	319
removeAllKeys: aCollection	Dictionary	327
removeAllKeys: aCollection ifAbsent: aOneParameterBlock	Dictionary	327
removeKey: key	Dictionary	327
removeKey: key ifAbsent: aBlock	Dictionary	328
~~remove: anObject ifAbsent: aBlock~~	Collection	319
select: aBlock	Dictionary Collection	328 319
size	Collection Object	319 295
values	Dictionary	328

Part 2 of 2.

Instance Interface

add: anAssociation
Add anAssociation to the receiver; return anAssociation.

Value of a	Value of b	Expression	Result in a	Answer
aDictionary: #a:2 #b:3	anAssociation: #c:4	a add: b	aDictionary: #a:2 #b:3 #c:4	anAssociation: #c:4

addAll: aDictionary
Add all of the key/value pairs in aDictionary to the receiver. Answer aDictionary.

Value of a	Value of b	Expression	Result in a	Answer
aDictionary: #x:2 #y:3	aDictionary: #e:6 #f:7	a addAll: b	aDictionary: #x:2 #y:3 #e:6 #f:7	aDictionary: #e:6 #f:7

asArray
Answer a new array whose elements are the values of the key/value pairs in the receiver.

Value of a	Expression	Result
aDictionary: #a:4 #b:2 #c:9	a asArray	anArray: 4 2 9

asBag
Answer a new bag whose elements are the values of the key/value pairs in the receiver.

Value of a	Expression	Result
aDictionary: #a:4 #b:2 #c:9	a asBag	aBag: 4 9 2

asByteArray
Answer a new byte array whose elements are the values of the key/value pairs of the receiver. The values must be integers in the range 0 to 255.

Value of a	Expression	Result
aDictionary: #a:4 #b:2 #c:9	a asByteArray	aByteArray: 4 2 9

asOrderedCollection
Answer a new ordered collection whose elements are the values of the key/value pairs of the receiver.

Value of a	Expression	Result
aDictionary: #a:4 #b:2 #c:9	a asOrderedCollection	anOrderedCollection: 4 2 9

asSet
Answer a new set whose elements are the values of the key/value pairs of the receiver.

Value of a	Expression	Result
aDictionary: #a:4 #b:2 #c:9	a asSet	aSet: 4 2 9

associationAt: key
Answer the association in the receiver which has the key key. It is an error if the key is not in the receiver.

Value of a	Expression	Result
aDictionary: #a:2 #b:3	a associationAt: #b	anAssociation: #b:3

associationAt: key ifAbsent: aBlock

Answer the association in the receiver which has the key key. If there is no such association, answer the result of evaluating aBlock.

Value of a	Expression	Result
aDictionary: #a:2 #b:3	a associationAt: #b ifAbsent: [nil]	anAssociation: #b:3
aDictionary: #a:2 #b:3	a associationAt: #x ifAbsent: [nil]	nil

associationsDo: aBlock

Evaluate aBlock with each association in the receiver. Answer the receiver.

See also: do:, keysDo:.

Value of a	Value of b	Expression	Result in b
aDictionary: #a:2 #b:3 #c:4 #d:5	aDictionary: (empty)	a associationsDo: [:a | a value even ifTrue: [b add: a]]	aDictionary: #a:2 #c:4

asSortedCollection

Answer a new sorted collection whose elements are the values of the key/value pairs of the receiver. Use the default sort block:

    [:a :b \| a < b]

(A sort block is a two-parameter block that returns true if the first argument is in the correct sort order with respect to the second.)

Value of a	Expression	Result
aDictionary: #a:4 #b:2 #c:9	a asSortedCollection	aSortedCollection: 2 4 9

asSortedCollection: aSortBlock

Answer a new sorted collection whose elements are the values of the key/value pairs of the receiver. Use aSortBlock for the ordering of elements. (A sort block is a two-parameter block that returns true if the first argument is in the correct sort order with respect to the second.)

Value of a	Expression	Result
aDictionary: #a:4 #b:2 #c:9	a asSortedCollection: [:j :k | j > k]	aSortedCollection: 9 4 2

at: key

Answer the value in the receiver that is associated with key. It is an error if the key is missing from the receiver.

Value of a	Expression	Result
aDictionary: #a:2 #b:3	a at: #b	3
aDictionary: #a:2 #b:3	a at: #x	An error

at: key ifAbsent: aBlock

Answer the value in the receiver that is associated with key. If the key is missing from the receiver, answer the value obtained by evaluating aBlock.

Value of a	Expression	Result in a	Answer
aDictionary: #z:2	a at: #b ifAbsent: [nil]	aDictionary: #z:2	nil
aDictionary: #z:2	a at: #b ifAbsent: [a at: #b put: 6]	aDictionary: #z:2 #b:6	6
aDictionary: #z:2 #b:3	a at: #b ifAbsent: [a at: #b put: 6]	aDictionary: #z:2 #b:3	3

at: key ifAbsentPut: anObject

Answer the value in the receiver that is associated with key. If the key is missing from the receiver then add anObject at key and answer anObject

Value of a	Expression	Result in a	Answer
aDictionary: #a:2 #b:3	a at: #b ifAbsentPut: 0	aDictionary: #a:2 #b:3	3
aDictionary: #a:2 #b:3	a at: #c ifAbsentPut: 6	aDictionary: #a:2 #b:3 #c:6	6
aDictionary: #a:2 #b:3	a at: #b ifAbsentPut: 6	aDictionary: #a:2 #b:3 #c:6	3

(Compare the last two examples with the last two examples of at:ifAbsent: just above.)

at: key ifPresent: aBlock

If the key is present in the receiver, answer the value obtained by evaluating the one-parameter block aBlock; else answer nil.

Value of a	Expression
aDictionary: #a:2 #b:3	a at: #b ifPresent: [:value l dict removeKey: #b]
aDictionary: #a:2 #b:3	a at: #b ifPresent: [:value l result := result + value]

at: key put: anObject

If key is missing from the receiver add a new association with key and anObject as the key/value pair. If key is present in the receiver, change the associated value to anObject. Answer anObject

Value of a	Expression	Result in a	Answer
aDictionary: #a:2 #b:3	a at: #b put: 4	aDictionary: #a:2 #b:4	4
aDictionary: #a:2 #b:3	a at: #c put: 6	aDictionary: #a:2 #b:3 #c:6	6

collect: aBlock

Answer a new dictionary of the same size as the receiver. The new dictionary contains one new key/value pair for each key/value pair in the receiver. The new values are obtained by invoking aBlock, passing each value of the receiver once, in the order of do:.

Value of a	Expression	Result
aDictionary: #x:3 #y:4	a collect: [:e l e + 1]	aDictionary: #x:4 #y:5

detect: aBlock

Answer the first value for which aBlock returns true; the block is passed the value part of the association. Raise an error if no element produces true.

Value of a	Expression	Result
aDictionary: #a:2 #b:3 #c:9	a detect: [:e l e odd]	3

detect: aBlock ifNone: errorBlock

Answer the first value for which aBlock returns true; the block is passed the value part of the association. Execute errorBlock if no element produces true.

do: aBlock

Invoke aBlock once for each key/value pair in the receiver, passing the value part to aBlock.

See also: associationDo:, keysDo:.

includes: anObject

Answer true if the receiver contains a key/value pair with a value part equal to anObject; answer false otherwise.

Value of a	Expression	Result
aDictionary: #a:2 #b:3 #c:9	a includes: 3	true

includesKey: key

Answer true if the receiver contains a key/value pair with a key of key; answer false otherwise.

Value of a	Expression	Result
aDictionary: #a:2 #b:3	a includesKey: #b	true

inject: initialValue into: aBlock

Evaluate aBlock once for each element in the receiver, passing two values to the block. In the first invocation, pass initialValue and the value part of the first key/value pair; in each successive invocation, pass the result of the previous invocation and the value part of the next key/value pair in the dictionary. Answer the result of the last evaluation of aBlock.

Caution: Dictionaries are optimized for indexing by keys; searching for values can be slow.

For more examples, see inject:into: on page 317.

Value of a	Expression	Result
aDictionary: #a:2 #b:3 #c:9	a inject: 0 into: [:v :e	v + e]	14

keyAtValue: anObject

Answer the key from the first key/value pair found in the receiver with a value of anObject. It is an error if the value is missing from the receiver.

Value of a	Expression	Result
aDictionary: #a:2 #b:3	a keyAtValue: 3	#b
aDictionary: #a:2 #b:3	a keyAtValue: 13	An error

keyAtValue: anObject ifAbsent: aBlock

Answer the key from the first key/value pair found in the receiver with a value of anObject. If not found, answer the value obtained by evaluating aBlock.

Caution: Dictionaries are optimized for indexing by keys; searching for values can be slow.

Value of a	Expression	Result
aDictionary: #a:2 #b:3	a keyAtValue: #b ifAbsent: [nil]	3
aDictionary: #a:2 #b:3	a keyAtValue: #c ifAbsent: [nil]	nil

keys

Answer a set containing the keys in the receiver.

See also: values

Value of a	Expression	Result
aDictionary: #a:2 #b:3	a keys	aCollection: #a #b

keysDo: aBlock

For each key in the receiver, evaluate aBlock. Answer the receiver.

See also: associationsDo:, do:.

Value of a	Value of b	Expression	Result in b
aDictionary: #a:2 #b:3 #c:7	aSortedCollection: (empty)	a keysDo: [:e | b add: e]	aSortedCollection: #a #b #c

If an ordered result is needed, it is necessary to sort the keys explicitly, since no assumptions can be made about the ordering of keys in a dictionary, nor of the ordering of keys passed by keysDo:.

occurrencesOf: anObject
Answer the number of occurrences of anObject in the values of the key/value pairs in the receiver.

Value of a	Expression	Result
aDictionary: #a:2 #b:3 #c:2	a occurrencesOf: 2	2

reject: aBlock
Answer a new dictionary that contains those associations whose values cause aBlock to return false.

See also: select:.

Value of a	Expression	Result
aDictionary: x:3 y:4 z:9	a reject: [:e | e even]	aDictionary: x:3 z:9

removeAllKeys: aCollection
For each element in aCollection that is a key in the receiver, remove the corresponding key/value pairs from the receiver. If aCollection contains values that are not keys in the receiver, or contains duplicate keys, raise an error.

Caution: Removal occurs one key at a time; if a key is missing or duplicated, execution stops at that point with possibly only part of the keys removed.

Value of a	Expression	Result
aDictionary: #a:2 #b:3 #c:6 #d:9	a removeAllKeys: #(a c)	aDictionary: #b:3 #d:9

removeAllKeys: aCollection ifAbsent: aOneParameterBlock
For each element in aCollection that is a key in the receiver, remove the corresponding key/value pairs from the receiver. If aCollection contains values which are not keys in the receiver, or contains duplicate keys, invoke the one parameter block for each.

Value of a	Expression	Result
aDictionary: #a:2 #b:3 #c:6 #d:9	a removeAllKeys: #(f a q c) ifAbsent: [:key | Transcript cr; show: 'Key missing: ', key printString]	aDictionary: #b:3 #d:9

The example will write two messages to the Transcript.

removeKey: aKey
Remove the key/value pair from the receiver that has the key aKey; answer the value. If aKey is not in the receiver, raise an error.

Value of a	Expression	Result in a	Answer
aDictionary: #a:2 #b:3 #c:6 #d:9	a removeKey: #c	aDictionary: #a:2#b:3 #d:9	6

removeKey: aKey ifAbsent: aBlock

Remove the key/value pair from the receiver that has the key aKey. If aKey is not in the receiver, evaluate aBlock.

Value of a	Expression	Result in a	Answer

aDictionary:
  #a:2 #b:3 #c:6 #d:9
	a removeKey: #c
	  ifAbsent: [ ]
		aDictionary:
		  #a:2#b:3 #d:9
			6

select: aBlock

Answer a new dictionary that contains those key/value pairs whose values cause aBlock to return true.

See also: reject:.

Value of a	Expression	Result
aDictionary: x:3 y:4 z: 9	a select: [:e	e odd]	aDictionary: x:3 z: 9

values

Return a collection holding the values of the key/value pairs in the receiver.

See also: keys.

Value of a	Expression	Result
aDictionary: #a:2 #b:3	a values	aCollection: 2 3

Class IdentityDictionary

Class IdentityDictionary is a concrete collection class whose elements are instances of class Association, which have key/value pairs. Values are accessed only by the key value. Only one key/value pair with the same key (as compared with ==) can exist in a dictionary.

Class Method Summary

There are no new public class methods.

Instance Method Summary

There are no new public instance methods. Inherited methods differ only in that comparisons for keys are performed with == rather than =. Multiple keys with the same value (using =) can exist in the dictionary.

Class Set

Class Set is a concrete collection class. Sets are unordered collections of any kind of object; only one of any given object is allowed in a set.

Class Method Summary

There are no new class methods.

Instance Method Summary

There are no new instance methods.

28

Collections: Sequenceable

SequenceableCollection is an abstract superclass of a group of collection classes that have an enforced internal orderings. All concrete subclasses can be indexed by integers; some enforce special orderings and some hold specialized kinds of objects.

The sequenceable collection classes are:

Kinds of Sequenceable Collections

All sequenceable collections can be indexed by positive integers. Indexes must not exceed the collection bounds; attempts to do so raise an error. Figure 78 summarizes sequenceable collections.

Class	Size	Ordering	Holds	Size answers	Note
Array	Fixed	Index	Any object	max size	
ByteArray	Fixed	Index	Integers: 0-255	max size	
Interval	None	Index	Calculated sequence	element count	Cannot set elements
OrderedCollection	Variable	Index	Any object	elements added	
SortedCollection	Variable	Internal	Any object	elements added	Sorted elements
String	Fixed	Index	Characters	max size	
Symbol	Fixed	Index	Characters	max size	

Figure 78: Comparison of **SequenceableCollection** Subclasses.

Additive Sequenceable Collections

AdditiveSequenceableCollection is the abstract parent class of indexable collection classes that can grow or shrink. Elements can be added, inserted, and removed as needed. Elements can be any object. The size of additive sequenceable collections is the count of the number of elements currently in the collection and not the number of room for elements. Thus, there are no uninitialized elements.

Ordered Collections

OrderedCollection is probably the most used of all collection classes except String. It's instances are indexable and are often used in place of arrays, since the maximum size does not have to be known at allocation time.

Elements can be inserted and deleted anywhere in the collection. Since elements can be added at the front and back, and removed from the front and back, ordered collections can be used as queues and stacks. Elements can be any object.

Sorted Collections

A SortedCollection can grow as elements are added. The elements are maintained in a sorted order. Elements can be any object provided they respond to the < message with a boolean, or an appropriate custom sort block is provided to indicate how elements should be ordered. Elements can be inserted and deleted.

Arrayed Collections

ArrayedCollection is the abstract parent class of collection classes that are indexable but that cannot grow or shrink; the maximum size of the collection must be known at allocation time. Elements cannot be inserted or deleted.

Arrays

Arrays have a fixed number of elements. Elements can be any object. Elements have an initial value of nil.

Byte Arrays

Byte arrays have a fixed number of elements. Elements can be any integer in the range 0 to 255. Elements have an initial value of zero.

Strings

Strings have a fixed number of elements. Elements can be any character with an internal value from 0 to 255. Elements have an initial value of Character value: 0.

Symbols

Symbols have a fixed number of elements. Elements can be any character with an internal value from 0 to 255.

It is guaranteed that any two symbols with the same value are also the same object. That is, if symbol1 = symbol2 then it always follows that symbol1 == symbol2. Symbols are identity objects.

Note: The comparison of symbols using == is quite fast, and is independent of the length of the symbol, since all that has to be compared is two object pointers, not two strings. It is as fast to use symbols as flags as it is to use numbers or booleans.

Caution: Symbols are typically used as keys into dictionaries and as names of methods. They should not be used for general-purpose strings. Symbols are remembered by the system. Using an excessive number of symbols can possibly cause the collection of remembered symbols to grow large. While details are release and platform dependent, it is best if symbols are only used where they are required.

Intervals

Intervals are collections that have computed values; they cannot be stored into. They represent values in some range of numbers such as all integers from 3 to 32 or all numbers from 1.0 to 10.0 in steps of 0.2. They are typically created by messages sent to integers, such as (1 to: 10) or (10 to: 100 by: 5).

Categories of Messages

Instance messages to sequenceable collections can be categorized into access, conversion, copying, iteration, replacement, searching, sorting, and testing. Methods shown in italics are inherited from Collection.

Access

Access methods in Collection are concerned with adding and removing objects in ways that do not specify positions or organization of the collection; in SequenceableCollection, access methods directly index elements of the collection.

add:	*Add an object*
addAll:	*Add objects in a collection*
at:	Answer element at index
at:Put:	Replace element at index
atAll:put:	Replace elements at indexes
atAllPut:	Replace all elements
first	Answer the first element
last	Answer the last element
remove:	*Remove an object*
remove:ifAbsent:	*Remove an object*
removeAll:	*Remove objects in a collection*

AdditiveSequenceableCollection, the parent of OrderedCollection and SortedCollection, adds:

after:	Answer the object after another
before:	Answer the object before another
removeAtIndex:	Remove the element at the index
removeFirst	Remove first element
removeLast	Remove last element

OrderedCollection adds:

add:after:	Add an element after another
add:afterIndex:	Add an element after an index
add:before:	Add an element before another
add:beforeIndex:	Add an element before an index
addAllFirst:	Add a collection at the front
addAllLast:	Add a collection at the back
addFirst:	Add an element at the front
addLast:	Add an element at the back

SortedCollection adds and removes:

~~at:Put:~~	Cannot change element at indexed point
~~atAll:put:~~	Cannot change elements at indexed points
~~atAllPut:~~	Cannot change all elements
~~replaceFrom:to:with:~~	Cannot replace elements
~~replaceFrom:to:withObject:~~	Cannot replace elements
~~replaceFrom:to:with: startingAt:~~	Cannot replace elements
sortBlock	Answer the sort block
sortBlock:	Set a new sort block

ArrayedCollection, the parent of Array, String and others, removes:

~~add:~~	Cannot add to fixed-size collection
~~addAll:~~	Cannot add to fixed-size collection

ByteArray adds:

byteAt:	Answer the byte at an index
byteAt:put:	Replace the byte at an index

Symbol removes:

~~at:put:~~	Cannot modify symbols
~~atAllPut:~~	Cannot modify symbols
~~atAll:put:~~	Cannot modify symbols

Conversion

Conversion operations convert collections to other collections, or to other values. (Remember that method names in italics are inherited from Collection).

asArray	*Convert to an array*
asBag	*Convert to a bag*
asByteArray	*Convert to a byte array*
asOrderedCollection	*Convert to an ordered collection*
asSet	*Convert to a set*
asSortedCollection	*Convert to a sorted collection*
asSortedCollection:	*Convert to a sorted collection, with sort block*

String adds:

asGlobalKey	Return key appropriate for global names
asLowercase	Convert upper-case to lower-case
asNumber	Convert a string of digits to an integer
asPoolKey	Return key appropriate for pool dictionary
asString	Answer the receiver
asSymbol	Convert to a symbol
asUppercase	Convert lower case letters to upper case

Copying

Copying creates a new instance that holds a copy of part or all of the receiver.

copy	*Whole collection*
copyFrom:to:	A subcollection
copyReplacingAll:with:	Substitution of subcollections
copyReplaceFrom:to:with:	Indexed substitution of a subcollection
copyReplaceFrom:to:withObject:	Indexed substitution of an element
copyReplacing:withObject:	One element replaces another
copyWith:	Add an object at the end
copyWithout:	Without a given element
reverse	All the elements reversed
, (comma)	Concatenate collections

String adds:

addLineDelimiters	Change backslash to line delimiters
subStrings	Break string up at white space
subStrings:	Break string up at specified character
trimBlanks	Remove leading and trailing blanks
trimSeparators	Remove leading and trailing white space

Iteration

All iteration methods pass each element of a collection to a block. Some build new collections from the results of the block invocations. (Method names in italics are inherited from Collection).

collect:	*A new collection, same size, new elements*
conform:	*Test each element*
detect:	*Answer first element for which a block is true*
detect:ifNone:	*As in detect: but traps error if none found*
do:	*Iteration across collection*
inject:into:	*Used for summing, products, etc.*
reject:	*New collection of elements failing a test*
reverseDo:	Iterate across collection backwards
with:do:	Iterate through two collections at once
select:	*New collection of elements passing a test*

Replacement

Replacement methods change groups of elements in the receiver.

replaceFrom:to:with:	Replace elements in indexed range
replaceFrom:to:with:startingAt:	Replace elements in indexed range
replaceFrom:to:withObject:	Replace elements in indexed range

SortedCollection removes:

~~replaceFrom:to:with:~~	Cannot replace elements in indexed range
~~replaceFrom:to:with:startingAt:~~	Cannot replace elements in indexed range
~~replaceFrom:to:withObject:~~	Cannot replace elements in indexed range

String adds:

bindWith:	Replace %1 in string with parameter
bindWith:with:	Replace %1 and %2 in string
bindWith:with:with:	Replace %1, %2, and %3 in string
bindWith:with:with:with:	Replace %1, %2, %3, and %4 in string
bindWithArguments:	Replace %1 to %n with arguments

ByteArray removes:

~~replaceFrom:to:withObject:~~	Cannot put general objects into a byte array

Searching

Searching methods return indexes of values or collections in the collection.

findFirst:	First index for which a block answers true
findLast:	Last index for which a block answers true
indexOf:	First index of a value (or error)
indexOf:ifAbsent:	First index of a value (or block result)
indexOfSubcollection:startingAt:	First index of subcollection (or error)
indexOfSubcollection: startingAt:ifAbsent:	First index of subcollection (or block result)

String adds:

indexOf:matchCase:startingAt:	Wild card string search
match:	Wild card string matching

Sorting

SortedCollection adds:

sortBlock	Answer the sort block
sortBlock:	Set the sort block

Testing

Testing methods can detect the presence of an element in a collection, determine how many of a given element are present, and test for emptiness and size.

=	*Compare elements of collection for equality*
==	*Compare collections for identity*
~=	*Compare elements of collection for inequality*
~~	*Compare collections for non-identity*
conform:	*Test each element*
detect:	*Answer first element for which block is true*
detect:ifNone:	*As in detect: but traps error if none found*
includes:	*Is a given element present?*
isEmpty	*Is the collection empty?*
notEmpty	*Is the collection not empty?*
occurrencesOf:	*How many of a given element are present?*
size	*How many elements in the collection?*

Interval adds:			
	increment		Answer the increment
Symbol adds:			
	argumentCount		Answer the number of colons
String adds:			
	sameAs:		Test strings for equality

Array Constants

Figure 79 shows the elements allowed in array constants, and the result they produce.

Constant	Notes	Examples	
		In array constant	As if written
Number	Integer	23	23
	Float	2.3e1	2.3e1
Character	All	$2	$2
String	All	'birthday cake'	'birthday cake'
Symbol	As a name	Richard	#'Richard'
	As a symbol	#Feynman	#'Feynman'
	As a quoted symbol	#'Lives'	#'Lives'
Array	As parenthesized list	(2 $r 4)	#(2 $r 4)
	As array constant	#(2 $r 4)	#(2 $r 4)
Byte array	As bracketed list	[2 3 4]	#[2 3 4]
	As byte array constant	#[2 3 4]	#[2 3 4]
Special characters: @ % & * - + =	\ < , > ? / ~	One at a time	@	#@
		%	#%
		&	#&
		*	#*
		-	#-
		+	#+
		=	#=
				#|
		\	#\
		<	#<
		,	#,
		>	#>
		?	#?
		/	#/
		~	#~
	Two or more at a time become groups of no more than two	+++	#++ #+
		///*	#// #/*
	Breaks up groups of letters or numbers	abc,def	#abc #, #def
		2+3	2 #+ 3

Figure 79: Elements Allowed in Array Constants.

Collections Returned

Figure 80 summarizes the class of instances answered by various messages. Entries in the table give the class of the answer returned by the messages listed down the left side, when sent to instances of the classes listed along the top. For example, the collect: message sent to an instance of class SortedCollection answers an instance of class OrderedCollection.

Table entries are one of the following symbols.

Abbreviation	*Class of Result*
A	Array
Bag	Bag
BA	ByteArray
OC	OrderedCollection
Set	Set
SC	SortedCollection
Str	String

Message	*Array*	*Bag*	*ByteArray*	*Interval*	*Ordered Collection*	*Set*	*Sorted Collection*	*String*	*Symbol*
,	A	x	BA	A	OC	x	SC	Str	Str
collect:	A	Bag	BA	A	OC	Set	OC	Str	Str
copyFrom:to:	A	x	BA	A	OC	x	SC	Str	Str
copyReplacingAll:with:	A	x	BA	A	OC	x	SC	Str	Str
copyReplaceFrom:to:with:	A	x	BA	A	OC	x	SC	Str	Str
copyReplaceFrom:to:withObject:	A	x	BA	A	OC	x	SC	Str	Str
copyReplacing:withObject:	A	x	BA	A	OC	x	SC	Str	Str
copyWith:	A	x	BA	A	OC	x	SC	Str	Str
copyWithout:	A	x	BA	A	OC	x	SC	Str	Str
reject:	A	Bag	BA	A	OC	Set	SC	Str	Str
replaceFrom:to:with:	A	x	BA	x	OC	x	x	Str	x
replaceFrom:to:with:startingAt:	A	x	BA	x	OC	x	x	Str	x
replaceFrom:to:withObject:	A	x	BA	x	OC	x	x	Str	x
reverse	A	x	BA	A	OC	x	OC	Str	Str
select:	A	Bag	BA	A	OC	Set	SC	Str	Str

Figure 80: Collection Class Answered by Various Methods. Entries in the table indicate the class of the answered collection. An x indicates an impossible answer.

Protocol Summary

Class Protocol Summary

Object class					
new	new:				
Collection class					
with:	with:with:	with:with:with:	with:with:with:with:		
SequenceableCollection class					
AdditiveSequencableCollection class		**ArrayedCollection class**			**Interval class**
OrderedCollection class	**SortedCollection class**	**Array class**	**ByteArray class**	**String class**	from:to:
	sortBlock:			**Symbol class**	from:to:by:

Instance Protocol Summary

Object				
= == ~= ~~	copy	printOn:	printString	size

Collection				
add:	asOrderedCollection	conform:	inject:into:	remove:
addAll:	asSet	detect:	isEmpty	remove:ifAbsent:
asArray	asSortedCollection	detect:ifNone:	notEmpty	removeAll:
asBag	asSortedCollection:	do:	occurrencesOf:	select:
asByteArray	collect:	includes:	reject:	

Sequenceable Collection				
,	copyReplacingAll:with:	copyWithout:	indexOfSubCollection:	replaceFrom:to:
at:	copyReplaceFrom:to:with:	findFirst:	startingAt:	with:startingAt:
at:put:	copyReplaceFrom:	findLast:	indexOfSubCollection:	replaceFrom:to:withObject:
atAll:put:	to:withObject:	first	startingAt:ifAbsent:	reverse
atAllPut:	copyReplacing:withObject:	indexOf:	last	reverseDo:
copyFrom:to:	copyWith:	indexOf:ifAbsent:	replaceFrom:to:with:	with:do:

AdditiveSequenceableCollection		ArrayedCollection			Interval
after:	removeFirst	~~add:~~	~~remove:~~	~~removeAll:~~	increment
before:	removeLast	~~addAll:~~	~~remove: ifAbsent:~~		
removeAtIndex:					

OrderedCollection	SortedCollection	Array	ByteArray	String	Symbol
add:after:	~~at:put:~~	No new protocol	byteAt:	< <= > >=	argumentCount
add:afterIndex:	~~atAll:put:~~		byteAt:put:	addLineDelimiters	~~replaceFrom:to:with:~~
add:before:	~~atAllPut:~~		~~replaceFrom:~~	asGlobalKey	~~replaceFrom:to:withObject:~~
add:beforeIndex:	~~replaceFrom:to:~~		~~to:withObject:~~	asLowercase	~~replaceFrom:to:with:startingAt:~~
addAllFirst:	~~with:~~			asNumber	~~at:put:~~
addAllLast:	~~replaceFrom:to:~~			asPoolKey	~~atAll:put:~~
addFirst:	~~withObject:~~			asString	~~atAllPut:~~
addLast:	~~replaceFrom:to:~~			asSymbol	
~~at:put:~~	~~with:startingAt:~~			asUppercase	
~~atAll:put:~~	sortBlock			bindWith:	
	sortBlock:			bindWith:with	

String (additional column):
- bindWith:with:with:
- bindWith:with:with:with:
- bindWithArguments:
- indexOf:matchCase:startingAt:
- match:
- sameAs:
- subStrings
- subStrings:
- trimBlanks
- trimSeparators

Class SequenceableCollection

Class SequenceableCollection is an abstract class that defines protocol for collections that store elements in a sequence that can be indexed by an integer.

Class Method Summary

Method	*Documented*	*See page*
new: count	Collection class Object class	315 289
with: element1	Collection class	315
with: element1 with: element2	Collection class	315
with: element1 with: element2 with: element3	Collection class	315
with: element1 with: element2 with: element3 with: element4	Collection class	315

Instance Method Summary

Method	*Documented*	*See page*
, aCollection	SequenceableCollection	342
=	SequenceableCollection Object	342 289
==	Object	289
~=	SequenceableCollection Object	343 289
~~	Object	290
add: anObject	Collection	315
addAll: aCollection	Collection	315
asArray	Collection	315
asBag	Collection	316
asByteArray	Collection	316
asOrderedCollection	Collection	316
asSet	Collection	316
asSortedCollection	Collection	316
asSortedCollection: aSortBlock	Collection	316
at: anInteger	SequenceableCollection	343

Part 1 of 3.

Method	Documented	See page
at: anInteger put: anObject	SequenceableCollection	344
atAll: aCollection put: anObject	SequenceableCollection	344
atAllPut: anObject	SequenceableCollection	344
collect: aBlock	Collection	316
conform: aBlock	Collection	317
copyFrom: intFrom to: intTo	SequenceableCollection	344
copyReplaceAll: subcollection with: aCollection	SequenceableCollection	344

copyReplaceFrom: intFrom
  to: intTo
  with: aCollection
	SequenceableCollection	345

copyReplaceFrom: intFrom
  to: intTo
  withObject: anObject
	SequenceableCollection	346

copyReplacing: targetObject withObject: anObject	SequenceableCollection	346
copyWith: anObject	SequenceableCollection	346
copyWithout: anObject	SequenceableCollection	347
detect: aBlock	Collection	317
detect: aBlock ifNone: aBlock	Collection	317
do: aBlock	Collection	317
findFirst: anObject	SequenceableCollection	347
findLast: anObject	SequenceableCollection	347
first	SequenceableCollection	347
includes: anObject	Collection	317
indexOf: anObject	SequenceableCollection	347
indexOf: anObject ifAbsent: aBlock	SequenceableCollection	347
indexOfSubCollection: aSeqColl startingAt: anInteger	SequenceableCollection	348

indexOfSubCollection: aSeqColl
  startingAt: anInteger
  ifAbsent: aBlock
	SequenceableCollection	348

inject: anObject into: aBlock	Collection	317
isEmpty	Collection	318
last	SequenceableCollection	348
notEmpty	Collection	318
occurrencesOf: anObject	Collection	319
reject: aBlock	Collection	319
remove: anObject	Collection	319
remove: anObject ifAbsent: aBlock	Collection	319

Part 2 of 3.

Method	Documented	See page
removeAll: aCollection	Collection	319
replaceFrom: intFrom **to: intTo** **with: aCollection**	SequenceableCollection	348
replaceFrom: intFrom **to: intTo** **with: aCollection** **startingAt: intIndex**	SequenceableCollection	348
replaceFrom: intFrom **to: intTo** **withObject: anObject**	SequenceableCollection	349
reverse	SequenceableCollection	349
reverseDo: aBlock	SequenceableCollection	349
select: aBlock	Collection	319
size	Collection Object	319 295
with: otherCollection **do: aBlock**	SequenceableCollection	349

Part 3 of 3.

Instance Interface

, aSeqColl

Answer a new sequenceable collection of the same class as the receiver that contains, in their original order, the objects in the receiver followed by the objects in **aSeqColl** (which must be some kind of sequenceable collection).

The size of the new sequenceable collection is the size of the receiver plus the size of aSeqColl.

Caution: A common error involves concatenating a character to a string:

string := string, stream next   " Attempt to concat character from stream"

Instead, do this:

string := string, stream next **asString**

Value of a	Value of b	Expression	Result
#(1 4 19)	#(3 76 4)	a, b	anArray: 1 4 19 3 76 4
'The winner is'	'Susan'	a, ' ', b	'The winner is Susan'
#(1 3 5)	aSet: 8 3 9	a, b	Error: set not seq. collection

= anObject

Answer true if:

- The receiver and anObject are instances of the same class; and
- The receiver and anObject answer the same value from the size message; and
- The values in the receiver and the values in anObject at the same index have the same values, using equal (=) for comparison.

Answer false otherwise.

Value of a	Value of b	Expression	Result
#(1 4 19)	#(1 4 19)	a = b	true

Value of a	Value of b	Expression	Result
#(1 4 19)	#(1 4 29)	a = b	false
'A String'	'A String'	a = b	true

Since elements are compared (using =) for equality, elements that are collections are also compared for equality. Thus the following evaluates to true.

```
" Test equality of created array and an array constant "
| a b |
a := Array with: 2 with: 3.
b := Array with: 1 with: a with: 4.         "b printString would show: (1 (2 3) 4)"
^ b = #(1 (2 3) 4)    "Answers true"
```
Example 280, Display

The following evaluates to false.

```
" Test equality of created array and an array constant "
| a b |
a := Array with: 2 with: 3.
b := Array with: 1 with: a with: 4.         "b printString would show: (1 (2 3) 4)"
^ b = #(1 (2 5) 4)    "Answers false"
```
Example 281, Display

Caution: Since a collection can contain a collection, it is possible that a comparison might try to run forever.

```
" This: RUNS 'FOREVER' or overflows stack  "
| a b |
a := Array new: 1.
b := Array new: 1.
a at: 1 put: b.
b at: 1 put: a.
^ a = b
"When you get tired of waiting, press your system's halt key(s)"
```
Example 282, Execute

~= anObject

Answer false if:

- The receiver and anObject are not instances of the same class; or
- The receiver and anObject answer different values from the size message; or
- Any values in the receiver and in anObject, at the same index, have different values, using equal (=) for comparison

Answer false otherwise. See the = method for additional information.

Value of a	Value of b	Expression	Result
#(1 4 19)	#(1 4 19)	a ~= b	false
#(1 4 19)	#(1 4 7)	a ~= b	false
'A String'	'A String'	a ~= b	true

at: anInteger

Answer the element in the receiver at index anInteger. It is an error if anInteger is not a valid index into the receiver.

Value of a	Expression	Result
anArray: 1 2 3 4 5 6	a at: 3	3
'abcdefgh'	a at: 3	$c
#(1 (2 3) 4)	a at: 2	An array: (2 3)

at: anInteger put: anObject

Replace the element in the receiver at index anInteger with anObject; answer anObject. It is an error if anInteger is not a valid index into the receiver.

Note: String and array *constants* are read-only and cannot be modified.

Value of a	Expression	Result
anArray: 1 2 3 4 5 6	a at: 3 put: 33	anArray: 1 2 33 4 5 6
anOrderedCollection: 1 2 3 4 5	a at: 3 put: 33	anOrderedCollection: 1 2 33 4 5
aString: 'abcdefgh'	a at: 3 put: $C	aString: 'abCdefgh'
(none)	'abcd' at: 3 put: $C	Error; read-only constant

atAll: aCollection put: anObject

Replace the elements in the receiver at the indexes in aCollection with anObject; answer the receiver. It is an error if any indexes in aCollection are not valid indexes into the receiver; such an error may leave the receiver partly updated.

Value of a	Value of b	Expression	Result
anArray: 1 2 3 4 5 6	#(5 2)	a atAll: b put: 9	anArray: 1 9 3 4 9 6
aString: ' 23'	#(1 2 3)	a atAll: b put: $0	'00023'

atAllPut: anObject

Answer the receiver with all elements replaced by anObject.

Expression	Result
(Array new: 5) atAllPut: 0	anArray: 0 0 0 0 0
(String new: 6) atAllPut: $0	'000000'

copyFrom: intFrom to: intTo

Answer a new collection of the same class as the receiver that contains the elements of the receiver from index intFrom through index intTo. The element at intFrom in the receiver will be at index 1 in the result, the element at intFrom+1 will be at 2, etc. The size of the result will be:

$$0 \max: (intTo - intFrom + 1)$$

Value of a	Expression	Result
anArray: 1 2 3 4 5 6	a copyFrom: 2 to: 4	anArray: 2 3 4
anArray: 1 2 3 4 5 6	a copyFrom: 4 to: 3	an empty array
'abcdefghij'	a copyFrom: 1 to: 4	'abcd'
#copyFrom:to:	a copyFrom: 1 to: 9	'copyFrom:'

copyReplaceAll: subCollection with: aCollection

Answer a new collection of the same class as the receiver that contains the elements of the receiver in the same order, but replacing all occurrences of the elements in subCollection with the elements in aCollection. The size of the result is:

$$receiver\ size + (n * (aCollection\ size - subCollection\ size))$$

where n is the number of times subCollection is found and replaced.

Value of a	Expression	Result
anArray: 0 1 2 0 4 3	a copyReplaceAll: #(0) with: #()	anArray: 1 2 4 3
'a b c d e'	a copyReplaceAll: ' ' with: ''	'abcde'
'abcba'	a copyReplaceAll: 'b' with: 'xx'	'axxcxxa'

copyReplaceFrom: intFrom to: intTo with: aCollection

Answer a new collection of the same class as the receiver that contains the elements of the receiver in the same order, except that elements from index intFrom through index intTo are replaced by the elements, in order, of aCollection.

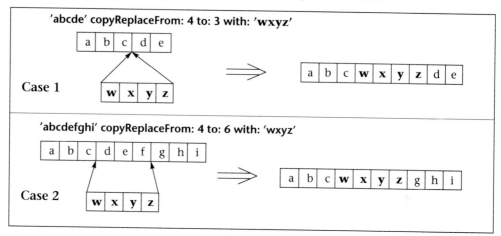

Figure 81: CopyReplaceFrom:to:with: with Replacement and Insertion.

There are two cases, as shown in Figure 81:

1) If intFrom is intTo+1, then the elements in aCollection are placed in a copy of the receiver just before intFrom. The operation can be an insert or an append, depending on the value of intTo.

   Insert: If intTo is less than the size of the receiver, then the elements in aCollection are inserted in a copy of the receiver just before intFrom.

   Append: If intTo is the size of the receiver, then the elements in aCollection are inserted at the end of a copy of the receiver.

2) Replace: Otherwise the elements in aCollection replace the elements in a copy of the receiver in the range from intFrom through intTo for (intTo-intFrom+1) characters.

The value of intFrom must be in the range one to the receiver size, and intTo must be in the range zero to the receiver size.

The size of the result is:

receiver size - (intTo - intFrom + 1) + aCollection size

Case	Value of a	Expression	Result
1	'196'	a copyReplaceFrom: 4 to: 3 with: '!'	'196!'
1	'196'	a copyReplaceFrom: 1 to: 0 with: 'x := '	'x := 196'
1	'abcdef'	a copyReplaceFrom: 3 to: 2 with: 'z'	'abzcdef'
2	'abcdef'	a copyReplaceFrom: 3 to: 3 with: 'z'	'abzdef'
2	'abcdef'	a copyReplaceFrom: 3 to: 4 with: 'z'	'abzef'
2	anArray: 1 2 3 4 5	a copyReplaceFrom: 3 to: 4 with: #(6)	anArray: 1 2 6 6 5
2	anArray: 1 2 3 4 5	a copyReplaceFrom: 3 to: 4 with: #(-3 -4)	anArray: 1 2 -3 -4 5

copyReplaceFrom: intFrom to: intTo withObject: anObject

Answer a new collection of the same class as the receiver that contains the elements of the receiver in the same order, except that elements from index intFrom through index intTo are replaced of anObject. This method is equivalent to copyReplaceFrom:to:with: if there is just one element in the collection

There are two cases:

1) If intFrom is intTo+1, then anObject is placed in a copy of the receiver just before intFrom. The operation can be an insert or an append, depending on the value of intTo.

   Insert: If intTo is less than the size of the receiver, then anObject is placed in a copy of the receiver just before intFrom.

   Append: If intTo is the size of the receiver then anObject is placed at the end of a copy of the receiver.

2) Replace: Otherwise anObject replaces the elements in a copy of the receiver in the range from intFrom through intTo for (intTo-intFrom+1) characters.

The value of intFrom must be in the range 1 to the receiver size and intTo must be in the range zero to the receiver size.

The size of the result is:

receiver size - (intTo - intFrom + 1) + 1

Case	Value of a	Expression	Result
1	'abcdef'	a copyReplaceFrom: 7 to: 6 withObject: $.	'abcdef.'
1	'abcdef'	a copyReplaceFrom: 3 to: 2 withObject: $z	'abzcdef'
2	'abcdef'	a copyReplaceFrom: 3 to: 3 withObject: $z	'abzdef'
2	'abcdef'	a copyReplaceFrom: 3 to: 4 withObject: $z	'abzzef'
2	anArray: 1 2 3 4 5	a copyReplaceFrom: 3 to: 4 withObject: 9	anArray: 1 2 9 9 5

copyReplacing: targetObject withObject: anObject

Answer a new collection of the same class and size as the receiver that contains the elements of the receiver in the same order, except that all elements with the value targetObject are replaced by anObject.

Value of a	Expression	Result
'abcdef'	a copyReplacing: $c withObject: $z	'abzdef'
' 23'	a copyReplacing: $ withObject: $0	'0000023'
anArray: 0 1 0 7 0 0 9	a copyReplacing: 0 withObject: 1	anArray: 1 1 1 7 1 1 9

(Note that the first parameter in the second example is a blank character.)

copyWith: anObject

Answer a new collection of the same class and size as the receiver that contains all of the elements of the receiver in the same order and with anObject appended to the end.

Value of a	Expression	Result
'abcdef'	a copyWith: $z	'abcdefz'
anArray: 2 5 9	a copyWith: 7	anArray: 2 5 9 7

copyWithout: anObject

Answer a new collection of the same class as the receiver which contains all of the elements of the receiver in the same order, except that all elements with the value anObject are removed.

Value of a	Expression	Result
'abcdef'	a copyWithout: $c	'abdef'
' 23'	a copyWithout: $	'23'
anArray: 0 1 0 7 0 0 9	a copyWithout: 0	anArray: 1 7 9

(Note that the parameter in the second example is a blank character.)

findFirst: aBlock

Answer the index of the first element for which aBlock answers true; else answer zero. The one argument block aBlock is evaluated for each element in the receiver, passing the element as a parameter. If the block answers true, then the index of the passed element is answered. If no element produces a true result, answer zero.

See also: indexOf:

Value of a	Expression	Result
'203-748-5943'	a findFirst: [:e | e isDigit not]	4
'0000023'	a findFirst: [:e | (e=$0) not]	6
anArray: 2 9 6 -3 8 45	a findFirst: [:e | e < 0]	4

findLast: aBlock

Answer the index of the last element for which aBlock answers true; else answer zero. The one argument block aBlock is evaluated for each element in the receiver taken in reverse order, passing the element as a parameter. If the block answers true, then the index of the passed element is answered. If no element produces a true result, answer zero.

Value of a	Expression	Result
'203-748-5349'	a findLast: [:e | e isDigit not]	8
'230000'	a findLast: [:e | (e=$0) not]	2

first

Answer the first element of the receiver. It is an error if the receiver is empty.

Value of a	Expression	Result
'abcdef'	a first	$a
''	a first	An error
anInterval: 3 to: 7	a first	3

indexOf: anObject

Answer the index of the first element of the receiver that is equal to anObject; else answer zero.

See also: findFirst:

Value of a	Expression	Result
'abcdef'	a indexOf: $c	3
#(1 2 3 4 5 6)	a indexOf: 8	0

indexOf: anObject ifAbsent: aBlock

Answer the index of the first element of the receiver that is equal to anObject; else answer the result of evaluating the zero argument block aBlock.

Value of a	Expression	Result
'12.34'	a indexOf: $. ifAbsent: [a size + 1]	3
'1234'	a indexOf: $. ifAbsent: [a size + 1]	5

indexOfSubCollection: aSeqColl startingAt: anInteger

Answer the index of the first element of the receiver that is the start of a subsequence matching aSeqColl; else answer zero. Start searching at index anInteger.

Value of a	Value of b	Expression	Result
'Mary had a little laptop,'	'had'	a indexOfSubCollection: b startingAt: 1	6
anArray: 5 1 9 3 4 11 91 3 4 7	#(3 4)	a indexOfSubCollection: b startingAt: 5	8
anArray: 5 1 9 3 4 11 91 3 4 7	#(3 7)	a indexOfSubCollection: b startingAt: 1	0

indexOfSubCollection: aSeqColl startingAt: anInteger ifAbsent: aBlock

Answer the index of the first element of the receiver that is the start of a subsequence matching aSeqColl; else answer the result of evaluating the zero argument block aBlock. Start searching at index anInteger.

Value of a	Value of b	Expression	Result
'Mary had a little laptop,'	'had'	a indexOfSubCollection: b startingAt: 1 ifAbsent: [0]	6
'Mary had a little laptop,'	','	a indexOfSubCollection: b startingAt: 1 ifAbsent: [a indexOf: $,]	25

last

Answer the last element of the receiver. It is an error if the receiver is empty.

Value of a	Expression	Result
'abcdef'	a last	$f
''	a last	An error
anInterval: 3 to: 11 by: 3	a last	9

replaceFrom: intFrom to: intTo with: aCollection

Replace the elements of the receiver, starting at the element at index intFrom, and continuing through the element at index intTo, with the elements of aCollection; answer the receiver. It is an error if intFrom and intTo are not valid indexes into the receiver, or if the size of aCollection is not (intTo-intFrom+1).

Value of a	Value of b	Expression	Result
'abcdef'	'xy'	a replaceFrom: 3 to: 4 with: b	'abxyef'

replaceFrom: intFrom to: intTo with: aCollection startingAt: intIndex

Replace the elements of the receiver, starting at the element at index intFrom, and continuing through the element with index intTo, with the elements of aCollection starting at intIndex; answer the receiver. It is an error if intFrom and intTo are not valid indexes into the receiver, or if the number of elements in the receiver to be replaced is not the same as the number of elements in aCollection at, and after, intIndex.

Value of a	Value of b	Expression	Result
'abcdef'	'xy'	a replaceFrom: 3 to: 4 with: b startingAt: 1	'abxyef'
'abcdef'	'uvwxy'	a replaceFrom: 3 to: 4 with: b startingAt: 2	'abvwef'

replaceFrom: intFrom to: intTo withObject: anObject

Replace the elements of the receiver, starting at the element with index intFrom, and continuing through the element with index intTo, with anObject; answer the receiver. It is an error if intFrom and intTo are not valid indexes into the receiver, or if intFrom is larger than intTo.

Value of a	Expression	Result
'abcdef'	a replaceFrom: 3 to: 4 withObject: $x	'abxxef'

reverse

Answer a collection with the same size and of the same class as the receiver, but with its elements in reverse order.

Value of a	Expression	Result
#(1 2 3 4 5 6 7 8 9 10)	a reverse	anArray: 10 9 8 7 6 5 4 3 2 1

reverseDo: aBlock

Evaluate aBlock with each element of the receiver, starting with the highest index and ending with the lowest index.

with: otherCollection do: aBlock

Evaluate the two-argument block aBlock for each element in the receiver, and the corresponding element at the same index in otherCollection. The receiver and otherCollection must both have the same size. Answer the receiver.

Example 283 multiplies two arrays.

```
" Multiply two arrays "
| a b prod |
a := #( 7 22 1 8 24 ).
b := (1 to: a size) asArray.
prod := OrderedCollection new: a size.
a with: b do: [ :e1 :e2 | prod add: e1 * e2 ].
^ prod       "Result: ( 7 44 3 32 120 ) "
```

Example 283, Display

Example 284 compares two strings and answers a third string, showing the differences.

```
" Compare two strings; answer a third showing the differences"
| a b str |
a := 'Mary has a little latpop, its screan is while as slow'.
b := 'Mary has a little laptop, its screen is white as snow'.
a size == b size
    ifFalse: [ self error: 'The strings are not same length' ].
str := ''.
a with: b do: [ :an :bn |
    an = bn
        ifTrue: [ str := str, an asString ]
        ifFalse: [ str := str, '*' ] ].
^ str
" Answers: 'Mary has a little la**op, its scre*n is whi*e as s*ow' "
```

Example 284, Display

Class AdditiveSequenceableCollection

Class AdditiveSequenceableCollection is an abstract class which is the parent of Ordered-Collection and SortedCollection. It describes indexed collections, which can have elements added and thus can grow.

Class Method Summary

There are no new class methods.

Instance Method Summary

Method	Documented	See page
after:	AdditiveSequenceableCollection	350
before:	AdditiveSequenceableCollection	350
removeAtIndex:	AdditiveSequenceableCollection	351
removeFirst	AdditiveSequenceableCollection	351
removeLast	AdditiveSequenceableCollection	351
size	AdditiveSequenceableCollection Collection Object	351 319 295

Instance Interface

after: anObject

Answer the element immediately following the first element in the receiver that is equal to anObject; the element immediately following has the next highest index. It is an error if the element found is the last in the receiver or if no element is found.

Value of a	Expression	Result
anOrderedCollection: 1 5 7 9 34	a after: 7	9

before: anObject

Answer the element immediately preceding the first element in the receiver that is equal to anObject; the element immediately preceding has the next-lowest index. It is an error if the element found is the first in the receiver or if no element is found.

Value of a	Expression	Result
anOrderedCollection: 1 5 7 9 34	a before: 7	5

removeAtIndex: anInteger

Remove the element of the receiver at position anInteger; answer the removed element. It is an error if anInteger is outside the range of the receiver.

Value of a	Expression	Result in a	Answer
anOrderedCollection: 1 5 7 9 34	a removeAtIndex: 3	anOrderedCollection: 1 5 9 34	7

removeFirst

Remove the first element of the receiver; answer the removed element. It is an error if the receiver is empty.

Value of a	Expression	Result in a	Answer
anOrderedCollection: 1 5 7 9 34	a removeFirst	anOrderedCollection: 5 7 9 34	1

removeLast

Remove the last element of the receiver; answer the removed element. It is an error if the receiver is empty.

Value of a	Expression	Result in a	Answer
anOrderedCollection: 1 5 7 9 34	a removeLast	anOrderedCollection: 1 5 7 9	34

size

Answer the number of elements added to the receiver. This is not the same as the number specified when the collection is created, since that number gives the maximum number of elements before the collection has to be resized.

Class OrderedCollection

Class OrderedCollection is a concrete class with instances that can act like arrays, queues, or stacks.

Class	Page
Collection	
SequenceableCollection	340
AdditiveSequenceableCollection	350
OrderedCollection	351
SortedCollection	356
ArrayedCollection	358
Array	360
ByteArray	361
String	362
Symbol	370
Interval	371

Class Method Summary

Method	Documented	See page
new: count	Collection class	315
with: element1	Collection class	315
with: element1 with: element2	Collection class	315
with: element1 with: element2 with: element3	Collection class	315
with: element1 with: element2 with: element3 with: element4	Collection class	315

Instance Method Summary

Method	Documented	See page
, aCollection	SequenceableCollection	342
=	SequenceableCollection Object	342 289
==	Object	289
add: anObject	Collection	315
add: anObject **after: targetObject**	OrderedCollection	354
add: anObject **afterIndex: anInteger**	OrderedCollection	354
add: anObject **before: targetObject**	OrderedCollection	354
add: anObject **beforeIndex: anInteger**	OrderedCollection	355
addAllFirst: aCollection	OrderedCollection	355
addAllLast: aCollection	OrderedCollection	355
addFirst: anObject	OrderedCollection	355
addLast: anObject	OrderedCollection	355
addAll:	Collection	315
after: anInteger	AdditiveSequenceableCollection	350
asArray	Collection	315
asBag	Collection	316
asByteArray	Collection	316
asOrderedCollection	Collection	316
asSet	Collection	316
asSortedCollection	Collection	316
asSortedCollection: aSortBlock	Collection	316
at: anInteger put: anObject	SequenceableCollection	344
atAll: aCollection put: anObject	SequenceableCollection	344
atAllPut: anObject	SequenceableCollection	344
before: anInteger	AdditiveSequenceableCollection	350
collect: aBlock	Collection	316

Part 1 of 3.

Method	Documented	See page
conform: aBlock	Collection	317
copyFrom: intFrom to: intTo	SequenceableCollection	344
copyReplaceAll: subcollection with: aCollection	SequenceableCollection	344

copyReplaceFrom: intFrom
   to: intTo
   with: aCollection
	SequenceableCollection	345

copyReplaceFrom: intFrom
   to: intTo
   withObject: anObject
	SequenceableCollection	346

copyReplacing: targetObject withObject: anObject	SequenceableCollection	346
copyWith: anObject	SequenceableCollection	346
copyWithout: anObject	SequenceableCollection	347
detect: aBlock	Collection	317
detect: aBlock ifNone: aBlock	Collection	317
do: aBlock	Collection	317
findFirst: anObject	SequenceableCollection	347
findLast: anObject	SequenceableCollection	347
first	SequenceableCollection	347
includes: anObject	Collection	317
indexOf: anObject	SequenceableCollection	347
indexOf: anObject ifAbsent: aBlock	SequenceableCollection	347
indexOfSubCollection: aSeqColl startingAt: anInteger	SequenceableCollection	348

indexOfSubCollection: aSeqColl
   startingAt: anInteger
   ifAbsent: aBlock
	SequenceableCollection	348

inject: anObject into: aBlock	Collection	317
isEmpty	Collection	318
last	SequenceableCollection	348
notEmpty	Collection	318
occurrencesOf: anObject	Collection	319
reject: aBlock	Collection	319
remove: anObject	Collection	319
remove: anObject ifAbsent: aBlock	Collection	319
removeAll: aCollection	Collection	319
removeAtIndex: anInteger	AdditiveSequenceableCollection	351
removeFirst	AdditiveSequenceableCollection	351
removeLast	AdditiveSequenceableCollection	351

Part 2 of 3.

Method	Documented	See page
replaceFrom: intFrom to: intTo with: aCollection	SequenceableCollection	348
replaceFrom: intFrom to: intTo with: aCollection startingAt: intIndex	SequenceableCollection	348
replaceFrom: intFrom to: intTo withObject: anObject	SequenceableCollection	349
reverse	SequenceableCollection	349
reverseDo: aBlock	SequenceableCollection	349
select: aBlock	Collection	319
size	Collection Object	319
with: otherCollection do: aBlock	SequenceableCollection	349

Part 3 of 3.

Instance Interface

add: anObject after: targetObject

Add anObject to the receiver immediately after the first element that is equal, using =, to targetObject; answer anObject. An element is immediately following another if its index is one greater than that of the other. It is an error if the receiver does not contain targetObject.

Value of a	Expression	Result on a	Answers
anOrderedCollection: 1 5 7 9	a add: 6 after: 5	anOrderedCollection: 1 5 6 7 9	6
anOrderedCollection: 1 5 7 9	a add: 6 after: 3	An error	

add: anObject afterIndex: anInteger

Add anObject to the receiver immediately after the index anInteger; answer anObject. It is an error if the index is outside the range of the receiver.

Value of a	Expression	Result	Answers
anOrderedCollection: 1 5 7 9	a add: 6 afterIndex: 2	anOrderedCollection: 1 5 6 7 9	6
anOrderedCollection: 1 5 7 9	a add: 6 afterIndex: 5	An error	

add: anObject before: targetObject

Add anObject to the receiver immediately before the first element that is equal to targetObject; answer anObject. An element is immediately before another if its index is one less than that of the other. It is an error if the receiver does not contain targetObject.

Value of a	Expression	Result in a	Answers
anOrderedCollection: 1 5 7 9	a add: 6 before: 5	anOrderedCollection: 1 6 5 7 9	6
anOrderedCollection: 1 5 7 9	a add: 6 before: 3	An error	

add: anObject beforeIndex: anInteger
Add anObject to the receiver immediately before the index anInteger; answer anObject.
It is an error if the index is outside the range of the receiver.

Value of a	Expression	Result in a	Answers
anOrderedCollection: 1 5 7 9	a add: 6 beforeIndex: 2	anOrderedCollection: 1 6 5 7 9	6
anOrderedCollection: 1 5 7 9	a add: 6 beforeIndex: 5	An error	

addAllFirst: aCollection
Add all of the elements of aCollection, in order, to the front of the receiver; answer
aCollection. This is similar to the expression (aCollection, receiver), except that the
expression answers a copy while addAllFirst: modifies the receiver.

Value of a	Value of b	Expression	Result in a	Answers
anOrderedCollection: $a $b $c	anOrderedCollection: $x $y	a addAllFirst: b	anOrdered Collection: $x $y $a $b $c	b

addAllLast: aCollection
Add all of the elements of aCollection, in order, to the end of the receiver; answer
aCollection. This is similar to the expression (receiver, aCollection), except that the
expression answers a copy while addAllLast: modifies the receiver.

Value of a	Value of b	Expression	Result in a	Answers
anOrdered Collection: $a $b $c	anOrderedCollection: $x $y	a addAllLast: b	anOrdered Collection: $a $b $c $x $y	b

addFirst: anObject
Add anObject at the front of the receiver; answer anObject.

Value of a	Value of b	Expression	Result in a	Answers
anOrderedCollection: $a $b $c	$x	a addFirst: b	anOrderedCollection: $x $a $b $c	b
anOrderedCollection: $a $b $c	anArray: 2 3	a addFirst: b	anOrderedCollection: (2 3) $a $b $c	anArray: 2 3

addLast: anObject
Add anObject at the end of the receiver; answer anObject.

Value of a	Value of b	Expression	Result	Answers
anOrderedCollection: $a $b $c	$x	a addLast: b	anOrderedCollection: $a $b $c $x	b
anOrderedCollection: $a $b $c	anArray: 2 3	a addLast: b	anOrderedCollection: $a $b $c (2 3)	anArray: 2 3

Class SortedCollection

Class SortedCollection is a concrete class that describes collections that are maintained in a sorted order. The elements are indexed and elements can be added and deleted.

Class Method Summary

Method	Documented	See page
new	SortedCollection class Object class	357 288
new: anInteger	SortedCollection class Object class	357 289
sortBlock: aTwoArgumentBlock	OrderedCollection class	357

Instance Method Summary

The collection returned from some methods such as collect:, reverse, and the copying methods are not instances of SortedCollection. See Figure 80, 'Collection Class Answered by Various Methods', on page 338.

Method	Documented	See page
~~at:put:~~	SequenceableCollection	344
~~atAll:put:~~	SequenceableCollection	344
~~atAllPut:~~	SequenceableCollection	344

~~replaceFrom:~~
  ~~to:~~
  ~~with:~~
	SequenceableCollection	348

~~replaceFrom:~~
  ~~to:~~
  ~~withObject:~~
	SequenceableCollection	349

~~replaceFrom:~~
  ~~to:~~
  ~~with:~~
  ~~startingAt:~~
	SequenceableCollection	348

sortBlock	SortedCollection	357
sortBlock: aTwoArgumentBlock	SortedCollection	357

Class Interface

new
Answer a new collection with room for a default number of elements and with the following default sort block:

> [:a :b | a < b]

Sort blocks are two argument blocks that answer true when the first argument is in proper sorted order with respect to the second argument, and false otherwise.

new: count
Answer a new collection with room for count elements and with the following default sort block:

> [:a :b | a < b]

Sort blocks are two-argument blocks that answer true when the first argument is in proper sorted order with respect to the second argument, and false otherwise.

sortBlock: aTwoArgumentBlock
Create a new sorted collection having room for a default number of elements; specify aTwoArgumentBlock as the sort block. Sort blocks are two argument blocks that answer true when the first argument is in proper sorted order with respect to the second argument, and false otherwise.

Example:

```
" Create a sorted collection that sorts in descending order  "
| sc |
sc := SortedCollection sortBlock: [ :a :b |  a > b ].
sc addAll: #( 2 1 5 6 7 3 ).
^ sc
   "Result: 7 6 5 3 2 1 "
```
Example 285, Display

Instance Interface

sortBlock
Answer the sort block of the receiver.

sortBlock: aTwoArgumentBlock
Change the sort block of the receiver so that aTwoArgumentBlock is the sort block. Sort the collection using the new sort block. Sort blocks are two-argument blocks that answer true when the first argument is in proper sorted order with respect to the second argument, and false otherwise.

Class ArrayedCollection

Class ArrayedCollection is an abstract class which is the parent of Array, ByteArray, String, and Symbol. It describes collections that are indexed but which cannot grow. Inherited messages that add elements to collections do not apply to ArrayedCollection and its subclasses.

Class Method Summary

Method	*Documented*	*See page*
new: count	Collection class Object class	315 289
with: element1	Collection class	315
with: element1 with: element2	Collection class	315
with: element1 with: element2 with: element3	Collection class	315
with: element1 with: element2 with: element3 with: element4	Collection class	315

Instance Method Summary

Method	*Documented*	*See page*
, aCollection	SequenceableCollection	342
=	SequenceableCollection Object	342 289
==	Object	289
~=	SequenceableCollection Object	343 289
~~	Object	290
~~add: anObject~~	Collection	315
~~addAll: aCollection~~	Collection	315
asArray	Collection	315
asBag	Collection	316
asByteArray	Collection	316
asOrderedCollection	Collection	316
asSet	Collection	316
asSortedCollection	Collection	316

Part 1 of 3.

Method	Documented	See page
asSortedCollection: aSortBlock	Collection	316
at: anInteger	SequenceableCollection	343
at: anInteger put: anObject	SequenceableCollection	344
atAll: aCollection put: anObject	SequenceableCollection	344
atAllPut: anObject	SequenceableCollection	344
collect: aBlock	Collection	316
conform: aBlock	Collection	317
copyFrom: intFrom to: intTo	SequenceableCollection	344
copyReplaceAll: subcollection with: aCollection	SequenceableCollection	344
copyReplaceFrom: intFrom to: intTo with: aCollection	SequenceableCollection	345
copyReplaceFrom: intFrom to: intTo withObject: anObject	SequenceableCollection	346
copyReplacing: targetObject withObject: anObject	SequenceableCollection	346
copyWith: anObject	SequenceableCollection	346
copyWithout: anObject	SequenceableCollection	347
detect: aBlock	Collection	317
detect: aBlock ifNone: aBlock	Collection	317
do: aBlock	Collection	317
findFirst: anObject	SequenceableCollection	347
findLast: anObject	SequenceableCollection	347
first	SequenceableCollection	347
includes: anObject	Collection	317
indexOf: anObject	SequenceableCollection	347
indexOf: anObject ifAbsent: aBlock	SequenceableCollection	347
indexOfSubCollection: aSeqColl startingAt: anInteger	SequenceableCollection	348
indexOfSubCollection: aSeqColl startingAt: anInteger ifAbsent: aBlock	SequenceableCollection	348
inject: anObject into: aBlock	Collection	317
isEmpty	Collection	318
last	SequenceableCollection	348
notEmpty	Collection	318
occurrencesOf: anObject	Collection	319
reject: aBlock	Collection	319
~~remove: anObject~~	Collection	319

Part 2 of 3.

Method	Documented	See page
~~remove: anObject ifAbsent: aBlock~~	Collection	319
~~removeAll: aCollection~~	Collection	319
replaceFrom: intFrom to: intTo with: aCollection	SequenceableCollection	348
replaceFrom: intFrom to: intTo with: aCollection startingAt: intIndex	SequenceableCollection	348
replaceFrom: intFrom to: intTo withObject: anObject	SequenceableCollection	349
reverse	SequenceableCollection	349
reverseDo: aBlock	SequenceableCollection	349
select: aBlock	Collection	319
size	Collection Object	319 295
with: otherCollection do: aBlock	SequenceableCollection	349

Part 3 of 3.

Class Array

Class Array is an concrete collection class with indexed instances that can hold any kind of object, but which cannot grow.

Class Method Summary

There are no new class methods.

Instance Method Summary

There are no new instance methods.

See the method summary of ArrayedCollection.

Class ByteArray

Class ByteArray is a concrete class that describes fixed-size indexed collections of bytes (8-bit unsigned integer values).

Class Method Summary

There is no new class protocol.

Instance Method Summary

Method	Documented	See page
byteAt: anInteger	ByteArray	361
byteAt: anInteger **put: aByteInteger**	ByteArray	361

~~replaceFrom: intFrom~~
  ~~to: intTo~~
  ~~withObject: anObject~~
	SequenceableCollection	349

Instance Interface

byteAt: anInteger

Answer the element at index anInteger, an integer in the range 0 to 255. This is equivalent to at:.

byteAt: anInteger put: aByteInteger

Set the element at index anInteger to aByteInteger, an integer in the range 0 to 255. This is equivalent to at:put:.

Class String

Class String is a concrete class that describes fixed-size indexed collections of characters.

Class Method Summary

There is no new class protocol.

Instance Method Summary

Method	Documented	See page
, aString	SequenceableCollection	342
= aString	String SequenceableCollection Object	364 342 289
== aString	Object	289
~=	String SequenceableCollection Object	365 289
~~	Object	290
< aString	String	365
<= aString	String	365
> aString	String	365
>= aString	String	365
addLineDelimiters	String	366
asArray	Collection	315
asBag	Collection	316
asByteArray	Collection	316
asGlobalKey	String	366
asLowercase	String	366
asNumber	String	366
asOrderedCollection	Collection	316
asPoolKey	String	366
asSet	Collection	316
asSortedCollection	Collection	316
asSortedCollection: aSortBlock	Collection	316
asString	String	366

Part 1 of 3.

Method	Documented	See page
asSymbol	String	366
asUppercase	String	367
at anInteger put: anObject	SequenceableCollection	344
atAll: aCollection put: anObject	SequenceableCollection	344
atAllPut: anObject	SequenceableCollection	344
bindWith: aString	String	367
bindWith: str1 with: str2	String	367

**bindWith: str1
  with: str2
  with: str3**
	String	367

**bindWith: str1
  with: str2
  with: str3
  with: str4**
	String	367

bindWithArguments: aCollection	String	367
collect: aBlock	Collection	316
conform: aBlock	Collection	317
copyFrom: intFrom to: intTo	SequenceableCollection	344
copyReplaceAll: subcollection with: aCollection	SequenceableCollection	344

copyReplaceFrom: intFrom
  to: intTo
  with: aCollection
	SequenceableCollection	345

copyReplaceFrom: intFrom
  to: intTo
  withObject: anObject
	SequenceableCollection	346

copyReplacing: targetObject withObject: anObject	SequenceableCollection	346
copyWith: anObject	SequenceableCollection	346
copyWithout: anObject	SequenceableCollection	347
detect: aBlock	Collection	317
detect: aBlock ifNone: aBlock	Collection	317
do: aBlock	Collection	317
findFirst: anObject	SequenceableCollection	347
findLast: anObject	SequenceableCollection	347
first	SequenceableCollection	347
includes: anObject	Collection	317
indexOf: anObject	SequenceableCollection	347
indexOf: anObject ifAbsent: aBlock	SequenceableCollection	347

**indexOf: aString
  matchCase: boolean
  startingAt: anInteger**
	String	367

Method	Documented	See page
indexOfSubCollection: aSeqColl startingAt: anInteger	SequenceableCollection	348

indexOfSubCollection: aSeqColl
    startingAt: anInteger
    ifAbsent: aBlock
	SequenceableCollection	348

inject: anObject into: aBlock	Collection	317
isEmpty	Collection	318
last	SequenceableCollection	348
match: aString	String	368
notEmpty	Collection	318
occurrencesOf: anObject	Collection	319
reject: aBlock	Collection	319

replaceFrom: intFrom
    to: intTo
    with: aCollection
	SequenceableCollection	348

replaceFrom: intFrom
    to: intTo
    with: aCollection
    startingAt: intIndex
	SequenceableCollection	348

replaceFrom: intFrom
    to: intTo
    withObject: anObject
	SequenceableCollection	349

reverse	SequenceableCollection	349
reverseDo: aBlock	SequenceableCollection	349
select: aBlock	Collection	319
sameAs: aString	String	368
size	Collection Object	319 295
subStrings	String	369
subStrings: aCharacter	String	369
trimBlanks	String	369
trimSeparators	String	369
with: otherCollection do: aBlock	SequenceableCollection	349

Instance Interface

= aString

Answer true if the characters in the receiver at each index, and the characters in aString at corresponding indexes, are equal, including case; answer false otherwise.

See also: sameAs:

Value of a	Value of b	Expression	Result
'Banana'	'banana'	a = b	false
'Banana'	'Banana'	a = b	true

~= aString

Answer false if the characters in the receiver at each index, and the characters in aString at corresponding indexes, are equal, including case; answer true otherwise.

See also: sameAs:

Value of a	Value of b	Expression	Result
'Banana'	'banana'	a ~= b	true
'Banana'	'Banana'	a ~= b	false

< aString

Answer true if the receiver is less than aString, ignoring case; answer false otherwise. The strings are compared up to the length of the shorter string. This comparison is designed for ordering strings for presentation to users.

Value of a	Value of b	Expression	Result
'Banana'	'Cabbage'	a < b	true
'1000'	'3000'	a < b	true
'1000'	'9'	a < b	true
'AA'	'aa'	a < b	false

<= aString

Answer true if the receiver is less than or equal to aString, ignoring case; answer false otherwise. The strings are compared up to the length of the shorter string. This comparison is designed for ordering strings for presentation to users.

Value of a	Value of b	Expression	Result
'Banana'	'Cabbage'	a <= b	true
'1000'	'3000'	a <= b	true
'1000'	'9'	a <= b	true
'AA'	'aa'	a <= b	true

> aString

Answer true if the receiver is greater than aString, ignoring case; answer false otherwise. The strings are compared up to the length of the shorter string. This comparison is designed for ordering strings for presentation to users.

Value of a	Value of b	Expression	Result
'Banana'	'Cabbage'	a > b	false
'1000'	'3000'	a > b	false
'1000'	'9'	a > b	false
'AA'	'aa'	a > b	false

>= aString

Answer true if the receiver is greater than or equal to aString, ignoring case; answer false otherwise. The strings are compared up to the length of the shorter string. This comparison is designed for ordering strings for presentation to users.

Value of a	Value of b	Expression	Result
'Banana'	'Cabbage'	a >= b	false
'1000'	'3000'	a >= b	false
'1000'	'9'	a >= b	false
'AA'	'aa'	a >= b	false

addLineDelimiters

Answer a new string, a copy of the receiver, in which each backslash character ($\) has been replaced with the current line delimiter. The current line delimiter is the value of LineDelimiter from the pool dictionary CldtConstants. It holds the platform-specific string for delimiting lines.

See the section on 'Line Delimiters' on page 138 for more information.

Value of a	Expression	Result
'Line 1\Line 2'	a addLineDelimiter	'Line 1 Line 2'

asGlobalKey

Answer a new instance of some class that holds a copy of the receiver. The new instance is appropriate for the platform-specific format of a global key in the dictionary Smalltalk.

asLowercase

Answer a copy of the receiver, with all upper-case characters converted to lower-case characters.

Value of a	Expression	Result
'OOPSLA is in the fall.'	a asLowercase	'oopsla is in the fall.'

asNumber

Answer an integer obtained from the receiver, which must contain only an optional leading minus sign and one or more digits in the range $0 to $9. It is an error for the receiver to contain any other characters, or to have a minus sign other than at the front; a zero is answered.

Value of a	Expression	Result
'123'	a asNumber	123
'-1'	a asNumber	-1
'FFE4'	a asNumber	0
' 23 '	a trimBlanks asNumber	23
'123 is a number'	a asNumber	123
'-1.2'	a asNumber	-1

asPoolKey

Answer a new instance of some class that holds a copy of the receiver. The new instance is appropriate for the platform-specific format of a pool dictionary key.

> CldtConstants at: 'Cr' asPoolKey

asString

Answer the receiver.

asSymbol

Answer a symbol containing a copy of the receiver.

Value of a	Expression	Result
'asFloat'	a asSymbol	#asFloat
'at:put:'	a asSymbol	#at:put:
'(a b c)'	a asSymbol	Same as: #'(a b c)'

asUppercase

Answer a copy of the receiver, with all lower-case characters converted to upper-case letters.

Value of a	Expression	Result
'abc123 def'	a asUppercase	'ABC123 DEF'

bindWith: aString

Answer a copy of the receiver, with all occurrences of the string '%1' replaced by aString. It is an error if any part of the string contains any of: %2, %3, ..., %9.

Value of a	Expression	Result
'File is "%1"'	a bindWith: fileName	'File is 'abraca.dab'''

bindWith: str1 with: str2

Answer a copy of the receiver, with all occurrences of '%1' replaced by str1 and all occurrences of '%2' replaced by str2. It is an error if any part of the string contains any of: %3, %4, ..., %9.

bindWith: str1 with: str2 with: str3

Answer a copy of the receiver, with all occurrences of '%1' replaced by str1, all occurrences of '%2' replaced by str2, and all occurrences of '%3' replaced by str3. It is an error if any part of the string contains any of: %4, %5, ..., %9.

bindWith: str1 with: str2 with: str3 with: str4

Answer a copy of the receiver with all occurrences of '%1' replaced by str1, all occurrences of '%2' replaced by str2, all occurrences of '%3' replaced by str3, and all occurrences of '%4' replaced by str4. It is an error if any part of the string contains any of: %5, %6, ..., %9.

bindWithArguments: aCollection

Answer a copy of the receiver, with all occurrences of '%n' replaced by the nth string in the collection aCollection. The value of n must be in the range 1 to 9. It is an error if any part of the string contains some %k, where k is an integer greater than aCollection size but less than ten.

```
" Binding values to %n in a string "
| bindee bindargs |
bindargs := #( 'Mary' 'lamp' 'light' 'snow' ).
bindee := '%1 had a little %2, its %3 was white as %4;'.
^ bindee bindWithArguments: bindargs
    "Answer: 'Mary had a little lamp, its light was white as snow;' "
```
Example 286, Display

indexOf: aString matchCase: boolean startingAt: anInteger

Answer an interval that describes the first occurrence of the pattern aString in the receiver. The search starts at index anInteger in the receiver. If boolean is true, then the search is sensitive to case.

The pattern can contain any characters. Except for the two special characters $# and $*, characters in the pattern match the same character in the receiver when boolean is true, and match the same character, but ignoring case, when boolean is false. The special characters, called wild card characters, are:

> \#   Matches any single character in the receiver.
>
> *   Matches zero or more characters in the receiver.

See also: match:, super>>indexOf...

In the following examples, the variable a holds the string:

'The tiger ate the food.'

Expression	Result	Matches
a indexOf: 'the' 　matchCase: false startingAt: 1	An interval: 　1 to: 3 by: 1	'The tiger ate the food.'
a indexOf: 'the' 　matchCase: true startingAt: 1	An interval: 　15 to: 17 by: 1	'The tiger ate the food.'
a indexOf: '#the' 　matchCase: true startingAt: 1	An interval: 　14 to: 17 by: 1	'The tiger ate the food.'
a indexOf: '*the' 　matchCase: true startingAt: 1	An interval: 　1 to: 17 by: 1	'The tiger ate the food.'
a indexOf: 't*e' 　matchCase: true startingAt: 1	An interval: 　5 to: 8 by: 1	'The tiger ate the food.'
a indexOf: 't#e' 　matchCase: true startingAt: 1	An interval: 　15 to: 17 by: 1	'The tiger ate the food.'

```
" Use from and to values of the interval obtained from
        indexOf:matchCase:startingAt:
        to copy elements of the matched string. "
| str pattern interval |
str := 'The tiger ate the food.'.
pattern := 't#e'.
interval := str indexOf: pattern matchCase: true startingAt: 1.
^ str copyFrom: interval first to: interval last
" Answer: 'the' "
```

Example 287, Display

match: aString

Answer true if the pattern in the receiver matches the whole of aString; otherwise answer false.

The pattern can contain any characters; except for the two special characters $# and $*, characters in the pattern match the same character in aString, ignoring case. The special characters, called wild card characters, are:

　　# 　　Matches any single character in the receiver.

　　* 　　Matches zero or more characters in the receiver.

See also: indexOf:..., super>>indexOf...

Value of a	Expression	Result
'Mississippi'	a match: 'Mississippi'	true
'M*i'	a match: 'Mississippi'	true
'Mi##issippi'	a match: 'Mississippi'	true
'*i*i*i*i'	a match: 'Mississippi'	true

sameAs: aString

Answer true if the receiver and aString are equal, ignoring case; answer false otherwise.

See also: =

Value of a	Value of b	Expression	Result
'Banana'	'banana'	a sameAs: b	true
'Banana'	'Banana'	a sameAs: b	true

subStrings

Answer an array containing the words in the receiver. A word is a group of characters separated by one or more of the separator characters: carriage return, line feed, form feed, tab, or blank.

Expression	Result
'The tiger ate the food.' subStrings	anArray: 'The' 'tiger' 'ate' 'the' 'food.'

Example 288 removes excess blanks and other separators from a string.

```
" Remove excess blanks from a string using subStrings "
| str1 str2 |
str1 := ' The    tiger    ate    the    food.  '.
str2 := ''.
str1 subStrings do: [ :s | str2 := str2, s, ' ' ].
^ str2              " Result: 'The tiger ate the food. ' "
```
Example 288, Display

subStrings: aCharacter

Answer an array containing substrings from the receiver. The substrings are a group of characters separated by aCharacter.

Expression	Result
'The tiger ate the food.' subStrings: $	anArray: 'The' 'tiger' 'ate' 'the' 'food.'

Example 289 breaks a path name at a backslash.

```
" Break a pathname into parts "
| path |
path := '\usr\dave\stbook\examples\seqcoll\breakpathname '.
^ path subStrings: $\
" Answers: ( 'usr' 'dave' 'stbook' 'examples' 'seqcoll' 'breakpathname' ) " Example 289, Display
```

trimBlanks

Answer a copy of the receiver with leading and trailing blanks removed.

Value of a	Expression	Result
' The tiger was not hungry. '	a trimBlanks	'The tiger was not hungry.'

trimSeparators

Answer a copy of the receiver with leading and trailing separator characters removed. The separator characters are space, plus Cr, Lf, Ff, and Tab, which are defined in the pool dictionary CLDTConstants.

Value of a	Expression	Result
' abc ', Cr, Lf	a trimSeparators	'abc'

Class Symbol

Class Symbol describes a special kind of string; symbols are identity objects.

Class Method Summary

There is no new class protocol.

Instance Method Summary

See String for the rest of the protocol of Symbol.

Method	Implemented	See page
argumentCount	Symbol	370
asString	Symbol String	370 366
asSymbol	Symbol String	370 366

~~replaceFrom: intFrom~~
  ~~to: intTo~~
  ~~with: aCollection~~
	SequenceableCollection	348

~~replaceFrom: intFrom~~
  ~~to: intTo~~
  ~~with: aCollection~~
  ~~startingAt: intIndex~~
	SequenceableCollection	348

~~replaceFrom: intFrom~~
  ~~to: intTo~~
  ~~withObject: anObject~~
	SequenceableCollection	349

Instance Interface

argumentCount
Answer the number of arguments in the method name held in the receiver. This is equivalent to the count of the number of colons in the receiver.

Value of a	Expression	Result
#argumentCount	a argumentCount	0
#indexOf:matchCase:startingAt:	a argumentCount	3

asString
Answer a string that has the same contents as the receiver.

asSymbol
Answer the receiver.

Class Interval

Class Interval is a concrete class that describes a sequence of numbers. While it acts like a collection when read from, it is not a collection; elements are represented by three numbers, one giving the start of a sequence, one giving the increment between elements, and one indicating a maximum element size.

Since intervals are read-only, messages such as comma (,), copy methods, collect:, reject:, and so on answer other types of collections, usually arrays; see Figure 80, 'Collection Class Answered by Various Methods', on page 338.

Class Method Summary

Method	Documented	See page
from: start **to: stop**	Interval	371

from: start
  to: stop
  by: step
	Interval	372

Instance Method Summary

See SequenceableCollection for the remaining protocol of Interval.

Method	Documented	See page
increment	Interval	372
size	Interval Collection	372

Class Interface

from: start to: stop
Answer an interval that starts at the number start, increments by 1, and ends on or before the number stop.

See also: Number>>to:

Expression	Equivalent to:
Interval from: 1 to: 10	1 to: 10
Interval from: 0.5 to: 2.3	0.5 to: 2.2

from: start to: stop by: step

Answer an interval that starts at the number start, increments by the number step, and ends on or before the number stop.

See also: Number>>to:by:

Expression	Equivalent to:
Interval from: 1 to: 10 step: 2	Interval from: 1 to: 10 step: 2
Interval from: 0.5 to: 2.3 step: 0.1	0.5 to: 2.3 step 0.1

Instance Interface

increment

Answer the increment of the interval.

Value of a	Expression	Result
1 to: 10 by: 3	a increment	3

size

Answer the size of the interval. The size of an interval is the number of values that the interval will answer.

Value of a	Expression	Result
1 to: 10 by: 3	a size	4

29

Common File System

This chapter describes the Common File System (CFS) classes, which are used for lower-level file access, including opening and closing file descriptors, reading and writing data, random access, errors, locking and sharing, testing and querying file and directory information, and platform file and directory issues.

See Chapter 13, 'Files', on page 143 for an introduction to and description of the use of CFS classes.

File streams, described in Chapter 31, 'File Streams', on page 407, are the preferred way to read and write files.

Two pool dictionaries are needed for file access.

CldtConstants	Holds names and values for various unprintable ASCII characters, and for line delimiters.
CfsConstants	Holds flags and error codes used with both low-level access and file streams.

The file classes are:

CfsFileStream and its subclasses are documented in Chapter 31, 'File Streams', on page 407.

Kinds of CFS Classes

Common File System classes include classes for examining directories and their entries, performing operations on files, and reporting errors.

CfsDirectoryDescriptor

Directory descriptors describe a whole directory and provide protocol for searching the directory, removing directories, and obtaining information about individual directory entries. Messages to CfsDirectory are:

chdir:	Change the current working directory
getcwd	Get the current working directory
mkdir:	Make a new directory
opendir:pattern:mode:	Open a directory stream
pathSeparator	The path separator character
pathSeparatorString	A string holding the path separator character
rmdir:	Remove a directory
rootDirectories	Answer a collection of the root directories

Instance messages of CfsDirectory are:

closedir	Close a directory stream
readdir	Get a directory entry
readdir:	Get a directory entry; reuse old instance
readdirName	Answer the name of the directory
rewinddir	Refresh and reset stream to the beginning

CfsError

Instances of cfsError are returned by file operations to indicate that an error has occurred. They all answer true to the isCfsError message, and provide protocol to find the error number and some descriptive text. Messages to instances of CfsError are:

errno	Answer the error number
identifier	Answer the name of the error number
isCfsError	Answer true
message	Answer the description of the error

CfsErrorProxy

Many file operations that return a cfsError when an error occurs, return a cfsErrorProxy instead of a cfsError to indicate that no error occurred; a cfsErrorProxy responds to only one message, isCfsError, and always answers false. Instances of CfsErrorProxy answer to one message:

isCfsError	Answer false

CfsFileDescriptor

File descriptors describe files, and contain the methods for file creation, opening, removing, querying, reading, or writing. Messages to CfsFileDescriptor are:

open:oflags:	Open a file
open:oflags:share:	Open a file with sharing
remove:	Remove the file from the file system

rename:new:	Rename the file
supportsLockType:	Query about lock support of platform
supportsShareMode:	Query about sharing support of platform

Instances of CfsFileDescriptor answer to these messages:

access	Answer the access mode: read, write, ...
close	Close the file
flush	Flush buffers to disk
lock:start:len:	Lock a section of the file
lseek:whence:	Seek to a position in the file
oflag	Answer the open flags
read:startingAt:nbyte:	Read from the file
rewind	Reset file position to the front
share	Answer the sharing mode
size	Answer the current file size
unlock:start:nbyte:	Unlock a section of the file
write:startingAt:nbyte:	Write to the file

CfsStat

CfsStat provides methods for obtaining information about files, such as file size, file type, and modification dates. Messages to CfsStat are:

| stat: | Answer an instance of CfsStat |

Messages to instances of CfsStat are:

isBlk	Answer true if this is a block special file
isChr	Answer true if this is a character special file
isDir	Answer true if this is a directory
isFifo	Answer true if this is a pipe or FIFO special file
isReg	Answer true if this is a regular file
isSpecial	Answer true if this is a special file
stat:	Update the receiver for a new path
stAtime	Answer the date and time of last access
stCtime	Answer the date and time of last status change
stDev	Answer the device ID of device holding file
stFtime	Answer the date and time of creation
stGid	Answer the group ID for the file
stIno	Answer the serial number of the file
stMtime	Answer the date and time of last modification
stNlink	Answer the number of links for the file
stSize	Answer the size of a regular file
stUid	Answer the user ID of the file

CfsDirectoryEntry

CfsDirectoryEntry, a subclass of CfsStat, provides methods for obtaining information about directory entries. It adds one instance message:

| dName | Answer the name of the directory |

CfsConstants Summary

This section places together various otherwise scattered tables of CfsConstants for easy location, and adds a table summarizing CFS error messages. The flags and constants are all in the CfsConstants pool dictionary.

File Open Flags

File open flags specify how to open a file. Only one of the first three flags can be given, but any of the last four can be *inclusive or*ed to it. Figure 82 shows these flags.

Flag	Description	Usage
ORDONLY	Open the file for reading only.	Choose just one of these flags.
OWRONLY	Open the file for writing only.	
ORDWR	Open the file for both reading and writing.	
OAPPEND	Set the file offset to the end of the file before *each* write.	*Inclusive or* zero or more of these flags to the one chosen above.
OCREAT	If the file does not exist, create a new one; if the file exists, just open it (unless OEXCL is also given; see below).	
OEXCL	Cause the open to fail if the file exists and OCREAT and OEXCL are both specified.	
OTRUNC	Truncate the file to a length of zero if it is successfully opened ORD-WR or OWRONLY.	

Figure 82: File Open Flags.

File Positioning Constants

File positioning constants specify how the file position is to be reset. Figure 83 shows these constants.

Flag	Description
SEEKSET	Set the position relative to the start of the file.
SEEKCUR	Set the position relative to the current position.
SEEKEND	Set the position relative to the end of the file.

Figure 83: File Positioning Constants.

File Error Constants

File error constants identify specific errors. The set of errors listed in Figure 84 summarizes all messages that are returned. Individual methods will list the only errors they return.

Constant	Description
EACCES *(Access)*	*Directories:* The directory has been removed, locked, or is otherwise inaccessible.
	Directories: A component of the path to the directory is invalid or inaccessible, or the path or directory name is too long.
	Directories: Read or search permission was denied for a component of the path.
	Files: The file cannot be accessed.
	Files: A component of the path to the file is invalid or inaccessible, or the path or directory name is too long.

Figure 84: File Error Constants.   Part 1 of 3.

Constant	Description
EBADF *(Bad file descriptor)*	*Directories:* The receiver is not a valid directory descriptor. *Files:* The receiver is not a valid file descriptor. *Locking:* The receiver is not a valid file descriptor. An attempt may have been made to set a shared (read) lock on a file open for writing, or to set an exclusive (write) lock on a file open for reading.
EBUSY *(Busy or locked)*	*Directories:* The specified directory is locked, or is in use, and this is considered by the platform to be an error. *Files:* The specified file is locked, or is in use, and this is considered by the platform to be an error. *Locking:* A conflicting lock already exists on all or part of the specified segment. *Reading:* The file is locked with a mandatory lock.
EEXIST *(File or directory does not exist)*	*Directories:* The specified directory already exists. *Directories:* The specified directory contains entries other than dot and dot-dot, and therefore cannot be removed. *Opening:* OCREAT and OEXCL were specified, the file already exists. *Rename:* The specified file is a directory that contains entries other than dot and dot-dot, and therefore cannot be removed.
EINVAL *(Invalid use)*	*General:* The method is being used incorrectly; an argument may be invalid. *Locking:* The platform does not support the specified type of lock, or an invalid argument was specified. *Seeking:* The arguments supplied are invalid. This error shall occur if a seek results in a negative file pointer position, or if an attempt is made to seek beyond the end of the file on a platform that considers it to be an error.
EISDIR *(Is Directory)*	The specified file is a directory, and the platform requires that a different operation be used to remove directories.
EIO *(Input or output)*	*General:* A low-level I/O error occurred, a platform-specific error occurred, or a platform function returned an undocumented error code.
ENFILE *(Number of files)*	*Files:* No more search handles are available. *Files:* The number of open files has exceeded a platform specific limit.
ENOENT *(No dir. entry)*	*Directories:* The specified directory does not exist. *Opening:* OCREAT was *not* specified and the file does not exist.
ENOSPC *(Not enough space)*	*Directories:* The file system does not contain enough space to hold the contents of the new directory or to extend the parent directory of the new directory. *Files:* There is insufficient free space remaining on the device containing the file. *Opening:* There is insufficient free space remaining on the device containing the file to create the required directory.
EPERM *(Permission)*	*Removal:* The client does not have permission to remove the file.
EROFS *(Read-only file system)*	*Directories:* The parent directory of the directory being created resides on a read-only file system or a locked or write-protected volume. *Directories:* The directory to be removed resides on a read-only file system or a locked or write-protected volume. *Files:* The file resides on a read-only file system, or a locked or write-protected volume. *Opening:* The path specifies a read-only file system or a locked or write-protected volume, and the file is to be created or opened with write access. *Removal:* The file to be removed resides on a read-only file system or a locked or write-protected volume.

Figure 84: File Error Constants. Part 2 of 3.

Constant	Description
EXDEV (External device)	*Rename:* The links named by old and new are on different file systems, and the file system does not support links between file systems.

Figure 84: File Error Constants. Part 3 of 3.

File Locking Constants

File locking constants specify how a file or segment of a file is to be locked. Figure 85 shows these constants.

Flag	Description
FRDLOCK	Specifies a shared (read) *advisory* lock, which prevents any other client from setting an exclusive advisory lock on any portion of the protected area. Noncooperating clients can read or write in protected areas.
FWRLOCK	Specifies an exclusive (write) *advisory* lock. An exclusive advisory lock prevents any other client from setting a shared *or* exclusive advisory lock on any portion of the protected area. Noncooperating clients can read or write in protected areas.
FMDLOCK	Specifies an exclusive *mandatory* lock, which prevents any other client from reading, writing, or locking any portion of the protected area.

Figure 85: File Locking Constants.

File Sharing Constants

File sharing constants specify how a file or segment of a file is to be shared. Figure 86 shows these constants.

Flag	Description
ODENYNONE	Other processes can open the file for any type of access: read-only, write-only, or read-write.
ODENYRD	Other processes can open the file only for write access.
ODENYWR	Other processes can open the file only for read access.
ODENYRDWR	Other processes cannot open the file for any kind of access; it is unspecified whether the current process can open it a second time.

Figure 86: File Sharing Constants.

Directory Search Flags

Directory search flags specify how a directory descriptor is to be searched. Figure 87 shows these constants.

Flag	Description
FREG	Match regular files.
FDIR	Match directories.
FSPECIAL	Match files that are neither regular files nor directories.

Figure 87: Directory Search Flags.

Protocol Summary

Class Protocol Summary

Object class				
= ==	~= ~~		new	new:
CfsDirectoryDescriptor class	**CfsError class**	**CfsErrorProxy class**	**CfsFileDescriptor class**	**CfsStat class**
chdir: getcwd mkdir: opendir:pattern:mode: pathSeparator pathSeparatorString rmdir: rootDirectories	No new protocol	No new protocol	open:oflag: open:oflag:share: remove: rename:new: supportsLockType: supportsShareMode:	stat: **CfsDirectoryEntry class** ~~stat:~~

Instance Protocol Summary

Object				
= ==	~= ~~	copy	isCfsError	printOn printString:
CfsDirectoryDescriptor	**CfsError**	**CfsErrorProxy**	**CfsFileDescriptor**	**CfsStat**
closedir readdir readdir: readdirName rewinddir	errno identifier message	No new protocol	access close flush lock:start:len: lseek:whence: oflag read:startingAt:nbyte: rewind share size unlock:start:len: write:startingAt:nbyte:	isBlk isChr isDir isFifo isReg isSpecial stat: stAtime stCtime stDev stFtime stGid stIno stMtime stNlink stSize stUid **CfsDirectoryEntry** dName ~~stat:~~

Class CfsDirectoryDescriptor

Class Method Summary

Method	Documented	See page
chdir:	CfsDirectoryDescriptor class	380
getcwd	CfsDirectoryDescriptor class	381
mkdir:	CfsDirectoryDescriptor class	381

opendir: aPathString
    pattern: aPatternString
    mode: flagInteger
	CfsDirectoryDescriptor class	381

pathSeparator:	CfsDirectoryDescriptor class	381
pathSeparatorString	CfsDirectoryDescriptor class	381
rmdir:	CfsDirectoryDescriptor class	382
rootDirectories	CfsDirectoryDescriptor class	382

Instance Method Summary

Method	Documented	See page
closedir	CfsDirectoryDescriptor	382
readdir	CfsDirectoryDescriptor	382
readdir: aCfsDirectoryEntry	CfsDirectoryDescriptor	382
readdirName	CfsDirectoryDescriptor	382
rewinddir	CfsDirectoryDescriptor	383

Class Interface

chdir: aPathString

Set the directory named by aPathString to be the current working directory. If successful, answer a cfsErrorProxy, else answer a cfsError that describes the error.

The errors can be: EACCESS EINVAL ENOENT EIO.

Expression
CfsDirectoryDescriptor chdir: '../src'

getcwd

Answer a string that specifies the absolute path name of the current working directory, else answer a cfsError describing the error that occurred. The last directory path set by chdir: is always answered by getcwd.

The errors can be: EACCESS EIO.

Expression
CfsDirectoryDescriptor getcwd

mkdir: aPathString

Create the directory named aPathString. If successful, answer a cfsErrorProxy; else answer a cfsError describing the error that occurred. The directory does *not* become the working directory.

See also: CfsFileDescriptor>>rename:new:, CfsFileDescriptor>>rmdir:

The errors can be: EACCESS EEXIST EINVAL ENOENT ENOSPC EROFS EIO.

Expression
CfsDirectoryDescriptor mkdir: 'archie'

openDir: aPathString pattern: aPatternString mode: flagInteger

Answer an instance of the receiver representing a directory stream over the directory named in the string aPathString. The stream will contain all those entries that match the pattern in the string aPatternString. The stream is positioned at the first matching entry. If there are no matching entries, or if another error occurs, answer a cfsError describing the error that occurred.

Patterns are strings made up of three kinds of characters.

Characters	Description
*	Matches zero or more arbitrary characters.
?	Matches one and only one arbitrary character.
All others	Other characters match themselves.

See the section on 'Searching Directories' on page 148 for more information about patterns.

The flags in flagInteger are one of, or are the *inclusive or* of two or more of the directory search flags in Figure 87, 'Directory Search Flags', on page 378.

The errors can be: EACCES EINVAL ENFILE ENOENT EIO.

Expression
CfsDirectoryDescriptor openDir: 'c:\' pattern: '*' mode: FREG | FDIR

pathSeparator

Answer the platform-specific path separator character to be used in path names on the current platform. It returns values such as $\, $/, or $:.

Expression
CfsDirectoryDescriptor pathSeparator

pathSeparatorString

Answer a one-character string that holds the platform-specific path separator character that is used in path names on the current platform. It returns values such as '\', '/', or ':'.

Expression
CfsDirectoryDescriptor pathSeparatorString

rmdir: aPathString

Remove the directory named in the string aPathString. The directory must be empty. Answer an instance of CfsErrorProxy if successful; else answer an instance of CfsError which describes the error that occurred.

The errors can be: EACCES EBUSY EINVAL ENOENT EEXIST EROFS EIO.

Expression
CfsDirectoryDescriptor rmdir: 'archie'

rootDirectories

Answer an array of strings that name the paths of the accessible root directories. The names contain platform-specific path separator characters. On Unix, the array holds one string ('\'), while on OS/2 or Windows the array holds several strings, such as: 'A:\', 'B:\', 'C:\', 'D:\'.

Expression
CfsDirectoryDescriptor rootDirectories

Instance Interface

closedir

Close the receiver's directory stream. Answer an instance of CfsErrorProxy if successful; else answer an instance of CfsError which describes the error that occurred.

The errors can be: EBADF EIO.

Value of a	Expression	Result
aCfsDirectoryDescriptor	a closedir	aCfsErrorProxy

readdir

Answer an instance of CfsDirectoryEntry, which describes the directory at the current position in the receiver's directory stream, and position the directory stream at the next entry. Answer nil if the current position was already at the end of the stream. If an error occurs, answer an instance of CfsError describing the error.

The errors can be: EACCES EBADF EIO.

Expression	Result
aCfsDirectoryDescriptor readdir	aCfsDirectoryEntry

readdir: aCfsDirectoryEntry

Answer the parameter, aCfsDirectoryEntry, filled in anew to describe the directory at the current position in the receiver's directory stream, and position the directory stream at the next entry. Answer nil if the current position was already at the end of the stream. If an error occurs, answer a cfsError describing the error.

The errors can be: EACCES EBADF EINVAL EIO.

Expression	Result
aCfsDirectoryDescriptor readdir: aCfsDirectoryEntry	aCfsDirectoryEntry

readdirName

Answer the name of the directory entry at the current position in the receiver's directory stream and position the directory stream at the next entry. Answer nil if the current position was already at the end of the stream.

Directory names containing empty names are skipped. It is unspecified whether the entries for dot ('.') and dot-dot ('..') are answered.

Expression	Result
aCfsDirectoryDescriptor readdirName	aString

rewinddir

Refresh the receiver so that it refers to the current state of the directory, then reset the position of the receiver's directory stream to the beginning of the directory. This is equivalent to closing the stream and then reopening it. If successful, answer a cfsError-Proxy; else answer a cfsError describing the error that occurred.

The errors can be: EACCES EBADF EIO.

Expression
aCfsDirectoryDescriptor rewinddir

Class CfsError

Class Method Summary

There are no new class methods.

Instance Method Summary

Method	Documented	See page
errno	CfsError	383
identifier	CfsError	384
isCfsError	Object	
message	CfsError	384

Instance Interface

errno

Answer the receiver's error number, an integer. It should be used only for comparison against error values defined in CfsConstants. Its numeric value should never be coded directly, since the error values are platform dependent.

Expression	Possible result
aCfsError errno	23

identifier

Answer the identifier representing the error reported by the receiver. The identifier is a string that is the value of the key in CfsConstants for this error. The identifier is platform independent and can be referenced in code. Prior to using the string as a key, convert it to a proper pool dictionary key with asPoolKey.

It is always true that, given aCfsError:

$$(\text{CfsConstants at: aCfsError identifier asPoolKey}) == \text{aCfsError errno}$$

Expression	Possible result
aCfsError identifier	'EACCES'

isCfsError

Always answer true.

Expression	Result
aCfsError isCfsError	true

message

Answer a string that holds a description of the error reported by the receiver.

Expression	Result
aCfsError message	aString

Class CfsErrorProxy

Class Method Summary

There are no new class methods.

Instance Method Summary

Method	Documented	See page
isCfsError	CfsError	384

Instance Interface

isCfsError

Always answer false.

Expression	Result
aCfsErrorProxy isCfsError	false

Class CfsFileDescriptor

Class Method Summary

Method	Documented	See page
open: pathString oflag: flags	CfsFileDescriptor class	386

open: pathString
   oflag: flags
   share: share
	CfsFileDescriptor class	386

remove: pathString	CfsFileDescriptor class	387
rename: oldPathString new: newPathString	CfsFileDescriptor class	387
supportsLockType: lockType	CfsFileDescriptor class	387
supportsShareMode: shareMode	CfsFileDescriptor class	387

Instance Method Summary

Method	Documented	See page
access	CfsFileDescriptor	387
close	CfsFileDescriptor	387
flush	CfsFileDescriptor	388

lock: lockType
   start: startInt
   len: lengthInt
	CfsFileDescriptor	388

lseek: offsetInt whence: seekType	CfsFileDescriptor	388
oflag	CfsFileDescriptor	389

read: stringOrByteArray
   startingAt: intPosition
   nbyte: anInteger
	CfsFileDescriptor	389

rewind	CfsFileDescriptor	389
share	CfsFileDescriptor	389
size	CfsFileDescriptor	389

Part 1 of 2.

Method	Documented	See page

unlock: lockType
    start: startInt
    nbyte: lengthInt
	CfsFileDescriptor	389

write: stringOrByteArray
    startingAt: intPosition
    nbyte: intLength
	CfsFileDescriptor	390

Part 2 of 2.

Class Interface

open: pathString oflag: flags

Create a file descriptor for the file described by pathString and open the file. Answer the file descriptor if the open is successful, else an instance of CfsError that describes the error. The open flags are shown in Figure 82, 'File Open Flags', on page 376.

The errors can be: EACCESS EBUSY EEXIST EINVAL ENFILE ENOENT ENOSPC EROFS EIO.

```
" Open a new file for writing; fail if it exists "
| file |
file := CfsFileDescriptor
        open: 'dropout.log'
        oflag: OWRONLY | OCREAT | OEXCL.
file isCfsError
    ifTrue: [ ^ self error: file message ].
file close
```
Example 290, Execute

open: pathString oflag: flags share: share

Create a file descriptor for the file described by pathString and open the file. Answer the file descriptor if the open is successful, else an instance of CfsError that describes the error. The open flags are shown in Figure 82, 'File Open Flags', on page 376.

The sharing options in the integer share are platform dependent. Some share modes may be invalid on some platforms. See Figure 86, 'File Sharing Constants', on page 378.

Flag	Description
ODENYNONE	Other processes can open the file for any type of access: read-only, write-only, or read-write.
ODENYRD	Other processes can open the file only for write access.
ODENYWR	Other processes can open the file only for read access.
ODENYRDWR	Other processes cannot open the file for any kind of access; it is unspecified whether the current process can open it a second time.

Figure 88: File Sharing Constants.

The errors can be: EACCESS EBUSY EEXIST EINVAL ENFILE ENOENT ENOSPC EROFS EIO.

```
" Open a file with exclusive read and write access "
| file |
file := CfsFileDescriptor
        open: 'examp291.fil'
        oflag: ORDWR | OCREAT
        share: ODENYRDWR.
file isCfsError
    ifTrue: [ ^ self error: file printString ].
file close
```
Example 291, Execute

remove: pathString

Remove the file named by pathString from the file system. Answer an instance of CfsError-Proxy if successful; else answer an instance of CfsError that describes the error.

The errors can be: EACCESS EBUSY EEXIST EINVAL EISDIR ENOENT EPERM EROFS EIO.

Expression
aCfsFileDescriptor remove: '\daves\stuff\'

rename: oldPathString new: newPathString

Change the path name of the file named by oldPathString to be newPathString. If the paths are not the same, the file will be moved; it is an error if there is already a file with the new name. If successful answer an instance of CfsErrorProxy; else answer an instance of CfsError that describes the error.

The errors can be: EACCES EBUSY EEXIST EINVAL EISDIR ENOENT ENOSPC EROFS EXDEV EIO.

Expression
aCfsFileDescriptor rename: 'oldname' new: 'newname'

supportsLockType: lockType

Answers true if the lock type is supported on the current platform; false otherwise. Valid values for lockType are shown in Figure 85, 'File Locking Constants', on page 378.

Expression
aCfsFileDescriptor supportsLockType: FMDLOCK

supportsShareMode: shareMode

Answers true if the current platform supports the share mode shareMode; answers false otherwise.

Expression
aCfsFileDescriptor supportsShareMode: ODENYRDWR

Valid values for shareMode are shown in Figure 86, 'File Sharing Constants', on page 378.

Instance Interface

access

Answer the receivers access mode, which can be one of the three values ORDONLY, OWRONLY, or ORDWR from the CfsConstants pool dictionary.

Expression
aCfsFileDescriptor access

close

Closes the file represented by the receiver with these steps: unlock all outstanding locks for this file that are owned by the current process; perform a flush; and close the underlying platform file. If successful, answer an instance of CfsErrorProxy; else answer an instance of CfsError that describes the error.

The errors can be: EBADF EIO.

Expression
aCfsFileDescriptor close

flush

Force all modifications made to the file to be written to the disk. This is required on platforms where the operating system buffers low-level I/O operations, but will have no effect on other platforms.

Depending on the platform, it may not be possible to force all changes to be written to the disk; however, flush will cause as much as possible to be written.

If successful, answer an instance of CfsErrorProxy, otherwise answer an instance of CfsError that describes the error.

The errors can be: EACCESS EBADF EIO.

Expression
aCfsFileDescriptor flush

lock: lockType start: startInt len: lengthInt

Lock a section of the file starting at startInt for lengthInt bytes. The starting position must be within the size of the file. The length must not cause startInt+lengthInt to exceed the size of the file, and the length must not be zero.

The lock type, lockType, can be one of the values shown in Figure 85, 'File Locking Constants', on page 378.

If successful, answer an instance of CfsErrorProxy; otherwise answer an instance of CfsError which describes the error.

Some lock types may be invalid on some platforms; a lock type is valid if the message:

CfsFileDescriptor supportsLockType: aLockType

answers true when passed one of the lock types as aLockType.

See the section on 'Locking' on page 154 for more information.

The errors can be: EACCES EBADF EBUSY EINVAL EROFS EIO.

Expression
aCfsFileDescriptor lock: FRDLOCK start: k1 len: k2-k1

lseek: offsetInt whence: seekType

Set the file offset for the file to be anInteger bytes from the position specified by seekType. The values for seekType are shown in Figure 83, 'File Positioning Constants', on page 376.

If successful, answer the resulting offset location in the file; otherwise answer an instance of CfsError that describes the error.

The value of offsetInt can be positive or negative, depending upon the seek type. It is an error to seek before the front of the file. Seeking cannot extend the file; attempts to seek past the end of the file are platform dependent.

See the section on 'Random Access' on page 152 for more information.

The errors can be: EBADF EINVAL EIO.

Expression
aCfsFileDescriptor lseek: pos whence: SEEKSET

oflag

Answer the open flags used to open the file.

Expression
aCfsFileDescriptor oflag

read: stringOrByteArray startingAt: intPosition nbyte: anInteger

Try to read anInteger bytes from the file into the buffer stringOrByteArray. Data is placed into the buffer starting at position intPosition, an index into the array. As much as an-Integer bytes can be read. It is an error if the buffer is not long enough for the maximum possible read. The bytes are copied without translation or modification into the buffer. If anInteger is zero, this method answers zero and has no other effect.

If successful, answer the number of bytes read from the file, which can be less than an-Integer; otherwise answer an instance of CfsError that describes the error.

See the section on 'Reading and Writing Files' on page 151 for more information.

The errors can be: EACCES EBADF EBUSY EINVAL EIO.

Expression
aCfsFileDescriptor read: buf startingAt: 1 nbyte: buf size

rewind

Reset the position of the file to be the beginning of the file. If successful, answer an instance of CfsErrorProxy; otherwise answer an instance of CfsError that describes the error.

The errors can be: EBADF EIO.

Expression
aCfsFileDescriptor rewind

share

Answer the share mode specified when the file was created. The result is an integer having one of the values in Figure 86, 'File Sharing Constants', on page 378.

See the section on 'Sharing Files' on page 155 for more information.

Expression
aCfsFileDescriptor share

size

Answer zero or a positive integer that specifies the size of the file, in bytes, as it currently exists. Note that this value can be different than that answered by the stSize message to an instance of CfsStat, since the latter reflects the size given in the directory, which may not reflect changes to the file made since it was opened.

The errors can be: EBADF EIO.

Expression
aCfsFileDescriptor size

unlock: lockType start: startInt len: lengthInt

Unlock a section of the file starting at startInt for lengthInt bytes. The values given, including the lock type, must *exactly* match parameters to a previously issued lock:start:len: message for the same file descriptor, and which successfully locked a section of the file. It is an error to unlock a section of the file that was not locked.

If successful, answer an instance of CfsErrorProxy; otherwise answer an instance of CfsError that describes the error.

The lock type, lockType, can be one of the values in Figure 85, 'File Locking Constants', on page 378.

See the section on 'Locking' on page 154 for more information.

The errors can be: EACCES EBADF EINVAL EIO.

Expression
aCfsFileDescriptor unlock: FRDLOCK startingAt: k1 nbyte: k2-k1

write: stringOrByteArray startingAt: intPosition nbyte: intLength

Try to write intLength bytes from the buffer stringOrByteArray into the file. Data is written from the buffer starting at position intPosition, an index into the array. All intLength bytes will be written. It is an error if the buffer is not at least intPosition+intLength-1 bytes long. The bytes are copied to the file without translation or modification. If intLength is zero, this method answers zero and has no other effect.

If successful, answer the number of bytes written to the file, which can be less than intLength; otherwise answer an instance of CfsError that describes the error.

See the section on 'Reading and Writing Files' on page 151 for more information.

The errors can be: EACCES EBADF EBUSY EINVAL ENOSPC EROFS EIO.

Expression
aCfsFileDescriptor write: buf startingAt: 1 nbyte: buf size

CfsStat

Class Method Summary

Method	Documented	See page
stat: aPathString	cfsStat class	391

Instance Method Summary

Method	Documented	See page
isBlk	CfsStat	391
isChr	CfsStat	391
isDir	CfsStat	391

Part 1 of 2.

Method	Documented	See page
isFifo	CfsStat	391
isReg	CfsStat	391
isSpecial	CfsStat	391
stat: aPathString	CfsStat	391
stAtime	CfsStat	392
stCtime	CfsStat	392
stDev	CfsStat	392
stFtime	CfsStat	392
stGid	CfsStat	392
stIno	CfsStat	392
stMtime	CfsStat	392
stNlink	CfsStat	392
stSize	CfsStat	392
stUid	CfsStat	392

Part 2 of 2.

Class Interface

stat: filePathString

Answer an instance of the receiver configured to answer statistics for the file named in filePathString. If an error occurs, answer an instance of CfsError that describes the error.

Instance Interface

isBlk

Answer true if the receiver is reporting information about a block special file, and false otherwise. (Not all platforms have block special files.)

isChr

Answer true if the receiver is reporting information about a character special file, and false otherwise. (Not all platforms have character special files.)

isDir

Answer true if the receiver is reporting information about a directory, and false otherwise.

isFifo

Answer true if the receiver is reporting information about a pipe or FIFO special file, and false otherwise. (Not all platforms have pipes or FIFO files.)

isReg

Answer true if the receiver is reporting information about a regular file, and false otherwise.

isSpecial

Answer true if the receiver is reporting information about a special file, and false otherwise. (Not all platforms have special files.)

stat: filePathString

Answer the receiver updated to answer statistics for the file named in filePathString. If an error occurs, answer an instance of CfsError that describes the error.

stAtime

Answer an array with two elements, the first a date and the second a time, which represent the date and time that the file was last accessed. Answer nil if not supported by the platform's file system.

stCtime

Answer an array with two elements, the first a date and the second a time, which represent the date and time that the file was last changed. Answer nil if not supported by the platform's file system.

stDev

Answer the device ID of the device containing the file. Answer nil if not supported by the platform's file system.

stFtime

Answer an array with two elements, the first a date and the second a time, which represent the date and time that the file was created. Answer nil if not supported by the platform's file system.

stGid

Answer the group ID for the file. Answer nil if not supported by the platform's file system.

stIno

Answer the serial number of the file. Answer nil if not supported by the platform's file system.

stMtime

Answer an array with two elements, the first a date and the second a time, which represent the date and time that the file was last modified.

stNlink

Answer the number of links for the file. Answer nil if not supported by the platform's file system.

stSize

Answer the size of the file. The file must be a regular file; the result is not defined for other kinds of files.

stUid

Answer the user ID of the file. Answer nil if not supported by the platform's file system.

CfsDirectoryEntry

Class Method Summary

Method	Documented	See page
~~stat: filePathString~~	cfsStat class	391

Instance Method Summary

Method	Documented	See page
dName	CfsDirectoryEntry	393

Instance Interface

dName

Answer a string holding the name of the directory.

30

Exception Handling

Exception handling lets programs recover from errors that would otherwise be fatal.

The exception classes are:

See Chapter 14, 'Handling Exceptions', on page 157 for an introduction to exception handling.

Kinds of Exception Classes

Blocks

Exceptions are handled by messages to blocks:

aBlock **when:** *anExceptionalEvent* **do:** *anExceptionHandlerBlock*

The when:do: message evaluates aBlock. If, during its execution, the exceptional event anExceptionalEvent is signalled, then the block anExceptionHandlerBlock is evaluated; it can take various actions, including retrying, resuming, or terminating processing. There can be no return statements in aBlock or in an exception handler block.

Exceptional Events

Exceptional events name a kind of exception and provide information about how to handle the exception when it occurs. Exceptions are signalled when detected; if an exception handler block has been defined for that exception, then the exception is trapped. IBM Smalltalk comes with four defined exceptional events. They are:

ExAll	The most general exception; catches all exceptions.
ExError	The exception signalled by error:. The error string is passed to the handler block.
ExHalt	The exception signalled by halt:. The halt message string is passed to the handler block.
ExUserBreak	The exception signalled by the system's user break handler.

These exceptions are all instances of class ExceptionalEvent and are held in the pool dictionary SystemExceptions.

Exceptional Event Collections

Exceptional event collections are collections of exceptional events:

ExError | ExUserBreak | ExHalt

They are used in a when:do: message:

aBlock when: **ExError | ExHalt** do: *anExceptionHandlerBlock*

Signals

Instances of Signal are passed to the exception handler block to describe the exception and provide protocol for handling it.

aBlock when: *anExceptionalEvent* do: [**:aSignal** | *exceptionHandlerCode*]

Categories of Methods

Blocks

Block's exception handling methods are:

when:do:	Run block and handle given exception
when:do:when:do:	Run block and handle given exceptions
when:do:when:do:when:do:	Run block and handle given exceptions
when:do:when:do:when:do:when:do:	Run block and handle given exceptions
when:do:when:do:when:do: when:do:when:do:	Run block and handle given exceptions

Block's exception termination methods are:

atEndOrWhenExceptionDo:	Block termination cleanup
whenExceptionDo:	Block error termination cleanup

ExceptionalEvent

Access methods
Access methods are:

defaultHandler	Answer the default handler block
defaultHandler:	Set the default handler block
description	Answer the description of the exception
description:	Set the description of the exception
parent	Answer the next most general exception
resumable	Answer true if the exception is resumable
resumable:	Set to true if the exception is resumable

Creation
New instances of ExceptionalEvent are obtained by asking an existing instance for a child of itself.

newChild	Create a new child of an existing exception

New instances of ExceptionalEventCollection are created with the | message.

		Create a new ExceptionalEventCollection

Signalling
Exceptions are signalled with one of four methods.

signal	Signal an exception
signalWith:	Signal an exception; pass one argument
signalWIth:with:	Signal an exception; pass two arguments
signalWithArguments:	Signal an exception; pass arguments

ExceptionalEventCollection

Exceptional event collections are formed with just one message.

		Concatenate another exception

Signal

Instances of Signal are passed to exception blocks.

Access

argument	The first argument from signal message
arguments:	All arguments from signal message
description	The description of the exceptional event
exception	The exceptional event itself

Termination
Termination methods end a handler block.

exitWith:	Exit all handlers with a value
handlesByDefault	Pass control to the default handler
resumeWith:with:	Resume execution at signalled place
retry	Retry whole block again
signal	Look for another handler in parent
signalWith:	Look for another handler in parent
signalWith:With:	Look for another handler in parent
signalWithArguments:	Look for another handler in parent

Protocol Summary

Class Protocol Summary

There is no new class protocol.

Instance Protocol Summary

Object			
printOn:			

Block (exception related)	ExceptionalEvent	Exceptional-EventCollection	Signal
atEndOrWhenExceptionDo:	|	|	argument
when:do:	defaultHandler		arguments
when:do:when:do:	defaultHandler:		description
when:do:when:do:when:do:	description		exception
when:do:when:do:when:do: when:do:	description:		exitWith:
	newChild		handlesByDefault
when:do:when:do:when:do: when:do:when:do:	parent		resumeWith:with:
	resumable		retry
whenExceptionDo:	resumable:		signal
	signal		signalWith:
	signalWith:		signalWith:with:
	sitnalWith:with:		signalWithArguments:
	signalWithArguments:		

Class Block

Class Method Summary

There are no class methods.

Instance Method Summary

Method	Documented	See page
atEndOrWhenExceptionDo: aBlock	Block	399
when: exception do: aBlock	Block	399
when: exception1 do: aBlock1 when: exception2 do: aBlock2	Block	400

Part 1 of 2.

Method	Documented	See page

when: exception1 do: aBlock1
   when: exception2 do: aBlock2
   when: exception3 do: aBlock3
	Block	400

when: exception1 do: aBlock1
   when: exception2 do: aBlock2
   when: exception3 do: aBlock3
   when: exception4 do: aBlock4
	Block	400

when: exception1 do: aBlock1
   when: exception2 do: aBlock2
   when: exception3 do: aBlock3
   when: exception4 do: aBlock4
   when: exception5 do: aBlock5
	Block	401

whenExceptionDo: aBlock	Block	401

Part 2 of 2.

Instance Interface

atEndOrWhenExceptionDo: endBlock

If *any* exception is raised during the evaluation of the receiver, evaluate endBlock: upon completion. The endBlock is not an exception handler block, but simply code that needs to be run when the receiver terminates.

If *no* exception is raised, evaluate endBlock after the receiver finishes.

See also: whenExceptionDo:

Example 292 assures that a stream is closed, no matter what happens.

```
" Make sure stream is closed no matter what "
| stream s |
s := ''.
stream := ReadStream on: 'It was a dark and stormy night'.
[ [ stream atEnd ]
    whileFalse: [ s := s, stream next asString ] ]
        atEndOrWhenExceptionDo: [ stream close ].
^ s
" Answers: 'It was a dark and stormy night' "                    Example 292, Display
```

when: anException do: anExceptionBlock

Evaluate the receiver; if an exception described by anException is raised, evaluate anExceptionBlock. A signalled exception is described by anException when:

- It is identical to anException; or
- the exception is an exceptional event collection containing the signalled exception; or
- either of the above is, or contains, an ancestor of the signalled exception.

```
" Capture a signalled event "
| e1 |
e1 := ExAll newChild.
[ e1 signal ]
    when: e1
    do: [ :sig |
        System message: 'e1'.
        sig exitWith: nil ]                    Example 293, Display
```

```
" A parent exception captures signal for a child "
| e1 e2 e3 |
e1 := ExAll newChild.
e2 := e1 newChild.
e3 := e2 newChild.
[ e2 signal ]
    when: e1
    do: [ :sig |
        System message: 'e1'.
        sig exitWith: nil ]
```
Example 294, Display

when: e1 do: b1 when: e2 do: b2

Evaluate the receiver; if an exception described by e1 or e2 is raised, evaluate the associated exception block b1, or b2. A signalled exception is described by anException when:

- It is identical to one of the exceptions; or
- the exception is an exceptional event collection containing the signalled exception; or
- either of the above is, or contains, an ancestor of the signalled exception.

In Example 295, message 'e1' is displayed, even though the exception signalled is e2, because the first when:do: specifies e1, and e1 is a parent of e2.

```
" Capture a signalled event "
| e1 e2 |
e1 := ExAll newChild.
e2 := e1 newChild.
[ e2 signal ]
    when: e1 do: [ :sig |  System message: 'e1'. sig exitWith: nil ]
    when: e2 do: [ :sig |  System message: 'e2'. sig exitWith: nil ]
" System message is 'e1' "
```
Example 295, Display

To prevent this, always put the when:do: clauses in order of least generality:

```
" Capture a signalled event "
| e1 e2 |
e1 := ExAll newChild.
e2 := e1 newChild.
[ e2 signal ]
    when: e2 do: [ :sig | System message: 'e2'. sig exitWith: nil ]
    when: e1 do: [ :sig | System message: 'e1'. sig exitWith: nil ]
" System message is 'e2' "
```
Example 296, Display

when: e1 do: b1 when: e2 do: b2 when: e3 do: b3

Evaluate the receiver; if an exception described by e1, e2, or e3 is raised, evaluate the associated exception block b1, b2, or b3. A signalled exception is described by anException when:

- It is identical to one of the exceptions; or
- the exception is an exceptional event collection containing the signalled exception; or
- either of the above is, or contains, an ancestor of the signalled exception.

when: e1 do: b1 when: e2 do: b2 when: e3 do: b3 when: e4 do: b4

Evaluate the receiver; if an exception described by e1, e2, e3, or e4 is raised, evaluate the associated exception block b1, b2, b3, or b4. A signalled exception is described by anException when:

- It is identical to one of the exceptions; or
- the exception is an exceptional event collection containing the signalled exception; or
- either of the above is, or contains, an ancestor of the signalled exception.

when: e1 do: b1 when: e2 do: b2 when: e3 do: b3 when: e4 do: b4 when: e5 do: b5
Evaluate the receiver; if an exception described by e1, e2, e3, e4, or e5 is raised, evaluate the associated exception block b1, b2, b3, b4, or b5. A signalled exception is described by anException when:

- It is identical to one of the exceptions; or
- the exception is an exceptional event collection containing the signalled exception; or
- either of the above is, or contains, an ancestor of the signalled exception.

whenExceptionDo: endBlock
If any exception is raised during the evaluation of the receiver, evaluate endBlock: upon completion. The endBlock is not an exception handler block, but simply code that needs to be run at the termination of the receiver.

If no exception is raised, endBlock is not evaluated.

See also: atEndOrWhenExceptionDo:

Class ExceptionalEvent

Class	Page
Object	
Block	300, 398, 500
ExceptionalEvent	401
ExceptionalEventCollection	404
Signal	404

Class Method Summary

There are no new class methods.

Instance Method Summary

Method	Documented	See page
I **anExceptionalEvent**	ExceptionalEvent	402
defaultHandler	ExceptionalEvent	402
defaultHandler: aHandlerBlock	ExceptionalEvent	402
description	ExceptionalEvent	402
description: aString	ExceptionalEvent	402
newChild	ExceptionalEvent	402
parent	ExceptionalEvent	403
resumable	ExceptionalEvent	403
resumable: aBoolean	ExceptionalEvent	403
signal	ExceptionalEvent	403
signalWith: anObject	ExceptionalEvent	403
signalWith: object1 with: object2	ExceptionalEvent	403
signalWithArguments: aCollection	ExceptionalEvent	404

Instance Interface

| anExceptionalEvent
Answer an instance of ExceptionalEventCollection containing the receiver and anExceptionalEvent.

Expression
ExError	ExHalt

defaultHandler
Answer the default handler of the receiver, or nil if none.

defaultHandler: aHandlerBlock
Set the default handler of the receiver to aHandlerBlock.

Expression
anException defaultHandler: [:sig	sig exitWith: nil]

description
Answer the description of the exceptional event.

Expression	Result
exSlippedOnBanana description	'An entity failed to resist gravitational forces when friction was lowered by an encounter with the peeling of a fruit.'

description: aString
Set the description of an exceptional event.

Expression
exSlippedOnBanana description: 'Banana peel caused a fall.'

newChild
Answer a new instance of ExceptionalEvent that is also a child of an existing instance, the receiver. The value returned is an exceptional event that can be signalled to raise the exception.

Example 297 creates three new exceptions: e1 is a child of ExAll, e2 is a child of e1, and e3 is a child of e2. A block that signals the e2 exception is executed. Since the when:do: message exceptions are ordered in the inverse of the hierarchy of exceptions, the signal invokes the handler for e2. Had the ordering been e1, e2, and then e3, the handler for e1 would have been invoked.

```
" Three children of ExAll  "
| e1 e2 e3 |
e1 := ExAll newChild.
e2 := e1 newChild.
e3 := e2 newChild.
[ e2 signal ]
    when: e3 do: [ :sig |  System message: 'e3'. sig exitWith: nil ]
    when: e2 do: [ :sig |  System message: 'e2'. sig exitWith: nil ]
    when: e1 do: [ :sig |  System message: 'e1'. sig exitWith: nil ]
" System message is 'e2' "
```
Example 297, Display

parent
Answer the parent of the receiver, or nil if the receiver has no parent. The parent is an exceptional event.

Expression	Result
ExHalt parent	ExAll

resumable
Answer true if the block in which the exception occurred can be resumed; answer false otherwise.

Expression	Result
ExAll resumable	false
ExHalt resumable	true

resumable: aBoolean
Set whether or not the exceptional event can be resumed from the point at which the receiver was raised.

Expression
exEngineOverrev resumable: partsFlewHereAndThere not

signal
Create an instance of Signal that describes the context in which the receiver was raised; then find and evaluate the appropriate handler, passing the instance of Signal as an argument. This message does not return.

Expression
ExAll signal
exSlippedOnBanana signal

signalWith: anObject
Create an instance of Signal that describes the context in which the receiver was raised and which contains anObject; then find and evaluate the appropriate handler, passing the instance of Signal as an argument. This message does not return.

Expression
exBounce signal: 'Hit left edge'
exSlippedOnBanana signalWith: 'Very ripe banana'

signalWith: object1 with: object2
Create an instance of Signal that describes the context in which the receiver was raised and which contains object1 and object2; then find and evaluate the appropriate handler, passing the instance of Signal as an argument. This message does not return.

Expression
exBounce signalWith: 'Hit left edge' with: Time now
exSlippedOnBanana signalWith: 'Very ripe banana' with: 'Left foot'

signalWithArguments: aCollection

Create an instance of Signal that describes the context in which the receiver was raised, and which contains object1 and object2; then find and evaluate the appropriate handler, passing the instance of Signal as an argument. This message does not return.

Expression
exBounce signalWithArguments: (Array with: 'Hit left edge' with: Time now)
exSlippedOnBanana signalWithArguments: #(ripe leftFoot)

Class ExceptionalEventCollection

Class	Page
Object	
Block	300, 398, 500
ExceptionalEvent	401
ExceptionalEventCollection	404
Signal	404

Class Method Summary

There are no new class methods.

Instance Method Summary

Method	Documented	See page
I **anExceptionalEvent**	ExceptionalEvent	404

Instance Interface

I **anExceptionalEvent**

Answer an instance of ExceptionalEventCollection containing the receiver and anExceptionalEvent.

Expression
anExceptionalEventCollection I ExHalt

Class Signal

Class	Page
Object	
Block	300, 398, 500
ExceptionalEvent	401
ExceptionalEventCollection	
Signal	404

Class Method Summary

There are no new class methods.

Instance Method Summary

Method	Documented	See page
argument	Signal	405
arguments	Signal	405
description	Signal	405
exception	Signal	405
exitWith: anObject	Signal	406
handlesByDefault	Signal	406
resumeWith: aKey with: aValue	Signal	406
retry	Signal	406
signal	Signal	406
signalWith: anObject	Signal	406
signalWith: object1 with: object2	Signal	406
signalWithArguments: aCollection	Signal	406

Instance Interface

argument
Answer the first argument passed when the exception was signalled, or nil if none was passed.

If the signalled exception is:

> exSlippedOnBanana signalWith: 'ripe' with: 'left foot'.

and the handler is, in part:

> [:sig | sig argument …

then sig argument answers 'ripe'.

arguments
Answer a collection containing all arguments passed when the exception was signalled, or nil if none were passed.

If the signalled exception is:

> exSlippedOnBanana signalWith: 'ripe' with: 'left foot'.

and the handler is, in part:

> [:sig | sig arguments …

then sig arguments answers the collection: ('ripe' 'left foot').

description
Answer the description of the signalled event. This is the same value that is the description of an exceptional event.

exception
Answer the exception that was raised.

If the signalled exception is:

> exSlippedOnBanana signalWith: 'ripe' with: 'left foot'.

and the handler is, in part:

```
[ :sig | sig exception …
```

then sig exception answers the exception exSlippedOnBanana.

exitWith: anObject
Terminate the when:do: expression; answer anObject as its result.

```
[ exSlippedOnBanana signal ]
    when: exSlippedOnBanana
    do: [ :sig | sig exitWith: 7 ].
        "Answers: 7 "
```

handlesByDefault
Exit the current handler block and invoke the exceptional event's default handler.

In Example 298, the handler in the when:do: passes control to the default handler.

```
" Default handler is run "
| ping |
(ping := ExAll newChild)
    description: 'ping signalled';
    defaultHandler: [ :sig |
        System errorMessage: sig description.
        sig exitWith: 'done' ].
[ ping signal ]
    when: ping
    do: [ :sig | sig handlesByDefault ]
    "Answers: 'done' "
```

Example 298, Display

resumeWith: key with: anObject
Build an association from key and anObject; resume execution of the block interrupted by the signal, answering the association as the result of the signal message. The values of key and anObject are completely arbitrary.

retry
Re-executes the receiver of the when:do: message. All handlers are reinstated. An endless loop can easily result from retry; be cautious when testing code.

signal
Terminate the current handler and begin a search for another handler. This message does not return. Other handlers might be the default handler for an exception, or another handler in another when:do: message executed earlier.

signalWith: anObject
Terminate the current handler and begin a search for another handler. The argument anObject is passed to the next handler in place of the arguments in the receiver. This message does not return.

signalWith: object1 with: object2
Terminate the current handler and begin a search for another handler. The arguments object1 and object2 are passed to the next handler in place of the arguments in the receiver. This message does not return.

signalWithArguments: aCollection
Terminate the current handler and begin a search for another handler. The arguments in aCollection are passed to the next handler in place of the arguments in the receiver. This message does not return.

31

File Streams

Streams can be opened on files, on collections, or on sources of random numbers. This chapter describes streams on files.

For an introduction to file streams, see the section on 'File Streams' on page 138.

The stream classes are:

Stream and its subclasses are documented in Chapter 37, 'Streams', on page 527.

Kinds of File Stream Classes

Class CfsFileStream is an abstract class that defines methods that all file streams must support, including fetching the next item from the stream, setting the stream position, and checking for the end of the stream.

CfsReadFileStream

Class CfsReadFileStream is a concrete class that streams across an input file. Operations include reading from the stream and skipping ahead to specified contents.

CfsReadWriteFileStream

Class CfsReadWriteFileStream allows both reading from and writing to a file stream.

CfsWriteFileStream

Class CfsWriteFileStream allows writing to a file, but not reading from it.

Categories of Messages

The following messages are supported by one or more file stream classes.

Iteration

Iterate through the stream to the end, or for random numbers, iterate forever.

do:	Read: Pass elements to a block

Positioning

Positioning methods query and set the read or write pointer to a new position.

atEnd	All: True if no more to read
position	All: Answer current position
position:	All: Set the position
reset:	All: Set position at front
setToEnd	All: Set position past last element
skip:	All: Skip the next n elements

Querying and Setting

Querying and setting methods answer or set stream state information.

atEnd	All: True if no more to read
bufferSize	All: Answer the size of the file buffer
bufferSize:	All: Set the size of the file buffer
fileDescriptor	All: Answer the file descriptor
isBytes	All: True if the stream works with bytes
isBytes:	All: Specify to work with bytes
isCharacters	All: True if the stream works with characters
isCharacters:	All: Specify to work with characters
isEmpty	All: True if file empty
lineDelimiter	All: Answer current line delimiter
lineDelimiter:	All: Set line delimiter
size	All: Answer size of file in bytes

Reading

Reading methods answer data from the stream.

close	All: Close the file
contents	Read: Answer the entire contents of the file
copyFrom:to:	Read: Copy into new collection
next	Read: Get next element
next:	Read: Get next n elements
nextLine	Read: Get next line
nextMatchFor:	Read: Compare next element with an object
peekFor:	Read: Compare next with an object
peek	Read: Peek at next element

upTo:	Read: Get elements up to a value
upToAll:	Read: Get elements up to a sequence
upToEnd	Read: Get elements up to the end

Skipping

Skip elements in the stream.

skip:	Read: Skip next element
skipTo:	Read: Skip ahead to a value
skipToAll:	Read: Skip ahead to a sequence

Writing

Writing methods modify a stream.

close	Write: Close the file
cr	Write: Output a line delimiter
flush	Write: Flush buffers to disk
next:put:	Write: Output n copies of a value
nextPut:	Write: Output a value
nextPutAll:	Write: Output contents of collection
space	Write: Output a space character
tab	Write: Output a tab character

Flags and Codes Summary

Open Flags

The file open flags, shown in Figure 89, specify how to open a file. One and only one of the first three flags must be given, but any of the last four can be *inclusive or*ed to it. The kind of file stream returned depends upon which of the first three flags is used.

Flag	Description	Usage
ORDONLY	Open the file for reading only.	Choose just one of these flags.
OWRONLY	Open the file for writing only.	
ORDWR	Open the file for both reading and writing.	
OAPPEND	Set the file offset to the end of the file before *each* write.	*Inclusive or* zero or more of these flags to the one chosen above.
OCREAT	If the file does not exist, create a new one; if the file exists, just open it (unless OEXCL is also given; see below).	
OEXCL	Cause the open to fail if the file exists and OCREAT and OEXCL are both specified.	
OTRUNC	Truncate the file to a length of zero if it is successfully opened ORDWR or OWRONLY.	

Figure 89: File Open Flags.

Error Codes

The errors returned by file streams are summarized in Figure 90.

Error	Description
EACCESS	The path or file name is too long, or some component of the path to the file is invalid or inaccessible.
EBUSY	The file is locked with a mandatory lock.
EEXIST	OCREAT and OEXCL were specified and the file already exists.
EINVAL	Probably an invalid argument.
ENFILE	The number of open files has exceeded some platform limit.
ENOENT	OCREAT was *not* specified and the file does not exist.
ENOSPC	Not enough space on the target device to create the directory entry.
EROFS	The file is read-only or is on a locked or write-protected volume, and the file is to be created, or opened with write access.
EIO	A low-level I/O error occurred, or a platform-specific error occurred, or a platform function returned an undefined error code.

Figure 90: Error Codes From File Streams.

Protocol Summary

Class Protocol Summary

Object class	
=	
CfsFileStream class	
on:	open:oflag:
CfsReadFileStream class	**CfsWriteFileStream class**
open:	open:
CfsReadWriteFileStream class	openEmpty:
openEmpty:	

Instance Protocol Summary

Object					
==	~~	size			
CfsFileStream					
atEnd	close	isBytes:	isEmpty	position	setToEnd
bufferSize	fileDescriptor	isCharacters	lineDelimiter	position:	skip:
bufferSize:	isBytes	isCharacters:	lineDelimiter:	reset	

CfsReadFileStream					**CfsWriteFileStream**
contents	next	nextMatchFor:	skipTo:	upToAll:	cr
copyFrom:to:	next:	peek	skipToAll:	upToEnd	flush
do:	nextLine	peekFor:	upTo:		next:put:
CfsReadWriteFileStream					nextPut:
					nextPutAll:
cr	next:put:	nextPutAll:	tab		space
flush	nextPut:	space			tab

Class CfsFileStream

CfsFileStream is an abstract class that defines methods for reading and writing bytes or characters to and from files.

Class Method Summary

Method	Documented	See page
on: fileDescriptor	CfsFileStream class	412
open: pathString oflag: openFlags	CfsFileStream class	412

Instance Method Summary

Method	Documented	See page
atEnd	CfsFileStream	412
bufferSize	CfsFileStream	412
bufferSize: anInteger	CfsFileStream	412
close	CfsFileStream	412
fileDescriptor	CfsFileStream	412
isBytes	CfsFileStream	413
isBytes: aBoolean	CfsFileStream	413
isCharacters	CfsFileStream	413
isCharacters: aBoolean	CfsFileStream	413
isEmpty	CfsFileStream	413
lineDelimiter	CfsFileStream	413
lineDelimiter: aSequenceableColl	CfsFileStream	413
position	CfsFileStream	414
position: anInteger	CfsFileStream	414
reset	CfsFileStream	414
setToEnd	CfsFileStream	414
size	CfsFileStream Object	414 295
skip: anInteger	CfsFileStream	414

Class Interface

The opening of file streams and the processing of errors from file streams often requires constants (such as ORDONLY or EBUSY) that are defined in the pool dictionary CfsConstants. All classes that use file streams should also use CfsConstants. The flags and codes are described in Figure 89, 'File Open Flags', on page 409.

on: fileDescriptor
Answer a new file stream that will stream over the file described by fileDescriptor, an instance of CfsFileDescriptor. The stream is positioned at the front. The kind of file stream returned depends upon the access mode of the file.

Access Mode	Answer
ORDONLY	An instance of CfsReadFileStream
OWRONLY	An instance of CfsWriteFileStream
ORDWR	An instance of CfsReadWriteFileStream

on: pathString oflags: flags
Answer a new file stream that will stream over the file named by pathString, and which is opened using the file open flags named flags. The stream is positioned at the front. The kind of file stream returned depends upon the access mode of the file.

Access Mode	Answer
ORDONLY	An instance of CfsReadFileStream
OWRONLY	An instance of CfsWriteFileStream
ORDWR	An instance of CfsReadWriteFileStream

Instance Interface

atEnd
Answer true if the position of the stream is just past the last item in the stream.

Expression
aCfsReadFileStream atEnd

bufferSize
Answer an integer that specifies the size of the file stream buffer in bytes.

Expression
aCfsReadFileStream bufferSize

bufferSize: anInteger
Set the size of the buffer to anInteger bytes; anInteger must be positive. Answer the receiver.

Expression
aCfsReadFileStream bufferSize: 10000

close
Close the file.

Expression
aCfsReadFileStream close

fileDescriptor
Answer the file descriptor of the file on which the file stream is open.

Expression
aCfsReadFileStream fileDescriptor

isBytes
Answer true if the file stream is working with bytes; answer false otherwise.

Expression
aCfsReadFileStream isBytes

isBytes: aBoolean
If aBoolean is true, set the file stream so that it works with bytes; if aBoolean is false, set the file stream so that it works with characters.

Expression
aCfsWriteStream isBytes: true

isCharacters
Answer true if the file stream is working with characters; answer false otherwise.

Expression
aCfsReadFileStream isCharacters

isCharacters: aBoolean
If aBoolean is true, set the file stream so that it works with characters; if aBoolean is false, set the file stream so that it works with bytes.

Expression
aCfsReadFileStream isCharacters: true

isEmpty
Answer true if the size of the file over which the stream is streaming is zero.

Expression
aCfsReadFileStream isEmpty

lineDelimiter
Answer the line delimiter of the file stream. The default line delimiter holds a platform-dependent character sequence; see lineDelimiter:.

Expression
aCfsReadFileStream lineDelimiter

lineDelimiter: aSequenceableCollection
Set the line delimiter for the file stream. The default line-delimiter holds a platform-dependent character sequence. The value can be changed to other platform-dependent values using pool variables, such as UNIXLineDelimiter, WINLineDelimiter, PMLineDelimiter, and LineDelimiter from the pool dictionary CldtConstants.

See the section on 'Line Delimiters' on page 138 for more information.

Expression
aCfsReadFileStream lineDelimiter: UNIXLineDelimiter

position

Answer the current position of the file stream on the file. The value returned is one less than the index in the file that will be returned next. Thus, a zero means that next will return the first element.

Expression
aCfsReadFileStream position

position: anInteger

Set the position of the stream to anInteger. The value is one less than the index of the element that will be referenced next. Thus, a zero means that next will return the first element.

Expression
aCfsReadFileStream position: (dict at: 'Page 3')

reset

Set the position to the front of the file.

Expression
aCfsReadFileStream reset

setToEnd

Set the position at the end of the file.

Expression
aCfsReadFileStream setToEnd

size

Answer the size of the file in bytes.

Expression
aCfsReadFileStream size

skip: anInteger

Increment the position in the file stream by anInteger. A positive value skips forward in the stream, and a negative value skips backward; anInteger must set the position to a value from zero to the size of the file.

Expression
aCfsReadFileStream skip: 12

Class CfsReadFileStream

ReadStream is an concrete class that defines methods for reading streams of objects.

Class Method Summary

Method	Documented	See page
on: fileDescriptor	CfsFileStream class	412
open: pathString	CfsReadFileStream class	416
open: pathString oflag: openFlags	CfsFileStream class	412

Instance Method Summary

Method	Documented	See page
atEnd	CfsFileStream	412
bufferSize	CfsFileStream	412
bufferSize: anInteger	CfsFileStream	412
close	CfsFileStream	412
contents	CfsReadFileStream	416
copyFrom: fromInteger to: toInteger	CfsReadFileStream	416
do: aBlock	CfsReadFileStream	416
fileDescriptor	CfsFileStream	412
isBytes	CfsFileStream	413
isBytes: aBoolean	CfsFileStream	413
isCharacters	CfsFileStream	413
isCharacters: aBoolean	CfsFileStream	413
isEmpty	CfsFileStream	413
lineDelimiter	CfsFileStream	413
lineDelimiter: aSequenceableColl	CfsFileStream	413
next	CfsReadFileStream	416
next: anInteger	CfsReadFileStream	417
nextLine	CfsReadFileStream	417
nextMatchFor: anObject	CfsReadFileStream	417
peek	CfsReadFileStream	417
peekFor: anObject	CfsReadFileStream	417
position	CfsFileStream	414

Part 1 of 2.

Method	Documented	See page
position: anInteger	CfsFileStream	414
reset	CfsFileStream	414
setToEnd	CfsFileStream	414
size	CfsFileStream Object	414 295
skip: anInteger	CfsFileStream	414
skipTo: anObject	CfsReadFileStream	418
skipToAll: aCollection	CfsReadFileStream	418
upTo: anObject	CfsReadFileStream	418
upToAll: aCollection	CfsReadFileStream	418
upToEnd	CfsReadFileStream	418

Part 2 of 2.

Class Interface

open: pathString

Answer an instance of CfsReadFileStream that will stream over the file named by path-String. The stream is positioned at the front.

Expression
CfsReadFileStream open: 'C:/data/1995/corp/goodstuf.dat'

Instance Interface

contents

Answer a collection containing the entire contents of the file. If isBytes is true, then the collection is a byte array, else the collection is a string.

Expression
aCfsReadFileStream contents

copyFrom: fromInteger to: toInteger

Answer a collection that holds the elements in the file from fromInteger to toInteger and in the same order. If isBytes is true, then the collection is a byte array, else the collection is a string. If toInteger is less than fromInteger, answer an empty collection. It is an error if the indexes are not valid for the file.

Expression
aCfsReadFileStream copyFrom: j to: k

do: aBlock

Starting with the next element in the stream, and for each element remaining in the stream, invoke aBlock passing the next element. If isBytes is true, then the element is an integer, else the element is a character.

Expression
aCfsReadFileStream do: [:elem	Transcript put: elem printString]

next

Answer the next element in the file stream; increment the position of the stream by one. It is an error if there are no more elements in the file stream. If isBytes is true, then the element is an integer, else the element is a character.

Expression
aCfsReadFileStream next

next: anInteger
Answer a collection containing the next anInteger elements; position the stream so that the element just behind the last element answered will be returned next. If there are less than anInteger elements, then all remaining elements are answered and the file will answer true to atEnd. If isBytes is true, then the collection is a byte array, else the collection is a string.

Expression
aCfsReadFileStream next: 12

nextLine
If a line delimiter exists in the remainder of the file stream, answer a collection containing all of the elements up to the next line delimiter. Position the stream just past the line delimiter.

If no line delimiter exists in the remainder of the file stream, answer all the remaining elements in the stream. Position the stream so that atEnd is true. If isBytes is true, then the collection is a byte array, else the collection is a string.

Expression
aCfsReadFileStream nextLine

nextMatchFor: anObject
Answer true if the next element in the stream is equal to anObject; answer false if there is a next element and it isn't equal to anObject. The position is advanced by one, even if no match was made. It is an error if the stream is at its end. If isBytes is true, then the element is an integer, else the element is a character.

Expression
aCfsReadFileStream nextmatchFor: $.

peek
If the file stream is not at its end, answer the next element. The position is not advanced. It is an error if the stream is at its end. If isBytes is true, then the element is an integer, else the element is a character.

Expression
aCfsReadFileStream peek

peekFor: anObject
Answer true if the next element in the file stream is equal to anObject; answer false if there is a next element and it isn't equal to anObject. The position is not advanced. It is an error if the stream is at its end. If isBytes is true, then the element is an integer, else the element is a character.

Expression
aCfsReadFileStream peekFor: $.

skipTo: anObject

If there is an element remaining in the file stream that compares equal to anObject, then set the stream position just past that object and answer true. If isBytes is true, then anObject is an integer, else it is a character.

If there is no object remaining in the file stream that compares equal to anObject, then set the stream position to its end and answer false.

Expression
aCfsReadFileStream skipTo: $.

skipToAll: aCollection

If there is a sequence of objects remaining in the file stream that compares equal to the sequence in aCollection, then set the stream position just past that sequence and answer true. If isBytes is true, then aCollection and the returned collection are byte arrays, else both are strings.

If there is no sequence of objects remaining in the stream that compares equal to the sequence in aCollection, then set the stream position to its end and answer false.

Expression
aCfsReadFileStream skipToAll: '.'

upTo: anObject

If there is an element remaining in the stream that compares equal to anObject, then set the stream position just past that object and answer a collection containing the elements up to but not including anObject. If isBytes is true, then anObject and the element must be integers, else they must be characters.

If there is no object remaining in the stream that compares equal to anObject, then set the stream position to its end and answer a collection containing the remaining elements.

Expression
aCfsReadFileStream upTo: $.

upToAll: aCollection

If there is a sequence of objects remaining in the file stream that compares equal to the sequence in aCollection, then set the file stream position just past that sequence and answer a collection containing the elements up to but not including the sequence. If isBytes is true, then the collection is a byte array, else the collection is a string.

If there is no sequence of objects remaining in the stream that compares equal to the sequence in aCollection, then set the stream position to its end and answer a collection containing the remaining elements.

Expression
aCfsReadFileStream upToAll: '.'

upToEnd

Answer a collection that holds all the remaining elements in the file stream. If isBytes is true, then the collection is a byte array, else the collection is a string. If the current position is at the end of the stream, answer an empty collection.

Expression
aCfsReadFileStream upToEnd

Class CfsReadWriteFileStream

ReadWriteStream is an concrete class defining methods for both reading and writing streams of objects.

Class Method Summary

Method	Documented	See page
on: fileDescriptor	CfsFileStream class	412
open: pathString	CfsReadFileStream class	416
open: pathString oflag: openFlags	CfsFileStream class	412
openEmpty: pathString	CfsReadWriteFileStream	420

Instance Method Summary

Method	Documented	See page
atEnd	CfsFileStream	412
bufferSize	CfsFileStream	412
bufferSize: anInteger	CfsFileStream	412
close	CfsFileStream	412
contents	CfsReadFileStream	416
copyFrom: fromInteger to: toInteger	CfsReadFileStream	416
cr	CfsReadWriteFileStream	420
do: aBlock	CfsReadFileStream	416
fileDescriptor	CfsFileStream	412
flush	CfsReadWriteFileStream	420
isBytes	CfsFileStream	413
isBytes: aBoolean	CfsFileStream	413
isCharacters	CfsFileStream	413
isCharacters: aBoolean	CfsFileStream	413
isEmpty	CfsFileStream	413
lineDelimiter	CfsFileStream	413
lineDelimiter: aSequenceableColl	CfsFileStream	413
next	CfsReadFileStream	416
next: anInteger	CfsReadFileStream	417
nextLine	CfsReadFileStream	417

Part 1 of 2.

Method	Documented	See page
nextMatchFor: anObject	CfsReadFileStream	417
next: anInteger **put: anObject**	CfsReadWriteFileStream	420
nextPut: anObject	CfsReadWriteFileStream	421
nextPutAll: aCollection	CfsReadWriteFileStream	421
peek	CfsReadFileStream	417
peekFor: anObject	CfsReadFileStream	417
position	CfsFileStream	414
position: anInteger	CfsFileStream	414
reset	CfsFileStream	414
setToEnd	CfsFileStream	414
size	CfsFileStream Object	414 295
skip: anInteger	CfsFileStream	414
skipTo: anObject	CfsReadFileStream	418
skipToAll: aCollection	CfsReadFileStream	418
space	CfsReadWriteFileStream	421
tab	CfsReadWriteFileStream	421
upTo: anObject	CfsReadFileStream	418
upToAll: aCollection	CfsReadFileStream	418
upToEnd	CfsReadFileStream	418

Part 2 of 2.

Class Interface

openEmpty: pathString
Answer an instance of CfsReadWriteFileStream that will stream over the file named by pathString. If the file exists, it will be truncated when it is opened. The stream is positioned at the front.

Instance Interface

cr
Write a copy of the file stream's line delimiter to the file.

See lineDelimiter: *on page 413 for information about line delimiters.*

Expression
aCfsReadWriteFileStream cr

flush
Write all data that might still be in buffers in memory to the underlying file. (Some platforms may not completely flush buffers until the file is closed.)

Expression
aCfsReadWriteFileStream flush

next: anInteger put: anObject
Write anInteger copies of anObject into the file stream; anObject must be a character or integer, depending on the setting of isBytes.

Expression
aCfsReadWriteFileStream next: 20 put: $-

nextPut: anObject
Write anObject into the file stream; anObject must be a character or integer, depending on the setting of isBytes.

Expression
aCfsReadWriteFileStream nextPut: $-

nextPutAll: aSequenceableCollection
Write the contents of aSequenceableCollection to the file stream; the collection must be either a string or a byte array, depending on the setting of isBytes.

Expression
aCfsReadWriteFileStream nextPutAll: 'nextPutAll: '

space
Write a space to the file stream.

Expression
aCfsReadWriteFileStream space

tab
Write a tab to the file stream.

Expression
aCfsReadWriteFileStream tab

Class CfsWriteFileStream

WriteStream is an concrete class that defines methods for writing streams of objects.

Class Method Summary

Method	*Documented*	*See page*
on: fileDescriptor	CfsFileStream class	412
open: pathString	CfsWriteFileStream class	422
open: pathString oflag: openFlags	CfsFileStream class	412
openEmpty: pathString	CfsWriteFileStream class	422

Instance Method Summary

Method	Documented	See page
atEnd	CfsFileStream	412
bufferSize	CfsFileStream	412
bufferSize: anInteger	CfsFileStream	412
close	CfsFileStream	412
cr	CfsWriteFileStream	423
fileDescriptor	CfsFileStream	412
flush	CfsWriteFileStream	423
isBytes	CfsFileStream	413
isBytes: aBoolean	CfsFileStream	413
isCharacters	CfsFileStream	413
isCharacters: aBoolean	CfsFileStream	413
isEmpty	CfsFileStream	413
lineDelimiter	CfsFileStream	413
lineDelimiter: aSequenceableColl	CfsFileStream	413
next: anInteger **put: anObject**	CfsWriteFileStream	423
nextPut: anObject	CfsWriteFileStream	423
nextPutAll: anObject	CfsWriteFileStream	423
position	CfsFileStream	414
position: anInteger	CfsFileStream	414
reset	CfsFileStream	414
setToEnd	CfsFileStream	414
size	CfsFileStream Object	414 295
skip: anInteger	CfsFileStream	414
space	CfsWriteFileStream	423
tab	CfsWriteFileStream	423

Class Interface

open: pathString

Answer an instance of CfsWriteFileStream that will stream over the file named by path-String. The stream is positioned at the front.

Expression
CfsWriteFileStream open: 'some.dta'

openEmpty: pathString

Answer an instance of CfsWriteFileStream that will stream over the file named by path-String. If the file exists, it will be truncated when it is opened. The stream is positioned at the front.

Expression
CfsWriteFileStream openEmpty: 'some.dta'

Instance Interface

cr
Write a copy of the file stream's line delimiter to the file. (See lineDelimiter: for information about line delimiters.)

Expression
aCfsWriteFileStream cr

flush
Write all data that might still be in buffers in memory to the underlying file. (Some platforms may not completely flush buffers until the file is closed.)

Expression
aCfsWriteFileStream flush

next: anInteger put: anObject
Write anInteger copies of anObject into the file stream; anObject must be a character or integer, depending on the setting of isBytes.

Expression
aCfsWriteFileStream next: 2 put: $-

nextPut: anObject
Write anObject into the file stream; anObject must be a character or integer, depending on the setting of isBytes.

Expression
aCfsWriteFileStream nextPut: $-

nextPutAll: aCollection
Write the contents of aCollection to the file stream; the collection must be either a string or a byte array, depending on the setting of isBytes.

Expression
aCfsWriteFileStream nextPutAll: 'asdf'

space
Write a space to the file stream.

Expression
aCfsWriteFileStream space

tab
Write a tab to the file stream.

Expression
aCfsWriteFileStream tab

32

Magnitudes

Magnitudes are objects that can be compared using greater-than and less-than operations; each has some kind of ordered values. Smalltalk implements numbers, dates, times, characters, and associations as magnitudes.

For an introduction to magnitude classes, see the section on 'Undefined Object' on page 54.

The Magnitude classes are:

Number and its subclasses are described in Chapter 33, 'Numbers', on page 449.

Kinds of Magnitudes

Associations

Associations are a key/value pair used in dictionaries. Keys are often symbols or strings, but can be most any object.

Characters

Characters are the individual letters, numbers, punctuation, and white space that make up strings. Characters are identity objects: it is always true that if two characters compare true with = that they will compare true with ==. This means that

> aChar copy == aChar

is always true.

Implementations may not all print the same characters but are guaranteed to print the Smalltalk character set (see the section on 'The Character Set' on page 31). Most implementations extend this character set, but do so differently. Collating sequences across platforms may differ; for best portability, make the least assumptions.

Dates

Dates represent calendar dates in the Gregorian calendar. The Gregorian calendar was adopted around the world from the 1500s through the 1700s, and is the one in use today in western countries and in science and technology.

The Gregorian calendar has 12 months with the number of days varying from 28 to 31, leap years every fourth year with century years an exception unless evenly divisible by 400. (The year 2000 is such an exception; it *is* a leap year.)

Times

Times are subdivisions of a single day. They represent hours, minutes, and seconds since midnight. Times can be subtracted and integers can be added to times.

Numbers

Numbers come in three types: fraction, float, and integer. They are described fully in the next chapter.

Categories of Magnitude Messages

This classification includes all classes described in this chapter; number and its subclasses are classified in the next chapter.

Access

There are no access methods in Magnitude.

Class Association adds:

key	Answer the key
key:	Set the key
key:value:	Set the key and value
value	Answer the value
value:	Set the value

Class Date adds:

dayName	The name of the day
dayOfMonth	The day of the month
dayOfYear	The day of the year
daysInMonth	Total days in the month
daysInYear	Total days in the year
daysLeftInMonth	Days left in the month
daysLeftInYear	Days left in the year.
firstDayOfMonth	New date holding first day in month
monthIndex	Number of the month in the year
monthName	Name of the month
year	Number of the year

Class Time adds:

hours	Hour as an integer
minutes	Minute as an integer
seconds	Seconds as number

Arithmetic

There are no arithmetic methods in Magnitude.

Class Date adds:

addDays:	Add an integer number of days to a date
subtractDate:	Subtract two dates; answer integer days
subtractDays:	Subtract integer number of days from a date

Class Time adds:

addTime:	Add a delta to a time
subtractTime:	Subtract two times; answer a delta

Conversion

There are no conversion methods in Magnitude.

Class Character adds:

asLowercase	Make it lower-case
asString	Make into a string
asSymbol	Make into a symbol
asUppercase	Make it upper-case
digitValue	Convert number character to integer
value	The internal code for the character

Class Date adds:

asSeconds	Number of seconds since the start of 1901

Class Time adds:

asSeconds	Number of seconds since midnight

Testing

Magnitude supports the full set of relational operations:

<	True if less than
<=	True if less than or equal
=	True if values equal
==	True if same object

>	True if greater than
>=	True if greater than or equal
~=	True if values not equal
~~	True if not same objects
between:and:	True if one value is between two others
max:	Answer highest of two values
min:	Answer lowest of two values

Class Character adds:

isAlphaNumeric	True if character is alphabetic or numeric
isDigit	True if character is numeric
isLowercase	True if lower-case
isSeparator	True if blank, line feed, carriage return, ...
isUppercase	True if upper-case

Protocol Summary

Class Protocol Summary

Object class				
==				
Magnitude class				
No new protocol				
Association class	Character class	Date class	Time class	*Number class*
key:value:	digitValue: value:	dateAndTimeNow nameOfDay: dayOfWeek: nameOfMonth: daysInMonth:forYear: newDay:month:year: daysInYear: newDay:year: fromDays: today indexOfMonth:	dateAndTimeNow fromSeconds: millisecondClockValue millisecondsToRun: now	(See the section on 'Numbers' on page 449)

Instance Protocol Summary

Object							
= == ~= ~~				copy	printOn:	printString	size
Magnitude							
< <= > >=				between:and:	max:		min:
Association	Character		Date		Time		*Number*
key key: key:value: value value:	asLowercase asString asSymbol asUppercase digitValue	isAlphaNumeric isDigit isLowerCase isSeparator isUppercase isVowel value	addDays: asSeconds dayName dayOfMonth dayOfYear daysInMonth daysInYear	daysLeftInMonth daysLeftInYear firstDayOfMonth monthIndex monthName subtractDate: subtractDays: year	addTime: asSeconds hours minutes seconds hours:minutes:seconds setFromSeconds subtractTime:		(See Chapter 33, 'Numbers', on page 449)

Class Magnitude

Magnitudes are objects with ordered values that can be compared using greater-than and less-than.

Class Method Summary

There are no new class methods.

Instance Method Summary

Method	Documented	See page
< aMagnitude	Magnitude	429
<= aMagnitude	Magnitude	430
= anObject	Object	289
== anObject	Object	289
> aMagnitude	Magnitude	430
>= aMagnitude	Magnitude	430
~= anObject	Object	289
~~ anObject	Object	290
between: min and: max	Magnitude	430
copy	Object	291
max: aMagnitude	Magnitude	430
min: aMagnitude	Magnitude	430
printOn: aStream	Object	294
printString	Object	295

Instance Interface

< aMagnitude

Answer true if the receiver is less than aMagnitude; answer false otherwise. The receiver and aMagnitude must be of the same subclass of Magnitude, or must be numbers.

Value of a	Value of b	Expression	Result
2	3	a < b	true
3	2	a < b	false
2	2	a < b	false

<= aMagnitude

Answer true if the receiver is less than or equal to aMagnitude; answer false otherwise. The receiver and aMagnitude must be of the same subclass of Magnitude, or must be numbers.

Value of a	Value of b	Expression	Result
2	3	a <= b	true
3	2	a <= b	false
2	2	a <= b	true

> aMagnitude

Answer true if the receiver is greater than aMagnitude; answer false otherwise. The receiver and aMagnitude must be of the same subclass of Magnitude, or must be numbers.

Value of a	Value of b	Expression	Result
2	3.7	a > b	false
3	2	a > b	true
2	2	a > b	false

>= aMagnitude

Answer true if the receiver is greater than or equal to aMagnitude; answer false otherwise. The receiver and aMagnitude must be of the same subclass of Magnitude, or must be numbers.

Value of a	Value of b	Expression	Result
2	3	a >= b	false
3	2	a >= b	true
2	2	a >= b	true

between: min and: max

Answer true if the receiver is greater than or equal to min and is less than or equal to max; answer false otherwise. The receiver and operand must be of the same subclass of Magnitude, or must be numbers.

Value of a	Value of b	Value of c	Expression	Result
5	1	9	a between: b and: c	true
1	5	9	a between: b and: c	false

max: operand

Answer the receiver, if the receiver is greater than operand; answer operand otherwise. The receiver and operand must be of the same subclass of Magnitude, or must be numbers.

Value of a	Value of b	Expression	Result
2	3	a max: b	3
3	2	a max: b	3

min: operand

Answer the receiver, if the receiver is less than operand; answer operand otherwise. The receiver and operand must be of the same subclass of Magnitude, or must be numbers.

Value of a	Value of b	Expression	Result
2	3	a min: b	2
3	2	a min: b	2

Class Association

Associations are objects with a key and an associated value.

Class Method Summary

Method	Documented	See page
key: newKey value: newValue	Association	432

Instance Method Summary

Method	Documented	See page
< anAssociation	Association Magnitude	432 429
<= anAssociation	Association Magnitude	432 430
= anAssociation	Association Object	432 289
== aMagnitude	Object	289
~= anAssociation	Association Object	432 289
~~ aMagnitude	Object	290
> anAssociation	Association Magnitude	432 430
>= anAssociation	Association Magnitude	433 430
between: min and: max	Magnitude	430
copy	Object	291
key	Association	433
key: newKey	Association	433
key: newKey value: newvalue	Association	433
max: aMagnitude	Magnitude	430
min: aMagnitude	Magnitude	430
printOn: aStream	Object	294
size	Object	295
value	Association	433
value: newValue	Association	433

Class Interface

key: newKey value: newValue
Answer a new instance of Association with the key set to newKey and the value set to newValue.

Expression	Result
zot := Association key: #Bill value: 22	#Bill:22

Instance Interface

< anAssociation
Answer true if the key of the receiver is less than the key of anAssociation; answer false otherwise.

Value of a	Value of b	Expression	Result
#a:4	#a:5	a < b	false
#a:4	#b:4	a < b	true

<= anAssociation
Answer true if the key of the receiver is less than or equal to the key of anAssociation; answer false otherwise.

Value of a	Value of b	Expression	Result
#a:4	#a:5	a <= b	true
#a:4	#b:4	a <= b	true

= anAssociation
Answer true if the key of the receiver is equal to the key of anAssociation and the value of the receiver is equal to the value of anAssociation; answer false otherwise.

Value of a	Value of b	Expression	Result
#a:4	#a:5	a = b	false
#a:4	#b:4	a = b	true

~= anAssociation
Answer true if the key of the receiver is not equal to the key of anAssociation or the value of the receiver is not equal to the value of anAssociation; answer false otherwise.

Value of a	Value of b	Expression	Result
#a:4	#a:5	a ~= b	true
#a:4	#b:4	a ~= b	false

> anAssociation
Answer true if the key of the receiver is greater than the key of anAssociation; answer false otherwise.

Value of a	Value of b	Expression	Result
#a:4	#a:5	a > b	false
#b:4	#a:4	a > b	true

>= anAssociation

Answer true if the key of the receiver is greater than or equal to the key of anAssociation; answer false otherwise.

Value of a	Value of b	Expression	Result
#a:4	#a:5	a >= b	true
#b:4	#a:4	a >= b	true

key

Answer the key of the receiver.

Value of a	Expression	Result
anAssociation: #Bill:22	a key	#Bill

key: newKey

Answer the receiver with the key set to newKey.

Value of a	Expression	Result
anAssociation: #Bill:22	a key: #Sam	anAssociation: #Sam:22

key: newKey value: newValue

Answer the receiver with the key set to newKey and the value set to newValue.

Value of a	Expression	Result
anAssociation: #Bill:22	a key: #Sam value: 39	anAssociation: #Sam:39

value

Answer the value of the receiver.

Value of a	Expression	Result
anAssociation: #Bill:22	a value	22

value: newValue

Answer the receiver with the value set to newValue.

Value of a	Expression	Result
anAssociation: #Bill:22	a value: 39	anAssociation: #Bill:39

Class Character

Characters represent the letters, numbers, and special characters of the ASCII character set, plus platform-specific characters.

Class Method Summary

Method	Documented	See page
digitValue: anInteger	Character	435
value: anInteger	Character	435

Instance Method Summary

Method	Documented	See page
< aMagnitude	Magnitude	429
<= aMagnitude	Magnitude	430
= aMagnitude	Object	289
== aMagnitude	Object	289
~= aMagnitude	Object	289
~~ aMagnitude	Object	290
> aMagnitude	Magnitude	430
>= aMagnitude	Magnitude	430
asLowercase	Character	436
asString	Character	436
asSymbol	Character	436
asUppercase	Character	436
between: min and: max	Magnitude	430
copy	Character Object	291
digitValue	Character	436
isAlphaNumeric	Character	437
isDigit	Character	437
isLetter	Character	437
isLowercase	Character	437
isSeparator	Character	438
isUppercase	Character	438
isVowel	Character	438

Part 1 of 2.

Method	Documented	See page
max: aMagnitude	Magnitude	430
min: aMagnitude	Magnitude	430
printOn: aStream	Object	294
size	Object	295
value	Character	438

Part 2 of 2.

Class Interface

digitValue: anInteger

Answer the character corresponding to a radix-36 digit whose internal value is anInteger, the character that will result in anInteger when sent the digitValue instance message. The operand, anInteger, must be an integer between 0 and 35. The answer will be one of $0...$9 or $A...$Z.

See also: inst>>digitValue

Value of a	Expression	Result
0	Character digitValue: a	$0
9	Character digitValue: a	$9
10	Character digitValue: a	$A
35	Character digitValue: a	$Z

The digitValue: message may be used to convert a binary integer value into a text string containing character digits of any radix up to 36. Example 299 illustrates digitValue: for base-16 numbers; this is essentially the same as printStringRadix: 16.

```
" Convert binary integer to string "
| str num n radix |
str := ''.
num := 32767.
radix := 16.
[ num > 0 ]
    whileTrue: [
        n := num \\ radix.
        num := (num / radix) truncated.
        str := (Character digitValue: n) asString, str ].
radix ~= 10
    ifTrue: [ str := radix printString, 'r', str ].
^ str
    "Answers: 16r7FFF"
```
Example 299, Display

value: anInteger

If anInteger is in the range 0-127, answer a character that represents the character at index anInteger in the ASCII character set. If anInteger is not in the range 0-127, answer a platform-specific character, or raise an error.

See also: inst>>value, Integer>>asCharacter

Value of a	Expression	Result
48	Character value: a	$0
57	Character value: a	$9
97	Character value: a	$a
90	Character value: a	$Z

Instance Interface

asLowercase
If the receiver is an upper-case letter, answer the corresponding lower-case letter; otherwise answer the receiver.

Value of a	Expression	Result
$A	a asLowercase	$a
$e	a asLowercase	$e
$(	a asLowercase	$(

asString
Answer a string that contains the receiver as its only element.

Value of a	Expression	Result
$a	a asString	'a'

asSymbol
Answer the symbol that uniquely identifies the receiver.

Value of a	Expression	Result
$a	a asSymbol	#a

asUppercase
If the receiver is a lowercase letter, answer the corresponding upper-case letter; otherwise answer the receiver.

Value of a	Expression	Result
$A	a asUppercase	$A
$e	a asUppercase	$E
$(	a asUppercase	$(

copy
Characters are identity objects which, like symbols and smaller integers, represent themselves. This means that any character having the value $a is not just equal to any other character having the value $a, but is the identical object. Thus, the copy method simply returns the receiver.

digitValue
Answer an integer representing the receiver that is considered as a radix-36 digit. A radix-36 digit is from the sequence 01…9ABC…XYZ.

Value of a	Expression	Result
$7	a digitValue	7
$A	a digitValue	10
$Z	a digitValue	35
$a	a digitValue	(error)

The digitValue message may be used to convert a text string, containing character digits of any radix up to 36, into a binary integer value.

```
" Binary integer from string "
| str num radix |
str := '12F4C'.
num := 0.
radix := 16.
```

```
        1 to: str size by: 1
            do: [ :n |
                num := num * radix + (str at: n) digitValue ].
        ^ num
            " Answers: 77644 "
```
Example 300, Display

For testing, replace the last line with:

```
" For testing, replace the last line above with: "
^ num printStringRadix: radix
```
Example 301, Display

isAlphaNumeric
Answer true if the receiver is a numeric digit ($0…$9) or an alphabetic letter ($a…$z or $A…$Z); answer false otherwise.

Value of a	Expression	Result
$7	a isAlphaNumeric	true
$A	a isAlphaNumeric	true
$e	a isAlphaNumeric	true
$/	a isAlphaNumeric	false

isDigit
Answer true if the receiver is a numeric digit ($0…$9); answer false otherwise.

Value of a	Expression	Result
$7	a isDigit	true
$A	a isDigit	false
$e	a isDigit	false
$/	a isDigit	false

isLetter
Answer true if the receiver is an alphabetic character ($a…$z or $A…$Z); answer false otherwise.

Value of a	Expression	Result
$7	a isLetter	false
$A	a isLetter	true
$e	a isLetter	true
$/	a isLetter	false

isLowercase
Answer true if the receiver is a lower-case alphabetic character ($a…$z); answer false otherwise.

Value of a	Expression	Result
$7	a isLowercase	false
$A	a isLowercase	false
$e	a isLowercase	true
$/	a isLowercase	false

isSeparator

Answer true if the receiver is a separator character; answer false otherwise. Separator characters are one of: carriage return, tab, line feed, space, or form feed. Separators are sometimes called white space.

Value of a	Expression	Result
$7	a isSeparator	false
$A	a isSeparator	false
$e	a isSeparator	false
$/	a isSeparator	false
$	a isSeparator	true

isUppercase

Answer true if the receiver is an upper-case alphabetic character ($A...$Z); answer false otherwise.

Value of a	Expression	Result
$7	a isUppercase	false
$A	a isUppercase	true
$e	a isUppercase	false
$/	a isUppercase	false

isVowel

Answer true if the receiver is one of: $A, $a, $E, $e, $I, $i, $O, $o, $U, or $u; answer false otherwise.

Value of a	Expression	Result
$7	a isVowel	false
$A	a isVowel	true
$e	a isVowel	true
$/	a isVowel	false
$y	a isVowel	false

value

Answer the numeric code of the character. If the code is in the range 0 to 127, then it is an ASCII code. If it is greater than 127, then it is a platform-dependent code.

See also: class>>value:, Integer>>asCharacter

Value of a	Expression	Result
$0	a value	48
$9	a value	57
$a	a value	97
$Z	a value	90

Class Date

Class Date describes objects that hold dates in the Gregorian calendar.

Day and Month Names

Day Names

Several methods below accept or return either the name of the day of the week or an index indicating the day of the week. Figure 91 gives the names and associated indexes.

Day Index	Day Name
1	#Monday
2	#Tuesday
3	#Wednesday
4	#Thursday
5	#Friday
6	#Saturday
7	#Sunday

Figure 91: Day Names.

Long and Short Month Names

Several methods below accept or return the name (or short name) of a month, or an index indicating the month. Figure 92 gives the names and associated indexes.

Index	Month Name Long	Month Name Short	Index	Month Name Long	Month Name Short
1	#January	#Jan	7	#July	#Jul
2	#February	#Feb	8	#August	#Aug
3	#March	#Mar	9	#September	#Sep
4	#April	#Apr	10	#October	#Oct
5	#May	#May	11	#November	#Nov
6	#June	#Jun	12	#December	#Dec

Figure 92: Long and Short Month Names.

Class Method Summary

Method	Documented	See page
dateAndTimeNow	Date	441
dayOfWeek: dayName	Date	441
daysInMonth: monthName forYear: anInteger	Date	441
daysInYear: anInteger	Date	441
fromDays: anInteger	Date	441
indexOfMonth: monthName	Date	441
nameOfDay: anInteger	Date	441
nameOfMonth: anInteger	Date	442

newDay: anInteger
  month: monthName
  year: anInteger
	Date	442

newDay: anInteger year: anInteger	Date	442
today	Date	442

Instance Method Summary

Method	Documented	See page
< aDate	Magnitude	429
<= aDate	Magnitude	430
= aDate	Object	289
== aDate	Object	289
~= aDate	Object	289
~~ aMagnitude	Object	290
> aDate	Magnitude	430
>= aDate	Magnitude	430
addDays: anInteger	Date	442
asSeconds	Date	442
between: min and: max	Magnitude	430
copy	Object	291
dayName	Date	443
dayOfMonth	Date	443
dayOfYear	Date	443
daysInMonth	Date	443
daysInYear	Date	443
daysLeftInMonth	Date	443
daysLeftInYear	Date	443
firstDayOfMonth	Date	444
max: aMagnitude	Magnitude	430
min: aMagnitude	Magnitude	430
monthIndex	Date	444

Part 1 of 2.

Method	Documented	See page
monthName	Date	444
printOn: aStream	Object	294
subtractDate: aDate	Date	444
subtractDays: n	Date	444
year	Date	444

Part 2 of 2.

Class Interface

dateAndTimeNow
Answer an array with two elements. The first element is a date representing the current date, and the second is a time representing the current time.

Expression	Value of element 1	Value of element 2
Date dateAndTimeNow	11/5/1994	11:43:26

dayOfWeek: dayName
Answer an integer between 1 and 7 that represents the day of the week of dayName; dayName must be a name in Figure 91, 'Day Names', on page 439.

Expression	Value
Date dayOfWeek: #Sunday	7

daysInMonth: monthName forYear: anInteger
Answer an integer between 1 and 31 that represents the day of the month of month-Name in year anInteger; monthName must be one of the symbols in Figure 92, 'Long and Short Month Names', on page 439.

Expression	Value
Date daysInMonth: #February forYear: 2000	29
Date daysInMonth: #November forYear: 1994	30

daysInYear: anInteger
Answer the number of days in year anInteger, either 365 or 366.

Expression	Value
Date daysInYear: 1994	365
Date daysInYear: 1996	366

fromDays: anInteger
Answer a date that is anInteger days after (or before, if negative) 1 January 1901.

Expression	Value
Date fromDays: 34241	10-1-94

indexOfMonth: monthName
Answer an integer between 1 and 12 that represents the month of the year of month-Name, which must be one of the symbols in Figure 92, 'Long and Short Month Names', on page 439.

Expression	Value
Date indexOfMonth: #January	1
Date indexOfMonth: #December	12

nameOfDay: anInteger

Answer a symbol representing the name of the day of the week, as given in Figure 91, 'Day Names', on page 439.

Expression	Value
Date nameOfDay: 7	#Sunday

nameOfMonth: anInteger

Answer a symbol representing the long name of the month, as given in Figure 92, 'Long and Short Month Names', on page 439.

Expression	Value
Date nameOfMonth: 12	#December

newDay: n month: monthName year: year.

Answer a date that represents the nth day of monthName in year. The monthName must be a name from Figure 92, 'Long and Short Month Names', on page 439. The year must be a positive integer.

Expression	Value
Date newDay: 2 monthName: #January year: 1995	1/2/1995

newDay: n year: year

Answer a date that represents the nth day of year. The parameter n must be an integer between 1 and 365 (or 366 if a leap year). The year in year must be a positive integer representing a four-digit year.

Expression	Value
Date newDay: 2 year: 1994	1/2/1994

today

Answer a date that represents today's date.

Expression	Value
Date today	11/4/1994

Instance Interface

addDays: anInteger

Answer a new date that represents the date anInteger days from the receiver.

Value of a	Expression	Result
9/25/1994	a addDays: 3	9/28/1994

asSeconds

Answer an integer that contains the number of seconds since 00:00 hours on 1 January 1901 until midnight of the day of the receiver. (This is the number of seconds from the start of the century until the end of the day of the date represented by the receiver.)

Value of a	Expression	Result
10/10/1994	a asSeconds	2959200000

dayName

Answer a symbol representing the name of the day of the week of the receiver. The answer will be one of the long symbols in Figure 91, 'Day Names', on page 439.

Value of a	Expression	Result
10/10/1994	a dayName	#Monday

dayOfMonth

Answer an integer between 1 and 31, representing the day of the month of the receiver.

Value of a	Expression	Result
9/25/1994	a dayOfMonth	25

dayOfYear

Answer an integer between 1 and 366, representing the day of the year of the receiver.

Value of a	Expression	Result
10/10/1994	a dayOfYear	283

daysInMonth

Answer an integer between 1 and 31, representing the number of days in the month of the receiver.

Value of a	Expression	Result
9/25/1994	a daysInMonth	30
2/1/1996	a daysInMonth	29

daysInYear

Answer an integer between 1 and 366, representing the number of days in the year of the receiver.

Value of a	Expression	Result
9/25/1994	a daysInYear	365

daysLeftInMonth

Answer an integer between 0 and 30, representing the number of days left in the month following the date of the receiver.

Value of a	Expression	Result
9/25/1994	a daysLeftInMonth	5

daysLeftInYear

Answer an integer between 0 and 365, representing the number of days left in the year following the date of the receiver.

Value of a	Expression	Result
9/25/1994	a daysLeftInYear	97

firstDayOfMonth
Answer a new date that represents the first of the month, for the month and year of the receiver.

Value of a	Expression	Result
9/25/1994	a firstDayOfMonth	9/1/1994
9/1/1994	a firstDayOfMonth	9/1/1994

monthIndex
Answer an integer between 1 and 12 that is the number of the month of the receiver.

Value of a	Expression	Result
9/25/1994	a monthIndex	9

monthName
Answer a symbol that represents the name of the month of the receiver. The symbol will be a long name from Figure 92, 'Long and Short Month Names', on page 439.

Value of a	Expression	Result
9/25/1994	a monthName	#September

subtractDate: aDate
Answer an integer containing the number of days between the receiver and aDate. The integer will be negative if the receiver represents an earlier date than aDate.

Value of a	Value of b	Expression	Result
9/24/1994	9/25/1994	a subtractDate: b	-1
9/25/1994	9/24/1994	a subtractDate: b	1
9/24/1994	9/24/1995	a subtractDate: b	-365

subtractDays: anInteger
Answer a new date that is anInteger days earlier (if positive) or later (if negative) than the receiver.

Value of a	Expression	Result
9/25/1994	a subtractDays: 1	9/24/1994

year
Answer an integer that contains the year of the receiver.

Value of a	Expression	Result
9/25/1994	a year	1994

Class Time

Values of Time represent a particular second since midnight.

Class Method Summary

Method	*Documented*	*See page*
dateAndTimeNow	Time	446
fromSeconds: anInteger	Time	446
millisecondClockValue	Time	446
millisecondsPerDay	Time	446
millisecondsToRun: aBlock	Time	447
now	Time	447

Instance Method Summary

Method	*Documented*	*See page*
< aMagnitude	Magnitude	429
<= aMagnitude	Magnitude	430
= aTime	Object	289
== aTime	Object	289
~= aTime	Object	289
~~ aTime	Object	290
> aMagnitude	Magnitude	430
>= aMagnitude	Magnitude	430
addTime: aTime	Time	447
asSeconds	Time	447
between: min and: max	Magnitude	430
copy	Object	291
hours	Time	447

hours: intHours
   minutes: intMinutes
   seconds: intSeconds
	Time	447

max: aMagnitude	Magnitude	430
min: aMagnitude	Magnitude	430
minutes	Time	448

Part 1 of 2.

Method	Documented	See page
printOn: aStream	Object	294
seconds	Time	448
setFromSeconds: intSeconds	Time	448
subtractTime: aTime	Time	448

Part 2 of 2.

Class Interface

Note: All examples use a 24-hour clock even if a particular locale uses a 12-hour clock, since results of some operations are clearer with a 24-hour clock.

dateAndTimeNow

Answer an array with two elements. The first element is a date representing the current date, and the second is a time representing the current time.

Expression	Value of element 1	Value of element 2
Date dateAndTimeNow	11/5/94	11:43:26

fromSeconds: anInteger

Answer a time that is anInteger seconds before midnight (if negative) or after midnight (if positive). If the absolute value of anInteger is greater than or equal to 86400, the number of seconds in a day, anInteger is taken modulo 86400.

Expression	Result
Time fromSeconds: 0	00:00:00
Time fromSeconds: 86400	00:00:00
Time fromSeconds: 86401	00:00:01
Time fromSeconds: 60*60 + 60 + 1	01:01:01

millisecondClockValue

Answer an integer indicating the number of milliseconds on the millisecond clock. The value returned is implementation-specific, but is guaranteed to always increase in value.

See also: millisecondsToRun:, Object>>bench:, Delay>>untilMilliseconds:, ProcessorScheduler>>signal:atTime:

Expression	Result
Time millisecondClockValue	243350593 (On the author's platform)

One use for this method is to time an operation. Get a value, then start the operation, say reading a record of a file; when done get another value and subtract the values. The result is approximately the number of milliseconds that the operation took.

```
" Time code with millisecond clock "
| start end msecs |
start := Time millisecondClockValue.
1000 timesRepeat: [ 100 factorial ].
end := Time millisecondClockValue.
msecs := end - start
    "Answer on authors platform: 18300 "
```

Example 302, Display

millisecondsPerDay

Answer 86400000, the number of milliseconds in a day.

Expression	Result
Time millisecondsPerDay	86400000

millisecondsToRun: aBlock

Answer an integer indicating the number of seconds required to evaluate **aBlock**.

See also: millisecondClockValue, Object>>bench:

Expression	Result
Time millisecondsToRun: [2000 factorial]	19812 (on the author's platform!)

now

Answer a time representing the current time. The resolution of the result is platform-specific.

Expression	Result
Time now	11:43:26

Instance Interface

Note: All examples use a 24-hour clock even if a particular locale uses a 12-hour clock, since results of some operations are clearer with a 24-hour clock.

addTime: aTime

Answer a time that represents the time at (aTime asSeconds) seconds after that of the receiver. Addition is modulo 24 hours; the largest value ever returned is **23:59:59**.

Value of a	Expression	Result
08:10:30	a addTime: 01:20:15	09:30:45
08:10:30	a addTime: 00:00:45	08:11:15
00:01:00	a addTime: 23:59:59	00:00:59

asSeconds

Answer an integer representing the number of whole seconds from midnight (**00:00:00**) up to the time of the receiver.

Value of a	Expression	Result
00:00:01	a asSeconds	1
00:01:01	a asSeconds	61
23:59:59	a asSeconds	86399

hours

Answer an integer that represents the number of whole hours since midnight (**00:00:00**) up to the time of the receiver.

Value of a	Expression	Result
01:59:32	a hours	8

hours: intHours minutes: intMinutes seconds: intSeconds

Answer the receiver reset so that it represents the time intHours hours, intMinutes minutes, and intSeconds seconds past midnight.

Expression	Result
Time new hours: 11 minutes: 48 seconds: 39	A time: 11:48:39

minutes

Answer an integer that represents the number of whole minutes since the start of the last hour of the receiver.

Value of a	Expression	Result
01:59:32	a minutes	59

seconds

Answer an integer that represents the number of whole seconds since the start of the last minute of the receiver.

Value of a	Expression	Result
01:59:32	a seconds	32

setFromSeconds: intSeconds

Reset the receiver so that it represents a time that is intSeconds seconds after midnight.

Value of a	Expression	Result
A time: 10:41:19	a setFromSeconds: 1331	A time: 11:11:11

subtractTime: aTime

Answer a time that represents the time at (aTime asSeconds) seconds before the receiver. Subtraction is modulo 24 hours; the largest value ever returned is 23:59:59.

Value of a	Expression	Result
A time: 08:30:30	a subtractTime: 01:20:15	A time: 07:10:15
A time: 08:10:30	a subtractTime: 00:00:45	A time: 08:09:45
A time: 00:01:00	a subtractTime: 23:59:59	A time: 00:01:01

33

Numbers

Class Number is a subclass of Magnitude. The Number classes include:

Kinds of Numbers

Numbers come in three types: integer, fraction, and floating-point. Their internal formats are platform specific; in fact, there may be multiple internal representations of a given number type for purposes of optimization.

Numbers are immutable; the internal representation cannot be changed from the outside. Instead, each operation returns a new number (or self). Some integers are identity objects as well.

Integer Numbers

Integer is an abstract superclass. On most platforms and releases, there are several different subclasses of class Integer, at least SmallInteger and LargeInteger. However, these subclasses are not exposed and are present for optimization purposes. The normal use of integers does not depend on such implementation details; conversions are automatically made as needed. Thus Integer is usually described and used as if it were not abstract.

Small integers are identity objects. That means all small integers with the same integer value, say 723, are the same object as all others with the same value. Thus, (722+1)==723 is always true. Small integers are those around zero, often with the range 2^{29}-1 to -2^{29}.

Larger integers may be implemented in one large integer class, in two classes (one for positive large integers and one for negative large integers), or in other ways. Such integers are *not* identity objects; as a result, it is possible to tell the difference between large and small integers using ==. (See the section on 'The Integer Long/Short Boundary' on page 454.)

Large integers are designed to grow to incredible sizes; on many platforms, they can have sizes up to as much as 64 kilobytes, and ranges from minus to plus 2^{524288} give or take a few. There is no interesting way to determine the maximum value of integers. As a result, integer overflow is not a thing Smalltalk programmers worry about much!

Integers support many bit operations, such as *and*ing, *or*ing, and masking. In these operations, the integer number is considered a bit string. (See the section on 'Inside Integers and Floats' on page 454.)

Fractions

Fractions are the ratio of two integers, and are typically created by a divide operation on two integers. Fractions have two components, a numerator and a denominator. Fractions are not identity objects, but their components can be.

Operations on fractions, including creation, always produce reduced results; that is, there are no common divisors of the numerator and denominator except 1. For example, the expression 3/9 produces the result (1/3); the expression (1/3)*(3/4) produces (1/4) rather than (3/12). Fractions are always reduced to the smallest values possible.

Fractions can be the ratios of very large integers; performance can become sluggish if fractions are indiscriminately and heavily used instead of floating-point numbers.

Floating-Point Numbers

Floating-point numbers use the platform's hardware support. However, when moving an image from one platform to another, Smalltalk takes care of any necessary conversion. IEEE formats are used on most platforms. Precision of floating-point numbers is platform and release dependent.

Categories of Messages

Number implements many kinds of messages; they can be classified in groups of related messages, as shown below. Messages inherited from Magnitude are not classified, although some are redefined in this chapter.

Arithmetic

Arithmetic messages include basic arithmetic and sign changing.

*	Multiply
+	Add
-	Subtract

/	Divide, without rounding or truncation
//	Divide, truncation towards negative infinity
\\	Remainder after division using //
abs	Absolute value
negated	Change the sign
quo:	Divide, with truncation towards zero
reciprocal	The reciprocal
rem:	The remainder after division using /
sign	The sign
sqrt	The square root
squared	The square

Class Integer adds:

factorial	Calculate factorial of a positive integer
gcd:	Greatest common divisor of two integers
lcm:	Least common multiple of two integers

Class Float adds:

fractionPart	Answer fraction part of float number
integerPart	Answer integer part of float number

Class Fraction adds:

denominator	Answer the denominator of the fraction
numerator	Answer the numerator of the fraction

Bits and Masking

All bit operations are on integers. Bits are indexed, with 1 at the right:

<<	Shift left
>>	Shift right
&	Logical and
|	Logical or
allMask:	True if all 1 bits in one are 1 bits in other
anyMask:	True if any 1 bits in one are 1 bits in other
bitAnd:	Logical and
bitAt:	Answer one bit at an index
bitInvert	Invert bits in receiver
bitOr:	Logical or
bitShift:	Shift bits left or right
bitXor:	Exclusive or
clearBit:	Set bit at index to zero
highBit	Bit index of high order bit
isBitSet:	True if indexed bit is 1
noMask:	True if no 1 bits in one are 1 bits in other
setBit:	Set bit at index to 1

Conversions and Rounding

Methods to convert and round in many ways are provided.

asFloat	Convert to a floating-point number
asFraction	Convert to a fraction
asInteger	Convert to an integer
ceiling	Convert to next highest integer

degreesToRadians	Conversion
floor	Convert to next lowest integer
radiansToDegrees	Conversion
rounded	Round to nearest integer
roundTo:	Round to nearest multiple of a number
truncated	Truncate to an integer
truncateTo:	Truncate to multiple of a number

Figure 93 compares the various integer rounding and truncation methods.

Method	Positive receiver	Negative Receiver
asInteger	Nearest integer	Same
ceiling	Smallest integer greater than or equal to	Same
floor	Largest integer less than or equal to	Same
rounded	Nearest integer	Same
roundedTo: f	Nearest multiple of number f	Same
truncated	Largest integer less than or equal to	Smallest integer greater than or equal to
truncateTo: f	Largest number less than or equal to the receiver that is a multiple of f	Smallest number greater than or equal to the receiver that is a multiple of f

Figure 93: Comparison of Rounding and Truncation Methods.

Figure 94 illustrates the various integer rounding and truncation methods on a number line.

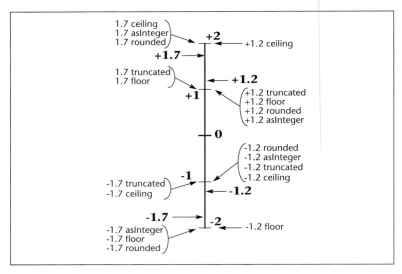

Figure 94: Rounding, Truncation, Ceiling, Floor, and Conversion. The values produced by sending ceiling, asInteger, rounded, truncated, and floor to four numbers are shown. The four numbers are two positive and two negative, with one of each being above the 0.5 mark and one of each below the 0.5 mark.

Generality

Two methods compare the generality of two numbers.

lessGeneralThan:	Test for generality
moreGeneralThan:	Test for generality

Instance Creation

Several methods create instances:

to:	Create interval with step size of 1
to:by:	Create interval with specified step size
@	Create a point

Iteration

Number classes provide for creation of intervals and for simple iteration.

to:by:do:	Iterate with specified step size
to:do:	Iterate with step size of 1

Class Integer adds:

timesRepeat:	Repeat a block some number of times.

Powers and Logarithms

Functions available include logarithms and powers to base e and arbitrary other bases.

exp	Natural log base raised to power
floorLog:	A truncated (integer) log
ln	Natural logarithm
log:	Logarithm to arbitrary base
raisedTo:	Number raised to a power
raisedToInteger:	Number raised to integer power

Printing

Class Number has no new printing methods; it inherits printOn: and printString from Object. These are overridden by each subclass to produce appropriately formatted output.

Class Integer adds:

printOn:base:	Print on a stream with given radix
printOn:base:showRadix:	Print on a stream with given radix
printStringRadix:	Format number in given radix
printStringRadix:padTo:	Format number in given radix; pad
printStringRadix:showRadix:	Format number in given radix; show radix?

Testing

Testing method answer true or false.

negative	Test for a negative number
positive	Test for a positive number or zero
strictlyPositive	Test for greater than zero

Class Integer adds:

even	True if even
isBitSet:	True if indexed bit is 1
odd	True if odd

Trigonometric

The basic trigonometric functions are supported, as are two conversion methods.

arcCos	Inverse Cosine
arcSin	Inverse Sine
arcTan	Inverse Tangent
cos	Cosine
degreesToRadians	Conversion
radiansToDegrees	Conversion
sin	Sine
tan	Tangent

Generality

For conversion purposes, numbers have a property called *generality,* which ranks the ability of a kind of number to 'hold more' than less-general numbers. The ranking, from most general to least, is: floating-point, fraction, large integer, and small integer. Details are implementation and platform dependent, but a set of messages (lessGeneralThan: and moreGeneralThan:) allow portable comparisons of generality.

Generality is used to determine how to perform mixed-class arithmetic. The addition of a number of one class to a number of another causes the number with the lowest generality to be converted to the class of the other number.

For example, in (2.3 + 7) the integer 7 is converted to a float, and then the addition is performed.

Inside Integers and Floats

The topics in this section are for advanced readers, or the insanely curious. Four topics are covered: how to find the size of small integers; how to use masking to simulate effects due to the size of a register; how to simulate sign propagation in registers; and how to find the number of digits of precision in a floating-point number.

The Integer Long/Short Boundary

Code like the following can be used to find the boundary between small and large integers:

```
" Find the boundary between long and short integers "
| minLong shortLen |
minLong := 1.
shortLen := 0.
[ minLong - 1 + 1 == minLong ]
    whileTrue: [
        minLong := minLong << 1.
        shortLen := shortLen + 1 ].
^ Array with: minLong with: shortLen
    "On the author's platform: (1073741824 30) "
```

Example 303, Execute

The minLong value is the smallest positive integer that requires long (positive) integer, and the shortLen value is the number of bits in a short integer. On the author's platform, OS/2 on an Intel 486, the values are 1073741824 and 30.

The key to this test is the expression (minLong - 1 + 1 == minLong). If minLong is a short positive integer, subtracting and adding one will produce a short integer with the same value, and, since short integers are identity objects, will produce exactly the same object. When minLong grows big enough to hold a long integer, the result after adding and subtracting will not be the same object.†

Example of Integers and Masking

This example is a quick and dirty random number generator adapted from *Numerical Recipes in C, Second Edition,* W. H. Press, et al, Cambridge University Press, 1992, pages 284-5.

While it does work, and can be used when poor-quality random numbers are acceptable, this example is intended to illustrate techniques of masking integers so that they act like integers in other languages, i.e., they act as if they overflow a register. Basically, an integer is *and*ed with the integer constant 16rFFFFFFFF to throw away all but the right-most 32 bits. Signed values require special handling; see the section on 'Signed Integers and Shifting' on page 456.

The generator itself is a one-liner:

        seed := (1664525*seed + 1013904223) bitAnd: 16rFFFFFFFF.

The variable seed can be set initially to any 32-bit value; for testing use 0. Each time it is recalculated, the previously calculated value is reused.

The *and* of 16rFFFFFFFF is necessary to simulate the loss of bits at the left that occurs in overflow when integers are limited to 32 bits.

Floating-point numbers in the range 0.0 to 1.0 are simply generated:

        float := (seed / 16rFFFFFFFF) asFloat.

The example below puts it all together and displays the first six generated values:

```
" Quick & Dirty Random Number Generator "
| seed int float maxShortInt |
seed := 0.
maxShortInt := 16r3FFFFFFF.        "Platform dependant"
Transcript cr.
6 timesRepeat: [
    seed := (1664525*seed + 1013904223) bitAnd: 16rFFFFFFFF.
    int := seed bitAnd: maxShortInt.  "Random short integer"
    float := (seed / 16rFFFFFFFF) asFloat.
    Transcript
        show: (seed printStringRadix: 16), ' ';
        show: (int printString), ' ';
        show: (float printString), ' '; cr ]

" The values in the transcript are:
16r3C6EF35F      1013904223      0.23606797
16r47502932      122693938       0.27856691
16rD1CCF6E9      298645225       0.81953376
```

---

† Adding, then subtracting, works only for positive integers; with negative integers, subtract first, then add.

```
16rAAF95334      720982836      0.6678669
16r6252E503      575857923      0.38407737
16r9F2EC686      523159174      0.62180749 "
```
Example 304, Execute

The mask 16r3FFFFFFF, assigned to maxShortInt, is minLong - 1. The constant 16rFFFFFFFF is 32 bits wide. The floating-point value is obtained by dividing the 32-bit wide seed by the maximum value that can be held in 32 bits (producing a fraction), and then converting to float; the result is in the range 0.0 to 1.0.

Signed Integers and Shifting

In some languages, such as C, it is not uncommon to convert a bit string into a signed number by shifting it left, so that the left-most one-bit is in bit position 32 (the sign bit), and then shifting back right to restore the proper value; the sign bit propagates as the right shifting is done. For example, to convert an unsigned byte into a signed number, C programmers often do this:

```
toSigned( unsigned char * ch )
{
    long int n;
    n := (ch << 24) >> 24;
    return n;
}
```

This does not work in Smalltalk, since the more a number is shifted, the bigger it gets; there is no sign position into which to shift a sign bit. The equivalent code is:

```
" Converting unsigned bytes to signed integers "
| ch n |
n := ch := 2r10101010.                    " 8-bit number "
(ch bitAt: 8) = 1
    ifTrue: [ n := ((ch bitXor: 2r11111111) + 1) negated ].
^ n
    " Answer: -86 "
```
Example 305, Display

Inside Floating-Point Numbers

Details of the floating-point implementation of a platform can be deduced by running some special code. This code is described in the book *Numerical Recipes in C*, Second Edition, by W. H. Press, et al., Cambridge University Press, 1992, pages 889-894. While written in C, it is easily converted to Smalltalk. Values answered include the radix in which calculations are performed (2 or 16 usually), the number of digits in the mantissa, number of bits in the mantissa, how many guard digits are used, and the largest and smallest usable floating-point numbers.

A quick and dirty check of the number of decimal digits and the number of hexadecimal digits are shown in Examples 306 and 307. Note that the actual number of bits might not be a multiple of four, so even the hexadecimal estimate is approximate.

```
" Quick and dirty number of decimal digits in float number "
(1/3) asFloat asFraction numerator printString size
" On the author's Intel 80486 the answer is 14 "
```
Example 306, Display

```
" Quick and dirty number of hexadecimal digits in float number "
((1/3) asFloat asFraction numerator printStringRadix: 16) size - 3      " '16r' size == 3 "
" On the author's Intel 80486 the answer is 12 "
```
Example 307, Display

Numeric Constants Summary

Numbers have the following general format, where square brackets delimit optional items, and digits represents one or more decimal (or base *radix*) digits.

$$[\textit{radix } \textbf{r}] [\text{-}] \textit{digits} [\text{.digits}] [\textbf{e} [\text{-}] \textit{digits}]$$

Figure 95 contains abbreviations used in Figure 96 which summarizes the formats of numeric constants. The format column shows blanks between parts of constants; these are for clarity in the table and should not be written in a constant.

Abbreviation	Stands for
digit	0 to 9 unless after an **r**, then 0 to *radix*-1, taken from the character sequence: 0 1 2 3 4 5 6 7 8 9 A B C ... X Y Z
digits	One or more of *digit:* 00 988765 010
sdigits	Optional minus sign followed by one or more of *digit*
radix	Positive base-10 integer in range 2 to 36: 2 4 9 16 36
exp	One or more decimal digits: 1 12 24
sexp	Optional minus sign followed by an *exp:* -2 12 -24
n_{10}	An integer in base-10 derived from *sdigits*
n_{radix}	An integer in base *radix* derived from *sdigits*
f_{10}	A floating-point number in base-10 derived from *sdigits.digits*
f_{radix}	A floating-point number in base *radix* derived from *sdigits.digits*

Figure 95: Abbreviations for Numeric Constants. The abbreviations above the dark line apply to the *Format* column in Figure 96; those below the line are used, in addition, in the *Result* column of Figure 96.

Kind	Format	Description	Result	Examples
Integer	*sdigits*	Signed integer	n_{10}	-238 14236
	sdigits **e** *exp*	Signed integer with exponent	$n_{10} * 10^{exp}$	2e8 -12e2
	radix **r** *sdigits*	Signed integer in base *radix*	n_{radix}	10r123 16rFF45
	radix **r** *sdigits* **e** *exp*	Signed integer in base *radix* with exponent	$n_{radix} * radix^{sexp}$	10r12e4 16rF5e2
Float	*sdigits.digits*	Signed float	f_{10}	3.14159 -100.0
	sdigits . digits **e** *sexp*	Signed float with exponent	$f_{10} * 10^{exp}$	0.31e-1 -1.0e-2
	radix **r** *sdigits.digits*	Signed float in base *radix*	f_{radix}	2r1101.1 16r2E1
	radix **r** *sdigits.digits* **e** *sexp*	Signed float in base *radix* with exponent	$f_{radix} * radix^{sexp}$	10r3.1e-1 16rD.Fe2
Fraction	*sdigits* **e** - *exp*	Fraction	$n_{10} / 10^{exp}$	234e-3 1e-1
	radix **r** *sdigits* **e** - *exp*	Fraction in base *radix*	$n_{radix} / radix^{exp}$	2r10e-3 16rFFe-4

Figure 96: Numeric Constants Summary.

Protocol Summary

Class Protocol Summary

There are no new class methods.

Instance Protocol Summary

Object			
=	~=	copy	printString
==	~~	printOn:	size

Magnitude			
<	>	between:and:	min:
<=	>=	max:	

Number			
*	asFraction	moreGeneralThan:	sign
+	asInteger	negated	sin
-	ceiling	negative	sqrt
/	cos	positive	squared
//	degreesToRadians	quo:	strictlyPositive
\\	exp	radiansToDegrees	tan
@	floor	raisedTo:	to:
abs	floorLog:	rasiedToInteger:	to:by:
arcCos	lessGeneralThan:	reciprocal	to:by:do:
arcSin	ln	rem:	to:do:
arcTan	log:	rounded	truncated
asFloat		roundTo:	truncateTo:

Integer		Float	Fraction
<<	factorial	fractionPart	denominator
>>	gcd:	integerPart	numerator
&	highBit		
|	isBitSet:		
allMask:	lcm:		
anyMask:	noMask:		
asCharacter	numerator		
bitAnd:	odd		
bitAt:	printOn:base:		
bitInvert:	printOn:base:showRadix:		
bitOr:	printStringRadix:		
bitShift:	printStringRadix:padTo:		
bitXor:	printStringRadix:showRadix:		
clearBit:	setBit:		
denominator	timesRepeat:		
even			

Class Number

Class Method Summary

There are no new class methods in Number.

Instance Method Summary

Method	Documented	See page
* aNumber	Number	461
+ aNumber	Number	461
- aNumber	Number	461
/ aNumber	Number	461
// aNumber	Number	462
< aMagnitude	Number Magnitude	463 429
<= aMagnitude	Number Magnitude	463 430
= aMagnitude	Number Object	463 289
== aMagnitude	Number Object	463 289
> aMagnitude	Number Magnitude	464 432
>= aMagnitude	Number Magnitude	464 432
@ aNumber	Number	464
\\ aNumber	Number	462
~= aMagnitude	Number Object	463 289
~~ aMagnitude	Number Object	464 290
abs	Number	464
arcCos	Number	465
arcSin	Number	465
arcTan	Number	465
asFloat	Number	465
asFraction	Number	465
asInteger	Number	466
between: min and: max	Magnitude	430
ceiling	Number	466
copy	Number Object	466 291
cos	Number	466
degreesToRadians	Number	467
exp	Number	467

Part 1 of 2.

Method	Documented	See page
floor	Number	467
floorLog: aNumber	Number	467
lessGeneralThan: aNumber	Number	467
ln	Number	467
log:	Number	468
max: aMagnitude	Magnitude	430
min: aMagnitude	Magnitude	430
moreGeneralThan: aNumber	Number	468
negated	Number	468
negative	Number	468
positive	Number	468
printOn: aStream	Object	294
printString	Object	295
quo: aNumber	Number	469
radiansToDegrees	Number	469
raisedTo: aNumber	Number	469
raisedToInteger: anInteger	Number	469
reciprocal	Number	470
rem: aNumber	Number	470
rounded	Number	470
roundTo: aNumber	Number	470
sign	Number	471
sin	Number	471
sqrt	Number	471
squared	Number	471
strictlyPositive	Number	471
tan	Number	471
to: stop	Number	472
to: stop by: step	Number	472

to: stop
  by: step
  do: aBlock
	Number	472

to: stop do: aBlock	Number	473
truncated	Number	473
truncateTo: aNumber	Number	473

Part 2 of 2.

Instance Interface

* aNumber

Answer a number that is the result of multiplying the receiver by aNumber. If the receiver and aNumber are not of the same class, the object with the lower generality is coerced to have the higher generality.

The class of the result may differ from the classes of both objects: multiplying fractions can result in an integer.

Value of a	*Value of b*	*Expression*	*Result*
2	3	a * b	6
2/3	4/5	a * b	8/15
2/3	3/2	a * b	1
2	3.0	a * b	6.0
2/3	3.0	a * b	2.0

+ aNumber

Answer a number that is the result of adding the receiver to aNumber. If the receiver and aNumber are not of the same class, the object with the lower generality is coerced to have the higher generality.

The class of the result may differ from the classes of both objects: adding fractions can result in an integer.

Value of a	*Value of b*	*Expression*	*Result*
2	3	a + b	5
2/3	4/3	a + b	2
2/3	1/2	a + b	7/6
2	3.0	a + b	5.0
1/2	3.0	a + b	3.5

- aNumber

Answer a number that is the result of subtracting aNumber from the receiver. If the receiver and aNumber are not of the same class, the object with the lower generality is coerced to have the higher generality.

The class of the result may differ from the classes of both objects: subtracting fractions can result in an integer.

Value of a	*Value of b*	*Expression*	*Result*
2	3	a - b	-1
4/3	1/3	a - b	1
2/3	1/3	a - b	1/3
4	3.0	a - b	1.0
3/2	1.0	a - b	0.5

/ aNumber

Answer a number that is the result of dividing the receiver by aNumber. If the receiver and aNumber are not of the same class, the object with the lower generality is coerced to have the higher generality. It is an error if aNumber is zero.

The sign of the result is positive if both objects have the same sign, and negative if the signs differ.

The class of the result may differ from the classes of both objects: dividing fractions can result in an integer, and dividing integers can result in a fraction.

Value of a	Value of b	Expression	Result
-2	-3	a / b	2/3
4/3	1/3	a / b	4
1/3	1/4	a / b	4/3
4	-2.0	a / b	-2.0
3/2	3.0	a / b	0.5

// aNumber

Answer an integer that is the result of dividing the receiver by aNumber, with truncation. If the receiver and aNumber are not of the same class, the object with the lower generality is coerced to have the higher generality.

It is an error if aNumber is zero.

The division is performed as with regular division (/); the result is then truncated toward *negative infinity*. In effect, it is:

(receiver / aNumber) floor

The sign of the result is positive if both objects have the same sign and negative if the signs differ. This differs from quo: which truncates toward *zero*.

The class of the result may differ from the classes of both objects: dividing fractions always results in an integer.

Value of a	Value of b	Expression	Result
-2	-3	a // b	0
4/3	1/3	a // b	4
4/3	1/5	a // b	6
4	-2.0	a // b	-2
3/2	3.0	a // b	0
5.6	1.0	a // b	5
-5.6	1.0	a // b	-6

\\ aNumber

Answer a number that is the remainder after division of the receiver by aNumber using //. If the receiver and aNumber are not of the same class, the object with the lower generality is coerced to have the higher generality. If aNumber is zero, an error is raised. The sign of the result is the same as the sign of aNumber.

The class of the result may differ from the classes of both objects.

Value of a	Value of b	Expression	Result
5	2	a \\ b	1
-2	-3	a \\ b	-2
4/3	1/3	a \\ b	0
4	-2.0	a \\ b	0
5.6	2.0	a \\ b	1.6

< aNumber

Answer true if the receiver is less than aNumber; answer false otherwise. If the receiver and aNumber are not of the same class, the object with the lower generality is coerced to the class with the higher generality prior to the comparison.

Value of a	Value of b	Expression	Result
2	3	a < b	true
2	3.0	a < b	true

<= aNumber

Answer true if the receiver is less than or equal to aNumber; answer false otherwise. If the receiver and aNumber are not of the same class, the object with the lower generality is coerced to the class with the higher generality prior to the comparison.

Value of a	Value of b	Expression	Result
2	3	a <= b	true
2	3.0	a <= b	true

= aNumber

Answer true if the receiver is numerically equal to aNumber; answer false otherwise (even if aNumber isn't a number). Numerical equality is platform specific, depending upon conventions regarding round-off error and representation of numbers. If the receiver and aNumber are not of the same class, the object with the lower generality is coerced to the class with the higher generality prior to the comparison.

Value of a	Value of b	Expression	Result
2	3	a = b	false
3	3	a = b	true
3	3.0	a = b	true
1e101	1e100	a/10 = b	true
1.0e30	1.0e30	a = b	true
1.2345678901234567	1.23456789012345678	a = b	true (See note)

Note: In the last line, both numbers exceed the precision available on the author's platform, and thus compare equal when they do not appear to be equal. Other platforms might get other results.

== aNumber

Answer true if the receiver and aNumber are the same object; else answer false.

Value of a	Value of b	Expression	Result	Notes
2	3	a == b	false	
3	3	a == b	true	
3	3.0	a == b	false	
1000	100	a/10 == b	true	Small integers; see page 449.
1e101	1e100	a/10 == b	false	Large integers; see page 449.
12.7	12.7	a+1-1 == b	false	

~= aNumber

Answer false if the receiver is numerically equal to aNumber; answer true otherwise (even if aNumber isn't a number). Numerical equality is platform specific, depending upon conventions regarding round-off error and representation of numbers. If the receiver and aNumber are not of the same class, the object with the lower generality is coerced to the class with the higher generality prior to the comparison.

Value of a	Value of b	Expression	Result
2	3	a ~= b	true
3	3	a ~= b	false
3	3.0	a ~= b	false
1e30	1e30	a ~= b	false
1e101	1e100	a/10 ~= b	false
1.0e30	1.0e30	a ~= b	false

~~ aNumber
Answer false if the receiver and aNumber are the same object; else answer true.

Value of a	Value of b	Expression	Result	Notes
2	3	a ~~ b	true	
3	3	a ~~ b	false	
3	3.0	a ~~ b	true	
1e30	1e30	a ~~ b	true	Large integers; see page 449.
1.0e30	1.0e30	a ~~ b	true	

> aNumber
Answer true if the receiver is greater than aNumber; answer false otherwise. If the receiver and aNumber are not of the same class, the object with the lower generality is coerced to the class with the higher generality prior to the comparison.

Value of a	Value of b	Expression	Result
3	2	a > b	true
3	3.0	a > b	false

>= aNumber
Answer true if the receiver is greater than or equal to aNumber; answer false otherwise. If the receiver and aNumber are not of the same class, the object with the lower generality is coerced to the class with the higher generality prior to the comparison.

Value of a	Value of b	Expression	Result
3	2	a >= b	true
3	3.0	a >= b	true

@ aNumber
Answer a point with the receiver as the *x* coordinate and aNumber as the *y* coordinate.

Value of a	Value of b	Expression	Result
2	3	a @ b	A point: (2@3)
7.01	2/3	a @ b	A point: (7.01@ (2/3))

abs
If the receiver is positive, answer the receiver; otherwise answer the receiver negated.

See also: negated, negative, positive, sign.

Value of a	Expression	Result
3.75	a abs	3.75

Value of a	Expression	Result
-3.75	a abs	3.75
-(2/3)	a abs	(2/3)

arcCos

Answer a floating-point number that is the inverse cosine of the receiver in radians. An error is raised if the absolute value of the receiver is greater than 1.0. It is true that (x cos arcCos = x), ignoring possible roundoff and computational error.

Value of a	Expression	Result
0.5	a arcCos	1.04719755
0.5	a cos arcCos	.5
1.2	a arcCos	Error

arcSin

Answer a floating-point number that is the inverse sine of the receiver in radians. An error is raised if the absolute value of the receiver is greater than 1.0. It is true that (x sin arcSin = x), ignoring possible roundoff and computational error.

Value of a	Expression	Result
0.5	a arcSin	0.52359878
0.5	a sin arcSin	.5
1.2	a arcSin	Error

arcTan

Answer a floating-point number that is the inverse tangent of the receiver in radians. It is true that (x tan arcTan = x), ignoring possible roundoff and computational error.

Value of a	Expression	Result
0.5	a arcTan	0.46364761
0.5	a tan arcTan	.5
1.0e30	a arcTan	1.57079633

asFloat

Answer a floating-point number that is numerically equal to the receiver.

Value of a	Expression	Result
3	a asFloat	3.0
3.0	a asFloat	3.0
5/2	a asFloat	2.5

asFraction

Answer a fraction that is numerically equal to the receiver. Floating-point numbers produce different results depending upon platform and implementation details.

Value of a	Expression	Result
3	a asFraction	3
3.5	a asFraction	(7/2)
4/3	a asFraction	(4/3)
123.456	a asFraction	(15432/125)
(none)	Float pi asFraction	(12566370614359 / 4000000000000)
(none)	Float pi asFraction asFloat = Float pi	true (but no guarantees!)

asInteger
Answer the integer that is nearest to the receiver according to the following expression:

(receiver + (receiver sign * 0.5)) truncated

The asInteger message is equivalent to rounded.

Value of a	Expression	Result
2.51	a asInteger	3
2.49	a asInteger	2
0.5	a asInteger	1
-0.5	a asInteger	-1
40000000000000000000 / 3	a asInteger	13333333333333327872

The last example shows the effect of the floating-point 0.5 in the definition. When high-precision fractions are converted, the maximum precision is that of the platform's floating-point numbers. If full precision is required, do this:

```
" Rounding Fractions "
| fract floor |
fract := 40000000000000000000/3.
floor := fract floor.
^ floor + (fract - floor) rounded
    " Answer: 13333333333333333333"
```
Example 308, Display

The bold lines show the rounding algorithm.

ceiling
Return the smallest integer that is greater than or equal to the receiver.

Value of a	Expression	Result
3	a ceiling	3
4.7	a ceiling	5
-9.3	a ceiling	-9
4/3	a ceiling	2
3/2	a ceiling	2

copy
Answer the receiver. It it thus always true that (aNumber copy == aNumber), even if aNumber is not an identity object.

Value of a	Expression	Result
3	a copy = a	true
3	a copy == a	true
3.0	a copy = a	true
3.0	a copy == a	true
3e30	a copy == a	true

cos
Answer a floating-point number, in the range -1.0 to 1.0, that represents the trigonometric cosine of the receiver. The receiver's value is represented in radians.

Value of a	Expression	Result
0	a cos	1.0
(none)	(Float pi / 4) cos	0.70710678

degreesToRadians

Answer a floating-point number that is the result of multiplying the receiver by the expression (Float pi /180).

See also: radiansToDegrees

Value of a	Expression	Result
1	a degreesToRadians	0.01745329
3/2	a degreesToRadians	0.02617993
90.0	a degreesToRadians	1.57079632
(none)	(180/Float pi) degreesToRadians	1.0

exp

Answer a floating-point number that is the irrational number *e* (2.718281...) raised to the power of the receiver.

See also: ln

Value of a	Expression	Result
1	a exp	2.71828183
3	a exp	20.08553692
(7/3) exp	a exp	10.312258

floor

Answer the largest integer less than or equal to the receiver.

Value of a	Expression	Result
3	a floor	3
3.99	a floor	3
3.01	a floor	3
-3.99	a floor	-4
-3.01	a floor	-4

floorLog: aNumber

Answer the largest integer less than or equal to the power to which aNumber must be raised to obtain the receiver. An error is raised if the receiver is less than or equal to zero, or if aNumber is less than or equal to 1.0.

lessGeneralThan: aNumber

Answer true if the receiver has a lower generality than that of aNumber; answer false otherwise.

Value of a	Value of b	Expression	Result
4	7	a lessGeneralThan: b	false
4	7/3	a lessGeneralThan: b	true
4	7.0	a lessGeneralThan: b	true

ln

Answer a floating-point number that represents the power to which the irrational number *e* (2.718281...) must be raised to obtain the receiver; this is the natural logarithm of the receiver. The receiver must be positive; an error is raised if it is not.

See also: exp

Value of a	Expression	Result
2.718281...	a ln	1.0
4	a ln exp	4.0
4	a ln	1.38629436

log: aNumber

Answer a floating-point number that represents the power to which aNumber must be raised to obtain the receiver. The receiver must be positive and aNumber must be greater than one; an error is raised if it is not.

Value of a	Value of a	Expression	Result
100	10	a log: 10	2.0
16	2	a log: 2	4.0
(none)	(none)	Float pi log: 2 sqrt	3.30299226

moreGeneralThan: aNumber

Answer true if the receiver has a higher generality than that of aNumber; answer false otherwise.

Value of a	Value of b	Expression	Result
4	7	a moreGeneralThan: b	false
7/3	4	a moreGeneralThan: b	true
4.0	7	a moreGeneralThan: b	true

negated

Answer a number of the same class that has the same magnitude but a different sign.

See also: negative, positive, sign

Value of a	Expression	Result
2	2 negated	-2
2.7	a negated	2.7
(3/13)	a negated	(-3/13)

negative

Answer true if the receiver is negative; answer false otherwise.

See also: positive, sign

Value of a	Expression	Result
2	a negative	false
-2	a negative	true
0	a negative	false

positive

Answer true if the receiver is positive; answer false otherwise.

See also: negated, positive, sign, strictlyPositive

Value of a	Expression	Result
2.8	a positive	true
-99	a positive	false
0	a positive	true

quo: aNumber

Answer an integer that is the result of dividing the receiver by aNumber, with truncation. If the receiver and aNumber are not of the same class, the object with the lower generality is coerced to have the higher generality. If aNumber is zero, an error is raised.

The division is performed as with regular division (/); the result is then truncated toward *zero*. In effect, it is:

(self / aNumber) truncated

The sign of the result is positive if both objects have the same sign, and negative if the signs differ.

This differs from //, which truncates toward *negative infinity*.

Value of a	Value of b	Expression	Result
-2	-3	a quo: b	1
4/3	1/3	a quo: b	4
4	-2.0	a quo: b	-2
3/2	3.0	a quo: b	0
5.6	2.0	a quo: b	2

radiansToDegrees

Answer a floating-point number that is the result of multiplying the receiver by the expression (180 / Float pi).

See also: degreesToRadians

Value of a	Expression	Result
1	a radiansToDegrees	57.29577951
3/2	a degreesToRadians	85.94366927
(none)	Float pi radiansToDegrees	180.0

raisedTo: aNumber

Answer a number that is the receiver raised to the power aNumber. An error raised if the receiver is less than or equal to zero.

Value of a	Value of b	Expression	Result
2	3	a raisedTo: b	8
2.0	3.0	a raisedTo: b	8.0
2.5	1.5	a raisedTo: b	3.95284708
(3/2)	(1/3)	a raisedTo: b	1.14471424

raisedToInteger: anInteger

Answer a number that is the receiver raised to the integer power anInteger.

Value of a	Value of b	Expression	Result
2	3	a raisedToInteger: b	8
2.0	3	a raisedTo: b	8.0
2.5	-2	a raisedTo: b	0.16
(3/2)	3	a raisedTo: b	(27/8)

reciprocal

Answer the reciprocal of the receiver.

Value of a	Expression	Result
2	a reciprocal	(1/2)
2.0	a reciprocal	0.5
(3/2)	a reciprocal	(2/3)

rem: aNumber

Answer the remainder that results from dividing the receiver by aNumber, with truncation. The sign of the remainder is the same as the sign of the receiver.

If the receiver and aNumber are not of the same class, the object with the lower generality is coerced to have the higher generality, and the result is of the class with the higher generality.

If aNumber is zero, an error is raised.

See also: \\

Value of a	Value of b	Expression	Result
6	3	a rem: b	0
-4	-3	a rem: b	-1
(5/4)	(1/3)	a rem: b	(1/4)
5	-2.0	a rem: b	1.0
(3/2)	3.0	a rem: b	1.5
5.6	2.0	a rem: b	1.6

rounded

Answer the integer that is nearest to the receiver, according to the following expression:

> (receiver + (receiver sign * 0.5)) truncated

The rounded message is equivalent to roundTo: 1.

Value of a	Expression	Result
2.51	a rounded	3
2.49	a rounded	2
0.5	a rounded	1
-0.5	a rounded	-1

roundTo: aNumber

Answer the number nearest to the receiver that is a multiple of aNumber. An error is raised if aNumber is zero.

See also: truncateTo:.

Value of a	Value of b	Expression	Result
9.7	2	a roundTo: b	10
8.3	4	a roundTo: b	8
-8.3	4	a roundTo: b	-8
12	(5/2)	a roundTo: b	(25/2)

sign

Answer 1 if the receiver is positive, 0 if the receiver equals 0, and -1 if the receiver is negative.

See also: abs, negative, negated, positive.

Value of a	Expression	Result
2	a sign	1
0	a sign	0
-2.2	a sign	-1

sin

Answer a floating-point number in the range -1.0 to 1.0 that represents the trigonometric sine of the receiver. The receiver's value is represented in radians.

Value of a	Expression	Result
0	a sin	0.0
(none)	(Float pi / 2) sin	1.0
(none)	(Float pi / 4) sin	0.70710678

sqrt

Answer a floating-point number that represents the square root of the receiver. An error is raised if the receiver is less than zero.

Value of a	Expression	Result
2	a sqrt	1.41421356
4	a sqrt	2.0

squared

Answer a number that represents the receiver multiplied by itself.

Value of a	Expression	Result
2	a squared	4
(3/2)	a squared	(9/4)
1.2	a squared	1.44

strictlyPositive

Answer true if the receiver is greater than zero; answer false otherwise.

See also: positive.

Value of a	Expression	Result
0	a strictlyPositive	false
-0.01	a strictlyPositive	false
0.001	a StrictlyPositive	true

tan

Answer a floating-point number that represents the tangent of the receiver (a value representing radians).

Receivers quite close to the asymptotes at (pi/2 + (n*pi)), where n is an integer, may answer unpredictable results. This series is: $\dots, \left(-\frac{3\pi}{2}\right), \left(-\frac{\pi}{2}\right), \left(\frac{\pi}{2}\right), \left(\frac{3\pi}{2}\right), \dots$

Expression	Result
0 tan	0.0
(Float pi / 4) tan	1.0
(Float pi / 4) negated tan	-1.0
(Float pi / 8) tan	0.41421356

to: stop

Answer an interval that represents an arithmetic progression from the receiver to the number stop in increments of one. The interval will be empty if stop is less than the receiver. Changes to variables used for stop do not affect the current execution. The last element in the sequence might not be stop; the last element is:

(stop - receiver) truncated + receiver

This method is a shorthand for the following:

Interval from: receiver to: stop

Expression	Values represented by interval
4 to: 8	4, 5, 6, 7, 8
-6 to: 0	-6, -5, -4, -3, -2, -1, 0
8.7 to: 9.5	8.7
1/3 to: 3	1/3, 4/3, 7/3

to: stop by: step

Answer an interval that represents an arithmetic progression from the receiver to the number stop in increments of the number step. The value of step can be positive or negative, but not zero. Changes to variables used for step (or stop) do not affect the current execution. The last element in the sequence might not be stop; the last element is:

((stop - receiver) // step) * step + receiver

The interval will be empty if:
- receiver < stop, and step < 0, or
- receiver > stop, and step > 0.

This method is a shorthand for the following:

Interval from: receiver to: stop by: step

Expression	Values represented by interval
4 to: 8 by: 2	4, 6, 8
0 to: -6 by: -3	0, -3, -6
8.7 to: 9.5 by: 0.5	8.7 9.2
1/3 to: 2 by: 1/3	1/3, 2/3, 1, 4/3, 5/3, 2

to: stop by: step do: aBlock

Evaluate aBlock for each element of an interval that represents an arithmetic progression from the receiver to the number stop in increments of the number step. The value of step can be positive or negative, but not zero. Changes to variables used for step (or stop) do not affect the current execution. The last element in the sequence might not be stop; the last element is:

((stop - receiver) // step) * step + receiver

The interval will be empty if:
- receiver < stop, and step < 0, or
- receiver > stop, and step > 0.

This method is a shorthand for the following:

(Interval from: receiver to: stop by: step) do: aBlock

to: stop do: aBlock

Answer the result of evaluating aBlock for each element in an interval that represents an arithmetic progression from the receiver to the number stop in increments of one. The interval will be empty if stop is less than the receiver. Changes to variables used for stop do not affect the current execution. The last element in the sequence might not be stop; the last element is:

(stop - receiver) truncated + receiver

This method is a shorthand for the following:

(Interval from: receiver to: stop) do: aBlock

truncated

If the receiver is positive, answer an integer that is the largest integer less than or equal to the receiver.

If the receiver is negative, answer an integer that is the smallest integer greater than or equal to the receiver.

Value of a	Expression	Result
2.3	a truncated	2
-2.3	a truncated	-2

truncateTo: aNumber

If the receiver is positive, answer the largest number, less than or equal to the receiver, that is a multiple of aNumber.

If the receiver is negative, answer the smallest number, greater than or equal to the receiver, that is a multiple of aNumber.

The value in aNumber can be positive or negative, and is ignored; the sign of the result is the sign of the receiver.

Value of a	Value of b	Expression	Result
9	4	a truncateTo: b	8
7.9	1.5	a truncateTo: b	7.5
23.45	3	a truncateTo: b	21
-23.45	3	a truncateTo: b	-21
23.45	-3	a truncateTo: b	21
-23.45	-3	a truncateTo: b	-21

Class Integer

Class Method Summary

There are no new Integer class methods.

Instance Method Summary

Method	Documented	See page
& anInteger	Integer	476
| anInteger	Integer	477
* aNumber	Number	461
+ aNumber	Number	461
- aNumber	Number	461
/ aNumber	Number	461
// aNumber	Number	462
< aMagnitude	Number Magnitude	463 429
<< anInteger	Integer	477
<= aMagnitude	Number Magnitude	463 430
= aMagnitude	Number Object	463 289
== aMagnitude	Number Object	463 289
> aMagnitude	Number Magnitude	464 430
>> anInteger	Integer	477
>= aMagnitude	Number Magnitude	464 430
@ aNumber	Number	464
\\ aNumber	Number	462
~= aMagnitude	Number Object	463 289
~~ aMagnitude	Number Object	464 290
abs	Number	464
allMask: anInteger	Integer	477
anyMask: anInteger	Integer	477
arcCos	Number	465
arcSin	Number	465
arcTan	Number	465
asCharacter	Integer	478
asFloat	Number	465

Part 1 of 3.

Method	Documented	See page
asFraction	Number	465
asInteger	Number	466
between: min and: max	Magnitude	430
bitAnd: anInteger	Integer	478
bitAt: anInteger	Integer	478
bitInvert	Integer	478
bitOr: anInteger	Integer	478
bitShift: anInteger	Integer	479
bitXor: anInteger	Integer	479
ceiling	Number	466
clearBit: anInteger	Integer	479
copy	Number Object	466 291
cos	Number	466
degreesToRadians	Number	467
denominator	Integer	479
even	Integer	479
exp	Number	467
factorial	Integer	479
floor	Number	467
floorLog:	Number	467
gcd: anInteger	Integer	480
highBit: anInteger	Integer	480
isBitSet: anInteger	Integer	480
lcm: anInteger	Integer	480
lessGeneralThan: aNumber	Number	467
ln	Number	467
log:	Number	468
max: aMagnitude	Magnitude	430
min: aMagnitude	Magnitude	430
moreGeneralThan: aNumber	Number	468
negated	Number	468
negative	Number	468
numerator	Integer	480
noMask: anInteger	Integer	480
odd	Integer	481
positive	Number	468
printOn: aStream **base: anInteger**	Integer	481

printOn: aWriteStream
  base: anInteger
  showRadix: boolean
	Integer	481

printStringRadix: anInteger	Integer	481
printStringRadix: anInteger **padTo: pad**	Integer	482

Part 2 of 3.

Method	Documented	See page
printStringRadix: anInteger showRadix: aBoolean	Integer	482
printOn: aStream	Object	294
printString	Object	295
quo: aNumber	Number	469
radiansToDegrees	Number	469
raisedTo: aNumber	Number	469
raisedToInteger: anInteger	Number	469
reciprocal	Number	470
rem: aNumber	Number	470
rounded	Number	470
roundTo: aNumber	Number	470
setBit:	Integer	482
sign	Number	471
sin	Number	471
sqrt	Number	471
squared	Number	471
storeOn: aStream	Object	295
storeString	Object	296
strictlyPositive	Number	471
tan	Number	471
timesRepeat: aBlock	Integer	483
to: stop	Number	472
to: stop by: step	Number	472
to: stop by: step do: aBlock	Number	472
to: stop do: aBlock	Number	473
truncated	Number	473
truncateTo: aNumber	Number	473

Part 3 of 3.

Instance Interface

& anInteger
Answer the bitwise *and* of the receiver and anInteger.

Value of a	Value of b	Expression	Result
1	1	a & b	1
0	1	a & b	0
0	0	a & b	0
2r101010	2r111000	a & b	2r101000

| anInteger
Answer the bitwise *or* of the receiver and anInteger.

Value of a	Value of b	Expression	Result
1	1	a | b	1
0	1	a | b	1
0	0	a | b	0
2r101010	2r111000	a | b	2r111010

<< anInteger
Answer the result of shifting the receiver left by the number of bits specified by anInteger. A negative value for anInteger results in right shifting. It is equivalent to:

> receiver bitShift: anInteger.

Value of a	Value of b	Expression	Result
2r00100	1	a << b	2r01000
2r00100	-1	a << b	2r00010
1	7	a << b	128

>> anInteger
Answer the result of shifting the receiver right by the number of bits specified by anInteger. A negative value for anInteger results in left shifting. It is equivalent to:

> receiver bitShift: anInteger negated

Value of a	Value of b	Expression	Result
2r00100	1	a >> b	2r00010
2r00100	-1	a >> b	2r01000
128	7	a >> b	1

allMask: anInteger
Answer true if all of the bits that are 1 in anInteger are 1 in the receiver; answer false otherwise. It is equivalent to:

> (receiver bitAnd: anInteger) = anInteger

Value of a	Value of b	Expression	Result
2r110011	2r110000	a allMask: b	true
2r110000	2r110011	a allMask: b	false
2r1111	2r0000	a allMask: b	true
2r1010	2r0101	a allMask: b	false

anyMask: anInteger
Answer true if any of the bits that are 1 in anInteger are 1 in the receiver; answer false otherwise. It is equivalent to:

> (receiver bitAnd: anInteger) ~= 0

Value of a	Value of b	Expression	Result
2r110011	2r110000	a anyMask: b	true
2r110000	2r110011	a anyMask: b	true
2r1111	2r0000	a anyMask: b	false
2r1010	2r0101	a anyMask: b	false

asCharacter

If the receiver is in the range 0 to 127, answer the character in the ASCII character set that is represented by the receiver; else (if the receiver is in the range 128 to 256) answer a platform-specific character; else (if the receiver is 257 or above, or negative) either answer a platform-specific character or raise an error.

Only those characters in the ASCII character set are guaranteed to display and print the same across platforms and implementations.

See also: Character>>value

Value of a	Expression	Result
88	a asCharacter	$X
200	a asCharacter	Platform-specific
600	a asCharacter	Platform-specific or error

bitAnd: anInteger

Answer the bitwise *and* of the receiver and anInteger.

Value of a	Value of b	Expression	Result
1	1	a bitAnd: b	1
0	1	a bitAnd: b	0
0	0	a bitAnd: b	0
2r101010	2r111000	a bitAnd: b	2r101000

bitAt: anInteger

Answer the bit in the receiver at the index anInteger. The index must be strictly positive (i.e., greater than zero). The rightmost bit (the least significant bit) is numbered 1, the next leftmost bit is numbered 2, etc.

Value of a	Value of b	Expression	Result
2r1000	1	a bitAt: b	0
2r1000	4	a bitAt: b	1

The value of a is:

...	7	6	5	4	3	2	1
...	0	0	0	1	0	0	0

bitInvert

Answer a value that is the receiver with all 1 bits changed to 0, and all 0 bits changed to 1. It is equivalent to the following:

    receiver bitXor: -1

Value of a	Expression	Result
1	bitInvert	-2
0	bitInvert	-1
7	bitInvert	-8

bitOr: anInteger

Answer the bitwise *or* of the receiver and anInteger.

Value of a	Value of b	Expression	Result
1	1	a and: b	1
0	1	a and: b	1

Value of a	Value of b	Expression	Result
0	0	a and: b	0
2r101010	2r111000	a and: b	2r111010

bitShift: anInteger

Answer the result of shifting the receiver left by the number of bits specified by anInteger. A negative value for anInteger results in right shifting.

Value of a	Value of b	Expression	Result
2r00100	1	a bitShift: b	2r01000
2r00100	-1	a bitShift: b	2r00010
1	7	a bitShift: b	256

bitXor: anInteger

Answer the bitwise *exclusive or* of the receiver and anInteger.

Value of a	Value of b	Expression	Result
1	1	a and: b	0
0	1	a and: b	1
0	0	a and: b	0
2r101010	2r111000	a and: b	2r010010

clearBit: anInteger

Set the bit in the receiver at the index anInteger to 0. The index must be strictly positive (i.e., greater than zero).

See also: setBit:.

Value of a	Value of b	Expression	Result
2r1101	1	a clearBit: b	2r1100
2r1101	2	a clearBit: b	2r1101

The value of a is:

...	7	6	5	4	3	2	1
...	0	0	0	1	1	0	1

denominator

Answer the integer 1.

even

Answer true if the receiver is a multiple of two.

Value of a	Expression	Result
1	a even	false
2	a even	true
0	a even	true

factorial

Answer the product of all of the integers from 1 to the receiver. It is an error if the receiver is not strictly positive.

Value of a	Expression	Factorial of receiver
4	a factorial	24
20	a factorial	2432902008176640000
40	a factorial	815915283247897734345611269596115894272000000000

gcd: anInteger

Answer the greatest common divisor of the receiver and anInteger. Answer 0 if both objects are zero. The sign of the answer is always positive.

See also: lcm:.

Value of a	Value of b	Expression	Result
12	4	a gcd: b	4
17	23	a gcd: b	1
60	-18	a gcd: b	6
-60	18	a gcd: b	6

highBit

Answer the index of the most significant non-zero bit in the absolute value of the receiver.

Value of a	Expression	Result
0	a highBit	0
2r10010110	a highBit	8
16rFFFF	a highBit	16
-8	a highBit	4

isBitSet: anInteger

Answer true if the bit in the receiver at the index anInteger is 1; answer false otherwise. The index must be strictly positive (i.e., greater than zero). This is equivalent to:

(receiver bitAnd: 1 << (anInteger - 1)) ~= 0

Value of a	Value of b	Expression	Result
2r1100	1	a isBitSet: b	false
2r1100	4	a clearBit: b	true

The value of a is:

...	7	6	5	4	3	2	1
...	0	0	0	1	1	0	0

lcm: anInteger

Answer the smallest integer that is a common multiple of the receiver and anInteger. The answer is always positive. Answer 0 if both objects are zero.

See also: gcd:

Value of a	Value of b	Expression	Result
12	4	a lcm: b	12
17	23	a lcm: b	391
60	-18	a lcm: b	180

numerator

Answer the receiver.

noMask: anInteger

Answer true if none of the bits that are 1 in anInteger are 1 in the receiver; answer false otherwise. It is equivalent to:

(receiver bitAnd: anInteger) = 0

Value of a	Value of b	Expression	Result
2r110011	2r110000	a noMask: b	false

Value of a	Value of b	Expression	Result
2r110000	2r110011	a noMask: b	false
2r110011	2r001100	a noMask: b	true

odd
Answer true if the receiver is not a multiple of two.

Value of a	Expression	Result
1	a odd	true
2	a odd	false
0	a odd	false
-3	a odd	true

printOn: aWriteStream base: anInteger
Write to the stream aWriteStream, at its current position, a sequence of characters that describes the receiver in radix anInteger. The format of the output is:

> brd

where 'b' is one or more decimal digits representing anInteger, 'r' is the character $r, and 'd' is one or more digits representing the receiver in radix anInteger. The radix must be in the range 2 to 36.

Value of a	Expression	Added to stream
17	a printOn: s base: 16	'16r11'
17	a printOn: s base: 8	'8r21'
17	a printOn: s base: 2	'2r10001'

printOn: aWriteStream base: anInteger showRadix: aBoolean
Write to aWriteStream, at its current position, a sequence of characters that describes the receiver in radix anInteger. If aBoolean is true, the format of the output is:

> brd

where 'b' is one or more decimal digits representing anInteger, 'r' is the character $r, and 'd' is one or more digits representing the receiver in radix anInteger. The radix must be in the range 2 to 36. If aBoolean is false, the output consists only of the 'd' part.

See also: Number>>printOn:

Value of a	Expression	Added to stream
17	a printOn: s base: 16 showRadix: false	'11'
17	a printOn: s base: 10 showRadix: true	'10r17'
17	a printOn: s base: 8 showRadix: false	'21'
17	a printOn: s base: 2 showRadix: false	'10001'
17	a printOn: s base: 2 showRadix: true	'2r10001'

printStringRadix: anInteger
Answer a character string that describes the receiver in radix anInteger. The format of the output is:

> brd

where 'b' is one or more decimal digits representing anInteger, 'r' is the character $r, and 'd' is one or more digits representing the receiver in radix anInteger. The radix must be in the range 2 to 36.

See also: Number>>printString

Value of a	Expression	Added to stream
17	a printStringRadix: 16	'16r11'
17	a printStringRadix: 10	'10r17'
17	a printStringRadix: 8	'8r21'
17	a printStringRadix: 2	'2r10001'

printStringRadix: anInteger padTo: count

Answer a character string that describes the receiver in radix anInteger. The radix is not included in the string. The radix must be in the range 2 to 36.

If the string that represents the number has less than count (an integer) digits, the digits will be padded on the left to length count with zeros. If it has more than count digits, no padding or truncation occurs. A minus sign occurs first in the string if the receiver is negative; if padding was done, it replaces the first padded zero.

Value of a	Expression	Result
17	a printStringRadix: 2 padTo: 7	' 0010001'
17	a printStringRadix: 2 padTo: 2	' 10001'
-17	b printStringRadix: 2 padTo: 7	' -010001'
-17	b printStringRadix: 2 padTo: 2	'-10001'

printStringRadix: anInteger showRadix: aBoolean

Answer a character string that describes the receiver in radix anInteger. If aBoolean is true, the format of the output is:

brd

where 'b' is one or more decimal digits representing anInteger, 'r' is the character $r, and 'd' is one or more digits representing the receiver in radix anInteger. The radix must be in the range 2 to 36.

If aBoolean is false, the output consists only of the 'd' part.

Value of a	Expression	Added to stream
17	a printStringRadix: 16 showRadix: false	'11'
17	a printStringRadix: 8 showRadix: false	'21'
17	a printStringRadix: 2 showRadix: false	'10001'
17	a printStringRadix: 2 showRadix: true	'2r10001'

setBit: anInteger

Set the bit in the receiver at the index anInteger to 1. The index must be strictly positive (i.e., greater than zero). This is equivalent to:

receiver bitOr: (1 << (anInteger-1))

See also: clearBit:.

Value of a	Value of b	Expression	Result
2r10101010	7	a setBit: b	2r11101010
2r0100	4	a setBit: b	2r1100

size

••• Answer the size of an integer as a number of 32-bit words allocated. Small integers are 0, long integers are 1 and up. For long integers, the maximum number size in bits will typically be (receiver size) * 32.

Caution: Some platforms may work differently; use this method only for exploration and testing, and not in production code.

timesRepeat: aBlock

Evaluate the zero-parameter block, aBlock, receiver times. If the receiver is not strictly positive, do nothing.

Example:

```
" Pad a string "
| pad str |
pad := 9.
str := '123456'.
(pad - str size)
    timesRepeat: [  str := '0', str ].
^ str
    "Result: 000123456"
```

Example 309, Display

Class Float

Instances of class Float are floating-point numbers.

Class	*Page*
Magnitude	429
...	
Number	459
Integer	474
Float	483
Fraction	484

Class Method Summary

Method	Documented	See page
pi	Float	483

Instance Method Summary

Method	Documented	See page
fractionPart	Float	484
integerPart	Float	484

Class Interface

pi

Answer a floating point number that represents the best approximation to π on the platform and implementation.

Example:

```
Float pi
    " Answers on the author's platform: 3.14159265"
```

Example 310, Display

Instance Interface

fractionPart

Answer a floating-point number that represents the fraction part of the receiver.

Value of a	Expression	Result
23.45	a fractionPart	0.45

integerPart

Answer a floating-point number that represents the integer part of the receiver.

Value of a	Expression	Result
23.45	a integerPart	23.0

Fraction

Fractions are the ratio of two integers.

Class	Page
Magnitude	429
...	
Number	459
Integer	474
Float	483
Fraction	484

Class Method Summary

There are no new class methods.

Instance Method Summary

Method	Documented	See page
denominator	Fraction	484
numerator	Fraction	484

Instance Interface

denominator

Answer the denominator of the receiver.

Value of a	Expression	Result
(5/21)	a denominator	21

numerator

Answer the numerator of the receiver.

Value of a	Expression	Result
(5/21)	a numerator	5

34

Points

Points represent a pair of values, such as points on an *x-y* plane, distances expressed as delta-*x* and delta-*y* on an *x-y* plane, or *x-y* vectors. They are usually created by the @ message to a number: 4@3 or by operations on points.

The Point classes are:

Class	*Page*
Object	
Point	488

Coordinate System

In the coordinate system for points, and for rectangles, the *x* values increase to the right and *y* values increase downwards from the origin. On the display screen, and in windows, the origin is in the upper-left corner. While this differs from mathematical conventions, and from the conventions of some platforms, it is uniform across all platforms and native to many. See Figure 97 for some sample points on a grid.

Categories of Point Messages

Operations on points can be categorized into access, arithmetic, comparison, rectangle creation, truncation and rounding, and other.

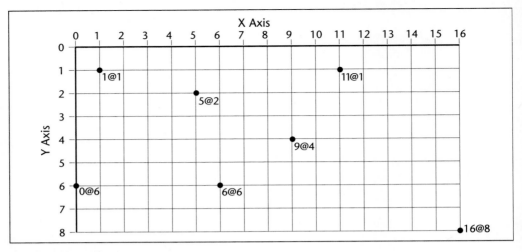

Figure 97: Coordinate System.

Access

Access operations are:

x	Return the *x* position
x:	Set the *x* position
y	Return the *y* position
y:	Set the *y* position

Arithmetic

Arithmetic operations are:

*	Multiply a point by a number
+	Add two points or a point and a number
-	Subtract two points or a point and a number
/	Divide a point by a number
//	Divide a point by a number with truncation
abs	New point with non-negative components
max:	Maximum of two points
min:	Minimum of two points
negated	Point with opposite signs

Conversions of numbers in points follows the normal rules of number conversion: thus, (2.0@3.0) = (2@3).

Comparison

Comparison operations are:

<	True if first point is left and above
<=	True if first point is equal or left and above
=	True if two points have equal values
>	True if first point is right and below
>=	True if first point is equal or right and below
between:and:	True if a point is between two other points

Comparison operations on points do not seem to obey the usual rules. It is possible for two points to answer false to all of these binary comparison operations. See Figure 98.

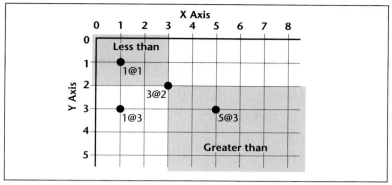

Figure 98: Points and Relationals. The grey areas show the ranges of points that are less-then and greater-than 3@2; they extend to infinity. The white areas are neither less-then nor greater-than. Thus, the point 1@3 is not less-than, greater-than, less-than or equal, or greater-than or equal. It is, however, certainly not-equal!

While points are not magnitudes, the fact that they respond to comparison operators, especially <, means that they can be put into sorted collections. However, the lack of a complete definition of ordering of points means that the sorting will not be very useful with the default sort ordering. It is suggested that a sort block should always be used with points. The following sort block sorts points by *x* position, and (if equal) by *y* position:

```
[ :p1 :p2 |
    p1 x = p2 x
        ifTrue: [ p1 y < p2 y ]
        ifFalse: [ p1 x < p2 x ]  ]
```

Rectangle Creation

Rectangle creation operations are:

corner:	Create a rectangle with a given corner
extent:	Create a rectangle with a given extent

Truncation and Rounding

Truncation and rounding operations are:

rounded	Point with rounded positions
truncated	Point with truncated positions
truncatededGrid:	Point with truncated positions
truncateTo:	Point with truncated positions

Other

Other operations are:

dist:	The distance between two points
transpose	A new point with *x* and *y* transposed

Protocol Summary

Class Protocol Summary

The following table summarizes the class protocols of Point.

Object class
Point class
x:y:

Instance Protocol Summary

The following table summarizes the instance protocols of Point.

		Object			
=	==	copy			
		Point			
*	<	between:and:	max:	transpose	x
+	<=	corner: aPoint	min:	truncated	x: aNumber
-	>	dist: aPoint	negated	truncatedGrid:	y
/	>=	extent:	rounded	truncateTo:	y: aNumber
//	abs				

Class Point

Class	Page
Object	
Point	488

Class Method Summary

Method	Documented	See page
x: xNumber y: yNumber	Point	489

Instance Method Summary

Method	Documented	See page
* aPointOrNumber	Point	489
+ aPointOrNumber	Point	490
- aPointOrNumber	Point	490
/ aPointOrNumber	Point	490
// aPointOrNumber	Point	491

Part 1 of 2.

Method	Documented	See page
< aPoint	Point	491
<= aPoint	Point	491
= aPoint	Point Object	492 289
~= aPoint	Point Object	492 289
== aPoint	Object	289
~~ aPoint	Object	290
> aPoint	Point	492
>= aPoint	Point	492
abs	Point	492
between: lowPoint and: highPoint	Point	493
copy	Point Object	493 291
corner: aPoint	Point	493
dist: aPoint	Point	493
extent: aPoint	Point	493
max: aPoint	Point	494
min: aPoint	Point	494
negated	Point	494
rounded	Point	495
transpose	Point	495
truncated	Point	495
truncatedGrid: aPointOrNumber	Point	495
truncateTo: aPointOrNumber	Point	495
x	Point	496
x: aNumber	Point	496
y	Point	496
y: aNumber	Point	496

Part 2 of 2.

Class Interface

x: xNumber y: yNumber
Answer a point that has an *x* value of xNumber and a *y* value of yNumber.

Value of a	Value of b	Expression	Result
x	y	Point x: a y: b	x @ y
4	2	Point x: a y: b	4 @ 2
2.5	3.2	Point x: a y: b	2.5 @ 3.2

Instance Interface

Note: The first line in most example tables shows the result of the method in symbolic terms.

* aPointOrNumber
Answer a new point that is the product of the receiver and a number or point representing a scaling factor.

If aPointOrNumber is a *number,* answer a new point that has an *x* coordinate that is the *x* coordinate of the receiver multiplied by the number, and has a *y* coordinate that is the *y* coordinate of the receiver multiplied by the number.

If aPointOrNumber is a *point,* answer a new point that has an *x* coordinate that is the *x* coordinate of the receiver multiplied by the *x* coordinate of the point, and has a *y* coordinate that is the *y* coordinate of the receiver multiplied by the *y* coordinate of the point.

Value of a	Value of b	Expression	Result
x1 @ y1	x2 @ y2	a * b	(x1*x2) @ (y1*y2)
2.5 @ 3.2	2	a * b	5.0 @ 6.4
2.5 @ 3.2	2 @ 3	a * b	5.0 @ 9.6

+ aPointOrNumber

Answer a new point that is the product of the receiver and a number or point representing a translation amount.

If aPointOrNumber is a *number,* answer a new point that has an *x* coordinate that is the *x* coordinate of the receiver added to the number, and has a *y* coordinate that is the *y* coordinate of the receiver added to the number.

If aPointOrNumber is a *point,* answer a new point that has an *x* coordinate that is the *x* coordinate of the receiver added to the *x* coordinate of the point, and has a *y* coordinate that is the *y* coordinate of the receiver added to the *y* coordinate of the point.

Value of a	Value of b	Expression	Result
x1 @ y1	x2 @ y2	a + b	(x1+x2) @ (y1+y2)
10 @ 15	2	a + b	12 @ 17
10 @ 15	2 @ 3	a + b	12 @ 18

- aPointOrNumber

Answer a new point that is the product of the receiver and a number or point representing a translation amount.

If aPointOrNumber is a *number,* answer a new point that has an *x* coordinate that is the *x* coordinate of the number subtracted from the receiver, and has a *y* coordinate that is the *y* coordinate of the number subtracted from the receiver.

If aPointOrNumber is a *point,* answer a new point that has an *x* coordinate that is the *x* coordinate of the point subtracted from the *x* coordinate of the receiver, and has a *y* coordinate that is the *y* coordinate of the point subtracted from the *y* coordinate of the receiver.

Value of a	Value of b	Expression	Result
x1 @ y1	x2 @ y2	a - b	(x1-x2) @ (y1-y2)
10 @ 15	2	a - b	8 @ 13
10 @ 15	2 @ 3	a - b	8 @ 13

/ aPointOrNumber

Answer a new point that is the receiver divided by a number or point representing a scaling factor.

If aPointOrNumber is a *number,* answer a new point that has an *x* coordinate that is the *x* coordinate of the receiver divided by the number, and has a *y* coordinate that is the *y* coordinate of the receiver divided by the number.

If aPointOrNumber is a *point,* answer a new point that has an *x* coordinate that is the *x* coordinate of the receiver divided by the *x* coordinate of the point, and has a *y* coordinate that is the *y* coordinate of the receiver divided by the *y* coordinate of the point.

Value of a	Value of b	Expression	Result
x1 @ y1	x2 @ y2	a / b	(x1/x2) @ (y1/y2)
2.5 @ 3.2	2	a / b	1.25 @ 1.6
2.5 @ 3.2	2 @ 4	a / b	1.25 @ 0.8

// aPointOrNumber

Answer a new point that is the integer quotient of the receiver and a number or point representing a scaling factor.

If aPointOrNumber is a *number,* answer a new point that has an *x* coordinate that is the *x* coordinate of the receiver integer divided by the number, and has a *y* coordinate that is the *y* coordinate of the receiver integer divided by the number.

If aPointOrNumber is a *point,* answer a new point that has an *x* coordinate that is the *x* coordinate of the receiver integer divided by the *x* coordinate of the point, and has a *y* coordinate that is the *y* coordinate of the receiver integer divided by the *y* coordinate of the point.

Integer division is as defined for the // message for the receiver's *x* and *y* coordinates, individually.

Value of a	Value of b	Expression	Result
x1 @ y1	x2 @ y2	a // b	(x1//x2) @ (y1//y2)
2.5 @ 3.2	2	a // b	1 @ 1
2.5 @ 3.2	2 @ 4	a // b	1 @ 0

< aPoint

Answer true if the receiver is above and to the left of aPoint; answer false otherwise.

See Figure 98 on page 487 for a picture of relationals for less-than (<).

Value of a	Value of b	Expression	Result
x1 @ y1	x2 @ y2	a < b	(x1<x2) & (y1<y2)
2 @ 3	4 @ 5	a < b	true
4 @ 5	2 @ 3	a < b	false

<= aPoint

Answer true if the receiver is neither below nor to the right of aPoint; answer false otherwise.

See Figure 98 on page 487 for a picture of relationals.

Value of a	Value of b	Expression	Result
x1 @ y1	x2 @ y2	a <= b	(x1<=x2) & (y1<=y2)
2 @ 3	4 @ 5	a <= b	true
4 @ 5	2 @ 3	a <= b	false
2 @ 3	2 @ 3	a <= b	true

= aPoint

Answer true if the *x* coordinate of the receiver is equal to the *x* coordinate of aPoint and the *y* coordinate of the receiver is equal to the *y* coordinate of aPoint.

Value of a	Value of b	Expression	Result
x1 @ y1	x2 @ y2	a = b	(x1=x2) & (y1=y2)
2 @ 3	4 @ 3	a = b	false
4 @ 5	5 @ 4	a = b	false
2 @ 3	2 @ 3	a = b	true
2 @ 3	2.0 @ 3.0	a = b	true

~= aPoint

Answer true if the *x* coordinate of the receiver is not equal to the *x* coordinate of aPoint or the *y* coordinate of the receiver is not equal to the *y* coordinate of aPoint.

Value of a	Value of b	Expression	Result
x1 @ y1	x2 @ y2	a = b	(x1=x2) & (y1=y2)
2 @ 3	4 @ 3	a = b	false
4 @ 5	5 @ 4	a = b	false
2 @ 3	2 @ 3	a = b	true
2 @ 3	2.0 @ 3.0	a = b	true

> aPoint

Answer true if the receiver is below and to the right of aPoint; answer false otherwise.

See Figure 98 on page 487 for a picture of relationals for greater-than (>).

Value of a	Value of b	Expression	Result
x1 @ y1	x2 @ y2	a > b	(x1>x2) & (y1>y2)
2 @ 3	4 @ 5	a > b	false
4 @ 5	2 @ 3	a > b	true
2 @ 3	2 @ 3	a > b	false

>= aPoint

Answer true if the receiver is neither above nor to the left of aPoint; answer false otherwise.

See Figure 98 on page 487 for a picture of relationals.

Value of a	Value of b	Expression	Result
x1 @ y1	x2 @ y2	a >= b	(x1>=x2) & (y1>=y2)
2 @ 3	4 @ 5	a >= b	false
4 @ 5	2 @ 3	a >= b	true
2 @ 3	2 @ 3	a >= b	true

abs

Answer a new point with *x* and *y* coordinates that are the absolute values of the *x* and *y* values of the receiver.

Value of a	Expression	Result
x @ y	a abs	(x abs) @ (y abs)
-2 @ 3	a abs	2 @ 3
-2 @ -3	a abs	2 @ 3
2 @ 3	a abs	2 @ 3

between: lowPoint and: highPoint

Answer true if the receiver is less than or equal to highPoint and greater than or equal to lowPoint; answer false otherwise.

See Figure 98 on page 487 for a picture of relationals.

See also: Rectangle>>containsPoint:

Value of a	Value of b	Expression	Result
x1 @ y1	x2 @ y2	x@y between: a and: b	((x@y) >= (x1@y1)) and: [(x@y) <= (x2@y2)]
2 @ 3	6 @ 8	4@5 between: a and: b	true
1 @ 1	4 @ 4	3@5 between: a and: b	false

This is similar, but not identical, to the rectangle message containsPoint:; between:and: answers true if the receiver is identical to highPoint, while containsPoint: will not.

copy

Answer a new point with the same *x* and *y* coordinates.

Value of a	Expression	Result
x @ y	a copy	x @ y
2 @ 3	a copy	2 @ 3

corner: aPoint

Answer a new rectangle with the receiver as the origin and aPoint as the corner. It is equivalent to the following message:

Rectangle origin: receiver corner: aPoint

Value of a	Value of b	Expression	Result
x1 @ y1	x2 @ y2	a corner: b	(x1@y1) corner: (x2@y2)
2 @ 3	4 @ 5	a corner: b	(2 @ 3) corner: (4@5)

dist: aPoint

Answer the distance between the receiver and aPoint. The distance is defined as the square root of the sum of the squares of the *x* and *y* distances between the receiver and aPoint.

Value of a	Value of b	Expression	Result
x1 @ y1	x2 @ y2	a dist: b	((x1-x2) squared + (y1-y2) squared) sqrt
0 @ 3	4 @ 0	a dist: b	5.0
2 @ 2	4 @ 4	a dist: b	2.82842712
1 @ 1	-1 @ -1	a dist: b	2.82842712
0 @ 0	3 @ 4	a dist: b	5

extent: aPoint

Answer a new rectangle with the receiver as the origin, and aPoint as the extent. It is equivalent to the following message:

Rectangle origin: receiver extent: aPoint

Value of a	Value of b	Expression	Result
x1 @ y1	x2 @ y2	a extent: b	(x1@y1) corner: ((x1+x2) @ (y1+y2))
2 @ 3	4 @ 5	a extent: b	(2 @ 3) corner: (6 @ 8)

max: aPoint

Answer a new point that is the lower-right corner of a rectangle formed by the receiver and aPoint. The new point has an *x* coordinate that is the maximum of the two *x* coordinates and a *y* coordinate that is the maximum of the two *y* coordinates. As a result it is possible that the answer is neither equal to the receiver nor to aPoint. Figure 99 illustrates the maximum of two points.

Value of a	Value of b	Expression	Result
x1 @ y1	x2 @ y2	a max: b	(x1 max: x2) @ (y1 max: y2)
2 @ 3	4 @ 5	a max: b	4 @ 5
2 @ 3	3 @ 2	a max: b	3 @ 3
0 @ 10	10 @ 0	a max: b	10 @ 10

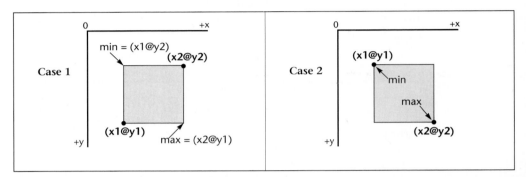

Figure 99: Comparison of Two Cases of min: and max: The input points are at the black dots. In Case 1, the minimum and maximum points are at different corners, and in Case 2, they are at the same corners as the input points.

min: aPoint

Answer a new point that is the upper-left corner of a rectangle formed by the receiver and aPoint. The new point has an *x* coordinate that is the minimum of the two *x* coordinates and a *y* coordinate that is the minimum of the two *y* coordinates. As a result it is possible that the answer is neither equal to the receiver nor to aPoint. Figure 99 illustrates the minimum of two points.

Value of a	Value of b	Expression	Result
x1 @ y1	x2 @ y2	a min: b	(x1 min: x2) @ (y1 min: y2)
2 @ 3	4 @ 5	a min: b	2 @ 3
2 @ 3	3 @ 2	a min: b	2 @ 2
0 @ 10	10 @ 0	a min: b	0 @ 0

negated

Answer a new point with *x* and *y* coordinates that have signs opposite those of the *x* and *y* values of the receiver.

Value of a	Expression	Result
x @ y	a negated	(x negated) @ (y negated)
-2 @ 3	a negated	2 @ -3
-2 @ -3	a negated	2 @ 3
2 @ 3	a negated	-2 @ -3

rounded

Answer a new point such that the new x coordinate is the receiver's x coordinate rounded, and the new y coordinate is the receiver's y coordinate rounded.

Value of a	Expression	Result
x @ y	a rounded	(x rounded) @ (y rounded)
2.4 @ 4.7	a rounded	2 @ 5

transpose

Answer a new point in which the receiver's x value is the new y value, and the receiver's y value is the new x value.

Value of a	Expression	Result
x @ y	a transpose	y @ x
2 @ 4	a transpose	4 @ 2

truncated

Answer a new point such that the new x coordinate is the receiver's x coordinate truncated, and the new y coordinate is the receiver's y coordinate truncated.

Value of a	Expression	Result
x @ y	a truncated	(x truncated) @ (y truncated)
2.4 @ 4.7	a truncated	2 @ 4

truncatedGrid: aPoint

Answer a new point with an x value that is the x value of the receiver truncated to the x value of aPoint, and a y value that is the y value of the receiver truncated to the y value of aPoint. This is exactly equivalent to truncateTo: as defined for point parameters.

Value of a	Value of b	Expression	Result
x @ y	tx @ ty	a truncatedGrid: b	(x//tx*tx) @ (y//ty*ty)
2.4 @ 4.7	1 @ 1	a truncatedGrid: b	2 @ 4
13.2 @ 8.3	2@2	a truncatedGrid: b	12 @ 8
13.2 @ 8.3	3 @ 3	a truncatedGrid: b	12 @ 6
13.2 @ 8.3	2.5 @ 1.5	a truncatedGrid: b	12.5 @ 7.5

truncateTo: aPointOrNumber

Answer a new point with truncated values.

If aPointOrNumber is a *point*, answer a new point with an x value that is the x value of the receiver truncated to the x value of aPoint, and a y value that is the y value of the receiver truncated to the y value of aPoint. This is exactly the same as truncatedGrid:.

If aPointOrNumber is a *number*, answer a new point with an x value that is the x value of the receiver truncated to the number, and a y value that is the y value of the receiver truncated to the number.

Value of a	Value of b	Expression	Result
x @ y	tx @ ty	a truncateTo: b	(x//tx*tx) @ (y//ty*ty)
2.4 @ 4.7	1 @ 1	a truncateTo: b	2 @ 4
2.4 @ 4.7	1	a truncateTo: b	2 @ 4
13.2 @ 8.3	2 @ 2	a truncateTo: b	12 @ 8
13.2 @ 8.3	2	a truncateTo: b	12 @ 8
13.2 @ 8.3	2.5 @ 1.5	a truncateTo: b	12.5 @ 7.5

x

Answer the *x* value of the receiver.

Value of a	Expression	Result
x @ y	a x	x
3 @ 5	a x	3

x: aNumber

Answer the receiver with the *x* value replaced with aNumber. Note that the object returned *is* the receiver, not a new point.

Value of a	Expression	Result
x1 @ y1	a x: x2	x2 @ y1
3 @ 5	a x: 4	4 @ 5

y

Answer the *y* value of the receiver.

Value of a	Expression	Result
x @ y	a y	y
3 @ 5	a y	5

y: aNumber

Answer the receiver with the *y* value replaced with aNumber. Note that the object returned *is* the receiver, not a new point.

Value of a	Expression	Result
x1 @ y1	a y: y2	x1 @ y2
3 @ 5	a y: 4	3 @ 4

Processes

Processes allow more than one thread of execution, with each process running separately and independently, except when explicitly synchronized.

The process classes are not part of a hierarchy. Class Block is also partly covered in two other chapters, those on blocks and exception handling.

See Chapter 15, 'Processes and Synchronization', on page 167 for an introduction to process classes.

The process classes are:

Categories of Classes and Methods

Block

Messages to blocks create processes. New messages are:

fork	Run the block in a separate process
forkAt:	Run in a separate process with a given priority
newProcess	Make a new, suspended process
newProcessWith:	Make a process with a given priority

Delay

Instances of class Delay are used to wait for some number of milliseconds. Class methods are:

forMilliseconds:	Delay for some milliseconds
forSeconds:	Delay for some seconds
untilMilliseconds:	Delay until some milliseconds have passed

Instance methods are:

resumptionTime	Answer when delay will resume
wait	Wait for delay to end

Process

Processes are instances of class Process. Instances of process answer to:

priority	Answer priority of a process
priority:	Set priority of a process
queueInterrupt:	Interrupt another process
resume	Resume execution of suspended process
suspend	Suspend a process
terminate	Terminate a process
yield	Yield the processor to another process

The resume, suspend, and terminate messages change the state of a process, as shown in Figure 100.

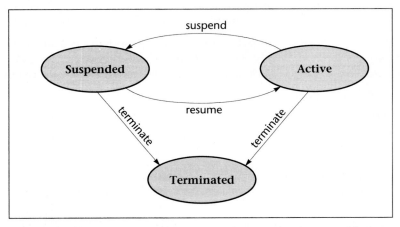

Figure 100: Process State Diagram. Ovals represent the three possible states of a process: suspended, active, and terminated. Arrows represent messages that change the process from one state to another. Messages not shown, such as resume sent a terminated process, are ignored.

ProcessorScheduler

There is but one instance of ProcessorScheduler; it is named Processor. Processor controls the processes in the system; its protocol allows control of priorities, the active process, and signalling semaphores at a given time.

Instance methods relating to the active process are:

activePriority	Get priority of the sender's process
activeProcess	Get the sender's process

Instance methods relating to signalling semaphores are:

signal:atTime:	Signal a semaphore at a given time

Instance methods relating to the priority of processes are:

highIOPriority	Priority of high-priority IO processes
lowIOPriority	Priority of low-priority IO processes
systemBackgroundPriority	Priority of system background processes
timingPriority	Priority of timing processes
userBackgroundPriority	Priority of user background processes
userInterruptPriority	Priority of user interrupts
userSchedulingPriority	Priority of user interface; default priority

Semaphore

Semaphores are special flags which are used to synchronize processes. Semaphore class methods are:

forMutualExclusion	New semaphore that has one signal
new	New semaphore that has never been signalled

Semaphore instance methods are:

critical:	Protect code that's updating a shared resource
signal	Add a signal to the receiver
wait	Suspend process until receiver has a signal

Priorities

There are seven defined priority levels, each mapped to an integer, with lower integer values meaning lower priority. See Figure 101.

Priority numbers should never be coded directly, nor should values outside the range 1 to 7 ever be used. Priorities in the three bold face lines are for user processes; other priorities should not be used without a thorough knowledge of how the system itself might be affected.

Priority	Message answering priority number	Description
1	Processor systemBackgroundPriority	System background processes
2	**Processor userBackgroundPriority**	**User background processes**
3	**Processor userSchedulingPriority**	**User scheduling priority**
4	**Processor userInterruptPriority**	**User interrupt priority**
5	Processor lowIOPriority	Low-priority IO processes
6	Processor highIOPriority	High-priority IO processes
7	Processor timingPriority	Timing process

Figure 101: Priorities. One of expressions in the center column should always be used to refer to the values of a priority, rather than coding the number directly. Bold entries are for user processes; others are typically for system use only.

Protocol Summaries

Class Protocol Summary

Object Class				
new	new:			

Block class	Delay class	Process class	ProcessScheduler class	Semaphore class
~~new~~ ~~new:~~	~~new~~ ~~new:~~ forMilliseconds: forSeconds: untilMilliseconds:	~~new~~ ~~new:~~	~~new~~ ~~new:~~	forMutualExclusion new ~~new:~~

Instance Protocol Summary

Object					
=	==				

Block	Delay	Process	ProcessScheduler		Semaphore
fork forkAt: newProcess newProcessWith:	resumptionTime wait	priority priority: queueInterrupt: resume suspend terminate	activePriority activeProcess highIOPriority lowIOPriority signal:atTime:	systemBackgroundPriority timingPriority userBackgroundPriority userInterruptPriority userSchedulingPriority	critical: hasSignals signal wait

---

Class Block

Class Method Summary

Method	Documented	See page
~~new~~	Object	288
~~new: anInteger~~	Object	289

Instance Method Summary

This is an incomplete list of Block methods; see Chapter 25, 'Blocks', on page 297.

Method	Documented	See page
fork	Block	501
forkAt: anInteger	Block	501
newProcess	Block	501
newProcessWith: aCollection	Block	501

Instance Interface

fork

Answer a new process and schedule it for execution with the same priority as the current active process. When it executes, the new process evaluates the receiver, a zero-parameter block.

forkAt: anInteger

Answer a new process with priority anInteger and schedule it for execution. When it executes, the new process evaluates the receiver, a one-parameter block.

newProcess

Answer a new process in suspended state, with the same priority as the current active process. The process can be started by sending it the message resume.

newProcessWith: aCollection

Answer a new process in a suspended state, with the same priority as the current active process. The process can be scheduled by sending it the message resume. When it executes, the new process evaluates the receiver with the parameters in aCollection; the number of arguments expected by the receiver must match the size of aCollection.

Class Delay

Class	Page
Object	
Block	300, 398, 500
Delay	501
Process	503
ProcessScheduler	506
Semaphore	507

Class Method Summary

Method	Documented	See page
~~new~~	Object	288
~~new: anInteger~~	Object	289
forMilliseconds: anInteger	Delay	502
forSeconds: anInteger	Delay	502
untilMilliseconds: anInteger	Delay	502

Instance Method Summary

Method	Documented	See page
resumptionTime	Delay	503
wait	Delay	503

Class Interface

forMilliseconds: anInteger

Answer an instance of Delay that, when sent the wait message, will suspend the active process for at least anInteger milliseconds. The value anInteger must be zero or positive.

```
" Delay a process for 30000 milliseconds "
| delay |
delay := Delay forMilliseconds: 30*1000.
[ delay wait. System message: 'I woke up. Yawn...' ] fork
```
Example 311, Execute

forSeconds: anInteger

Answer an instance of Delay that, when sent the wait message, will suspend the active process for at least anInteger seconds. The value anInteger must be zero or positive.

```
" Delay a process for 30 seconds "
| delay |
delay := Delay forSeconds: 30.
[     delay wait.
     System message: 'You call that a nap? 30 whole seconds!' ] fork
```
Example 312, Execute

untilMilliseconds: anInteger

Answer an instance of Delay that, when sent the wait message, will suspend the active process until the millisecond clock has reached at least the value anInteger milliseconds. The value anInteger must be zero or positive, and should be less than the current millisecond clock value, but not more than 86,400,000 milliseconds, the number of milliseconds in a day.

Values of the millisecond clock can be obtained from the expression Time millisecondClockValue and the number of milliseconds in a day can be obtained from the message Time millisecondsPerDay. The values in the millisecond clock are release and platform dependent; assume only that there is some value which is logically incremented every millisecond.

For more information on the millisecond clock, see the section on 'Millisecond Clock' on page 61 and the method millisecondClockValue in class Time on page 446.

See also: ProcessScheduler>>signal:atTime:, Time>>millisecondsToRun:

In the following example, a process waits until a given time on a wall clock.

```
" Delay until a given wall clock time "
| wallThen milliNow milliThen delay |
" Fake a time that happens to be in 30 seconds "
wallThen := Time now addTime: (Time new hours: 0 minutes: 0 seconds: 30).

milliNow := Time millisecondClockValue.
milliThen := milliNow +
```

(1000 * (wallThen subtractTime: Time now) asSeconds).

```
delay := Delay untilMilliseconds: milliThen.
[      delay wait.
       System message: 'Uhhhgg... Yawn... What time is it?' ] fork
```
Example 313, Execute

Instance Interface

resumptionTime
Answer the value of the millisecond clock at which this delay will end. It is possible that the value will represent a time that is in the past.

wait
Suspend the current process for at least the delay period; resume the process at some time after the period has expired. There is no guarantee that a process will resume at exactly the end of the delay process, since other processes might be dispatched first; it is guaranteed that the waiting process will not be dispatched until the delay period is over.

Note that the delay period can be zero if the instance of Delay was created by the untilMilliseconds: method long enough ago that the specified time has passed.

Class Process

Class	Page
Object	
Block	300, 398, 500
Delay	501
Process	503
ProcessScheduler	506
Semaphore	507

Class Method Summary

Method	Documented	See page
~~new~~	Object	288
~~new: anInteger~~	Object	289

Instance Method Summary

Method	Documented	See page
priority	Process	504
priority: anInteger	Process	504
queueInterrupt: aBlock	Process	504
resume	Process	505
suspend	Process	505
terminate	Process	505
yield	Process	505

Instance Interface

priority
Answer the priority of the receiver. The value is an integer. See Figure 101 on page 499.

priority: anInteger
Attempt to set the priority of the receiver to be anInteger. If the priority can be changed, the change will not take effect until the next context switch. Some platforms may not support changing priorities in all cases; if so, do nothing.

The new priority should not be coded as an integer, but either as a value obtained from the priority message, above, or a value obtained from messages to Processor. See Figure 101, 'Priorities', on page 499.

queueInterrupt: aBlock
Queue a block for another process to run as soon as it is able to do so. The block can perform any action, but is typically used to pass exceptions to another process or to simulate interrupts. The block runs as a part of the other process.

Example 314 uses queueInterrupt: to set the variable seconds. The alternative is to use semaphores to synchronize use of the variable.

```
" Using the queueInterrupt: Message "
| semi seconds p running |
semi := Semaphore new.
seconds := 5.
running := true.
p := [
            [running]
                whileTrue: [
                    (Delay forSeconds: seconds) wait.
                    Transcript cr; show: Time now printString,
                        ' delay is ', seconds printString ].
            Transcript cr; show: 'Finished.'
        ] fork.

[ (Delay forSeconds: 15) wait.
        p queueInterrupt: [ seconds := 3 ].
        (Delay forSeconds: 15) wait.
        p queueInterrupt: [ seconds := 10 ].
        (Delay forSeconds: 15) wait.
        p queueInterrupt: [ running := false ] ] fork

" The Transcript shows:
01:07:53 PM delay is 5
01:07:58 PM delay is 5
01:08:04 PM delay is 3
01:08:07 PM delay is 3
01:08:10 PM delay is 3
01:08:13 PM delay is 3
01:08:17 PM delay is 3
01:08:20 PM delay is 10
01:08:30 PM delay is 10
01:08:40 PM delay is 10
Finished.  "
```

Example 314, Execute

Example 315 uses queueInterrupt: to issue a signal to an exception in another process.

```
" Using the queueInterrupt: Message for interrupts "
| exception p |
exception := ExAll newChild.
p := [
        [ 1000 timesRepeat: [ 100 factorial ] ]
        when: exception
        do: [ :sig |
                Transcript cr; show: 'Interrupted'.
                sig exitWith: nil ].
        Transcript cr; show: 'Finished.'
    ] forkAt: Processor userBackgroundPriority.

[ (Delay forSeconds: 5) wait.
        p queueInterrupt: [ exception signal ] ] forkAt: Processor userInterruptPriority

" Transcript shows:
Interrupted
Finished.  "
```

Example 315, Execute

resume

Set the receiver so that it is ready to execute; when, and if, the process is actually executed depends on its priority, and the priorities of other processes.

suspend

Set the receiver so that it is suspended and will not be executed until it receives a later resume message.

terminate

Terminate the receiver. Execution of the receiver will stop immediately at some undefined point in the code; the execution cannot be restarted.

yield

Place the receiver at the back of the queue of processes, at the same priority, that are waiting to execute. If the receiver is the current process, give up execution and let the next available process execute.

The yield message should be used in processor- or I/O-intensive processes, so that other processes get a chance to run. It is typically not needed in processes that frequently wait on semaphores, or that wait for human input, since such waiting allows other processes to execute.

Class ProcessScheduler

Class Method Summary

Method	*Documented*	*See page*
~~new~~	Object	288
~~new: anInteger~~	Object	289

Instance Method Summary

Method	*Documented*	*See page*
activePriority	ProcessorScheduler	506
activeProcess	ProcessorScheduler	506
highIOPriority	ProcessorScheduler	506
lowIOPriority	ProcessorScheduler	506
signal: aSemaphore **atTime: anInteger**	ProcessorScheduler	507
systemBackgroundPriority	ProcessorScheduler	507
timingPriority	ProcessorScheduler	507
userBackgroundPriority	ProcessorScheduler	507
userInterruptPriority	ProcessorScheduler	507
userSchedulingPriority	ProcessorScheduler	507

Instance Interface

activePriority
Answer the priority of the currently active process; the active process is the one sending this message. This answers the same value as would the priority message sent to the active process itself:

> Processor activeProcess priority

activeProcess
Answer the currently active process; the active process is the one sending this message.

highIOPriority
Answer the priority of the process monitoring the local network devices and other time-critical input/output processes. User processes should not use this priority.

lowIOPriority
Answer the normal priority of input/output processes. User processes should not use this priority.

signal: aSemaphore atTime: anInteger

Signal the semaphore aSemaphore at the time anInteger, which is some number of milliseconds from midnight.

See also: Time>>millisecondsToRun:, Delay>>untilMilliseconds:

systemBackgroundPriority

Answer the priority of a system background process; this process only runs when there are no other processes in the system. User processes should not use this priority.

timingPriority

Answer the priority of the process monitoring the real-time clock. User processes should not use this priority.

userBackgroundPriority

Answer the priority of a user background process. User processes should use this priority for tasks that should not interfere with user interaction.

userInterruptPriority

Answer the priority of any process forked by the user processes, which should be executed immediately. User processes use this priority for tasks that are more important than user interaction.

userSchedulingPriority

Answer the priority of the user interface process, and the default priority for any process forked by the user interface. User processes use this priority for tasks that should compete with user interaction; typically, it is a bad idea to run processes at this priority, not only because they interfere with user interaction, but they also get interrupted by user interaction.

Class Semaphore

Class Method Summary

Method	Documented	See page
forMutualExclusion	Semaphore	508
new	Object Semaphore	288 508
~~new: anInteger~~	Object	289

Instance Method Summary

Method	Documented	See page
critical:	Semaphore	508
signal	Semaphore	508
wait	Semaphore	508

Class Interface

forMutualExclusion
Answer a new instance of the receiver, which behaves as if it has received one signal message and no wait messages. The first process to wait on this semaphore will not block.

new
Answer a new instance of the receiver, which acts as if it has never received any signal or wait messages.

Instance Interface

critical: aBlock
Evaluate aBlock when the receiver has no other critical blocks executing. Answer the result of evaluating aBlock.

This message has the effect of acquiring a semaphore, executing a block, and releasing the semaphore, all in a single operation.

signal
Send a signal to the longest waiting process on the receiver. If there are no such processes, the signal is remembered; a count of remembered signals is maintained.

wait
Suspend the active process until the receiver receives a signal message, and the active process has been waiting the longest of all processes waiting on the semaphore. If the receiver has been signalled and has a positive signal count, do not wait.

36

Rectangles

Rectangles represent a pair of points on an *x-y* plane. They are usually created by operations on points such as extent: or corner:.

The Rectangle classes are:

Class	Page
Object	
Rectangle	513

Categories of Messages

Operations on rectangles can be categorized into access, areas, comparisons, scaling and translation, and truncating and rounding.

Access

Access operations on corner points retrieve the current point or reset a point in the current instance.

bottomLeft	Answer the point at the bottom-left corner
bottomLeft:	Set the point at the bottom-left corner
bottomRight	Answer the point at the bottom-right corner
bottomRight:	Set the point at the bottom-right corner
corner	Answer the point at the bottom-right corner
corner:	Set the point at the bottom-right corner
origin	Answer the origin (the top-left corner)
origin:	Set the origin (the top-left corner)
origin:corner:	Set the origin and corner

origin:extent:	Set the origin and extent
topLeft	Answer the point at the top-left corner
topLeft:	Set the point at the top-left corner
topRight	Answer the point at the top-right corner
topRight:	Set the point at the top-right corner

Access operations on edges, extents, and center points retrieve the current value or reset a value in the current instance.

bottom	Answer the y coordinate of the bottom edge
bottom:	Set the y coordinate of the bottom edge
bottomCenter	Answer point at the center of the bottom edge
center	Answer a point at the center
extent	A point holding the height and width
extent:	Set the height and width relative to the origin
height	Answer the height
height:	Set the height relative to the origin
left	Answer the x coordinate of the left edge
left:	Set the x coordinate of the left edge
leftCenter	Answer the point at the center of the left edge
right	Answer the x coordinate of the right edge
right:	Set the x coordinate of the right edge
rightCenter	Answer point at the center of the right edge
top	Answer the x coordinate of the top edge
top:	Set the x coordinate of the top edge
topCenter	Answer the point at center of the top edge
width	Answer the width
width:	Set the width relative to the origin

Areas

Area operations return the area of a rectangle, or the area outside but within another rectangle.

area	Answer the area of the rectangle
areasOutside:	A collection of rectangles outside the receiver

Comparison

Comparison operations compare the points in a rectangle.

==	Identity of rectangles
=	Equality of value of origin and corner points

Scaling and Translation

Scaling and translation operations scale, translate, move, merge, and inset rectangles.

expandBy:	New rectangle expanded from another
insetBy:	New rectangle inset from another
insetOriginBy:cornerBy:	New rectangle inset from another
intersect:	New rectangle that's an intersection of both
merge:	New rectangle just big enough to hold both
moveBy:	Move rectangle by a delta
moveTo:	Move rectangle to a new origin
scaleBy:	New rectangle scaled in x and y
translateBy:	New rectangle translated by x and y

Testing

Testing operations test intersection and containment.

contains:	True if one rectangle contains another
containsPoint:	True if a rectangle contains a point
intersects:	True if one rectangle intersects another

Truncation and Rounding

Truncation and rounding operations operate on the points within a rectangle.

rounded	Rectangle with rounded positions
truncated	Rectangle with truncated positions

Coordinate System

In the coordinate system for rectangles (and for points), *x* values increase to the right and *y* values increase downwards from the origin. On the display screen, and in windows, the origin is at the upper-left corner. While this differs from mathematical conventions, and from the native operating system conventions of some platforms, it is uniform across all platforms. See Figure 102 for a rectangle on a grid and an illustration of rectangle terminology.

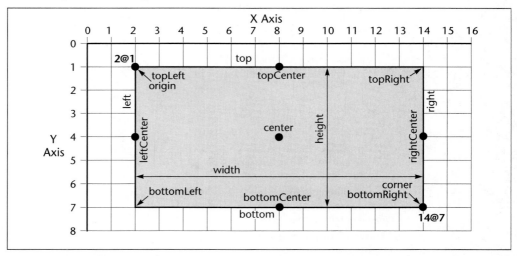

Figure 102: Rectangle Coordinates. The rectangle (4@1 corner: 12@7) is drawn on a grid that maps the coordinate system. All words are terms used with rectangles; some points have more than one name, such as origin and topLeft.

It is sometimes useful to remember the letters L-T-R-B, which stand for left, top, right, and bottom, the sides of a rectangle clockwise from the left side. This is the order of points in a rectangle using "corner" notation: left@top corner: right@bottom.

Normalization

Normalization of rectangles means reorganizing the order of the points in the rectangle such that the smallest *x* value and the smallest *y* value are always returned by origin, and the largest values by corner.

Smalltalk does not do normalization. It is possible that operations on rectangles can produce unnormalized results. The rectangle 4@7 corner: 12@1 (bottomLeft and topRight in Figure 102) is not normalized; the origin message to it will answer 4@7.

To normalize a rectangle, do this:

```
" Answer a new rectangle that is the normalized version of another rectangle "
| rect |
rect := 10@12 corner: 2@4.
^    (rect origin min: rect corner) corner:
     (rect origin max: rect corner)
     " Answers: 2@4 corner: 10@12 "
```

Example 316, Display

A faster method, intended to be added to class Rectangle, normalizes the instance itself:

```
" Rectangle method to normalize a rectangle "
! Rectangle publicMethods !

normalize
     " Answer the receiver adjusted to be in normalized form "
     | a b |
     (a := origin x) > (b := corner x)
          ifTrue: [
               origin x: b.
               corner x: a ].
     (a := origin y) > (b:= corner y)
          ifTrue: [
               origin y: b.
               corner y: a ].
     ^ self  ! !
```

Example 317, FileIn

After Example 317 is filed in, try these:

```
" Normalizing Rectangles "
(12@12 corner: 2@2) normalize
"Answer: 2@2 corner: 12@12"
```

Example 318, Display

```
" Normalizing Rectangles "
(9@1 corner: 1@9) normalize
"Answer: 1@1 corner: 9@9"
```

Example 319, Display

```
" Normalizing Rectangles "
(1@1 corner: 2@2) normalize
"Answer: 1@1 corner: 2@2"
```

Example 320, Display

Protocol Summary

Class Protocol Summary

Object class		
Rectangle class		
left:right:top:bottom:	origin:corner:	origin:extent:

Instance Protocol Summary

Object				
= ==	~= ~~	printString	printString	
Rectangle				
area	contains:	insetOriginBy:cornerBy:	origin:	topCenter
areasOutside:	containsPoint:	intersect:	origin:corner:	topLeft
bottom	corner	intersects:	origin:extent:	topLeft:
bottom:	corner:	left	right	topRight
bottomCenter	expandBy:	left:	right:	topRight:
bottomLeft	extent	leftCenter	rightCenter	translateBy:
bottomLeft:	extent:	merge:	rounded	truncated
bottomRight	height	moveBy:	scaleBy:	width
bottomRight:	height:	moveTo:	top	width:
center	insetBy:	origin	top:	

Class Rectangle

Rectangles are pairs of points that describe an aligned rectangle on a grid.

Class	*Page*
Object	
Rectangle	513

Class Method Summary

Method	*Documented*	*See page*

left: leftNum
  right: rightNum
   top: topNum
    bottom: bottomNum
	Rectangle	515

origin: originPoint **corner: cornerPoint**	Rectangle	515
origin: originPoint **extent: extentPoint**	Rectangle	515

Instance Method Summary

Method	Documented	See page
=	Rectangle Object	516 289
==	Object	289
~=	Rectangle Object	516 289
~~	Object	290
area	Rectangle	516
areasOutside: aRect	Rectangle	516
bottom	Rectangle	517
bottom: aNumber	Rectangle	517
bottomCenter	Rectangle	517
bottomLeft	Rectangle	517
bottomLeft: aPoint	Rectangle	517
bottomRight	Rectangle	518
bottomRight: aPoint	Rectangle	518
center	Rectangle	518
contains: aRect	Rectangle	518
containsPoint: aPoint	Rectangle	518
copy	Rectangle Object	519 291
corner	Rectangle	519
corner: aPoint	Rectangle	519
expandBy: aValue	Rectangle	519
extent	Rectangle	519
extent: aPoint	Rectangle	520
height	Rectangle	520
height: aNumber	Rectangle	520
insetBy: aValue	Rectangle	520
insetOriginBy: originValue cornerBy: cornerValue	Rectangle	521
intersect: aRect	Rectangle	521
intersects: aRect	Rectangle	522
left	Rectangle	522
left: aNumber	Rectangle	522
leftCenter	Rectangle	522
merge: aRect	Rectangle	522
moveBy: aPoint	Rectangle	523
moveTo: aPoint	Rectangle	523
origin	Rectangle	523
origin: aPoint	Rectangle	523
origin: originPoint corner: cornerPoint	Rectangle	523
origin: originPoint extent: extentPoint	Rectangle	523
right	Rectangle	524
right: aNumber	Rectangle	524

Part 1 of 2.

Method	Documented	See page
rightCenter	Rectangle	524
rounded	Rectangle	524
scaleBy: ptOrNum	Rectangle	524
top	Rectangle	524
top: aNumber	Rectangle	524
topCenter	Rectangle	525
topLeft	Rectangle	525
topLeft: aPoint	Rectangle	525
topRight	Rectangle	525
topRight: aPoint	Rectangle	525
translateBy: ptOrNum	Rectangle	525
truncated	Rectangle	526
width	Rectangle	526
width: aNumber	Rectangle	526

Part 2 of 2.

Class Interface

Note: The first line in the tables of examples for most methods contains a symbolic description of the operation.

left: leftNum right: rightNum top: topNum bottom: botNum

Answer a new rectangle with sides at the specified positions.

Expression	Result
Rectangle left: l right: r top: t bottom: b	l@t corner: r@b
Rectangle left: 2 right: 3 top: 4 bottom: 6	2@4 corner: 3@6

origin: originPoint corner: cornerPoint

Answer a new rectangle with an origin of originPoint and a corner at cornerPoint.

Expression	Result
Rectangle origin: l@t corner: r@b	l@t corner: r@b
Rectangle origin: 2@4 corner: 3@6	2@4 corner: 3@6

origin: originPoint extent: extentPoint

Answer a new rectangle with an origin of originPoint and an extent of extentPoint. The x value of the extent is added to the x value of the origin to determine the x value of the corner, and the y value of the extent is added to the y value of the origin to obtain the y value of the corner. See Figure 103.

The message:

    Rectangle origin: orig extent: ext

is equivalent to:

    Rectangle origin: orig corner: (orig x + ext x) @ (orig y + ext y)

Expression	Result
Rectangle origin: l@t extent: x@y	l@t corner: (l+x)@(t+y)
Rectangle origin: 2@4 extent: 1@2	2@4 corner: 3@6

Figure 103: Ways To Create A Rectangle. The input points are at the black dots. In Case 1, the minimum and maximum values are at different corners, and in Case 2 they are at the same corners as the input points.

Instance Interface

= aRect
Answer true if the origin and corner points of the receiver are equal to the origin and corner points of aRect, using the = method for point comparison.

Expression	Result
(2@4 corner: 3@5) = (2@4 extent: 1@1)	true

~= aRect
Answer false if the origin and corner points of the receiver are not equal to the origin and corner points of aRect, using the ~= method for point comparison.

Expression	Result
(2@4 corner: 3@5) = (2@4 extent: 1@1)	true

area
Answer the area of the receiver. The area is defined to be the width times the height, where width is the value returned by the width message to the receiver, and height is the value returned by the height message to the receiver.

Caution: The area can be negative for rectangles that are not normalized.

Value of a	Expression	Result
l@t corner: r@b	a area	(b-t) *(r-l)
(2@2 corner: 5@5)	a area	9
(1@1 extent: 3@4)	a area	12
(2@4 corner: 1@5)	a area	-1

areasOutside: aRect
Answer a collection of rectangles containing the parts of the receiver outside of aRect. For all points in the receiver, but outside aRect, exactly one rectangle in the collection will contain the point; thus these rectangles satisfy the following constraints:

- The rectangles do not intersect.
- No rectangle intersects aRect.

If the receiver is completely outside aRect, return the receiver. If the receiver is completely within aRect, return an empty collection.

The corner point, and the bottom and right edges, are not included in a rectangle (see includesPoint: for details). Thus (2@2 corner: 3@3) and (2@3 corner: 3@4) have no common points.

The number of rectangles returned can vary from zero to four.

Expression	Result

(2@2 corner: 4@4)
   areasOutside:
      (2@2 corner 3@3)
	A collection holding:
	   3@2 corner: 4@4
	   2@3 corner:3@4

(2@2 corner: 5@5)
   areasOutside:
      (3@3 corner 4@4)
	A collection holding:
	   2@2 corner: 3@5
	   3@2 corner: 5@3
	   4@3 corner: 5@5
	   3@4 corner: 4@5

bottom
Answer the y coordinate of the receiver's bottom horizontal edge.

Value of a	Expression	Result
l@t corner: r@b	a bottom	b
2@4 corner: 3@6	a bottom	6

bottom: aNumber
Answer the receiver with the y coordinate of the receiver's bottom horizontal edge set to aNumber.

Value of a	Expression	Result
l@t corner: r@b	a bottom: B	l@t corner: r@B
2@4 corner: 3@6	a bottom: 8	2@4 corner: 3@8

bottomCenter
Answer the point at the center of the receiver's bottom horizontal edge.

Value of a	Expression	Result
l@t corner: r@b	a bottomCenter	(r-l)/2+l @ b
2@4 corner: 3@6	a bottomCenter	2@6

bottomLeft
Answer the point at the bottom-left corner of the receiver.

Value of a	Expression	Result
l@t corner: r@b	a bottomLeft	l@b
2@4 corner: 3@6	a bottomLeft	2@6
3@6 corner: 2@4	a bottomLeft	3@4

bottomLeft: aPoint
Answer the receiver with the coordinates of the bottom-left corner set to aPoint.

Value of a	Expression	Result
l@t corner: r@b	a bottomLeft: L@B	L@t corner: r@B
2@4 corner: 3@6	a bottomLeft: 1@5	1@4 corner: 3@5

bottomRight

Answer the point at the bottom-right corner of the receiver. The bottomRight and corner messages are equivalent.

Value of a	Expression	Result
l@t corner: r@b	a bottomRight	r@b
2@4 corner: 3@6	a bottomRight	3@6

bottomRight aPoint

Answer the receiver with the coordinates of the bottom-right corner set to aPoint. The bottomRight: and corner: messages are equivalent.

Value of a	Expression	Result
l@t corner: r@b	a bottomRight: R@B	l@t corner: R@B
1@4 corner: 3@6	a bottomRight: 6@6	1@4 corner: 6@7

center

Answer the point at the center of the receiver.

Value of a	Expression	Result
l@t corner: r@b	a center	((r-l)/2+r) @ ((b-t)/2+t)
2@2 corner 4@4	a center	3@3

contains: aRect

Answer true if all of the points in aRect are points in the receiver; answer false otherwise.

Value of a	Value of b	Expression	Result
2@2 corner: 6@6	3@3 corner: 4@4	a contains: b	true
2@2 corner: 6@6	5@5 corner: 6@6	a contains: b	true
2@2 corner: 6@6	5@5 corner: 7@7	a contains: b	false
2@2 corner: 6@6	2@2 corner: 6@6	a contains: b	true

containsPoint: aPoint

Answer true if the point aPoint is in the receiver; answer false otherwise. The receiver contains aPoint when:

- aPoint is equal to, or is below and to the right of, the receiver's origin; and
- aPoint is above and to the left of the receiver's corner.

This definition includes none of the points on the right and bottom edges, but includes points on the top and left edges. The points returned by topRight, bottomLeft, and corner are thus not included.

Value of a	Value of b	Expression	Result
2@2 corner: 6@6	3@3	a contains: b	true
2@2 corner: 6@6	6@6	a contains: b	false
2@2 corner: 6@6	7@7	a contains: b	false
2@2 corner: 6@6	2@5.9999	a contains: b	true
2@2 corner: 6@6	2@6	a contains: b	false

This is similar, but not identical, to the point message between:and: which answers true if the receiver is identical to highPoint, while containsPoint: will not.

copy

Answer a copy of the receiver with identical corner and origin points. The copy message is equivalent to:

> Rectangle origin: receiver origin corner: receiver corner

Note that the points in the receiver and its copy are identical objects; thus:

> receiver origin == receiver copy origin

and:

> receiver corner == receiver copy corner

corner

Answer the bottom-right corner of the rectangle.

Value of a	Expression	Result
l@t corner: r@b	a corner	r@b
2@4 corner: 3@6	a corner	3@6

corner: aPoint

Answer the receiver with the bottom-right corner set to aPoint. This message is equivalent to the bottomRight: message.

Value of a	Expression	Result
l@t corner: r@b	a corner: R@B	l@t corner: R@B
2@4 corner: 3@6	a corner: 6@7	1@4 corner: 6@7

expandBy: aValue

Answer a new rectangle that is the receiver expanded by aValue, which is a rectangle, point, or number containing a delta distance by which the receiver is to expand. This method is equivalent to insetBy: except that the signs are reversed. See Figure 104.

If aValue is a *rectangle,* then the new rectangle origin is the origin of the receiver minus the origin of aValue, and the corner is the corner of the receiver plus the corner of aValue.

If aValue is a *point* or *number,* then the origin of the new rectangle is the origin of the receiver minus aValue, and the corner is the corner of the receiver plus aValue.

Negative values cause the coordinate to be inset.

Value of a	Value of b	Expression	Result
2@2 corner: 4@4	1	a expandBy: b	1@1 corner: 5@5
2@2 corner: 4@4	1@2	a expandBy: b	1@0 corner: 5@6
2@2 corner: 6@6	-1@-1	a expandBy: b	3@3 corner: 5@5
2@2 corner: 4@4	1@2 corner: 3@4	a expandBy: b	1@0 corner: 7@8

extent

Answer the extent of the receiver; the extent is a point with the *x* value holding the receiver's width, and a *y* value holding the receiver's height.

See also: width, height

Value of a	Expression	Result
l@t corner: r@b	a extent	(r-l) @ (b-t)
2@2 corner: 4@5	a extent	2@3
4@5 corner: 2@2	a extent	-2@-3

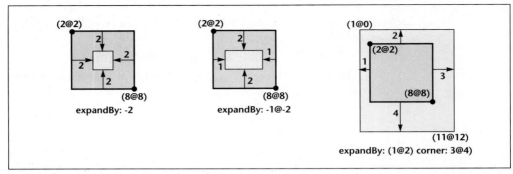

Figure 104: Expanding a Rectangle. Three examples of expandBy: used to both inset and expand the rectangle (2@2 corner: 8@8). The original rectangles are a darker grey; the resulting rectangles are a lighter grey.

extent: aPoint
Answer the receiver with the extent set to aPoint. The origin is not changed.

Value of a	Expression	Result
l@t corner: r@b	a extent: X@Y	l@t corner: (l+X)@(t+Y)
2@2 corner: 4@4	a extent: 3@4	2@2 corner 5@6

height
Answer the height of the receiver; the height is the corner *y* value less the origin *y* value.

Value of a	Expression	Result
l@t corner: r@b	a height	b-t
2@1 corner: 3@6	a height	5
4@4 corner: 2@2	a height	-2

height: aNumber
Answer the receiver with the height set to aNumber. The origin is not changed. The *y* value of the corner is set to the receiver's *y* value plus aNumber; the *x* value is unchanged.

Value of a	Expression	Result
l@t corner: r@b	a height: H	l@t corner: r@(t+H)
2@1 corner: 3@6	a height: 3	2@1 corner: 5@4

insetBy: aValue
Answer a new rectangle that is the receiver inset by aValue which is a rectangle, point, or number containing delta distances by which the receiver is to be inset. This is equivalent to expandBy: except that the signs are reversed. See Figure 105.

If aValue is a *rectangle,* then the new rectangle origin is the origin of the receiver plus the origin of aValue, and the corner is the corner of the receiver minus the corner of aValue.

If aValue is a *point or number,* then the origin of the new rectangle is the origin of the receiver plus aValue, and the corner is the corner of the receiver minus aValue.

Negative values cause coordinates to be expanded.

Value of a	Value of b	Expression	Result
l@t corner: r@b	*L@T corner: R@B*	*a insetBy: b*	*(l+L)@(t+T) corner: (r-R)@(b-B)*
1@1 corner: 6@6	1	a insetBy: b	2@2 corner: 5@5
1@1 corner: 6@6	1@2	a insetBy: b	2@3 corner: 5@4
1@1 corner: 6@6	-1@ -1	a insetBy: b	0@0 corner: 7@7
1@1 corner: 6@6	1@2 corner: 2@1	a insetBy: b	2@3 corner: 4@5
1@1 corner: 6@6	4@4	a insetBy: b	5@5 corner: 2@2

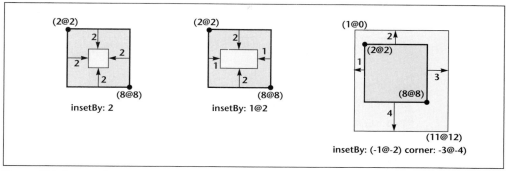

Figure 105: Inset a Rectangle. Three examples of insetBy: used to both inset and expand the rectangle (2@2 corner: 8@8). The original rectangle is darker grey; the result is lighter grey.

insetOriginBy: originValue cornerBy: cornerValue

Answer a new rectangle that is the receiver with its origin inset by originValue, and its corner inset by cornerValue. The values are points or numbers containing delta distances by which the receiver is to expand.

The origin of the new rectangle is the origin of the receiver plus originValue, and the corner is the corner of the receiver minus cornerValue.

Negative values cause coordinates to be expanded.

Value of a	Expression	Result
l@t corner: r@b	*a insetOriginBy: L@T cornerBy: R@B*	*(l+L)@(t+T) corner: (r-R)@(b-B)*
1@1 corner: 6@6	a insetOriginBy: 1 cornerBy: 2	2@2 corner: 4@4
1@1 corner: 6@6	a insetOriginBy: 1@2 cornerBy: 2@1	2@3 corner: 4@5
1@1 corner: 6@6	a insetOriginBy: -1 cornerBy: -2	0@0 corner: 8@8
1@1 corner: 6@6	a insetOriginBy: 4 cornerBy: 2	5@5 corner: 4@4

intersect: aRect

Answer a new rectangle that describes the area of overlap (or lack of overlap) of the receiver and aRect. If the two rectangles have no points in common, then the result has either zero or negative width or height.

See also: intersects:, merge:

Value of a	Value of b	Expression	Result
1@1 corner: 6@6	1@1 corner: 2@2	a intersect: b	1@1 corner: 2@2
1@1 corner: 6@6	5@5 corner: 7@7	a intersect: b	5@5 corner: 6@6
1@1 corner: 6@6	6@6 corner: 7@7	a intersect: b	6@6 corner: 6@6

Value of a	Value of b	Expression	Result
1@1 corner: 6@6	7@7 corner: 8@8	a intersect: b	7@7 corner: 6@6
1@1 corner: 6@6	0@0 corner: 2@2	a intersect: b	1@1 corner: 2@2

intersects: aRect

Answer true if the receiver and aRect have any points in common; answer **false** otherwise. Note that the bottom-right corner of a rectangle is not within the rectangle; see containsPoint: for more information.

Value of a	Value of b	Expression	Result
1@1 corner: 6@6	1@1 corner: 2@2	a intersects: b	true
1@1 corner: 6@6	5@5 corner: 7@7	a intersects: b	true
1@1 corner: 6@6	6@6 corner: 7@7	a intersects: b	false
1@1 corner: 6@6	7@7 corner: 8@8	a intersects: b	false
1@1 corner: 6@6	0@0 corner: 2@2	a intersects: b	true

left

Answer the *x* coordinate of the receiver's left side.

Value of a	Expression	Result
l@t corner: r@b	a left	l
1@2 corner: 3@4	a left	1

left: aNumber

Answer the receiver with the *x* coordinate of the receiver's left edge set to aNumber.

Value of a	Expression	Result
l@t corner: r@b	a left: L	L@t corner: r@b
2@4 corner: 5@6	a left: 3	3@4 corner: 5@6

leftCenter

Answer the point at the center of the left vertical edge.

Value of a	Expression	Result
l@t corner: r@b	a leftCenter	l @ ((b-t)/2)+t
3@4 corner: 5@6	a leftCenter	3@5

merge: aRect

Answer a new rectangle that is the smallest rectangle containing the receiver and aRect. The origin of the new rectangle is the minimum of the origin of the receiver and the origin of aRect, and the corner is the maximum of the origin of the receiver and the corner of aRect. Minimum and maximum are as defined by the min: and max: messages of point.

See also: intersect:

Value of a	Value of b	Expression	Result
1@1 corner: 6@6	1@1 corner: 2@2	a merge: b	1@1 corner: 6@6
1@1 corner: 6@6	5@5 corner: 7@7	a merge: b	1@1 corner: 7@7
1@2 corner: 6@6	2@1 corner: 7@7	a merge: b	1@1 corner: 7@7
1@1 corner: 2@2	3@3 corner: 4@4	a merge: b	1@1 corner: 4@4

moveBy: aPoint

Answer the receiver with aPoint added to the origin and aPoint added to the corner; the extent remains unchanged. While this is similar to translateBy:, this method modifies the receiver, and translateBy: returns a new rectangle.

See also: translateBy:

Value of a	Value of b	Expression	Result
l@t corner: r@b	X@Y	a moveBy: b	(l+X)@(t+Y) corner: (r+X)@(b+Y)
1@1 corner: 2@2	3@3	a moveBy: b	4@4 corner: 5@5

moveTo: aPoint

Answer the receiver with the origin set to aPoint and the extent unchanged.

Value of a	Value of b	Expression	Result
l@t corner: r@b	X@Y	a moveTo: b	X@Y corner: (X+r-l)@(Y+b-t))
1@1 corner: 2@2	3@3	a moveTo: b	3@3 corner: 4@4
1@2 corner: 4@5	2@1	a moveTo: b	2@1 corner: 5@4

origin

Answer the origin of the receiver.

Value of a	Expression	Result
l@t corner: r@b	a origin	l@t
3@4 corner: 5@6	a origin	3@4

origin: aPoint

Answer the receiver with the origin set to aPoint. The corner remains unchanged.

Value of a	Expression	Result
l@t corner: r@b	a origin: L@T	L@T corner: r@b
3@4 corner: 5@6	a origin: 2@3	2@3 corner: 5@6

origin: originPoint corner: cornerPoint

Answer the receiver with the origin set to originPoint and the corner set to cornerPoint. The message to class Rectangle having the same name returns a new rectangle, while this message changes values in, and returns, the receiver.

See also: class>>origin:corner:

Value of a	Expression	Result
l@t corner: r@b	a origin: L@T corner: R@B	L@T corner: R@B
1@1 corner: 6@6	a origin: 2@3 corner: 7@9	2@3 corner: 7@9

origin: originPoint extent: cornerPoint

Answer the receiver with the origin set to originPoint and the corner set so that the extent is extentPoint. This differs from the message with the same name to class Rectangle in that it returns a new rectangle, while this message changes values in, and returns, the receiver.

See also: class>>origin:extent:

Value of a	Expression	Result
l@t corner: r@b	a origin: L@T extent: W@H	L@T corner: (L+W)@(T+H)
1@1 corner: 6@6	a origin: 2@3 extent: 5@6	2@3 corner: 7@9

right

Answer the *x* coordinate of the receiver's right vertical side.

Value of a	Expression	Result
l@t corner: r@b	q right	r
1@2 corner: 3@4	a right	3

right: aNumber

Answer the receiver with the *x* coordinate of the right vertical edge set to **aNumber**.

Value of a	Expression	Result
l@t corner: r@b	a right: R	l@t corner: R@b
2@4 corner: 5@6	a right: 7	2@4 corner: 7@6

rightCenter

Answer the point at the center of the right vertical edge.

Value of a	Expression	Result
l@t corner: r@b	a rightCenter	r @((b-t)/2+b)
3@4 corner: 5@6	a rightCenter	5@5

rounded

Answer a new rectangle such that the origin and corner are the origin and corner of the receiver, with each coordinate rounded to the nearest integer.

Value of a	Expression	Result
2.4@3.6 corner: 8.1@9.6	a rounded	2@4 corner: 8@10

scaleBy: ptOrNum

Answer a new rectangle with values of the receiver scaled by **ptOrNum**. Scaled values are obtained by multiplying the origin and corner points by **ptOrNum**, which can be either a point or a number.

Value of a	Expression	Result
l@t corner: r@b	a scaleBy: xs@ys	(l*xs)@(t*ys) corner: (r*xs)@(b*ys)
2@2 corner: 4@4	a scaleBy: 2	4@4 corner: 8@8
2@2 corner: 4@4	a scaleBy: 3@4	6@8 corner: 12@16

top

Answer the *y* coordinate of the receiver's top horizontal edge.

Value of a	Expression	Result
l@t corner: r@b	a top	t
2@4 corner: 3@6	a top	4

top: aNumber

Answer the receiver with the *y* coordinate of the top horizontal edge set to **aNumber**.

Value of a	Expression	Result
l@t corner: r@b	a top: T	l@T corner: r@b
2@4 corner: 3@6	a top: 5	2@5 corner: 3@6

topCenter

Answer the point at the center of the receiver's top horizontal edge.

Value of a	Expression	Result
l@t corner: r@b	a topCenter	((l-r)/2+l) @ t
2@4 corner: 5@6	a topCenter	3.5@4

topLeft

Answer the point at the top-left corner of the receiver; this message is equivalent to the origin message.

Value of a	Expression	Result
l@t corner: r@b	a topLeft	l@t
2@4 corner: 3@6	a topLeft	2@4

topLeft: aPoint

Answer the receiver with the coordinates of the top-left corner (the origin) set to aPoint. The corner is not changed.

Value of a	Expression	Result
l@t corner: r@b	a topLeft: L@T	L@T corner: r@b
2@4 corner: 3@6	a topLeft: 1@2	1@2 corner: 3@6

topRight

Answer the point at the top-right corner of the receiver.

Value of a	Expression	Result
l@t corner: r@b	a topRight	r@t
2@4 corner: 3@6	a topRight	3@4

topRight: aPoint

Answer the receiver with the coordinates of the receiver's top-right corner set to aPoint.

Value of a	Expression	Result
l@t corner: r@b	topRight: R@T	l@T corner: R@b
2@4 corner: 3@6	a topRight: 2@5	2@5 corner: 2@6

translateBy: ptOrNum

Answer a new rectangle with coordinates of the receiver translated by ptOrNum, which can be either a point or a number. Translation of the receiver's values is done by adding ptOrNum to the origin and to the corner. While this is similar to moveBy:, this method returns a new rectangle and moveBy: modifies the receiver.

See also: moveBy:

Value of a	Expression	Result
l@t corner: r@b	a translateBy: X@Y	(l+X)@(t+Y) corner: (r+X)@(b+Y)
2@4 corner: 3@6	a translateBy: 2@5	4@9 corner: 5@11
2@4 corner: 3@6	a translateBy: -1	1@3 corner: 2@5

truncated

Answer a new rectangle such that the origin and corner are the origin and corner of the receiver, with each coordinate truncated to the nearest integer.

Value of a	Expression	Result
l@t corner: r@b	a truncated	(l@t) truncated corner: (r@b) truncated
2.4@3.6 corner: 8.1@9.5	a truncated	2@3 corner: 8@9

width

Answer the width of the receiver; the width is the *x* value of the corner less the *x* value of the origin.

Value of a	Expression	Result
l@t corner: r@b	a width	r-l
2@2 corner: 3@5	a width	1

width: aNumber

Answer the receiver with the width set to aNumber. The origin is not changed. The *x* value of the corner is set to the receiver's *x* value plus aNumber; the *y* value of the corner is unchanged.

Value of a	Expression	Result
l@t corner: r@b	a width: W	l@t corner: (l+W)@b
2@1 corner: 4@6	a width: 3	2@1 corner: 5@6

37

Streams

Streams are objects that support sequential access to collections and files. A stream can be opened on a collection, a file, or a source of random numbers.

The stream classes are:

See Chapter 12, 'Streams and File Streams', on page 135 for an introduction to streams. CfsFileStream and its subclasses are documented in Chapter 31, 'File Streams', on page 407.

Kinds of Stream Classes

Class **Stream** is an abstract class that defines methods that all streams must support, including fetching the next item from the stream, iterating with do:, and checking for the end of the stream.

PositionableStream

Class PositionableStream is an abstract class that defines methods for read and write streams. The stream can be on any sequenceable collection. Operations include retrieving the contents (the possibly modified original collection), setting and retrieving the position, and skipping elements.

Positionable streams have a collection across which they stream, starting with the first element and continuing to the last, unless explicitly changed. Streams keep an internal position for the previous element. Figure 106 shows positions in an eight-element stream.

Positionable streams can be opened on any kind of indexed collection.

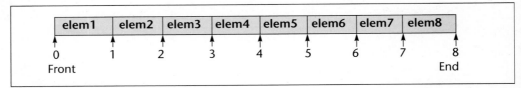

Figure 106: Positions of Streams and Elements. Position zero indicates the front of the stream, position 1 occurs just after element 1, etc.

ReadStream

Class ReadStream streams across any sequenceable collection. The collection is not modifiable. Operations include reading from the stream and skipping ahead to a specified sequence.

WriteStream

Class WriteStream allows writing to a sequenceable collection, but not reading from it. Setting the write position truncates items past that point. Write streams are frequently used to construct strings that will be displayed or printed.

ReadWriteStream

Class ReadWriteStream allows both reading and writing a stream. Setting the read/write position does not truncate the collection.

EsRandom

Instances of class EsRandom produce a stream of machine-generated pseudo-random floating-point numbers of good quality. The random number generator is self-seeding, using the system clock; it is not possible to override the self-seeding process.

Categories of Messages

The following messages are supported by one or more stream classes.

Compatibility

Compatibility methods allow the same code to process both open file streams and open positionable streams.

close	Positionable: Do nothing
flush	Write: Do nothing

Iteration

Iterate through the stream to the end or, for random numbers, iterate forever.

do:	All: Pass elements to a block

Positioning

Positioning methods set the read or write pointer to a new position.

position	Positionable: Answer current position
position:	Positionable: Set the position
reset:	Positionable: Set position at front
setToEnd	Positionable: Set position past last element

Querying and Setting

Querying and setting methods answer or set stream state information.

atEnd	Read: True if no more to read
isEmpty	Positionable: True if collection empty
lineDelimiter	Positionable: Answer current line delimiter
lineDelimiter:	Positionable: Set line delimiter

Reading

Reading methods answer data from the stream.

copyFrom:to:	Read: Copy into new collection
next	Read: Get next element
next:	Read: Get next *n* elements
nextLine	Read: Get next line
nextMatchFor:	Read: Compare next with an object
peek	Read: Peek at next element
peekFor:	Read: Compare next with an object
upTo:	Read: Get elements up to a value
upToAll:	Read: Get elements up to a sequence

Skipping

Skipping methods skip elements in the stream.

skip:	Read: Skip next element
skipTo:	Read: Skip ahead to a value
skipToAll:	Read: Skip ahead to a sequence

Writing

Writing methods modify a stream.

cr	Write: Output a line delimiter
next:put:	Write: Output *n* copies of a value
nextPut:	Write: Output a value
nextPutAll:	Write: Output contents of collection
space	Write: Output a space character
tab	Write: Output a tab character

Protocol Summary

Class Protocol Summary

Object class			
Stream class			
EsRandom class	*PositionableStream class*		
	on:	on:from:to:	
	ReadStream class	**WriteStream class**	
		with	with:from:to:
		ReadWriteStream class	

Instance Protocol Summary

Object						
==	size					
Stream						
atEnd	do:	next				
EsRandom	*PositionableStream*					
~~size~~	close	isEmpty	lineDelimiter	position	reset	setToEnd
	contents		lineDelimiter:	position:		upToEnd
	ReadStream		**WriteStream**			
	copyFrom:to:	peekFor:	cr	~~next~~	nextPut:	space
	next:	skip:	~~do:~~	next:put:	nextPutAll:	tab
	nextLine	skipTo:	flush			
	nextMatchFor:	skipToAll:	**ReadWriteStream**			
	peek	upTo:	copyFrom:to:	nextMatchFor:	skip:	upTo:
		upToAll:	next	peek	skipTo:	upToAll:
			next:	peekFor:	skipToAll:	truncate
			nextLine			

Class Stream

Class Stream is an abstract class that describes the protocol of all streams except file streams.

Class Method Summary

There are no new class methods.

Instance Method Summary

Method	Documented	See page
atEnd	Stream	531
do: aBlock	Stream	531
next	Stream	531
size	Stream Object	532 295

Instance Interface

Note: Positions in stream examples are shown by the character › before the next element in the stream.

atEnd
Answer true if the position of the stream is just past the last item in the stream.

Value of a	Expression	Result
aStream: 1 2 3 6 7 ›8 10 11	atEnd	false
aStream: 1 2 3 6 7 8 10 11›	atEnd	true

do: aBlock
Evaluate aBlock for every element in the stream, starting with the next element and continuing to the end.

Value of a	Value of sum	Expression	Result in sum
aStream: ›1 2 3 4 5	0	a do: [:e I sum := sum + e]	15
aStream: 1 2 3 ›4 5	0	a do: [:e I sum := sum + e]	9

next
Answer the next element in the stream and advance the position by one. It is an error if no more elements remain.

Value of a	Expression	Answer	Value of a that results
aStream: 6 7 8 ›10 11	a next	10	aStream: 6 7 8 10 ›11
aStream: 6 7 8 10 ›11	a next	11	aStream: 6 7 8 10 11›

size

Answer the size of the collection that the stream is on.

Expression	Answer
(Stream on: 'abcdefghijklmnopqrstuvwxyz') size	26

Class PositionableStream

PositionableStream is an abstract class defining protocol for reading and writing streams of objects.

Class Method Summary

Method	Documented	See page
on: aCollection	PositionableStream class	533

on: aCollection
  from: intFirst
  to: intLast
	PositionableStream class	533

Instance Method Summary

Method	Documented	See page
atEnd	Stream	531
close	PositionableStream	533
contents	PositionableStream	533
do: aBlock	Stream	531
isEmpty	PositionableStream	533
lineDelimiter	PositionableStream	533
lineDelimiter: aSeqColl	PositionableStream	533
next	Stream	531
position	PositionableStream	534
position: anInteger	PositionableStream	534
reset	PositionableStream	534
setToEnd	PositionableStream	534
size	Stream Object	532
upToEnd	PositionableStream	534

Class Interface

Note: Positions in stream examples are shown by the character › before the next element in the stream.

on: aCollection

Answer a new stream that will stream over the collection aCollection. The stream is positioned at the front.

Value of a	Expression	Result
anArray: 1 2 9 8 3 7	Stream on: a	aStream: ›1 2 9 8 3 7

on: aCollection from: intFirst to: intLast

Answer a new stream that will stream over a copy of a subsequence of the sequenceable collection aCollection. The subsequence is obtained as if by the copyFrom:to: method of the collection. The stream is positioned at the front. It is an error if intFirst or intLast are not integer indexes into the collection, or if intLast is less than intFirst-1.

Value of a	Expression	Result
anArray: #(1 2 9 8 3 7)	Stream on: a from: 2 to: 5	aStream: ›2 9 8 3

Instance Interface

close

This method does nothing; it is provided for compatibility with file streams.

contents

Answer a copy of the collection over which the stream is streaming.

Value of a	Expression	Result
aStream: 1 2 3 6 7 8 10 11	a contents	aCollection: 1 2 3 6 7 8 10 11

isEmpty

Answer true if the size of the collection over which the stream is streaming is zero.

Value of a	Expression	Result
aStream: 1 2 3 6 7 8 10 11 ›	a isEmpty	false
(none)	(Stream on: #()) isEmpty	true

lineDelimiter

Answer the line delimiter of the stream.

For information on line delimiters, see the section on 'Line Delimiters' on page 138.

Value of a	Expression	Result
a Stream	a lineDelimiter	Platform dependent

lineDelimiter: aSequenceableCollection

Set the line delimiter for the stream. The value can be changed to other platform-dependent values using pool variables such as UNIXLineDelimiter, WINLineDelimiter, PMLineDelimiter, and LineDelimiter from the pool dictionary CldtConstants.

For information on line delimiters, see the section on 'Line Delimiters' on page 138.

Value of a	Expression	Result
a Stream	a lineDelimiter: WINLineDelimiter	a Stream

Line delimiters do not have to be strings, just as streams do not have to be over strings. For example, it is possible to have a line delimiter of an integer zero that is used to delimit sequences of non-zero integers.

```
" Line delimiter of #(0) "
| w |
w := WriteStream on: (Array new: 1).
w lineDelimiter: #(0).
w nextPutAll: #( 1 2 3 4 5 ).
w cr.
w nextPutAll: #( 9 8 7 6 ); cr.
^ w contents
    "Answer: 1 2 3 4 5 0 9 8 7 6 0"
```

Example 321, Display

position

Answer the current position of the stream on the collection. The value returned is one less than the index of the element that will be returned next. Thus, a zero means that next will return the first element.

Value of a	Expression	Result
aStream: 1 2 3 6 7 8 ›10 11	a position	aStream: 6

position: anInteger

Set the position of the stream to anInteger. The value is one less than the index of the element that will be referenced next. Thus, a zero means that next will return the first element.

Value of a	Expression	Result
aStream: 1 2 3 6 7 8 ›10 11	a position: 0	aStream: ›1 2 3 6 7 8 10 11
aStream: 1 2 3 6 7 8 ›10 11	a position: a size	aStream: 1 2 3 6 7 8 10 11 ›

reset

Set the position to the front of the collection.

Value of a	Expression	Result
aStream: 1 2 3 6 7 8 ›10 11	a reset	aStream: ›1 2 3 6 7 8 10 11

setToEnd

Set the position at the end of the stream.

Value of a	Expression	Result in a
aStream: 1 2 3 6 7 8 ›10 11	a setToEnd	aStream: 1 2 3 6 7 8 10 11 ›

upToEnd

Answer a sequenceable collection that contains the elements from the current position to the end of the stream. Set the position at the end.

Value of a	Expression	Answer	Result in a
aStream: 1 2 3 6 7 8 ›10 11	a upToEnd	aCollection: 10 11	aStream: 1 2 3 6 7 8 10 11 ›

Class ReadStream

ReadStream is an concrete class defining methods for reading streams of objects.

Class Method Summary

Method	Documented	See page
on: aCollection	PositionableStream class	533
on: aCollection from: intFirst to: intLast	PositionableStream class	533

Instance Method Summary

Method	Documented	See page
atEnd	Stream	531
close	PositionableStream	533
contents	PositionableStream	533
copyFrom: fromInteger to: toInteger	ReadStream	536
do: aBlock	Stream	531
isEmpty	PositionableStream	533
lineDelimiter	PositionableStream	533
lineDelimiter: aSeqColl	PositionableStream	533
next	Stream	531
next: anInteger	ReadStream	536
nextLine	ReadStream	536
nextMatchFor: anObject	ReadStream	536
peek	ReadStream	537
peekFor: anObject	ReadStream	537
position	PositionableStream	534
position: anInteger	PositionableStream	534
reset	PositionableStream	534
setToEnd	PositionableStream	534
size	Stream Object	532
skip: anInteger	ReadStream	537
skipTo: anObject	ReadStream	537

Part 1 of 2.

Method	Documented	See page
skipToAll: aSeqColl	ReadStream	537
upTo: anInteger	ReadStream	537
upToAll: aSeqColl	ReadStream	538
upToEnd	PositionableStream	534

Part 2 of 2.

Instance Interface

Note: Positions in stream examples are shown by the character › before the next element in the stream.

copyFrom: fromInteger to: toInteger

Answer a sequenceable collection that holds the elements from fromInteger to toInteger, and in the same order. If toInteger is less than fromInteger, answer an empty collection. It is an error if the indexes are not valid for the collection. It is equivalent to:

> receiver contents copyFrom: fromInteger to: toInteger

Value of a	Expression	Answer
aReadStream: 1 2 3 4 5 6 7 8	a copyFrom: 3 to: 5	aCollection: 3 4 5

next: anInteger

Answer a sequenceable collection containing the next anInteger elements; position the stream so that the element just behind the last element answered will be returned next. If there are less than anInteger elements, then answer the remaining elements, and set the stream to its end.

Value of a	Expression	Answer	Result in a
aReadStream: 1 2 3 ›4 5 6 7 8	a next: 3	aCollection: 4 5 6	aReadStream: 1 2 3 4 5 6 ›7 8
aReadStream: 1 2 3 4 5 6 ›7 8	a next: 3	aCollection: 7 8	aReadStream: 1 2 3 4 5 6 7 8 ›

nextLine

If a line delimiter exists in the remainder of the stream, answer a sequenceable collection containing all of the elements up to, but not including, the next line delimiter. Position the stream just past the line delimiter.

If no line delimiter exists in the remainder of the stream, answer all the remaining elements in the stream. Position the stream so that atEnd is true.

Line delimiter	Value of a	Expression	Answer	Result in a
'\'	aReadStream: '›abc\def'	a nextLine	'abc'	aReadStream: 'abc\›def'
'\'	aReadStream: 'abc\›def'	a nextLine	'def'	aReadStream: 'abc\def›'
#(0)	aReadStream: ›4 5 0 7 8 0	a nextLine	aCollection: 4 5	aReadStream: 4 5 0 ›7 8 0

nextMatchFor: anObject

Answer true if the next element in the stream is equal to anObject; answer false if there is a next element and it isn't equal to anObject. The position is advanced by one, even if no match was made. It is an error if the stream is at its end.

Value of a	Expression	Answer	Result in a
aReadStream: 1 2 3 ›4 5 6 7 8	a nextMatchFor: 4	true	aReadStream: 1 2 3 4 ›5 6 7 8
aReadStream: 1 2 3 ›4 5 6 7 8	a nextMatchFor: 5	false	aReadStream: 1 2 3 4 ›5 6 7 8

peek

Answer the next element in the stream if it is not at its end. The position is not advanced. It is an error if the stream is at its end.

Value of a	Expression	Answer	Result in a
aReadStream: 1 2 3 ›4 5 6 7 8	a peek	4	aReadStream: 1 2 3 ›4 5 6 7 8

peekFor: anObject

Answer true if the next element in the stream is equal to anObject; false if there is a next element and it isn't equal to anObject. The position is not advanced. It is an error if the stream is at its end.

Value of a	Expression	Answer	Result in a
aReadStream: 1 2 3 ›4 5 6 7 8	a peekFor: 4	true	aReadStream: 1 2 3 ›4 5 6 7 8
aReadStream: 1 2 3 ›4 5 6 7 8	a peekFor: 5	false	aReadStream: 1 2 3 ›4 5 6 7 8

skip: anInteger

Set the stream position forward or backward anInteger elements. It is an error to skip past the end or before the front.

Value of a	Expression	Result in a
aReadStream: 1 2 3 ›4 5 6 7 8	a skip: 3	aReadStream: 1 2 3 4 5 6 ›7 8
aReadStream: 1 2 3 ›4 5 6 7 8	a skip: -2	aReadStream: 1 ›2 3 4 5 6 7 8

skipTo: anObject

If there is an object remaining in the stream that compares equal to anObject, then set the stream position just past that object and answer true.

If there is no object remaining in the stream that compares equal to anObject, then set the stream position to its end and answer false.

Value of a	Expression	Answer	Result in a
aReadStream: 1 2 3 ›4 5 6 7 8	a skipTo: 7	true	aReadStream: 1 2 3 4 5 6 7 ›8
aReadStream: 1 2 3 ›4 5 6 7 8	a skipTo: 3	false	aReadStream: 1 2 3 4 5 6 7 8 ›

skipToAll: aCollection

If there is a sequence of objects remaining in the stream that compares equal to the sequence in aCollection, then set the stream position just past that sequence and answer true.

If there is no sequence of objects remaining in the stream that compares equal to the sequence in aCollection, then set the stream position to its end and answer false.

Value of a	Expression	Answer	Result in a

aReadStream:
  1 2 3 ›4 5 6 7 8
	a skipToAll: #(6 7)	true	aReadStream:
			  1 2 3 4 5 6 7 ›8

aReadStream:
  1 2 3 ›4 5 6 7 8
	a skipToAll: #(2 4)	false	aReadStream:
			  1 2 3 4 5 6 7 8 ›

upTo: anObject

If there is an object remaining in the stream that compares equal to anObject, then set the stream position just past that object and answer a collection containing the elements up to, but not including, anObject.

If there is no object remaining in the stream that compares equal to anObject, then set the stream position to its end and answer a collection containing the remaining elements.

Value of a	Expression	Answer	Result in a
aReadStream: 1 2 3 ›4 5 6 7 8	a upTo: 7	aCollection: 4 5 6	aReadStream: 1 2 3 4 5 6 7 ›8
aReadStream: 1 2 3 ›4 5 6 7 8	a upTo: 3	aCollection: 4 5 6 7 8	aReadStream: 1 2 3 4 5 6 7 8 ›

upToAll: aCollection

If there is a sequence of objects remaining in the stream that compares equal to the sequence in aCollection, then set the stream position just past that sequence and answer a collection containing the elements up to, but not including, the sequence.

If there is no sequence of objects remaining in the stream that compares equal to the sequence in aCollection, then set the stream position to its end and answer a collection containing the remaining elements.

Value of a	Expression	Answer	Result in a
aReadStream: 1 2 3 ›4 5 6 7 8	a upToAll: #(6 7)	aCollection: 4 5	aReadStream: 1 2 3 4 5 6 7 ›8
aReadStream: 1 2 3 ›4 5 6 7 8	a skipToAll: #(2 4)	aCollection: 4 5 6 7 8	aReadStream: 1 2 3 4 5 6 7 8 ›

Class WriteStream

WriteStream is an concrete class defining methods for writing streams of objects.

Class	Page
Object	
Stream	531
PositionableStream	532
ReadStream	535
WriteStream	538
ReadWriteStream	541
EsRandom	545

Class Method Summary

Method	Documented	See page
on: aCollection	PositionableStream class	533

on: aCollection
  from: intFirst
  to: intLast
	PositionableStream class	533

with: aCollection	WriteStream class	539

with: aCollection
  from: intFirst
  to: intLast
	WriteStream class	539

Instance Method Summary

Method	Documented	See page
atEnd	Stream	531
close	PositionableStream	533
cr	WriteStream	540
contents	WriteStream PositionableStream	540 533
~~do: aBlock~~	Stream	531
isEmpty	PositionableStream	533
flush	WriteStream	540
lineDelimiter	PositionableStream	533
lineDelimiter: aSeqColl	PositionableStream	533
~~next~~	Stream	531
next: anInteger put: anObject	WriteStream	540
nextPut: anObject	WriteStream	540
nextPutAll: aCollection	WriteStream	540
position	WriteStream PositionableStream	540 534
position: anInteger	PositionableStream	534
reset	PositionableStream	534
setToEnd	PositionableStream	534
size	Stream Object	532
space	WriteStream	541
tab	WriteStream	541
upToEnd	PositionableStream	534

Class Interface

Note: Positions in stream examples are shown by the character › before the next element in the stream.

with: aWriteableCollection
Answer a new instance of the receiver that streams over the collection aWriteableCollection. The stream is positioned at its end.

Value of a	Expression	Result
#($a $b $c $d)	WriteStream with: a	aWriteStream: $a $b $c $d ›

with: aWriteableCollection from: startInteger to: endInteger
Answer a new instance of the receiver that streams over a copy of that portion of the collection aWriteableCollection that starts at the position startInteger and ends with the position endInteger. The stream is positioned at its end.

Value of a	Expression	Result
#($a $b $c $d)	WriteStream with: a from: 2 to: 3	aWriteableStream: $b $c ›

Instance Interface

cr
Write the stream's line delimiter to the stream at its next location. While cr sounds like it applies only to strings, it will write any line delimiter to any stream.

See also: lineDelimiter, lineDelimiter:

Value of a	Line delimiter	Expression	Result
aStream: 1 2 3 ›	#(-1)	a cr	aStream: 1 2 3 -1›
aStream: 'abc'	'\'	a cr	aStream: 'abc\'

contents
Answer a copy of that portion of the collection, over which the stream is streaming, that precedes the current position.

Value of a	Expression	Result
aWriteStream: 1 2 3 6 7 ›8 10 11	a contents	aCollection: 1 2 3 6 7

flush
Do nothing. The flush message provides compatibility with file streams.

next: anInteger put: anObject
Store anObject into the next anInteger locations in the write stream. Advance the position by anInteger. This is equivalent to:

anInteger timesRepeat: [:n | receiver nextPut: anObject]

Value of a	Expression	Result
aWriteStream: 'Smith›'	a next: 5 put: '.'	aWriteStream: 'Smith.....›'
aWriteStream: 1 2 3 ›	a next: 3 put: 4	aWriteStream: 1 2 3 4 4 4 ›

nextPut: anObject
Store anObject into the next location in the write stream. Advance the position by one.

Value of a	Expression	Result
aWriteStream: 'Smith›'	a nextPut: $.	aWriteStream: 'Smith.›'
aWriteStream: 1 2 3 ›	a nextPut: 4	aWriteStream: 1 2 3 4 ›

nextPutAll: aCollection
Store the elements of aCollection into the next locations in the write stream. Advance the position by (aCollection size).

Value of a	Expression	Result
aWriteStream: 'Smith›'	a nextPutAll: '.'	aWriteStream: 'Smith.›'
aWriteStream: 1 2 3 ›	a nextPutAll:#(4 5)	aWriteStream: 1 2 3 4 5 ›

position: anInteger
Set the position of the stream to anInteger, effectively truncating any elements beyond the new position. The value is one less than the index of the element that will be referenced next. Thus, a zero means that next will return the first element.

Value of a	Expression	Result
aStream: 1 2 3 6 7 8 ›10 11	a position: 2	aStream: 1 2 ›

space

Store a space character into the next location in the write stream. Advance the position by one. This is equivalent to:

receiver nextPut: $

Value of a	Expression	Result
aWriteStream: '234'	a space	aWriteStream: '234 '

tab

Store a tab character into the next location in the write stream. Advance the stream position by one.

Class ReadWriteStream

ReadWriteStream is an concrete class defining methods for both reading and writing streams of objects.

Class Method Summary

Method	Documented	See page
on: aCollection	PositionableStream class	533

on: aCollection
   from: intFirst
   to: intLast
	PositionableStream class	533

with: aCollection	WriteStream class	539

with: aCollection
   from: intFirst
   to: intLast
	WriteStream class	539

Instance Method Summary

Method	Documented	See page
atEnd	Stream	531
close	PositionableStream	533
cr	WriteStream	540
contents	ReadWriteStream	542

Part 1 of 2.

Method	Documented	See page
copyFrom: fromInteger **to: toInteger**	ReadWriteStream	542
do: aBlock	Stream	531
flush	WriteStream	540
isEmpty	PositionableStream	533
lineDelimiter	PositionableStream	533
lineDelimiter: aSeqColl	PositionableStream	533
next	Stream	531
next: anInteger	ReadWriteStream	543
next: anInteger put: anObject	WriteStream	540
nextPut: anObject	WriteStream	540
nextPutAll: aCollection	WriteStream	540
nextLine	ReadWriteStream	543
nextMatchFor: anObject	ReadWriteStream	543
peek	ReadWriteStream	543
peekFor: anObject	ReadWriteStream	544
position	PositionableStream	534
position: anInteger	PositionableStream	534
reset	PositionableStream	534
setToEnd	PositionableStream	534
size	Stream Object	532
skip: anInteger	ReadWriteStream	544
skipTo: anObject	ReadWriteStream	544
skipToAll: aSeqColl	ReadWriteStream	544
space	WriteStream	541
tab	WriteStream	541
upTo: anObject	ReadWriteStream	544
upToAll: aSeqColl	ReadWriteStream	545
upToEnd	PositionableStream	534

Part 2 of 2.

Instance Interface

contents
Answer a copy of *all* of the collection over which the stream is streaming.

Value of a	Expression	Result
aReadWriteStream: 1 2 3 6 7 ›8 10 11	a contents	aCollection: 1 2 3 6 7 8 10 11

copyFrom: fromInteger to: toInteger
Answer a sequenceable collection that holds the elements from fromInteger to toInteger, and in the same order. If toInteger is less than fromInteger, answer an empty collection. It is an error if the indexes are not valid for the collection. It is equivalent to:

receiver contents copyFrom: fromInteger to: toInteger

Value of a	Expression	Answer
aReadWriteStream: 1 2 3 4 5 6 7 8	a copyFrom: 3 to: 5	aCollection: 3 4 5

next: anInteger

Answer a sequenceable collection containing the next anInteger elements; position the stream so that the element just behind the last element answered will be returned next. If there are less than anInteger elements, then all remaining elements are answered, and set the stream to its end.

Value of a	Expression	Answer	Result in a
aReadWriteStream: 1 2 3 ›4 5 6 7 8	a next: 3	aCollection: 4 5 6	aReadStream: 1 2 3 4 5 6 ›7 8
aReadWriteStream: 1 2 3 4 5 6 ›7 8	a next: 3	aCollection: 7 8	aReadStream: 1 2 3 4 5 6 7 8 ›

nextLine

If a line delimiter exists in the remainder of the stream, answer a sequenceable collection containing all of the elements up to, but not including, the next line delimiter. Position the stream just past the line delimiter.

If no line delimiter exists in the remainder of the stream, answer all the remaining elements in the stream. Position the stream so that atEnd is true.

line delimiter	Value of a	Expression	Answer	Result in a
'\'	aReadWriteStream: '›abc\def'	a nextLine	'abc'	aReadWriteStream: 'abc\›def'
'\'	aReadWriteStream: 'abc\›def'	a nextLine	'def'	aReadWriteStream: 'abc\def›'
#(0)	aReadWriteStream: ›4 5 0 7 8 0	a nextLine	aCollection: 4 5	aReadWriteStream: 4 5 0 ›7 8 0

nextMatchFor: anObject

Answer true if the next element in the stream is equal to anObject; answer false if there is a next element and it isn't equal to anObject. The position is advanced by one, even if no match was made. It is an error if the stream is at its end.

Value of a	Expression	Answer	Result in a
aReadWriteStream: 1 2 3 ›4 5 6 7 8	a nextMatchFor: 4	true	aReadWriteStream: 1 2 3 4 ›5 6 7 8
aReadWriteStream: 1 2 3 ›4 5 6 7 8	a nextMatchFor: 5	false	aReadWriteStream: 1 2 3 4 ›5 6 7 8

peek

Answer the next element in the stream if it is not at its end. The position is not advanced. It is an error if the stream is at its end.

Value of a	Expression	Answer	Result in a
aReadWriteStream: 1 2 3 ›4 5 6 7 8	a peek	4	aReadWriteStream: 1 2 3 ›4 5 6 7 8

peekFor: anObject

Answer true if the next element in the stream is equal to anObject; false if there is a next element and it isn't equal to anObject. The position is not advanced. It is an error if the stream is at its end.

Value of a	Expression	Answer	Result in a
aReadWriteStream: 1 2 3 ›4 5 6 7 8	a peekFor: 4	true	aReadWriteStream: 1 2 3 ›4 5 6 7 8
aReadWriteStream: 1 2 3 ›4 5 6 7 8	a peekFor: 5	false	aReadWriteStream: 1 2 3 ›4 5 6 7 8

skip: anInteger

Set the stream position forward or backward anInteger elements. It is an error to skip past the end or before the front.

Value of a	Expression	Result in a
aReadWriteStream: 1 2 3 ›4 5 6 7 8	a skip: 3	aReadWriteStream: 1 2 3 4 5 6 ›7 8
aReadWriteStream: 1 2 3 ›4 5 6 7 8	a skip: -2	aReadWriteStream: 1 ›2 3 4 5 6 7 8

skipTo: anObject

If there is an object remaining in the stream that compares equal to anObject, then set the stream position just past that object and answer true.

If there is no object remaining in the stream that compares equal to anObject, then set the stream position to its end and answer false.

Value of a	Expression	Answer	Result in a
aReadWriteStream: 1 2 3 ›4 5 6 7 8	a skipTo: 7	true	aReadWriteStream: 1 2 3 4 5 6 7 ›8
aReadWriteStream: 1 2 3 ›4 5 6 7 8	a skipTo: 3	false	aReadWriteStream: 1 2 3 4 5 6 7 8 ›

skipToAll: aCollection

If there is a sequence of objects remaining in the stream that compares equal to the sequence in aCollection, then set the stream position just past that sequence and answer true.

If there is no sequence of objects remaining in the stream that compares equal to the sequence in aCollection, then set the stream position to its end and answer false.

Value of a	Expression	Answer	Result in a
aReadWriteStream: 1 2 3 ›4 5 6 7 8	a skipToAll: #(6 7)	true	aReadWriteStream: 1 2 3 4 5 6 7 ›8
aReadWriteStream: 1 2 3 ›4 5 6 7 8	a skipToAll: #(2 4)	false	aReadWriteStream: 1 2 3 4 5 6 7 8 ›

upTo: anObject

If there is an object remaining in the stream that compares equal to anObject, then set the stream position just past that object and answer a collection containing the elements up to, but not including, anObject.

If there is no object remaining in the stream that compares equal to anObject, then set the stream position to its end and answer a collection containing the remaining elements.

Value of a	Expression	Answer	Result in a
aReadWriteStream: 1 2 3 ›4 5 6 7 8	a upTo: 7	aCollection: 4 5 6	aReadWriteStream: 1 2 3 4 5 6 7 ›8
aReadWriteStream: 1 2 3 ›4 5 6 7 8	a upTo: 3	aCollection: 4 5 6 7 8	aReadWriteStream: 1 2 3 4 5 6 7 8 ›

upToAll: aCollection

If there is a sequence of objects remaining in the stream that compares equal to the sequence in aCollection, then set the stream position just past that sequence and answer a collection containing the elements up to, but not including, the sequence.

If there is no sequence of objects remaining in the stream that compares equal to the sequence in aCollection, then set the stream position to its end and answer a collection containing the remaining elements.

Value of a	Expression	Answer	Result in a
aReadWriteStream: 1 2 3 ›4 5 6 7 8	a upToAll: #(6 7)	aCollection: 4 5	aReadWriteStream: 1 2 3 4 5 6 7 ›8
aReadWriteStream: 1 2 3 ›4 5 6 7 8	a skipToAll: #(2 4)	aCollection: 4 5 6 7 8	aReadWriteStream: 1 2 3 4 5 6 7 8 ›

Class EsRandom

EsRandom is an concrete class that defines methods for reading streams of random numbers.

Class Method Summary

There are no new class methods.

Instance Method Summary

Method	Documented	See page
atEnd	EsRandom Stream	546 531
do: aBlock	Stream	531
next	EsRandom Stream	546 531

Instance Interface

atEnd
Answer false. There are always more elements to return.

next
Answer the next random number in the stream.

38

System Interfaces

There are a number of interesting messages to various system classes that are not otherwise covered in this book. This chapter is an accumulation of such classes and methods. The coverage of the classes in this chapter is not at all complete; interesting methods have been extracted, but the bulk of the protocol is ignored.

Classes documented in this chapter are:

Kinds of Classes

EmSystemConfiguration

Class EmSystemConfiguration has one instance, which is referenced by the global variable System. All messages to a system configuration must be sent to this one instance.

EmSystemConfiguration implements a hodge-podge of messages, including easy-to-use prompters, saving the image, exiting the system, and forcing a garbage collection.

EsCompiler

Class EsCompiler compiles source code into methods. There are only a few public methods, all of which allow evaluation of source code.

Class EsCompiler is available only in the development environment and is not a part of the runtime package distributed with applications. Only tools designed for use within the development environment can use these methods.

Messages

Class Message holds the arguments and the selector from a message send; instances of Message are created when certain errors occur to describe the failed message send. Class DirectedMessage is similar, but knows about the receiver of the failed message send.

Details describing when such messages are created, and when and how they are sent, are platform dependent. Messages are documented here because such objects show up in debugger tracebacks, and are passed as parameters to system-generated messages such as doesNotUnderstand:.

Message

An instance of class Message is provided by the underlying system (often called the 'virtual machine') when a message send cannot complete. It provides access to the message selector and the arguments of the message.

DirectedMessage

An instance of class DirectedMessage is provided by the underlying system when a message cannot complete. It contains all that an instance of Message does, plus it provides the object to which the message was directed. It also allows the message to be sent again.

UndefinedObject

Class UndefinedObject has one instance named nil. Its protocol is limited. The one instance is used as a value wherever a 'non-value' is needed, including to fill otherwise uninitialized memory.

Class EmSystemConfiguration

Class Method Summary

There are no new class methods.

Instance Method Summary

Method	Documented	See page
availableMemory	SystemConfiguration	549
commandLine	SystemConfiguration	549
confirm: aString	SystemConfiguration	549
confirmYesNoCancel: aString	SystemConfiguration	549
errorMessage: aString	SystemConfiguration	550
exit	SystemConfiguration	550
globalGarbageCollect	SystemConfiguration	550
imageFileName	SystemConfiguration	550
message: aString	SystemConfiguration	550
prompt: aString	SystemConfiguration	550
prompt: aPromptString answer: anAnswerString	SystemConfiguration	550

Instance Interface

availableMemory

Answer the available memory. The globalGarbageCollect message should be sent first to reclaim unused memory. Platforms may allow Smalltalk to extend the memory area when it runs out; thus, it is possible that availableMemory will indicate little memory remaining, even though (in reality) much more can be allocated.

" **Get the size of the maximum available memory** "
System globalGarbageCollect.
^ System availableMemory   *Example 322, Display*

commandLine

Answer the command line used to start IBM Smalltalk as an array of strings, the first of which is the path name of the executable file that started the current execution. The exact contents of the answer are release and platform dependent.

Expression	Result
System commandLine	An array: ('E:/IBMST/PMIMAGE/ES.EXE' ...)

confirm: aString

Ask a question; the user confirms with the Yes or No buttons: if Yes, it answers true; and if No, it answers false.

Expression
System confirm: 'Continue destroying all data?'

confirmYesNoCancel: aString

Ask a question; the user confirms with the Yes, No, or Cancel buttons: if Yes, it answers true; if No, it answers false; and if Cancel, it answers nil.

Expression
System confirmYesNoCancel: 'Continue destroying all data?'

errorMessage: aString
Beep and display a message; the user confirms with the OK button.

Expression
System errorMessage: 'The sky is falling!'

exit
Exit the Smalltalk system. The image is not saved. There is no confirming prompt.

Expression
System exit
(System confirm: 'Exit Smalltalk without saving image?')   ifTrue: [System exit]

globalGarbageCollect
Perform a full garbage collection.

Expression
System globalGarbageCollect

imageFileName
Answer the name of the file that holds the image.

Expression	Result
System imageFIleName	'image'

message: aString
Display a message; the user confirms with the OK button.

Expression
System message: 'Hello, world!'

prompt: aString
Display the string and ask for a line of input; two buttons, OK and Cancel, are shown. Pressing OK terminates the dialog and answers whatever is typed by the user, or an empty string if nothing was typed. Pressing Cancel terminates the dialog and answers nil.

Expression
System prompt: 'Enter network name'

prompt: promptString answer: defaultString
Display promptString and asks for a line of input; the value in defaultString is displayed as a default. Two buttons, OK and Cancel, are also displayed. Pressing OK terminates the dialog and answers whatever is typed by the user, or the default if nothing was typed. Pressing Cancel terminates the dialog and answers nil.

Expression
System prompt: 'A sandwich walked into a bar and ordered a drink.'   answer: 'Sorry, we don''t serve food.'

Class EsCompiler

EsCompiler compiles Smalltalk code into methods.

Class Method Summary

Method	Documented	See page
evaluate: sourceString	EsCompiler	551
evaluate: sourceString **for: aClass**	EsCompiler	551
evaluate: sourceString **for: aClass** **ifFail: aBlock**	EsCompiler	552

Instance Method Summary

There are no new instance methods.

Class Interface

evaluate: sourceString

Answer the result of evaluating sourceString, a string containing Smalltalk code, if it could be compiled. If the compilation fails, answer nil. The method is compiled in the context of nil, the only instance of UndefinedObject. The code must not have a method header; one is added with the name Doit.†

If the code has no return statement, answer the last value in the method, and not the usual default answer of self.

This method performs the function of the Evaluate menu item. It is equivalent to:

EsCompiler evaluate sourceString for: nil ifFail: [:climErr | nil]

Examples:

" **Compile and evaluate an expression** "
EsCompiler evaluate: '2 + 3'   *Example 323, Display*

" **Compile and evaluate an expression; trace its execution**"
EsCompiler evaluate: 'self halt. 10 factorial'   *Example 324, Display*

evaluate: sourceString for: anObject

Answer the result of evaluating sourceString, a string containing Smalltalk code, if it could be compiled. If the compilation fails, answer nil. The method is compiled in the

---

† Pronounced Do-it, not dot, dut, or doyt. Doit is an old-time Smalltalk term that is going out of favor and is being replaced by Evaluate, which has elegance but no charm. The old term remains in the innards of the system, at least for now.

context of anObject. The code must not have a method header; one is added with the name Doit. This method is equivalent to:

EsCompiler evaluate sourceString for: aClass ifFail: [:climErr | nil]

Examples:

" **Compile and evaluate an expression in a given context** "
EsCompiler evaluate: '2 + 3' for: nil   *Example 325, Display*

" **Compile and evaluate an expression in a given context, using self**"
EsCompiler evaluate: 'self + 3' for: 2
    " Answers: 5 "   *Example 326, Display*

evaluate: sourceString for: anObject ifFail: aBlock

Answer the result of evaluating sourceString, a string containing Smalltalk code, if it could be compiled. If the compilation fails, evaluate aBlock and answer the result. The method is compiled in the context of anObject. The code must not have a method header; one is added with the name Doit.

Examples:

" **Compile an expression containing an error** "
EsCompiler evaluate: '2 + + 3'
    for: UndefinedObject
    ifFail: [:climErr | System errorMessage: climErr message]   *Example 327, Display*

The parameter passed to the block is an instance of ClimCompilerError. It responds to these messages:

Message	*Description*
context	Answer anObject.
message	Answer a string holding the error message.
sourceString	Answer sourceString.
startPosition	Answer the index into the source string of the first character of the error location; may answer nil if the start position cannot be determined.
stopPosition	Answer the index into the source string of the last character of the error location; may answer nil if the stop position cannot be determined.

See Chapter 19, 'Example: The DoIt Browser', on page 223 for an example of this method and of the use of instances of ClimCompilerError.

Class Message

Class Method Summary

There are no new class methods.

Instance Method Summary

Method	Documented	See page
arguments	Message	554
arguments: anArray	Message	554
selector	Message	554
selector: aSymbol	Message	554

Instance Interface

In the examples below, the value of a is an instance of Message received by a does-NotUnderstand: method invoked by the invalid message in the first column.

A typical doesNotUnderstand: method, along with a class in which it can be run, is shown in Example 328:

```
" A doesNotUnderstand: example "
Object subclass: #DoesNot
    instanceVariableNames: ''
    classVariableNames: ''
    poolDictionaries: ''!

!DoesNot publicMethods !
doesNotUnderstand: a
    Transcript cr;
        show: a arguments printString;
        cr;
        show: a selector printString.
    Transcript cr;
        show: a class printString.
    super doesNotUnderstand: a! !
```
Example 328, FileIn

Evaluate Example 329 to execute Example 328. An instance of DoesNot does not understand theMessage:.

```
" An instance of DoesNot does not understand theMessage "
DoesNot new theMessage: 'argument1'
```
Example 329, Execute

arguments

Answer a collection (an instance of some SequenceableCollection subclass) that holds the parameters of the message, or nil if there are no parameters.

Invalid message	Expression	Result
DoesNot new asdf	a arguments	#()
DoesNot new asdf: 4 qwer: 8	a arguments	#(4 8)

arguments: anArray

Set the arguments array.

selector

Answer a symbol that names the selector of the message, or nil if there is no selector.

Invalid message	Expression	Result
DoesNot new qwer	a selector	#qwer
DoesNot new asdf: 4 qwer: 8	a selector	#asdf:qwer:

selector: aSymbol

Set the message selector.

Class DirectedMessage

Class Method Summary

There are no new class methods.

Instance Method Summary

Method	Documented	See page
arguments	Message	554
arguments: anArray	Message	554
selector	Message	554
selector: aSymbol	Message	554
receiver	DirectedMessage	555
receiver:	DirectedMessage	555
send	DirectedMessage	555

Instance Interface

receiver

Answer the object to which the failed message was sent.

receiver:

Set the object.

send

Resend the message. This is equivalent to the message:

```
aDirectedMessage receiver
    perform: aDirectedMessage selector
    withArguments: aDirectedMessage arguments
```

Class UndefinedObject

Class Method Summary

There are no new class methods.

Instance Method Summary

Method	Documented	See page
isNil	UndefinedObject	555
notNil	UndefinedObject	555

Instance Interface

isNil

Answers true.

notNil

Answers false.

Indexes

Indexes

The indexes provide a variety of ways to find information. In addition to a general index, the method index includes all method definitions in Part IV, and three class indexes organize the classes in Part IV by name, chapter, and hierarchy.

General
>   An index of terms, concepts, and features covering the whole book.

Methods
>   An index of method names from Part IV.

Classes by Name
>   An index of classes in Part IV organized by the name of the class.

Classes by Chapter
>   An index of classes in Part IV organized by the name of the chapter in which the class is defined.

Classes by Hierarchy
>   An index of classes in Part IV organized by class hierarchy.

Index

General

C

callbacks 188
cascaded message 40
CFS. *See* Common File System
CfsConstants 108
CfsConstants pool dictionary
    143, 373, 376–378
CfsErrorProxy 139
CG. *See* Common Graphics
CgConstants pool dictionary
    108, 109
character set 31
characters 58, 434–438
    constants 34
class
    creating 85
    definition 10
    external format 90
    instance variables 101, 102
    library 5
    tree 12
    variables 101, 102
    viewing hierarchy 127
CLDT. *See* Common Language
    Data Types
CldtConstants pool dictionary
    109, 138, 143, 207, 373
collections 65–84, 309–329, 331–
    372
    boundary checking 68
    comparison 310, 332
    creating 67
    fixed-size 71
    kinds 65
    of collections 72
    sequenceable 331–372
    summary table 66
    variable-size 76–82
colors 186
command line 549
comments 31
Common File System 3, 373–393
Common Graphics 4
Common Language Data Types
    3
Common Language
    Implementation 4
Common Process Model 4
compiler 5, 108, 228, 548, 551–
    552
constants 32–35, 337, 457
containment hierarchy 158, 181

coordinate system 485, 511
copying 115–117
CPM. *See* Common Process
    Model
critical section 171
current working directory 145

D

data hiding 7, 20, 85–98
dates 58, 439–444
debugging 5, 26, 130–132, 133
delaying 167, 501–503
dependents 283–285
dictionaries 66
dictionary 82, 321–328
    identity 328
Display 24
Doit 49, 131
DoIt Browser 223–233
drawable 193
drawing 197–202

E

Employee class 14, 85–91
encapsulation 20
Engine class 12
errors 26
    capturing 164
    file 139, 153
    See also exception handling
Evaluate 24
evaluating code 49, 132
events 188–190
ExAll 157, 396
exception handling 157–166,
    395–406
exceptional event collections
    159, 396, 404
exceptional events 157, 160,
    396, 401–404
    ExAll 157, 396
    ExError 157, 396
    ExHalt 158, 396
    ExUserBreak 158, 396
    signalling 160–161
exceptions
    building 162–163
    handling 159
ExError 157, 396
ExHalt 158, 396
exiting Smalltalk 550

expressions 38–41
    binary 39
    cascaded 40
    keyword 39
    mixed 39
    unary 39
external class format 90
ExUserBreak 158, 396

F

false 38, 106, 303–308
file directory 144, 380–383
    creating 145
    current 145
    existence 147
    removing 145
    searching 148, 378
file errors 139
file locking 153, 378, 387, 388, 389
    advisory 154
    mandatory 154
    regions 154
file names 143
file selection prompter 119, 124
file sharing 153, 155
file streams 138
filein 5, 90
fileout 5, 90
files 143–156, 373–393
    deleting 146
    error constants 376
    error handing 153
    locking constants 378
    open flags 376, 409
    opening 150–153
    patterns 148
    positioning constants 376
    random access 152
    reading 151
    removing 146
    reset to beginning 153
    sharing constants 378
    writing 151–153
FinancialInstrument class 12
fixed-size collections 71, 358–372
floating-point 57, 450, 483–484
    constants 33, 457
    precision 456
flow of control 42
fonts 199
fork 168
fractions 33, 57, 450, 484
    constants 33, 457

R

radix 457
random access 152
random numbers 135, 142, 208, 545
random streams 142
rectangles 62–63, 509–526
  normalization 512
recursion 46
refinement 11–19, 21, 87, 93–97
relative path names 144
return statement 50
Richardson, Dan 213
root directories 144

S

scientific notation 32, 457
scope of variables 105
self 9, 38, 46, 106, 228
semaphores 170–178, 507–508
sequenceable collection 340–349
sets 67, 80, 329
side effects 107
signal
  instance of Signal 158
  to exceptional event 158
Silberschatz, A. 178
SingleDeposit class 91–93
Smalltalk dictionary 38, 106
Smith, David N. 22
sort blocks 79
sorted collections 67, 78, 356–357
  sort blocks 79
source code 127
special variables 38, 101, 106
statements 41–42
  return 50
stereograms 205–213
stream filters 235–246
streams 135–142, 527–546
  on collections 135
  on files 135, 407–423
  positionable 136
  random 142
strings 67, 73, 362–369
  comparison 74
  constants 34
  example 208
subclass subclass type 117
super 38, 46, 88, 106

symbols 67, 74, 370
  constants 34
System 547
system configuration 547
system interrupt key 163
SystemExceptions pool
    dictionary 109

T

Tannenbaum, Andrew 178
Taylor, David A. 22
text prompter 119, 123
times 60, 445–448
TimeValueOfMoney class 9–11
Transcript 29, 124, 126
true 38, 106, 303–308

U

unary expression 39
unary header 47
unary message 36, 46
undefined objects 555
underscore 32
Ungar, David 118
UNIXLineDelimiter 138
user interfaces 179–202
  See also widgets 179
user interrupt key 163

V

van Gobble de Gook, Hendrick
    Wilhelm 130
variableByteSubclass subclass
    type 118
variableLongSubclass subclass
    type 118
variables 38, 101–110
  assignment to 40
  block locals 101, 104
  block parameters 101, 103
  class 101, 102
  class instance 101, 102
  global 84, 101, 106
  instance 101, 102
  local 46, 48
  method locals 101, 104
  method parameters 101, 102
  pool 101, 102
  pool dictionary keys 107
  resolution order 102
  scope and lifetime 105
  side effects 107

  special 38, 101, 106
  type 21
variable-size collections 76–82
variableSubclass subclass type 117
variableWordSubclass subclass type
    118
VisualAge. *See* IBM VisualAge

W

white space 31, 35
White, I. 98
widgets 179–202, 223
  callbacks 188
  creating 182
  destroying 183
  events 188–190
  geometry 190–193
  hierarchy 182
  layout 190–193
  managing 182
  mapping 182
  realizing 182
  resources 183
WinLineDelimiter 138
Wirfs-Brock, R. 98
working directory 145
workspace 206–208
workspaces 23, 124–126
WritingInstrument class 93–97

Index

Methods

Index

Classes by Name

Index

Classes by Chapter

Index

Classes by Hierarchy

Obtaining Code for Examples

Files containing the complete code of the numbered examples in the book can be obtained in a number of ways.

Free via FTP

The file is available at no charge via FTP (File Transfer Protocol) over the Internet from Benjamin/Cummings Publishing Co. Issue the command:

    ftp bc.aw.com

and log in as anonymous. Use your e-mail address as your password. Once logged in, change to the directory for Smith by typing:

    cd bc/smith

Before retrieving the source code, it is a good idea to look at the readme file to see what is new with the Smith file since this book went to press. The command:

    get README

will retrieve this file. Quit FTP to log off and read the file. (Although the README file can be read on-line, it is courteous not to tie up the login for reading.) Then log back on when you are ready to download.

You can also get a listing of available filenames using either the ls command, or the dir command. Assuming that you are in the proper subdirectory, these commands require no arguments.

FTP and file extraction can be complicated. Instructions vary depending on your system: Macintosh, DOS, OS/2, Windows, and Unix all work a little differently. If you are new to using FTP, it is best to consult your favorite local network wizard.

Using On-Line Services

CompuServe

A CompuServe™ userid is required and there is a charge for general access to the service, but no extra charge for the software. As of this writing, IBM uses CompuServe for customer support for the VisualAge and Smalltalk products. The file is available on the IBM Smalltalk and IBM VisualAge forums in three formats.

The file names all have the form DNSSL*n* which stands for David N. Smith, Smalltalk Language book. The number, *n*, indicates the version of the file; updates, including errata for the book and corrections to the examples, if any, will have higher numbers.

DNSSL*n*.ZIP	The files are contained in a PKZIP™ archive. Download this file if you run under Windows or OS/2; use the PKZIP program to extract the files. PKZIP is available elsewhere on CompuServe.
DNSSL*n*.SIT	The files are contained in a STUFFIT™ archive. Download this file if you are using a Macintosh for CompuServe access; use the STUFFIT program (or the UNSTUFFIT program) to extract the files. UNSTUFFIT is available elsewhere on CompuServe.
DNSSL*n*.TXT	The files are concatenated together to form one long text file. The use of an editor that will read very large files is necessary to split the file into its parts. The first part of the file contains instructions.

Other Services

The files listed above will be available on other on-line services, including America Online, e-World, and Delphi. Details are not available at press time. The files will have the same names unless the service requires a different naming scheme. Check your service's Smalltalk or object-oriented programming area.

By Mail

A diskette holding the machine-readable materials is available by mail at a nominal charge. It is available only on a 3.5 inch diskette; the diskette is formatted for use on DOS, Windows, and OS/2 only; other formats are not available.

Within the USA

By *credit card*, in the USA, call 1-800-447-2226. Ask for the program code diskette to accompany the book, *IBM Smalltalk: The Language*, by David N. Smith. Reference Product ISBN #0-8053-0907-1. The price is $10.00, plus shipping, handling, and state and city sales taxes. Visa, MasterCard, and American Express are accepted.

By *check*, in the USA, fill out the coupon located at the end of this section. The price is $10.00, (shipping and handling is included), plus state and city sales taxes.

In Canada

In Canada contact:

Addison-Wesley Publishers Ltd.
P.O. Box 580
26 Prince Andrews Place
Don Mills, Ontario, CANADA M3C 2T8

Phone 416-447-5101, Fax 416-443-0948

Ask for the Program Code diskette to accompany the book, *IBM Smalltalk: The Language*, by David N. Smith. Reference product ISBN 0-8053-0907-1.

International Orders

Outside Canada and the USA, contact:

Addison-Wesley Publishing Company
International Publishing Company
Jacob Way
Reading, Massachusetts, 01867

Phone 617-944-3700 ext. 2405

Telex 989572 ADWES UD

Fax 617-942-2829

Ask for the Program Code diskette to accompany the book, *IBM Smalltalk: The Language*, by David N. Smith. Reference product ISBN 0-8053-0907-1.

Obtaining Program Code by Mail

A diskette containing the program code of the numbered examples in this book is available by mail. The program code may be obtained from other sources as well, as indicated in the Preface of the book.

To obtain a 3.5 inch diskette (suitable for Windows and OS/2), and pay by check, fill out the coupon below. Remove this entire page from the book, or make a copy of this page, fill in the required information, and insert into an envelope, along with your check made out to *Benjamin/Cummings*, place appropriate postage on it, and mail. Please include state sales tax with your order. Shipping and handling are included for orders prepaid by check.

Offer available in the United States only.

Please send me the program code diskette to accompany the book *IBM Smalltalk: The Language* by David N. Smith.

Diskette ISBN 0-8053-0907-1.

Diskette Price:	$10.00
Your State Sales Tax:	_____
Check Total:	_____

Make check payable to: *Benjamin/Cummings*.

Ship to:

Name	_____
Street/Box	_____
City	_____
State	_____
Zip Code	_____

Allow 2-3 weeks from receipt of coupon for delivery.

Mail this form to:

Benjamin/Cummings Publishing Company, Inc.
Jacob Way
Reading, Massachusetts
01867

Obtaining Program Code by Mail

A diskette containing the program code of the numbered examples in this book is available by mail. The program code may be obtained from other sources as well, as indicated in the Preface of the book.

To obtain a 3.5 inch diskette (suitable for Windows and OS/2), and pay by check, fill out the coupon below. Remove this entire page from the book, or make a copy of this page, fill in the required information, and insert into an envelope, along with your check made out to *Benjamin/Cummings*, place appropriate postage on it, and mail. Please include state sales tax with your order. Shipping and handling are included for orders prepaid by check.

Offer available in the United States only.

Please send me the program code diskette to accompany the book *IBM Smalltalk: The Language* by David N. Smith.

Diskette ISBN 0-8053-0907-1.

    Diskette Price: $10.00

    Your State Sales Tax: _____

    Check Total: _____

Make check payable to: *Benjamin/Cummings*.

Ship to:

    Name   _____

    Street/Box _____

    City   _____

    State   _____

    Zip Code   _____

Allow 2-3 weeks from receipt of coupon for delivery.

Mail this form to:

    Benjamin/Cummings Publishing Company, Inc.
    Jacob Way
    Reading, Massachusetts
    01867